Rudi Van de Velde

Hospital Information Systems –

The Next Generation

With 173 Figures

Springer-Verlag
Berlin Heidelberg GmbH

Prof. Rudi Van de Velde
Academisch Ziekenhuis
Informatieverwerking
Vrije Universiteit Brussel
Laarbeeklaan 101
1090 Brussel, Belgium

ISBN 978-3-642-77619-9 ISBN 978-3-642-77617-5 (eBook)
DOI 10.1007/978-3-642-77617-5

Originally published by Springer-Verlag Berlin Heidelberg New York 1992
Softcover reprint of the hardcover 1st edition 1992

Typesetting: Camera-ready by author
27/3145 – 5 4 3 2 1 0 – Printed on acid-free paper

Foreword

Since the publication of *Hospital Computer Systems*, edited by Morris F. Collen in 1974, many reviews have appeared presenting sound analyses and evaluations of the latest developments and design of hospital information systems (HIS). Many of them were published within the IMIA Working Group 10 which is devoted to HIS but still an updated and critical overview was lacking which reviews what has been achieved since then and which also takes a inspired glance into the future. As the quotation from Romain Rolland introducing this latest work by Rudi van de Velde states *"I love and admire the past but I would like the future to be even better."* Hence, it is noteworthy to point out that this book includes topics ranging from "Trends in Medical Informatics, Setting the Scene" to "HIS in the Years Ahead" and dealing separately with hospital management concerns and medical applications.

Hospital management is the field wholly supported by the HIS, since it deals with transactions issued by the team of patient care professionals about the patients and, as such, handles computer communications between the more or less autonomous substructures of the hospital, including central and costly resources such as laboratories, radiology departments and pharmacies, and links medical and administrative services (as Marion J. Ball already pointed out when she undertook to categorize the HIS). We should also keep in mind that a HIS may be open to outside users under certain conditions and not only used within a closed system: for example, local general practitioners, primary care services, or insurance companies.
The so-called *medical computing applications*, on the other hand deal with less standardized approaches, as is unfortunately usually the case within HIS. They must be more tailored (they were formerly considered to be heterogeneous), specialized, and "local" and therefore, closer to the subsystems which are now called "ward information systems" (WIS) and are built around a more or less extensive use of workstations. Obviously, it is feasible to integrate HIS and WIS only if they can cope with open computer architectures and new software engineering rules for development and implementation. The book by Rudi van de Velde provides a balanced discussion of all the client-server architectural features of an open system that accommodates both HIS and WIS and aims for better integration.

In a brief review, the book also explains why, despite the fact that the feasibility of designing and implementing HIS on a centralized computer architecture had been recognized the desire to preserve the purity of design led to rejection of the idea as compatible with what are nowadays often still rejected as sometimes "heterogeneous, foreign bodies" such as medical systems. Initially, these systems were dedicated, off-line systems, and although after some degree of development, for a number of the most successful ones, particularly those used in clinical laboratories, attempts were made to link up with a true HIS or with other similar dedicated medical subsystems, they never quite became true, full-scale HIS.

Finally, the book shows new ways of using object-oriented HIS modeling and new, sound software engineering trends in open architectures to better manage the possibilities of expanding these systems: this is necessary to keep them vital, responsive, and capable of fulfilling as many of the users' expectations as possible. Dr Van de Velde's vision is of a promising future for new designs and implementations with the new family of modern HIS.

Prof.Dr. J-R Scherrer
Division of Informatics
University Hospital of Geneva and Faculty of Medicine
Geneva,Switzerland
March 1992

Preface

The current health care system is in a state of transition. This transition is caused by a growing expectation of the population for health care delivery, by changing government regulations combined with reduced budgets and finally by an emerging sophisticated technological evolution towards an electronically, based patient medical record. As hospitals take the first place in terms of medical services and expenditures, the hospital information systems on which they rely for the collection and communication of huge volumes of medical data will continue to play an increasing role in the near future.
The emphasis of this book concerns the broad spectrum of applications that computers have in medicine in general and in the hospital area in particular, in order to sustain all health care actors involved in the selection, implementation or management of hospital information systems. Above all, it attempts to provide both a conceptual framework for hospital information systems, showing how applications can fit together and a practical inspiration for this emerging domain.
This book has arisen on the one hand from my 15 years of personal experience of hospital information systems' design and implementation at the university hospital of Brussels, and on the other hand it is based on the lectures given at the faculty of medicine at the University of Brussels. Therefore, it is not meant as an encyclopaedic reference work, but it should be of great value as beginning textbook for medical students, clinicians and executives involved in that exciting, fast-moving domain looking for an introduction. In fact, computers are playing an essential role in medicine today and may soon be a necessary part of a physician's education. Readers without prior computer knowledge should have no difficulties in understanding this text.

The book follows a logical progression organized into four parts : the first one sets the scene of health care and gives a description of trends in medical informatics. It includes also some fundamental principles of computer science. The second part focuses on hospital management systems, discussing departmental information systems such as radiological, laboratory, nutrition and nursing. The third part covers more medically oriented applications : cardiology, image management, telemedicine, etc. Finally, the last part provides general conclusions and some guidelines. Although technology is evolving rapidly, the major concepts highlighted in the book will not change for a time. Therefore, the basics described here provide a good understanding for tomorrow's technology over the next decade.

It is my sincere hope that the reader's time will be spent well.

Some of the readers may be more familiar than myself with certain themes or have other opinions than those presented in the book. I invite them to exchange ideas and points of view.

For those desiring additional information I refer to the extensive bibliography.

Acknowledgments

A book of a certain size is only possible thanks to the contributions of many individuals. Many people with whom I had lots of discussions had an indirect but influential effect upon the content of the book.
I gratefully acknowledge and express my appreciation for the proofreading of individual chapters to :

Prof. R.Gardner, Ph.D.	*University of Utah,Salt Lake City,USA*
Prof.Lenhard,M.D.	*Johns Hopkins Hospital,Baltimore,USA*
Prof.P.de Vries-Robbé M.D.	*University of Nijmegen,The Netherlands*
Prof. J.R. Scherrer M.D.	*University Hospital of Geneva, Switzerland*
Prof.L.Tielemans M.D.	*University Hospital of Brussels, Belgium*
Prof. A. Hasman Ph.D.	*University of Maastricht, The Netherlands*
Prof.G.J.E. De Moor M.D.	*University Hospital Gent, Belgium*
C. Florin Ir.	*Hewlett Packard,Geneva, Switzerland*
L. De Keyser M.D.	*Digital Europe, Belgium*
J.Andre	*TDS, Europe*
Prof.A. Albert Ph.D.	*University of Liege, Belgium*

Of course I also wish to mention the valuable contributions of W. Vyncken, M.D., Van Bellen S., M.D., R. Luypaert, Ph.D., L. Huyghens, M.D., P. De Wilde, M.D., Y. Taeymans, M.D. and Prof. S. Lauwers, M.D.

I would particularly like to thank Ms. De Vos Nelly for her excellent work in typing and editing during the preparation of the manuscript. Without her efforts this book would never have seen daylight. And I should not forget Hooge Machteld who completed the book's illustrations.

Finally I thank my wife, Nancy, and my children, Kristof and Kathy, for all the hours that I stole from them, their understanding, support and encouragement that was crucial in writing this book. They do not understand a lot of computers, but they know that hospital information systems are important to me and that is enough.

To all these people goes my deepest gratitude.

Rudi Van de Velde
Affligem, December1991

Contents

Trends in Medical Informatics: Setting the Scene

Part 1

"I love and admire the past
But I would like the future to be even better"

Romain Rolland

1

The Current Health Care System : In a State of Transition

1.1 Setting the Scene

Hospitals and other medical care facilities have not been immune to an information fever, which has been steadily spreading in recent years. But a healthy dose of data, organised to fulfill some carefully defined needs and made accessible to those who require it, is anything but a disease. It is a constructive response by hospitals to the increasing pressures being exerted on them.

The current European health care system is measured by its 800.000 physicians and 15.000 hospitals having more than 3 million beds for a population of about 320 million. Health care services, growing at a rate of 8% per year and amounting to over 8% of the GNP form one of the most rapidly expanding economic sectors in Europe. There are several important challenges which require attention in the scenario for health care in Europe [BAR 90]:

Growing need for health care

- Increasingly older population requiring more health services
- Growing demands for quality health care
- Increasing expectations that services will be provided

Growing offer of health care

- Ability to provide life saving and life-enhancing services
- Improving the range and quality of offered care

Limits on increases in spending for health care

- Need for greater education and support for patients/customers
- Declining pool of individuals available to staff health services
- Declining number of working-age tax payers
- Political constraints on the availability of funds to provide health services

The greatest challenge facing hospitals today is to harmonise the quality of care with the need for reduction of costs. Health care costs have continuously increased over the past 2 decades, forcing governments to change reimbursement policies and reducing hospital budgets, often by reducing staff. There is a growing gap between the expectations from patients of the care available to them and the limited resources to provide it. Therefore, hospitals have to provide care for sicker patients with fewer resources. They have to seek a higher allocation of scarce resources, focusing awareness on the cost implications of delivered care. Under these conditions, the health care provider needs better and timely information to make accurate decisions. In the health care sector, hospitals take first place in terms of medical services and expenses. Hospital information systems (HIS) on which they rely for the collection and communication of data will play a very important role in the next decade. They are becoming transaction intensive and database dependent. These systems are big business, and hospitals will acquire more software as they become increasingly dependent on automation. At the present time, hospitals spend 1% - 3% of their budget for information technology. Some predict that this percentage will increase to 8% in the years ahead.

> ***The goal of a HIS is to use computers and communications equipment to collect, store, process, retrieve and communicate patient care and administrative information for all hospital-affiliated activities, to satisfy the functional requirements of all authorized users and to provide decision support to the central government and politicians.***
> *following* M.F. Collen.

Most current hospital information systems are based on a concept of either hierarchical and centralized or fragmented and distributed information systems, the latter with poor integration between the various components.
Sometimes they have been designed for delivering very quickly operational and administrative information but providing insufficient or late management information to hospital managers. Alternatively, if they are able to produce both types of information, a serious decrease in computer performance occurs due to the "*Von Neumann*" bottleneck of monolithic computer applications. In addition, due to the high specialisation of some hospital applications (e.g. imaging work, radiotherapy) and also to the extreme complexity of the health care sector, there is insufficient communication among such applications.

The current health care system is in a state of transition. This transition is *first technological* from a paper based patient medical record to an electronic patient medical record and *second organisational* with a transfer of activities from hospital to ambulatory care. So, hospital information systems have to become more clinical oriented, less administrative and much closer to the process of providing patient care. The following patterns are emerging :

- More workstations and computers
- More systems networked
- More systems accessed from outside the hospital
- More systems functioning 24 h a day

With the integration between information systems and diagnostic support systems hospitals are becoming highly information intensive, and an increasing share of operating costs is directly related to this. Also, to improve health care management, information systems are essential. Management is to be concieved as a *feed back system* which controls daily operations in order to achieve optimal patient care.

1.2 Trends in Medical Informatics

Medical informatics is the integration of two well-established disciplines: *medicine and informatics*. It is concerned with a broad range of issues in the management of medical information in biomedical research and clinical practice.
Medicine today largely relies on the collection, management and communication of large amounts of information gathered from many different sources: imaging departments, laboratories, nursing homes, hospitals. Even more complex are the patterns of medical information, which have different formats, such as:

- Alphanumerical results (e.g laboratory results)
- Text results (e.g discharge summaries)
- Signals (e.g monitors)
- Images (e.g X-radiography)
- Video (e.g endoscopy, ultrasound)

Each person involved in patient care in the hospital requires specific user-tailored information. During the next few years we will observe two trends : the hospital's reliance on computerized information will increase, and hospital information systems will support inside communications between all surrounding medical-oriented and management-oriented applications, and outside communications by exchanging medical information (interhospital, general practitioners, specialists, etc.).
As care is often provided at different geographical locations, there is also a need for communication, based on both fixed and mobile systems. The requirements on medical communications that involve vital decisions are great for availability, confidentiality, quality, integrity and security.

The introduction of new technologies in medicine during the past decade has resulted in :

- *Less invasive* therapy equipment : lithotriptor, gamma-cameras, etc...
- *Powerful diagnostic* tools in the medical imaging field: magnetic resonance imaging (MRI), ultrasound imaging (US), etc...
- *Advanced patient monitoring* in acute care and cardiology, e.g. electrocardiographs, arrhythmia monitors
- *Integration of these instruments* into coherent and consistent information systems

The processing and transmission of pictorial information in medicine (radiology, pathology) need special attention as we are steadily moving toward a diagnostic environment that will provide all patient images. On the other hand, it must be clear that images are not enough, and the need for information derived from clinical information systems is obvious. To improve the result of a specific examination, physicians need information from many more sources than just past and present images. The integration of information is necessary for any system to survive but will become increasingly difficult due to the continuing changes in technology and practice patterns.

In summary, computer processing power is growing exponentially and storage capacity linearly, while our needs also grow as a function of our insight and requirements. The concept of Open Systems is gaining momentum. Cost-efficiency and openness that prevent vendors to "lock in" their customers are the real benefits of the Open Corporation.

Three experimental rules can express trends in information technology (Fig.1.1):

- *Processor performance* : Major improvements in processor architecture (reduced instruction set processors, parallel processors) have led to exponential performance increases, predicted by B.Joy in 1983 *(Joy's Law).*
- *Processor memory* : G. Amdahl proposed that for every MIPS (million instructions per second) needed, 1 Mbyte of additional memory must be available (Amdahl Law). The increased performance of large computers was forecast some time ago by G. Meyers.
- *Communications* : A third empirical law postulates that a direct relationship exists between the evolution of microelectronics and the required transmission rate of networks (Ruge Law)

We can conclude that with new technologies medical information systems are evolving to a point at which they will provide physicians with rapid timely access to various "views" of their patients and will support medical decision making. This will come through a convergence of four components:

- Networks and distributed clinical information systems
- Image management and communication systems
- Knowledge-based decision support systems
- Integration of diverse functions in single workstations

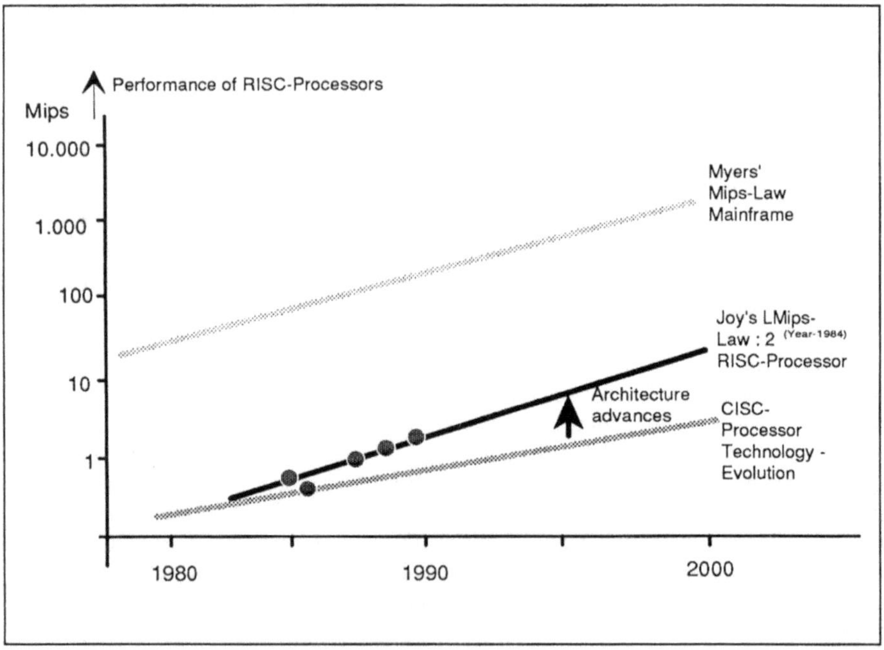

Fig. 1.1 Enhanced performance of computing power. In all probability Joy's Mips Law will remain valid far into the 1990s [ING 90].

(Source Reprinted with permission of Ingolf Ruge in *The growing influence of microelectronics on telecommunications.* Siemens Review, Fall 1990,p.16.)

2

Health Care Actors : Objectives and Requirements

2.1 Organisational Trends

Until the 1960s most hospital organisations had a strong hierarchical structure. It was assumed that the success of an organisation was directly connected with the quality of the top medical or administrative management. Practically everything was regarded in its relation to the organisation. The development of computer usage took place in the same manner. The mainframe computer was used for administrative tasks such as bookkeeping, salaries and patients invoicing. Personal computing was still out of the question.

Later, towards the end of the 1970s and at the beginning of the 1980s, a change took place. Hospitals began to see the importance of informatics as well. It was the time in which the need of quick decisions was becoming more and more urgent. It was also important that a quick and flexible stream of information be put into operation. Hierarchical structures gave way to smaller, decentralised units, departments requiring tailor-made computers: the rise of the mini-computers had become a fact.

In the 1980s this trend towards smaller units and decentralisation developed further into the smallest possible unit: the individual. Each individual (administrator, nurse, physician) becomes essential, is involved in taking decisions, needs information, in short, has a number of tasks in which a personal computer can be very useful. The window which is to give access to the "hospital database" has to be user-friendly, capable of personal computing activities and transparent, and therefore the PC workstation becomes pre-eminent. It is "the personal computing tool to empower the individual".
In fact, this is where the change from an industrial society to an information society is happening. In organisations, more integration and cooperation of the various levels will be seen. Instead of a vertical structure, we will have a horizontal one in which small units are to take the initiative and participate. The necessity of responding quickly in our changing society will increase. Communication requirements, computing power and storage capacity are constantly growing.

In the 1990s the health care industry will continue to be driven by the three primary issues that emerged in the 1980s : the need to improve productivity, profitability and quality of care. One way to manage this situation is to make staff more productive

through automation. The key word for the future of health care information systems is integration.
Evolution here is driven by the objectives and requirements of four main actors hospital management, health care providers, health care authorities and patients sometimes characterised by fundamental contradictions and mutual incompatibilities between the objectives and requirements of each group.
The largest information flows between actors in the health care sector are (Fig.2.1) requisitions, results reporting and medical certificates to insurance or social security.

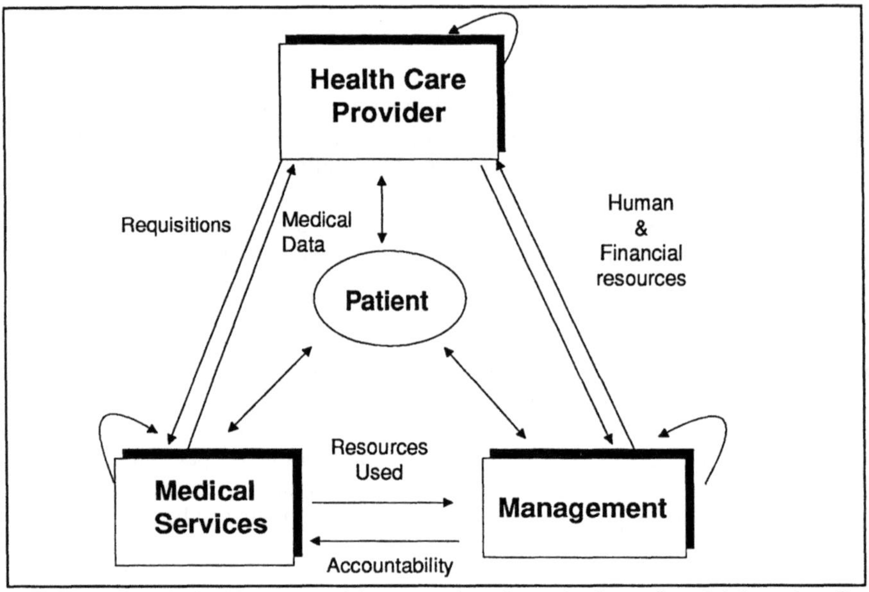

Fig.2.1 Generic health care model representing the main "actors" and information flows surrounding the patient

2.2 Objectives and Requirements for the Hospital Management

Better management begins with better information; this is well understood nowadays, yet information policy continues to fail in many places. It is not sufficiently well planned, the user is not taken into account, problems are tackled in a fragmented way, one forgets to define a strategy, objectives are not formulated, and the requirements are not adequately investigated. However, the most important cause of failure has not yet been mentioned: *the information policy is too often left to information scientists.* This has gradually drawn the attention of members of hospital management, who recognise the importance of information as the "fourth production factor" beside raw materials, capital and labour.

However, until recently the computer department was the exclusive domain of technicians. They started with calculators to carry support logistic activity. They were located in computer centres isolated from other departments of the hospital. Applications were limited to administrative activities like bookkeeping, invoicing, personnel and patient administration. The role of these specialists, information

scientists, programmers, analysts or EDP managers, was clearly defined. Often they opposed changes to this monopoly situation, and an ivory tower mentality was common.
Information is too important to be left to specialists. The supply of information is no longer a matter of logistics. It has developed into an issue of strategic management. Besides, the final user cannot be neglected. In the triangle *information technology - management- end user,* he is essential to the success of the system.
Man, who is after all, the primary concern in the implementation of successful systems, was more or less kept in the dark as to the place he was to take within the information system. The user's fear and false expectations can be adequately overcome by means of a specially adapted education, training and coaching for all. Data processing has now been opened to the non-professional users of informatics. In some hospitals two "worlds" (data processing departments vs. users) were created which almost independently developed information systems. Conflicting interests, overlaps and internal competition were the order of the day, with all the consequences involved.

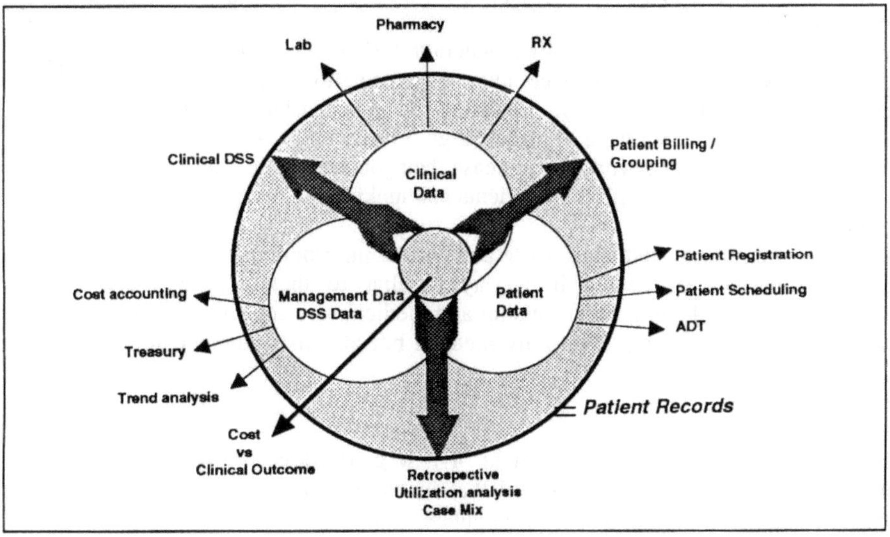

Fig. 2.2 Global view of a hospital information system (HIS) : spheres of interest and application domains; DSS, Decision Support Systems; APT, Appointment

Today, the first task of a hospital from a management point of view is to operate as a *global company,* and this is the way some hospital managers define it. It needs to share information in all medical and other departments. This information is neither administrative nor medical. It is "*hospital information*" and is the mutual combination of patient demographic, medical and administrative data (Fig.2.2). Five major strategies are important to achieve this:

- o To keep *patient care requirements above administrative matters* and generate financial information as a byproduct of patient care activity, not as the end product
- o To have *a secure, reliable, on-line clinical information system*

- To connect and manage *distributed information resources*
- To *facilitate* the hospital use of *information technology* and introduce new technology wherever cost effective
- To establish *stewardship for implementation* of enterprise-wide solutions and standards

2.3 Objectives and Requirements for the Clinical User

Currently nursing operations are still largely not computerised. In fact, first generation HIS have forgotten the real users in hospitals. Nurses, whose salaries account for 30% -40% of a hospital's operating budget, spend 25%- 40% of their time performing clinical and especially communication tasks as indicated by studies since the 1960s. They still use clipboards for recording measurements and observations, although many of these measurements come from automated sources. Repetitive transcriptions, telephone and paper communications are the primary processes to improve because nurses spend too much time on paper instead of being with the patient.

An important reason to convert first generation HIS into fully integrated clinical information systems is to enhance nursing information management. A nursing shortage is seen in every country. Realising that this can lead to a reduction in the quality of patient care, we have to place a high priority on the nurse's job satisfaction. Freeing nurses from paperwork can increase their job satisfaction, as well as enabling them to spend more time with their patients and making the nurse's contribution more visible.

Physicians and nurses need appropriate and correct information at the right place and the right time and presented in a way familiar to them. They have urgent communication needs with other nursing and medical services and ancillary services (laboratory, radiology,etc.). Not only medical but also management information is needed.

The second reason for the development of new generation HIS is the desire for a longitudinal electronic medical record that would follow a patient from birth and register all inpatient and outpatient encounters. Such a system can give access to all demographics, nursing records, medications, physician orders and patient progress. A synergy would be created with compatible systems to support multiple health care users and help them to manage patient information. Every user would be encouraged to contribute his particular information, and no user must enter all of it. For instance, many elements in the electronic medical record can be used and controlled by several persons within the hospital. If we take a closer look at patient medication :

- A medication is *ordered* by a *physician* (medication, dosage, usage)
- This medication is *prepared* by a *pharmacist* (delivery time, contra-indications)
- The medication is *delivered* by *nurses* (intake, time), and
- The charges are registered by an *administrative* clerk (cost).

The third reason supporting this development is the pressure towards a more cost-effective health care. Although health care is priceless in terms of its benefit to individuals, modern medicine has a price that society must pay. Even if technology can save lives and speed up diagnosis and treatments, the large capital investment required for sophisticated technical equipment, combined with high operating costs, has to be recovered. *As everywhere else, technology is partly the solution and partly the problem.* MRI, CT and position emission tomography (PET) reveal aspects of the body never seen before. Lasers, lithotriptors, pacemakers and implantable defibrillators treat conditions that otherwise might require drugs or major surgery. In the case of HIS, cost effectiveness will come from an open architecture providing not only the facilities for integrating multiple vendors but also creating a synergy among its different parts.
One technical challenge is that of creating standard communications protocols, such as defined by HL-7 (Health Level Seven Standards Committee) and IEEE-MEDIX standards (Institute of Electrical and Electronics Engineers, Medical Data Interchange Committee), which will probably evolve in the coming years.

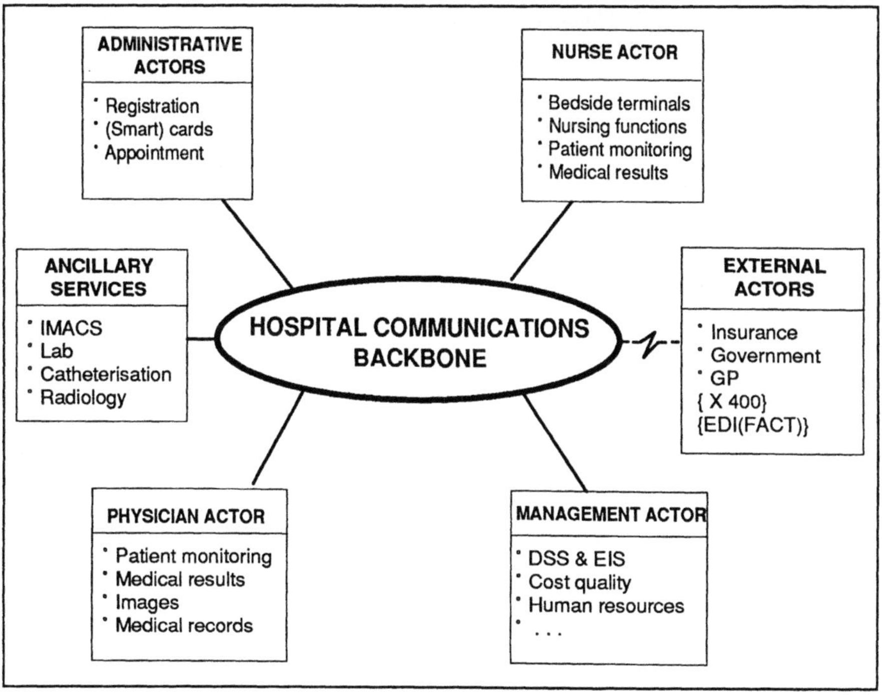

Fig.2.3 Logical representation of the integrated hospital of the future depicting the main actors in the health care environment; main functions and important features

2.4 Objectives and Requirements from the Patient

Due to the fact that there is a greater sense of well-being among people, the level of morbidity has decreased at all ages, and a greater life expectancy with a better quality of life is expected. Patients have high expectations of faster, less aggressive, non-

invasive and whenever possible more ambulatory care with preventative measures. However, there is a gap between the resources that are available and the expectations. In addition, the mobility of people has increased tremendeously. The consequence is that patients receive care at different locations, from different health care providers or in various institutions. Thus, the need for hospitals to exchange medical information intramural and extramural and with patients at home has increased (Fig.2.3).
This combination of communication and information systems can help provide better care, at a lower cost, with reduced stays in hospital.

2.5. Objectives and Requirements from Health Care Authorities

Health care authorities at all levels are looking for less expensive care and need decision-making support tools to optimise the use of available resources.
Insurance organisations demand indications of quality, cost of diseases per unit of production as well as procedures to improve productivity.
Resource management systems (case mix management, clinical audit, budgeting and monitoring, productivity management) are elements to make more strategic and operational decisions in a context of scarce resources.

3

The Genesis of Hospital Information Systems : A Look at the Past and the Future.

3.1 Introduction

Over the past 30 years the development of HIS has occurred in different phases. This chapter takes a look at the past and present aspects of HIS and the elements that will be of influence in shaping the future of the next generation of HIS.
It is clear that health care organisations may vary from country to country and that even within a country hospitals may vary substantially, so it is obvious that this review is a general one, focussing on the most important trends.
As stated, present HIS are targetted at efficient hospital and patient management rather than at patient care. Some installations have replaced medical records by electronic systems accessible by physicians, and there are strong indications that this will become commonplace.

3.2 First Generation

In the 1960s the first generation of HIS focussed primarily on automating more administrative functions where information processing systems were easy to install. Almost all of them were designed around central systems and were limited by the capabilities of computing hardware and software available at that time.
These HIS used batch-oriented mainframe computers to produce patient bills, salaries and financial outputs. Generally, first-generation HIS were technology driven, although medical benefits were stressed from the beginning.

In the 1970s the first on-line applications made their entrance for admission/discharge/transfer (ADT) systems. Hospitals started to use multiple computer systems. Laboratory systems appeared and were installed most of the time on a separate minicomputer system having little integration with the central system as the intention was to gather patient data as close as possible to the source. No or little integration was available around these "islands of automation".
Due to the architecture of computers many systems displayed degradation in performance when placed under heavy loads, resulting in unacceptable response times. The user interface for these systems was often very cumbersome and limited by the display technology available at the time.
Hierarchical menu-driven display structures often require from the user intensive question and routing dialogues to retrieve information. They were due to third-generation computer languages rigid extensive programming.

In summary, first-generation HIS can be characterised as locally developed applications and almost dedicated to administrative functions. Hospitals built their data processing and communications infrastructure one brick at a time, and they often bought different bricks (Table 3.1)

3.3 Present Situation in Europe

Present day HIS are still mostly administrative-oriented, but in most hospitals they cross departmental and speciality boundaries. In contrast to the first systems, they are management oriented, based on communication networks to integrate various sub-systems.
Initially, few software vendors could satisfy all departmental needs and provide a comprehensive HIS, except for ADT and finance. Therefore, many hospitals had their first encounters with distributed processing in the late 1970s. Those distributed systems ran their applications independently of the central mainframe and later sent their results. Many specialised software vendors have greatly improved the efficiency of ancillary systems such as laboratory, pharmacy, intensive care unit (ICU).
Two approaches have now emerged to satisfy most hospital information processing needs. One is the centralized approach oriented around a single database, with all hospital applications operating on the same database (examples : BAZIS/ Leiden, the Netherlands; AZ-VUB/Brussels, Belgium; DIOGENE/Geneva, Switserland), the second is revealing and is the distributed approach communicating data between a number of dedicated systems, (DIOGENE, AZ-VUB).
Most European HIS were initially developed for a group of regional hospitals or a single large hospital. Examples of such exist in many countries such as the Netherlands (BAZIS), France (Staff), Spain (Insalud/Dias), Germany (AKDB), Belgium (Caritas). However, it has been very difficult to install these systems over a large geographic area or in another country. Commercial HIS vendors have faced similar problems, with the exception of a few large American companies. The difficulties reside mostly in the cost of software changes to adapt to local administrative and clinical practices, in addition to the support of multi-lingual systems.

3.4 Next Generation

At large hospitals the use of HIS is becoming routine. Health care professionals have also changed their attitude towards information technology, partly by demystification of personal computing and also due to financial pressures. Consequently, systems become gradually more clinically oriented, first with independent systems and then with HIS designed to support communication of medical information. The trend towards clinical information systems requires integration of departmental systems. Integrated environments have been widely accepted as a way to increase productivity. An integrated environment is a system in which all users beneficiate from the same user interface; it is a system that unites all scattered data files into one logical view and finally it provides users with the facility to share common functions.

Table 3.1 Phases in automation in hospitals since the 1960s. The four paradigms of Computing; LSI, Large Scale Integration; VLSI, Very Large Scale Integration; RDBMS, Relational Data base Management System; OODBMS, Object Oriented Data base Management System; ADT, Admission, Discharge, Transfer; LAB, Laboratory

DECADE	1960s	1970s	1980s	1990s
Computer				
Processing	Batch	On-line & Transactional	Desktop	Networks & Cooperative Computing
Hardware	Mainframe	Mini & Terminals	PC's and Workstations	Portable
Languages	Assembler Fortran	Cobol PL/1	C Pascal Prolog	Object Oriented
Technology	Medium-scale Integration	LSI	VLSI	Ultra large Scale
User				
Interface	None/ Line by line	Character Terminal	Windowing Pointing devices	Multi-media
Profile	Experts	Computer Scientists	Individuals	Groups
Status	Submissive	Dependent	Independent	Freedom
Data				
Type	Alphanumeric	Text	Graphical & Images	Voice & Multimedia
File system	Flat-file	Index-sequential Direct	Database: Codasyl - RDBMS	DDBMS OODBMS
Scope	Centralized Multi-purpose	Decentralized Single-purpose	Integration	Decentralized Multi-purpose
Applications				
Nature	Calculation	Access	Representation and Search	Knowledge & Communication
Focus on	Administration	Capturing charges	Optimizing management	Providing patient care
Scope	Centralized-Multi-purpose	Decentralized-Single-purpose	Integration	Decentralized-Multi-purpose
Portfolio	Financial	LAB, ADT	Radiology, Order Entry, pharmacy	Medical & Decision support

On the other side, because of the complexity of implementing health care IS, the number of self-made systems will decrease while the number of vendor made systems will continue to rise (Fig.3.1).

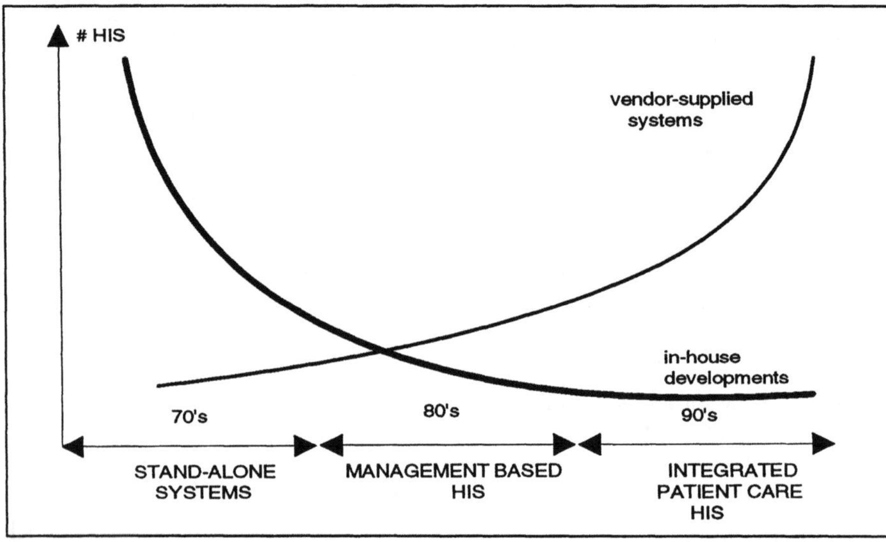

Fig. 3.1 Evolution of vendor supplied systems versus in-house developments of hospital information systems (HIS)

Experiences demonstrate that no single vendor can assemble the expertise and tools needed to build all dedicated departmental medical systems. Instead, developers concentrate on a few functional areas, and hospitals will continue to install a variety of systems. Some technical advances have made it easier for hospitals to install and support software packages from multiple vendors, and it is a fact that during the past few years offers of comprehensive systems have decreased. On the other hand, there is a rise in the number of companies focussing on market niches.

Therefore, the primary role for the next generation of HIS will be to centralise patient information originating from heterogeneous, multi-vendor departmental systems and to replace the current manual medical record. To achieve this goal, the system must automate most record-keeping activities of physicians and nurses.

As it is obvious that IS are more efficient and accurate when data are entered at the source, the idea of bedside terminals has been explored for patient-centred clinical information systems. However, only carefully designed user interfaces, extensive availability and short response times will encourage physicians and nurses to use the system daily. Otherwise, they will continue to use paper and pen for manual medical records.

Hospitals which have experienced decentralisation for some years are realising that they have a variety of information systems but few *hospital-wide* applications and no *comprehensive view* of their organisation (e.g. in terms of delivery of management information). Similar to large multinational companies which operate several markets but keep a global view, hospitals are in fact also global companies for which agreement on common cultural and technical standards is essential.

In fact, the main challenge for the next generation of HIS is to provide integration of patient information for nurses and physicians in their routine practice. The main problem that arises is *how do you decentralise and at the same time keep strong controls ?* The concept of Open Systems is gaining momentum. Cost-efficiency and openness that prevent vendors to "lock in" their customers are the real benefits of the Open Corporation. Technical advances allow decentralisation of processing, fault tolerance, user friendly interfaces and short response times. These fit better the nature of human beings.
In the future, hospitals will be more decentralised, but they will require more coordination. About Mainframes: there are two schools of thought, one predicts the end of the Mainframe era others contends that the Mainframe will always reside as a central data repository. The real answer is nor black or white but can be declared by the changing role of the Mainframe. In fact the Mainframe changed its role from a *total* computing resource delivery system to a less important role. It becomes one of several computer nodes connected to the network. One notices today a reduction of the market share for mainframes, but not a disappearance [FRE91].
The concept of downsizing -often initiated outside MIS- is based on four basic issues: cost savings, technological advances, the changing role of the end-user and improvements in networking (Fig.3.2).

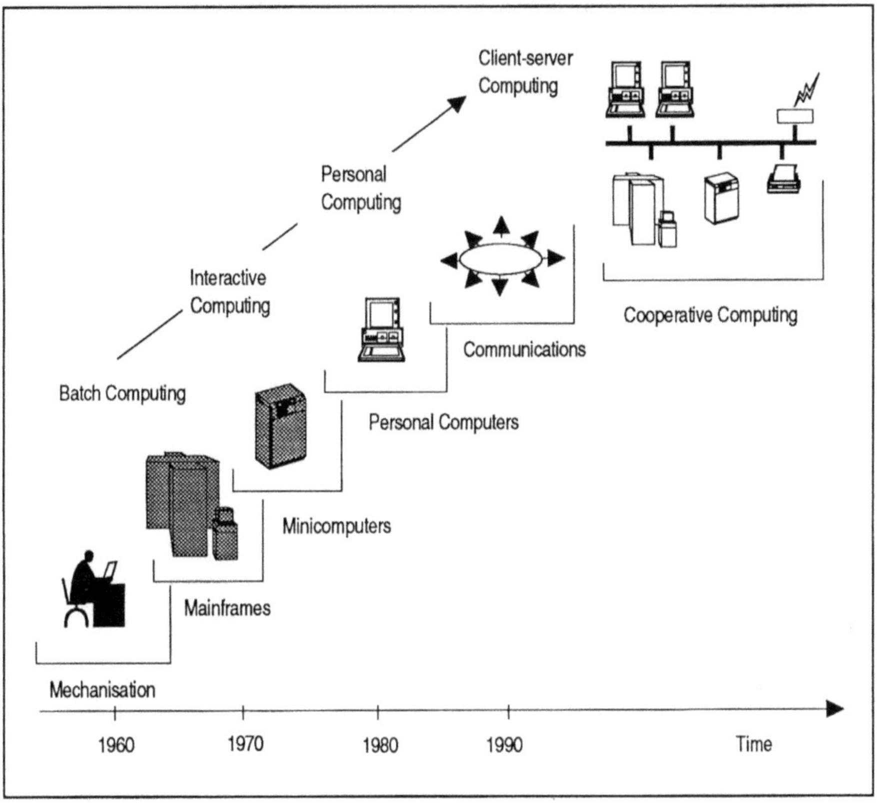

Fig. 3.2 Evolution of computing from the late 1960s until the 1990s in hospitals : influence of an evolving technology

In summary, the next generation of HIS will be built around the medical record and support nursing activities. It will ensure the production of managerial information as a byproduct, in contrast with present systems. They will be more user driven.
The IT department will evolve to an integrator and coordinator role because of hospital requirements and technological evolution. It will coordinate multi-disciplinary teams, and as a technology expert, it will recommend standards and global directions.

On the technical side HIS in the future will change from a central multipurpose system or dedicated (single purpose) *systems to a network of distributed systems combining the advantages of both approaches*: ***the era of cooperative hospital computing is revealing.***

In the following sections an architecture for the next generation of HIS will be discussed. From a technical viewpoint this may be viewed as a series of layers, each with a specific functional purpose, each supporting higher layers of the structure. To the greatest extent possible, every layer will be independent of the others to permit changes without disturbing the overall structure. Each layer provides a key component of the functionality needed to build a distributed but integrated HIS.

4

Computer System Fundamentals

4.1 Computer Generations : Past, Present and Future

The history of computers started with a census. In 1890 Herman Hollerith, the father of the punch card, built the equipment for the counting, sorting and tabulating of the results of the census, in the USA. It was not until the 1930s that the sub-functions (punching, reading, counting and sorting) were combined into one system. The whole was connected with the punch card equipment and came under central control.

Shortly before and during the Second World War the developments in the FRG and the USA were closely connected with military applications. Towards the end of the 1940s Von Neumann, a mathematician at the American Institute of Applied Science, together with a number of colleagues developed the architecture of the current computer systems. The program is filed into the memory of the computer. The machine has possibilities for the control of its own processing, the carrying out of calculations and simple input and output operations. It also has a small memory from which the commands and data could be loaded into the registers of the processor, after which these could be processed in the right order. This architecture proved to be extraordinarily successful and could easily stand the test of time, for at present computers still work for the greater part with the same concept. This mode of operation developed into the so-called Von Neumann principle. Until recently, all computers had been based on this principle, the microcomputers (the personal computer, PC) as well as the mini-computers and the bigger brothers, the mainframes. The Von Neumann machine can only process one program at a time, but as a result of multi-programming and time-sharing techniques, the user gets the impression that he is able to work on it with several other users at the same time.

Very recently, a completely different architecture for parallel computers was designed, namely, neural networks which will be capable of validating information and solving concrete problems. Besides, the fifth generation of informatics is said to be even more userfriendly than its predecessors. The old family Von Neumann computer has reached to its fourth generation. About every 10 years a new computer generation comes into being (Tables 4.1, 4.2).

A **first-generation computer** is to be recognised by its size. The monster, built around electron tubes, had to be placed in a room with a height of two floors. In order to cool the whole off a little, an air current was blown through it permanently. The central memory of the computer consisted of magnetisable iron rings: ferrite cores. The original computer software programs have been written in machine language (a series of little zeros and little ones) which have been baked in as hardware proper. Whenever one is talking about the first-generation computer hardware, one can safely speak about "ironmongery". They were exclusively used as calculating machines.

From the 1960s, during the **second computer generation**, electron tubes were replaced by transistors. At the same time the first real computer language was introduced: the assembler language. Files were created which are supplied to the program separately. In these files the information prepared for computer use was stored. Usually this was done by means of a form: a list on which the contents of the information could be recorded in recognisable zones thanks to the indication via section headings. For the storage of files one began to turn to the familiar computer-accessible data carriers: the punch card, punch tape, magnetic tape.
In the second generation the computer became "all purpose", it could cope with all tasks. Besides calculation, it was also supplied with administrative functions.

The **third computer generation,** born during the 1970s, is, strangely enough, a product of the *"golden Sixties"*. Under the pressure of constant economic growth, things were suddenly seen from a much more ambitious viewpoint. The result was that computing centres shot up like mushrooms. The current appearance of informatics was mainly defined by this development. At the beginning of the 1970s there appeared within the too spacious computer rooms the standard computer peripheral devices: magnetic tape drives, terminals, printers, etc. This peripheral equipment is still used at present, and has hardly changed its appearance.
Toward the end of the decade the general use of the *chip* materialised as well. The process of miniaturization and increase of capacity of the data equipment was started off. A chip is a miniaturised memory element consisting of integrated circuits embedded in a silicon semiconductor. The basic raw material for chips is silicon oxide, which is extracted from very pure sand. At that time, *mini computers* appeared on the scene. First employed as process computers exclusively designed for process control, later on they too became "all purpose". In the field of software, higher programming languages like FORTRAN, ALGOL, COBOL and PL1 were developed. Concurrently the first data bases, inspired by the much larger access and filing possibilities of magnetic discs, were designed. The third-generation software was, moreover, characterised by an initial, though timid, interest in the methodical development of data systems. The methodologies had a phased approach, were practical and structured from bottom upwards. Also, telecommunication at the informatics level got into its stride. Real-time, time sharing and other multi-programming techniques, solely contributing to user friendliness, were applied. The involvement of the end-user was encouraged only to a very limited extent. However, in spite of all the new technology, the computer still did not reach the man in the street.

It is only during the **fourth computer generation** that the actual end-user of the computer is given proper attention. In the field of hardware the final user is

momentarily overwhelmed with a complex choice of personal computers and work stations.
Miniaturisation and increase of capacity continued: smaller chips with bigger performances are made. By way of illustration, the size of the storage capacity corresponding to the storage of one million of units (1 megabyte) amounted to $11m^3$ in 1959, while in 1984 this capacity had been reduced to $8cm^3$. In the field of cost reduction the same spectacular developments occurred: what, in 1950 was still an "expensive machine", taking up a whole room, is now surpassed in capacity by the cheapest pocket calculator, of which the most expensive element is the small battery of 1.5 V.
Besides very sophisticated graphic screen workstations, laser and ink-jet printers make their entry. Telematics applications give a new dimension to remote computer control. Large network systems are set up, there is the relative success of videotex systems (Minitel), and there is the Telefax rage.
"Ready-made software" is at our disposal. Apart from the almost traditional word processing, we are offered, among other things, electronic mail, database systems, calendar administration, decision making systems, electronic files. In parallel, two sorts of computer languages are successful: Pascal, ADA and "C" (offshoots from third-generation "higher computer languages") and the so-called 4GL languages like UNIFACE, ACCELL, FOCUS, MAPPER, JAM and LINC which, contrary to their predecessors, are of the non-procedural type. Characteristic of the 4GL languages and methodologies are their data orientation, their iterative course and their top-down approach. For the user the system will be easier to handle. And if these fourth generation software tools are applied efficiently, a considerable increase of productivity may be the result. The designing, developing, testing, implementing and maintaining of system relations can be supported via Computer Aided Systems Engineering or CASE.

With the **fifth computer generation** a completely new type of computer is announced: the parallel computer or neural computer. It is composed of different parallel-connected processing units, which are linked to each other like the synapses in our nervous system. They are the "grain of sand" in the brain, and yet they still remain far distant from the human brain. Nature is not anywhere near being overtaken, not even as far as compactness is concerned. One does calculate in gigabits and giga-instructions per second (1 giga = one billion) it is true, but a human chromosome contains an estimated 20 gigabits of information. A respectable supercomputer remains inferior to our brain matter. After 30 years of life, the human memory still contains many hundreds of gigabits. Compared with all this, neural computers amount to nothing, not even in case the fifth generation of hardware is equipped with artificial intelligence software so that it can reason, associate and learn. As forerunners of this fifth generation "knowledge base" systems there are expert systems and other decision-making tools, whose concept is still being designed. They especially aim to support of the average system user. Other notable novelties are, among other things: the Josephson connections, the optronics (optic electronics, of which the optical disc and the optic fibre are the most striking representatives), the integration of data, image and sound via multi-functional work stations included in integrated networks (ISDN, value added networks).

Table 4.1 Overview of computer generations and their relationship to new software developments

	Software				Involvement	
GENERATION	**Languages**	**Information Access Method**	**Engineering**	**System Software**	**Usage**	**Main Actors**
I	Machine languages	Sequential	Nihil	Proprietary	Passive and exclusive	Hardware constructor
II	Symbolic assembly	Sequential (SAM)	Process oriented	Proprietary	Account-control Administrative	Programmer
III	Procedural : FORTRAN ALGOL COBOL PL/1	Direct/ISAM Database -Hierarchical - Network	Process oriented Phased approach Bottom-up	Proprietary Multiprogramming TOS DOS	Broader scope Management-oriented	Software engineers
IV	C, PASCAL ADA Not procedural: FOCUS, MAPPER,ACCEL, UNIFACE Artificial Intelligence	Database - relational Documentation SW Packages Decision support	Iterative Top-down Users involved CASE tools Expert systems Artificial Intelligence	Virtual memory OS MS DOS (PC) MVS (IBM) BS2000 (SIEMENS) VMS (DEC) UNIX	Cooperative computing User-friendly (all knowledge domain information center)	Information scientists Reliable end-users
V	Natural language	OO-DBMS Knowledge base	User centered		Towards all users	All end-users

Table 4.2 Overview of computer generations and their relation with new hardware developments

	CPU			Peripherals			(Tele) Communications		
GENE-RATION	**Type**	**Circuit**	**Memory Internal**	**Memory External**	**Printers**	**Terminals**	**Medium**	**Link (net)**	**Type of Operations**
I	Mainframe (Von Neumann)	Vacuum tube	Electro-mechanical Ferrite			Console typewriter			Batch
II	Mainframe (Von Neumann)	Transistors		Magnetic tape card drum	Chain	Console typewriter			Batch
III	IBM 360 Mainframe mini (Von Neumann)	I.C.	Chips ROM RAM PROM EPROM	Magnetic card tape disk	Matrix Daisywheel	Teleprinter Telex Terminal Mark sensing	Cable of copper	Telex Public (dial-up) Leased	Conversational Real-time Time-sharing
IV	IBM 370 Mainframe Supermini Micro PC (Von Neumann)	VLSI	VMOS Bubble	Winchester disc Floppy disc Streamer IC card	Photocom-position Thermal Ink-jet Laser	Badge Telefax Workstation Image workst. Optical reader (Language recognition)	Cable of copper Beam Connection	Videotex Packet-Switching (DCS)	Network (LAN, WAN, MAN)
V	Neural networks	Josephson circuits		Optical disc High density		Integrated work station (ISDN)	Optical fibre		ISDN network

4.2 Concepts of Computer Systems

4.2.1 The Hardware Level

Almost all computer systems produced in the past 40 years are based on the Von Neumann architecture. John Von Neumann designed a computer architecture consisting of five entities the input unit, the output unit, the arithmetic and logical unit (ALU), the memory and the control unit (Fig.4.1). This architecture, based on the "stored program concept" enables instructions and data to be stored in the same internal memory unit and processed by the ALU in the same way.
The computer executes the program instructions at a certain speed (clock speed, machine cycles). The main memory holds program instructions and data. These find every instruction to be executed next in the instruction counter (address) and places (instruction fetch) the content of this instruction in the instruction register.
The next phase (execution phase) is the execution of the instruction stored in the instruction register by the ALU, copying in the meantime the address of the next instruction into the instruction counter.
The problem of this type of architecture is that data and instructions use the same paths in both directions and bottlenecks (waiting queues) occur under heavy load. Alternatives to solve this problem are supplied by techniques such as "parallel computing" that result in an non-linear performance increase, or the use of solid data cache memories that stand in the same relation to internal memory as internal memory to the concept of "virtual memory" on disk. (Virtual memory, is memory residing on magnetic disk and extending the amount of storage in main memory. The backing-storage area is known as swapping area)

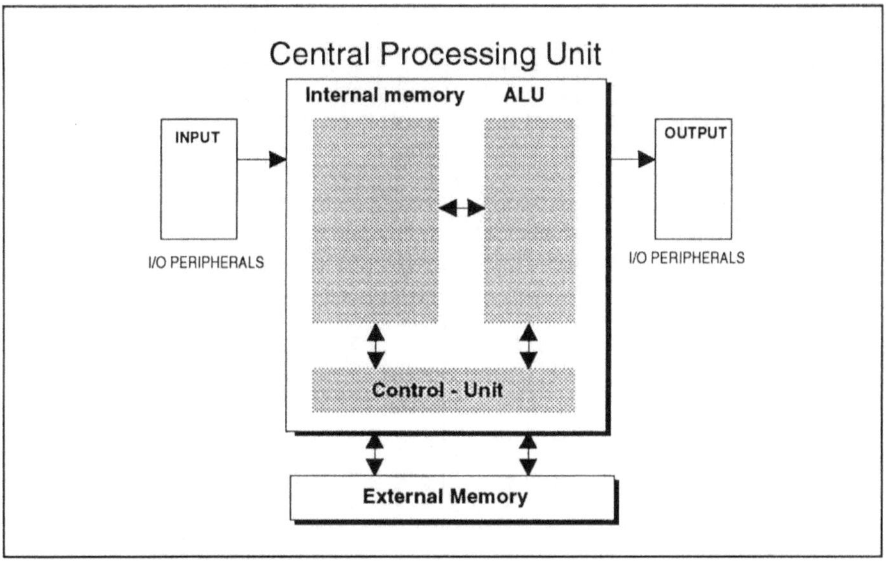

Fig.4.1 General architecture of computer systems, based on the Von Neumann architecture ALU,arithmetic and local unit

Some important features determining the performance of a computer system are :

- the *bitpath:* indicates how wide a "chunk" of information the processor can handle at one time
- the *clock speed*: indicates how fast the CPU processes data internallly
- the *bus architecture*: indicates the way the processor interacts with and is connected to system memory (memory bus) and input/output (I/O) peripherals (I/O bus and expansion slots) such as fixed disk drive or network interface

Most personal computers use a single-bus architecture, with all internal and external components linked to a single bus line, by plugging the appropriate interface into an open slot. The basic function of this interface is translating between internal and external data forms. This architecture creates a number of problems with a multiple-user system.

To eliminate bottleneck problems found in single-bus architecture some constructors separate memory and I/O paths, optimising in that way the data transfers between the CPU and the internal memory, improving system performance. Hereby the I/O control is transferred to a special device (I/O controller, channel) rather than wasting the main processor's time. This I/O controller contains its own processor and can work simultaneously with the CPU. Completion and execution of I/O commands are sent over the control bus, data over the data bus.

Another method to improve the system performance (i.e. data access from magnetic disk) and speed up transactions is by locating data quickly in "cache" memory rather than the slower system memory (dynamic RAM-DRAM). The cache memory consists of a cache memory controller and a certain amount of dedicated high speed memory (high-speed static RAM). The cache controller assists the processor in managing memory interactions, and the cache memory therefore stores frequently requested data or instructions improving the so-called "hit-ratio". Ideally, a cache contains a copy of the most heavily accessed portions of main memory in order to obtain a high "hit" rate.

A register can be thought of as a storage location within the CPU(microprocessor), from which data can be read or into which they can be stored temporarily. Some types of registers are general purpose registers, instruction registers, instruction counter, work register.

4.2.2. Operating Systems

No computer system is able to work without an "operating system" (OS). The core of the OS, the kernel, is loaded each time the computer is turned on, and reacts to interrupts (from external devices) and to requests from other processes. The routine that loads the kernel (OS) into main memory is called a boot (*bootstrap*).In general terms the OS is the interface between the applications (designed by users) and the hardware (designed by the manufacturers). The main features of an OS are :

- *Supervising and controlling computer resources* such as memory,disks, tapes, printers, monitors,etc
- *Scheduling tasks* in order to optimise CPU performance
- *File management*:allows users to perform allocation and naming of files and directory management.
- *Monitoring user requests*

- *Providing some general tools* to streamline the operations of the system : back-up, recovery, spooling, caching, etc.

We can divide the OS into two strategically important operating systems :

- *Single-user.* Only one application runs at a time. It consists of the following modules: Users communicate with an OS through a command processor. The input/output control system (IOCS) translates logical I/O requests into physical I/O operations. Files and programs are accessed through the file system.For example, MS-DOS

MS-DOS is a single-user,single-tasking operating system whose limitations are a maximum of 640K/application without expanded memory support.It can only address 1 MB memory, two addressing techniques are available : (a) **expanded memory** originally developed to increase memory addressability in a single-tasking environment. It "outwits" MS-DOS and allow applications to break the OS 1 MB addressing barrier; (b) **extended memory,** the memory added above 1 MB, extending up to 256 MB typically used by non-DOS applications.

- *Multi-user.* In a multi-user environment several application programs reside in main memory simultaneously (i.e.*multiprogramminng*), but the CPU is only active for one application program at a time,in that way reducing the time a resource is idle. There are two primary modes of operation: batch multiprogramming and interactive multiprogramming (also called "timesharing"). The later deals with sessions, initiated with a logon and ended with a logoff.

  A typical multiprogramming OS, contains modules to perform the following functions : memory manager (e.g.:virtual memory principle), resource manager (e.g.: deadlock), command processor, scheduler (time management), input/output control system, spooler (a module that collects jobs on a disk for further processing), file management system. For example, UNIX.

UNIX is often called a "de facto standard operating system". Hundreds of different vendors offer nowadays UNIX-based systems and software, and the UNIX market is still growing. The emergence of UNIX as a popular operating system and combining it with networking to build a system that is network oriented and "*open*" (*concept of open systems*) is gaining momentum especially in Europe and is closely linked : (a) to the development of a new generation of processors : RISC processors, Motorola 680X0 and INTEL 80X86 processors; (b) to the urgent need for standardization, scalability and portability, preventing vendors to "lock in" their customers.

Because UNIX is available on mainframes, mini-computers, work stations and personal computers and supports system-to-system communications (in a network), it makes them very suitable for hospitals.

The key features of a UNIX system are :

- *Portability,* the possibility of running on different computer systems. Besides the UNIX system itself, the applications software written for UNIX is also portable.
- *Multi-user operation,* UNIX is a multi-user system designed to support a group of simultaneous users.
- *Background processing,* provides a user with the facility to initiate a task and then proceed to other tasks.

- *Hierarchical file system,* organising the information in a hierarchical way reflecting the natural structure of data.
- *UNIX Shell,* a powerful command interpreter.
- *Pipes,* a well-known facility to combine several simple programs to perform more complex functions, eliminating the need for new software development.
- *UNIX utilities,* including several programs like : SORT, text processing, filters, spooling, editors.

4.2.3 MUMPS

MUMPS first developed at the Massachusetts General Hospital in Boston stands for Massachusetts General Hospital Utility Multi-Programming System. Although the language started in a hospital, many users are applying MUMPS to business. Originally developed for medical applications, the comprehensive string processing and information management syntax of MUMPS are important features contributing to its widespread use. It is most often used for on-line, interactive applications where immediate data retrieval and prompt response are of importance.

A wide variety of MUMPS application software is available in the public domain. The US Department of Health and Human Services supports the distribution and maintenance of the COSTAR (Computer Stored Ambulatory Record) system originally developed at Massachusetts General Hospital. This system contains modules for patient scheduling query and report generation.
A general purpose, database management system called "File Manager" is available through the MUMPS Users Group. This package of standard MUMPS routines was developed by the Veterans Administration and is currently used for patient identification, pharmacy, laboratory, pathology, mental health, dietetics, radiology, nuclear medicine and administrative systems. The package can be used as a stand-alone, programmerless system or as a set of utility programs for use in system development [MUG 84].

The standard MUMPS computer language is a general purpose, interpretive, high-level programming language designed for interactive data management applications. Despite its interpretative nature, current implementations of MUMPS permit good throughput as compared with other languages. Users report that response time for most applications is immediate.
Its string-handling features and hierarchically structured database suit it for medical, word processing and business applications where large, complex files must be designed, constructed and maintained. MUMPS has a comprehensive set of commands, functions and operators which facilitate the manipulation of textual data, and the use of string subscripts speeds application development.

Programs can be transported between different computers running standard MUMPS. This means that the user is not restricted to a single hardware manufacturer or software producer. A number of competing alternative suppliers of standard MUMPS systems are available for each category or size of system, from the microcomputer level up through the middle ranges of capability to the large mainframe level. Other well-known commercial systems based on MUMPS are ANTRIM, SUNQUEST (Laboratory Systems), SMS and MEDITECH (hospital applications). Although MUMPS has been quite successful in the past, we see that many organisations and vendors nowadays are gradually replacing MUMPS-driven applications with applications oriented towards newer software tools and less cumbersome displays.

4.2.4 File Systems and the Future

HIS are characterised as data-intensive applications that manage and share large amounts of multi-media data among many users: alphanumerical data (e.g. laboratory data, patient demographic data), graphical data (e.g. ECG,EEG), text data (e.g. discharge letters), images (e.g. RX),etc. File systems are thus extremely important in any software system.
A file system is a collection of files stored on a storage device, usually a disk. There are two main types of storage, primary and secondary (primary storage, RAM memory; secondary storage, megnetic disks). The logical representation of a file is very different from its physical representation. The logical representation is what you see on the display when you retrieve the file. The physical representation is how the file is actually organised on the disk. Its content will usually be scattered around the disk.

UNIX file system: UNIX provides a file system with hierarchically ordered files and directories. At the top of the hierarchy is a directory. It may contain the names of the files and/or the names of other directories. The file system divides the disk into 1MB blocks. The contents of a UNIX file may be scattered on a disk. When you access a file in a UNIX system the UNIX file system fetches the blocks in the proper order, resulting in the logical representation of your file. The I-node mechanism converts the physical representation to the logical.
The I-node (generally available in main memory) refers to data in the first ten blocks. If a file is longer than 10 blocks, the locations af subsequent data blocks are stored in an indirect block. The location of the indirect block is stored in the Inode (11th position). Beyond this limit UNIX handles files with a double-indirect (12th position in Inode) and triple-indirect block (13th position in Inode).

If we take a look at the file structure of most HIS, over 80% still use files or older database technology (hierarchical, network DBMS); only a few hospitals have moved to relational database management systems (RDBMS).
Since the early 1960s three types of file structures have emerged, flat files, record files and database management systems (Table 4.3).

Table 4.3 Comparison between classic file system, RDBMS and OODBMS

	CLASSICAL	RDBMS	OODBMS
Type	Record	Relational	Object
Model	Reduced data model	Data-model	Object model
DML	3GL	SQL 4GL	Object-oriented C++, Smalltalk,... 4GL - 5GL
Functionality	-	+	++
Flexibility	-	+	++
Performance	++	+	++
Productivity	-	+	+++
Security	-	+	+

DML, Data Manipulation Language; SQL, structured query language;
GL, Generation Language ; RDBMS, Relational Data Base Managment System;
OODBMS, Object Oriented Data Base Management System

Flat files the earliest method for storing data is in essence a long stream of bits that is read, written or updated, always starting at the beginning of the file and progressing until the end. Everything (information access, update, write, etc) which has to be done with the file you have to write yourself.

Record files are characterised by another granularity: they store the data in records, that is, a collection of fixed-length chunks, providing access to any of these records. These record files can be classified according to the type of access: sequential, index-sequential or direct (random).
They have good performance as they minimise the access time for secondary storage to maximise the information returned. All data must fit into those predefined, hard-coded data structures which are quite different from the real (world) structure of data. Therefore, they are characterised by a lack of flexibility, productivity and functionality. As data are tightly integrated with the application, it leads to data redundancy, and as a consequence the integrity of data held in more than one place is difficult to maintain. Moreover, one has to supply personally the recovery mechanism in case of hardware or software failure.

Database Management Systems (DBMS) on the contrary solve a lot of these problems, as they separate the data from the application. It should provide built-in, multi-user sharing, data independence, integrity and security mechanisms (back-up, recovery).
DBMS are characterised by the combination of seven basic services :

- Robust security
- Centralized data integrity (e.g. referential integrity: maintaining accurate database relationships)
- User and group management
- Permission management
- Storage mangement

- Online backup and restore
- Automatic crash recovery

Three types of database organisations have emerged since the late 1960s : hierarchical (father-child) DBMS (e.g. DL/1 and IMS from IBM), network DBMS (e.g. IDMS/R from CA) and for the present time a variety of relational DBMS (e.g. DB2 from IBM, ORACLE, Sybase, Informix).
The data manipulation language (DML) of commercial RDBMS language that permits uniform database access and data interchange is based on SQL (structured query language). The SQL versions are all "more or less" compatible with each other. At the same time, a lot of integrated fourth-generation languages have emerged with report writers and form builders that make it easy to prototype and build applications. Thus, what RDBMS offer in flexibility and productivity, they lack in performance, especially compared with classic file systems.

Distributed Database Management Systems *(DDBMS)*: As single-site databases on mainframes become too expensive, slow and limited hospitals will move from those central monolithic systems around mainframes toward a network of locally but globally accessible heterogeneous databases on different computer systems. This will lead to the emergence of distributed data base management systems (DDBMS).
In a truly distributed database environment, databases will be divided into horizontal and vertical fragments so that those pieces are physically located in the place where the data will be used, but logically look like one database to the user.
The most important requirement in achieving this distributed database system environment is the availability of a two-phase commit. A two-phase commit makes sure that the replication session is completed without interruption at each node of the network before the updates are committed to the network.

A new emerging trend is appearing in the early 1990s, the advent of **object oriented DBMS** (OODBMS) that aims to offer the best of previous file structures, namely, the superior performance of classic files with increased flexibility and productivity, accompanied by all related security and recovery mechanisms. Some commercial systems are already available, e.g. ONTOS, GEMSTONE, VERSANT, O2,....
The main difference between OODBMS and conventional databases is that object databases store objects, rather than tables, hierarchies or networks. Just as a relational database keeps track of different data organised in tables and their relationships, an object-oriented DBMS keeps track of different objects and their relationships.
By increasing the capability of software building blocks who offer more than just storing or retrieving data attributes object databases provide more features to represent complex application domains. Because OODBMS can encapsulate both data and behaviour within an object, they provide much richer data models and mechanisms to define complexity.
Our guess is that OODBMS have a bright future, but are still in their infancy as OODBMS-vendors keep modifying their strategies while many leading companies are conducting research at this time. In some years from now hospitals will realize that they need more than RDBMS.

In summary Fig.4.2 gives a representation of the application architecture from the 1970s towards the end of the 1990s, evolving in terms of place of user representation, process logic, semantic rules and file structure.

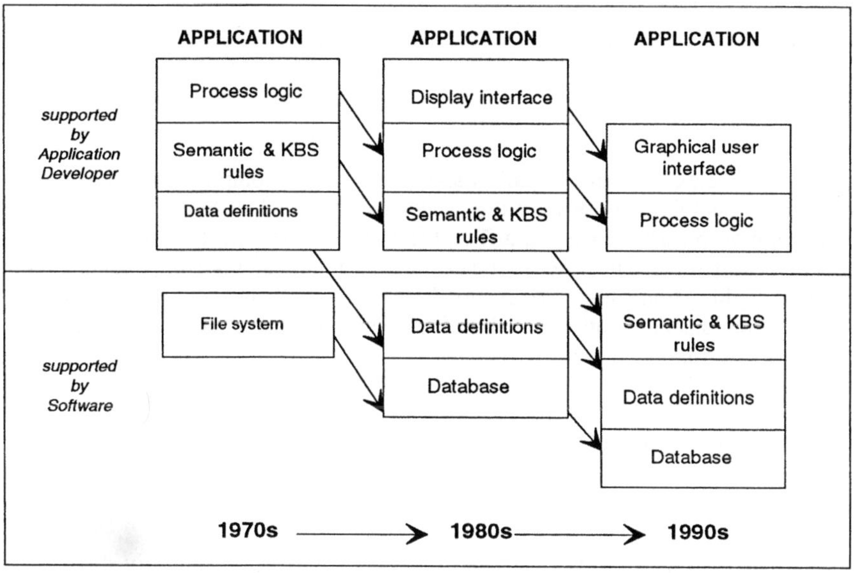

Fig.4.2 Representation of the application architecture evolving in terms of place of user representation, process logic, semantic rules and file structure

5

Standardization in Medical Informatics

As physicians are extreme individualists and medicine is a complex discipline and art continuously evolving towards more specialisation and sub-specialisation, the formalisation of this art is long and difficult [DEM 90]. Because the present tower of Babel of incompatible hardware, software and communications components cannot provide a stable foundation to respond to the challenge of integration and communication, standardization has therefore been recognized as a crucial issue in Health Care information systems (IS).

5.1 The Need for Standards

° ***Open Systems***

A decade ago, information was "locked-up" into big systems and very difficult to exchange with others. The rapid progresses in hardware technology and declining cost have resulted in distributed computing, the decentralisation of computing power to end-users. The breadth of choice offered to users has its drawbacks. The effectiveness of an IS depends also on the possibilities to communicate the information it contains. The capability of different vendors' products to communicate with each other or to use similar software has been well-recognised as limited.
For these reasons many organisations and vendors have decided to support the "*open system*" effort to develop global industry-wide standards for multi-vendor operating environment and networking. Open systems will change the IS community. The words "open" and "standards" will be on the lips of most IT managers in the 1990s. Two forces are driving open systems, firstly the cost effectiveness of multi-vendor products and secondly the need to connect current " islands of automation" existing in hospitals.

Open systems are systems that communicate with the outside world using standard protocols. Because they use standards, they can be interconnected and work in a multi-vendor environment. This is crucial, because no single vendor is able to meet the needs of the entire hospital. For a user who is configuring a computer system or network, the benefit of open systems is the freedom to choose the best component for each function from the offerings of all manufacturers. Overall advantages are: shared data, reduced integration costs, protection of software investments, reduced maintenance costs and greater freedom in selecting suppliers.
Three elements of open systems generating these benefits are:

- *Portability:* easy transportation of applications from one computer to another
- *Scalability:* choice of various systems optimised to perform specific functions
- *Interoperability*: interworking and data interchange between heterogeneous systems including some proprietary systems

The OSI Reference Model

The corner stone of open systems was set in 1983 when the International Organization for Standardization (ISO) published its Open Systems Interconnection (OSI) Reference Model (Fig.5.1). The OSI model organised communications functions into seven layers. The first three layers define communication between network nodes, the remaining four layers,"end-to-end"services. The layers may be split further into the transmission of data and the applications. An important reason for dividing the OSI model into seven layers is that having multiple layers enables standards and product developers to change one layer without affecting others. These layers are the following :

Interconnection layers

1.Physical: To provide the interface to the physical communication medium. It establishes the physical connection between computer equipment and the network.

2.Data-link: To transmit a stream of bits (frame) from one network node to another with indication of errors and a limited form of error correction. It packages the raw bits into *message frames* for transmission, and unpackages it on receipt.

3.Network: Concerned with *routing* and relaying between multiple sub-networks. It determines the most economical path (internetworking, bridges between networks) packets will take through the network.

Internetworking layer

4.Transport: To provide *end-to-end* transmission of data to a required quality of service (e.g. error-free). In fact it controls the transmission quality and ensures that the network facilities are used effectively. Depending on the class of transports available, this layer provides flow control, retransmission of lost or wrong data, and suppression of duplicated data.

5.Session: Establishes and controls the dialogue between the two systems. A connection between users is called a *session.* It acts as the liaison between user and network.

6.Presentation: Concerned with the *syntax* of information transfer between end-systems. It translates the messages to and from the format used on the network, so that it is comprehensible to the sending and receiving programs (varying data formats of different vendors).

7.Application: Concerned with the *semantics* of information transfer.
The application layers are responsible for receiving the message from the sending program in the first computer and handing it over to the receiving program of the second computer. It provides information services such as file transfer, remote file access.

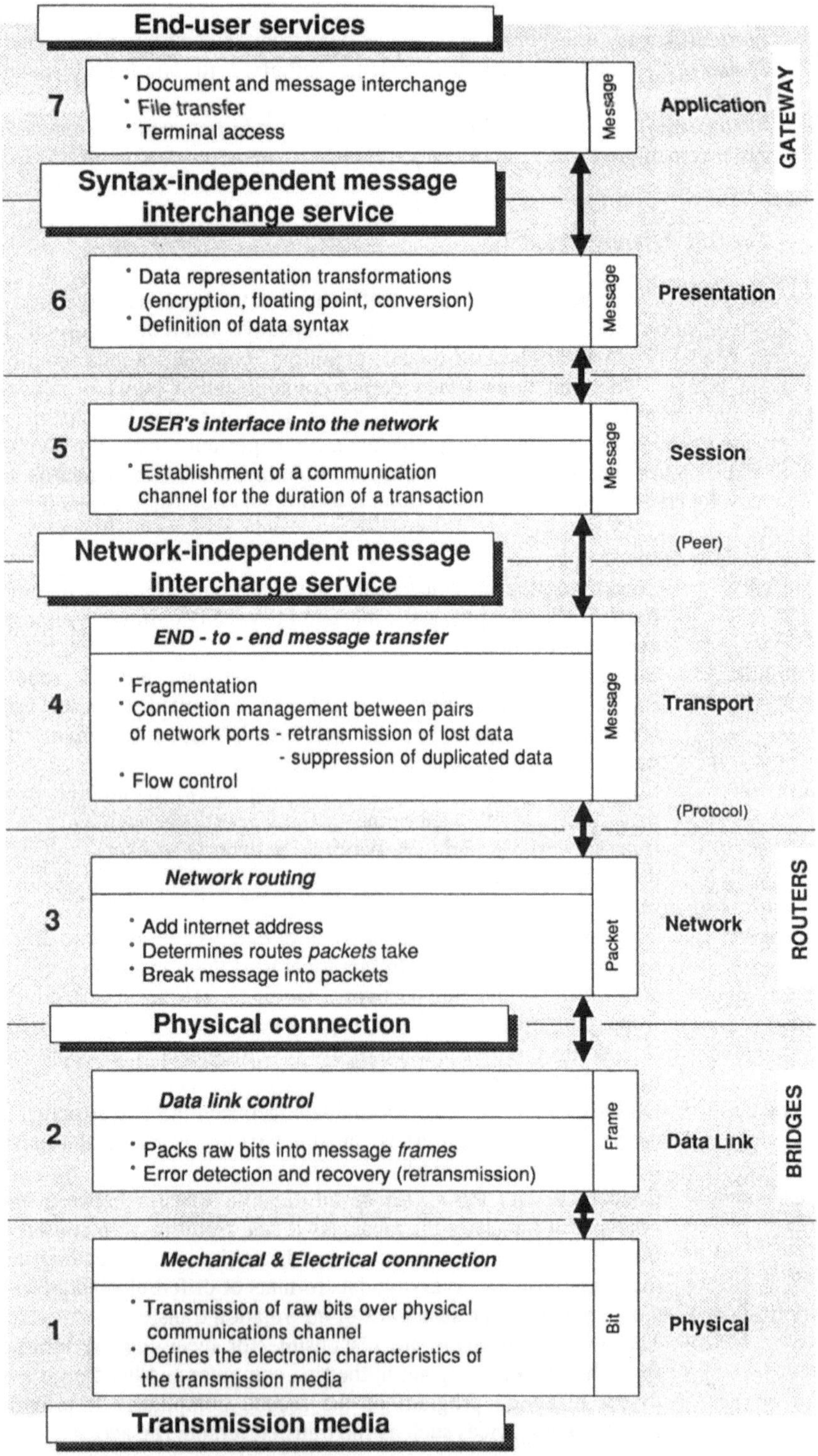

Fig.5.1 The Open Systems Interconnection (OSI) Reference Model

A major concept which derives from layering is "enveloping" that is, the data from each layer is encapsulated in protocol information by the next lower layer and so on. Each layer uses the services of the next lower layer and provides services to the layer above. No layer has access to any other layer except those immediately above or below it. These services are defined in outline in the Basic Reference Model and in detail in the relevant standard. An entity in any one layer may communicate with an entity in the corresponding layer of another OSI end-system using a protocol (i.e. logical communication between peer-entities). Any number of protocols may be defined in any one layer (i.e. physical layer protocols include X.21, CSMA/CD, Token Ring, Token Bus, FDDI).
Any organisation can have an open system by implementing these standard protocols. The movement toward this model as the global standard for open systems has steadily gained momentum.

5.2 Standardization Bodies

° ***International Standardization Bodies***
The most important standardization organisations at the international level are the International Standardization Organisation (ISO), the International Electrical Committee (IEC) covering the electrical and electronic hardware and the International Telegraph and Telephone Consultative Commitee (CCITT) covering telecommunications standards.
A special standard specifying how the base standards should be used to carry out particular functions are called functional or standards profiles and are covered on the international level by the Special Group on Functional Standardization (SGFS) which has a similar and corresponding organisation in Europe, the European Workshop for Open Systems (EWOS) (Table 5.1).
Furthermore, each country in Europe has its own national standardization bodies.

Table 5.1 Overview of important corresponding standardization organisations at the international and European level; ISO, International Organization for Standardization; IEC, International Electrotechnical Commission; CCITT, International Telegraph and Telephone Consultative Commission; SGFS, Special Group on Functional Standardization; CEN, Comité Européen de Normalisation; CENELEC, Comité Européen de Normalisation Electrotechnique; ETSI, European Telecommunications Standard Institute; EWOS, European Workshop on Open Systems; EGMED, Experts Group Medical

Standards	International level	European level
General	ISO	CEN ----> CEN TC 251
Electrical	IEC	CENELEC
Telecom	CCITT	ETSI
Functional	SGFS	EWOS ----> EWOS EGMED

° ***European Sandardization Bodies***

Early in 1990, CEN, the European Committee for standardization (responsible for the production of European standards which respond to the specific needs of the member states), with the aim of promoting an OSI (Open Systems Interconnection) reference model in Europe, set up a technical committee (TC) for the development of standards for health care informatics, designated CEN/TC 251 (medical informatics). A major goal of this committee is to develop standards for communication among independent, heterogeneous medical IS so that clinical and management data produced by one computer system (for example, a referral laboratory) could be transmitted to another system (e.g. the computer system in the ordering physician's practice). Such standards could lead to many improvements and efficiences in clinical care, research and administration. CEN believes that some of the issues related to such standardization require cooperation and harmonisation among world-wide efforts, including the many initiatives in the USA.

The creation of CEN/TC251 on the one hand officially responsible for the general coordination of all standardization activities in health care informatics, and the existing ambitious AIM (Advanced Informatics Medicine) research program established by the Commission of European Communities (CEC) will be very important to the future of medical informatics and to all further standardization efforts.

The TC 251 decided to constitute the following Working Groups; which cover the following items:

° Health Care Information Modelling and Medical Records
° Health Care Terminology, Semantics and Knowledge Bases
° Health Care Communications and Messages
° Medical Imaging and Multi-Media
° Medical Devices
° Health Care Security, Privacy, Quality and Safety
° Intermittently Connected Devices

Supported in this initiative by the CEC and the EFTA, ITSTC [CEN formed together with ETSI (European Telecommunication Standards Institute) a joint Information Technology Steering Committee] defined the principle of "functional standards" prepared by EWOS (European Workshop for Open Systems). A functional standard corresponds to a minimum basic set of sub-component standards, which are essential for the functioning of a particular application. EWOS not an official standardization organisation is an open forum, a satellite of CEN/CENELEC [DEM 91].

The European Federation of Medical Informatics (EFMI), comprised of nineteen national scientific societies for Medical Informatics in Europe, created a working group EFMI WG3 on standards in Health Care Informatics.

° ***USA Standardization Bodies***

In order for the European request from CEN/TC251 to obtain a unified USA response, ANSI worked with the US Department of Health and Human Services Agency for Health Care Policy and Research (AHCPR) in order to play a coordinating role for the different USA standard efforts.

At his meeting on March 11 in 1991, ANSI staff offered the suggestion that the health care informatics community may wish to consider the possibility of forming an *ANSI standards planning panel* to meet their needs for national coordination and to oversee USA input into international and regional efforts in this area. The proposed scope will be the definition of health care informatics standards covering the following domains:

1. Health care models and electronic health care records
2. Interchange of health care data, images, sounds and signals within and between organisations/practices
3. Health care codes and terminology
4. Communication with diagnostic instruments and health care devices
5. Representation and communication of health care protocols, knowledge and statistical databases
6. Additional areas of concern or interest with regard to health care information

The proposed purpose was explained as follows: [ANS 91]

To perform the functions of a Standards Planning Panel per Section C2.1 of the ANSI Procedures for the Development and Coordination of American National Standards in the field of healthcare informatics standards. Specifically, the planning panel would coordinate the word of the standards groups for healthcare data interchange and healthcare informatics (e.g., IEEE, ASTM, HL7, ACR/NEMA) and other relevant standards groups (e.g., X3, X12) toward achieving the evolution of a unified set of non-redundant, non-conflicting standards that are compatible with ISO and non-ISO communications environments. In addition, it shall interact with and provide input to CEN/TC 251 (Medical Informatics) in a coordinated fashion and explore avenues of international standards development (e.g., ISO and IEC).

5.3 Medical Standardization Groups

The most important medical standardization groups discussed hereafter are (Fig.5.2) : Health Level 7 (HL-7), MEDIX IEEE P1137, ASTM E31, IEEE P 1073 (MIB) and ACR NEMA.

5.3.1. Health Level Seven

In 1986 a standardization commission in the USA started with the development of a standard specifically devoted to health care corresponding to the 7th layer of ISOs OSI model and recognized as such by vendors in the USA. A voluntary user/vendor/consultant committee (70% vendors, 20% hospitals, 10% consultants) was established in 1987 for the purpose of simplifying the implementation of interfaces between computer applications from different vendors.

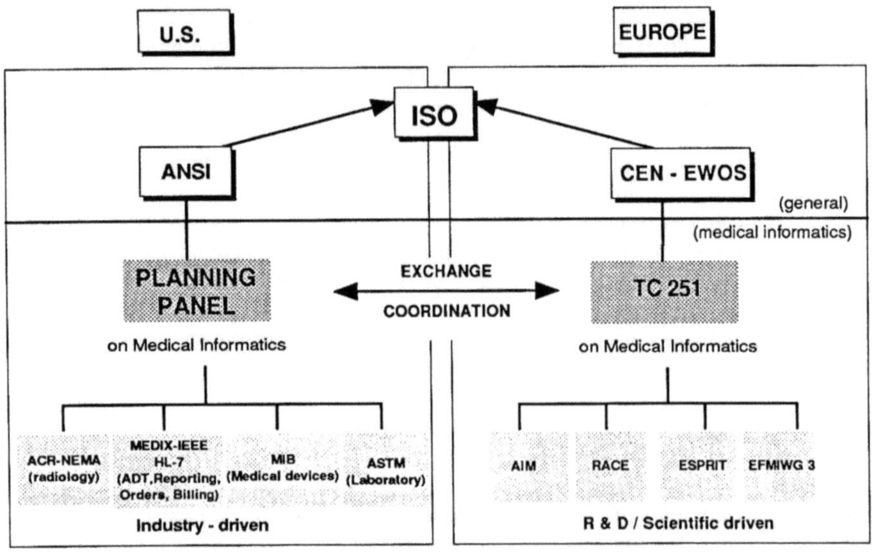

Fig.5.2 Schematical representation of the most important medical standardization groups in health care

In order to solve the problem of data exchange between different hardware and software platforms, Health Level Seven (HL-7) has been defined as an emerging standard whose format and protocol allow health care institutions to exchange key sets of data originating from different clinical or administrative application systems. This protocol (HL-7) aims to standardise health care data exchange for ADT, orders, result reporting and billing data. By simplifying the interface implementation it reduces interface costs (it reduces the N(N-1)/2 problem to a N problem if one wishes to connect N different systems) and provides users with greater choice in application systems. HL-7 defines specifications at the functional application level for messages. Important in the HL-7 context is the *trigger-event*, i.e. the assumption that an event in the real world creates the need for data to flow among systems, for example: admitting a patient, placing an order. When messages are transferred, the HL-7 standard specifies that it must be "acknowledged" at the application level from the receiving system when committed to the database of the receiving application.

In the HL-7 standards (version 2.0, 1988) the overall structure for the following interfaces are defined :

- Admission, discharge, transfer and registration
- Order entry
- Generalised queries
- Finance message specifications
- Ancillary data reporting transaction set
- Data dictionary reports
- Lower level protocol

HL-7 defines the specific data messages that are exchanged among applications and the procedures used for their exchange. It focusses more on the data content and interrelationship of messages, including the communication of certain error conditions. As such it operates at the seventh level of the ISO model. Three levels depending upon the sophistication of a particular communication environment are defined [AND 90] .

Abstract Message Level. This level specifies the data fields that will be sent within a message, the valid response messages and the treatment of application-level errors or the failure of the underlying communication system. It is suitable for using the HL-7 standard in environments that provide maximum protocol functionality (that is, within the OSI model or proprietary networks such as SNA LU6.2 and RPC). The abstract message level within HL-7 corresponds to OSI layer 7.

Encoding Rules. The second level within HL-7 is applicable to environments that support a robust transport level but do not fully meet higher level requirements. The transport level assures that data are sent successfully between two computers. At this level, the HL-7 standard specifies the exact string of bytes that will be sent from one application to another, rather than just listing the fields abstractly, as at the abstract message level. To determine the exact representation of the message, HL-7 "encoding rules" are applied to the abstract message definition. This level of the HL-7 standard corresponds most closely to OSI layers 5 and 6 (e.g. session and presentation layers).

Lower Level Protocol. For the HL-7 standard to be applied in the least robust environments, which do not provide even basic transport reliability (that is, point-to-point RS-232 links, modems and LANs linked to host computers via RS-232 communications links), the lower level protocol may be applied to fulfill the most basic requirements. This protocol provides a data format and procedures for breaking a message, which may consist of thousands of characters, into a number of smaller blocks, each containing a checksum and character count. Individual blocks must be acknowledged by the lower level protocol, and a complete message is provided to an application only when all blocks have been received. The lower level protocol corresponds to OSI levels 3 and 4, network and transport layers. OSI levels 1 and 2 correspond to services that are always provided by the communications devices themselves, even in the least robust environments considered by HL-7.

5.3.2 MEDIX IEEE P1157

Another scientific engineering and educational group is the IEEE P1157 Medical Data Interchange Committee (MEDIX), which is in the process of developing standards for communication of medical data between heterogeneous health care IS. As a matter of fact, HL-7 and MEDIX are working to converge as a goal for the HL-7 3.0 standard.

This working group has developed a reference model for data exchange upon which the architecture is based. It defines the information content and information semantics, not based on a particular ancillary service since the health care environment does not have a single decomposition of function/services performed.
The data model is explicit and uses object-oriented modelling techniques. The overall architecture is based upon a client-server model of interaction. Medical applications (i.e. clients) interact with an aggregation of medical objects on a server through the facilities of an agent, in response to a "triggerevent".

Objectives:

- Support communications both within and between medical centres, among patient care settings, ancillary services and administration. The eventual scope includes all health care communications.
- Do not assume any specific decomposition of the health care system into sub-systems and structure the standard in a flexible manner so that multiple sub-sets of features are allowed, in order to minimise constraints upon system implementations which conform to the standard. The standard focuses on interface specification, not on implementation.
- Provide a framework allowing migration of applicable health care standards into a common reference model. Ideally, we want just one set of worldwide health care communication standards. A mechanism is needed to allow existing work to converge to a single harmonised set of international standards.
- Define a standard set of interface transactions which allow health care information systems to interchange data.
- Specify standard representations of transaction data items, while allowing for domain specific variations.
- Ensure data integrity, consistency , security, reliability and ownership.
- Ensure compatibility of multiple vendor systems at the applications interface level through the use of ISO/OSI standard protocols and functional standards. The use of OSI will allow the health care community to take advantage of the enormous investment in time and resources which has been made in developing OSI standards and in making them available commercially.
- Ensure that successive protocol versions are compatible. Any standard developed today must provide facilities for evolution of the standard while ensuring that successive versions are backwards compatible.

5.3.3 ASTM E31

Under the ASTM (American Society for Testing and Materials) E31 (computerisation) committee a number of working groups have been set up with the mission to develop standards that will enhance the orderly growth of computerisation in medicine. The E31.11 sub-committee has the charter of the exchange of clinical data in general. The first standard produced by E31.11 was ASTM E1238.88 for the exchange of clinical laboratory data between, for example, laboratories and physician's offices or HIS. The first revision of ASTM E1238 extends this to additional clinical data items. It deals principally with the message syntax and not with the semantics (codes) or communications profiles, as opposed to EUCLIDES (see chapter on telemedicine).

Other relevant ASTM E31 sub-committees are E31.12 (medical informatics) which has focused on developing recommendations for electronic patient records (ASTM E1239 is a guide to the definition of patient registration fields), E31.14 which is developing standards for interfacing instruments in the clinical laboratory to computers and E31.15 which is to tackle the problem of exchanging medical decision logic, based on the Arden Syntax.

5.3.4 IEEE P1073 (MIB)

The IEEE P1073 Medical Information Bus (MIB) provides an OSI compliant standard for communication between bedside medical devices. For more information we refer to the chapter on medical devices.

5.3.5 ACR-NEMA

The American College of Radiology (ACR) and the National Electrical Manufacturers Association (NEMA) have defined a standard method for transferring medical images and associated information between devices manufactured by various suppliers in the ACR NEMA standard publication no.300-1988 "Digital imaging and communications"[ACR 88]. For more detailed information relating to this standard, we refer to the chapter on image communication systems.

6

Most Important Trends in the 1990s

6.1 Introduction

It is clear that in medical informatics we are moving toward a diagnostic environment in which health care providers will have the possibility to access in a transparent and integrated way all medical data including text, numeric data and image data. The trend is clear: the transformation of patient records into a completely electronic form. What most people nowadays do not realise is that this evolving technology will provide much more than a simple access to these medical data. As physicians and nurses have an overview of all the medical data, they will develop a broader understanding of the full implications of the disease processes which have been diagnosed.

Today's HIS are characterised by a rapidly growing number of users and a growing volume of data in different formats. This large number of users causes a sharp increase in the demand for main memory and CPU performance, which will affect the response time. The performance load increases still further if high-level programming languages (such as 4GL, report writers) are used. The constantly expanding volume of data, due to the evolving trend for digitalisation of more and more medical information, has a great effect on the increase of secondary storage devices.
This will come through a convergence of several separate requirements: the need to archive huge amount of data, to transport these data in a very fast way, to have sufficient processing power to process that information, to integrate knowledge-based decision support systems with the data stored in RDBMS and to provide it via a user-friendly interface. Together they will evolve into a hospital (clinical) information system, with intelligent workstations at the end to communicate with a central repository.
In the following paragraphs the current technology and a perspective of future technology related to medical informatics will be discussed in terms of hardware as well as software.

6.2 The Need for Increased Processing Power : RISC/CISC/Multi-Processors

The computers working by the Von Neumann principle, all have the same problem: when information is transferred from memory to registers, the processor itself is doing nothing while not being available for other tasks. This delay is called "Von Neumann's bottleneck". Much of recent computer research is spent on the solution of

this limitation or, in any case, to the restriction of its influence. On the one hand, this research has led to the development of a new generation of chips, the so-called RISC (reduced-instruction-set computer) chips. One of the consequences of this processor technology is that reading instructions from the memory is done in a different way, as a result of which, this kind of operation can proceed faster. On the other hand, there is increasing interest in parallel processing. Parallel processing is an attempt to increase the capacity of a computer by using several processors which carry out tasks simultaneously that, generally speaking, should have been carried out sequentially by a single processor. Of course, this description leaves much to the imagination. For instance, there is no explanation of what a task is or of how the processors are connected to each other.
In the next sections the characteristic features and points in favour of this new technology are briefly considered.

RISC versus CISC
It has been found that when using complex instructions the well-known 80/20 rule will apply. With 20% of the instructions available, 80% of the program is carried out. The 20% in question will, moreover, mainly consist of simple instructions. In other words, the complex instructions of an extensive instruction set are seldom used, and to a large extent they are lumber. When this is left out, then the microcode of the processor can disappear, too, and simple instructions will remain. If, subsequently, each instruction can be processed in one clock-pulse, then an enormous gain in speed will be attained.

The idea of building a processor based on the 80/20 rule originated in the laboratories of IBM about 20 years ago. The idea occurred of having the limited instructions directly built into the semiconducting material of the processor, in fact, similarly to the way in which a microcode is registered on the processor. These instructions can be called up directly, as a result of which the processor works faster. By supplying the processor with a large number of registers as well, it will be possible to carry out many operations simultaneously. The result is a RISC processor (Reduced Instruction Set Computer).
Furthermore, an increase in speed can be attained by means of so-called *pipelining*. With this, feature the next instruction is already being obtained from the memory during the processing of the current instruction. This technique is also used with the counterpart CISC systems (Complex Instruction Set Computer).

The elementary difference between CISC and RISC is that, with CISC, a complicated task can be specified with one instruction, but it will take a comparatively long time to carry out this instruction. With RISC, more instructions are necessary to specify a complicated task. However, as it is possible for compilers to generate machine code efficiently, and as this code can be processed quickly, RISC produces a gain in time compared with CISC.
The result of this is a computer with a better price/performance relation, more MIPS (million instructions per second) for less money. Prognostications estimate that the price/performance relation of RISC hardware will improve by 40%-50% each year.

For CISC systems this growth is still 20% at present. More is not to be expected, as this technology has reached the limits of what is physically possible.

Yet the processor is not the determining factor in the speed of RISC. All specialists agree that a good compiler is the most essential part of the RISC concept. *The point is how to transpose program lines into an efficient machine code. The better the compiler, the fewer lines of machine code will be generated.*
The development of the compiler technique was a prerequisite for the break-through of RISC. With the technique of 10 years ago a program was still translated into endless lines of machine code. By this, the gain in speed of a RISC processor was as good as undone. Nowadays, with the above-mentioned compilers the number of machine code lines can be strongly limited. That RISC will completely supersede the traditional systems is not likely. The computer architecture of the future is more likely to be a combination of RISC and CISC, in which the best of both is interwoven.
There is no exact definition of RISC. The processors brought on the market by the manufacturers differ greatly from each other. A standard does not exist either, as to the number and sort of instructions. There are manufacturers producing RISC chips with 90 instructions; others have more than a 150.

About Compilers
In order to understand something of both architectures, let us look at the heart of a computer. The heart of this machine (whether this is a PC, a workstation, a microcomputer or a mainframe) is formed by the processor. With a microprocessor all functions are on a semiconductor material layer. A processor works with various registers, storage locations on the chip itself, based on transistors in which results are stored that will be used for further processing.
In fact, a transistor is no different from a switch it has two states: on or off. In binary code this gives the values one or zero. A certain binary code may be an instruction by which a processor will multiply two numbers. Another code may be an instruction to temporarily file the result of the multiplication into a register. Such instructions are called machine code. According to the speed with which transistors can switch, a computer can process an endless stream of instructions, by human standards, per unit of time.
Nobody has any longer on a keyboard next to the barespace, only a 1- or 0-key for quickly putting a number of instructions into a computer. Yet in former days programs actually used to be put into the memory with switches, bit by bit. Nowadays, if one wants to write a program, one uses a long series of binary code computer languages such as COBOL, FORTRAN, Lisp or C. With these languages, program lines can be written which are reasonably understandable. For instance, the following lines of Basic:

```
10 for I  =  1 to 100
20 sum    =  sum+I
30 next I
```

Anyone with a little experience in programming knows that this means: read the series of numbers 1 to 100 and add these numbers. However, a processor cannot do

anything with this text. Only using a translation procedure the instructions can be processed into a binary code. This translation is executed by a compiler. For each computer language there is a separate compiler, which in its turn is tuned to a special processor and to a special control system. Consequently, the variety in compilers is great.
As a result of the further development of the compiler technique very complicated instructions can now be sent to the processor, by which the execution of more than one task is initiated. In order to steer the latter in the right direction, the processor has a separate processing logic for each instruction. This has been realized by fixing a number of transistors into a specific logic circuit, and so, this formula is called *microcode.*

Multi-processor Systems

A processor works at a certain speed, the clock frequency, measured in megahertz (MHz). Per clock pulse a step is taken in the processing of the instructions. A complex instruction will require a number of these clock pulses, which takes more time and so costs time. It is true that by raising the clock frequency a large gain in time can be achieved, but this too is subject to a maximum. A number of alternative ways exist to increase the throughput of computers. Let's take a look at the most important one.

Interleaved memory, pipelining are alternative ways to increase the speed of single processors. For some applications this is not good enough. The answer is to link many processors in a parallel computer. A distinction should be made between a number of programs working simultaneously, the distribution of tasks with co-processors and the splitting up of one single set into several processes working simultaneously.

A Number of Tasks in One Machine. The first case is referred to as *multi-tasking,* one program is working in the foreground (the set with which the user is working at that moment) and at the same time several programs are running in the background (for instance the sorting of a database and the printing of a spreadsheet diagram). In principle, multitasking only works on one CPU. It is indeed possible , by means of clever software, to split up the CPU into a number of separate microprocessors. Thus, for instance, an Intel 80386 CPU with the PC operating system can begin to behave like a series of independent 8086-microprocessors. Yet it all remains multi-tasking, and with the increase of the number of working programs the system's performance is diminished considerably.

Co-processors. The distribution of tasks by means of co-processors is of much longer standing. In order to relieve the CPU, graphic tasks are delegated to the graphic co-processor and the number crunching to the mathematic co-processor. Up until now, this technique yielded good results. Yet this is not really an example of parallel processing either, for the system does not exactly work on the same task as a unity. The co-processor simply takes over a certain process task and then the CPU remains free for other assignments.

Parallel Processors. With parallel processing, all processors are working simultaneously on various tasks within the same process(program). The tasks are not dealt with in order, sequentially, but alongside each other, in parallel. The aim is to execute as many computing steps per unit of time as possible. The more computing steps per second taking place, the greater the speed of the system. Parallel processing usually is performed using a number of microprocessors in one system. Each processor will then carry out its own task within the process to be dealt with at that moment. Parallel processing within one single chip is possible, for instance via pipelining or concurrent evaluation techniques, but it will make the system inflexible.

The technique. Two kinds of multi-processor systems can be distinguished. **Tightly coupled systems** all processors have access to the common memory, mostly, by sharing one operating system. Communication among the processors occurs via common data structures in the memory. With **loosely coupled systems**, each processor has its own memory and a copy of the operating system. Communication among the processors takes place via a parallel bus. Here, it is the tightly coupled system which will be further discussed, paying special attention to the difference between symmetric and asymmmetric ones.
The kernel is always placed in the memory, co-ordinating the activities of the processors; it is in fact, the "manager" of the computer. However, the problem in a system with a number of processors is that there are possibly several "managers" in the system. Then you can say that one of the managers becomes "general manager", assigning certain tasks to this managers, or that each manager keeps his own responsibilities, but that there has to be mutual agreement on who takes care of which tasks.

Symmetrical asymmetrical. There are two approaches to multiprocessing: asymmetric and symmetric architectures. Asymmetric systems incorporate at least one main CPU, which is mainly responsible for executing the operating system, while the other processors are treated as slave processors dedicated to special functions such as disk I/O, network I/O or memory management.
In symmetric multiprocessors all processors are equal and have no pre-assigned tasks. They share a common bus, the same interrupt structure, and access to common memory and I/O channels. The general trend in both hardware and software is towards symmetric multiprocessing. To date only UNIX supports symmetrical multiprocessing.
Load balancing is a very important point in multiprocessor systems. The aim is to distribute the entire load over the processors, without, for instance, one processor being occupied all the time, while other processors are doing nothing.

Neural computers

Neural computers are another "end-of-century" machine which aim to raise performance levels by a factor 100 to 1000 and show an even much higher degree of parallelism. Inspired by the working of the human brain, which is composed of about 40 billion neurons, theoretical models have been built whose artificial neurons as active or inactive binary elements simultaneously make decisions on the basis of the global state of the network.

6.3 The Need for Archiving Huge Amounts of Data

The problem arising in the health care environment is that due to the increase of computerised diagnostic and therapeutic medical procedures the amount of generated information registered about a patient has drastically increased over the last decade. In the last several years most large data centres have reported 30%-60% annual growth rates for disk storage devices. Due to the fact that most medical decisions are based on access to patient information, the most important function for the diagnostic, therapeutic and nursing process is very fast access to a huge amount of data. Tomorrow's computers will need their power to access much greater amounts of data at much higher speed.
For the moment there is no industry comparable with the health care environment, which puts such high demands on the archiving of information on computer media, for the following reasons:

- Various formats of information that have to be stored : data, text, image and voice
- The quantity of information storage : transient and (mostly) long-term information
- High requirements put on the accessibility and availability of data

It is estimated that actually only 15% of the hospital data is stored on existing computer storage media: memory chips, magnetic and optical hard disks and magnetic tape (Fig.6.1 and Table 6.1).

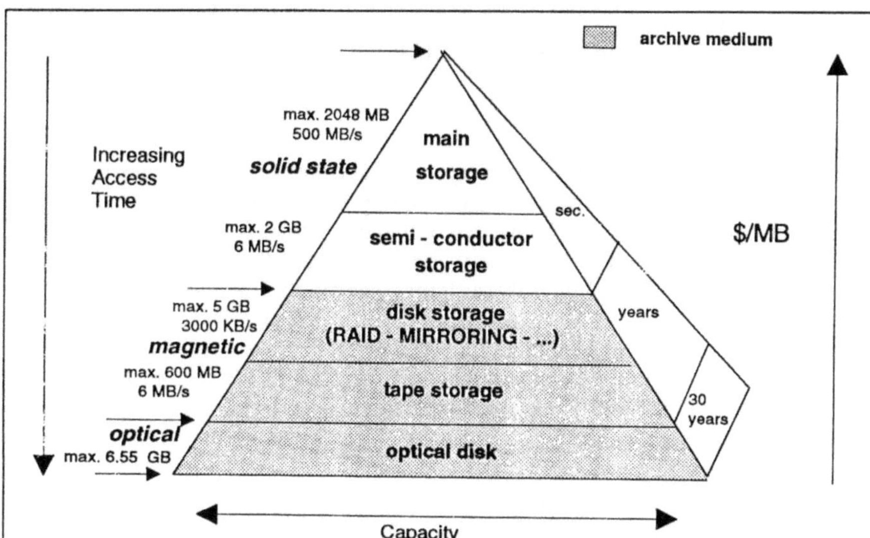

Fig.6.1 Hierarchical representation of different memory types in terms of capacity, speed of access and price

Memory Chips

Compared with other storage media semi conductor memories are the most expensive but fastest available storage devices. The density of memory chips is evolving from circuit paths of 0.8 micron in width down to the 0.1 micron range. The consequence is that billion-bit (gigabit, Gb) memory chips will usher in the next decade. CMOS (Complementary Metal-oxide-silicon) technology already prefers them for its integrative capability and reduced power consumption. As we know that space gained implies increased capacity, memory chips static and dynamic random access memory (RAM) chips on one hand, read-only (ROM/EPROM) on the other will evolve in the same way as the increasing power of microcomputers and the speed of local area networks. It is obvious that these devices will facilitate the introduction of image and voice applications in the health care sector.

Another alternative as extension for CPU memory especially used in mainframe environments is a semiconductor storage module. A semiconductor storage is composed of big assembly of DRAM chips, up to 512MB, and connected to main CPU as if it were a magnetic disk.

Magnetic Disks

The magnetic disk is still an attractive media for the permanent storage of large amounts of data for on-line access, due to the fact that their storage capacity is much greater and less expensive than semiconductor storage. In magnetic disk storage there are two areas which will have a great impact on performance : the development of read-write heads capable of travelling closer to the disk surface (air cushions of 25 micron thick with thin film techniques) and the increase of archiving density on the disk. These techniques go hand in hand, because a reduction in head elevation enhances storage density and reduces data access time.

Optical Storage Technologies

Since its introduction in 1983, the optical disk has always been associated with the notion of future information technology. WORM (Write Once Read Many times) disks, as the name suggests, can be written only once. The optical medium consists of rotating disk, coated with a polymer in which a laser beam burns holes (pits), representing ones and zeros. Inversely, a shining laser beam can optically detect those ones and zeros.

The optical disk has several advantages :

- High capacity of optical storage, 6.8 GB per disk at the present time, due to track density (15000 tracks per inch, more than 10 times the density of a magnetic disk)
- Portability
- Multi-media capability such as image, data and sound
- Highly reliable, less contamination, optical head is 1000 times further away from the disk surface than the flying magnetic disk head
- Reduced cost of information access
- Direct access
- Unerasable

The most potential disadvantage is its reduced retrieval speed. The data transfer rates for magneto-optical (MO) disks vary between 500KB/s for write and 650KB/s for read operations. The WORM disks between 250 KB/s for write and 500 KB/s for read.

Although optical disks offer major advantages, they have been plagued by a lack of standards. Optical disks are available in different sizes, 3.5-inches, 5.25-inches and 14-inches.

Optical storage technologies come in three forms:

- **CD-ROM**

  Compact Disk - Read Only Memory is an interesting component in the dissemination of information. A lot of information such as multi-media encyclopaedias are being published. There is no doubt that the optical disk will be the data archiving medium of the 1990's.

- **WORM**

  Write Once Read Many times disks can be written only once and the data are protected from changes. In WORM technology a high power laser makes a permanent physical mark on the recording surface. The disks are 12 inches (30,5cm) and are CLV (Constant Linear Velocity) or CAV (Constant Angular Velocity) format and read by a low power laser. WORM disks are very suitable for applications in which permanence is top-priority and security is also important (estimated shelf-life of 100 years), e.g. electronic medical records.

- **MO**

  The magneto-optical disk is based on a concept of a laser beam to read and write data from and to an erasable and rewriteable magnetic medium. Magneto-optical recordings have the advantage of removability and combine the advantage of magnetic and optical disks. It can replace magnetic disks as soon as better access times have been achieved. Average access time is becoming shorter every year (75 ms), and the recording density is improving. For the moment memory capacity of magnetic-optical disk is not so extensive (650 MB) because it's diameter is only 5 1/4 inches (13,5 cm).

Magnetic Tape

At the present magnetic tape is the cheapest archiving medium, although it is characterized by some serious inconveniences, sequential access and criability.

For the moment, the digital data recorder of a 12-inches tape unit (which is an improved digital VTR for coded digital date recording), is a promising file media from the viewpoints of capacity (120 GB), low media cost and considerably fast speed.

Another alternative is a helical scan magnetic cartridge unit. The 8-mm Helical Scan Tape Drive represents the latest in tape back-up technology. This tape drive uses compact cartridges to store up to 5 GB of user data on one tape. Different tape lengths are available for added flexibility, ranging in capacity from 270 MB up to the 5 GB maximum. The small size of these tapes contrasts with the space required to store large tape libraries.

By mounting the heads on a rotating drum (1800 rpm) with an axis of 6° from the vertical, while the tape moves slowly in the same direction, the tracks are written diagonally (as portions of a helix) across the tape. Hence the name, helical scan (Fig.6.2). Cross-talk is minimised because alternate tracks on the tape have their data written at different angles.

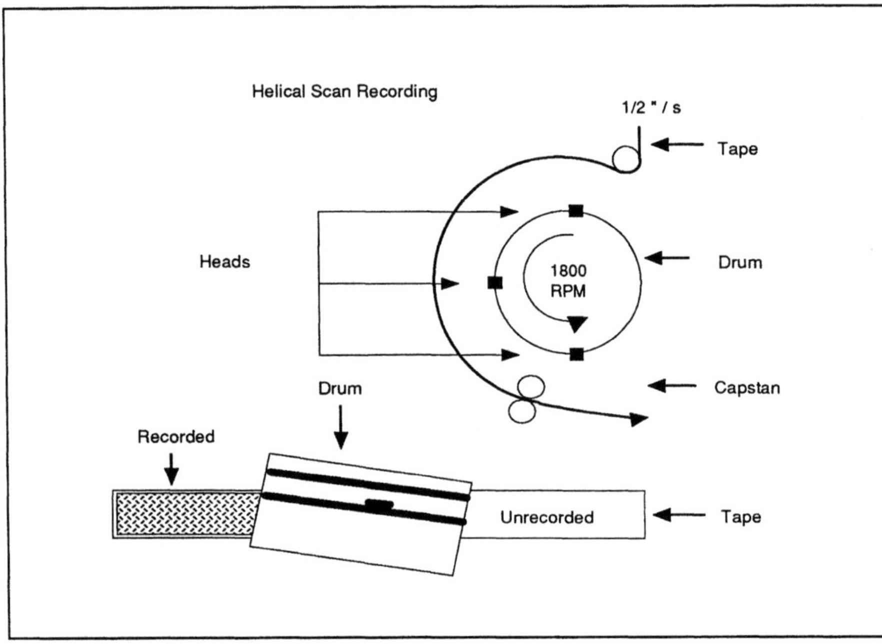

Fig.6.2 Principle of helical scan recording

Table 6.1 Comparison of existing storage devices, in terms of capacity, speed, price and throughput

	Storage Device	Capability (MB)	Access Time (ms)	Media Cost ($/MB)	Through-put (KB)
	Dram Chips Disk	512	0.3		
Disk	Magetic disk	6000	15	10	3000
	Optical disk	6800	90	0.2	650
	Optical magetic disk	650	75	0.7	1000
Tape	Magnetic tape	145	100000	0.2	750
	Magnetic tape cartridge	5000	170000	0.15	500
	DAT	1200			160
	Optical tape	50000		0.05	
Card	Optical card	2.5	100	0.01	8
	IC card	0.032			
	Laser Film	30			

DAT, digital audio tape ; DRAM, direct random access memory; IC, integrated circuit

6.4 The Need for Communication. Local Area Networks

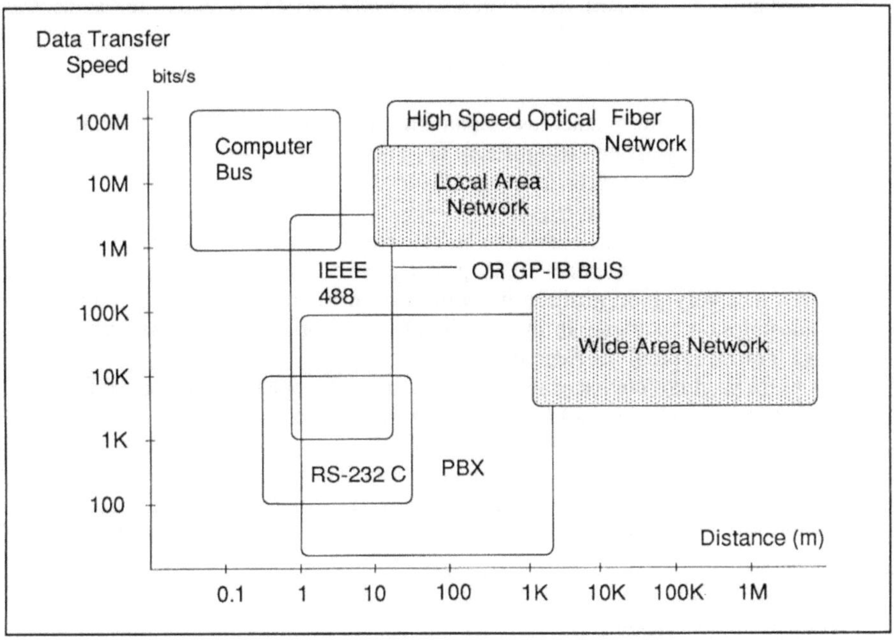

Fig.6.3 Position of local area network (LAN) technology compared with other computer networks in terms of distance and data speed

The explosion of personal computers, combined with the evolution of functions towards more intelligent workstations results in a user-friendly and more efficient environment and leads to a distributed computer landscape. This *downsizing* has a lot of advantages as the user sees one integrated corporate system instead of those islands of automation. This is one of the most important requirements of a local area network (LAN): to encompass the entire HIS.

A LAN provides a high-speed transmission facility which can be used by all users within the institution regardless of the type of hardware they use (PC, MAC, workstation, computer) and the type or nature of information to be transferred. As a link between multiple computer systems, the LAN is managed by a supervisor called a LAN-SERVER station. This server is a microprocessor system with the following main tasks :

- Managing network activity (load, fault recovery)
- File sharing (authorisation, security)
- Data transfer handling
- Exchange with the outside world (via bridges and gateways)
- Printer sharing

The elements by which a LAN is characterised are :

- *Cable*: (un) shielded twisted pair, thin or thick coax or optical fiber
- *Topology*: describing the geometric form of a network

- bus (e.g. Ethernet) all network nodes listen to all transmissions, selecting certain ones based on address identification
- star (e.g. Arcnet) all workstations are wired directly to a central workstation, called a hub.
- ring (e.g. Token ring) all network nodes are wired in a ring

° *Access method*:
- carrier sense multiple access/collision detection (CSMA/CD IEE 802.3)
- Token passing (Token Ring IEE802.5, Token Bus 802.4;)

° *Transmission type*: baseband or broadband

Figure 6.3, illustrates various communication systems in terms of distance and speed. High-speed fiber optic network (FDDI) promises very fast speed over long distances. LAN takes in a very good position but will have difficulty in supplying the medical image transmission backbone in the hospital, because of a lack of optimized control for image transmission of the huge data volumes.
Today's users need not choose a single LAN transport mechanism to the exclusion of any other, but each solution still has distinct characteristics (Tables 6.2).

Table 6.2 Comparison of key characteristics of several network types

Medium	Ethernet	Token Ring	FDDI	ARCNET	LOCAL TALK
Cabling supported	thin coax, thick coax, unshielded, twisted pair, optical fiber	(un)shielded, twisted pair (T3),T1	Optical fiber	(un)shielded twisted pair	(un)shielded twisted pair Fiber
Topologies supported	Bus, star	Ring (star)	Ring,star (Tree)	Star	(star) bus
Transmission speed	10 Mbps	4 Mbps, 16 Mbps	100 Mbps	2.5 Mbps (20 Mbps)	230 Kbps
Standard supported	IEEE 802.3	IEEE 802.5	IEEE 802.8		
Major characteristics	average, intermittent data traffic	intermittent data traffic	Heavy data traffic, very secure but still costly	average data traffic	Low data traffic
Max nodes	1.023	255	-	255 (2.047)	255
Min. Frame	72 B	21 (26) B	-	8.75 (12.50)	-
Max. Frame	1.50 KB	4.5 (18) KB	-	0.50 (4.13)	-

The 100-Mbps FDDI offers users the increased speed and performance reliability of fiber-optic cable without the expense of taking the fiber all the way to each workstation.

A disadvantage of Ethernet is (since it is a bus rather than a ring topology) that if you cut the cable anywhere, the network is gone. Also, under heavy loads, throughput decreases because of the collision detection (CSMA/CD) access method. CSMA/CD controls the simultaneous release of data from two workstations by halting transmission for a random time at times when data packages could collide on the network. Transmission can be slowed, but collisions are not always avoided.
The 16-Mbps Token Ring shows more potential for the future than Ethernet, but not everyone is using all its features. The throughput varies, and the way the driver is written makes a big difference. Whether it catches up to Ethernet's market share depends a lot on the players in the market.

6.5. The Need for Cooperative Computing

Client-Server : The Computer Paradigm of the Future

As in each organisation the cost aspect is of overriding importance; in the world of computers this is significant as well. Once a computer with a specific capacity has been installed in a hospital, the user requirements for processing capacity will increase every year (10%-40% per year, depending on the organisation), and soon the available computer capacity will be insufficient. The question thus posed is: will the computing capacity of the existing machine be doubled or will a second machine be installed (in the context of an analogous applied technology)? In the 1960s and 1970s this question could be answered by "**Grosch's law**" which determined that for mainframe computers a "twice" as powerful computer costs the square root of two (half as powerful) computers (Fig.6.4). Thus, it was appropriate to aim at connecting as many users as possible to computers of maximum size. Hence the coming into existence of large monopolistic central computing centres in the 1960s to 1970s.

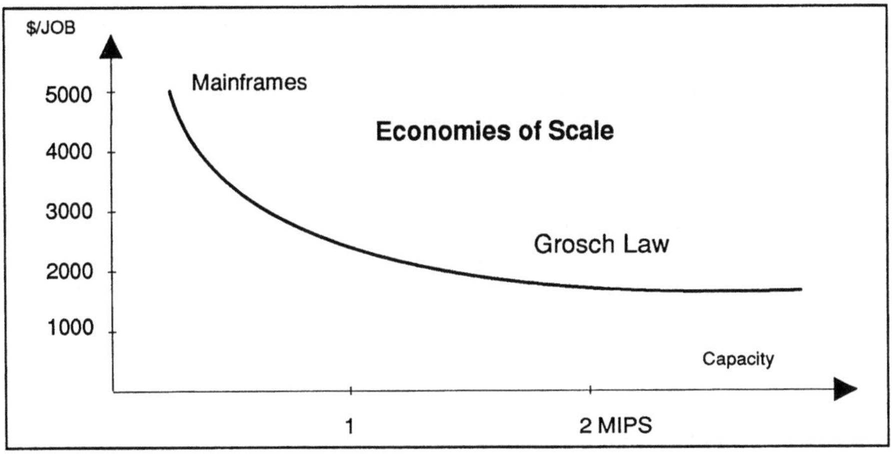

Fig.6.4 Relation of computing capacity versus costs per job in the 1960s and 1970s, as governed by Grosch's law

The advantages of this central approach were:

- ° Users had been released from the "control" of this central system (back-up, security)
- ° Information could be made easily accessible for any authorised user
- ° Expensive peripheral equipment was available to anyone

These are the intrinsic advantages of a centralist approach, which, on the contrary, will constitute the obstacles in a decentralised data processing environment.
What, then, is the motivation for decentralisation? Here three factors can be emphasised :
Economic transition factors due to which, as a result of technological evolution, several curves depending on the group (capacity) of the machine originate, inside which Grosch's law still remains valid (Fig.6.5)

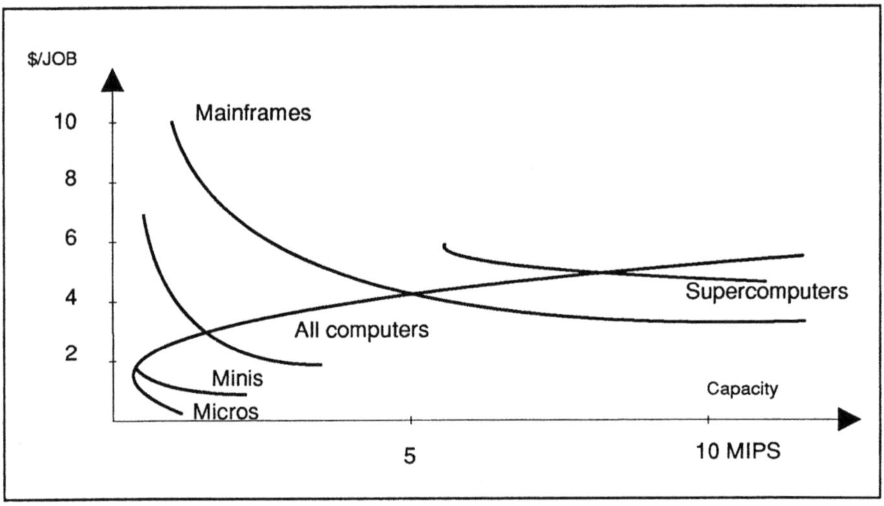

Fig.6.5. Actual situation of Grosch's law revised: CPU computing capacity versus the cost of computing. Main conclusion is "it is most effective to accomplish any task on the least powerful type of computer capable of performing it...."
(Source Philip Ein-Dor Communications of the ACM 28 Feb. 1984)

It is now generally assumed that, in order to minimise the hardware costs, a particular application should be executed on the smallest computer able to cope with this job within the specified time. So, does this mean the end of large computer systems and an invasion of PCs? No! A "heavy" tariffing/invoicing program on a PC would take up days and only be of academic use. On the other hand, word processing on a PC is cheaper than on a supercomputer.
New technical possibilities as a result of an advancing miniaturisation and, running parallel to it, a falling cost price mean that the dumb terminals of yesterday are being replaced by intelligent work stations with :

- ° User-friendly graphical user interfaces (GUI) via bit-mapped displays and pointing devices (mouse, light-pen)

- User-friendly and productivity-increasing software tools like 4th generation languages (UNIFACE, JAM, ACCEL, PROGRESS), relational data base systems (Sybase, Oracle, Ingres, PROGRESS), case tools, object-oriented computer languages

The demand for a greater user autonomy constitutes a last motivation, including more freedom and of course a better user interface simulating the normal working environment.

The advantages of a centralist approach are exactly the disadvantages of decentralisation. It will be computer networks which will be set the task to compensate the disadvantages that go with this decentralisation to a generally higher assessment.

The Rationale Behind Client-Server Computing

Not long ago, the choices you had in arranging a computer system were limited. The speed of processors, the connectivity and software capabilities were all limiting factors. If one thinks of the 1960s as the era of batch processing, the 1970s as the era of time-sharing and the 1980s as the era of personal computing, the 1990s will become clearly the era of networking computing (the client-server architecture) and the building of distributed applications to run on such systems.

Future networks perform an open-ended integration of what was good about mainframes (that they tied people together /centralised integration) and what was good about micro-computers (giving the advantages of stand alone processing), delivering finally the advantages of interaction and coordination.

Four major waves have been pushing computing technology:

- *The first was mainframe-centred computing,* reflecting the demand of the time. It emphasized centralised decision-making and centralised control of corporate computing and database resources. The network management architecture was centralised with the mainframe at the centre. These point-to-point networks, are a relatively easy topology to manage.
- *The second wave brought decentralized computing* to departments.
  Independent mission-critical applications units were developed within the hospital or acquired from vendors. Laboratory systems and financial systems, and ADT systems are the most important. Those applications provided by multiple vendors were installed on heterogeneous computer systems; in most cases there was no integration or communication at all. In some hospitals a network was established (the enabling technology was the X.25 packet switching protocol, or TCP/IP internet working protocol or SNA in the IBM world or DECNET), characterised by the construction of point-to-multi-point logical networks. This configuration added several orders of magnitude to the complexity of network management.
- *The third wave characterised by desktop computing* extends the trend to decentralise decision-making even further. The use of PC LANs for linking the PCs together combined with the use of different network management tools for each networking technology made the task of managing the network extremely difficult. The LANs were not expensive, but the scope was limited and the software was also less mature. Although it was possible to make available a large pool of software to users, these LANs were characterized by the lack of "corporate" thinking in which users essentially share files instead of information.

- *The fourth wave, or the next advance in computing capability* is noted by Sanford C. Bernstein as the *networking computing age.* This type of computing goes further than basic file-sharing, using PCs as terminals.

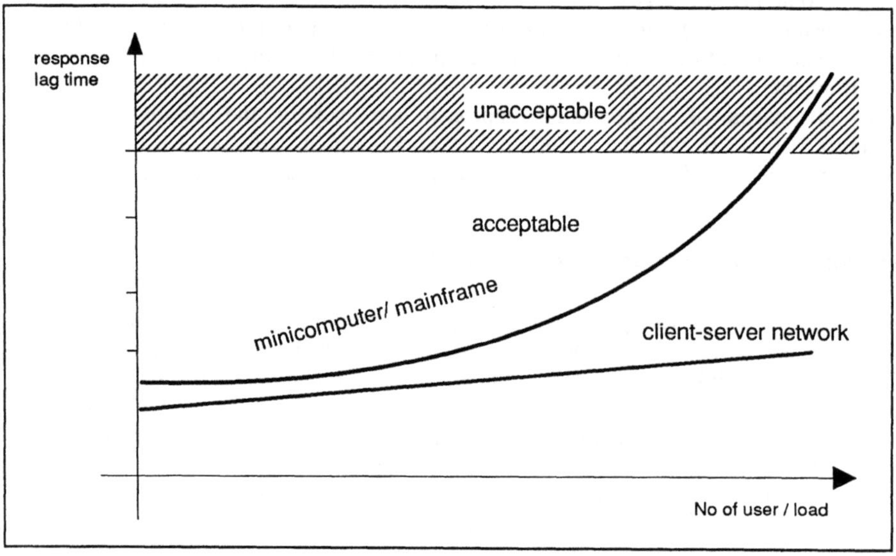

Fig. 6.6 Impact of a client-server architecture in function of an increasing number of users, compared with a mini computer/mainframe

For years, serious hospital databases were monolithic creatures running only on one large machine accessed by dumb terminals. As more and more departmental computers are networked, there is a growing need for users to access databases across the network without having to worry about where the information is stored. In the late 1980s, databases evolved so that an application, called a *client*, on one machine could run against a (database) *server* on another machine. At first this client-server database architecture was found on minis, but later on the client function was moved down to microcomputers and LANs. The objective of the client-server is to offload as much processing as possible on the client and leave the server with the shared information and the software for managing it [FRA 90].

This form of parallel processing is extremely effective, as properly designed client-server networks cause very little degradation, even under heavy loading conditions that would increase response time on monolithic computer systems to an unacceptable level (Fig.6.6). Last but not least, there is also a cost benefit factor as the total costs are less than the equivalent in a mainframe configuration, and too substantial to be ignored in health care information processing.

Client /server computing is different from:

- Traditional PC-LAN network OS, where the applications are only executed at the desktop
- Traditional mainframe applications in which the data base and the application run only on the host

True client/server computing involves applications that split processing tasks between :

- *Front-end portion :* clients (PC or UNIX workstations), usually on a LAN, which handles local data manipulation and maintains the user interface. It handles the users requests, present the results as requested. It is the interface between the user and the server.
- *Back-end portion* : one or several servers (from X86 PC 680X0, to mainframe) which offer to the user a set of standardised services (database servers, other number-intensive processing servers, mail services)

Thus the user has a graphical user interface (GUI) and application processing at the desktop, along with the benefits of cooperative processing with larger systems [FRA 90]. The benefits and characteristics of this distributed, networked heterogeneous computing environment are as follows :

- *Distributed*: The cost to add incremental computing is reduced since the environment is comprised of multiple "smaller" elements versus an environment composed of a large computer
- *Networked*: Enterprise environments are a reflection of a networked society. The technology is scalable so that small hospitals also benefit.
- *Heterogeneous* and dynamic: Computers from different vendors operate and participate in a non-proprietary, open system environment.

As hospitals have acquired more and more computer systems over the years, the network will evolve as a powerful resource that can unite scattered machines. Our users have told us that they want a network to "*connect anything, anywhere, anytime*".

Network Computing Components

Components of networking computing are :

- *Application servers* providing computational resources for executing the application
- *Information servers* containing multi-media filing systems and databases
- *A I servers* including expert systems and neural networks
- *Utility/administration servers* including:
  - File and print services (such as LAN servers)
  - Directory services : user account servers who manage a global registry that contains user (login) account information
  - Network management server providing a view of the network environment including resource utilisation and available capacity description of resources being used by each user application
  - Automatic back up and software distribution system updating services
  - MAIL servers

The Art of Decomposing

In the past all applications were processed by one mainframe. In order to define a distributed architecture one of the fundamental problems is to decide where to locate software, data and computers all over the network. The decision rules are organisational, economic, functional and technical. All of them change in the course of time. The natural location of application software and data is on a personal host when dedicated to a single user and on a common host when shared by several (functional) departments. However, for technical and economical reasons, they are often installed further upstream from the user because :

- For large databases, heavy batch processing and number crunching, this is still economical today
- For reasons of security, responsibility and common use of data

Implementation Scenario

In most systems one will not go in one step from a star network to the future network. So the computer centre has to evolve continuously, rather than step by step, towards its ultimate function: providing the heart of the information services and safeguarding the hospital information. Although many *tasks* of the computer centre are decentralised to local systems, it continues to grow exponentially in computer performance (30%/year) and storage capacity (20%/year) as a result of common databases expanding and more users wishing to access them. A possible evolutionary approach could be accessed in different phases as illustrated in Fig.6.7.

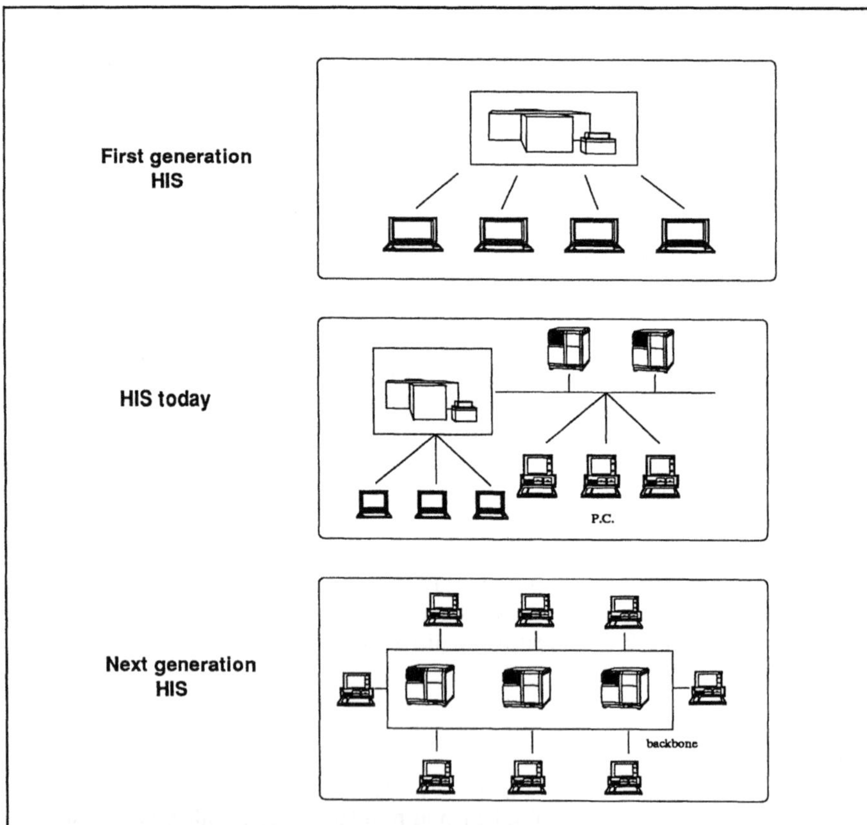

Fig.6.7 From a centralised towards a distributed HIS: an evolutionary approach in different phases. First phase , 1st generation perfect star; next phase, central system connected to sattellites; third phase , second generation of HIS

6.6 The Undeniable Importance of the User Interface

Historically, the clinician-computer interface has always been a problem due to:

- Difficulties in using the keyboard data entry
- Difficulties in finding time to learn to use a system
- Reliance on dictation and handwritten notes

By using a simple set of commands and working with on-line forms that closely resemble each hospital's form and look familiar to them, nurses and physicians are able to enter the data for which they are responsible. In fact, nurses and physicians want a system that conforms to them; they do not want to adjust to the system. Easy to learn and easy to use are most important issues.

User interfaces have advanced from line to screen, from screen to window, from window to bit-mapped (graphical).

As physicians and nurses are in fact nowadays still occasional computer users, who don't like to spend much time on computer education, user training has to be minimised and user productivity optimised through the adoption of a consistent Graphical User Interface (GUI). This term, almost unknown some years ago, has made its way into the daily vocabulary of researchers and software vendors. Providing a consistent GUI to an application reduces learning time and allows the use of software of greater complexity and increases the usability, productivity and effectivity.

More and more users buying applications software are also buying a "*look and feel*" associated with that specific application. They are asking to have this portability among different platforms (i.e. computer hardware) and different user interfaces.

Regardless of individual preference towards a GUI, it is sure that we are confronted with a plethora of at times conflicting standards*(Motif, OPEN-look, Next-Step, DecWindows, MS-windows, Presentation manager, MAC multifinder).* This is the most difficult problem to solve.

An approach for addressing this problem of application portability across multiple platforms is to split up an application into three parts, providing the possibilities to change one part without affecting the other areas: application,representation and data layer. The *application layer* consists of the core functionality of the application that can be described in a "presentation-independent" way. The *presentation layer* specifies the collection of interaction objects defined for a given user interface. The *data layer* performs the traffic with the database system. This concept gives also rise in the implementation of client-server architecture . Those systems can be classified according to several approaches: (event-driven) declarative, object-oriented approach, data-driven and interactive layout systems [SEA 90]. Object Oriented (OO) paradigms are ideal for developing GUI, as functions and data are called and activated at the click of a mouse button.

The workstation is the window to the environment and to its applications. It presents a graphical metaphor to the user, conveying not just the applications available but also the resources of the environment, through the use of pointing devices (mouse, trackballs). The character-mode application will depart the scene, leaving place for more human oriented GUI applications. Instead of having a bunch of applications we will have an integrated environment that let the user switch from one application to another in an integrated, transparent way, like people think and work.

GUI design considerations

The design of GUIs must cover the sometimes conflicting work settings, requirements and needs of various health care professionals who interact with the system. They will strongly influence the success and acceptance of every system. The more the design encapsulates and understands the medical (user) requirements, the closer the system will amalgamate with the application domain (Fig.6.8). As building a "good" interface in a hospital environment is a big challenge (compared to previous cumbersome display technology), there is a small but, rapidly growing set of GUI software tools available (Neuron Data, XVT, Tele soft,...) aimed at helping developers building better interfaces.

Unlike in traditional data processing environments, where more emphasis was put on clean, structured top-down programming styles, actual developments are characterized by "user-centred" driven designs, where much more attention is given to the value of the user interface. Therefore, the design of the user interface with his "objects" and "processing" features involving the end-user right from the beginning is a very suitable approach (tool) in the design of applications, that closely relates to the paradigm of OO programming.
The notion of user-centred design has been mentioned in human factors research, for instance in Norman 1986 [NOR 86] and is inseparably connected with the notion of user-friendliness.
It is important to stress the fact that this user-centered design requests:

- An iterating design methodology in close cooperation with all the users involved (multi-diskiplinary approach),defining how selected objects behave and look [WEN 91]
- An immediate start with the design of the user interface scenario from the beginning of the project instead of considering this activity as the last step in the engineering process, as was normally the case

The user interface scenario together with the information requirements will afterwards be the foundation upon which the technical implementations will be based and upon which the prototype (data and functional model) will map the concept into reality in the next phase. In parallel with those activities, the design of the data model can be undertaken, which must fit into the high level design of the hospital information model.
A consequence of this evolution (actual representation facilities require a lot of information and instantaneous processing power) is the appearance of cooperative processing as a new quality of information processing. As it becomes impossible to run all applications on a central host due to the sequential bottleneck of the Von Neumann computer architecture of most of the computers in use today [BIR 91] dedicated distributed architectures are appearing. The client-server architecture emerges, in which clients (e.g. workstations) request services from servers (data base server, X-server, print server, application server). In fact, more and more a liberation of the software from the hardware is materialising, as programming efforts are becoming much more expensive than hardware investments, due to the drastic price cuts for chips.

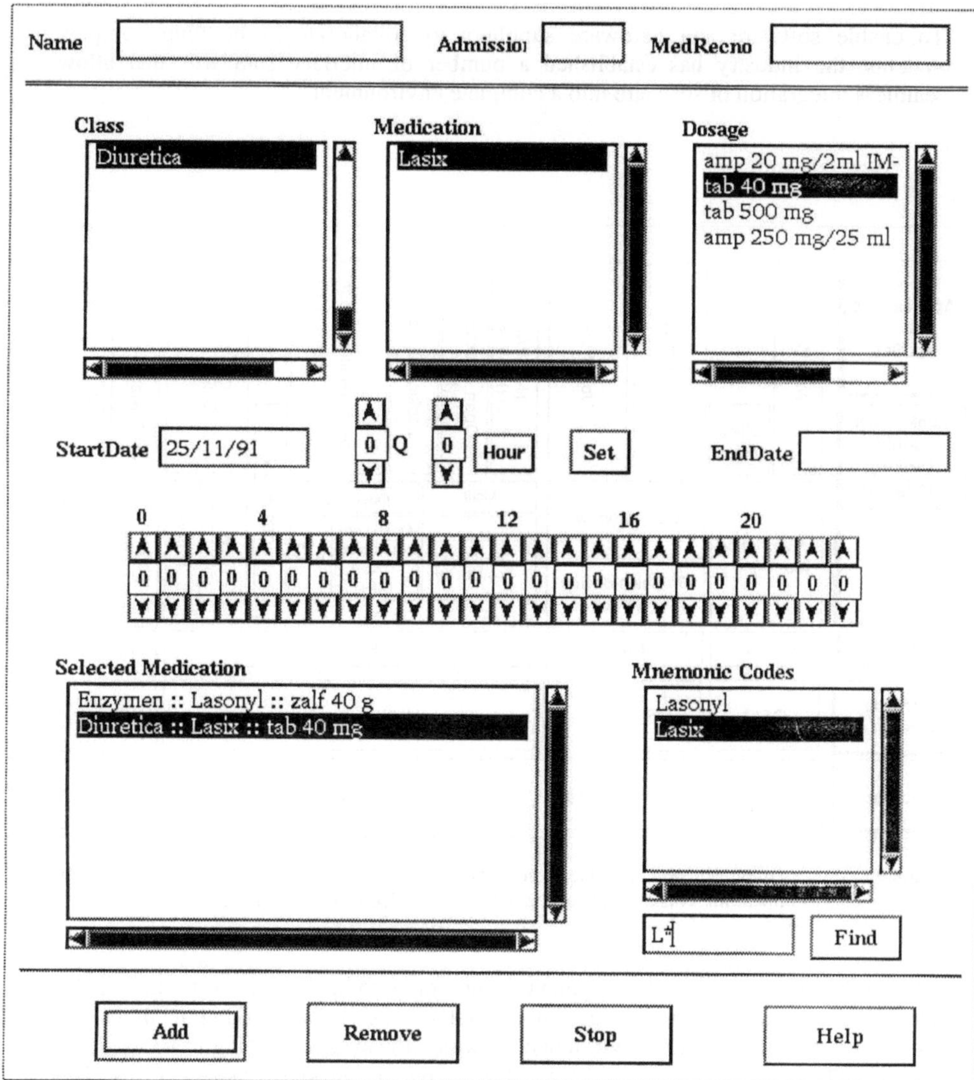

Fig. 6.8 Example of a GUI, for medication ordering .
(Source Department medical informatics , AZ-VUB University Hospital of Brussels)

There are several layers to any GUI : a low-level imaging model, a window system that keeps track of which part of the screen belongs to which application (window manager) and the toolkit offering the user the look-and-feel (Fig. 6.9).

The beauty of a multi-tasking environment with multi-windowing and a standardised look-and-feel between applications from different vendors (orientations) is that when new software is added the user does not have to learn a new way of working because he resides in the "same work environment". The X-window system, as part of the workstations standard software, gives access to software on other computers located elsewhere on the network.

To enable software and hardware suppliers to collaborate in building complex systems, the industry has established a number of interface standards that allow seamless integration of software into a complete environment.

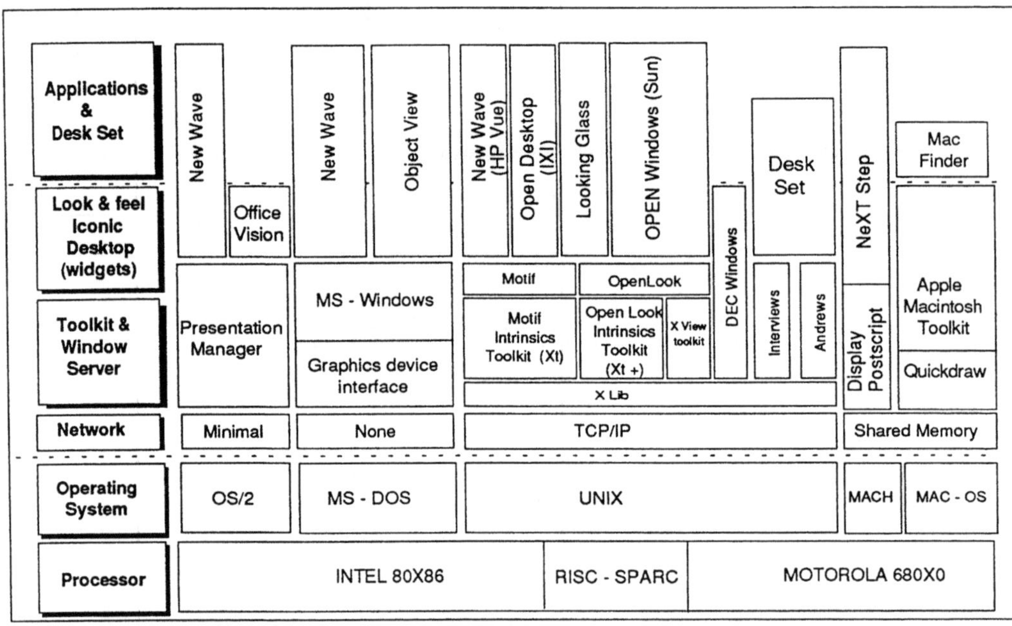

Fig.6.9 Graphical user interfaces nowadays. Subdivision over 5 layers : processor, operating systems, network, window server, iconic desktop and application.

The problem in systems development is not only to make the user's knowledge explicit (or extracting knowledge) to understand the tasks, working methods and organisation of the hospital environment in which the system is going to be used, but the crucial issue is to *develop the user's knowledge and produce new concepts*. This can be done through prototyping and optimizing the interaction between the user and systems developer in an iterative way, evolving into a more efficient organisational change. The helix symbolises the iterative element of the experimental approach to systems development. In the case of the helix, the organisational structure is depicted (Fig.6.10).

The quality of this user interface is determined by two elements:

- *The degree of experience of the system developer*
- *The hardware and software platform used*

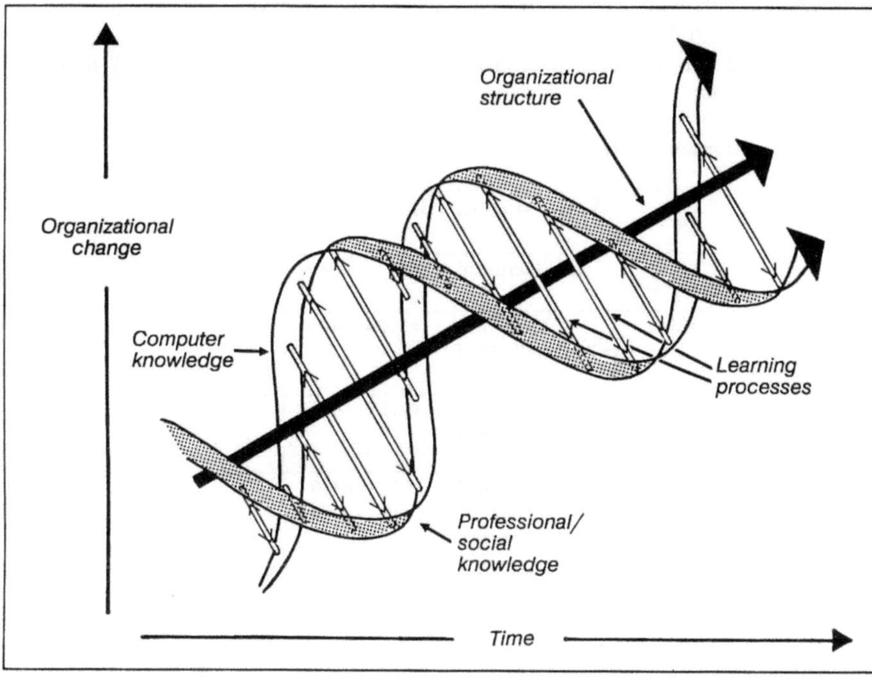

Fig.6.10 The double-stranded, learning process- driven, systems development helix [N0E 89]
(Source Reprinted with permission from Noehr C., Bernstein K. in *Can HIS be developed without organizational change ? The creative potential in user participation.* In MEDINFO'89 edited by Barber B., D. Cao, D. Qin, G. Wagner, Elsevier Science Publisher, 1989, pp. 337)

Although the basic philosophies for graphical user interfaces in contrast with earlier applications, relying on long modal command sequences are very similar, two concepts can be distinguished [RAN 90] (modal means that if an application is in a particular dialogue, the rest of the application cannot be used simultaneously with or independently of the previous dialogue). *The selection precedes command* method requires that the user selects an object and identifies afterwards the action he wants to execute on it. *The direct manipulation method,* executes its action immediately (mouse dragging, window resizing). All of these systems rely on the mouse as the pointing device. Two types of menus can be distinguished : pop-up and pull-down. The first one appears at a certain pointer position, the later one is invoked by pressing the select button in the menu bar. Pop-up windows, pull-down windows and the use of "pointing" devices are necessary and obvious for the user with minimal training. In some application colour can be used to achieve this goal.

The Choice of the User Workstation

The question arises, what kind of user work station we are going to use (table 6.4)? Will it be an ASCII-terminal-PC, MAC, workstation or X-terminal ?

The answer is relatively simple: use the least powerful type of computer. The economics are worth discussing.

- First, we can compare the basic costs (including host ports and network connections)

Table 6.3 : Comparison between the basic cost of different types of workstations.

Work station	Basic cost ($) - (1992)
ASCII terminal	**600 - 2000**
MAC II fx PC/486 (33 MHz)	**4500 - 10000**
MAC II si PC/386 (33 MHz)	**3000 - 6000**
X-terminal Workstation diskless-disk	**2500 - 6000** **5000 - 20000**

- Second, we can compare strategies for allocation of the computing budget for a server

Server type	Internal Memory	Storage	Mips	Basic cost
PC (486)	8 MB	1GB	12	$ 15.000
WS (RISC)	64 MB	1GB	25	$ 30.000
Mainframe	64MB	100GB	25	$ 2.000.000

- Third, a single CPU with terminal user support is a Von Neumann machine; it processes a single instruction stream, switching rapidly between users programs to provide service. However, a collection of workstations can execute all applications programs in parallel.

So one has to make a decision between a one, or a multiplatform systeem :

- *PCs/MACs:* with various software products to provide windows for secretaries and physicians, coupled with accompanying cut and paste facilities
- *Workstations/X-terminals :* at the high-end for extensive users (physicians, ICU,..).
- *ASCII-terminals :* For other users it may be simpler and more cost effective to meet users' need with a terminal. Ten terminals with a 10 MIPS host will probably be more economical and offer better performance than 10 workstations, 90% of which are idle or underused. Because a lot of users in a hospital do not need the capabilities of a PC/workstation it is not cost-effective to install a workstation at places used in a very limited way or used only 10 %

of the time, e.g. admission clerks, kitchen, inventory-warehouse, data-entry financial department.

In fact the computer power need to manage and support the medical user environment of a hospital work station will be a compact desktop unit with:

- 16-19 inch screen
- high-resolution colour or monochrome screen (where necessary)
- a Posix compliant OS
- 10 MIPS processing power
- minimum of 8 MB RAM per user

This processing will come from X86 or 680X processors offering some DOS compatibility, or from the latest generation of RISC processors.

Some users will have X-terminals coupled to shared computing systems (rather than work stations maintenance). For the user, the choice of underlying technology will be irrelevant they will just see their screen, keyboard and mouse.

Table 6.4 The choice of the user work station, in relation to different criteria

Criteria	Terminal	Diskless Workstation	X -terminal (X-term)	PC/MAC
Most important Bottlenecks	CPU (Network)	Network	Network and CPU of the client	Network
High number of displays	System slows down	System slows down (less than previous)	System slows down	System won't slow down
Processing power	None	Applications can run locally	X-client software (depends on someone else MIPs)	Application can run locally
Network	None	Node on a network	Node on a network	Node on a network
Software versions	Independent	Diskless workstations from different vendors require different software versions	Regardless of the vendor everyone uses the same software copy.	Application software versions need to be replicated automatically
Guidelines for choice	Simple, non-window applications	Applications require complex graphics with locally processing power	Applications access lots of data and functions. Non-modal operations preferred. If users don't utilize those MIPS all the times, X-terminals can be the best way of utilizing MIPS	User requires existing popular SW tools (Lotus, Excel, Word) Price may be important.

6.7. The Need for Higher Productivity Software Tools

Over the last decade the ratio of hardware to software costs has changed dramatically. There has been a complete flip in the relative costs of hardware to software development. Some 80% and more is actually spent on software rather than on hardware, and much of this expenditure is on maintaining existing software. Rather than developing applications from scratch , a lot of programming efforts are put into programming modifications and maintenance. It is a well-known fact that the initial development costs are much lower than compared with maintenance investments.
One of the most important data processing investments are still software investments. Although users can minimise those investment risks by buying application software, they cannot eliminate them completely (see chapter 8: The Make or Buy Decision).

In the next two chapters the current status and perspectives of software development tools will be discussed in detail.

6.8 Conclusion

In summary, there is no possibility in sight that transmission capacities will not be sufficient to cover our needs, there will be no shortage of archiving capacity considering the new technologies for optical and magnetic disks, and there is no problem of intelligent graphical user work stations. The questions to be answered are:

- The problem of integration
- The problem of software lag
- The urgent need for standardisation on different levels

7

Modelling Health Care Systems

7.1 The Software Dilemma

Hospital managers are beginning to realise that hospitals are relying more and more on their IS and that the IS development group challenges the issue not only to produce better systems but also to be more responsive to user needs and reduce software development and maintenance time. This is simple to recognise, but so difficult to attain.

Nowadays we can observe that application software does not keep pace with the constantly changing needs of healthcare environment or with a dynamic evolving technology. The result is that because of low productivity, large application backlogs everywhere and poor quality, the cost of building and maintaining applications becomes more outrageous. The Wall Street Journal summarised it as follows ;

"Oil and software are the two principal obstacles to economic progress."

Over the past decade significant advances have been made in data storage and user interface components of computer applications. Attempts to improve the real bottleneck, the "process logic component" of applications (the "thinking" portion of applications), have resulted in only marginal improvements. As software developments did not follow technological advances, analysis and design techniques are becoming extremely important. The emphasis has been gradually shifted from coding to analysis and design, a natural consequence of recognising the role of the user. More emphasis is put on software engineering, but this still has far to go before it reaches the maturity of other engineering disciplines. We must stress the fact that when speaking about engineering techniques we always have in mind formulas, algorithms, scientific calculations, etc. Software engineering in contrast has few aspects in common with these engineering techniques and puts more emphasis on the human aspect of communications, knowledge extraction, human interactions, etc.

Five objectives are important to achieve in this domain:

- Development flexibility (productivity)
- Quality increase
- Maintenance flexibility
- Scalability
- Transportability

In the past, several techniques have been adopted with almost religious fanaticism, believing that each of them was the final solution. First came structured techniques, then came CASE tools and fourth generation languages (4GL), and now we have

entered the decade of object orientation that will solve all our problems as claimed by some object-oriented preachers (Table 7.1). Brooks [BRO 88] argued in his article "No silver bullet" that there are no "magic" solutions to the difficult problems associated with software engineering.
The problem with current code generators and 4GL tools -also thought to be the ultimate solution- is that they do not solve the problem at all and do not allow the developer to directly model the health care environment.
4GL are languages which generate 3GL programs by form-filling, screen-painting, specifying variable names or constants. As they increase productivity and reduce maintenance by a factor of 1 to 3, it is a well-known fact that they consume more computing, compared with equivalent 3GL coding, and suffer from performance decrease and inflexibility in design. On the other hand, for comprehensive medical applications, application developers must still translate an application area into procedural, sequential computer code that is by and large incomprehensible and difficult to implement and maintain.
Code generators offer the advantage, starting from a predefined product or prototype, of generating output code in third generation language (3GL). Some CASEtools are integrated with existing 4GL, so that they can generate 4GL code.

Table 7.1 Schematical representation of different tools aimed to improve software productivity

CLASS OF PRODUCT	ADVANTAGES
3 GL and 4GL front ends to RDBMS	More descriptive programming approach Superior maintenance economics Higher productivity
Object-oriented tools and languages	Higher productivity by reusability Performance Rich method for real world representation
CASE tools	Descriptive approach Directly produces program code

7.2 The Software Development Process. The Software Life Cycle

Like all (living) things : software is planned, created (born), used (lives) and finally deleted or replaced (dies). So application software has a life, during which it undergoes many changes, and at a certain time a trade-off point is reached at which maintenance investments are no longer productive. The software then re-enters the planning-design-implementation-support cycle, termed the "software life cycle". This approach, commonly referred as the "waterfall" model, is divided into four main phases: the requirements and analysis phase, the design phase, the implementation phase and the maintenance phase (Fig. 7.1).
Starting from the requirements formulation defined in the planning phase the analysis is started. De Marco offers the following definition [DEM 78], *"Analysis is the study of a problem, prior to taking some action"*. The analysis phase answers the question of **what** the system should do to satisfy the user and gives an analysis of the actual

and future user requirements and specifications. It resides in the real world and is completely defined in the language of the users.
The design phase explains **how** the requirements of the former stage can be resolved. It is a phase of progressive decomposition toward more detail on the functional and information level. It is essentially a creative process, referred to as the broad design and including the definition of a conceptual model (e.g. ER model) and logical model (by refinement).
The third stage is the implementation phase concentrating on the technical implementation of the IS on the functional level (application architecture, programs), the information level (data architecture, database systems) and the technical level (network architecture, hardware components of the system).
Finally the life cycle is terminated with the maintenance phase needed for errors late detected or caused by continuously changing environmental or internal requirements.

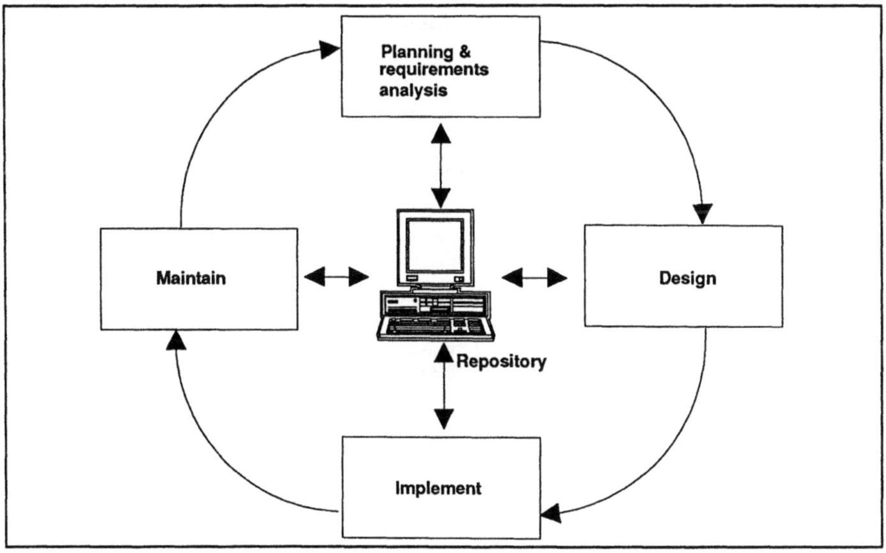

Fig. 7.1 The software development cycle

The software life cycle is mostly implemented based on a view of the real perceivable world in terms of a functional decomposition and design methodology using a top-down analysis. It has been shown that this development process was too inflexible and not appropriate for many applications, especially in the medical field. One phase must be completed before entering in a top-down fashion into the next stage. The iterative feature is only possible between two successive steps (Fig. 7.2).
Meyer [MEY 88] summarises the flaws of this top-down system design methodology as follows:

- Top-down design takes no account of evolutionary changes
- In top-down design, the system is characterised by a single function, a questionable concept.
- Top-down design is based on a functional mind set, and consequently the data structure aspect is often completely neglected.
- Top-down design does not encourage reusability.

Two trends are emerging, which are in fact complementary [MUR 90] :

- Software engineers are modifying the classic "waterfall" model of software into an alternative model in which specifications are written in a computer-executable language, to allow them to validate the formal method and to generate the code automatically in the design phase. Many features of this are found in CASE tools.
- Another relatively new emerging trend in software engineering is object-oriented analysis (OOA), object-oriented design (OOD) and object-oriented programming (OOP) especially aimed to increase the overall development and maintenance of software by encapsulation of attributes and corresponding processes as an intrinsic whole over several objects. The next section will address some very important concepts of object orientedness.

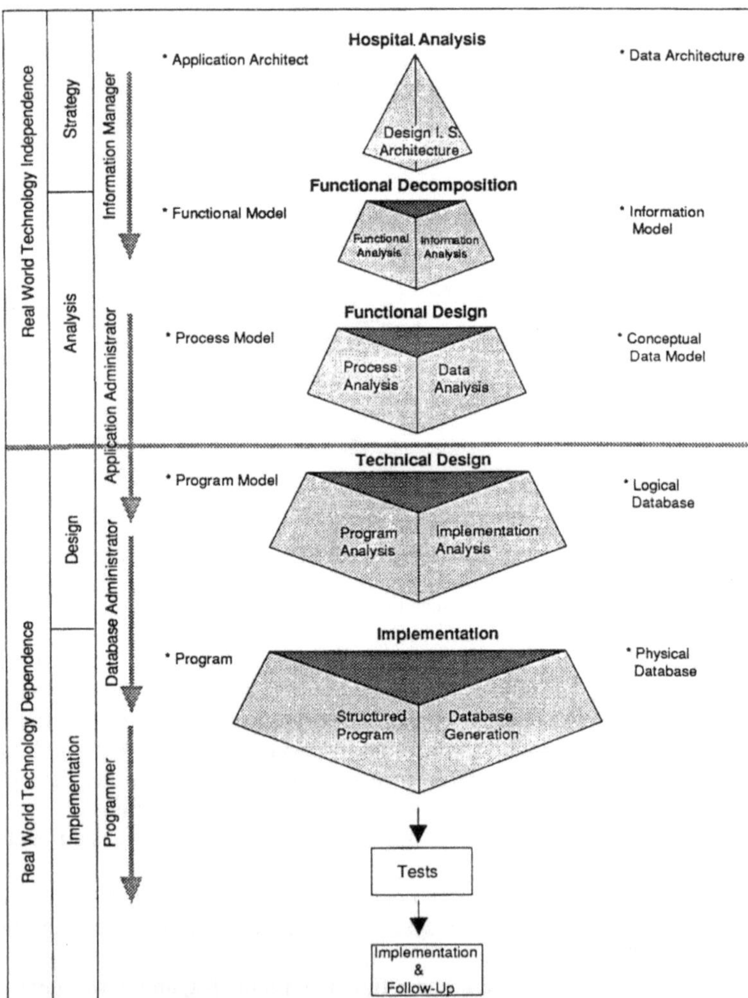

Fig. 7.2 The waterfall model proceeding through different successive steps is the oldest and most well known software development process

7.3 Changing the Way Applications Are Developed

7.3.1 Creators Not Users

As the user becomes more and more important, design of IS 'in response to pressure from end-user departments' has shifted from "technical driven" approaches towards more "user-driven" approaches. More and more people are aware that the real problems of IS design are found on a higher level than the technical platform. It is especially important to stress that the information development process is a political, technical and organisational issue as well.
As different groups (actors) are involved in this creative process they are often characterised by conflicting objectives, priorities and values. Implementation of new systems can sometimes disrupt the classic way of working in terms of authority, work and communication patterns. One must be realistic to recognise and anticipate this reality.
These conditions stipulate that high requirements are stressed for new software development tools and methodologies. The term design is given its original meaning again: the consequent creation of the functionality of a technical system from the standpoint of its users. To cope with this evolving complexity, two new important development environments are emerging, complementary with each other: CASE tools, and OOD methodology and programming languages.

7.3.2 Computer -Aided Software Engineering

CASE is known as the process of assisting the systems development life cycle by applying automated productivity tools. The output of every phase generated by a computer is the input of the next phase in the life cycle process. All information related to the project is stored in a "project database", often called a repository. This approach offers the advantage of producing much greater consistency among computer-aided tasks, reducing the learning process, and increasing overall productivity.
Yet the "term" CASE covers for the moment more than it really is, as most tools consist in fact of drawing tools, text editors, simple syntax checkers and cross-reference generators. Moreover, besides accompanying high financial investments, most tools also need a substantial amount of training and support. So the scope of CASE tools should be broadened, to sustain the complete systems development life cycle.
Compared with other areas of data processing, there is a general lack of agreement upon what CASE products should do. There is even not a standardised definition available describing and comparing the different items deliverable, produced as output (documentation) in each phase of the software life cycle. Most CASE tools are in fact hard-wired to a specific analysis or design method. A very excellent discussion on these items can be found in the article of Davis [DAV 88].
Generally speaking, the options for systems analysis and design methodologies vary depending upon the approach chosen, from more functional modelling-driven methodologies (e.g. Yourdon development methodology, functional decomposition) towards a more data-driven oriented methodology (e.g. Jackson structured development, ER model) to 'as of this writing' few OOD tools (OOATool, Object

International, USA). Let us examine the different approaches that often can be found nowadays in most analysis and design methodologies.

7.3.2.1 The functional modelling approach

This approach is concerned with describing at various levels of abstraction how a system "behaves". Several kinds of graphical representation techniques exist, such as functional decomposition diagrams (FDD), action diagrams (James Martin), state transition diagrams. They all have in common that they describe what processes are needed to run a selected complete area and how these processes interrelate and are decomposed [MAR 86]. By successive decomposition, functions, processes and procedures are defined.

- Functions are determined at the top levels of the information strategy planning; *examples are patient scheduling, inventory control and quality assurance.*
  - A function is a group of activities which together support the objectives of the organisation
  - It is advancing and continuous
  - It is not based on the organisational structure
  - It defines what is done, not how
- Processes are indicated at the level below this; *examples are admit patient, create order and administer drug.*
  - A process is a specific activity that is repeated continuously
  - It can be described by terms of input and output
  - It is not based on the organisational structure
  - It defines what is done, not how
- Procedures are designed at the level below processes.
  - It defines how a process is carried out
  - It is technology dependent
  - To execute a process, multiple types of procedures can be carried out

An alternative method closer to the real world is the top-down data flow diagram method (DFD, from Gane and Sarson) that provides a graphical representation of the sources and flow of data and also the processes transforming the data.

7.3.2.2 The information modelling approach

This approach is concerned with describing at various levels of abstraction the real-world entities (information models), the data structures (conceptual models) and finally the tables and fields (logical/physical models). Again, different representation methodologies exist such as the entity-relationship model (ER model) described by Chen [CHE 80], NIAM representation development by Nyssen [WIN 87], data structure diagrams (Excelerator),etc.

In designing the data architecture of an IS two questions have to be resolved : what information should be stored in the database system, and how should these entities be organised ? The first issue is resolved by analysis, while the latter is addressed through the design of a conceptual data model.

The database design can be divided into two major phases :

- **A content-oriented or infological phase** specifying the semantic or conceptual aspects of information, resulting in a conceptual data model. It aims at representing those information needs 'for example, by objects' which are of interest for the specific application and their mutual relationships. As it is an infological model it is completely independent of underlying techniques, like the database model, internal data model and storage structure of data.
- **A technique-oriented or technological phase**, specifying the logical aspects of information, resulting in a logical data model specifying the attributes of every object.

  As Coad and Yourdon argued in their book, *Object-oriented analysis* [COA 91], they come to the following conclusions :
  - The analysts rush off to do data flow diagrams.
  - After a while, out of synch in time and content, another team works on an information model (this team is called the "database group").
  - The second team receives extensive subject matter understanding.
  - The first team likes the insight but resists the massive changes they must (having grabbed for functionality first).
  - The functional (DFD) team wins out, and the results of the two teams never get reconciled ("Oh, we'll put it together in the design").

7.3.3 Reverse Engineering

Nowadays, many applications have already been automated and represent in that way large investments. Reverse engineering is another method that starts from the existing software system and defines and (re)designs the new system from the old one in-stead of starting from scratch, reducing the risk factor of failure considerably in that way.

7.4 The Object-Oriented Paradigm

The OO-approach aims to increase the overall development and quality of software based on the concepts of reusability and extensibility. The former provides the ability for software products to be reused in whole or in part for new applications, while the latter provides the ability for software products to be adapted continuously to changes in specifications.

Information engineering has just started to use object-oriented methodologies (OOM) as a replacement of pure process-oriented methodologies (e.g. structured analysis and design) and pure data-oriented information engineering. Whatever style will emerge in the future, a structured approach is mandatory in every engineering methodology; in that way OOM is not something radically new as claimed by some "00 preachers" (N.WIRTH).

7.4.1 Object Oriented Analysis

OOA is a relatively young method. Its aims are :

- To shorten the widening gap that exists between more data-oriented techniques (e.g. ER diagrams) and more functionally oriented (e.g. DFD) analysis techniques in order to improve the internal consistency of reusable analysis and design results and facilitate the effective communication of those results.

- To reduce this complexity 'as clinical IS are very complex' by understanding and modelling the real world (application domain) as a collection of concepts and entities, the former one representing classes (persons, procedures, etc.) and the latter one representing objects by specialisation (patients, nurses, physician, medical procedures, etc.), each characterized by their attributes and functionalities.
- To specify two kinds of objects: classes and instances which reflect the problem domain and the system's responsibilities within it, that is to say : their *behaviour* (roles and responsibilities), their *attributes* (state) and also the way in which they *communicate* with each other.

Between objects, "message-passing mechanisms" and inside objects, "methods" (services) specifying the required behaviour and how those objects should react to these messages will be implemented. Message passing is the act of sending a message to invoke a method. A class is an abstract model of its instances and is a way of grouping objects having the same properties and behaviour. A class describes data structure, a list of operations that can be applied to the data structure and an interface giving facilities to access the features from the classes outside.

Objects are instances of a class and concrete or abstract entities from the real perceivable world, concerning which users intend to register and manage information and define events and activities. Objects can be identified in terms of real-world objects, although abstract nouns also represent objects. Concrete objects are patients, health care providers and medical services, while abstract objects are diagnosis, patient orders, medical procedures, etc. Inheritance relations between classes are used to express specialisations and generalisations of the concepts (methods) represented by the classes. For instance, if we take the general class **person** it can be specialised into three subclasses, **physician**, **patient** and **nurse**, implying that **patient objects** will inherit properties of the class person (see also the OO model example in a later chapter) (Fig. 7.3.).

7.4.2 Object-Oriented Design

OOD goes one step further and defines additional details reflecting a specific implementation to fulfil those responsibilities. According to Meyer [MEY 88], OOD is the method which leads to software architectures based on the objects every system or subsystem manipulates (rather than the 'function' it is meant to ensure). In contrast to the "waterfall" model which is based either on the functions that they must ensure (functional decomposition) or on the data oriented approach (data flow approach), the 00 paradigm at it simplest, according to Henderson-Seller and Edwards [HEN 90], takes the same components of a software system (data and procedures) but de-emphasises the procedures, stressing instead the encapsulation of data and procedural features together (Fig. 7.4.).

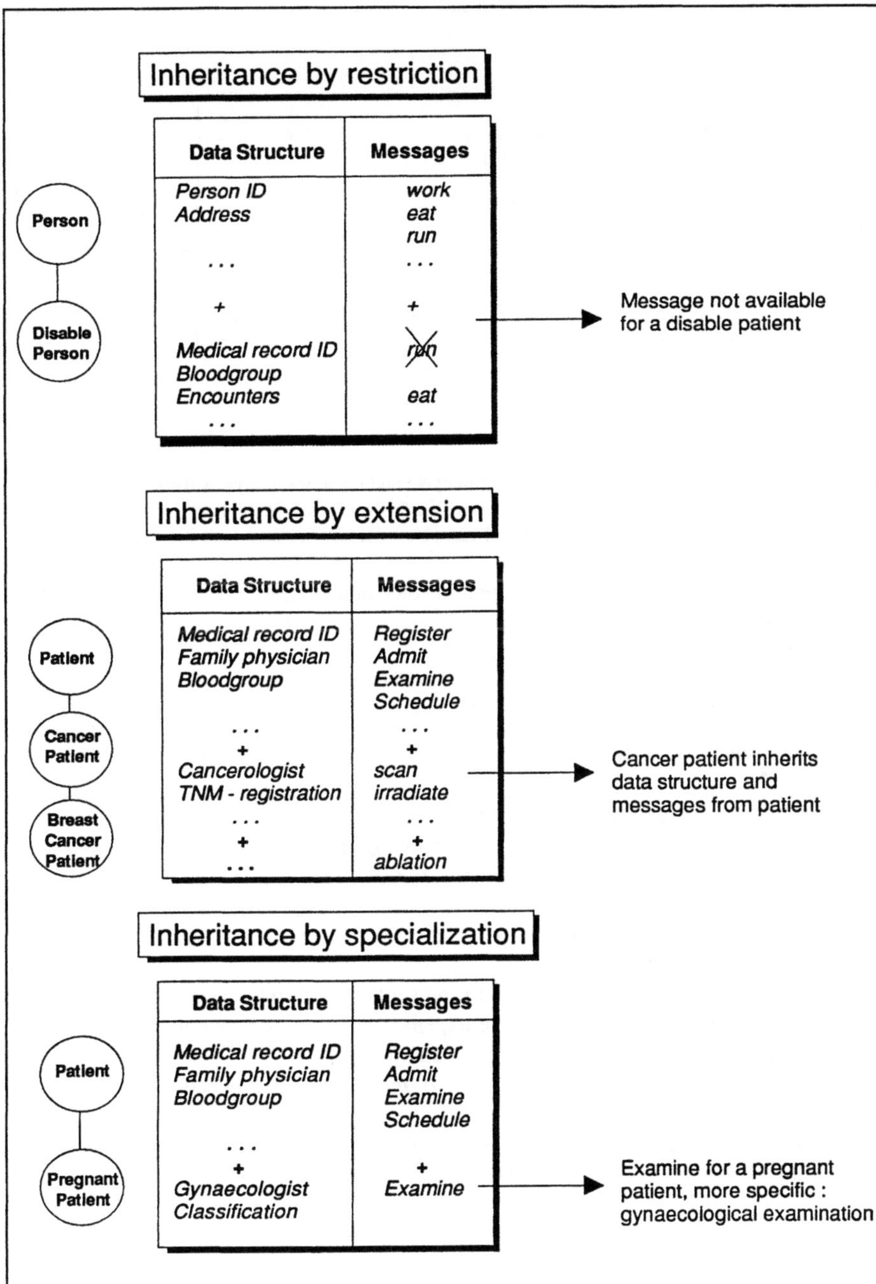

Fig. 7.3 An example depicting a patient-pregnancy 00 model :class and object, structure and service layers. Inheritance by extension (identify gynaecologist, define diagnosis, order medication); Inheritance by specialisation (gynaecological examination) and Inheritance by restriction.

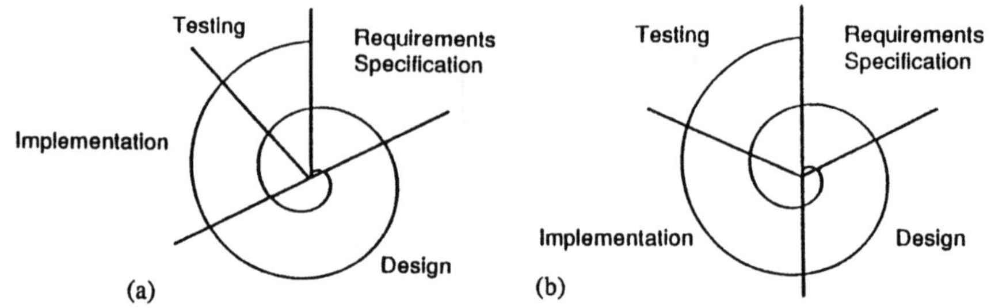

Fig. 7.4 *Left*, object-oriented software life cycle and *right*, traditional software life [WIR 90]
(Source reprinted with permission from Wirfs-Brock R., Wilkerson B, Wiener L. in *Designing object-oriented Software*, New Jersey, Prentice-Hall Inc, 1990, pp 8-9)

Henderson-Seller defined several stages in the object-oriented life cycle by the analysis and design stages (Table 7.2.).

Table 7.2 Summary of proposed seven-point methodological framework for object-oriented (OO)) systems development [HEN 90]..
(Source reprinted with permission from B.Henderson et al. in *The object oriented systems life cycle - Communications of the ACM*, Vol 33,9, sep.1990 pp 142-159)

1.	*Undertake 00 system requirements specification.* High-level analysis of the system in terms of objects and their services.
2.	*Identify the objects, their attributes and the services (operations) each can provide (interface).*
3.	*Establish interactions between objects in terms of services required and rendered.* This is the equivalent of the DFD representation, in which data flow relates to messages and/or message arguments, since data are encapsulated in the object and do not flow in the same way as data in DFD.
4.	*Use of "lower level" entity-data flow diagrams* (or information flow diagrams (EDFD/IDFD). The analysis phase merges into the design phase and a more successive internal refinement of objects is executed.
5.	*Concurrently bottom-up concerns.* Objects will be constructed originating from libraries containing more primitive objects.
6.	*Develop hierarchy of objects.* This stage tries to develop a logical hierarchy of objects in order to detect missing anes.
7.	*Aggregation and/or generalisation of classes.* At this stage the components continue to be worked on, until they are general and generic enough to be stored in a library of components.

7.4.3. Object-Oriented Programming Languages

OOP requires that data and related processes are isolated. Together they make a single object. Programs become a collection of objects that exchange messages between one another to trigger events. The procedures belonging to an object are called methods. Within an object all activities occur sequentially. Different objects execute in parallel an may interact through messages. In contrast to traditional languages in which the sequence of events is program-driven and the user reacts to the program, in OOPs it is controlled by the user.
OO languages (OOL, e.g. Small talk, Eiffel, Actor or hybrid languages such as C++ and objective C) support the most key features of OO thinking such as encapsulation, inheritance, abstraction and message connections.

7.4.4. Considerations

Traditional systems describe applications in terms of their functionality, OO systems describe applications in terms of objects involved.
The main advantage of the OO paradigm is the reusability and homogeneity of objects in terms of data and services, cutting down development and maintenance time. The key characteristics of OO technology are :

- **Encapsulation**: objects encapsulate data, related procedures and an interface that provides the only way to access the features of the class from the outside.
- **Message connections**: objects request other objects to take action via messages corresponding to methods defined for that object inside. To initiate a method a message is sent to the object.
- **Abstraction** : the principle of ignoring those features of an object not relevant for the current problem domain. We distinguish procedural and data abstraction.
- **Inheritance**: object classes are created by inheriting the structure of existing classes. All objects in one class (the instances of the class) have exactly the same structure.
- **Polymorphism** : every object is allowed to have several types and can respond to the same message in different ways (e.g. admission of a patient as inpatient, admission of a patient as outpatient)
- **Dynamic binding** : the ability to refer to the effective type of an object at run time.

Finally it is important to stress that even if you are using 3GL or 4GL, OOA and OOD methodologies and their concepts can be exploited effectively even without using OOL. On the other hand, OOL have many more facilities for expressing the OOA and OOD results and semantics.
Perhaps, this evolutionary approach can 'with the objective to introduce OOL over time' be considered as a more pragmatic and realistic approach as many hospitals are sitting on an expensive software investment of application software written in 3GL or 4GL code based upon hierarchical or network DBMS. For the time being there are not enough programmers using OOL, although this may change over a period of several years.

8

The Make or Buy Decision

It is unlikely that any one software vendor has sufficiently experienced people to understand the information needs of all hospital departments. Also, information needs differ in similar departments of differents hospitals.
One can buy stand-alone systems, but they are designed to do 'just that' stand alone. These systems can benefit from each other's data but have not been designed to benefit from each other's functionality.

In the 1970s and 1980s hospitals mostly developed their own customized systems to meet their needs. Due to the proliferation of a continuously evolving technology and the accompanying shifts in skill requirements and to the declining health care budgets most hospitals are obliged to rely on specialized consulting and software firms to fill in the gaps in their applications systems portfolio.
Every hospital IS manager will be forced to choose between developing the applications internally or acquiring the software externally, or a combination of both.
The make or buy analysis is far from a black-and-white proposition. Just as no hospital can maintain a complete staff of doctors from every medical speciality, no hospital has enough financial resources to establish an information department containing skills from every niche within the computer area and from every specialised application area to build a complete HIS which covers all user needs.
The most effective IS departments are those which can find the right mix of proprietary internal systems and external systems and decide which IS skills to retain and develop in-house and which to acquire from outside. Let us focus briefly on both sides.

8.1 The Buy Side

The IS department is in a position to take a very important role in the final decision for the best long-run course according to :

- Functionality benchmarks which should provide some indication of what the proposed software can and cannot do (take care not to be enthusiastic about a package with fancy graphics and user interfaces, but little functionality)
- Level of support
- The systems integration question, which is often the most important issue on the buy side, can lead to high expenses and integration difficulties

It is also important to stress whether you would like to acquire a vendor-based HIS and to provide the time and personnel needed to evaluate, select, negotiate and implement a new system, which may vary (depending upon the size) from 6 to 16 months. Also the time needed to train hospital personnel to use the system adds further to the complete cost.

8.2 The Make Side

On the make side, an internally developed system should fit the users' needs almost perfectly, although unforeseen some difficulties may arise on the make side such as :

- Maintenance costs, which are difficult to quantify
  (post-implementation and first enhancements list from users after implementation)
- The risk of a serious design flaw discovered too late in the project

8.3 Planning for Acquisition of an Information System : Some Remarks

If hospitals are plannning to buy software, then it is highly advisable 'in order to avoid the common misconception that externally acquired software automatically eliminates all problems' to create a formal request for proposal (RFP) for the decision afterwards of whether to make or buy. The aim of the RFP is to define goals and objectives for the application sytem. Therefore system requirements and related measurement criteria (performance) must be determined in order to make an evaluation as objectively as possible. Important also are site visits to customers with already installed systems to learn from their experience. Finally, the information engineering department should be cooperating with the users in the selection process of the system. Both are indispensable, the former to judge the technical aspects and the latter for a clear understanding of their service to establish the functional requirements. A responsible user group should be nominated in order to illuminate discussions.

In acquiring a vendor-provided system a well-defined RFP can insure :

- Significantly shorter developmental time frames, compared with a self-developed sytem
- Higher probability of success
- Continued vendor support
- Possible lower overall cost

The requirements must be defined on several levels :

- **Functional expectations** that cover in detail (depending on their relative importance) an exhaustive list of functions necessary for the hospital's staff. It is advisable to rank these functions according to different levels of importance.
  As most of the time vendors do not have specific knowledge of the (your) hospital, it is important to ask detailed rather than general questions. Vendors always try to interpret questions in the most advantageous way. Do not ask if a function is available but ask for an explanation 'how' a function is treated/executed.
- **Technical considerations** : An important factor to consider is whether the proposed/desired solution is in pace with the current technology :
  - Is the application platform hardware independent ?

- Is the performance of the system under peak load sufficient for your needs ?
- How is the risk of hardware and or software failure minimised (high-availability, start-up time after recovery, recovery and back-up procedures, etc.) ?
- Is the system able to provide long-term growth in term of increased functionality, increased number of system users, larger patient (data) volumes ?

- **Vendor considerations** : Because of the instability of the (hospital) software industry nowadays, hospitals must be aware of the risk that vendors often leave the industry scene or are merged with other companies. Hospitals must protect themselves against these discontinuities. A proven vendor should have a number of customers with systems already in use and also important is the number of sales in the previous 12 months. He should prove his financial and operational stability in terms of continuing support and maintenance facilities after installing the sytem. Site visits to hospitals with installed sytems are useful to evaluate the vendor's promises.
- **Integration capabilities** : Recognising that the success of a future (departmental) HIS depends upon its facility to integrate the application system with other systems, the capabilities for interfacing to other systems must be carefully studied ; e.g. on-line (real-time) interface and additional costs for a smooth interface. Interface specifications must be given in detail.
- **Financial expectations** : In order to avoid misunderstandings, the vendor should specify :
  - Cost necessary to implement the system (hardware and software)
  - Cost for the maintenance on several bases (8-h, 24-h)
  - Cost for user training and education (per person) and documentation
  - Cost for additional modifications
- **Agreement considerations** (contractual document) form one of the most important and careful steps in the acquisition of a vendor system before the final decision has been taken that is, the written agreement, in order to reduce the risks and misunderstandings on both sides. Although most vendors propose their own contract it is worthwhile studying it carefully and eventually modifying it.

  The "written" features to be covered in this contract are :
  - Time frame : installation data, education period, testing period, production period, final approval
  - Integration and modification capabilities : the vendor agrees or not to provide the interface and/or modifications. Don't forget to write down what was asked and promised.
  - Costs related overrunning the time limit (penalties), modification
  - Regular charges : licence price, maintenance price (source code included or not)
  - Price for new improvements to the software : what does the vendor mean by upgrade ?

As a vendor's standard contract mostly excludes the agreements made previously in the RFP, it is advisable to write down the prior agreements, including the requirements in the RFP, to obtain a full commitment of the vendor before the final purchase.

Perhaps one of the most important steps in the selection process is to define an *evaluation team,* that should not only consist of the effective users of the system but also of representatives of all the key areas of the hospital that will feel the consequences of the system to be implemented. That is the (real) users and also hospital managers as they will need (derive) management information for steering and strategic activities. This team will in fact lead the project towards the successful implementation of the system and will carry the responsibility to establish the budget, define the requirements, evaluate operational and performance criteria and monitor (evaluate) the implementation activities, up to the users' training.
Finally, in making the choice for a "brand new" system with few (none) customers, several risks can arise and one should keep in mind, as stressed by Carney [CAR 87] the following wisdom :

> *A pioneer must be willing to take risks in order to gain a competitive advantage and be willing to accept the risk of failure.*
> *A leader is one who does not want to be in the first wave of technological innovation but is willing to pay the additional price in going with the most advanced technology.*
> *A follower is one who prefers to implement proven technology.*

9

Computer Safety in Healthcare Systems

9.1 The Need for Security Administration

Because health care IS contain varying degrees of sensitive patient information and are potentially life-threatening they should be treated accordingly and conform to stringent safety regulations. Due to the fact that information technology will play a constantly increasing role in hospitals, there is also a parallel increase in the risk of misuse or failure (loss) of IS and data stored about patients in centrally DBMS caused by hardware or software weakness or by users violating certain mechanisms.
Security refers to the protection of IS against unauthorised disclosure, alteration or destruction. This involves three features: information systems must always be available at users wish, authorised users must be able to do the things they are permitted to and the integrity of the system must be guaranteed.
In order to guarantee the safety of medical information systems, a security policy has to be defined, and software quality requirements have to be set up by analysing the possible threats. One can classify three basic risks on the data and systems levels :

- **Integrity loss**. Integrity involves ensuring that the things users are trying to do are correct. Therefore we have to define rules, avoiding alteration by systems errors originating from the hardware or software.
- **Confidentiality loss**. We have to define resistance to unauthorised access.
- **Availability loss**. Unauthorised impairment of functionality.

This demands also a security administrator who manages the security domain according to the previously established security policy and defines within the hospital the functional requirements on all the systems. In order to achieve a certain level of security some security functions have to be defined.
The way these security features are handled on the software, hardware and user levels defines the security policy of the environment. Let us refer therefore to the criteria for the Evaluation of Trustworthiness of Information Technology Systems (GISA, German Information Security Agency, 1989) [GIS 89] (Fig. 9.1) :

- **Authentication and identification**. This feature specifies the identification and authentication of objects (i.e. users, user groups, other computer systems) prior to any interaction. One must decide what actions to take if identification and authentication fail. Secure user identification procedures must be defined to control access to health care IS. Authentication of users is ideally a combination of :
    - Something you have (cards)
    - Something you are (biometrics e.g. fingerprints)
    - Something you know (PIN, personal identification code with each card)

  - Something you do (e.g. voice recognition, handwriting combined with stroke analysis)
- **Access rights**. After identification and authentication, every object that needs to manipulate certain types of information (for update, read, write, delete, etc.) must be administered rights (administration and verification of rights) to do that. So every time an object wishes access (i.e. to what information and which actions he may undertake), his right must be verified. In a health care environment, some rights are not static but granted depending upon the content of certain (medical) attributes (e.g. only referring physicians may have access to medical results of patients for which they are responsible). The security officer will grant and revoke access rights to objects down to the level of a single user.
- **Audit accountability** (requirements and audit). This function ensures that a log is provided every time an attempt is made by an object to exercise some rights. The content of the log may vary depending upon the policy of the organisation. The following data can be registered : user identification, time of access, location of the workstation, success or failure of the attempt, type of action and content of the information before and after access.
- **Object reuse**. Some elements such as peripheral storage devices can be used concurrently by several objects (users, computer system). In order to avoid security conflicts one must be assured that no residual information of a former transaction remains accessible for other users.
- **Error recovery**. Hardware or software failures can cause disrupted data to enter into the system or lose data and reduce in that way the liability of the IS. In order to repair the damage while guaranteeing as little loss of data as possible, recovery mechanisms have to be provided :
  - On a continuous basis by the following actions :
    - Check-point mechanism (RDBMS)
    - Before and after images (RDBMS)
  - On a periodical basis
    - Back-up and restore
    - Forward and backward recovery
- **Fault tolerance** (continuity of service). As health care IS are potentially life-threatening in case of disruption, the availability of specified data and functions within an overall acceptable response time must be guaranteed on a 24 h basis. Some possible alternatives facing this problem may be fault-tolerant systems (hardware) or duplicates (shadow databases).
- **Data communication security**. In order to ensure an effective communication of sensitive medical data (for example lab results or RX results that are transmitted between physicians or medical units) that could be subject to security threats, protection mechanisms to inhibit attacks are needed in order to guarantee the integrity of the message and the validity of the original message. Note that for data communication security, encryption algorithms and associated key management procedures must be defined to ensure :
  - Message authentication to secure the originator of the data stream
  - Peer-entity authentication to ensure that during data communication the desired partners communicate with each other
  - Message content confidentiality

Besides these, a trusted system must exhibit an appropriate level of quality assurance by being able to meet certain criteria :

- Quality of specification of the system components to be evaluated
- Quality of software development methodology
- Quality of operational behaviour to evaluate whether or not the security functions behave correctly under operational conditions
- Quality of user/system documentation
- Quality of the security policy

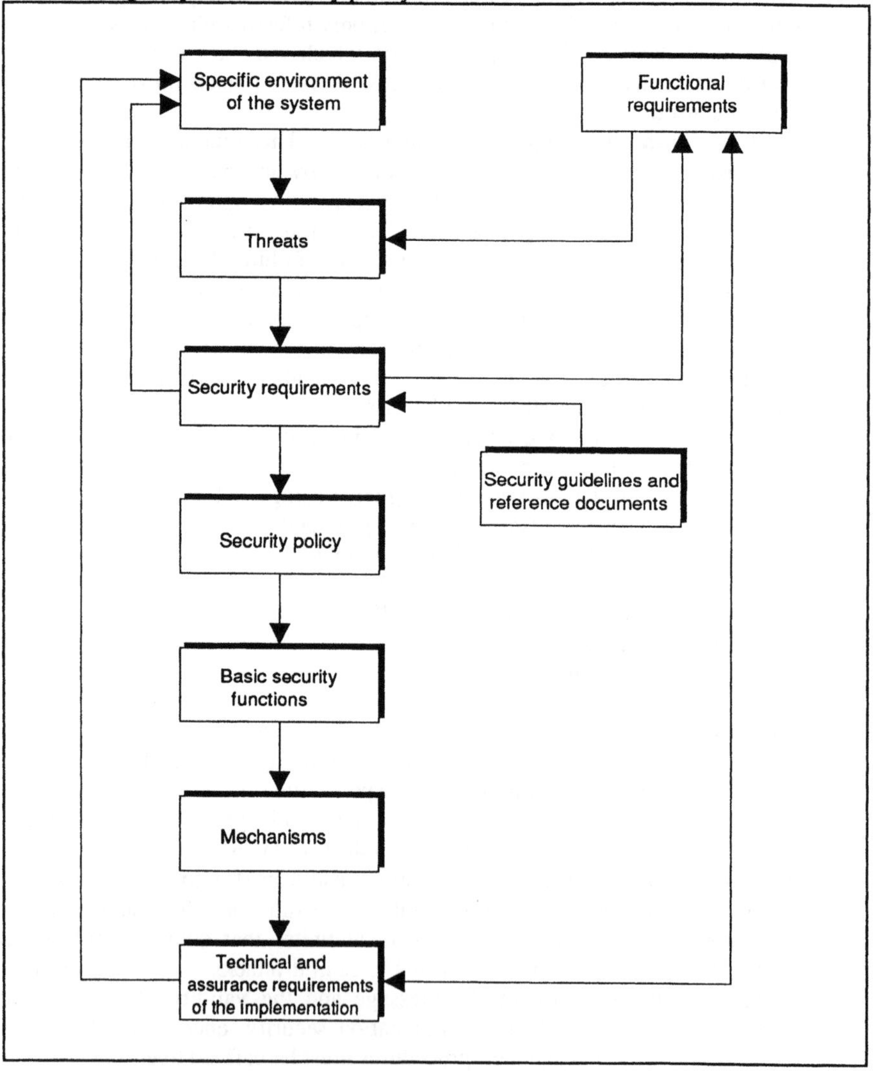

Fig. 9.1 Dependency relationships involved in the specification of a security policy and the necessary implementation assurance [GIS 89]

(Source GISA German Information Security Agency 1989 in *IT - Security Criteria : Criteria for the evaluation & Trustworthiness of Information Technology Systems* - Koln, Bundesanzeiger, p.7)

9.2 Security, Integrity and Recovery Mechanisms in Database Systems

Security

In relational database management systems security is handled by two mechanisms, SQL GRANT and REVOKE commands, that specify which users have access (i.e. select, insert, update, delete) and to which objects. A second security mechanism is the use of VIEWS to provide selections of subsets of data within database systems related to the application domain of every user. Authorisation and identification mechanisms are defined by the login mechanism (which requires each user to have an established name) and a password on the system or in each database.
A transaction is a logical unit of work and a unit of recovery. Thus, the transaction either executes completely or is cancelled. Recovery refers to the mechanism that puts the database back on its feet after a system failure. The COMMIT and ROLLBACK operations assure the consistency of the database. The former indicates a successful end of the transaction (i.e. a logical unit of work has successfully been completed or committed), while the latter indicates an unsuccessful end (roll it back). By means of a transaction log in which changes to the database are recorded, it is possible to undo an update or restore a situation by using the before images (roll backward). Executing a commit or rollback operation establishes a synchronisation point representing the boundary between two consecutive transactions.
However, in a distributed database system environment a protocol is necessary to ensure that a given transaction applying to more than one "resource manager" is either accepted completely (commit) or rejected (roll back). This protocol is called "two-phase commit".

Integrity

In the database world, integrity refers to the accuracy or correctness and consistency of the data in the database. There are several kinds of data integrity.Three important ones to mention are domain constraints, entity integrity and referential integrity.

Back-up and recovery

Previous security/recovery mechanisms refer to operations executed at transactional level "atomic" failures, but the system must also be prepared to recover from "global" failures. Such failures can be divided into two broad categories :

- System failures, which affect all transactions (batch and on-line) actually in progress (e.g. power failure, fire, etc.)
- Media failures, which affect only one particular device, causing the non-functioning of a part or of the complete database (e.g. disc controller failure, disc crash, etc.)

Besides special precautions on the hardware level (no-break group, duplication on some components, fault-tolerant systems) the back-up and recovery mechanism is the most important one in use. Although very system-dependent, they are generally characterised by logging all changes made to the database on a transaction log (tape or disc). When a failure occurs the transaction log can rebuild the "history" starting from the last copy of a complete database restored from a back-up, using the after images (roll forward).

9.3 Fault-Tolerant Information Systems in Hospitals

As hospitals never close and are operational 24 h a day, a main element in the global security policy is to guarantee a highly reliable and available IS.
In the past, several hospitals have attempted to achieve full reliability and availability by duplicating hardware for use as standby in the case of failure of one computer system. This approach was not cost-effective as the resulting up-time increased to 97% (at most) and was not sufficient compared with the financial and personnel investments.
To meet this challenge some computer companies started in the early 1980s to develop fault-tolerant computer systems, e.g. Tandem, Stratus. Meanwhile, OLTP (on-line transaction processing) requirements have risen so high (health care, banking, airways, etc.) that most computer companies are offering or announcing fault tolerance in the long-run.
Although the concepts of fault tolerance may vary from company to company, the most relevant characteristics of such systems are (Tandem) :

- Multiple, independent, parallel but not redundant processors using non-shared memory
- A suitable operating system capable of handling this architecture
- Dual-port disc drives and (duplicate) mirrored disc volumes (all data that a program writes on one disk are replicated on a second one)
- Facilities of incremental system growth without causing incompatibilities

Another approach is the use of RAID (Redundant Array of Inexpensive Drives). They are using multiple low cost drives as a group to improve performance and provide in that way a degree of redundancy and fault-tolerance.
It is clear that as for the next decade the market share of such systems will increase and become of great importance for the health care industry.

9.4 The Phenomenon of Computer Viruses

When talking about security it is inevitable to consider computer viruses, as the panic in the PC world has raised a lot of questions about them, how they work and what can be done against them.
Computer viruses work like biological viruses, which when placed in contact with uninfected cells inject genetic material into them resulting in a continuous multiplication of those viruses. When a computer virus, i.e. a piece of software, is placed on a computer system it copies itself into other specific programs in a "hidden" way and instructs the infected programs to infect other programs. At a certain event (date, program execution, etc.), special functions are executed by the computer virus, causing deletion of files, display of all kind of irrelevant messages, etc.
Viruses need not only reside in executable code, they can also reside in real data. Some important computer viruses are Trojan horse, time bombs and computer virus [WIN 89]. A Trojan horse is a piece of software built into a host program which is not capable of invading repeatedly into other programs. It executes an extra functionality.

A time bomb is comparable with a Trojan horse but executes the extra functionality only when certain conditions are fulfilled. A computer virus is a Trojan horse or a time bomb invading or copying itself repeatedly in other programs, without compromising the functionality of host programs.
In PCs they aim to delete data or prevent users for working with the system. In multi-user systems viruses can be used to obtain privileges of other users (super-user). The best way to protect against viruses is to define a security policy for the organisation : do not use "illegal" software and make regular separate backup records of source and data.

Hospital Management Systems

Part 2

" The reasonable man adapts himself to the world, the unreasonable man adapts the world to him. All progress depends on the unreasonable man . "

George Bernard Shaw

10

Architecture of a Hospital Information System

10.1 Hospital Information Systems : A Definition

A hospital information system (HIS) can be defined as an open system which attempts to integrate and communicate the outside and inside flow of information within a hospital and provide the functions common for all applications (Fig 10.1). The areas embraced by a HIS will functionally include, medical information systems, patient administration systems and financial/management systems.

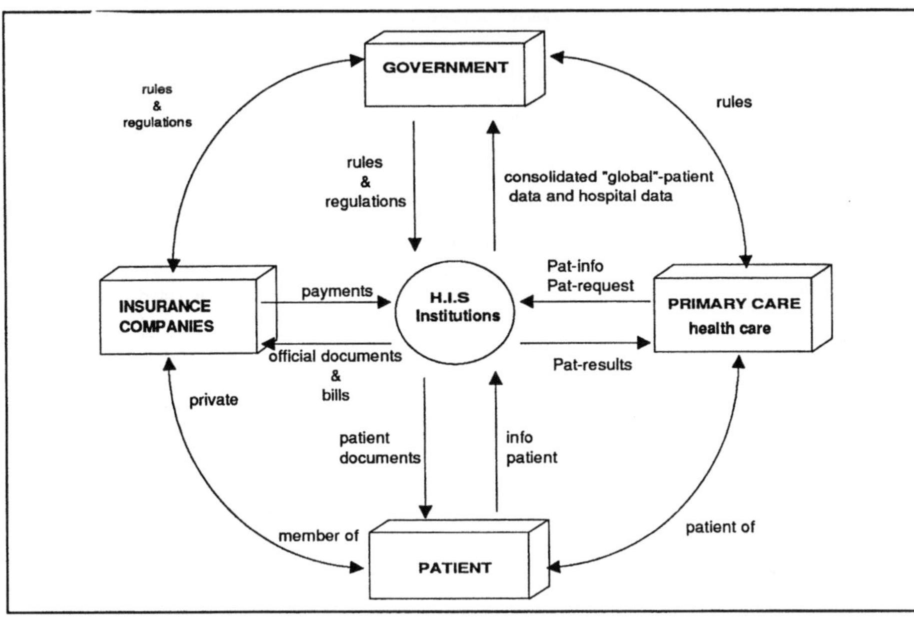

Fig.10.1 Representation of a HIS and its external links *"A hospital information system attempts to integrate and communicate the outside and inside information flow...."*

A HIS serves essentially as a *medium for communication* between the diverse collaborating functional sub-systems or units in a hospital [KEY 88]. It acts therefore as a *skeleton* to facilitate the integration of various systems operating at sub-system level.

Each of these subsystems will operate in some more or less stand-alone fashion. Some subsystems will operate at a lower level such as monitoring applications (e.g. ICU).
As nowadays hospital information systems have to communicate with a broad range of IS using various IT technologies on the hardware and software levels, they have to tie diverse subsystems together to unify the view for the end-user as part of the need for integration on "all" levels. This interface or front-end function may be part of the HIS or may be a stand-alone function replicated on every departmental node. The first one has the advantage of centralising all functions or data which are transferred; the second one has the advantage of having less impact on the performance and availability of the central HIS.

Table 10.1 Description of a hospital information system in terms of the main functions (11) by which it supports the organisation as a whole [VEL 89]

Management oriented	Patient oriented	
Financial-economical	**Patient - management**	**Medical**
1. Financial general ledger accounts receivable accounts payable budget control **2. Material and technical Management** stock control inventory maintenance planning energy control purchase / order management **3. Personnel system** personnel management loans and salaries **4. Patient billing** insurability medical act administration **5. Strategic planning and study** executive IS cost accounting retrospective utilization analysis	**6. Outpatient & Inpatient** patient registration ER registration patient scheduling **7. Inpatient** inpatient (pre-)admission admission registration bed census **8. Result reporting and order entry** order entry & communication result reporting	**9. Nursing** care - planning charting nurse staffing food supply **10. Diagnostic** radiology function laboratory ° cardiology ° pneumology laboratory ° chemistry ° haematology ° microbiology ... **11. Therapeutic** operatingroom radiotherapy pharmacy intensive care OB-gynaecology ...

The hub of a HIS is composed of a central database where all interconnected departmental systems can store (archive) and retrieve their data, created or produced earlier from other "feeder " systems. Administrative and medical data are gathered in the central HIS as well. In health care the same database can be used by a variety of health care actors varying from medical to administrative personnel for medical, administrative and management purposes (Table 10.1) [WIE 81].

Due to the fact that this database provides a broad range of services, it has to be designed very carefully. The information stored in the HIS database can be divided into two main groupings (Table 10.2) :

° *Data related to the patient,* (patient oriented) further subdivided into patient-medical data and patient-administrative data.
Medical data are all those concerning the medical status of the patient, and composed of all diagnostic patient-related data and all therapeutic patient-related data such as measured physiological results therapeutic data and the patient's medical records. They vary from, text and image patterns to voice data (future).
Patient-administrative data can further be subdivided into :

- Patient identification data: information that identifies the patient as unique such as name, date of birth, sex, place of birth, race etc.
- Patient demographic data: information that can change during the patient's life cycle in the HIS database, address, job, marital status, etc.
- Patient-episode data: information referring to a concrete episode in the hospital, episode identification number, location, type of episode, etc.
- Patient-financial information related with the price of performed examinations or procedures
- Patient-encounter data: information referring to a concrete encounter in the hospital
- ...

° *Data related to the hospital,*(management and planning oriented) further subdivided into financial and clinical oriented data . As patients are indirectly generating clinical and financial data, both types of data are the input for future-oriented planning and management functions.Clinical data are used for clinical monitoring functions (quality assurance,DRG,resource utilization,...).
Financial data are those necessary to run the hospital in general on a short and mid-long term.These data are a collection of all data necessary to manage and control the daily operation of the hospital. It contains the natural data classes of an organisation, such as general ledger, accounts receivable, payable, personnel, general ledger and budgeting .Integrating both types of information enables a hospital to operate on a more cost efficient way and to use this information for future-oriented strategic planning functions as input for executive decision support systems. They are most alphanumeric,graphical, less text and very little image data.

Table 10.2 Description of a hospital information system in terms of the main information entities [VEL 89]

Clinical subsystem : patient central		***Patient-Record***
Medical information	**Medical-administrative information**	***Real-Time ---> Short-Term***
Diagnostic ° laboratory ° radiology ° nuclear medecine ° EEG,ECG,EMG, respiratory. Therapeutical ° operation history ° radiotherapy ° intensive care ° physiotherapy ° nursing ° medication	° Admission data ° Patient demographic data ° Orders ° Planning and appointment data ° Patient diets ° Material deliveries	
Hospital : Communication system - Repository system		
° General accounting ° Accounts receivable ° Accounts payable ° Personnel data ° Loans and salaries ° Budget control ° Inventories	° Case mix ° Resource allocation data ° Simulations / Models ° Retrospective utilization data ° Cost / Quality information	***Mid-Long Term ---> Future***
Financial information	**Strategic information**	
Management subsystem : hospital central		***Hospital Record***

10.2 Design Objectives of A Hospital Information System

The most important design goals of HIS are :

° *To have **a common registration** of total patient information **at the point** of each transaction.* The capture of data is recognised to be a key concern in designing a comprehensive HIS. Important elements are:

- Patient data from birth to death

- Open-ended data retention
- Text, graphics, image, voice, signal and alphanumerical data
- Electronic computer-bases patient record: the technology exists to create the CPR although no one has done it completely as yet.

° *To have the possibility* ***to access information*** *from any location at any time*
Maximum benefits (improved quality care with reduced costs) are only realised when the primary creators and consumers of information interact directly with a system. Important features are :

- On-line access
- Bedside (terminals)
- Physician offices
- Outpatient clinics
- Portable, wireless devices

° *To recognise the* ***health care provider as major user*** *and thus ease of use*
The greater the need to share data and functions by all health care providers, the more we need integration and the better we achieve a cost efficient HIS. Important features are :

- User interface simplicity
- Comprehensive functionality
- Access to information in a variety of ways
- Access to other databases
- Expert systems
- Turning data into information

° *To recognise* ***integration*** *as a "conditio sine qua non".*
Although the patient is not a direct user of a HIS, he is the main driving force towards integration as he wishes to be seen as a whole. "His and Integration is a tautology, as a HIS without integration is no HIS" [EHL 91].

° *To recognise that a HIS must be* ***cost efficient.*** The main guidelines are:

- Open system design
- Standards
- Off the shelf hardware and software
- Efficient design
- Modularity

° *To provide tools for evaluating health care* ***cost and quality***
As the quality of patient care is as important as the reduction of overall costs for survival, the HIS should deliver meaningful hospital information (i.e. a mix of medical and administrative data) to assist hospital executives in solving the dilemma of quality versus cost. In fact the financial system will be a byproduct of patient care in contrast to HIS of the first generation.

° *To recognise the clinical* ***communications hub of a HIS***
The core business of a hospital is patient care. The process of that care involves the patient, his or her chart and the health care professional. Systems are becoming patient oriented instead of management oriented.

° *To recognise that technology must meet* ***the user's and application needs***
A generic solution may not always be an appropriate and/or adequate platform. The presentation of data should be customized to the type of user because user

needs will not change to fit the systems requirements.

- *To establish **the basis** for hospital controlled and developed applications*
  An application platform has to be established upon which other applications can be build.
  All hospitals are the same, but each is different, therefore unique needs are best addressed by the institution.
- *To guarantee **backward compatibility** of new software releases*
  It is preferable to implement application enhancements in an evolutionary rather than a revolutionary way. New and enhanced capabilities while continuing to support existing applications, has to be provided.
- *To guarantee **high availability** of the system*
  - Fast response time
  - Reliability and
  - Confidentiality

10.3 The Integration Challange

10.3.1 Moving from Data Exchange to Information Sharing.

Like other industries, hospital computerisation is often characterised by "islands of automation", that is applications run on a variety of large and small proprietary computers. Some computer systems are dedicated to a single application. As a result, patient information is often scattered among various heterogeneous systems in different locations with little or no transfer of information from one system to the other. Hospital users are increasingly demanding a coherent information system rather than the collage of disparate systems that they too often find today. Complaints about "data diarrhoea", too many facts, are common.
As medicine today contains many specialities, communication requirements are growing in exponential relation to the rate of sub-specialisation in health care. Most of these phenomena are driven by the emerging technological evolution, and this in turn results in less cohesion and greater degradation of medical care. As the patient remains the same and wishes to be seen as a whole the integration on the operational level (=medical care) and informational level (=medical data) must be assured.

In a hospital environment integration has always been identified as a goal easy to recognise but so difficult to attain. It is the key for effective improvement of the hospital operation in the medical, administration and financial fields, presenting the organisation for all "actors" as a unified whole. It is the most important trend in medical informatics in the coming years.
The aspect of integration in the HIS database deserves special attention, as it facilitates multiple users accessing a critical mass of data upon their specific view, accomplishing in that way multiple functions and providing a synergistic effect for :

- The executive who wants accurate data because costs and charges are involved and have to be controled for case-mix analysis, profitability,...

- The physician who wants accurate data to optimise the health care process and to detect anomalies originating from different systems, without having to learn multiple system sign-ons protocols
- The nurse who desires accuracy to offer optimal care by using automated patient charts

So every user is encouraged to contribute their particular data items to establish the HIS-database upon which multiple users can rely; no single user can enter all of the data [CLA87].

10.3.2 Levels of Integration

Integration can be achieved on four levels.

Data integration stands for the fact that data are stored only once and (centrally or distributed) presented to authorised users in a familiar way. An important aspect belonging to data integrity is "validity checks", covering the following features :

- Range checks
- Pattern checks
- Consistency checks
- Computed checks
- Spelling checks

A trade-off has to be achieved between physical and logical integration, for performance reasons. Sometimes it is better to duplicate some data elements in order not to influence the user response time.

The concept of data integrity derived from the perceivable real world is further composed of three integrity levels: syntactic, semantic and pragmatic integrity (Fig.10.2) [STE 85]. While for most applications syntactic integrity is system controlled, semantic and pragmatic integrities are more difficult to manage and more user controlled (Fig.10.3). On the other hand, for clinical data the need for pragmatic and semantic integrity is higher than the need for syntactic integrity and demands disproportionately far more efforts.

It is clear that at a certain level (semantic, pragmatic) data integrity is only possible by integrating two techniques, knowledge-based and database systems,(Fig.10.4).

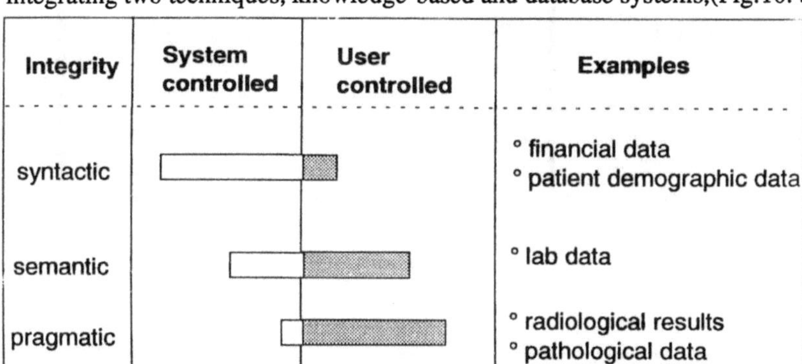

Fig.10.2 Representation of data integrity divided into its syntactic, semantic and pragmatic issues

Functional integration, a topic on the lips of many persons nowadays, is concerned with the unique management of hospital functions in order to reduce redundancy on the application code generation site, for multiple reasons such as maintenance and definition.

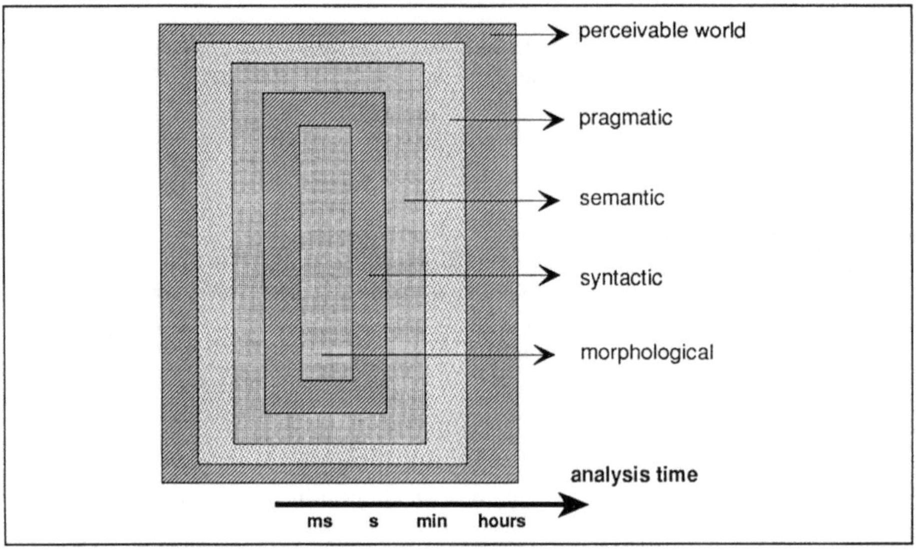

Fig.10.3 Types of analysis. Pragmatic analysis explains the internal representation with the context; semantic analysis explains the internal representation of the sentence; syntactic analysis (parser) defines the structure of a sentence, verb, noun, etc.; lexical analysis indicates if the word is a verb or noun; morphological analysis defines the structure of a word into radical, prefix, suffix, etc.

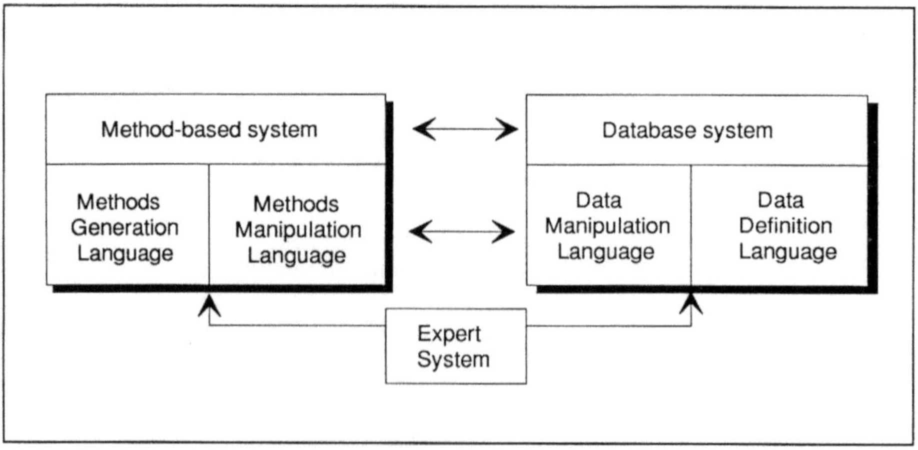

Fig10.4 Data integration at certain levels (pragmatic and semantic) is only possible by integrating knowledge and data

Management integration. Although not often mentioned it is desirable that the management of hospitals also be guided in the same integrated way. Starting from the strategic directions and guidelines defined by the upper management, every medical service, patient care and administration service should be aware of his defined "territory" and the scope of his domain without degeneration into conflicting and competing hierarchical services. Especially as we enter the decade of decentralisation, coordination of all institutional activities over the complexities of political consequences is most desirable and a "must".

Technical integration involves dealing with the aspect that it is most desirable to have the possibility to inter-connect hardware devices from different origins (interconnectivity) and have portable applications (portability). The hospital end-user aims to have one work station at his desk providing him a "window" to the hospital environment and his applications, resembling as much his classic desk environment. Users demand products (= applications) that have the same look and feel on different platforms (workstations, computer). Figure 10.5 illustrates several approaches. For these topics we refer to previous chapters concerning open system standard philosophy and graphical user interfaces.

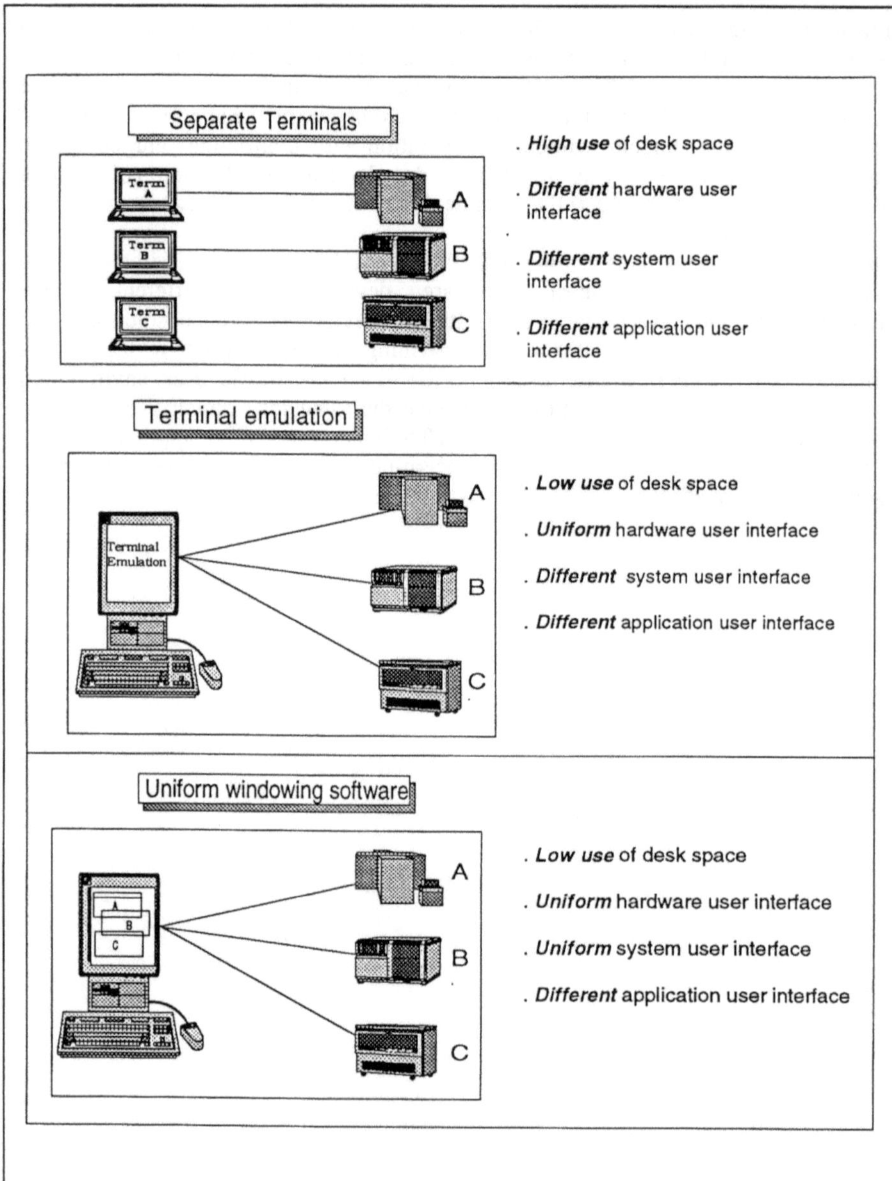

Fig.10.5 Several levels of technical integration oriented towards the end-user. Terminal emulation software allows the user to communicate separately with other computers from different vendors. Windowing provides the user the facility to communicate concurrently with other heterogeneous applications.

10.4 The Urgent Need for a Broadly Accepted Framework

Building an IS that the health care environment supports as a whole is an extremely complicated undertaking. An unique break-down of health care IS in each country or at a European level is not obtainable, due to different policies, strategies and objectives. The question of how data and functions are distributed among (organisational) locations in the health care community is a complex one due to many, sometimes (varied) subjective reasons.

The major obstacles to the progress that might be made in the area of HIS arise almost entirely from the lack of a well-accepted overall (structure) framework within a HIS and the total non-uniformity of data definition in this field. These factors have severely hampered the integration of systems, their transportability and the commercial development of software solutions in this area.

If we aim to exchange data from one health care level to another and vice versa (health care provider, departmental level, hospital level, regional level, national level), feedback is necessary in order to continue to motivate users (data originators/feeders) and to control the quality of data.

Especially in the health care environment the notion "*integration*" is on the lips of many persons, so that all the IS have to relate to each other, and this does not happen without coordination of separate parts within one framework.

There is a growing need to recognise that standardisation activities in medical informatics is a must, in order to ensure the interchangeability of information among health care organisations and also to ensure the transportability of IS to make them economically viable. Health care systems are expensive to develop and to maintain and tend to be installed on an international basis. A number of initiatives are undertaken nowadays in that direction on the national and international level, towards the definition of a standard architecture. For instance, inside the ESPRIT (European Strategic Programme for Research and Development in information Technology) programme a consortium has been founded, called RICHE (Réseau d'Information et de Communication Hospitalier Européen) to construct a framework for open information and communication systems for health care in Europe.

The general objectives of the RICHE project are to develop :

- A modular European reference architecture and a global data model for overall open information and communication systems for hospitals in their local environment that show the relationships between the various parts of the architecture
- Detailed architecture and data models for selected hospital functions in line with the reference architecture
- Standards for intra- and inter-operational exchange of data and for connection with external systems
- A number of working prototypes in order to demonstrate the feasibility for application of the architecture and data models

- A conformance classification for products and systems in the RICHE framework
- RICHE is not limited to the hospital domain

10.5 Heading for Harmony

Driving forces towards standardisation are the Healthcare Information Standards Committee (HISCC) in the USA and the centre for European Normalisation on the European continent (CEN) and its sub-committee on health care (CEN/TC251, technical committee). CEN/TC251 has created several work groups based on its programme of work as presented in its document "Directory of the European Standardisation Requirements for Health Care Informatics and Programme for the Development of Standards" [CEN 91]. Seven work groups have been nominated, of which working group 1, Healthcare Information Modelling and Medical Records, especially deals with issues concerning HIS. It aims to construct a framework not limited to the hospital domain for open information and communication systems for health care in Europe. A universal framework will focus on using the best efforts of different international committees to harmonise them in a unified framework.

As medical, managerial and administrative requirements in the health care sector vary within the same organisations in the same country, and also between different countries, it is clear that such defined standards may not represent a rigid bureaucratic framework. It was decided to start with a high level view of the health care environment and, by successive refinement, to progress into greater detail. In the design process of a health care (HC) IS, different phases are described in the CEN document: the HCI framework, HCIS architecture and Common Conceptual Schemas (Fig. 10.6). They are interrelated because the output of each phase is the input for the next one.

10.5.1 The Health Care Information Framework

The *HCI framework* produces a high-level model of the health care environment and is a logical mapping between the real world, in particular the health care environment, and its health care Information systems Architecture. This framework -representing the main health care subsystems, their connections, rules etc...- is the basis for an evolutionary development of heterogeneous computer supported health care information and communication systems.

A key feature of the framework is its reliance on the use of abstractions. In this way the framework -at its most abstract level- reflects the fundamental and essential features of health care processes and information, and can be seen as applicable to all HC entities. It defines the general information structure enables the exchangeability of information.

The European Health Care framework will maintain and build upon the diversity of national Health Care systems in the european countries. An harmonized description/structure of planning documentation (Policies, Strategies, Budgets, Health Care status Reports, etc.) will be provided to ensure comparisons between european countries.

The main rationale for a standardized health care information framework is:

- To act as a contract between the users and procurers on the one hand and developers and providers of IS on the other hand.
- To ensure that all applications and (computerized) data bases are developed to support the health care organisation as a "Whole" as opposed to just "a Single" organisation or department.
- To obtain economies of scale -originating from enhanced portability-, as healthcare information systems are expensive to develop and to maintain, and tend to be installed on an international basis
- To define a common basic understanding that allows all health care information systems to interchange data

This framework is technology-independent and understandable by health care decision/policy makers and users.

10.5.2 The Health Care Information System Architecture

Starting from the different health care areas defined in phase 1, the Health Care Information System Architecture *(HCIS architecture)* aims to describe for *each selected health care area* (e.g. hospitals, ambulatory health care services, GP, laboratories,...) the different sub-systems (sub-areas) of which they are composed in terms of specific functions and information needs.

This phase:
- Requires intensive user involvement
- Remains independent of technology
- Identifies areas for system design
- Creates a data model (ER model)
- Creates a process model and links to the data model

By choosing the classes and objects that are common to several countries, and common to several subsystems, one obtains the basic pieces on which the architecture can be build up. The HCIS describes the healthcare information in terms of common objects and classes.

10.5.3 Common Conceptual Schemas

Finally, for some common areas and/or applications identified in the overall HCIS architecture, a detailed conceptual and logical description representing the standard nucleus for those selected areas/and or applications of the data and processes will be identified. Those conceptual schemas can be locally enlarged according to their specific needs. This leads in the final phase to a consistent physical implementation. It enables subsequent consistent implementations in different physical environments.

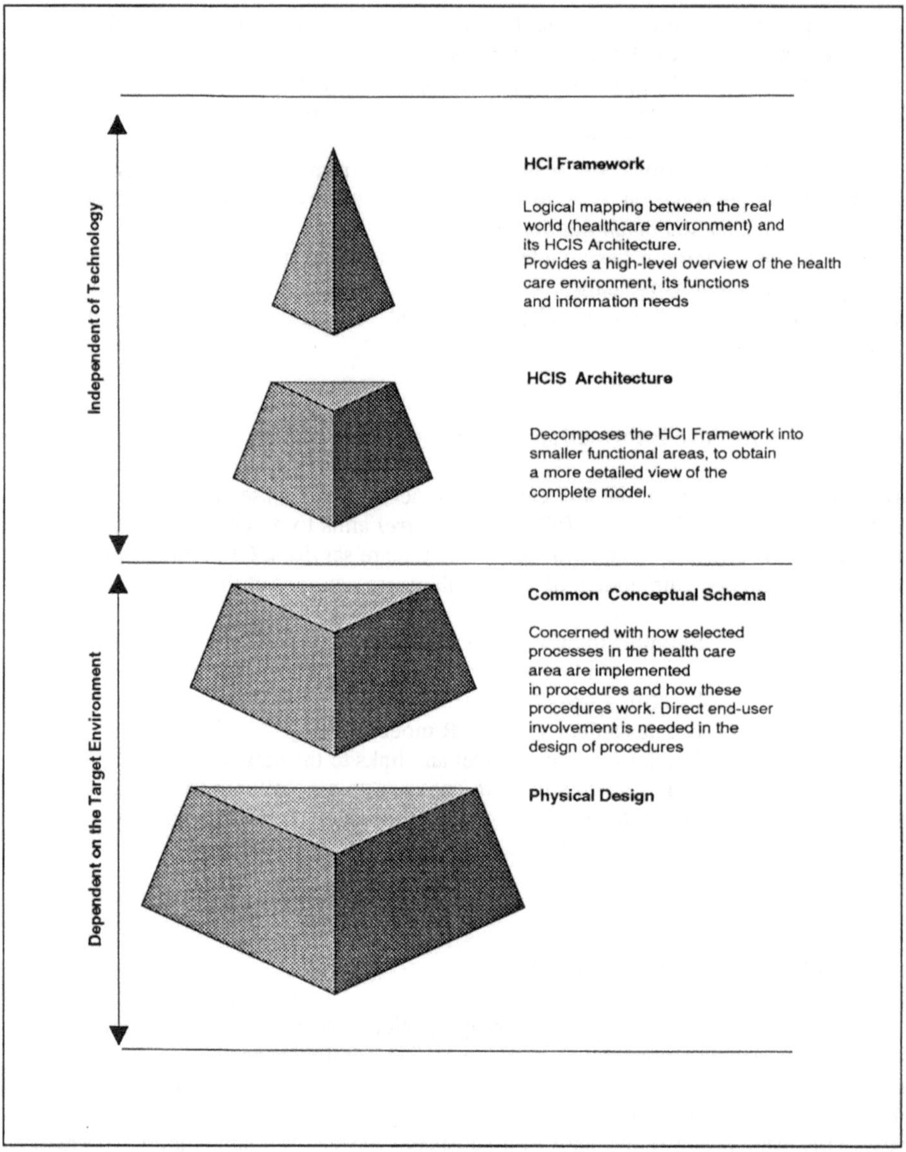

Fig10.6 Representation of different phases towards the definition of a standardised architecture as proposed in the CEN document "Directory of the European Standardisation Requirements for Health Care Informatics and Programme for the Development of Standards" [CEN 91]

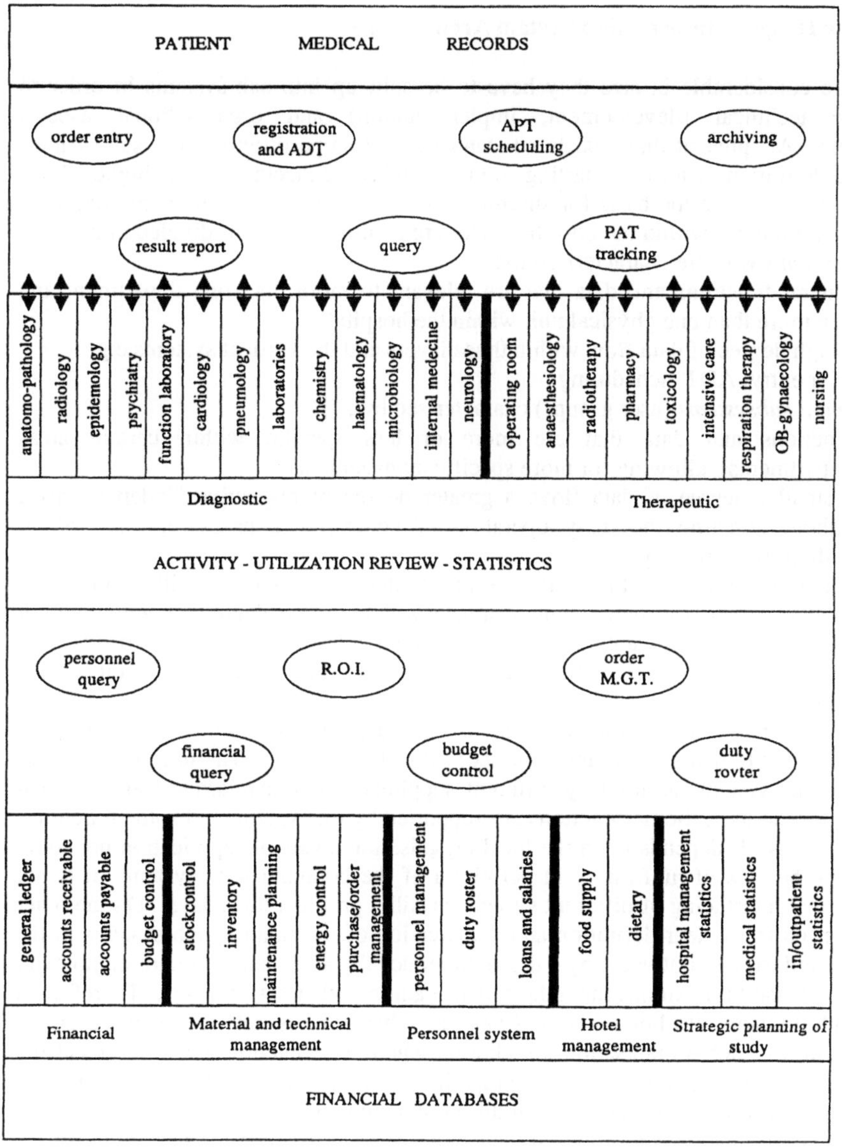

Fig.10.7 Hospital information systems architecture : representation in terms of horizontal (common) systems and vertical (departmental) sub-systems, covering administrative and medically, oriented application domains. *APT*, appointment; *PAT*, patient; *ROI*, return on investment; *MGT*, management; *ADT*, admission discharge transfer.

10.6 The Hospital Information System Architecture

As HIS are considerable in size they have to be split up into sub-systems in order to make the technical (development, implementation) and organisational aspects manageable. At present there exists no standard for this partitioning into sub-systems nor on the definition of terms. Starting from the HCIS architecture on the highest level as input, which will be the basis for sharing data for the implementation of consistent systems, several areas within the hospital sector are identified and sub-divided into :

Common systems who are characterised by:

- General functions and data that are relevant to more than one department and span more than one physical unit within the hospital
- A high degree of data flow within those layers and the vertical systems,e.g. order entry, ADT, scheduling

Departmental subsystems (user groups) characterised by :

- Functions and data that are more or less specific within certain areas (departments), allowing for more specific management
- A smaller degree of data flow, a greater degree of respective "independence", without affecting the daily operation of control data bases, e.g. labsystem, cardiology, radiology

Departmental systems are those that support the functional activities and data management of a specific department characterised by some degree of autonomy of management within a hospital environment but which could also work more or less as a stand-alone unit outside the boundaries of a hospital, covering medical and administrative areas.

The question of how data and functions are distributed among "locations" in hospitals is a complex one due to many, sometimes (varied) subjective reasons. The decomposition of a HIS into sub-systems as used by different suppliers is not standardised and is often confusing for the user. Some functions are supported by one system and some functions, by both systems. It depends upon the local organisation, available application portfolio, etc. Given the lack of uniformity in definition of the boundaries of systems, it is not surprising that interfacing of different systems is still a problem nowadays. On the other hand, the need for a clear definition and demarcation of information sub-systems in the health care industry is motivated by a desire to reduce the level and degree of complexity of the IS and also to maximise the independence among other sub-systems. Therefore, a general sub-division into horizontal and vertical subsystems is most convenient, giving the freedom to each organisation to choose where its function must be localized (Fig.10.7). The final goal is to obtain compatibility, integrability and cost reduction for integration of different sub-systems from different manufacturers.

Four main criteria have been proposed which can be used to guide the definition of the various information sub-systems which comprise the total IS of the business.

Flexibility. It is imperative for each sub-system to be flexible enough to respond to changing business conditions affecting it, without creating a need to modify any of the other sub-systems. In this way, the stability of each sub-system will be enhanced due to its ability to respond to various changes imposed on it both from inside and outside the business.

Separability and uniqueness. The components of each sub-system must be separate and unique from the other sub-systems so that each can be analysed independently in detail. The condition is designed to minimise greatly the number of interconnections among sub-systems. Furthermore, each system has to respond to its own goals in total autonomy.

Comprehensibility. The motivation for this requirement is to ensure that each sub-system is of a manageable size so that it takes less time and effort not only to understand but also to design, implement and maintain.

Integrability. The purpose of this condition is to ensure that each proposed sub-system is capable of being easily integrated with other sub-systems to achieve a fully IS system for the hospital.

To summarize, the HIS (ambulatory care, pharmacy, laboratories, private medical specialists) is a complex structure (Fig.10.8), it is advisable to decompose the hospital reference framework into smaller, functional areas in order to:

- Reduce the level of complexity of the whole system
- Obtain a more detailed view of the complete model
- Integrate the local (design implementation) into the complete model of the health care system
- Obtain maximum integration, offering information sharing and higher productivity between departmental systems

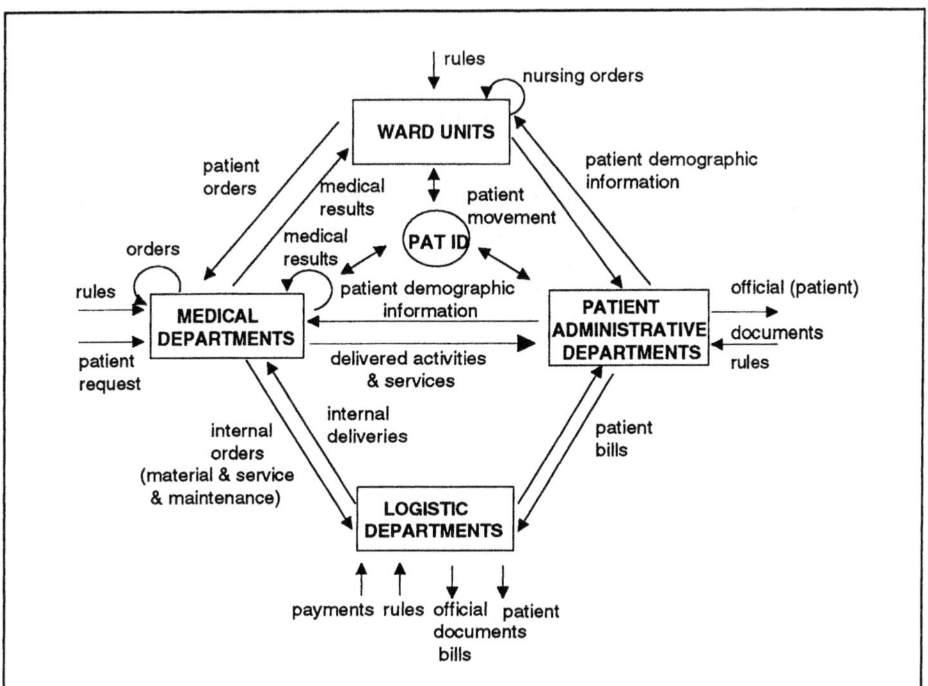

Fig.10.8 General model of a HIS architecture, depicting information flows between the most important internal and external organisational units

10.7 A Generic Model for a Hospital Information System

10.7.1 Application-Driven Versus Object-Driven Approach.

In developing a HIS based on centralised databases, we can follow two approaches, the *"application driven"* and the *"object driven"* [VEL 87]. The application-driven approach defines separate databases and systems for each new application, resulting in the generation of application databases. This approach causes a proliferation of databases and often duplicate data, and even worse it does not give the major advantages of database operations. Sometimes this solution, in which data are embedded in the function, is even more expensive than a conventional file organisation system due to severe maintenance problems and inflexibility.
On the other hand, object databases (often called data classes) are built from organisational objects rather than applications or functions by looking at the information needs. It is a part of object-oriented thinking and stresses the reusability of data and functions as explained previously.
As data structures, based on a good, profound analysis, are very stable and do not change with time as often as organisational procedures or functions, objects which can be largely independent of specific applications will give the best long-term results and need to be planned carefully by top-down development.
Although thorough data analysis is required, they offer more advantages in the long term because, maintenance costs will decrease and new application development will be faster as it provides long-term stability for the information resources of the hospital and the number of applications will grow disproportionally to the number of object databases

Covering an almost complete hospital information domain the system can be built around the following objects : *patients, medical acts, products* (medication), *health care actors, medical results* (medical record) and *equipments* (facilities). Depending upon the end-user's needs, every data-entity must further be split into :
-*Operational data* containing the day-to-day operations, reflecting the current state of the hospital
-*Management data* desirable for planning and other analytical purposes, containing extracts from the operational data; they can be down-loaded to PCs.

10.7.2 Generic Limited HIS Model

A generic "limited HIS model" has been proposed. This model defines an *00 model* (Fig.10.9) dealing with objects as communicating entities and an *entity relationship diagram* (Fig.10.10) consisting of data entities representing the information layers. The latter describes the *static behaviour* of the application domain and its relationships. The OOM describes the *dynamic behaviour* of the application domain, encapsulating the state (data) and behaviour (functions) that manipulate the state of the object. Every object performs a useful and meaningful role in the system operation. Communication is represented by means of message connection mechanisms.

The representation notations have been based on the OOA methodology of Coad and Yourdan [COA91]. The most important message connections are represented and explained hereafter. The majority of the class and objects has no explicit services; they all have implicit services (create, connect, access and release), which are not normally shown.

Let us explain the limited HIS model (Fig.10.9) : (The names highlighted in italic and bolt hereafter represent the objects) a *PERSON* with health problems comes to the *HOSPITAL* to see a physician. On the first visit to the *HOSPITAL* as a *PATIENT,* the *PERSON* sends a message that let him register as a *PATIENT* (create patient) **(1)**. Each time the patient has a medical problem and comes to the hospital for observation or treatment, he sends a message **(2)** to create and initialise a new *ENCOUNTER* event (as inpatient or outpatient). Patient encounters to the hospital are grouped by episodes of care, and multiple encounters within an *EPISODE* are possible. An *EPISODE* is created at the request of a *PHYSICIAN,* grouping all the patient's related medical data for a specific treatment, admission, diagnosis. When making an appointment or scheduling a pre-admission, the system can manually or automatically link this *ENCOUNTER* with a new existing specific or last active EPISODE. Episodes are accessible chronologically, active only, or closed.
This message connection represents values (data, time). Hereafter, every time the *PATIENT* visits the hospital for a new admission, a message is sent to *PATIENT* to validate (update) its attributes **(3)**.
During this in- or outpatient *EPISODE,* a physician records the patient's physical and mental health state by sending a message to create a *MEDICAL_ORDER* **(4)**. The new *MEDICAL_ORDER* in turn sends a message to create a new *MEDICAL_ACT_ORDER_ ITEM* for the specific order **(5)**, **(6)**. To create a *MEDICAL_ACT_ORDER_ITEM* messages must be sent to both the *PHYSICIAN* and the *NURSE* so that they can execute it and supply feedback of the result of the medical act.
A nurse executes the administering of medication following certain prescription rules **(7)**.
The different objects, their description and life cycle are briefly discussed hereafter.
(The numbers, 1 to 6 represent the messages in the OOM
Subject domains : **1,** subject patient
2, subject medical act
3, subject product
4, subject resources)

10.7.3 The OO-MODEL

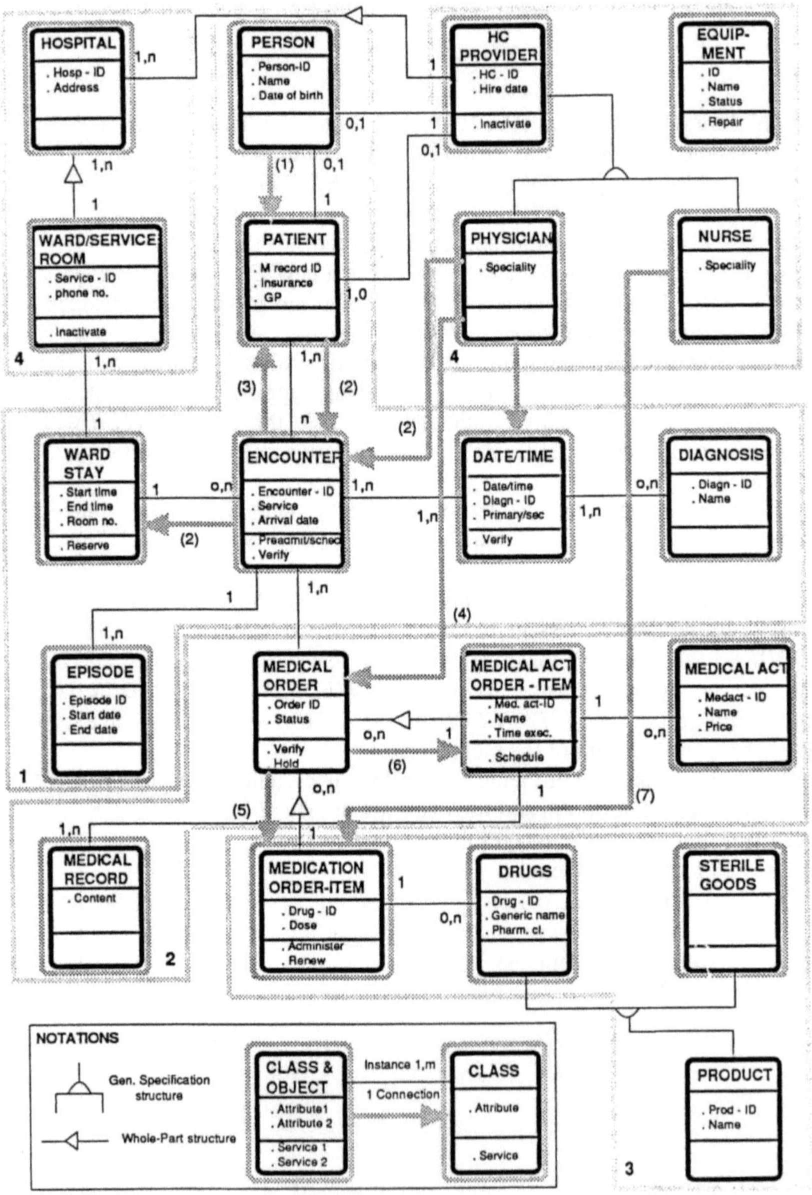

Fig.10.9 HIS-00 model subject, class and object structure (attribute and service layers)

10.7.4. The ER-Model

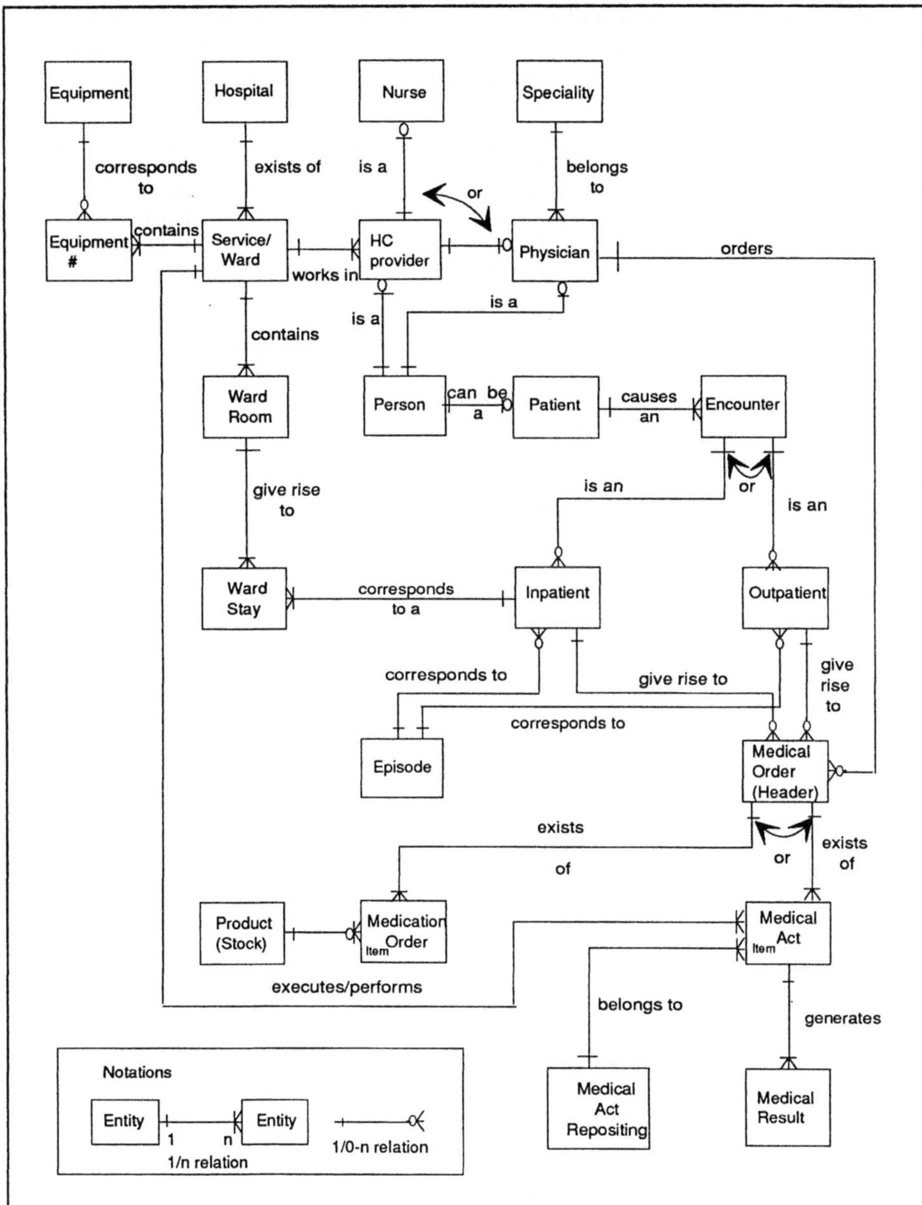

Fig.10.10 Hospital Information System: ER-Entity-Relationship diagram (reduced)

10.7.5 Object descriptions

This section presents in more detail the most important objects of the corresponding HIS-OO model : the information they encapsulate (data structure) and the operations (methods) they include applicable to manipulate its data, depicted by means of a "*life-cycle*" diagram.

OBJECT	**EPISODE**		
DESCRIPTION	Episode is an abstraction of an encounter by a specific patient with a specific facility which as an associated duration; encounter is a sub-class of EPISODE . An episode can be a certain period corresponding to different encounters during which the patient is treated for a specific disease		
ATTRIBUTE	***P-KEY***	***DOMAIN***	***F-KEY***
Medical record ID		Patient-ID	**PATIENT**
Episode ID	**P**	String	
Start date		Date	
End date		Date	
Episode status		Code	
LIFE CYCLE			
STATE		***ACTION***	***NEXT STATE***
Null		Register	Active
Active		Change Delete End	Active episode Cancelled Inactive episode
Inactive		Undo Archive	Active Archived episode
Any, non-null		Retrieve	Some, Non-null

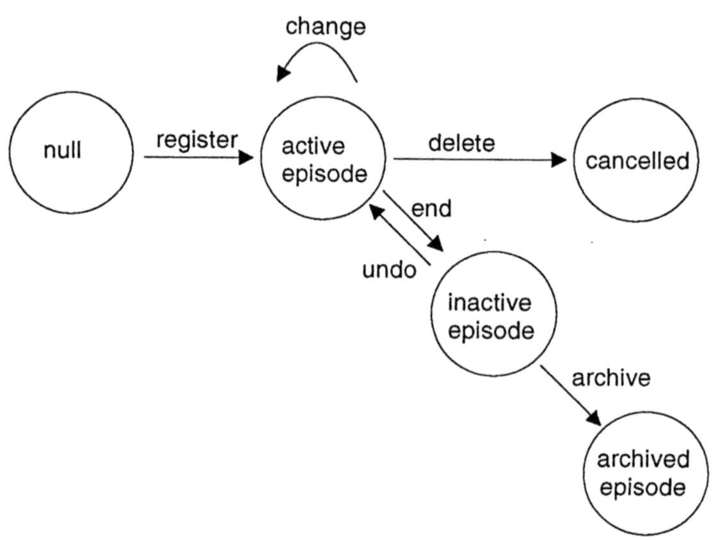

OBJECT		**PERSON**	
DESCRIPTION	Object defining an individual with all common attributes; it is a (super) class of objects PATIENT and health care provider		
ATTRIBUTE	***P-KEY***	***DOMAIN***	***F-KEY***
Person ID	P	String	
Last name		String	
First name		String	
Address		String	
Phone		String	
Marital status		Code	
Nationality		Code	
Dat of birth		Date	
Sex		Sex code	
LIFE CYCLE			
STATE		***ACTION***	***NEXT STATE***
Null		Create	ID unknown Active
ID unknown		Retrieve Modify Delete	ID unknown Active Null
Active		Retrieve Delete Change Inactivate	Active Null Active Inactive
Inactive		Retrieve Delete Change Activate	Inactive Null Inactive Active
Any, Non-null		Retrieve	Same, Non-null

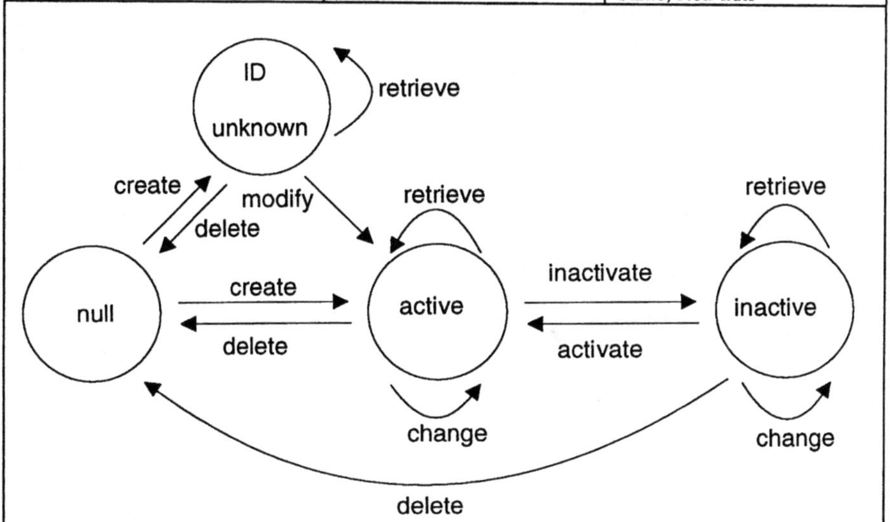

OBJECT		**PATIENT**	
DESCRIPTION	A single person representing the recipient of patient care Duration of the patient object extends over multiple (outpatient) visits and multiple admissions (inpatient) It is the abstraction of a person in the role as patient		
ATTRIBUTE	***P-KEY***	***DOMAIN***	***F-KEY***
Person ID		String	**PERSON**
Insurance		String	**INSURANCE**
Bloodgroup		String	
Medical record ID	**P**	Patient ID	
Spouse/other		Relationship code	**PERSON**
General practitioner		Physician ID	**PHYSICIAN**
First visit		Date/time	
LIFE CYCLE			
STATE		***ACTION***	***NEXT STATE***
Null		Register	ID unknown Active
ID unknown		Retrieve Update Delete	ID unknown Active Null
Active		Retrieve Delete Modify Inactivate	Active Null Active Inactive
Inactive		Retrieve Delete Change Activate	Inactive Null Inactive Active
Any, Non-null		Retrieve	Same, Non-null

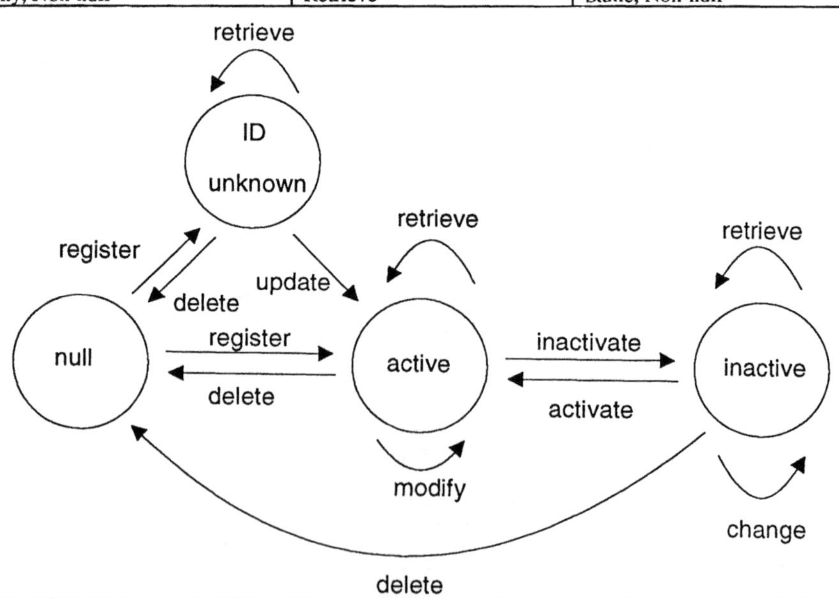

OBJECT		**(PATIENT)_ ENCOUNTER**	
DESCRIPTION		**Object associated with each patient visit as inpatient/ outpatient) to a health care provider or service; it can cover a hospitalisation period or an outpatient episode**	
ATTRIBUTE	***P-KEY***	***DOMAIN***	***F-KEY***
Patient		Parient ID	**PATIENT**
Encounter ID	**P**	String	
Encounter status		State of object	
Attending physician		Physician ID	**H_CARE_PROVIDER**
Attending service		Service ID	**SERVICE**
Referring physician		Physician ID	**H_CARE_PROVIDER**
Referring service		Service ID	**SERVICE**
Episode ID		String	**EPISODE**
Family physician/GP		Physician ID	**H_CARE_PROVIDER**
Arrival date/time		Date/time	
Departure date/time		Date/time	
Accident		Code	
Scheduled date/time		Date:time	
Sharge status		Code	
Episode ID		Episode ID	**EPISODE**

LIFE CYCLE		
STATE	***ACTION***	***NEXT STATE***
Null	Preadmit/Req. outpatient (OP) Admit/Req. OP	Pending Active
Pending	Admit/Reg. OP Cancel Modify	Active Null Pending
Active	Discharge Change Transfer (OP <---> IP) Cancel	Discharged Active Active Cancelled
Discharged	Undo/Renew Archive	Active Archived
Any, Non-null	Retrieve	Same, Non-null

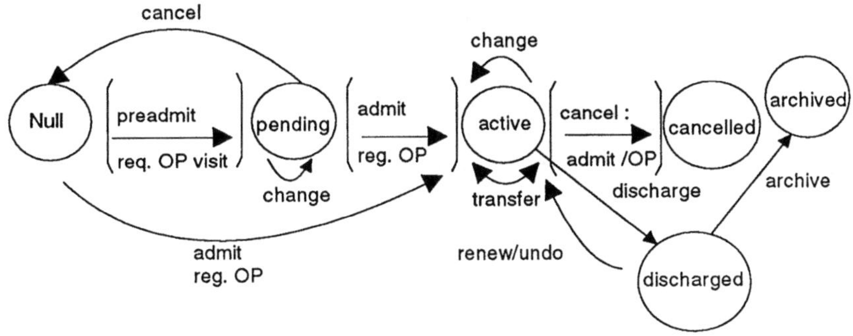

OBJECT	**MEDICAL_ORDER**
DESCRIPTION	A medical order object is a medical activity placed for a patient by/on behalf of a referring health care provider (refering physician, nurse) to a service (or provider) for an explicit set of medical services in order to: - change the medical status of a patient - to increase or refine the information on the patient needed in a diagnostic/therapeutic environment

ATTRIBUTE	***P-KEY***	***DOMAIN***	***F-KEY***
Order ID	**P**	String	
Patient		Patient ID	**PATIENT**
Report destination		Service ID	**SERVICE**
Comment text		String	
Order date/time		Date/time	
Operator identifier		Person ID	**PERSON**
Signature authority		Physician ID	**H_CARE_PROVIDER**
Order status		Code	
Ordered by		Physician ID	**H_CARE_PROVIDER**
Referring location		Location ID	**SERVICE**

LIFE CYCLE

STATE	***ACTION***	***NEXT STATE***
Null	Place request Create order	Unverified/Waiting list Active accepted
Unverified	Verify Change	Accepted Unverified
Accepted	Discontinue (d/c) Modify Hold Cancel Schedule	Discontinued (d/c'd) Accepted Held Cancelled Scheduled
Held	Resume	Accepted
Scheduled	Cancel	Cancelled
Discontinued	Delete	Null
Any, Non-null	Retrieve	Same, Non-null

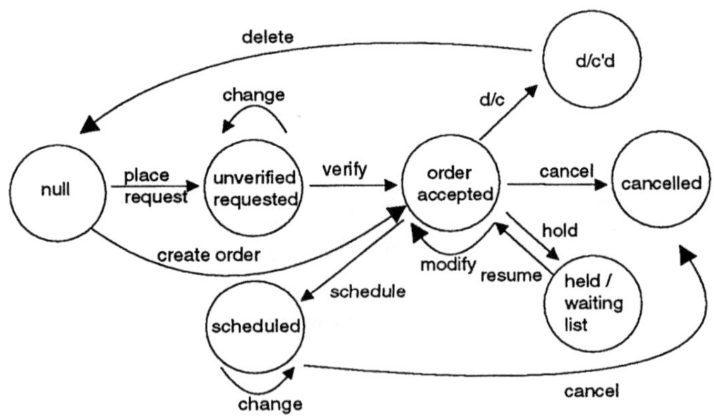

OBJECT		**MEDICATION_ITEM**	
DESCRIPTION	This object covers the detailed pharmacy order, initiated by a physician order and administered by nurses. A medication-item is part of the general medical (medication) order		
ATTRIBUTE	***P-KEY***	***DOMAIN***	***F-KEY***
Order ID	**P**	String	
Prescription type		Code	
Medication routing		Code	
Duration of prescription		String	
Drug ID	**P**	String	**DRUG**
Drug dose		String	
Who administered		Operator ID	**PERSON**
When administered		Date/time	
Who verified		Person ID	**PERSON**
When verified		Date/time	
Order start date/time		Date/time	
Order stop date/time		Date/time	
Order frequency		String	
Patient instruction		String	
LIFE CYCLE			
STATE		***ACTION***	***NEXT STATE***
Null		give medication	Completed
Order scheduled		Start administering	Active/In progress
Active		Complete Discontinue Administer Delete	Completed Discontinued Dose given/registered Cancelled
Completed		Renew	Scheduled
Any, non-null		Retrieve	Same, non-null

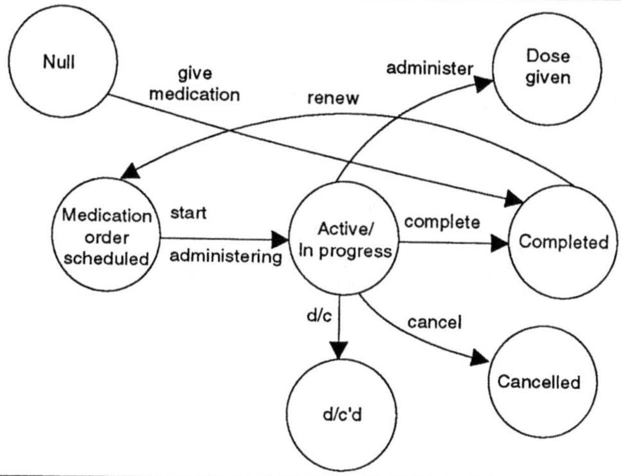

OBJECT		MEDICAL_ACT_ITEM	
DESCRIPTION	A medical act is an object that can be considered as an activity performed on a patient on behalf of a referring health care provider which changes the patient's health status or completes the information we have about the patient; acts include consultation, drug administration, nursing act, meal, laboratory test, associated/preparatory acts, therapeutical acts		
ATTRIBUTE	*P-KEY*	*DOMAIN*	*F-KEY*
Medical act	**P**	Medical act Id	**MEDICAL_ACT**
Order ID	**P**	String	
Specialty		String	
Name medical act		String	
Charge code		Code	
Associated preparation act		Medical act ID	**MEDICAL_ACT**
Type of act		Code	
Medical act start time		Date/time	
Medical act stop time		Date/time	
Who performed		Person ID	**PHYSICIAN**
When performed		Date/time	
LIFE CYCLE			
STATE		*ACTION*	*NEXT STATE*
Null		Start act (urgently)	Active
Order scheduled		Start execution act	Active/ In progress
Active		Complete Discontinue Report	Performed Discontinued Preliminary report
Performed		Redo	Active
Any, non-null		Retrieve	Same, non-null

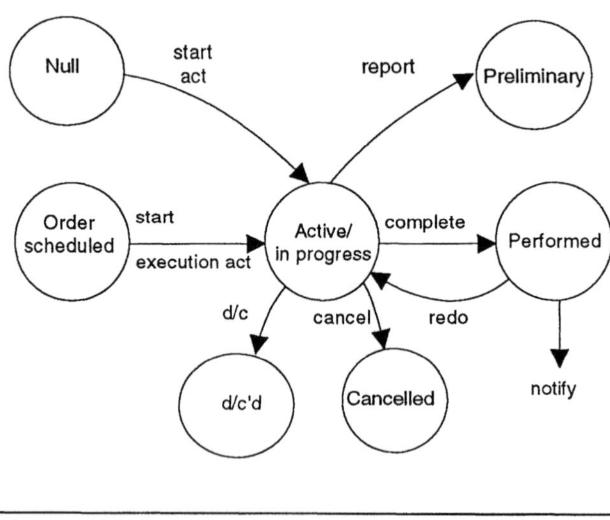

OBJECT		MEDICAL_RESULT	
DESCRIPTION		The medical result is generated by the execution of a particular medical_act (diagnostic or therapeutic) by a health care provider	
ATTRIBUTE	***P-KEY***	***DOMAIN***	***F-KEY***
Result Id	**P**	Result ID	
Status result		Status	
Result value		String	
Medical act		Medical act ID	**MEDICAL_ACT_ITEM**
Abnormal indication		Code	
Date generated		Date/time	
Date verified		Date/time	
Date reported		Date/ttime	
Operator ID		PersonID	**PERSON**
Patient		Patient ID	**PATIENT**
Order ID		Order ID	**MEDICAL_ORDER**

LIFE CYCLE		
STATE	***ACTION***	***NEXT STATE***
Null	Start Act	In progress
In progress	Enter result Report	Unverified Preliminary (result)
Unverified Completed	Verify/over-read Report	Verified Preliminary
Verified	Correct Reject Delete Report	Verified Null Cancelled Final
Any, non-null	Retrieve	Same, non-null

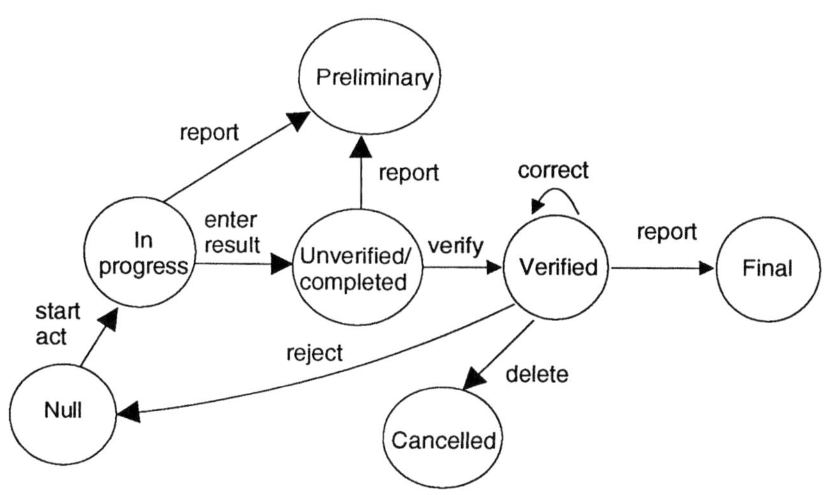

OBJECT		SERVICE	
DESCRIPTION	The service object is an abstraction of a specific service unit in a specific facility on which a service is performed; a service can be a ward unit, an outpatient unit, medical support service, logistic unit, etc.		
ATTRIBUTE	***P-KEY***	***DOMAIN***	***F-KEY***
Service Id	**P**	String	
Service type		String	
Service name		String	
Phone number		Number	
Building ID		String	
Room numbers		String	
Chief of service		Person ID	**PERSON**
LIFE CYCLE			
STATE		***ACTION***	***NEXT STATE***
Null		Create	Active
Active		Change Delete Inactivate	Active Null Inactive
Inactive		Activate Delete	Active Null
Any, non-null		Retrieve	Same, non-null

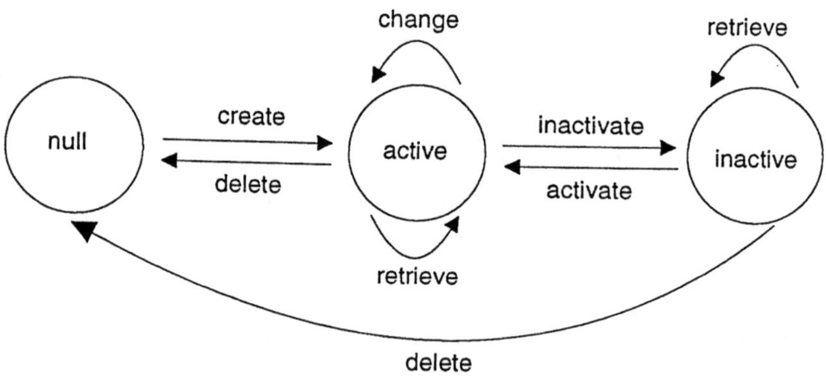

OBJECT		**HEALTH_CARE_PROVIDER**	
DESCRIPTION	Object defining the health care provider and his attributes; health care provider is a sub-class of PERSON and a superclass of PHYSICIAN and NURSE		
ATTRIBUTE	***P-KEY***	***DOMAIN***	***F-KEY***
Person ID	**P**	Person ID	**PERSON**
Health care provider ID		String	
Medical unit		Code	**SERVICE**
Title		String	
Status		Code	
LIFE CYCLE			
STATE		***ACTION***	***NEXT STATE***
Null		Create	Active
Active		Change Delete Inactivate	Active Null Inactive
Inactive		Activate Delete	Active Null
Any, non-null		Retrieve	Same, non-null

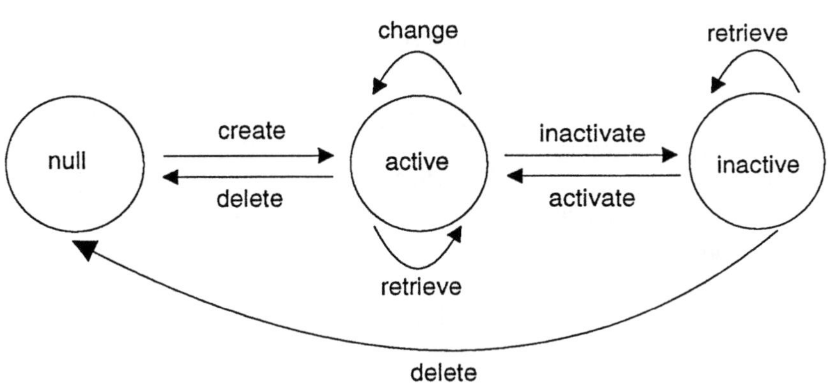

OBJECT		**EQUIPMENT**	
DESCRIPTION		The equipment object is an abstraction of a specific (medical) equipment used/installed at a specific service unit	
ATTRIBUTE	***P-KEY***	***DOMAIN***	***F-KEY***
Equipment ID	**P**	string	
Equipment name		String	
Equipment type		String	
Equipment		String	
Equipment status		Code	

LIFE CYCLE		
STATE	***ACTION***	***NEXT STATE***
Null	Create(activate)	Active
active	Use/schedule Inactivate	Active Out of service
Out of service	Repair	Active
Active	Delete/sell	Null
Out of service	Delete/sell	Null
Any, non-null	Retrieve	Same,non-null

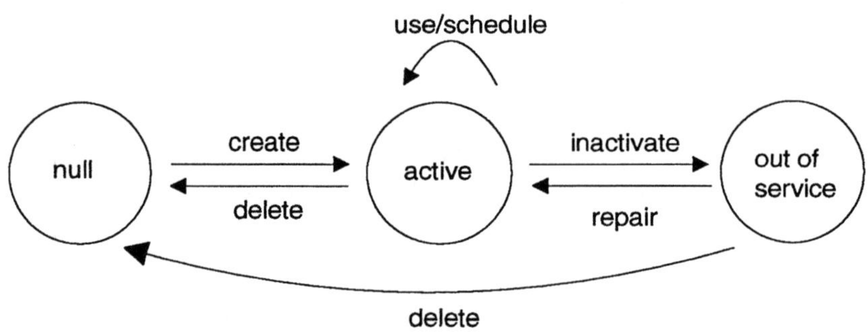

11

The Patient Management System

11.1 Introduction

The patient management system is the core sub-system of every HIS that streamlines the administrative functions related to patients and gathers the basic data of interest about patients for a variety of activities (admissions, patient care, nursing etc.). It includes the registration of patient demographic data, admission, discharge, transfer data for inpatients and visiting outpatients. In fact, it establishes the foundations of the central HIS database towards the electronic medical record system and serves as a repository for other "feeder" systems.

11.2 Inpatient Management

The inpatient management module streamlines all the functions from ADT, bed census, scheduling and insurance verification for patients in beds.
It is clear that selected departments (Food department, House keeping, Pharmacy, etc.) will automatically be notified of all of the following activities.
The *admission system* is one of the first functions that interacts with the patients and their family, leading to registration of the essential patient identification (if not already registered before) and admission data as the basis for other sub-systems for different patient classes.
The *pre-admission system* allows registration of all relevant patient data prior to admission of the patient in order to reduce the waiting time at the effective admission. Patients admitted through this system can be managed by the patient waiting list management system.
The *patient location* traces the patient within the hospital and can be retrieved on-line in a number of ways :

- By name
- By ward unit
- By phonetic search
- By physician (attending or referring)
- By admission/discharge/transfer date

Transfer and discharge. An efficient patient administration system must also keep track of the different changes of patient locations during his/her hospital stay.
The transfer function offers the possibility of keeping track of patient movements from one location (bed, room, ward unit) to another, while the discharge function registers the time and status of a patient leaving the hospital. Part of this module is

also the registration when a patient is allowed home for the weekend. It is clear that this information is transmitted to all services throughout the institution.

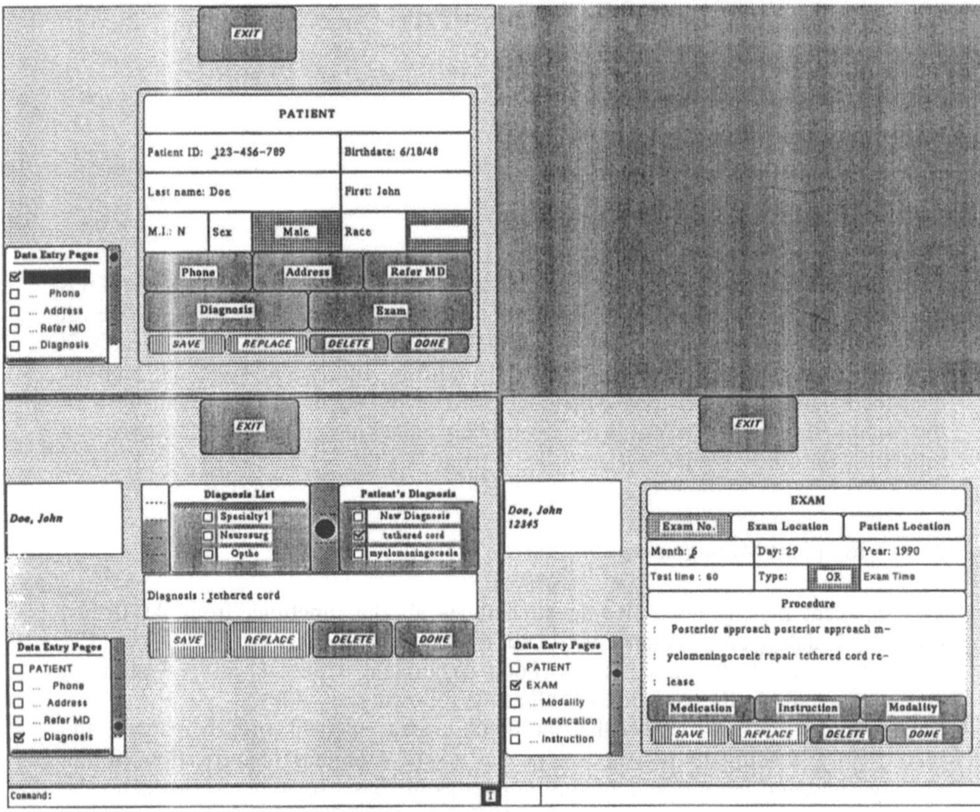

Fig.11.1 Typical demographics display. The *upper left window* shows the menu of items used to enter or display a patient. The *lower left window* shows the menu of items used to enter or display the patient's diagnoses. The *lower right window* shows the menu of items used to enter or display an exam ination result.

(**Source** Reprinted with the persmission form Don Krieger, Gerald Burk and Robert J. Sclabassi University of Pittsburgh, Neuronet, *Computer*, March 1991, p. 52)

Bed Activity

In an hospital it is very important to trace patients in order to assist in an optimal resource (bed) allocation. At any time users can receive up-to-the minute *real-time bed census* information for the entire institution by ward unit or by medical speciality. The bed information displayed real-time includes :

- Available beds
- Reserved beds
- Occupied beds
- Isolation beds

Each occupied bed shows the patient's name, age, sex, admission date and attending physician.

When the demand for inpatient places (beds) significantly exceeds the immediate capacity of the hospital, there will be a need of a computerised *waiting list system.* The waiting list function assists the hospital and its staff so that the maximum number of patients can receive care service in the shortest amount of time. When a patient has to be admitted due to an urgent medical condition but not serious enough for an emergency admission and there is no bed available, he enters the waiting list.
Afterwards, patients can be selected according to various criteria, e.g.one-day surgery cases, admission priority cases and waiting time
When admitted, patients will move from the waiting list to the inpatient system.

11.3 Outpatient Management

The outpatient management module streamlines all the functions related to outpatients. It establishes the foundations for appointments, charge capture, etc.
The main functions are :

Patient registration. For all outpatients presenting them for the first time to the institution, all relevant patient identification and demographic data as the basis for further registrations of the medical history are recorded. At the same time a unique permanent patient identification (medical) record number has to be assigned, permitting the easy and unambiguous retrieval of all relevant patient information and avoiding the creation of duplicate patients (Fig.11.1).

Outpatient/inpatient transfer. Especially in the emergency department patients registered as outpatients must be easily transferred from one status to another (from outpatient to inpatient and vice versa).

11.4 Reports

Many standard reports have to be generated on demand or automatically at multiple locations including :
Operational information
- Patient admission, discharge and transfer lists (by type)
- Patient admission documents
- Patient legal/insurance sheets
- Patient lists by referring/attending physician
- Embossed plates
- Automatic printing of GP letters (discharge letter)
- Patient labels
- Waiting list reports

Management information
- Overview of admission, movements and discharge of patients sorted by various headings (by service, by date, by date of patient)
- Data for the production of bed/service census reports and statistical reports
- Billing data

It is worthwhile to transfer some reports as standard ASCII files to intelligent workstations (PC, MAC) so that users have the possibility to view and print them according to their personal requests or integrate them with some popular end-user tools.

11.5 Resource Utilization Parameters in Hospitals

There are different parameters in use in hospitals, nowadays related to the patient management system, which give an indication of the resource utilisation within those organisations. These parameters are based on the following terms:

- Total number of beds, B_T (or by service , i B i)
- Number of patients admitted by year, Ay (or by month , Am)
- Number of patients discharged by year, Dy (or by month , Dm)
- Number of inpatient- days in 1 year, Py (or by month , Pm)

The definition of an inpatient-day differs from country to country.
We can define the following parameters:

- *Average length of stay* (L_A) is calculated in various ways, according to the hospital or country

$$L_A = \frac{P_Y}{A_Y} \qquad L_A = \frac{P_Y}{D_Y} \qquad L_A = \frac{P_Y}{1/2 \cdot (Ay + D_Y)}$$

- *Average occupation rate* (O_A)

$$O_A = \frac{P_Y}{365 \cdot B_T} \times 100$$

It is worthwhile mentioning that the average occupation rate is not always a good representation of effective bed utilisation. For instance: services with an increased turnover rate, tend to have a reduced average occupation rate, compared to services with low turnover rate.
In this expression Py/365 corresponds to the average number of beds occupied by day (average daily occupation rate).

11.6 Patient Cards: An Overview

In most health care institutions patients are provided with personal identification cards (ID) containing data such as name, sex, date of birth and medical record number (Fig. 11.2). In most cases, plastic ID cards are used for print processing or for data. Otherwise ID cards with a magnetic strip or with bar code are used and nowadays in some places (very seldom) integrated chip cards (IC cards) or optical cards are appearing (Table 11.1). Today, many roles for patient cards have been identified. The most important functions are identification card, emergency card, insurance card, pharmacy card, minimum basic data set (MBDS) card and medical record card, the fullest expression of the patient card concept.

Communication of medical patient data is becoming more and more important , as people become more mobile. Thus, portable medical records included in patient data cards is one essential element in a distributed medical information environment. All portable media will be discussed for completeness, although some of them are not suitable as a mobile storage device.
In the very near future, applications based on certain types of data cards will appear in special domains (cardiology pacemaker, nephrology renal dialysis). Patient data cards (PDC) can facilitate medical data transfer and information exchange. The success of this portable medical record assumes the implementation of standards defining contents (diversity in medical language, encoding, dataset structure, hardware function) and confidentiality.

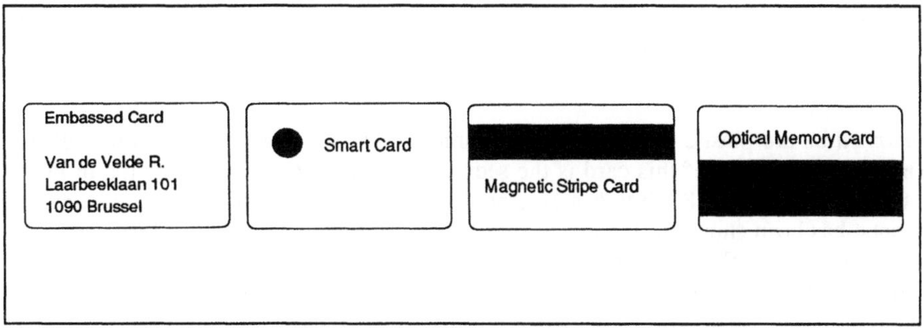

Fig. 11.2 Patient data cards can improve admitting procedures, medical history taking and data communication within the hospital. Application domains include demographic information, insurance data, medical history, medical encounters, identification of patient, referral information, improved hospital-patient relationship, pharmacy history and interaction, speciality. Possible forms include cardiology card, pediatric card, dental card.,etc..

Embossed card is a plastic card mostly used for patient identification and demographic information, by electromechanical embossing. It cannot be read electronically. The security can only (partially) be guaranteed by a signature of the cardholder.

OCR card is of plastic or paper (various formats) identified with OCR-A or OCR-B and can be read electronically. It has a limited capacity for data storage and the same purposes as an embossed card. Confidentiality is poor.

Bar-code card is of plastic or paper (various formats) with bar-code data. It can be read electronically and has a limited capacity for data storage. Confidentiality is poor. Nowadays a new type of bar code data capture has been announced : the Portable Data File (PDF 417). PDF 417 opens up many important new applications. It can hold the data needed to complete a transaction with no need to rely on the availability of external databases. Features include : high density (100 char. per cm sq) - encryption options- large capacity (2000 alphanumeric characters).

Magnetic cards are plastic (or paper) cards for storage of limited (maximum 200 characters for the moment) amounts of data and are useful for the storage of patient identification data. However, they suffer from a number of several disadvantages apart from the limited storage capacity:

- Data can easily be corrupted through improper handling
- The magnetic stripe can be damaged
- Data can easily be read by anyone

By using adequate encryption techniques the latter two are easily solved. The price of a read/write magnetic card reader varies between $ 200 and $ 800 and needs a separate computer system. A magnetic card sells for less than $ 1 .
Because of the maturity of this technology and the read/write card devices already installed, magnetic cards will dominate the card industry for years, despite the limited amount of information stored on the magnetic stripe, and function more or less as a gateway to the huge amount of data in database systems.

Smart cards are plastic cards with a small microprocessor and memory chip built in. The main advantage of this card is the security option they offer through the in-built intelligence. Up to 128 Kbits can be stored with existing technologies. Considerable interest has been shown in the use of these cards for medical purposes. Two sorts are available: the simple-chip version (processor and memory are one chip) and the two-chip version (processor and memory separate). Due to the fact that the intelligence is incorporated in the card, card readers are not expensive, in contrast to the price of the card which varies between $ 10 and $ 30. When produced in large quantities, the cost will drop ($ 5).
The other type is a *memory card* that is available in different versions:

- ROM-CARD; write once (totally), read only memory
- PROM-CARD; write once (one programmable memory unit), read only memory
- EEPROM-CARD, electronically erasable and programmable read only memory card
- S-RAM CARD, static random access (read/write) memory

Because these cards contain a battery, they are quite thick and are more easily damaged. Smart cards will emerge and move into everyday use. For further in-depth study, we refer to the work of R. Bright, Smart cards: principles, practice, application [BRI 88].

Optical memory cards or laser cards are another important product of the optical storage technology (Fig 11.3). Comparable with a credit card, it contains an optical recording strip. It exists in two versions: "write once" card (WORM) and read only memory type (ROM card). The price of the card varies between $ 10 and $ 30, while the corresponding card readers/writers are 4 times less expensive than magnetic card readers and 20 times more expensive than optical card readers. It has the advantages of durability and permanence, high recording density and greater resistance to alteration and fraud compared with magnetic cards.
As the information is recorded optically, data cannot be destroyed by magnetic or electric fields. Therefore, it is most useful for recording patient identification and treatment (insurance information) history, and also other important vital medical data

(treatment history, drug information, allergies). A semi-conductor laser beam of a few microns in diameter is applied to the optical recording layer of the plastic card to create (burn) pits and record data in rasters.
These data are read afterwards by illuminating with a low-power laser beam and detecting the reflected light (changes in reflectivity of the pits) with a photosensor. It has at present a storage capacity of 2 MB (equivalent to 100 typed sheets of A4 paper) and is anticipated to increase several more MB in the near future. This is the only card for the moment that can memorise text, voice image and data.

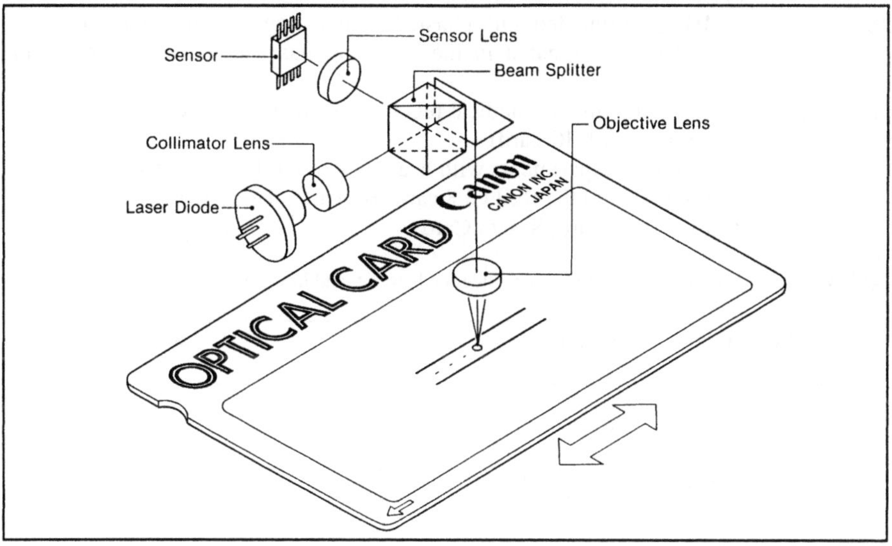

Fig.11.3 A semi-conductor laser beam of a few microns in diameter is applied to the optical recording laser of the plastic card to form pits and record data. The recorded data are read by illuminating with a low-power laser beam and detecting the reflected light with a photo- sensor. Data can be added to but not erased. [Source : courtesey of Canon Inc.]

Security Considerations

As the capacity of optical cards and smart cards increases constantly, huge amounts of data, could be stored on them, which are susceptible to physical destruction, unauthorised alteration of data or possibility of physical loss. Consequently, a periodical back-up for the data on another medium (magnetic disc, magnetic tape, optical disc) becomes a must.
With respect to confidentiality (privacy), a policy has to define who is the owner of the card, who is authorised to have access to it, their rights, etc. We refer for detailed reflections on this subject to the chapter on security policies in health care systems.

The general acceptance of a patient data card will depend upon the possibility of its acting as a bridge between various health care actors not only on the national level, but also across national borders. Therefore, a common agreement based on standards is absolutely essential to realise this acceptance. The ISO technical committee concerned with information technology is JTC1, and the sub-committee relating to portable records is JTC1/SC17. For the moment, experiments are being carried out in several countries:

UK	Maternity records on optical memory cards. (London) Exeter care card project on Bull CP8 smart cards
Japan	Optical cards for mass health examination (Kagawa medical school) Perinatal care with IC memory card
USA	AMHTS (automated multiphasic health testing and services) center optical card originated in the USA but has become very popular in Japan
Switzerland	General practitioner medical record card (IC memory card)
Sweden	Pharmacy card (IC card)
France	The current experiments with health smart cards use microprocessor technology and the Bull CP8 card (Biocarte, Transvie Card, Dialyse Card, Santal Card, Sesam Card)

Table 11.1 Comparison of magnetic versus integrated circuit and laser cards

Parameter	Magnetic	IC	Laser
Physical support	Magnetic stripes	IC chips	Optical layer
Memory capacity	JIS: 576 bits OSI: 1200 bits	256 Kbits 64 Kbits	2 MB
Reading/writing	Serial by magnetic head	Random access	Random and sequential by laser beam
Information	Alphanumeric	Alphanumeric	Alphanumeric, coded graphics and images
Power	Passive	Active	Passive
Security	Easy to read and alter information	Difficult to read and alter information; internal protection	Easy to read; security enhanced by codification
Adverse environment	Affected by magnetic and electric fields	Affected by static electricity	
Present use	Widespread	Limited use	Testing phase
Development possibilities	Limited in terms of security and capacity	Wide range	Limited by no rewriting; wide capabilities
Main features	Inexpensive; widely used; limited security and capacity	Capable of intelligent computations; internal security	Very large memory; resistant to environmental factors; write once

11.7 Hospital Information Systems in Europe

11.7.1 An Integrated Hospital Information System in Geneva (DIOGENE)

The DIOGENE HIS at the University Hospital of Geneva is built around a central mainframe computer housing a unique database. Except for a proliferation of personal microcomputers generally not connected to other computers, the DIOGENE system, with a single team of computer scientists, is responsible for all the computer-based functions and information in the hospital. The hospital comprises 5 buildings and has 1600 beds, 35 000 inpatients per year, 450 000 outpatients per year and 5500 employees (including physicians). The DIOGENE project was approved in 1973, with a budget of 25 million Swiss francs over a period of 10 years.

The system was introduced for administrative applications, including personnel management, in 1974. Invoicing was added in 1977, patient admissions in 1978 and general accounting in 1979. The system was progressively extended to all the wards in 1979 and 1980. Extensions to the radiology department and laboratories occurred from 1979 to 1982. Interactive medical encoding by interns and residents was added in 1985. The system soon included new emergency laboratories (1986), monthly and yearly medical statistics on patients (1987), the pharmacy (1987), integrated outpatient clinics in surgery (1987) and medicine (1988) and the medical bacteriology laboratory (1988).

The Operator Pool and the DIOGENE Telestation

From the ward, the nurses communicate with the HIS through a telestation. The telestation consists of a telephone linked to the operator pool, a television monitor to visualise transactions, an identification-badge reader for access control and a printer. The nurse orally transmits instructions to an operator who then executes the transaction. The nurse follows the transaction's progress by watching the television monitor in the ward. The advantages of telestations in the wards are ease of use, even for newcomers and occasional users, reductions in initial and follow-up training times, permanent user support, use of simple and familiar equipment (a telephone and TV screen), control of transactions at the ward level, and protection of data confidentiality by positive and selective user identification.

The operator pool ensures that a person with knowledge of the computing system is present for the support of users on a 24-h basis. At peak periods, up to 9 operators answer calls from as many as 120 wards. Instead of forcing all users to learn a highly specialised language that permits dialogue with the computer, the system has a human operator perform the translation from natural language. In their experience, this approach gives users a degree of freedom they would not have otherwise. The operator pool offers continuous training (when personnel are new or when there are changes in procedures) as well as information capture and updating of access rights.

Hospital Computing Facilities

The computing centre is built around two Control Data Corporation mainframe computers, a CYBER 180/855 and a CYBER 180/840. The system contains 24 disc drives (16 GB), 6 magnetic tape drives (1600/6250 bytes per inch), 4 front-end processors to link the mainframe computers to the network, 9 satellite computers operating under UNIX (four SUN machines, four HP-9000/825-845s and one VAX-750), 113 ward unit stations, 454 connected personal computers and terminals, 202 remote printers (beside the ward unit stations), 8 remote fast printers and 237 asynchronous lines of communication.

The Network

The Intersat network links every computer in the DIOGENE system with every other computer and with every terminal and printer. Various types of computers are connected on the network, including large computers (CYBER), UNIX machines (VAX and SUN), personal workstations (IBM personal computers and compatibles) and small, low-cost network nodes. The nodes are made up of microprocessor-based systems that act as interfaces between the network and groups of terminals and printers. There is no hierarchy among the elements that make up the network. The communication protocol permits communication between any two elements, such as two terminals or a terminal and a program.

Medical Encoding by Physicians

The medical records application holds the diagnoses and procedures for each patient during the course of hospitalisation. Succinct medical summaries provide data on the activities of the various medical services and facilitate clinical research. A pilot interactive system for recording diagnoses and procedures was installed in two medical departments in 1985. Interactive capturing of data at different terminals is progressively replacing the traditional manual method, which used preprinted coding sheets.

Physicians have interactive terminals in their offices. After finding a patient's name on the list of patients in the ward, the physician registers the diagnoses.

Three strategies for the establishment of diagnoses have been tried. The first involves surveying the list of the most frequently used terms for a specific service (up to 400 such terms are organised according to the user's needs, in groups of up to 10 terms). The second involves choosing the code that corresponds to the appropriate diagnosis for a particular patient within a comprehensive alphabetical directory (comprising 7600 terms) and then entering this code at the terminal so as to check its translation into full text. The third strategy involves surveying, on the terminal screen, the complete tree of the International Classification of Diseases in order to identify the appropriate diagnosis. The same method is used to capture surgical procedures (2100 related terms defined). For each procedure, the physician also enters the date and name of the surgeon.

Because the medical record includes demographic information supplied by the admissions service, as well as the history of the patient's stay provided by the nurses, a summary of the patient's stay can be made available. Such summaries, in narrative form, contain information that could subsequently be made available for statistical and scientific investigation (e.g. calculation of case mix and retrieval of all cases with certain characteristics). The physician responsible for a medical service automatically receives a list of discharged patients who were under his or her care and whose summaries are not yet complete. Physicians are authorised to obtain an exhaustive coding of data on all patients. When signing the letter of discharge, the chief

physician can check whether the coded information corresponds to the contents of the letter of discharge.
The aims of the documentation system are as follows: statistical analyses of diagnoses and surgical procedures, monitoring and comparing the activities of the medical services, retrieval of cases for inclusion in retrospective studies, case presentation for teaching, analyses of health care costs with respect to disorder and aetiological study.

Discussion
The change from traditional coding on forms to a system of interactive capture of information in text form has resulted, as would be expected, in considerable improvement in the quality and availability of information at this hospital. The DIOGENE HIS has been in place for 11 years. The success of the project from the users' standpoint has been demonstrated by continual requests for more features and a resulting need to enlarge the system. Indeed, integrated, centralised systems will not last long unless they can evolve and grow toward distributed and open architectures.
The need for growth is critical, and migration to a second-generation HIS has been under study since 1986. New hardware, including the new generation of UNIX/RISC machines, and new software (Ingres RDBMS, C, C++, Eiffel) have been selected, and a financial plan, together with a description of the objectives of the DIOGENE 2 system, has been submitted to the government of Geneva. The project was approved, with a 4-year budget, in May 1989 [SCH 90].

11.7.2 An Integrated Hospital Information System in Brussels (A.Z.-VUB)

The University Hospital of Brussels (AZ-VUB) established in 1979 is a full-service, 800-bed university hospital that provides care for 23000 inpatients, supports over 300 000 outpatient visits and receives 32000 emergency patients a year. The hospital's central IS which is a on-line 24 h a day (400 terminals) and performs 10000 transactions per hour during peak periods runs on an AMDAHL computer system under the IBM VM/ O.S. [VEL91]. The actual in-house developed HIS, is based on a IDMS/R codasyl DBMS. This HIS was created completely in-house and focused primarily on automating the more administrative and managerial tasks. It covers the following systems: ADT, general ledger, patient billing, laboratories, radiology, food administration, patient appointment and scheduling, inventory, pharmacy and personnel management.
Using the intrinsic integration experience from this first generation of HIS, it will be the precursor to tomorrow's on-line medical record; therefore, the product envisioned for the second generation HIS is a direct outgrowth of the path set in the past.

The architecture of the next generation of HIS is based on a set of layers, founded on an open software technology (fig. 11.4). This open software technology is based on operating systems and not machines. Machines are constantly replaced as newer ones render older ones obsolete. A technology based on machines requires successive cycles of re-education: progression at the price of retrogression. Operating systems

evolve continuously. A technology based on operating systems also evolves continuously.
After a thorough analysis of RDBMS available under UNIX, the AZ-VUB selected the Sybase RDBMS to run on a UNIX super-mini-computer using C, C++, OSF-Motif, Windows 3.0. as graphical metaphor. As physicians and nurses are occasional computer users who do not like to spend much time on computer education, user training has to be minimised and user productivity optimised through adoption of a consistent graphical user interface (GUI). Sybase databases contain actual patient files in 3 GB of storage.

The Architecture of the Distributed Information System

A long term database (LTDB) has been implemented including all inpatients, outpatients, active patients, previous episodes of care, medical and related administrative data to fulfil that need. Other shared institutional files are also centralised there. In fact, the LTDB consists of a patient identification database, a database holding the read-only dictionaries with relatively static information, a database holding all the scheduled appointments for in- and outpatients and a database holding previous clinical data for each ancillary service. This is essential for fulfilling the function of a total historical patient medical record. The LTDB is surrounded by a knowledge layer, which registers metadata as well as some procedural rules concerning the underlying application clients.

The second objective was to integrate patient appointment scheduling, ADT and nursing systems. Nursing is starting to take a strong business orientation in terms of measuring productivity. Thus the second component is made of "short-term" databases maintained by particular clinical systems (departments) for the management of detailed current clinical information about active patients. Access to the database is very carefully controlled, so that only authorised users have permission for certain operations. Sybase-stored procedures provide a higher level of security than standard SQL. Medical data become available in the LTDB after it has been validated
real-time in the short term database (STDB) rather than as part of a periodic "batch" update. Each of these data-bases must have access to and coordinate with the central LTDB.

The Hardware Architecture : Client-Server Networks

Workstations and servers communicate via the high-speed, fiber-optic network. In the past all applications were processed by two (sometimes one) mainframes. In order to define a distributed architecture one of the fundamental problems is to decide where to locate software, data and computers all over the network. The decision rules are organisational, economic, functional and technical. All of them change in the course of time. The natural location of application software and data is on a personal host when dedicated to a single user and on a common host when shared by several (functional) departments. Components of our networking computing are :

- Application servers providing computational resources for executing the application (X86 PC' s, 680XO UNIX WS)

- ° File Servers containing multi-media filing systems (Pyramid UNIX multi-processor)
- ° AI servers, expert systems
- ° Utility/administration servers including (X86 PC' s, 680XO UNIX WS) :
  - ° File and print services (such as LAN servers)
  - ° User account servers which manage a global registry containing user (login) account information
  - ° Network management server providing a view of the network environment including resource utilisation, available capacity and description of resources being used by each user application
  - ° Management facilities: automatic back-up, automatic software distribution system updating applications

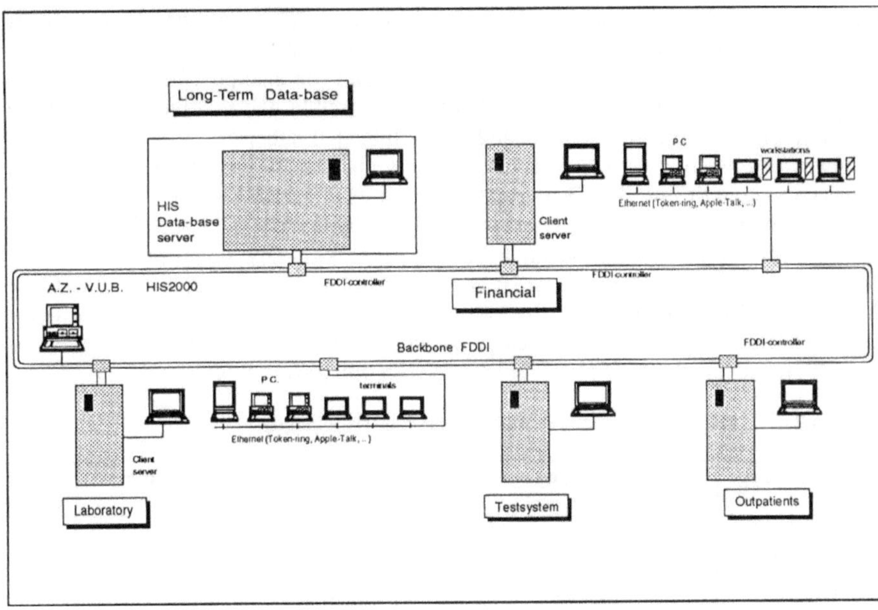

Fig. 11.4 Architectural representation of the distributed clinical information system of the University Hospital in Brussels (AZ-VUB) [VEL 91]

Implementation Scenario

The AZ-VUB will not go in one step from a star network to the future network. The computer centre evolves continuously rather than step by step towards its ultimate function: providing the heart of the information services and safeguarding the hospital information. Although many tasks of the computer centre are decentralised to local systems, it continues to grow exponentially in computer performance (20%) and storage capacity (15%) as a result of common databases expanding and the demand from more users to access them.

The implementation scenario for our next generation is phased as follows: first phase, perfect star (--->)1990; next phase, the central system connected to satellites (from 1990 ---->1992); and finally in the last phase, distributed HIS (from 1993). The benefits and characteristics of this computing environment are:

- Distributed: the cost to add (or delete) incremental computing is reduced since the environment is comprised of multiple "smaller" elements versus an environment composed of a large computer.
- Networked: enterprise environments are a reflection of a networked society. The technology is scalable so that small hospitals can also benefit.
- Heterogeneous and dynamic: computers from different vendors operate and participate in a non-proprietary, open-system environment.

11.7.3 Hospital Bar Coding

The need for better and more precise information gathering is widely accepted in health care but difficult to attain, due to the complexity of the health care sector. The use of a bar code is often a powerful solution. The bar code is a vehicle for the storage and retrieval of information, based on elementary physics that light is reflected by light areas and absorbed by dark areas [JAC 89].
Its technology is already widely used in industry and can also provide many benefits for specific applications to hospitals. It offers a feasible and relatively inexpensive way to improve quality and to manage large volumes of data .
As always, a wide variety of bar-coding systems are in use, such as Code 39, Universal Product Code (UPC), European Article Number (EAN), etc. The 13-digit EAN barcode is based on every product available for sale and is a unique identification number which cannot be confused with any other product. This problem was recognised in the USA, and in 1983 the Health Industry Bar Code Council (HIBCC) was founded. Its purpose is to develop and publish standards for implementing bar codes in health care. Although the HIBCC standard is based on Code 39, it accepts the need for co-existence with other symbologies.

Table 11.2 Some characteristics of different bar code symbologies

Type	Numeric	Alpha numeric	Full ASCII	Fixed length	Self - checking	Discrete	Check characters
Plessey	yes						2
Discrete 2/5	yes				yes	yes	
Interleaved 2/5	yes				yes		1 (optional)
3 of 9 code	yes	yes	yes		yes	yes	1 (optional)
Codebar	yes				yes	yes	
UPC/EA	yes			yes			1
Code 11	yes					yes	1 or 2
Code 93	yes	yes	yes				2
Code 128	yes	yes	yes		yes		1

There exist various potential uses of bar coding in several domains. They can be generalised as follows :

- *Tracing objects*, e.g. sterilised materials, blood bank
- *Receipt and delivery of products,* e.g. pharmaceutical products
- *Archive management and lending,* e.g. X-ray film folders and patient files
- *Registration and input,* e.g. medical acts, food requisition

The input medium available for reading bar codes can vary depending upon the application. They can be mobile such as a hand terminal eventually provided with a keyboard; this offers the advantage of gathering data off-line. Or the input device is connected immediately to a terminal (workstation), replacing the classic key strokes by light pen. For some applications high-quality scanning devices are necessary. Therefore, laser scanners are in use. Although more expensive than light pens they have the advantage of being very sensitive and offer for instance the possibility of reading labels which are not flat.

Usefulness of Bar coding in Hospitals

Following the classification discussed above, some examples of health care bar coding are discussed briefly.

° *Bar coding of sterilised materials.* Every article sterilized in the hospital is provided with a unique bar-codelabel (registration number). Afterwards the departments to which the sterilized goods are supplied are also registered. A last step could be recording the patient to whom the sterile article is applied. In case of problems, every article can be traced.

° *Bar coding of pharmaceutical products.* Every drug can be registered at delivery to the ward unit and administration to the patient by means of a mobile bar code and reader. Especially with unit-dose packages of drugs supplied with a bar-code identification, this is a safe and complete registration system that increases the quality of patient care and decreases work of input.

° *Bar coding of X-ray film folders and patient files.* Patient files and film folders for in and outpatients are uniquely identified with a bar code. The film folders and patient files transferred from the archive to physicians or ward units are registered via a bar code light pen or laser scanner. In this way, the user knows at any time the exact location of the object.

° *Bar coding of data entry.* A last example could be the registration of input forms on which each element is pre-printed with unique bar code identifiers (medical acts, patientmeal menus, nurses' care provided,etc).

12

Order Entry And Result Reporting Management Systems

12.1 Introduction

One of the most important objectives of a patient care information system (PCIS) is to establi the communication links between wards and functional departments for inpatients a outpatients. The messages are mainly composed of result reports, outpatients and inpatie orders (examinations, procedures), prescriptions (blood transfusion, medication) and are for t moment characterised mostly by manual systems. Automating order entry and result reporti functions, usually rather labor-intensive, reduces communication errors (reduce telepho traffic) and enables physicians and nurses to allocate their time to more professional task Integration of this sub-system with the nursing information system can relieve the nurse fro tedious clerical work.

The order entry and result reporting sub-system is therefore a major part of the daily activiti of physicians and nurses. It aims to integrate all type of orders and results for all select ancillary departments and transmit information about orders and results between referri (originating) and executing (processing) services. Procedures and examinations for ancilla services, medications, diets, etc. can be ordered by authorised users from any workstati throughout the hospital. At the same time, duplicate order checking can be done.

An order can be a request for a diagnostic or therapeutic act (RX, surgical intervention, etc), medication order for the pharmacy, request for material, laboratory examination or blood, fo from the kitchen, linens from housekeepings, supplies from central supply, etc. After placing order, a positive acknowledgement (or confirmation message) has to be sent back, indicating t corresponding status of the order.

The most important data elements of an order entry system include:

- Order number supplied by the ordering service to the order
- Ancillary order number assigned by the ancillary department to the order
- Status code indicates the processing status (requested, in process, requested to sto fulfilled)
- Priority indicates how soon the order needs to be executed
- Order comment (abbreviation) indicates family (group of examinations) procedures
- Order call-back phone number given for reporting a status or result
- Results copies is a composite item referring to the people who need copies of the results
- Ordering physician responsible for the order
- Order date/time

- Order frequency code identifying the frequency of order execution
- Entered by using the code of the person who actually keyed the order/result in
- Originating location
- Ancillary service taking care of executing/processing the order
- Executing physician carrying out the order
- Executing date/time

12.2 The Order Entry Module

12.2.1 Order Entry Methods

For the moment, most ordering systems are based on manual procedures while some hospitals are using automated order entry programs as a sub-system from a comprehensive HIS. They are mostly directed towards nurses, although some commercial systems (TDS healthcare, LDS knowledge data systems, etc.) try to involve physicians directly in placing their orders on a workstation instead of writing them on paper and allowing the nurses or other clinical workers transcribe them with all the possible mistakes that can occur.
As stated by Prokosch and Pryor [PROK 88] the input of data is a critical area of design. It must be simple, fast, unambiguous and feasible and yet structured enough to insure correctness. The successful implementation of an order entry program depends not only on a careful planning process but mainly on the design and evaluation of the order-entry interface. A variety of frameworks (structures) for personal orders (related to one physician, nursing unit, medical service) and more general orders has to be designed carefully. An integrated "*order dictionary*" system composed of a common terminology of medical acts, medication orders, diet orders, etc. as part of a modern HIS is more advisable. If we look at the possible approaches of existing order entry programs we can divide them into two categories:

- *Freetext order entry* (pure electronic mail)
  The information exchange (i.e. freetext orders) communicated by an electronic mail system is probably from the users standpoint and from the technical aspect for design and implementation the easiest means of order processing but has some serious disadvantages. Data are unstructured and uncontrolled; sometimes data entry is more time-consuming and useless for future data analysis because the content of the orders can only be interpreted by human beings and not by computers for the moment. Human language interpretation will probably be the scope of future fifth computer generations.

- *Menu-based order entry*
  Users are guided through pull-down, pop-up menus assisting them in the selection of specific orders by domain (pull-down,pop-up) and of certain values through value list ranges (pop-up). These types of order entry processing programs are most suitable for future data analysis for decision support functions as part of a modern HIS (Fig 12.1). Combined with a centralised storage of data in the HIS database, they provide the user with a tremendous advantage allowing consistency and priority checking of all these orders. For the near future, it provides a way to extend these order entry systems towards intelligent data acquisition order entry programs [PRO 88].

Although the fact that current data entry systems are far removed from such concepts (referrir to chapter 27), expert systems and decision support facilities will be more and more integrat in future HIS, providing "intelligent" data entry modules, supporting the physician wi information suggestions and advice derived from clinical data stored in the HIS database. However, the general acceptance of such intelligent data entry order systems is dependent upon number of important factors: the quality of the supporting knowledge base, the speed of th inference mechanism, which has an impact on the response time, and the ease of data entry ar operation for the occasional user (GUI).

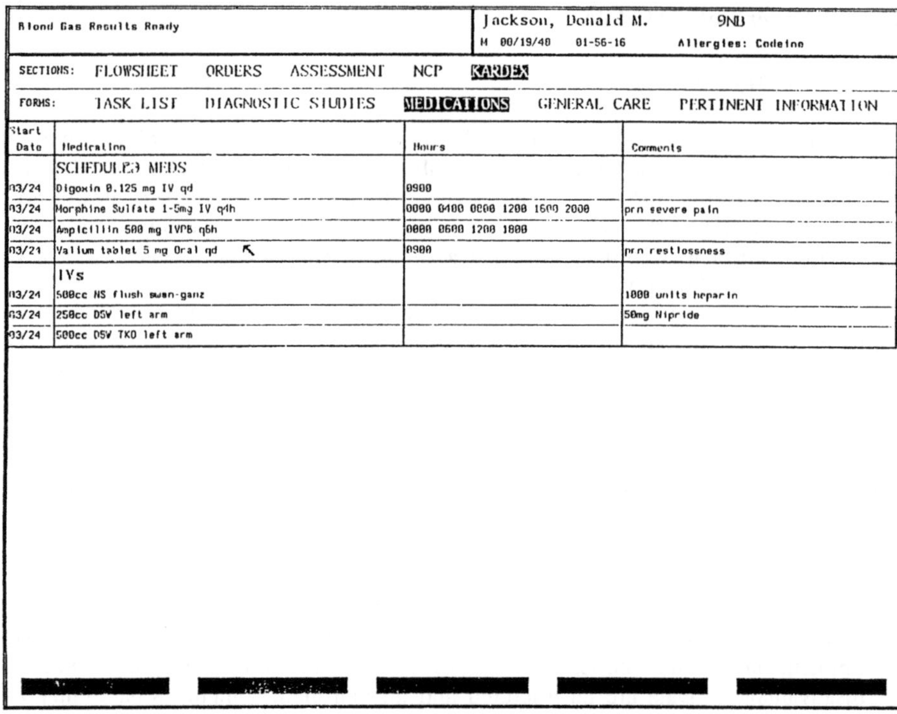
Blood Gas Results Ready | Jackson, Donald M. 9NB
M 00/19/40 01-56-16 Allergies: Codeine
SECTIONS: FLOWSHEET ORDERS ASSESSMENT NCP KARDEX
FORMS: TASK LIST DIAGNOSTIC STUDIES MEDICATIONS GENERAL CARE PERTINENT INFORMATION

Start Date	Medication	Hours	Comments
	SCHEDULED MEDS		
03/24	Digoxin 0.125 mg IV qd	0900	
03/24	Morphine Sulfate 1-5mg IV q4h	0000 0400 0800 1200 1600 2000	prn severe pain
03/24	Ampicillin 500 mg IVPB q6h	0000 0600 1200 1800	
03/24	Valium tablet 5 mg Oral qd	0900	prn restlessness
	IVs		
03/24	500cc NS flush swan-ganz		1000 units heparin
03/24	250cc D5W left arm		50mg Nipride
03/24	500cc D5W TKO left arm		

Fig. 12.1 Medication order entry window. with built-in formulary provided in list
(source reprinted with permission from EMTEK Health Care Systems Inc., Tempe, Arizona, USA)

12.2.2 Collection, Processing and Tracking of Orders: Guidelines

In a "state-of-the-art" HIS, orders should be entered by the physicians themselves by makin choices from standardised and personalised menus. The procedures have to be fast, accurate an flexible. Orders have to be able to be entered from any work station that communicates with th HIS, including terminals located in remote facilities and in physicians' offices. Orders also ha to be entered before admission and activated at admission time, to avoid delays, errors an omissions. Department order sets and personal order sets must be part of the system.

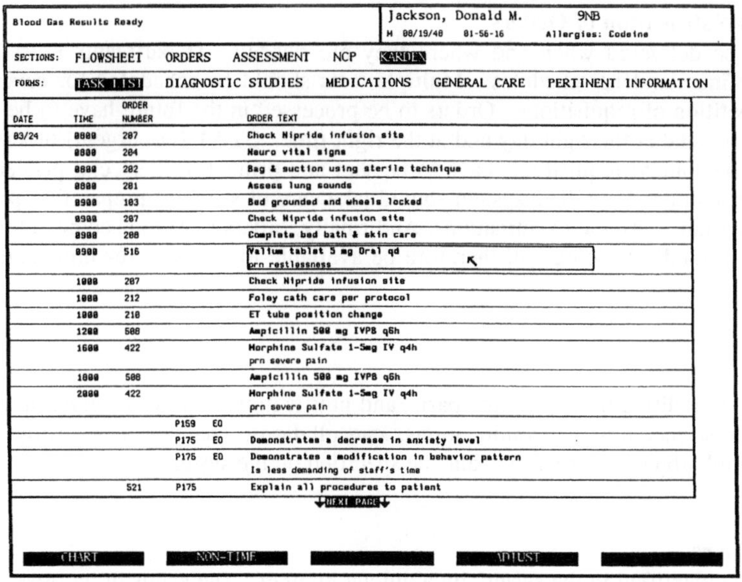

12.2 The nursing task list presents a chronological list of the nursing activities that must be performed in the coming shift.

rce reprinted with permission from EMTEK Health Care Systems Inc., Tempe, Arizona, USA)

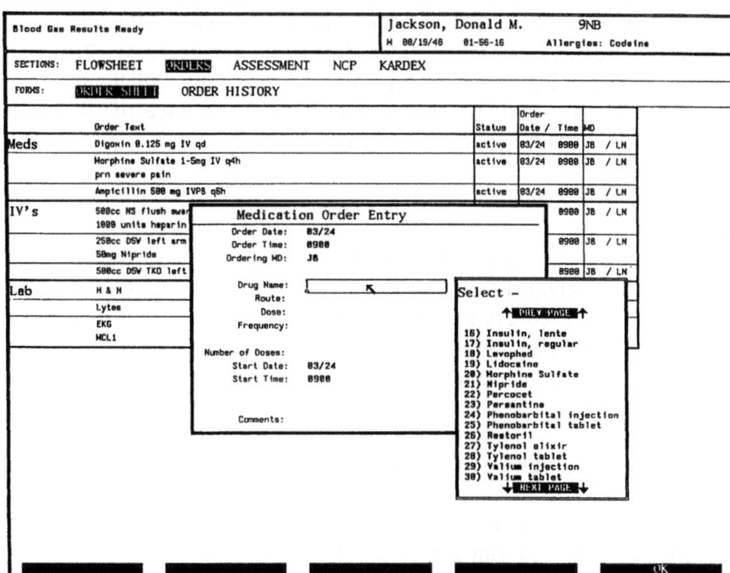

. 12.3 Physicians can rapidly enter orders for their patients by choosing items from structured lists.

urce reprinted with permission from EMTEK Health Care Systems Inc., Tempe, Arizona, USA)

Scheduling and Notification of Orders

Orders have to be delivered when and where they are needed. Departments must have the possibility to define standard schedules. Multiple tests should be scheduled for several days, avoiding the repetition of requisitions. Orders to be processed in the future have to be held and automatically generated at the right day and at the right time. STAT (i.e. urgent) orders have to be processed immediately; requisitions have to be sent and printed on a special printer or on a printer equipped with an alarm. The system should take care of standard preparation procedures associated with certain tests and examinations. And finally, orders have to become automatically part of the patient medical record and therefore be available to all users for immediate review and process.

Modifications

Orders have to be modified on a real-time basis, and notifications have to be given immediately to all departments, including discontinuations, cancellations, changes, suspensions and re-activations. Completion of an order may also be specified on the system.

Tracking of Orders

Orders have to be identified in the system by a unique number. The status of an order has to be provided permanently and immediately to the medical staff. This will eliminate almost all phone calls and inquiries about status and results. Orders have to be retrieved and presented in a format specified by the department or by the user (by order number, by date, chronological or reverse, for a specific date or for a number of days, since admission, etc). Results should also be presented in the form of spreadsheets and graphics (Fig.12.2 and Fig.12.3). The availability of an electronical medical record integrated with this system gives clinicians the possibility to look through various episodes of care and by succesive refinement to trace the orders and related results within a specific active (passive) episode of care.

Contingency Routing

Ancillary departments need to specify contingencies to route, to hold and to re-route orders based on time, day, type of patient, type of order, location, emergency, etc. If a laboratory is closed at night and another one covers emergency, STAT orders have to be automatically re-routed to the laboratory that is open. Also, if a hospital has two locations for the same type of services, the system should be able to route the request to the facility nearest to the patient.

A complete order management system should also produce several kind of documents, e.g.

- List of new orders
- Daily orders summary: list of all orders made since midnight the previous day and of all orders remaining current. Interim copies should be available at any time
- Current order summary

Such systems require a 24-h system availability. It means that systems cannot be taken down for back-ups and have to be available to medical staff 24 h per day, 7 days per week. Back-ups have to be done on line.

The qualitative and quantitative benefits of such systems are enormous :

- Elimination of transcription errors, duplicate orders and data losses
- Speed and accuracy
- Standardisation of procedures and terminology
- Personalisation through the use of departments, specialities and doctors' order sets
- Status tracking, suppression of phone calls
- Remote and distributed access
- Scheduling
- Automatic byproducts

Case : LDS Hospital in Salt Lake City

At the LDS Hospital in Salt Lake City an intelligent medication ordering application in a pharmacy system as part of a comprehensive HIS-HELP system was implemented. (Fig.12.4.). The task of this order entry module is the selection of a drug using key words and the entry of the associated ordering parameters, which are dose, route and schedule.

At a 550-bed care teaching faculty, a 10-month study was performed showing the difference expert system technology can make in the use of this type of drug monitoring incorporated in the HELP system.

Table 12.1 The Help system drug alerts, their causes and actions taken
(source reprinted with permission from 3M Health Care in The Help Patient Care System. A design overview p. 29)

Type of alert	Number of alerts	Percentage of total alerts	Percentage of alerts resulting in therapy changes
Drug - drug	199	28.9	79.9
Drug-allergy	112	16.2	56.3
Drug-aboratory	310	44.9	79.7
Drug-disease	0	0.0	0.0
Drug-dose	50	7.3	94.0
Drug-diet	9	1.3	77.8
Drug-route	2	0.3	100.0
Drug-interval	3	0.4	66.7
Alternate drug	5	0.7	100.0
TOTALS :	690	100.0%	77.1%

Total number of patients monitored = 13737; Total number of drug alerts = 5% of all patients monitored

From Table 12.1 we see that although many people think of drug alerts in the context of drug-to-drug or drug-to-allergy interactions, the most important type of alert results from drug-to-laboratory interactions. On the other hand, 77% of the alerts resulted in therapy changes, indicating the need for awareness before the drugs are administered.

```
Frame :          4.6.22
Title :          Suggested order for ceftazidime injection
Type :           Initialization
Author :         H.U. Prokosch
Drug Name :      ceftazidime ==== mgm, injection
Modified :       06 / 12 / 88
Compiled :       06 / 15 / 88

Variable Declaration :
     creatinine  WHICH IS        |- 13 1 1 1  7 ~ Creatinine Channel 7 -|  OR
                                 |- 13 1 4 1 13 ~ Creatinine SMAC -|;

     creatinine^clearance  WHICH IS
          ( 140 - age ) * weight / ( creatinine * 72 )          IF sex = "male"
       OR
          0.85 * ( 140 - age ) * weight / ( creatinine * 72 )  IF sex = "female";

Initialize Defaults :
     Route :  intravenous piggyback
              intravenous
              intramuscular

     Dose and Schedule :
              IF creatinine^clearance < 5.0 THEN
              BEGIN
                   dose^value = 500;
                   schedule = "q 48 hrs";  min^interval = 24;  max^interval = 48;
              END
              ELSE IF  .....
                         .
                         .
                         .
              ELSE IF  creatinine^clearance >= 31    AND
                       creatinine^clearance <  50    THEN
              BEGIN
                   dose^value = 500;
                   schedule = "q 48 hrs";  min^interval = 24;  max^interval = 48;
              END
              ELSE  IF .....
                         .
                         .
                         .
              min^dose = 250;
              max^dose = 2000;

Comments :
     Third generation antibiotic.
     Decrease dose in renal failure.
```

Fig. 12.4 Intelligent order entry program, an example of a predictive knowledge frame for the order of a ceftazidime injection [PRO 88]

(source reprinted with permission of H.V. Prokosch, Pryor T.A. : *Intelligent Data Acquisition in order entry programs.* In Proceedings 12th annual Symposium on Computer Applications in Medical Care [Washington D.C. 1988, IEEE Computer Society Press, pp. 454 - 458)

The order entry module includes the following actions :

- On-line ordering of medications
- Display of order history
- Immediate notification to the transport service
- Staffing analysis by care level and ward unit

The order entry module includes for inpatients and outpatients as well :

- Order entry: create order by authorised user. The order entry system can use the logon name of the user as ordering operator.
- Create personal order set by user/type/department: allows a user to create personal orders corresponding with his profile and store them.
- Create order for verification: allows creation of orders by non-authorised users for verification and authorisation afterwards.
- Order verification: allows authorised users to verify and release orders in status 'hold' as created previously.
- Order hold/release: orders can be placed in hold status and released afterwards
- Order discontinue/ renew: orders can be discontinued and renewed afterwards
- Order inquiry: to review orders by patient/by status/by department in chronological order
- Print orders on special destination printers: historical order,by status, by department (referring)

12.3 Result Entry Module

After the results have been registered by ancillary departments they have to be disseminated through the hospital. The result reporting module is an essential step in the patient care process after the result entry. These reports can be released at several places to different authorised users :

- By on-line query by patient, department or test
- By type of report (individual report, global, cumulative)
- By result reporting at the patient's nursing unit for inpatients
- By result reporting at the patients referring service/physician for outpatients

For instance, preliminary lab reports can be disseminated to ER departments or ER patients, clearly marked as "preliminary" or "partial" results. For legal and integrity reasons there are six important requirements for an electronically based result message system:

(1) The referring object (physician, services) must be identified
(2) The request must be dated and/or timed
(3) The creator of the result must be identified
(4) Each result must be dated and/or timed
(5) Each result must be identified and approved by a computer signature
(6) The information may not be altered after the computer signature has been added; changes should only be allowed by the creator or with his approval

The department which is responsible for result entry needs to have release controls for providing results depending on their status, i.e.

- Preliminary reports
- Partial reports
- Verified/complete reports

At the same time, the status of the corresponding order has to be adjusted, e.g. in process or completed.
The result entry module includes for inpatients and outpatients;

- Results entry
- Results verification and authorisation
- Result reporting by patient (cf. historical, cumulative), by department, by status (partial/urgent, completed, etc.).

Case : The TDS Health Care System
One of the most well-known vendors 'especially in the USA' in nursing station /order entry/ results reporting systems besides HBO, SMS, McDonnell Douglas is TDS health care systems. The system automates and streamlines many of the procedures typically performed manually in hospitals, such as patient scheduling, care planning, tests and medications ordering and results reporting.
The TDS health care system is designed to be used directly by the medical staff, the nurses and other caregivers, using light pen menu selection technology. By merely pointing the light pen, health care professionals scroll through customised screens built following their personalised standard formats and terminology to create orders, retrieve results and perform many other data management functions.The technology platform of the TDS system is based on IBM 370 mainframe architecture. The Health Care System consists of the following main modules : patient administration, order management, results processing and nursing.

The core of the TDS health care system (TDS7000) is a function-rich patient care system that indefinitely stores and manages all care data in the form of a Permanent Patient Record (PPR). As many as 16 million individual detailed patient records (each capable of storing more than 65000 episodes) are available on-line to care providers and managers from anywhere in the health care facility or system. The PPR also divides that long-term record into episodes of care according to institutionally defined criteria. Clinicians can view any episode (or all episodes) of care on-line in real time. Access to the PPR is protected by a user-code system referred to as the user's electronic signature.

Through workstation graphic capabilities and clinical spreadsheets, physicians and nurses review patient care data from multiple perspectives to identify abnormal trends across multiple episodes. This automated access to "lifetimes" of care sets the stage for improved quality, reduced cost and more effective management outcomes.

Integrated with the PPR is a resource and appointment scheduling application that automates patient schedules for all resources in every facility and department. By building a thorough history of activities, hospital management can detect significant trends and track resource utilisation.

The entry of orders into the system is done primarily by making selections in customised menus. This allows staff and physicians to enter orders quickly and accurately. All orders are automatically made a part of the PPR. As such, they are available throughout a patient's stay for quick, on-line review or reprinting.

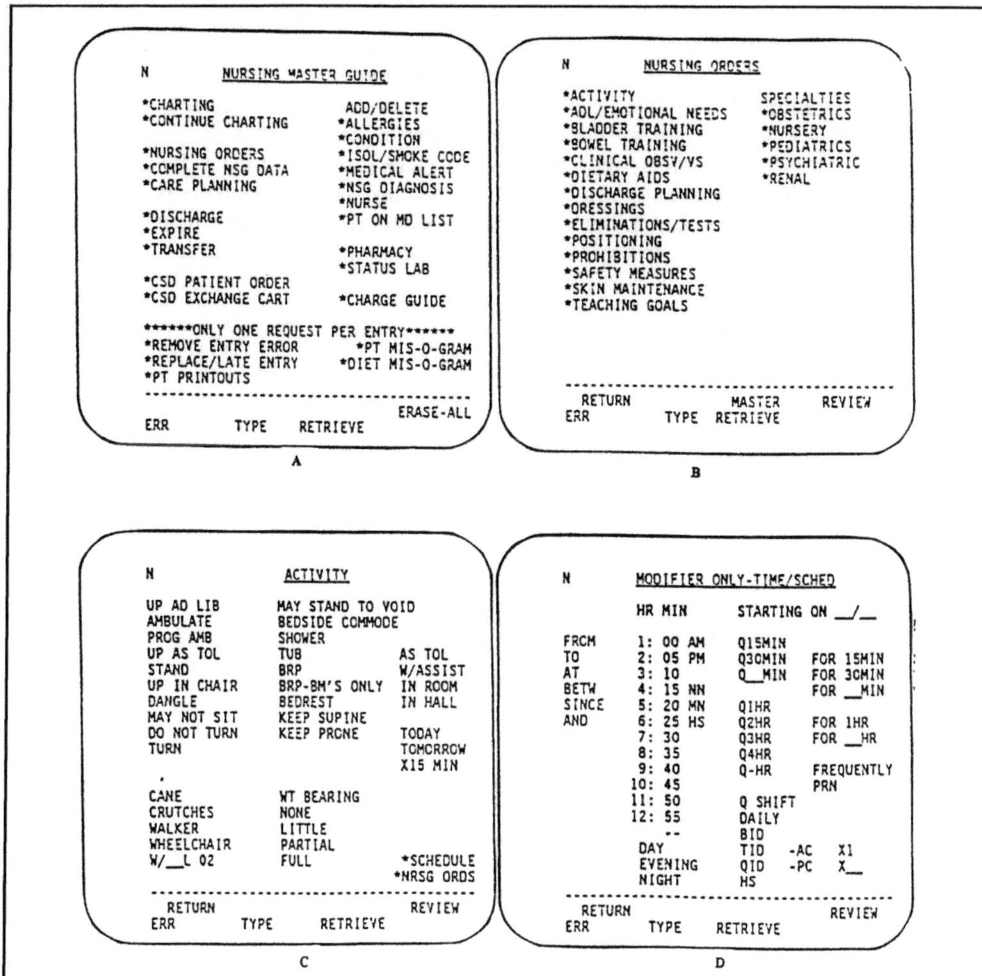

Fig. 12.5 (a) A typical nursing master guide screen allows access to many patient care activities. If the nurse elects to use the NURSING ORDERS pathway as included in the nursing master guide, a screen (b) will appear. As an example, if the nurse selects ACTIVITY, a screen (c) will appear. After making the needed activity selections, the nurse selects SCHEDULE. The new screen will be displayed (d).

(source reprinted with permission of TDS-health Care System)

Lab and radiology procedures, medications and IV fluids, diets and various diagnostic and therapeutic procedures may be ordered by authorised personnel and physicians from any workstation that communicates with the system. This includes all terminals within the hospital, workstations in clinics and remote facilities and even workstations set up in physician offices.

Routine admission orders ("profiles") may be entered for pre-admitted patients and activated at the time of admission, thus avoiding costly delays in the initiation of treatment. Physicians can enter in the sytem "personal order sets" which contain common orders for this speciality.
For example, the initiation of physician's routine preoperative orders can be reduced to a matter of seconds with a few light pen selections. Department order sets offer the same benefits for protocols and unit-specific orders. In adition, the system provides also the facility to prevent costly duplicate orders as on-line, up-to-the-moment displays of current orders is given for each patient and each department during the order-entry process. All orders are automatically made a part of the PPR. As such, they are available throughout a patient's stay for quick, on-line review or reprinting. (Fig. 12.5.).

13

Patient Appointment and Scheduling

13.1 Patient Appointment Systems : Different Viewpoints

Although there is quite a lot of interest in optimal scheduling of patient appointments over a long time [HOL 67] [VIS 78] [ZWI 81] [PET 84], few (user-friendly) systems have been installed up to now. There could be more interest depending upon the viewpoint. Patients (=demand side) and physicians (=supply side) have different time orientations. As physicians deal with many patients, but one at a time, the personal efficiency of health care providers in general must be increased, providing better communications, better feed-back information (trends, evolution, etc.). As physicians and the hospital appear to the patient as a single entity, and as on the other side the patient wishes to be seen as one person, and does not like to receive fragmented care (as is often the case in large institutions), he is afraid of losing his individuality in the large flow of patients. That is the application domain in which patient appointment systems will play a fundamental role in the years ahead, as an interface between patient information-related sub-systems and medical record-related sub-systems. In fact, it is a logic step with the availability of a patient IS to plan future medical diagnostic acts or treatments for physicians and medical facilities in advance.
So when dealing with patient appointment systems we have to define the objectives expected of the system by the hospital. (Table 13.1)
The expectations of patient appointment systems are concentrated in the areas of time and scope. The area of time involves providing an optimal time-scheduling function for all the resources needed to treat inpatients and outpatients. The area of scope requires that the patient appointment and scheduling systems offer a foundation upon which the order entry and result reporting sub-system, the medical record and nursing IS may be built up. This comprehensive view, which is "total systems" thinking, aims to bring the patient, the physician and the medical record together at an appointed time [DAV 67].

The main objectives of a patient appointment and scheduling sub-system have been arranged round four different viewpoints:

The patient's viewpoint:

- Optimisation of waiting periods (reduction of waiting time)
- Keeping the period of time between the request for a medical act and the execution of this act as short as possible
- Expectations of a more individual oriented care, preserving continuity of treatment

The administrator's viewpoint:

- Increase of communication between the various services by means of decentralised appointment planning
- More patients versus a constant number of employees
- Reduction of the time necessary for collecting, processing and supplying information
- Fewer authorities engaged in the administration of appointments

The manager's viewpoint:

- Personnel can be deployed in a more efficient way by means of planning
- Space and medical equipment can be exploited efficiently
- No peak pressure by irregular streams of patients (Fig 13.1)
- Improved ability to gather significant and useful statistical information on the administrative and medical level as well
- The ability to produce detailed cost-accounting studies, relating to activity procedures, patients and resources used (personnel, material)

The physician's viewpoint:

- The physician expects to have administrative work done by clerical personnel (reduce telephone traffic)
- He or she is concerned with the variety of medical situations to be dealt with
- Ability to be informed more efficiently about the medical status of the patient

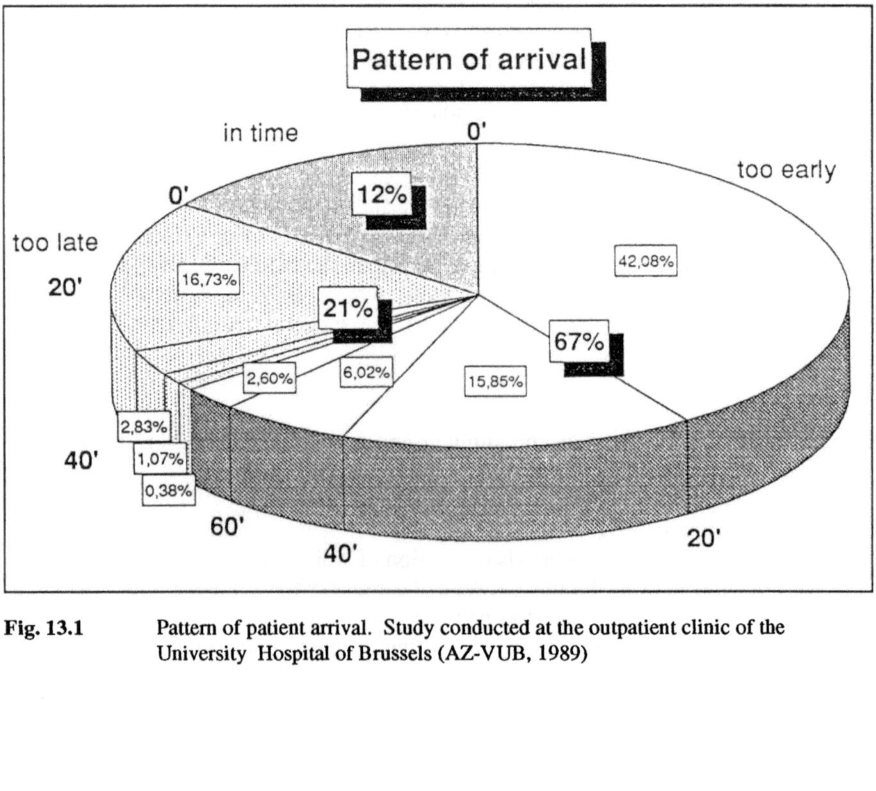

Fig. 13.1 Pattern of patient arrival. Study conducted at the outpatient clinic of the University Hospital of Brussels (AZ-VUB, 1989)

Table 13.1 Points of difference between manual and automatic systems for appointment administration

Manual patient appointment system	Automatic distributed appointment system
Appointments can only be made in the secretariat of the unit in question.	Appointments can be made from any terminal.
For different services different secretariats should be approached.	The patient has to approach one place only.
Appointments can only be made during working hours.	Appointments can be made night and day.
If a patient forgets his appointment dates, it will be difficult to retrace this information.	Appointment dates of patients are always available via terminal.
The cancelling of an appointment involves a lot of search work.	The cancelling of an appointment hour automatically generates messages to all patients with names and addresses.
For several appointments per patient an intensive telephone traffic is required.	Telephone traffic is reduced.
Statistical information only available via intensive efforts.	Statistical information can easily be inferred from the recorded data.
Many mistakes appear to be made in the field of identification of patients.	Mistakes are reduced.
Mail reminders have to be carried out manually	Mail reminders are automatically printed. This is especially useful for certain therapeutic services which schedule patients on a recurring basis of weeks or months into the future.
Communication with central medical archives via copying system.	Communication is automatically established.

13.2. Minimal Requirements of a Patient Appointment and Scheduling System

According to different viewpoints, the requirements of patient appointment and scheduling systems can be established. They are grouped and discussed at the patient, service-planning, management, information supply and integrational levels.

At the patient level:

1. In a planning system it should be possible to make appointments for outpatients, inpatients and external patients in advance.
2. A centralised and a decentralised appointment scheduling mechanism or a combination of both forms must be possible.
3. The patients have to be identified in a simple way, so that appointments can even be made by telephone. The following possibilities of access to the central database should be available: soundex (phonetic), family name, date of birth, administrative number.
4. If more than one examination is planned the system should assist in :
   - Choosing the most optimal way
   - Drawing attention to the incompatibility between certain examinations, for example, IVP after an examination of the stomach or CT scan after an examination of the stomach with contrast.
5. Every time an appointment is assigned, the scheduled event (date, time, place) with all additional information should be printed on an appointment card for the patient.
6. If an appointment was planned for a patient, it should be possible to carry through alterations in a patient's case history (inpatient versus outpatient).
7. Extra attention has to be paid to patients who must be seen as quick as possible, because of high medical priority (e.g. patients sent by the emergency unit or inpatients). For some medical services it is therefore advisable to plan a few unallocated appointment slots at regular intervals. Another alternative here is to allow overbooking, but this can lead to excessive pressure on physicians and technicians, who have to see more patients in the same time interval (time slot).

At the service-planning level:

1. It should be possible to draw up individual schedules (appointment diaries) per appointment unit. An appointment unit can be: a doctor, a medical instrument (CT,MRI,ECG,etc.) a medical service or a combination of these.
2. Depending on the circumstances, the planning can be adjusted. Thus, it should be possible to cancel and transfer an appointment unit for a certain period.
3. A computerised patient scheduling system can be executed in a manual or in an automatic mode. In the "manual mode", the secretary highlights the patient and enters examinations, preferred time and physician (or room), according to the type of examination and priorities.
   When an "automatic scheduling mode" is selected, the system will present the first available time slot for the first physician (or examination room) available, based on predefined criteria. Here, rooms, physicians and examinations are defined with the interrelations between them.
4. The user who interacts with the patient appointment and scheduling system must be provided with a high level (reliable and fast) graphical user interface that gives him access to the system by customised displays resembling his familiar agenda (Fig. 13.2) as much as possible.

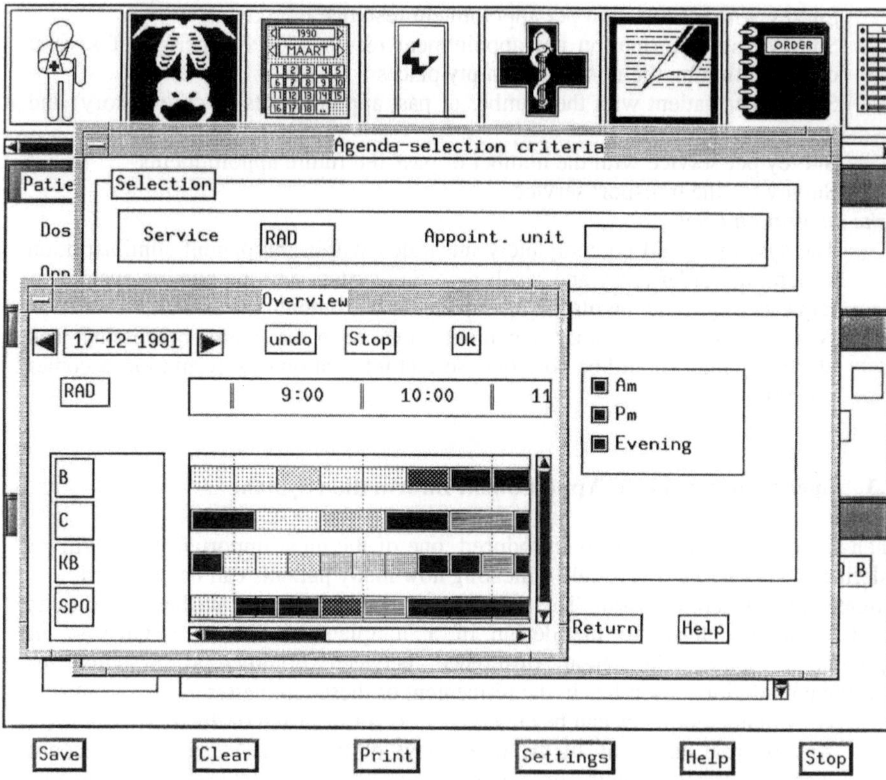

Fig.13.2.: Representation of the graphical user interface as implemented in the patient appointment and scheduling system of the hospital of the Free University of Brussels (Dept. of medical informatics, AZ-VUB)

At the management level:

The system should be able to provide control information about the visiting pattern. For a certain period of time the following information should be made available:

- Planned and real visits (inpatients versus outpatients)
- Unplanned and emergency visits
- First and subsequent visits (what was the percentage of new patients seen in each clinic ?)
- Activity profile statstics
- Planned and real opening hours (how long did it take to see the physician?)
- Sum totals per physician, speciality, working day, period, apparatus
- Percentage of occupation (what is the waiting time?)
- Trends per numbers of patients per speciality
- Referrals via external physicians (general practitioners, specialists)
- What is the referral ratio?

At the information supply level:

Real-time surveys (or lists) replacing the appointment card system should be available in the following forms:

- Survey with information per appointment resource per day
- Survey with information per appointment resource over a period of several days mentioning the number of empty places
- Survey per patient with the number of past appointments (= case history) and future appointments
- Survey per service with the number of past and future appointments
- Survey for the transport service

At the integration level:

- The system should be completely integrated within the patient administration system, the order entry and result reporting system and the nursing system, as requests/orders can be placed for inpatients and outpatients as well.
- A connection with other technical tools such as word processing and electronic mail should be possible, so that integration of information becomes possible.

13.3 Specifications for an Appointment Information System

When an appointment system is introduced, one of the most important tasks will be to define an appointment schedule indicating how many patients can be expected or treated in a certain time slot. The definition or specification of all these conditions for the computer leads to the design of a 'template' similar to a page in an appointment diary. The great difference between commercial systems for appointment administration lies in the refinement of these templates:

- How many templates can be created per doctor or group of doctors?
- Are external data (day of the week, days of leave, etc.) taken into account when templates are being drawn up?
- Does the possibility exist to introduce flexible consulting hours?
- Is it possible to reserve parts of appointments periodically (for instance, for the maintenance of equipment)?
- The time which can be covered? With some systems this is limited to a maximum of 3 months, while some consultations have to be given on an annual basis.

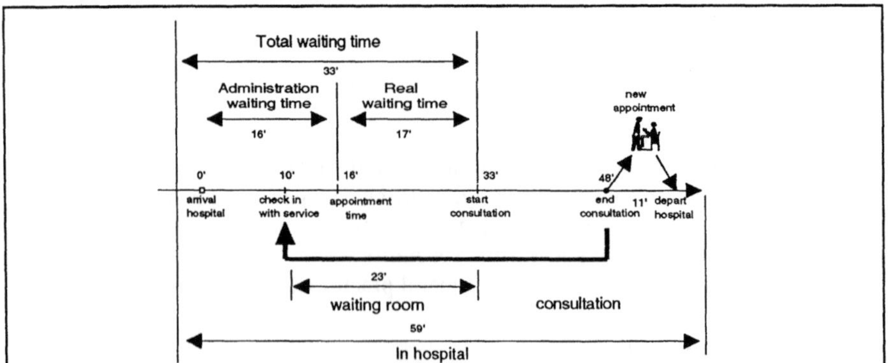

Fig. 13.3. : Waiting-time situation : study conducted in the Orthopaedics Clinic, University Hospital of Brussels (AZ -VUB 1989)

Sometimes it is also advisable, from the point of view of patient service, to register for later processing the actual time as well as the length of the consultation for each patient. The previous illustration of a waiting-time situation is based on registered data of 12000 patients coming from the University hospital in Brussels (700 beds, 300000 polyclinic visits per year, 1988) (Fig. 13.3). This shows that the patient on average:

- Enters the hospital 15 min earlier than agreed
- Is present 6 min before the time agreed for the doctor's consultation
- Has to wait 24 min after the time agreed for the consultation, which takes up about 10 min

Appointment Systems

Depending on the method of working of the physician to be consulted or the service in attendance, several types of appointment schedules can be introduced, at which we will now have a closer look.

- *Several patients at each point of time*: **two-at-a-time**
  At one point of time, two (or several) patients are summoned. This system is advised for doctors who limit themselves to a very short consultation and so have a higher occupation percentage.
- *Fixed duration of examination: individual system*: **individual system**
  With the individual appointment schedule, one appointment per unit of time is made. The individual appointment per hour is recommended for on average longer consultations, in case of a large deviation of consultation intervals (from 15 min to an hour). The system reduces the waiting time for patients and allows them to arrive closer to the time they will be seen.
- *Several patients at the same time*: **block appointments (pure block system)**
  This appointment schedule summons all patients at the same specified time when a clinic starts. Patients are taken care of on a first-come, first-served basis. The patient is not given an appointment for a specific hour, but all the patients are told to come at the same time. The advantage for the physicians is that they will always have patients, and in case a patient does not arrive or comes too late the physician continues working and will not be kept waiting for the patients; on the other hand, the advantages for the patients are less obvious because they have to wait their turn. This type of block appointment system will work fine if the number of patients to be seen is relatively small or if the average time that a physician spends with each patient is small.
- *Completely free consulting hours*
  This is often found with general practitioners. The patient comes within the duration of a consultation. Again, first-come, first-served basis is the rule.
- *Individual appointment schedule with a variable length of consultation*
  This is comparable with the individual appointment schedule, but the length of each consultation depends on the patient and on the medical treatment. It is recommended for medical services or physicians who need a rather long and varying time interval, dependant upon each patient, treatment or medical act (for example, psychiatrists).

Choosing the Ideal Appointment Schedule

From the preceding points it can be concluded that basically the selected appointment schedule depends on two factors [SCH 73]: the average length of an examination (treatment) and the deviation length of an examination (treatment). From this it can be inferred that for examinations of very short duration the pure block (group) schedule is better. For consultations of longer duration, the individual appointment schedule is preferred. Furthermore, the general conclusion that can be drawn is that the more personal the appointment (with a particular doctor at a specified time), the lower the "no-show" rate of the patient and the better the punctuality of both doctors and patients. It should be mentioned that one appointment per unit of time has to be aimed at, because this causes the waiting time of the patients to be reduced to a minimum.

Subsequently, it should be checked regularly whether an adjustment of the chosen schedule is necessary. This can be done, for instance, by roughly measuring the waiting times once a year.

Parameters to be considered

For assigning an appointment to a patient, a number of parameters should be known to begin with. It is also important to adapt the patient's personal wishes to the available places (slots) in the screen, which defines the procedure of an appointment. Let us consider hereafter the parameters in establishing an appointment (Fig. 13.4):

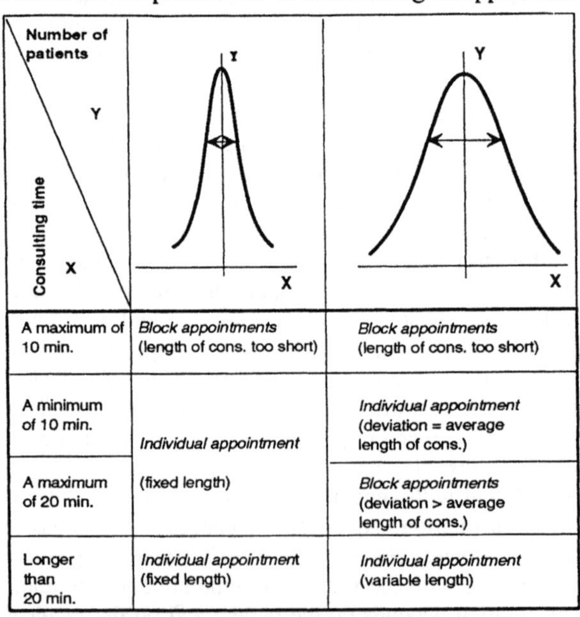

A maximum of 10 min.	*Block appointments* (length of cons. too short)	*Block appointments* (length of cons. too short)
A minimum of 10 min.	*Individual appointment* (fixed length)	*Individual appointment* (deviation = average length of cons.)
A maximum of 20 min.		*Block appointments* (deviation > average length of cons.)
Longer than 20 min.	*Individual appointment* (fixed length)	*Individual appointment* (variable length)

Fig. 13.4 Outline schedule of possible appointment systems in relation to the deviation; X, length of examination ; Y, number of patients

- *The length of a consultation/treatment*
  The total average length of the specified examination/treatment in that service (i.e. the interval between the time a patient enters and the time the medical service is ready for the next patient) must be known in advance.
- *The appointment time*

The required time for consultation (according to the attending doctor's advice and according to the patient's wishes) in the short-term or in the long-term must be given. It has been found that recently made appointments are better kept by patients. Therefore, it is necessary with long-term appointments to send a reminder to the patient, mentioning date, hour and service where he is expected (and any documents that should be brought).

- *Additional examinations/treatments*
  It should be known whether or not the patient has to undergo any additional examinations. Therefore, the patient flows to and between medical departments should be organised in such a way that the (out)patient's number of visits to the outpatients' department can be limited to a minimum, their length being optimal.
- *Activities arranged in the morning*
  Belonging to this group are all activities for which the patient has to have an empty stomach and all other activities occurring in combination with an examination on an empty stomach. Obviously, it is advisable to make appointments for all these activities on the same morning.
- *Interval*
  In some cases an intervening period between various consultations is necessary, for instance blood tests or cardiology tests in nuclear medicine.
- *Desired physician*
  Some patients always request the same physician; either this must be reported to the computer as a parameter again and again, or the system memorises this information.

13.4. Points of Consideration

When one decides to introduce an automatic system for appointment administration, it is important to answer a few questions beforehand; the main questions to be posed are:

- Who is going to assign the appointments (centralised versus decentralised)?
- Is overbooking allowed? If so, for which type of patients/ examinations/ treatments?
  Who is to decide on this?
- Are we going to work with qualifying periods if, for specific reasons, an appointment cannot be assigned?
- How are we going to deal with the cancellations of particular appointments?
- Who is going to draw up the appointment schedules per doctor/service?

On the other hand, one should be aware of the disadvantages attached to automation as well:

- What is to be done in the case of a computer failure?
- How is the security to be settled?

An alternative for a decentralised on-line system for appointment administration is one that to works semi-automatically; appointments are assigned by hand to be added to the computer by an operator later on.

Which is the optimal solution depends on the hospital and is weighted with respect to arguments such as the size of the institution (scattered over various buildings? yes or not) and the cost price of the communication network.

14

Operating Theatre Management Information System

14.1 History

Operating theatres are expensive and consume large sums in terms of personnel, equipment, material and medication. On the other hand, they provide a major source of revenue. Due to the importance of such huge departments in the institution, the hospital manager wants to be informed about their effectiveness. Surgery is a scientific and technical discipline; to be efficient, surgery practice requires a continuous acquisition of new technologies and adaptation of the organisation.In most hospitals single-discipline operating rooms per hospital division have evolved into physically closed multi-discipline operating rooms (surgery blocks) in which effective resource management has become an important and critical issue for the efficient use of personnel, instrumentation, time and inventories [BAR 87]. Hospital executives place a high priority on the proper functioning of their OR systems. Nowadays operating theatres hold a key position in hospital management.

In the late 1970s few hospitals had installed an operating room (OR) IS. Because of the fact that at that time almost no vendors offered such an application, existing OR IS were mostly developed in-house. They functioned merely as semi-automated appointment books. In the mid-1980s a few vendors were appearing in the marketplace with OR IS, at first focussing on appointment scheduling and charging then later on personnel management, inventory control and equipment management. Nowadays, however, these systems have evolved towards complete OR IS handling complex functions such as appointment scheduling, inventory management, utilisation review, personnel management, etc.. In fact, OR systems are still in their infancy in most hospitals, and OR users and vendors need to be educated and informed mutually about their benefits and possibilities. On the other hand, vendors and hospitals must determine what they really want. This situation will change rapidly in the near future.

In Europe and the USA (Joint Commission on Accreditation of Hospitals -JCAH) more stringent standards of quality assurance for patient care are advocated [BAL 89]. The emphasis is on care monitoring and generic screening for quality assurance outcome criteria standards. As this is costly, difficult and time-consuming with manual systems, computers will be necessary to monitor patient care, capturing data at the source, manipulating that data, detecting errors and providing meaningful information to improve the quality of patient care.

The most important features provided by an OR IS are:

- Scheduling surgical procedures
- Preparing work flow in advance

- Reporting tool for analysis of utilisation of surgical suites
- Documenting OR procedures, including instruments and supplies needed for each surgical intervention
- Capturing operating costs by case
- Personnel management
- Linking and integrating with other hospital departments (ADT, laboratory)
- Instrument management
- Inventory management (materials and medication)
- Patient transportation notification
- Registration of clinical data (OR record, anaesthetic record, infectious surveillance)
- Monitoring the use of antibiotics for surgical patients

14.2 Scheduling of Surgical Procedures

The primary motivator for implementing OR IS is the scheduling of surgery cases. An optimal scheduling process is composed of the assignment of a patient with the specific surgical procedure(s) to a group of staff members for an operating room at a specific time. It starts with the input of patient data, (multiple) surgical procedure(s) and (multiple) surgeon(s). It can, for instance, act as a framework on which the operator can place the case (spreadsheet) in the operating room of choice, covering (depending upon the surgical procedure) a number of time slots. Another alternative is, although extremely difficult to achieve, leaving the scheduling process to a completely automatic rule-driven allocator. As poor turn-around time, OR inefficiency and scheduling conflicts are often a problem for most ORs', careful selection of a scheduling template is very important. The University Hospital of Brussels (AZ-VUB) handles this problem by using a block scheduling system, in which specific surgical specialties obtain blocks of time. The other free blocks are left for emergency interventions and/or filled in on a first-come, first-serve basis.

It is desirable that these scheduling modules have the ability to check for case and supply conflicts. Some surgical procedures demand special instruments, or conflicts can arise in booking the surgeon in one room while scheduling an instrument in another.

When the schedule is completed and verified, a surgeon-specific case list of the instruments and supplies needed for each intervention is produced. At the same time, several units can be informed: admission department (automatic pre-admission), ward (bed census), radiology (requested examinations), pathology (lab tests), etc. Cases added after this time are treated as on the flight, or urgent.

The day before the final intervention, the OR manager can arrange a final adjustment and editing of the agenda of the day. A worksheet (case cart) is also printed out, indicating the supplies and instruments needed by the scheduled surgeon for the pending operation. It is fed from an integrated medical act database which contains all relevant data related to every surgical procedure.

14.3 Automated OR Record and Anaesthesia Record

When a patient enters the OR every "event" can be registered into the computer: time of entry, start time of anaesthesia, incision time, end of the surgical procedure, postoperative time period, projected return to the ward unit, etc. The system can automate monitoring the patient's progress through surgery and the perioperative nursing process. One of the most interesting benefits is that these progress milestones can be followed at a distance by other departments or ward units without continually telephoning to the OR for information for themselves or for the family, to discover in what phase the case is at that moment. Currently, only a few hospitals have implemented this technology [HAR 90] (Fig. 14.1.).

The emergence of automated computerised systems, which automatically gather data arriving from patient monitors in real-time and provide the facility to enter other data manually, has prompted the development and assessment of computerised anaesthesia records. The anaesthesia record is composed of three parts: the preoperative assessment of the patient's health situation, perioperative data and postoperative data. We will briefly define in this section the scope of this record. The essential data contained herein can be summarised as follows:

° *Patient demographic data:* name, age, sex, place, patient-hospital ID, ward unit.

° *Preoperative data*:
  - Lab-results (haematology, biochemistry)
  - Drug history and premedication (transfusions)
  - Allergy or toxin cases
  - Blood pressure
  - Length/weight
  - Previous surgery
  - Respiratory data (X-radiograph of thorax, lung function tests)
  - Cardiovascular data (ECG, cardiac rate, hypertension, cardiac pathology)
  - Neurological data (epilepsy, psychiatric disorders)
  - Metabolic and endocrine data

° *Perioperative data (intraoperative data) (Fig.14.2.)*
  - Operative procedures (surgical speciality, operating theatre, utilisation, date, time, start time, finish time, urgency of surgery)
  - Medical personnel involved (surgeon(s),anaesthesist(s), nurses, technicians)
  - Anaesthetic techniques [duration, type of anaesthetic, possible complications, patient classification (ASA, APACHE)]
  - Medical instruments (patient monitors) used
  - Drug and fluid administration (and antibiotics)
  - Equipment used
  - Fluid balance (blood loss, drainage, urinary output, IV fluids)
  - Monitored physiological parameters (Table 14.1.)
  - Observations made during the surgical intervention such as complications encountered

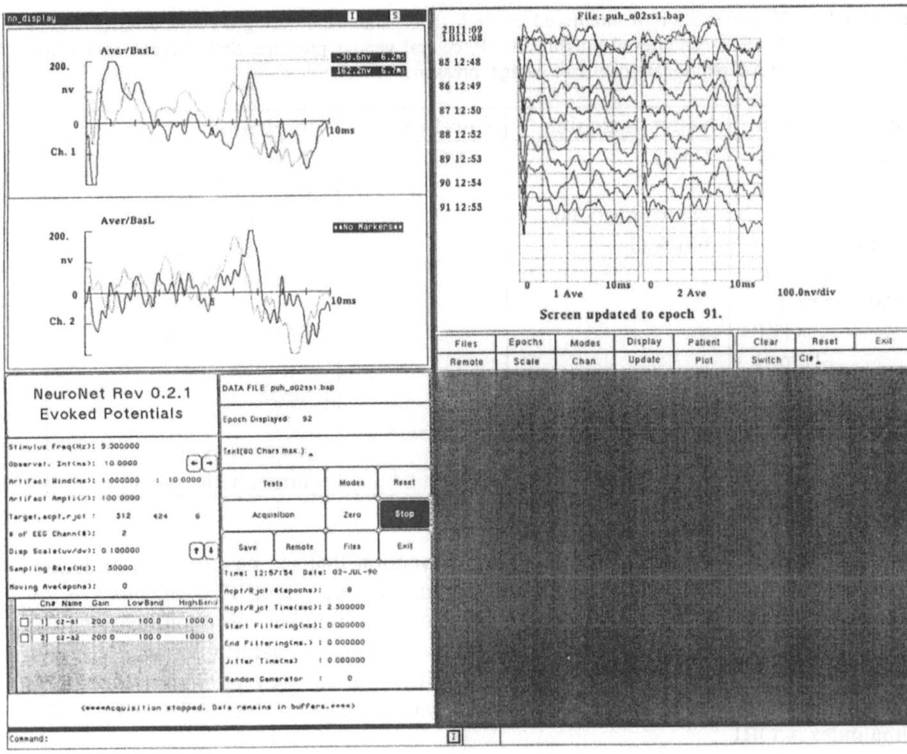

Fig. 14.1. Typical operating room display during evoked response monitoring. The *upper left panel* shows the current, partially completed, evoked response (*solid line*) superimposed on a baseline evoked response from the beginning of the case (*dotted line*). Note that the current response is delayed by 0.5 ms compared with the baseline. The *lower left panel* shows all the parameters and controls for acquiring evoked responses. Note that the stimulus frequency is 9.3 Hz and the observation interval is 10 ms. These are typical parameters for acquiring brain stem, auditory evoked responses as shown here. The *upper right panel* shows a waterfall display of evoked responses acquired over the past several minutes.

(Source reprinted with permission from Don Krieger, Gerald Burk, and Robert J. Sclabassi, University of Pittsburgh, Neuronet, *Computer*, March 1991, p. 50)

- *Postoperative data:*
  - Prescriptions for blood, antibiotics, analgesia, drugs
  - Fluid balance
  - Oxygen therapy
  - Specific examinations to be ordered (biochemistry, RX)
  - Nosocomial infectious diseases
  - Surgery protocol composed by surgeon

Table 14.1. Representation of monitored physiological parameters during a surgical intervention; MAP, mean arterial pressure; CVP, central venous pressure; Sa02,oxygen saturation; PCW, pulmonary capillary wedge pressure

Cardiovascular	Neuromuscular	Cerebral	Respiratory
ECG/heart rate	EMG	EEG	Respiratory rate
Blood pressure			End-tidal CO_2
	Neuromuscular		O_2 concentration
MAP(inv./noninv.)	blockade		N_2O, O_2, expired
Pulse rate			Inspirated O_2 ,N_2O
Cardiac output			
CVP			Expired tidal volume
Temp1			
Temp2			SaO_2
PCWP			
			Inspired/expired anaesthetic agent

To evaluate the overall risk of the surgical intervention that the patient is to undergo, indices of risk based on several different parameters are used. The objective is to perform the operation on the patient with the least number of complications or secondary effects [TOR 90]. An index of risk is a numerical value with which it has been shown that it is possible to associate a value of risk. Several indices are used depending upon the scope and application domain envisioned, e.g. ASA, APACHE, trauma index, CORI.

14.4 Inventory Management

Most ORs have no automatic inventory control mechanism, resulting in extravagant quanities of supplies or tools. Automated OR inventory control can be of help to a hospital in cutting costs. "OR nurses tend to hoard supplies because of the fear of not having something the surgeon needs. They are trying to avoid angering the surgeon, "concludes S. Scott of Atwork corporation. An automated inventory control system can help solve such problems, give an indication when a minimum level of quantity is reached for re-ordering, check expiration dates, prevent overstocking and reduce the cost of inventory.

Whenever a surgical procedure is performed, an automatic updating of the inventory system must be carried out and new supply orders have eventually to be generated.

14.5 Charge Capturing

After the surgical procedure has been fulfilled, the responsible nurse or physician must verify the case cart with the procedures performed, the items delivered and the medication administered. Other information relating to the surgical procedure such as serial number and lot number of a prothesis are also registered into the system. Finally, all the input data are transferred to the billing system and (following to the legal rules) charged to the patient. On the other side, the same data are fed into the inventory management system.

De Klokkengberg Medisch Centrum
Department of CardioThoracic Anesthesia

PT. NAME:
ID #: 57055667/201/154
PT. AGE: 64
PREOP DX: AORTASTEN.
POSTOP DX:
PROCEDURE: AVR
ANESTHES: LACHI TJ ARA
SURGEONS: V. GELDORP

DATE: 02/10/1989
ANES. BEG: 07:45
OPER. BEG: 08:36
OPER. END: 12:45
ANES. END: 12:50
ASA RISK:
PREMEDIC: MORFINE/SCOPOLAM
PT WT / HT: 64 164

ETT: RUSH DIAM 9.0
IV: VIALON 14G LI ARM
AL: MEDICUT 20 G LI A RA
CVL: RE I UG INT INTRODUCE
PA: SWAN GANZ 7.5 FR
POS: RUGLI GGI NG
HYP: HYPOTHERMIE

TIME	07:46	07:49	07:50	07:55	08:00	08:05	08:10	08:15	08:20	08:25	08:30
FENTA		1						2.5->			
ETOM											
PAVUL		8									
MIDAZ		5		10							
MANDO				2							
SUFEN											
GAS-%				FOREN							
FIO2%	22.0	22.0	100.0	22.0	88.0	85.0	64.0	63.0	63.0	63.0	63.0
TV(l)											
SAO2				100	99	99	99	99	100	100	100
ETCO2	0.0	0.0	0.0	0.0	22.0	26.6	22.0	25.5	22.5	26.6	15.9
RATE											
SvO2											

TIME	08:35	08:38	08:40	08:45	08:50	08:55	09:00	09:05	09:07	09:10
FENTA										
ETOM										
PAVUL										
MIDAZ										
MANDO										
SUFEN										
GAS-%			1.50			0.00				
FIO2%	63.0	63.0	63.0	61.0	60.0	62.0	64.0	65.0	65.0	65.0
TV(l)										
SAO2	100	100	100	98	INTERF	98	98	98	98	98
ETCO2	19.0	16.7	15.2	14.4	18.2	17.4	13.6	16.7	12.9	13.6
RATE										
SvO2										

TIME	07:46	07:49	07:50	07:55	08:00	08:05	08:10	08:15	08:20	08:25	08:30
		ST-II		MAN/10		TNT/3		DOPA/3		ADA/3	
SYS	0	155	169	161	118	123	123	119	166	149	143
DIA	0	73	75	74	57	59	56	56	74	62	61
MAP	0	105	116	105	81	83	80	80	107	94	91
HR	65	69	71	62	55	57	56	53	57	54	52
MPA	0	0	0	0	0	21	20	21	27	26	24
CVP	0	0	0	0	0	5	6	6	6	5	5
PCWP									23		
CO									6.90		
SVR									1169		
PVR									46		
ST		X XX	X XX	0.00	-0.10	-0.10	0.00	-0.10	0.10	-0.10	-0.10
EKG	SR	SR	SR	SR	SR	SR	SR	SR	SR	SR	SR
TEMP	23.4	23.5	23.5	23.5	24.5	24.3	24.2	24.4	35.4	35.3	35.2
UO										225	

TIME	08:35	08:38	08:40	08:45	08:50	08:55	09:00	09:05	09:07	09:10
								DRUK/H		TNT=0
SYS	137	141	150	149	136	107	96	105	73	114
DIA	57	65	63	68	63	52	52	50	40	57
MAP	86	92	95	100	93	73	68	69	49	50
HR	49	50	50	62	62	62	62	64	61	63
MPA	24	25	26	39	35	24	20	19	16	20
CVP	5	5	5	8	6	5	5	5	7	5
PCWP				23						
CO										
SVR										
PVR										
ST	-0.10	-0.10	-0.10	-0.10	-0.30	-0.40	-0.10	0.20	0.10	0.10
EKG	SR	SR	SR	SR	SR	SR	SR	SR	SR	SR
TEMP	35.1	35.0	35.0	34.9	34.3	34.4	34.3	34.2	34.2	34.2
UO										

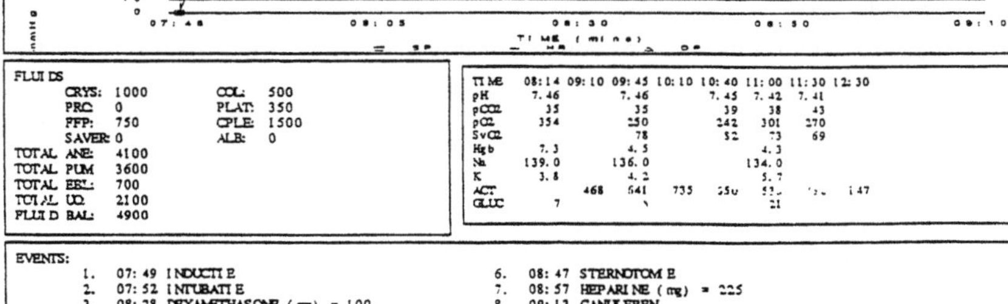

FLUIDS
CRYS: 1000 COL: 500
PRC: 0 PLAT: 350
FFP: 750 CPLE: 1500
SAVER: 0 ALB: 0
TOTAL ANE: 4100
TOTAL PUM: 3600
TOTAL EBL: 700
TOTAL UO: 2100
FLUID BAL: 4900

TIME	08:14	09:10	09:45	10:10	10:40	11:00	11:30	12:30
pH	7.46		7.46		7.45	7.42	7.41	
pCO2	35		35		39	38	43	
pO2	354		250		242	301	270	
SvO2			78		52	73	69	
Hgb	7.3		4.5			4.3		
Na	139.0		136.0			134.0		
K	3.8		4.2			5.7		
ACT		468	641	735	[illegible]	[illegible]	[illegible]	147
GLUC	7		[illegible]			21		

EVENTS:
1. 07:49 INDUCTIE
2. 07:52 INTUBATIE
3. 08:28 DEXAMETHASONE (mg) = 100
4. 08:28 GENTAMYCINE (mg) = 60
5. 08:36 BLOEDVERW KOUDE/ANTISTOF
6. 08:47 STERNOTOMIE
7. 08:57 HEPARINE (mg) = 225
8. 09:13 CANULEREN
9. 09:32 CARDIOPL: warm 200/Koud 700
10. 10:51 ONTLUCHTEN

Fig. 14.2. Overview of medical data gathered during a patient's surgical intervention **(source** reprinted with the permission of Computil, Belgium)

14.6 The Integration Issue

As stated initially, integration is one of the most important issues for a hospital as we enter the 1990s. Interfacing or integrating the OR system with other areas of the HIS is a must. The most important application domains with which OR systems have to be interfaced are:

- ADT department, with which they need to exchange patient data (patient identification and demographic data) and to which they must sent notifications in the future
- Radiology department to have immediate access to radiology requests and reports for "preops"
- Laboratory departments in order to place laboratory orders and have access to lab results for "preops"
- Infection control department

There are several possibilities in linking the OR with the admissions department :

- The admitting department is notified of a request for a bed reservation, while the OR schedules the patient for surgery.
- The admitting department performs the OR scheduling and bed reservation.
- The O.R. performs the scheduling and bed reservation.

14.7 Documentation of the Operating Room

It is necessary to have a number of "resource files" (or dictionary) describing the resources to be managed. The most important files are:

- Surgical procedure file, which gives the definition of each procedure in terms of estimated duration, preparation time, clean-up time, equipment supplies and tools necessary for the intervention, preferred OR, maximum number of times the procedure is allowed to be performed per day, charge data, medical speciality of the act, required presence of another surgeon, name abbreviation
- OR file, which contains a description of each OR, specifying classes of procedures that can be executed, agenda (daily availability times), available equipment
- Supply file including item's code, supplier, cost, charge, re-ordering level, quantity on hand
- Staff member file specifies for every member (surgeon, anaesthesiologist, nurse) personal information and availability

14.8 Reporting Tools

In order to achieve an optimal resource allocation, statistics and management reports are necessary as a feed-back system. Typical reports include:

- Daily surgical analysis which gives on a selected date an overview of all performed procedures organised according to difficult criteria (by speciality, by patient types)

- Supply and equipment utilisation report which gives the total costs and consumption for each supply item on a monthly basis (implants logs) or equipment utilisation
- Incision time analysis report which gives the time required for each surgical procedure, in order to adjust this information in the surgical procedure file
- Monthly surgical analysis report, compared with previous year(s) or months, which gives the number of surgical cases performed, organised according to different criteria [by patient type (inpatient, outpatient), by surgical class].
- Other reports such as trend utilisation and revenue reports by surgical speciality, average cost per case, wound classifications

15

Automation in Nutriton

15.1 Introduction

At the moment the furnishing of food in most hospitals is characterised by:
- A large degree of centralisation
- Proportioning and composition of meals on the assembly line
- Transport by means of ready-made dinner trays

The consequence is that ordinary patients and diet patients are obliged to eat "pot-luck". Criticism of the existing hospital establishment [PLU 84] [BIJ 82] [IBF 81] [SWI 82] [WHE 84] for social reasons to improve the provision of services (more options), and therapeutic reasons (dietary rules) has led to a pursuance of better care for the patient in various fields, also within the sector of food supply. In this sector, a large quantity of data has to be handled, and in principle this could be carried out by hand if sufficient manpower was available to get everything done within the desired space of time. If not, then the introduction of automation within this sector is an obvious solution.

15.2 Aims

The aims of a computer-based meal distribution system are:
- To offer options to patients, within the limitations of their diet
- To arrange the time of menu choice for patients as close as possible to the time they take their meal
- Flexibility in adapting diets
- Improvement of communication between nursing units and hotel sector
- A better control of the distribution of food
- Check-up and analysis of nutritional values

15.3 Preceding Concepts

In this paragraph some important concepts are explained briefly:

Meals

Chronologically, we distinguish the following meals:
- Breakfast between 0630 - 0830 hours (bread, butter, filling, drink)

°Provision between meals

° Lunch between 1200 - 1300 hours (soup, protein, sauce, vegetables, potatoes, dessert)

°Provision between meals

° Dinner between 1700 - 1800 hours (bread, butter, filling, drink)

°Provision between meals

Possible provisions between meals include drinks (tea, coffee, milk, etc.), an extra small dish (fruit, yoghurt, soup) or a complete meal.

Diet Food

With regard to the composition of food a distinction is made between normal food and diet food: the latter is food which is different from normal food for medical reasons.

Diet Order and Advice

Via a diet order, the doctor prescribes the diet for the patient. This diet prescription is imparted to the dietician (nutritian), who together with the patient translates it into dietary advice, depending on the individual wishes and needs of each patient. Per diet order, various forms of advice are possible, because demands are made only with respect to the nutrient quality over the complete day and not with respect to the quality of this nutrient in each separate dish. So it is sensible for each hospital to formulate a standard dietary advice per diet order.

Menus and Menu Components

The pattern according to which meals are composed is called a menu. The menu is composed of menu components which, depending on the time of the year, are seasonal and, within this cycle, correspond to a nutrient component. So the arrangement of the menus is done in cycles. Such a cycle is comparable with the seasons. As not all menu components and/or nutrient components are available throughout the year, it is necessary to split up the year into cycles. Nutrient components, in their turn, are composed of basic system parts (ingredients), for example:

Menu component	Bread	Milk
Nutrient component	Grey bread	Chocolate milk
	White bread	Whole milk and cream
	Brown bread	
Ingredients	Flour	Milk
	Salt	Chocolate
	Dough	Sugar

It will be obvious that to lay down all these data -possible diets (simple and compound), allowed components per diet, arrangement of components per menu cycle- an amount of once-only work which should not be underestimated is required..

Meal Cards (=Menu Choice)

Starting from the feeding and/or dietary profile of each patient, and taking into account the allowed nutritional components per patient for this diet and the menu cycle, a personalised meal card is composed, on which various dishes are listed from which the patient in question can choose.

15.4 Organisation of the Kitchen

Collecting the Patients' Choices

The dietary rules (dietary advice) are placed in the computer system per patient. Depending on the organisation of the hospital, these can be registered centrally (by the food supply department) or not (by nursing staff). Obviously, for patients receiving ordinary food, nothing, special is indicated (fig. 15.1).

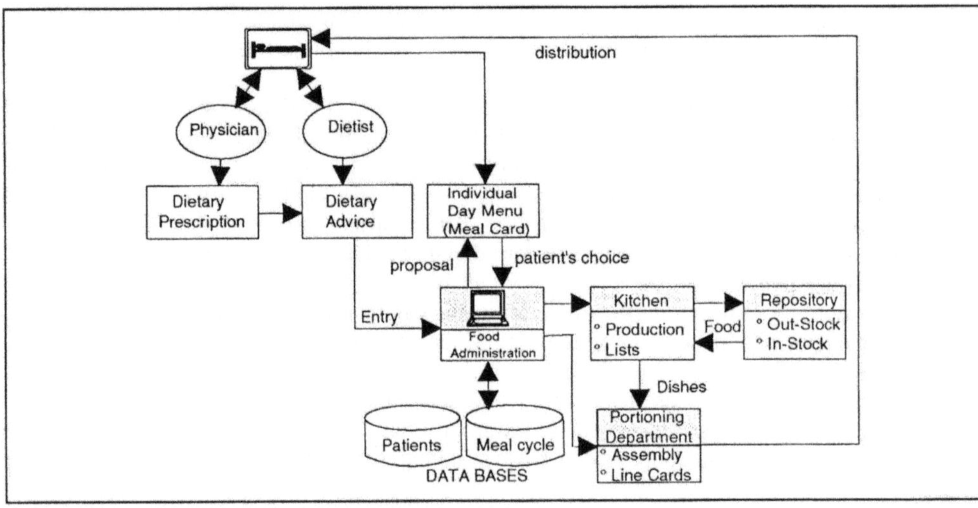

Fig.15.1 **Illustration of automation in nutrition: information flow**

Starting from the admitted patients (and also the patients who are expected) and the cycle time with the available nutritional components, individualised meal cards are printed (sometimes called patient card, menu choice card or food card). The patient makes his choice and can be assisted by the dietician or the nurse. This choice is reported to the computer, which at the same time carries out a number of checks such as the maximum size of allowed portions, permitted menu components, etc.

There are several alternatives of gathering this information: by using barcode-identified mealcards, registered with transportable barcode readers, or hand-held portable computers (limited display). The registration of the patient choices can also be made by optical character recognition (preprinted forms), but this has the disadvantage that the freedom in composing the meal cards is reduced, unless they are printed by means of a laser printer, resulting in variable "preprinted" forms. Input through the terminals is the most conventional but most time-consuming way. Based on this gathered information , it is possible to print:

-*Assembly line cards.* These are used in the kitchen on the assembly line in preparing and portioning patients' meals. The cards have been composed in such a way as to take into account

the place of the scooping bowls.
- *Total production lists.* Based on the total number of applications, production lists (sometimes called preparation lists) are printed, indicating the number of portions and half-portions per menu component (idem for the provisions between meals). These can then be subdivided further at ingredient level and if integrated with a stock-keeping system, the necessary orders to suppliers can be drawn up.
-*Compose cooking lists.* Subsequently, from these preparation lists cooking lists can be composed, on which the dishes to be cooked are given, with the quantities in kilograms or litres, for instance, 10 l of cream soup, 4 l of tomato soup, 2 l of onion soup.

Preparation Systems in the Kitchen
Two kinds of preparation systems are found:
- *Linked,* in which the dishes are eaten immediately after preparation
- *Unlinked,* in which, after preparation, the meals are frozen or deep-frozen and warmed up for consumption in the central kitchen or departmental kitchen. This is a less energy-friendly method of working, as energy is wasted (once to freeze the food, once to heat it up again) but requires fewer people for meal distribution.

Distribution Systems
Generally, two systems of food distribution are found in hospitals:
- *Centralised.* The meals are prepared in the central kitchen and portioned individually per patient, based on the assembly line cards. Each part of the meal has its position on the assembly line.
- *Decentralised.* These meals are also prepared centrally, but they are transported to the nursing units in portions for several persons, and portioned there on the spot.

Considerations
A big problem is keeping meal cards up-to-date in accordance with the actual number of patients present. Thus, for optimal functioning it is necessary for this system to be "strongly" (i.e. real-time) integrated with the patient administration system. Also, "standbys" have to be built into the system, for registering unscheduled admissions (for example via the emergency service). It is, therefore, necessary to keep the interval of time between the registration of information and the production of assembly line cards and cooking lists as short as possible.

15.5 Nutritional Value Analysis and Evaluation

The nutritional (food) database forms the heart of the nutrient analysis and dietary counselling program. It is a compendium of nutritional data containing brand name and generic food compositions concerning all nutritional components.
Each nutritional component is characterised by:
- Amount normally supplied to a patient
- Corresponding amount of calories
- Amount of proteins
- Fat content (saturated, monounsaturated, polyunsaturated)
- Amount of carbohydrates

- Amount of salt
- Amount of calories, etc.

For the analysis and evaluation of the food supplied to a patient, all the nutritional components chosen and taken by the patient can be fed into the computer over a period of 1-7 days, after which, via a program, an analysis is made of the nutritional value. Then, the results can be represented in tables or graphically. On the other hand, it is possible, based on the physician's prescription, to discuss the menu with the patient in question and to check whether the nutritional value of the totality of the nutritional components taken/chosen has been adapted to the doctor's prescriptions or directions. Nowadays, for this a number of microcomputer-based programs are on the market, which make a flexible and comprehensive nutrient analysis. These systems are based on a food database including information on foods by common name, brand name, calories and amounts of nutrients. These databases also include values for total energy, protein, saturated fat, unsaturated fat, poly-unsaturated fat, complex carbohydrates, potassium, cholesterol, sugar, vitamin A and C, iron, etc. Some important packages to mention are: Nutri-call (Camde Corp.), Dine system (Dine Systems, Inc.), The Food Processor (ESHA Research Nutrition Systems), Nutrologic Wizard (CSPI), Nutrilogic (HMC software), Nutripak (Nutritional Data Resources).

15.6 Functional Requirements of an Automated Nutrition System

Hereafter, the most important functions of an automated nutrition systems are briefly summarised :

Administrative Functions

- Registration of diets per patient
- Registration of patients' choices/meal cards
- Registration of urgent choices
- Questioning of patient diets

Production Functions

- Production of meal cards
- Production of assembly line cards
- Production of cooking lists
- Statistical surveys
- Analysis of nutritional value of patient intake over several days

Repository

- Management of nutritional components
- Management of ingredients
- Management of ingredients/nutritional components
- Management of cycles
- Management of menu components

To conclude, the efficiency of an automated nutrition system for patients depends heavily on the "flexibility" by which nutrition data can be gathered on the one side and mainly by the degree of integration of this system with the patient management system on the other. Preprinted meal choice forms (read by barcode or mark sense techniques) as commercialised in many existing packages nowadays do not provide the flexibility nor the user friendliness as required.

16

Laboratory Information Systems

16.1 History

Until the late 1960's, most laboratories performed their tests manually. The first laboratory information systems (LIS) were developed about 20 years ago. They were primarily designed to facilitate the work flow within laboratories to generate patient laboratory reports. They were also intended to reduce the turnaround time for laboratory test results and to cope with a growing demand for laboratory determinations in private and hospital practice. Clinical laboratory departments were a perfect domain for the application of computer technology. Because of the similarities to industrial production (serial manufacturing, automation, large volumes of data; Fig. 16.1) LIS produced immediate and actual benefits resulting in :

- An increase of performed test requests
- Accuracy and quality of tests performed
- Optimised access and availability of medical data for authorised users

Clinical laboratories can be divided into a number of medical specialities depending on the kind of analyses performed :

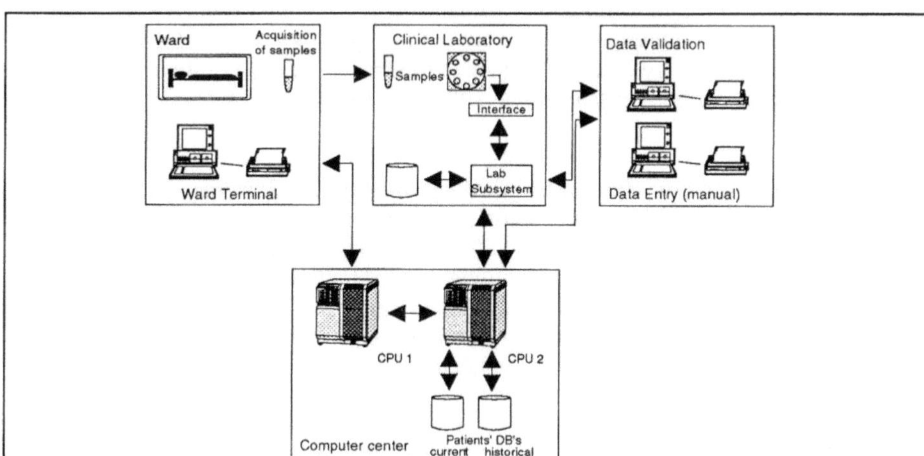

Fig.16.1 Data flow in processing laboratory test requests

Laboratory	Task summary
Chemistry	Quantitation of chemicals in body fluids
Hematology	Characterisation of blood elements
Microbiology	Isolation and identification of infectious agents
RIA	Radioimmunoassays
Cytology	Identification of malignant cells in body fluids
Immunology	Measurement of antigens or antibodies in body fluids
Surgical pathology	Diagnosis of lesions removed at surgery or by biopsy
Blood bank	Preparation and transfusion of blood products

Although early LIS were primarily designed to automate manual operations, they were not ideally suited to produce strategic management information:

- As a means of monitoring the request of laboratory tests by physician and patient or by pathology
- As a means of calculating the cost/benefit ratio of laboratory services

Due to the fact that in many countries health care costs are constantly being reduced and LIS did have a great influence on increasing health care expenses, changing social regulations made them shift from profit to cost centres in many hospitals.

The benefits of an evolving network technology, which makes it possible in real-time to connect analysers with central LIS databases, and the availability of user-friendly report generators and 4GL, which provide users with the ability to design their own reports, made it possible to exploit the strategic value of LIS for administrative and medical purposes as well. These features are characterising modern LIS in contrast with those commercially available in the early 1970s.

Today laboratory professionals are aware of the importance of the effectice application of information technology, that will gravitate towards distributed on-line processing, away from the batch oriented systems of the 1970s and 1980s.

Objectives of State-of-the-Art Laboratory Information Systems

The most important objectives of a complete LIS consist of the following features :

- Complete integration with the HIS for initiating the patient order (related to patient data) and result reporting and billing (related to the electronic medical record)
- To decrease the turnaround time of tests (improved laboratory productivity)
- To monitor test quality (improved quality control)
- To monitor the work flow in the laboratory (management statistics)
- To control laboratory inventory
- To assure high availability. In order to cause minimal laboratory disruption, a back-up system must be installed to assure that the LIS is operating 24 h a day with preventive maintenance schedules.

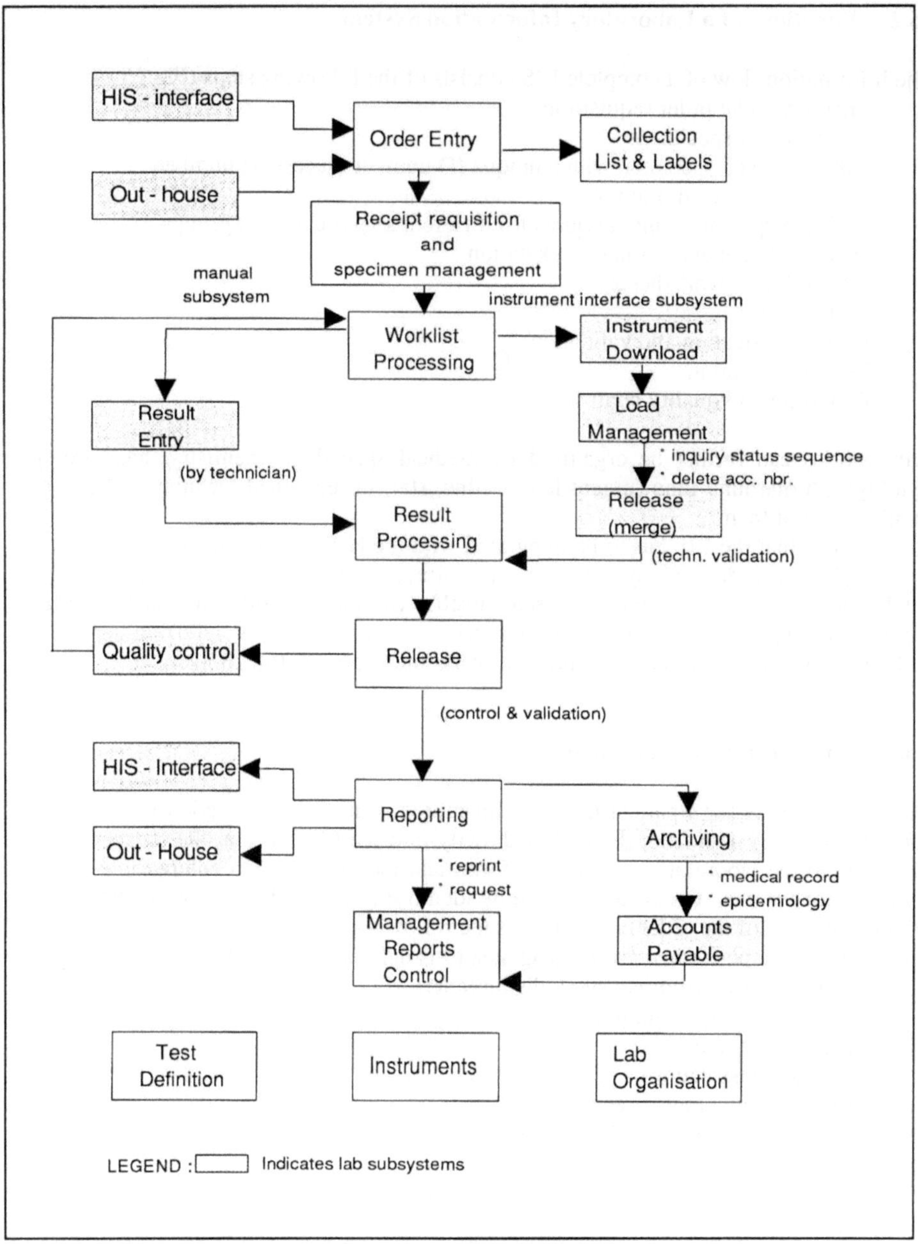

Fig. 16.2 Information flow of a laboratory information system.

16.2 Functions of a Laboratory Information System

The information flow of a complete LIS consists of the following steps (Fig.16.2):

- Creation of the order requisition
- Collection of specimens
- Labelling each specimen with a unique ID number (accession number)
- Transport to the laboratory
- Dividing specimens into aliquots for different analytical work groups
- Delivery to the appropriate workstation
- Production of worksheets
- Test analysis
- Result verification and validation
- Report generation
- Reporting and quality control

Laboratories can further be organised by medical speciality (chemistry, haematology, cytology), turnaround time (urgent lab, routine, stat) or analytical technique (RIA), or a combination of them.
It is obvious that the LIS has to be integrated with the HIS so that patient data relating to the ADT and order sub-systems can be directly transmitted to the LIS without duplication within the laboratory system itself. Similarly, results are made available through the reporting system to the appropriate nurse stations or referring services in order to reduce phone calls and to prevent work interruptions (Fig.16.3).

16.3 Order Entry Management

Physician's orders for a patient may be transmitted from the ward station to the LIS via the order entry system from the HIS or directly into the LIS. If not, the request may be delivered to the laboratory on a request form, and the order is then entered into the LIS by laboratory clerks. Orders are entered by identifying the medical record number of the patient. As part of the order entry process the following data elements may be required :

- Tests to be performed (verified against tests defined in the system)
- Testing priority (routine, stat,today,urgent)
- Collection method and time
- Specimen source
- Notes and instructions
- Date and time order is received

Depending upon the organisation of the laboratory, two methods of specimen collection are used:

- *Specimen immediately available.* Specimen labels are (pre)printed (or available) for specimen tubes at collection time. These labels contain a system (unique) assigned access number for tests as well as patient data. These test procedures may start immediately for any order received when specimen is available.

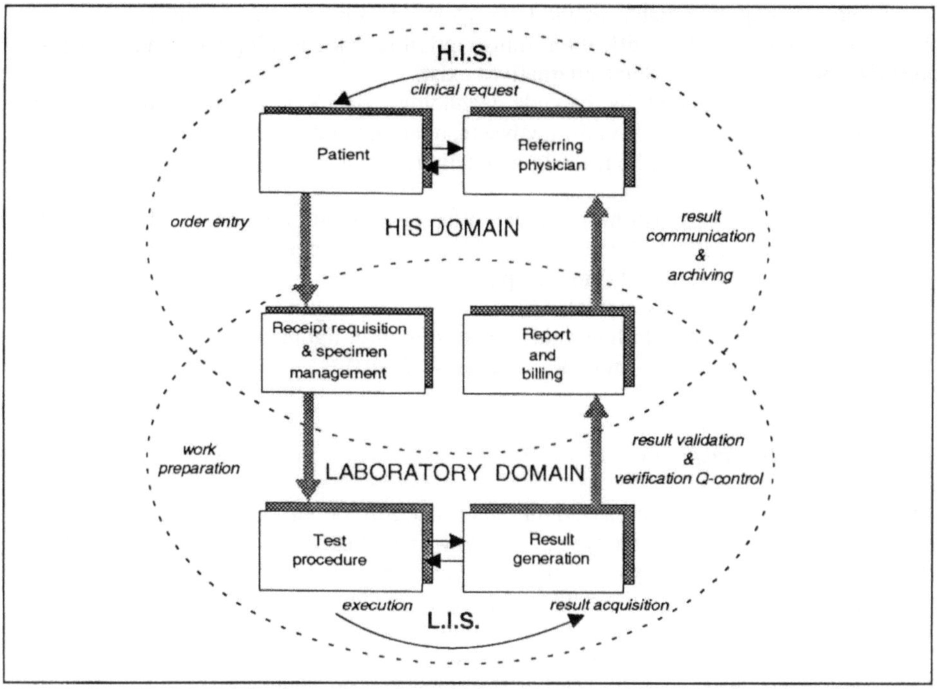

Fig.16.3 The key elements of a laboratory information system (LIS), representing the main flows and relationships

° *Specimen to be collected.* Tests which are ordered with the indication that collection is required are evaluated according to several user-defined criteria. The orders are consolidated, and minimum specimen requirements are calculated. Tests may be combined into one tube according to the type of tests required, or they may be assigned to individual tubes. Labels may then be printed which include the system assigned access number, patient identification data, specimen type and container requirements. Labels are printed in a specified location sequence and may be produced according to collection groups. These groups are identified as :

STAT orders
Timed collections
Nursing station collections
Routine collections
Serial collections

Afterwards, specimen collections according to the nursing station sequence are performed guided by the information printed on the labels. If the patient is unavailable, the request for the patient may be rescheduled for another collection run or may be cancelled. Otherwise, if the specimen was successfully drawn, then the collection is verified in the system so that the information can be passed to the results processing phase.

Today, no completely reliable method for identification of patients and specimens is available. Specimen misidentification, transcription errors and illegible handwriting are potential sources of errors. Some alternatives exist.

- Labels can be coded by barcode technology or OCR identification and read automatically afterwards in the analysers, relating patients and specimen.
- The request forms can be filled in manually or replicated with patient identification data by using embossed cards.
- Request forms can also be generated after on-line introduction of requested test procedures by patient. Barcoded patient wrist bands are not widely used.

Several methods exist for identifying the patient:

- Normal data entry by terminal
- Data entry combined with pointing devices (mouse, lightpen)
- Optical reading (cards, bar code, mark sense sheets)

16.4 Results Management

After specimens have been collected and distributed to the various laboratory units, test procedures may start. Upon the type of results we can distinguish two categories of tests: ones that register numerical values and ones that require visualisation and interpretation, e.g. biopsied tissues (pathology) or cultured organisms (microbiology).
The nature of the results determine the procedure to be used for result acquisition.
Test procedures can be executed in several ways :

- *Tests performed manually and individually* are those which do not necessarily occur in any specified sequence. It is more convenient for the technologist to evaluate the specimen individually as in the case of microbiology cultures or differential counts.
- *Tests performed on analysers individually* (by specimen) *or in batch* with (without) the inclusion of controls and standards refer to processing of tests in a specified sequence, which may include controls or standards periodically spaced among the patient specimens depending upon the automated instrument, if used. According to a pre-defined user-selected sequence the system will automatically position controls and standards among the patient specimens. The worksheets may then be printed to provide a hard copy media on which to record testing results. The formats of the worksheets are selected by the laboratory. The specimens (patients) are placed in the turntable of the analysers in the same position as occurring on the work list (position identification). By linking the computer to autoanalysers, human transcription errors and turnaround time are reduced, by associating each result with a particular specimen.

It is essential that specimens are correctly identified. In using automated instruments a method called "*positive specimen identification*" can be used. That is, the specimens are

identified in such a way that the corresponding patient is recognised automatically. Every specimen cup is identified by a magnetic (magnetic strip), optical (barcode) or mechanical (embossed) device at generation time (dispatching) of the cups.
The advantages are:

- Correct patient identification
- No "*position identification*" needed in which every position on a worksheet corresponds to the specimen of a particular patient
- No worksheet required

When results are entered into the system, an immediate edit and verification check is performed. The result is checked against the expected format (number of digits and/or decimal places or alphabetic characters) as well as validation ranges. The latter include verification against warning limits, outside of which a result may be considered as invalid or outlying. For reporting, results are also compared with age/sex-specific reference range. Patient results falling outside the reference (or so-called "normal") are indicated on the report as abnormal. *Delta checking* is also considered useful; that is the latest available test result for that particular procedure will be compared with the result currently being entered. Additional capabilities available in results entry include :

- Predefined messages
- Free text messages
- Default results (results which are typically obtained for the test)

After results have been entered and have passed the format and validation checks, they may be verified and released for ultimate reporting. Therefore patient tests can be retrieved by status whether they are pending, entered, released or completed, and verified by an authorised person.

16.5 Data Acquisition

As computers become cheaper and more powerful, more sophisticated systems are embedded in analytical and other medical instruments as a move to more targeted hardware and software turnkey solutions. Current LIS are interfaced to a variety of automated instruments, allowing the LIS to receive numerical test results in real time sent by the instrument for review, correction and release for subsequent reporting. Patient samples and quality controls are automatically processed.
Often those instruments are typically connected to a concentrator functioning as an intelligent controller to monitor in real time the signals from multiple instruments, consolidate and pre-process data where needed and forward the data to the laboratory computer. The control of analysers by the computer is important, because in this way instruments are becoming more user-friendly to operate. The trend is towards highly automated stand-alone analysers. This provides a store-and-forward capability in the event of downtime on the main computer.

There are two types of results in a LIS : numerical and interpretative textual data. Due to the fact that the management of textually oriented tests (less automated) in laboratories are more difficult to implement, the penetration of LIS into microbiology, cytology and surgical pathology has been slower than into comparable laboratories with numerical results. In particular, for some interpretative tests the number of steps depend on the interpretation made during the test execution. Results entered that way into the LIS are subject to the same edit and verification checks that are applied to results entered manually.

16.6 Results Reporting

Multiple reporting capabilities are provided for inpatients and outpatients to support the various reporting needs of the laboratory and hospital. All patient result reports include basic heading information such as patient name, age, sex, hospital location, date and time of report printing, referring physician and page numbering :

- *Cumulative reports* include all laboratory work for an inpatient since admission or a pre-defined date. They are usually produced on a daily basis or on request.
- *Interim reports* reflect all changes to the inpatient's laboratory testing process since the last cumulative report. Interim reports may be printed as required several times per day.
- *STAT reports* are automatically printed whenever tests ordered as STAT are completed, immediately upon result verification. The reports are printed on dedicated printers which may be located in the laboratory or in a critical area, e.g. ICU, ER (emergency room).
- *Discharge reports* are available for production after a patient is discharged from the hospital and all testing procedures have been completed.

16.7 Quality Control

One of the major benefits of installing a laboratory computer data processing system is a greater degree of quality control over laboratory data. All the information entered into the computer may be screened and subjected to a number of different verification and validation techniques in order to draw the attention of the laboratory staff to incorrect and suspicious results, malfunctioning of the laboratory equipment and clerical-type errors.

Maintenance of high quality standards in a laboratory practice is an important objective made more and more difficult by an increasing workload. An important concern for the laboratory personnel is the correct operation of testing equipment. By comparing measured and expected results from *control samples* an indication is given whether testing equipment is working properly. Positions on worksheets are reserved for control samples. In the LIS, all procedures for which control samples or standard samples are to be included in the specimen (patient) testing process are identified. Laboratory staff assign a code number to the control and then define the name of the control, batch number and type of quality control reference. Multiple control levels (e.g. normal, high or low controls) may be allocated to one worksheet. Each control is then further defined to include the assay mean, standard deviation and desired level of precision. The user also defines the acceptable control limits and validity limits to be used as a cross-check when quality control results are entered into the system. Some additional features are included to handle special situations as required.

Logically, the validation of data may be divided into four categories [ALB 80]. The first level is applied to the test request: the suitability of the sample is checked, and the patient, request and sample identification are validated to ascertain their existence and plausibility.
The second category of validation is concerned with the single results. On input, the format of the results is checked, and if the results were entered manually, then they are verified. This is followed by two range checks for plausibility and likelihood.
Another category of checks, based on statistical quality control techniques, is used to validate the performance of the laboratory equipment and staff. The quality control is applied on several levels using known and blind samples; a distinction is made between the short and long-term aspects of quality control. The most important is the "short-term" quality control whose main objective is to gain assurance that the test has been done correctly under acceptable conditions. This scheme is further subdivided into the "bench" quality control performed by the technician before execution of the analyses and"blind" quality control administered by a quality control officer who submits fictitious test requests through the system. The results of these samples are subsequently retrieved by the system and compared against the warning and action limits. The quality control results are reported and inspected before the results are authorised.
The "long-term" quality control scheme is intended to monitor the consistency of testing over a period of time and hopefully to detect changes before they seriously affect the results. It is a well-known fact that the cumulative sum technique is well suited for this purpose.
Lastly, the individual results are examined in the context of the allowable biological variation. This is done in two ways: first, the mutual compatibility of the results obtained from one sample is tested by a set of experimentally established rules, and second, statistical techniques are used to uncover a possible inconsistency of the current and previous results obtained from the same individual (Delta checks).

The quality control reports may be produced as part of an end of the day process or on demand. The information for each result linked to a quality control code number includes the calculated standard deviation, mean and coefficient of variation. A modified Levy-Jennings graph is also produced to chart the quality control trends and shifts for a specified period of time.

17

Radiology Information Systems

17.1 Natural Couples

In medicine, there is a clear trend towards the increasing use of noninvasive imaging techniques to determine the optimal diagnostic and therapeutic procedures for patients. Radiology departments have grown in importance and have become huge organisations in terms of personnel, technologically advanced medical equipment for medical specialties and the imaging procedures performed daily. The costs and revenues of this department have to be monitored very carefully.

It is obvious that radiology departments nowadays are also seeking methods to provide efficient, qualitative, medical and administrative services to patients, physicians and technologists. In this chapter, the general concepts of radiology information systems (RIS) are emphasised as well as the aspects of integration between HIS and RIS with their alphanumerical data on the one hand, and image management and communication systems (IMACS) with their huge amount of image data, including the management of image databases and traffic on the other hand. Most existing RIS are oriented towards the management of classically film-based services. The evolution towards a digital image management system will be gradually. The realisation of the so-called IMACS is just in its starting phase, which makes the situation more or less comparable with that for HIS in the 1970s. The main difference is the tremendous volume of data to be stored and transported, which follows from the large volume of data contained in images, although the variety of tables in the image database of IMACS is much lower than in a HIS.

Table 17.1 A comparison of hospital information system (HIS) and image management and communication systems (IMACS). GB, gigabyte; MB, megabyte; WS,Workstation; B, byte; R, radiology

Feature	HIS	RIS	IMACS
Size of data base (GB)	1- 20	1 - 5 GB	1000 - 20.000
Number of tables (n)	400	30	20
Length of tables	10 - 1000 B	10-1000 B	1 - 6 MB
Response time (s)	< 3	< 3	> 3
Number of WS (n)	100	10	10
Types of WS	cheap numerical	limited bitmapped	expensive bit-mapped

As IMACS are becoming increasingly important, it is interesting to compare the differences and similarities of both systems (Table 17.1). It is obvious that the alphanumerical data available in the HIS are a prerequisite and will be indispensable for managing the image database [VEL91].
We are moving towards a diagnostic imaging environment that will provide all medical patient images. It is clear that images do not stand alone, and the need for information derived from previous radiological examinations and from other clinical IS is obvious. To maximise the value of a specific examination physicians need information from many sources other than past and present images. So, the issue of "integration", necessary for any system to survive, deserves extra attention (Fig. 17.1). This might be clarified by keeping in mind that a clinical user needs an integrated overview of all relevant patient data, image data from IMACS and alphanumerical data from HIS and RIS at the right time and in the right place. The physician acquires images through the IMACS from patients identified by the HIS coupled with numerical and text data in medical reports about examinations from the RIS at the relevant time and place, perceiving all these subsystems as one logically related system.

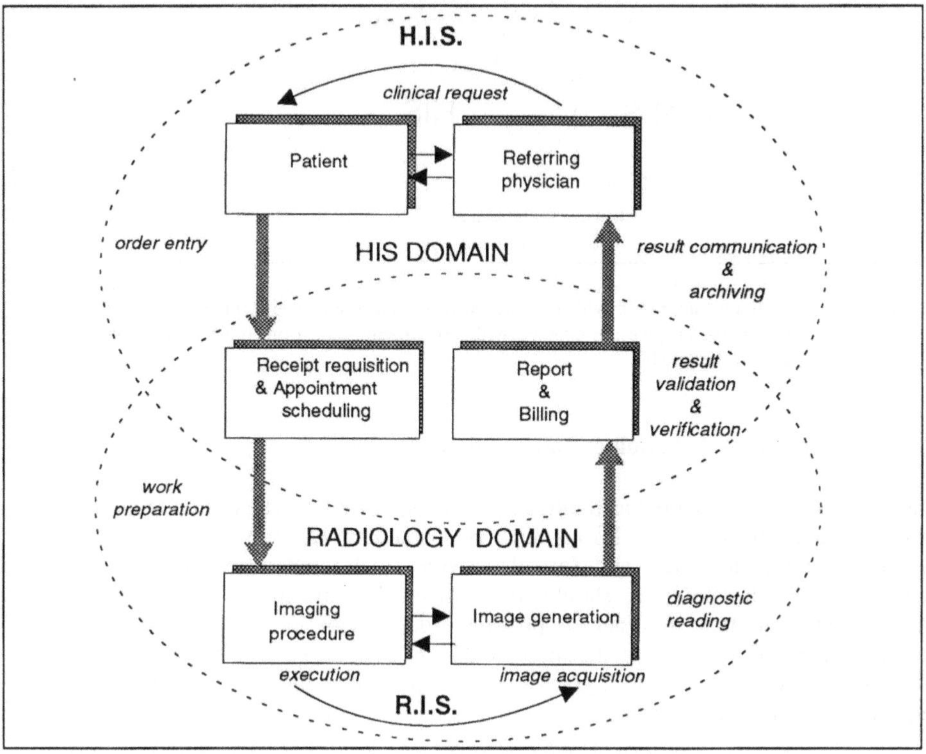

Fig. 17.1 The key elements of a radiology information system (RIS), representing the main flows and relationships

An IMACS is not viable when it is not integrated both with the RIS and with the HIS. The RIS has to be integrated with the HIS to make use of the single central hospital (alphanumerical) database. An IMACS can be connected with the HIS (possibly integrated) and have a common part with the RIS, which is in fact included in the HIS, if the RIS is an integrated part of the HIS. Of course, there will be a part of the HIS with no relation to IMACS and RIS, and vice versa (Fig 17.2).
Both users at the image acquisition end and users at the hospital clinic end and information scientists should thus be involved in setting up IMACS in a multi disciplinary approach. It is clear that the coupling of IMACS and HIS -so- called integration- should be realised as early as possible, as the information in the HIS database may serve to manage large image databases, probably of many terrabytes in size.

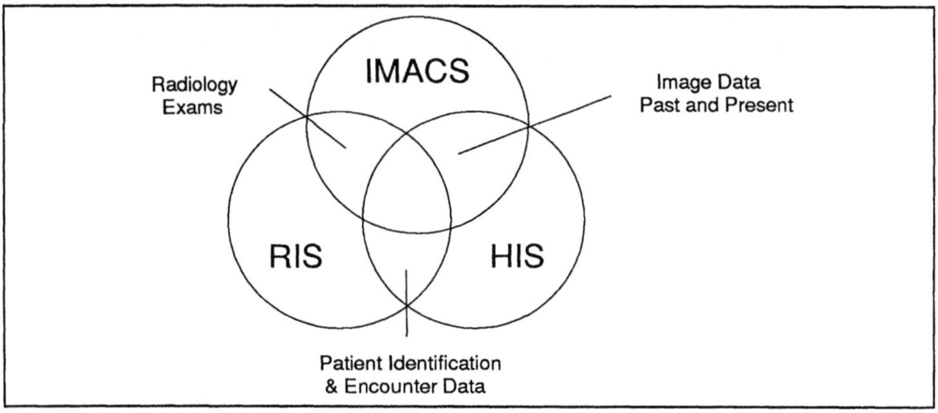

Fig. 17.2 Optimal integration will be achieved if the management of images (IMACS) stored in the image archive are coupled with examination data from the RIS and with patient data from the HIS

17.2 Constituents of Radiology Information Systems

The RIS has to be considered as the front end of each IMACS. The current goal of a RIS should be to use the computer for registration, scheduling, reporting and communication of all relevant patient data and for all activities and functions within the imaging department. Furthermore, it should be horizontally integrated with the nursing communication system in order to provide order scheduling. Let us consider the individual parts of an RIS in some more detail. In Fig. 17.3 a data flow diagram of an RIS is presented, and Table 17.2 gives an overview of the main activities in a RIS from requisition to reporting activity.

Table 17.2 Overview of the main activities and related sub-systems in RIS/HIS/PACS environment CPU, central processing unit; IMACS,image management and communication systems

Action	Sub-system	Computer Peripheral
1. Clinical request	HIS	Terminal
2. Appointment and scheduling	HIS & RIS	Bit-mapped workstation
3. Image acquisition	RIS & IMACS	IMACS workstation (local CPU)
4. Image processing and manipulation	IMACS	IMACS workstation (local CPU)
5. Interpretation and reporting and approval	RIS - IMACS	IMACS workstation
6. Communication to referring physician	IMACS - HIS	Simple viewing station
7. Archiving	IMACS - HIS	Long storage archive
8. Retrieval history	HIS-IMACS	Simple viewing station

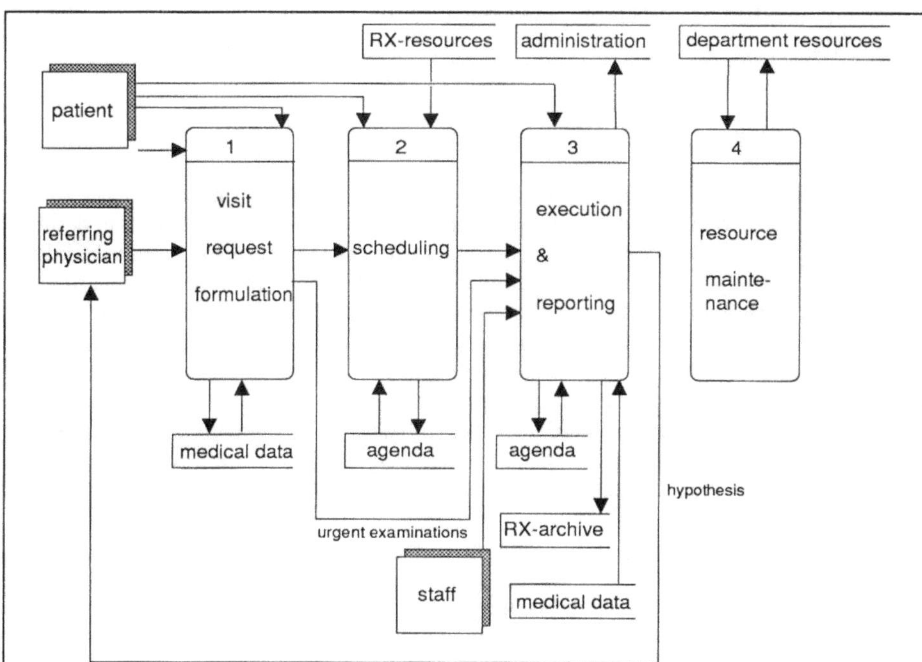

Fig. 17.3 Data flow diagram of a radiological information system (DFD methodology following C. Gane and T. Sarson)

17.2.1 Examination Requisition

The radiology process starts with the creation of the examination requisition by the referring physician for future diagnosis and treatment. The patient identification and demographic data have to be retrieved if registered previously in the ADT system from the HIS in a transparent user environment via several search facilities, such as phonetic search and medical record number, and coupled to the requisition. If the patient is not registered, the admission function has to be included in the RIS and fed to the HIS. This requisition requires:

- Patient selection
- Identification of the patient's clinical problem
- Identification of the imaging studies that have to be carried out for the patient
- Possible (pre-)fetching of previous radiology examination results
- The automatic validation of the request with previous or future, similar or duplicate examinations, which have to be flagged
- The indication of conflicts between examinations

Various documents have to be printed for preparing and streamlining the work. These documents include transportation sheets, indicating where transporters have to move the patient; flash cards to identify the patient's imaging study; and examination preparation cards (work lists) to be used by the radiologists at the time of examination to assemble information on e.g. drugs used and patient's time of arrival and departure. Some institutions use barcode labels to assist them in the fast retrieval and registration of patient data.

17.2.2 Scheduling

After the requisition has been entered into the system, the examination has to be scheduled for a certain examination room and time. Scheduling criteria are defined according to the specific needs of the department. It is obvious that the basic scheduling mechanism in an appointment system forms the basis of this in the radiology department, i.e. length of examination, scheduling templates, slot length, available resources, agenda and GUI [VEL 87]. Scheduling systems in radiology vary substantially, but all have the common feature of booking appointments in advance for various examinations. The scheduling procedure involves the following activities:

- Transmission of orders entered by nursing stations or referring services directly into the department schedule prior to receiving the paperwork from the floors
- Maintaining the daily patient schedule by room, providing a better distribution of workload
- Preventing, permitting or highlighting overbookings
- Preventing duplicate, conflicting or incompatible examination scheduling with previous or future examinations, if not already detected at a previous stage
- Indicating the sequence of examinations
- Retrieving active cases by any one of a wide range of selection criteria such as patient, room number, radiologist or referring physician

- Supporting of automatic label printing for flash cards and film tracking
- Calculating the workload of each section in real time
- Supporting automatic transportation notes
- Printing the daily schedule by appointment time, resource (i.e. examination room), or in-patient location
- Requisition of the radiologist's approval before certain examinations can be scheduled

17.2.3 Acquisition

The acquisition phase includes the creation of images and their registration in the IMACS. The examination preparation cards (or work lists) indicate to the technician which examinations have to be performed. Before starting the examinations, patient identification data have to be coupled with the images, either by using the flash cards (labels) for conventional films or electronically for digital imaging modalities such as computer tomography (CT) scans or magnetic resonance (MR) images. Each image has further to be identified by a unique identifier coupled with the examination. Historical images are sometimes needed during the execution of the examination.

The patient tracking module registers the time started and ended for each examination performed for that patient. A registration of time intervals allows the hospital to look for trends and to drive for an improvement in patient flow. It can also form the basis for generating productivity and utilisation reports. An alternative method is the use of barcodes. Before the patient arrives, requisition orders or the work list can be printed using barcodes. The requisitions are barcoded with the patient identification number and other instructions such as examination code and patient's medical record number. When the technician is carrying out the procedure, he may read the data at a glance, adding his confirmation and change, if necessary.

17.2.4 Diagnostic Reporting

After completion of the examination, the next stage is the interpretation, generation and communication of the results to the referring physician. During reporting, the previous reports included in the patient's medical record are often consulted. This report-generation process is the least developed component of every RIS system [GRE 90]. Nowadays, transcription by secretaries of dictated reports in combination with text processing facilities and stored radiological tests is by far the most common and preferred system used for report generation by radiologists, as they provide the highest freedom for expression and the fastest way of report generation for radiologists. Up to now several other experiments and methods of report generation have been tried over the years, not always with success. One of these is based on a dialogue between the computer and radiologist (e.g. the Missouri automated radiology system, MARS). The report is built up by making iterative selections from a standard thesaurus (library) of terms, which are subdivided into examination type, anatomy and diagnosis [LEH 73].

Another technique has emerged through the development of touch-sensitive terminals on which diagnostic possibilities are indicated. The physician may prepare his report by touching the appropriate items on a touch-sensitive screen. These systems have not been well accepted in Europe. Commercial systems were produced by CGR and Siemens (e.g. SIREP) [WHE 79]. Another approach utilises mark-sense sheets [MAN 73] or some form of coded or mnemonic input by the radiologist (RAPORT system). Report generation systems using structured (coded) reports are only successful in domains in which the content and organisation of reports are well structured.

Some experiments are being carried out currently using more sophisticated voice recognition methods for data entry methods in report generation. A speech recognition system produces machine-readable reports from dictated phrases using (for the moment) a lexicon of 1000 to 7000 words (e.g. Kurzweill systems). *Speech recognition* is the ability to input data directly into the computer, to recognise spoken words and to digitise these correctly. *Voice recognition* is the ability to uniquely identify the user, based upon analysis of the particular speech patterns. It is clear that -although very promising- this technology does not seem to be ready yet for general use as report generation since surrounding noise and pronunciation are still obstacles in voice recognition. Speech recognition performance is concerned with a number of features: the speaking rate (discrete speech versus continuous speech), the size of the vocabulary the computer is expected to recognise and the consideration whether the computer will recognise utterances from any speaker (speaker dependent versus speaker independent).

Every procedure can further be coded according to the diagnosis, using for example the American College of Radiology (ACR) classification. This can be an integral part of the diagnostic reporting sub-system and is highly desirable for retrieving cases according to medical diagnoses. Radiologists may use system terminals to apply approval codes (electronic signature) and do final editing of the reports themselves, even from remote locations. Reports remain on-line for any designated period.

17.2.5 Teaching File

For teaching and research purposes, a number of cases are indicated as valuable and stored in a database of diagnostic information, i.e. a teaching file. Afterwards, it is possible by specifying certain criteria to retrieve all desired information for teaching and research purposes.

17.2.6 Results Reporting: Mailing Facility

After the results have been created and verified (if necessary), they will be sent to the referring physicians or to the patient's location (inpatient or outpatient department).
It is most desirable to do this with mailing facilities.

17.2.7 Film and Patient Tracking

To reduce the loss incured by unreturned film loans, a film management and lending system is still necessary. The main objectives of a film-tracking system are:

- To support the operational functions of archive management
- To keep track of X-radiographs
- To provide for check-out of a film jacket (e.g. via barcoding) to any temporary location or referring physician outside or inside the department
- To provide for check-in from any temporary location
- To provide an on-line film location inquiry in order to locate the film quickly, as the films for a patient can be scattered over different locations. Some hospitals use barcode readers as automatic data entry for this purpose.

For future IMACS systems, it is worthwhile to compare the transactions within a film library and an IMACS system (Table 17.3) [MAT 89], [MAT 90]. Since digital images are not "returned", there is no transaction similar to returning films to the film room. Occasionally, however, the radiologist may wish to store a newly made transformed image or annotated overlay. Furthermore, images copied from archival to intermediate storage do not have to be copied back to archive storage after being used.

Table. 17.3: Comparison of classical film library management systems versus IMACS system

Film library transaction	IMACS transaction
Inactive file-room to active file-room	Archival to intermediate storage
New films to active file-room	Image generators to IMACS viewing station
Active file-room to light-box	Intermediate storage to IMACS viewing station
Light-box to active file-room	None
Active file-room to inactive file-room	Movement of new images from intermediate to archival (storage)
Active file-room to borrowers	Intermediate storage to remote display
Borrowers to active file-room	None

17.2.8 Management Reports and Billing

Finally, the system has to provide billing data to be processed by a general billing module. The effective management of a radiology department requires tools which are adequate to understand the operation of the department thoroughly, to have enough accurate data to suggest changes to the operation and to monitor the effectiveness of these decisions once new actions have been taken. So, the system has to provide comprehensive statistical information. The framework for management reporting can be divided into three categories:

1. Daily Management

- The daily log lists patients in chronological order and by department section
- The new patient report lists all new patients by origin
- The incomplete activity report lists incomplete exams that have been performed but not transcribed and approved. It helps determine the efficiency of the department.
- The system maintains teaching files according to the physician and ACR code

2. Operation Management

- The room productivity reports provide valuable utilisation data for work flow monitoring
- The facility and equipment utilisation reports provide information for equipment usage
- The revenue report summarises clinical fees by cost centre
- The activity report lists all departmental activities by type of examination and by patient type

3. Personnel Management

- Technologist productivity reports
- Physician productivity reports

17.2.9 Inventory Tracking

A departmental inventory tracking module is necessary to provide the user with the ability to notify the system of changes in inventory and to monitor the current availability of goods. This capability can be used to identify consumption trends as well as to measure the costs of maintaining inventory levels. Economic order quantities are determined for all products in the system.

17.2.10 Equipment Maintenance

Information about preventive and unscheduled maintenance is maintained for a user-defined set of equipment. The information recorded includes: equipment identifier, manufacturer, services, dates of all maintenance, type of maintenance, problems, cost of repair, part replaced and time down. Query reports may be run to summarise or select maintenance records using any of the data recorded as a sort or selection criteria.
In Fig.17.4 an entity-relationship diagram of a RIS is presented.

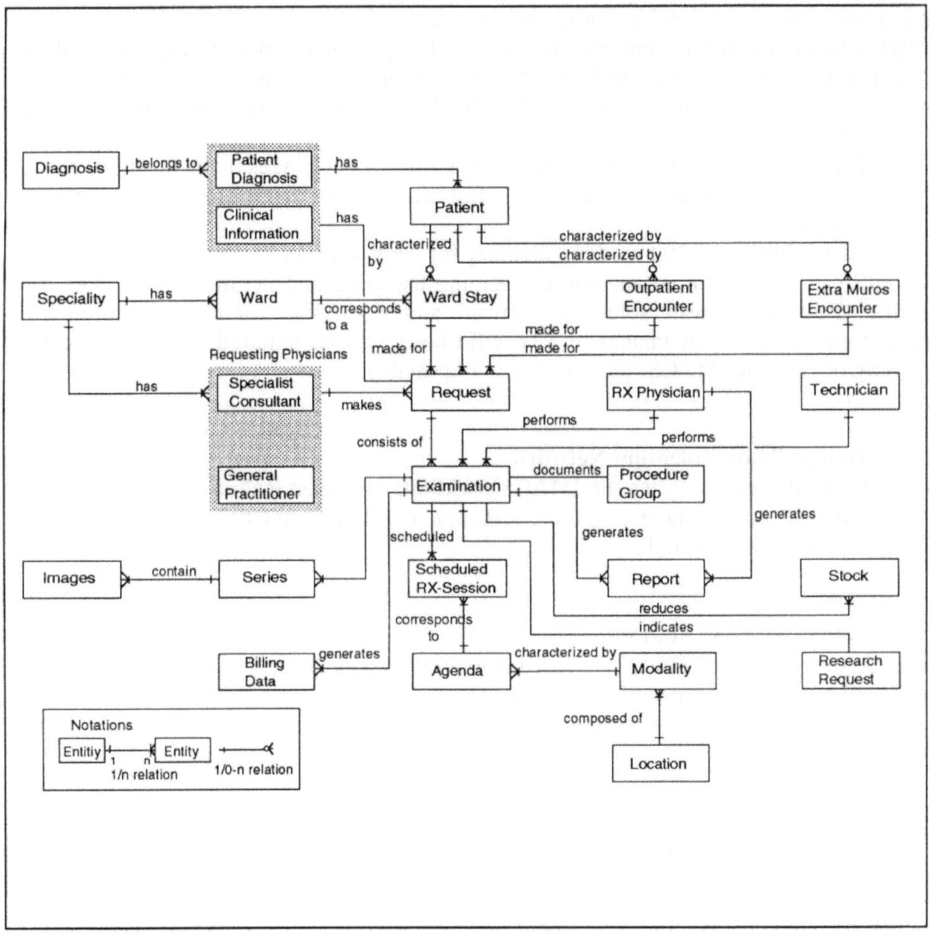

Fig. 17.4 Entity-relationship representation of a radiological information system; (RX, radiology department)

17.3 Relationship of IMACS to HIS

17.3.1 Image Acquisition Nodes

As part of the examination identification, a unique identification of the patient is required. Such will be present in the HIS and must be copied to the imaging modalities (IM) for the acquisition of digital images coupled to the IMACS. The best moment to couple the examination identification to the image is when the image is created. Because a visit can consist of one or more examinations the RIS has to be extended with the

notions of *folder* and *sub-folder* for image storage.
Rough overall calculations indicate that the total digital image storage capacity will be measured in terabytes. Even with a reduction factor of 10, this is still a tremendous amount of data. It is more or less accepted that the physical storage structure should be layered into three parts:

- A relatively slow but huge archive containing all the images in the hospital
- A faster but smaller intermediate buffer with images that are needed in the very near future
- A small but very fast working memory for daily routine

The HIS can play an important role in deciding the place and the moment to store the images. Besides hardware solutions, software and algorithms that manage the correct and in-time allocation of images to a specific layer will be required. Without a close coupling of HIS and IMACS, this strategy is impossible.

17.3.2 Image Communication Network

A standardised network forms the IMACS backbone and must include a link to the HIS for control and management purposes, although this link could be physically isolated from the image transport link.

17.3.3 Image Viewing Stations

Since there are many different types of image users in a hospital, it may be expected that there will be different types of stations for the display of images. The HIS has also an important role in the proper presentation of both alphanumerical and image data in an integrated way.

17.4 Distributed Radiology Systems: A Possible Architecture

Early RIS ran mainly on separate, independent mini-computer systems or sometimes on the central computer facility. Compared with other departments, radiology departments are characterised by the need for more computational and especially more communicative needs. The advantages of a RIS are presented in Table 17.4.
In a real computer network environment a configuration hierarchy could contain the following components (see also Fig. 17.5):

- A centralised cluster of one (or more) hospital information computer systems, utilised by other departmental feeder systems for demographic patient data and the long-term archiving of longitudinal medical records
- A centralised radiology application server to collect intermediate radiology data and function as an interradiology communication vehicle
- Microcomputers and workstations with high-quality, bit-mapped screens in different imaging areas for communication with the rest to collect data to generate reports and to perform medical functions such as viewing or image manipulation.

Indeed, the RIS is the front end of the IMACS system and of other hospital data sources.

Table 17.4 Overview of the main features and advantages of a radiological information system

Improvement	Cause
For the patient	Reduced waiting time
Patient result reporting	Flexible report formats
	Decrease in turnaround time
	Decrease in lost results
Resource management	Appropriate workload in advance by theatre
	Inventory control record
Administration	Accurate billing input
	Accurate workload
	Optimalisation of workflow
Personnel performance	Increased efficiency
Film management	Increased film control
	Loan lists
	Automatic link with IMACS

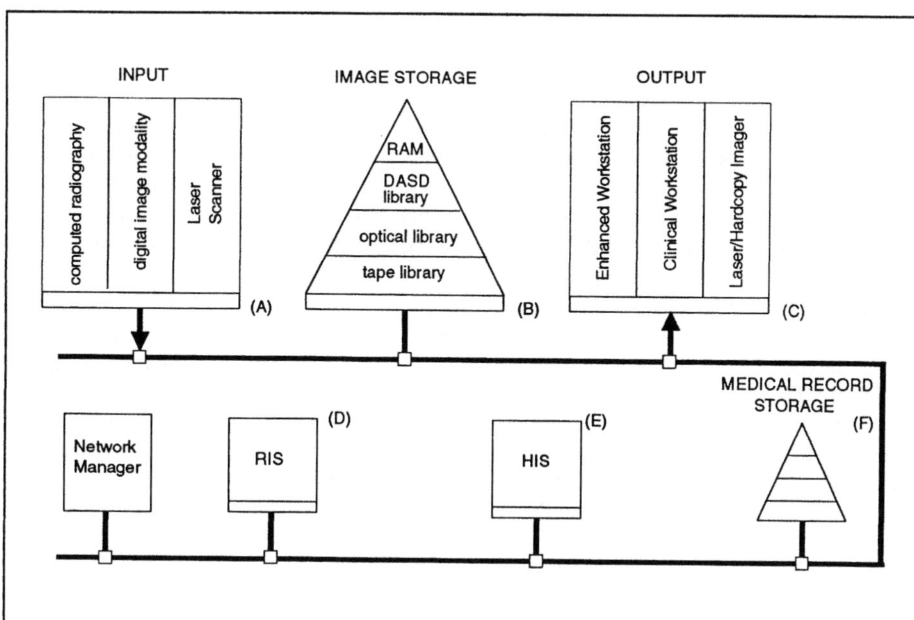

Fig.17.5 Distributed Radiological Information System : a possible architecture

18

Oncology Information Systems

18.1 Introduction and Objectives

Setting up an IS for the treatment of patients diagnosed as having cancer must accomplish a number of requirements [LEN 84]:

- Manage the patient database such as patient registration, census, appointments, demographic information
- Organise and visualise patient clinical data for inpatient and outpatients in an integrated way, collected at each clinic visit for outpatients, and during admission for inpatients
- Schedule patient care activities and therapy according to clinical algorithms. As most cancer treatments need chronological sequences of actions over a certain period, the computer can assist the health care provider with scheduling and planning
- Maintain clinical data for retrospective analysis, including a hospital-wide tumour registry system

In the care process of cancer patients, several established methods of treatment are available. The most important and well-known are radiotherapy, medical treatment (chemotherapy, immunotherapy, hormone therapy) and surgical interventions, individually or in several combinations. As patients suffering from cancer need specialised clinical management, automated data systems have been implemented, focussing on the particular requirements of cancer and medical providers. Some well-known systems are the Oncology Center Information System (OCIS) managed by the Johns Hopkins Oncology Center [LEN 84] and, for radiotherapy, the MKS system developed at the Radiation Oncology Center (ROC) of the Wayne State University, Detroit, Michigan, USA.

In the next sections the main constituents of an oncology IS for a comprehensive cancer centre are briefly discussed. Background information is combined with the environmental and structural information needed to develop an understanding of an oncology IS. The tools to meet the clinical information needs listed above are presented. They form the clinical data management system for effective management of laboratory data, pharmacy, blood transfusion, daily care plan, etc.

Clinical data management handles information derived from inpatient and outpatient visits. Special attention has to be paid to the representation of data. In medicine, data are divided into several categories : tabular (i.e. data organised in a table in clinically useful ways), graphical and special. The tabular data (compare laboratory cumulative results) can be arranged in two ways, listing the data in columns and the times in rows and vice versa. Another useful way of medical data representation is the graphical one, marking and focussing attention on certain events or abnormalities.

The most important types of clinical data used in an oncology information system are:

- *Laboratory data* including results from chemistry, haematology and microbiology, organised in various ways; data from chemistry and haematology are represented in tabular form (chronological), while bacteriological reports are organised by type, specimen and organism.
- *Pharmacy information* represents overviews of medications administered (given, not given and scheduled doses) to the patient in a tabular, chronological form. As part of the pharmacy system drug profiles are maintained by the patient for managing the prescription of future drug orders, and functioning as a reminder of scheduled doses to be given. In the OCIS system from the Johns Hopkins Oncology Center [ENT 89], additional special reports contribute to clinical functions of the pharmacy such as : pain management (identifies all patients receiving pain medication), antibiotic screening (identifies all patients receiving antibiotics to ensure appropriateness of the medication treatment) and a so-called chemotherapy card for chemotherapy patients indicating all chemotherapy undertaken and investigational drug doses administered. The record contains the drug identification data, administration, dose, volume and form (finally a cumulative dose indication).
- *Radiology reports*, available, on-line, are especially necessary for radiotherapy, 3D planning, follow-up, staging.
- *Blood transfusion data* describe the blood products used and given to the patient (red blood cells, platelet transfusion therapy). And evaluation of the transfusion outcome (increase of red blood cells, post-transfusion platelet count, i.e. the observed increment, transfusion reactions).
- *Therapy planning*. A therapy consists normally of a number of treatments (cycles, sessions) over a certain period of time. Associated with the sequence of treatments is the ordering of specific tests and procedures (radiology, laboratory) at certain moments to monitor the patient's status and provide an early warning in order to intervene as quickly as possible for the benefit of the patient. All the information for a certain therapy is contained in a "protocol" which simply represents a set of formal rules for treatment of the cancer as well as for disease- or treatment-related complications. It includes criteria for accepting a patient with the corresponding treatment and also includes information to evaluate the outcome of the treatment [BLU 86].
- *Daily care plans* (for physicians, nurses, paramedical staff) can be composed for inpatients and outpatients, identifying all therapies, tests and reminders scheduled for that day, as patients are connected to a specific therapy (defined within a protocol). The current daily care plan must make allowances for the patient's current status and also the status of the previous plan. They can be modified if necessary and adapted to the situation. Outpatient care plans are more difficult to realise, because outpatients usually do not visit the center on a daily basis, but every few days or on a weekly basis.
- *Supporting functions*. Besides the above mentioned activities, a number of other so-called supporting functions are necessary to help manage the cancer centre in an administrative and medical way.
  - Electronic mail to prevent sometimes labor-intensive telephone communicaton
  - Patient appointment and scheduling systems for inpatients and outpatients; appointments are made to see a physician or a nurse or have a procedure or therapy done.

- ° Patient census management includes functions to register admission data, therapy start time, outpatient visits, billing data,etc.
- ° Order entry module to place order requests for procedures, tests, medication, etc.

° *Tumour registry* represents a classification and codification of all patients having cancer and specifies tumour types, diagnosis and treatment. Each record contains the patient identification, organ of origin (e.g. lung tumour) or tumour class e.g. lymph node involvement, tumour location, stage (TNM classification if available, FIGO, etc.) histology including grade and prognostic score system (if available) for each primary and secondary tumour, with time events.

° *Abstract* of the patient's medical record, includes important medical and administrative data in condensed form for rapid reference during treatment (patient history, tumour codification, diagnosis, morphology)

° *Surgical* pathology reports concern the analysis of certain sources or abnormal morphologies.

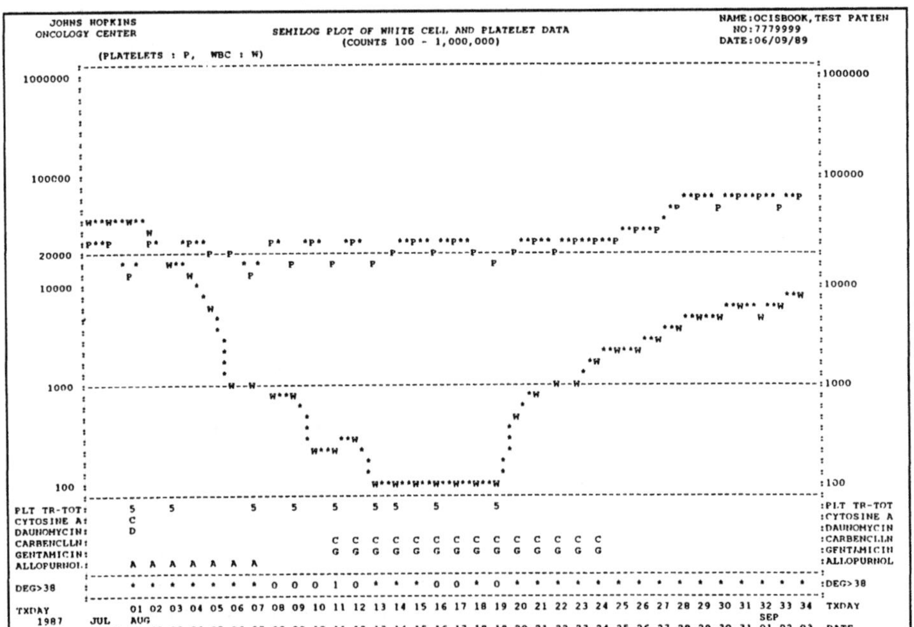

Fig.18.1 Semilogarithmic plot of white cell and platelet data on a log scale from 100 to 1 000 000.; below the plot events are shown for the administration of chemotherapy [ENT 89]

(Source: reprinted with the permission from Lenhard R.E. Data management in Clinical decision making in Enterline J.P., Lenhard R.E., Blum B.I., *A clinical Information System for Oncology*, New York, Springer-Verlag, 1989, p. 29.)

18.2 Chemotherapy

Chemotherapy is a medical treatment (by means of chemical substances given to the patient) which aims to destroy cancer cells selectively. The chemotherapy drug doses are frequently calculated on the basis of milligrams per square meter of the patient's body surface area. Computer programs can assist with the dose calculation, deriving the surface from the height and weight of the patient, but can be overridden afterwards as necessary. A chemotherapy record is created, containing all drug doses and the chemotherapy administered. This record covers the different drugs administrated, date of administration dose, volumes and form (Fig.18.1,18.2).

JOHNS HOPKINS ONCOLOGY CENTER 2S HISTORY NC: 777 77 77
NAME: PATIENT,SAMPLE
DATE: 07/15/86

COMP FLOW

		08JUL86	09JUL86	10JUL86	11JUL86	12JUL86	13JUL86	14JUL86
J8410		DAY 19	DAY 20	DAY 21	DAY 22	DAY 23	DAY 24	DAY 25
J8530		DAY 19	DAY 20	DAY 21	DAY 22	DAY 23	DAY 24	DAY 25
PAT STATUS								
TEMP-MAX	DEG C	38	39.4	37.8	38.1	38.0	38.0	37.8
TEMPERATUR	DEG C	37.9*	38.5*	37.8	37.4	38.0*	38.0*	37.2
MAX BP	MM HG	130/62	150/70	140/90	168/70	150/70	154/78	150/60
MAX PULSE		122	110	120	100	110	120	120
MAX RESPIR		28	24	32	30	26	28	28
BODY WT AM	KG		85.4	86.1	84.0	84.8	84.5	84.3
BD SUR AR	M SQ		2	2.01	1.99	2	2	1.99
FVC							1.8	2.0
CARE LEVEL		4	4	4	4	4	4	4
FLUID (IV)	ML	4120	3410	2990		4130	3595	3965
FLUID (PO)	ML	120	0	567		2075	1130	1310
TOTL INTAK	ML	4240	3410	3557		6205	4725	5275
URINE OUT	ML	4425	2000	4050		6795	4620	3300
LIQ STOOL	ML	0	0	0		0	0	30
EMES OUT	ML	0	0	325		0	520	100
TOTL OUT	ML	4425	2000	4375		6795	5140	3430
IN/OUT DIF	ML	-185	1410	-818		-590	-415	1845
BLD PROD								
PLT TR-TOT		13			11			
PLT TRN-PH		13			11			
HEMATOLOGY								
WBC	#/CU	044*	099*	300*	300*	300*	300*	200
RBC	M/CU	2.89*	3.55	3.51	3.11*	3.48	3.79	3.00
HGB	G/DL	8.5*	10.4*	10.2*	9.1*	10.6*	11.6*	9.1
HCT	%	25.5*	32.1*	30.6*	26.8*	32.0*	34.4*	26.5
RETICLCYTE	%		0.1*					
PLATELETS	/MM3	76000*	56000*	41000*	78000*	54000*	39000*	32000
ABS NEUT				22	6			28
CHEMISTRY								
SER NA	MEQ/L	134*	142	144	145	145	147	146
SER K	MEQ/L	4.8	4.5	4.1	3.6	3.6	3.8	3.7
DIR BILI	MG/DL	0.6*			1.1*			
DIAGNOSTIC TESTS								
URINE K	NEQ/L					53		
URINE CL	NEQ/L					97		
MEDICATION								
HYDRCRTSNE	MG		50	50	50	50	50	50
FLUCYTOSIN	GN			2	2	2	2	2
ACYCLOVIR	MG	1500	2000	3000	3000	3000	3000	3000

Fig.18.2 Portion of a sample of a comprehensive flowsheet in the Oncology Center Information System [ENT 89]

(Source Reprinted with permission from Stuart G.J., Blum B.I., Lenhard R.E. Clinical data Management. In *A Clinical Information System for Oncology,* Enterline J.P., Lenhard R.E., Blum B.I. eds, Springer Verlag, 1989, pp. 85)

18.3 Radiotherapy

Radiotherapy is a treatment for patients diagnosed as having cancer in which high-energy ionising radiation is used for the destruction of tumours. The goal is to obtain a maximum and uniform dosage of radiation in the tumour and a minimum dosage outside the site to be treated. This is very important for very sensitive areas such as brain tissues spinal cord, lung and liver. The problem is that the ionising radiation cannot be so focused in such a way that with one radiation beam the tumour receives a maximum dose. Therefore, several exposures from a number of beams, originating from different directions and having various intensities are needed in order to achieve a maximum uniform dosage of radiation over the tumour. This type of appplication is very appropriate for automation, because of the large amount of calculations needed and the possibility for fine tuning by trial and error methods, resulting in optimal isodose curves from these different beams.
A number of treatment machines (X-ray emitters, gamma-emitters or electron emitters) are in use nowadays, depending upon the type of radiotherapy.
High-energy radiotherapy machines intended for irradiation of deep-seated tumours emit X- ray or gamma radiation. With this type, the maximum absorbed dose occurs below the skin surface due to the "build-up" effect, so no burning. The absorption will be less depth dependent , so that at 17 cm depth the dose of the beam will be around 50% of that for a 15-MeV beam (Fig.18.3). Treatment is carried out using the X-rays from electron linear accelerators operating in the range of 4 to 25 MeV or the gamma-radiation of Cobalt-60 therapy machines. The (electron) linear accelerator is the most commonly employed. The principle is that electrons accelerated by high power radiowaves reach energies of from 4 to 25MeV, hit a target while emitting X-rays (photons) that can be directed from any angle through the patient to treat deeply localised tumours [AIR 88].

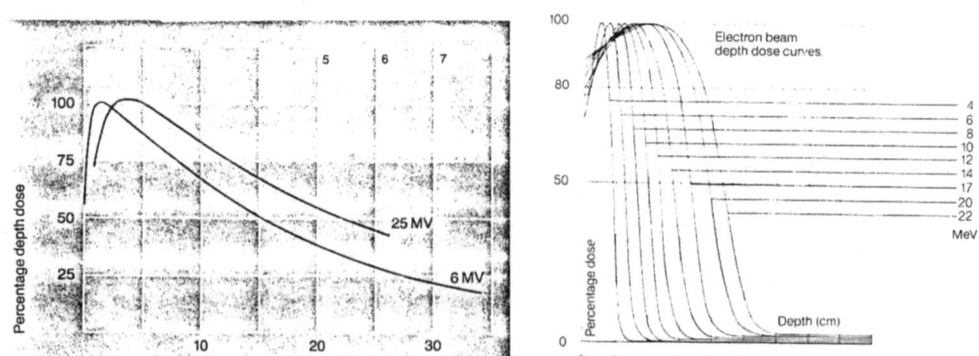

Fig.18.3 Independent diaphragm motion : distribution of deep-dose with photons (***left***) and electrons (***right***)

[**Source** : courtesy of Philips Medical Systems in *Linear accelerator for radiation therapy (SL15)*]

On the other hand, it is also possible to produce electron beams in the energy range from 4 to 35 MeV. Treatment with electrons is characterised by a rather high degree of absorption in tissue, so that skin tissue receives up to 80% - 95% of the intensity of the beam. Electrons are characterised by a sharp cut-off of dose beyond a certain depth, thereby sparing tissues beyond this depth. The depth range of electrons depends on their energy.
In high-energy radiotherapy, several beams of radiation with different intensities and directions are necessary to maximise the dose in the tumour and to limit exposure of normal tisssues below the level of tolerance. This radiotherapy treatment can be divided into several phases : the treatment planning phase, the simulation phase and the effective irradiation of the patient, including quality control (Fig.18.4).

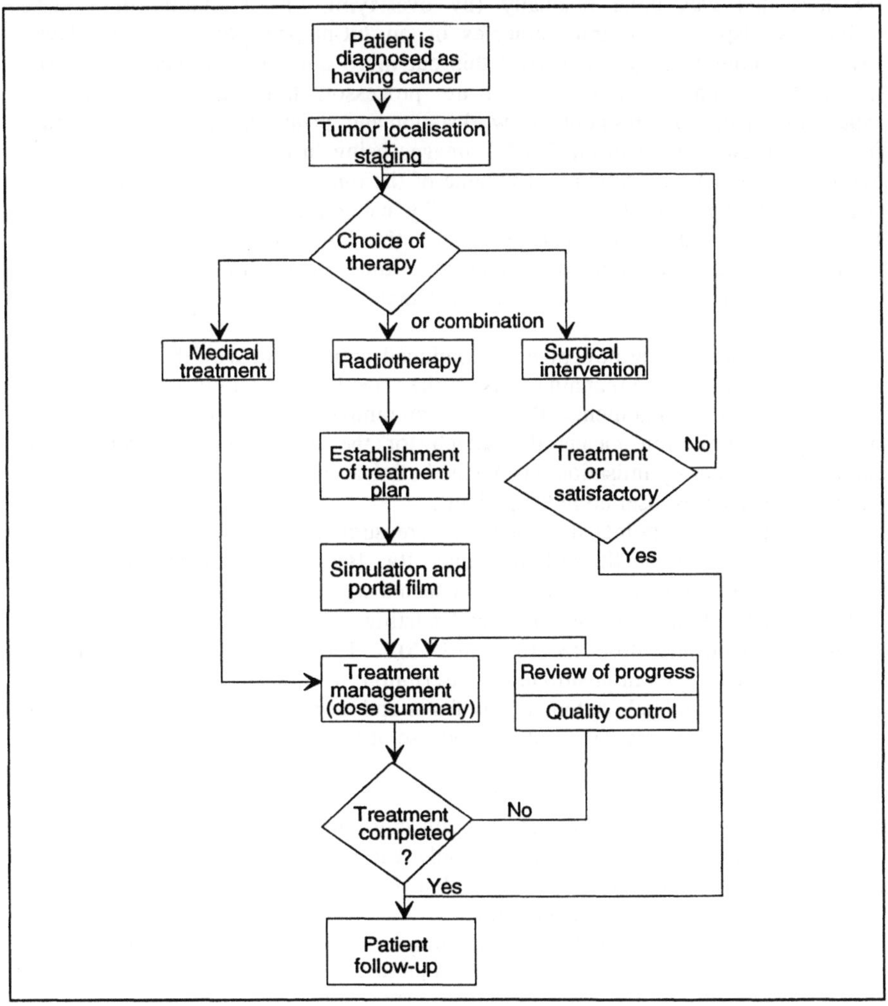

Fig.18.4 Generic basis cycle and flowchart in the treatment of cancer patients

18.3.1 Treatment Planning

A treatment plan results in drawing radiation distribution or *isodose curves* for a patient, taking into account the individual anatomy and exact tumour location. The goal is to determine the location and contours of the tumour, its extent and relation to other organs, to calculate the best irradiation scheme and to find the optimal way of delivering the prescribed 3D (space-time) dose distribution to the patient using the available modalities. A computerised dose planning system assists the physician in calculating in advance the radation absorbed by the tumour.

The dedicated (embedded) treatment planning computer combines the isodose curves of different beams together to produce by accumulation the resultant dose. In the early days this was done manually (by overlaying or summation of isodose distributions displayed on transparancies or on bit-mapped displays nowadays). Nowadays, a computer system carries this out more quickly and accurately. The components of such a computer system are processor, digital tablet (digitiser) for manual entry of the patient's contour, workstation and printer/plotter to obtain a hard copy of the final plan. Current 2D CT images being in digital form already, are providing (as input) the contour and volume of the tumour to be treated from which physical parameters, radiation beam size (by using differently sized or variable collimators), beam direction, their weighting (i.e. duration of irradiation), beam wedging, tissue compensators and sequences, time of treatments, are derived. Formerly, these calculations were performed manually and were very tedious and long.

The process of calculating new plans is continued until a plan with the best score is obtained. The result of the planning phase is the selection of beam positions and size to be used in future treatments. Research programmes involving optimisation are continuing. Optimisation means the search for the best treatment plan by the computer. Computer optimisation has reached clinical applicability in *brachytherapy* (irradiation by sources inserted in the patient).

At a large number of points the intensities are summated to produce 2D isodose curves, which are contour lines of equal intensity. Because all calculations are done automatically, the results can be adjusted in such a way that the radiation distribution is optimal. The optimal isodose curves and relating parameters are stored as part of the patient's electronic dose record (Fig.18.5). The advantage of radiotherapy automation is that errors in positioning transcription of the contours and calculations can be corrected completely automatically faster and more accurately, where as in the past only a few positions were calculated because of the time involved.

Nowadays, many radiotherapy centres are concentrating a lot of their effort into the calculation of 3D dose models. There are only a few commercial products available due to the expensive processing power needed (fast memories, fast processors), lack of standards and slow speed of calculation.

3D dose distribution is calculated by extracting contours of regions of interest from a series of CT scans, reconstructing the 3D contour and interactively determining the position and intensity of the source of radiation [FUS 89] (Fig.18.6).

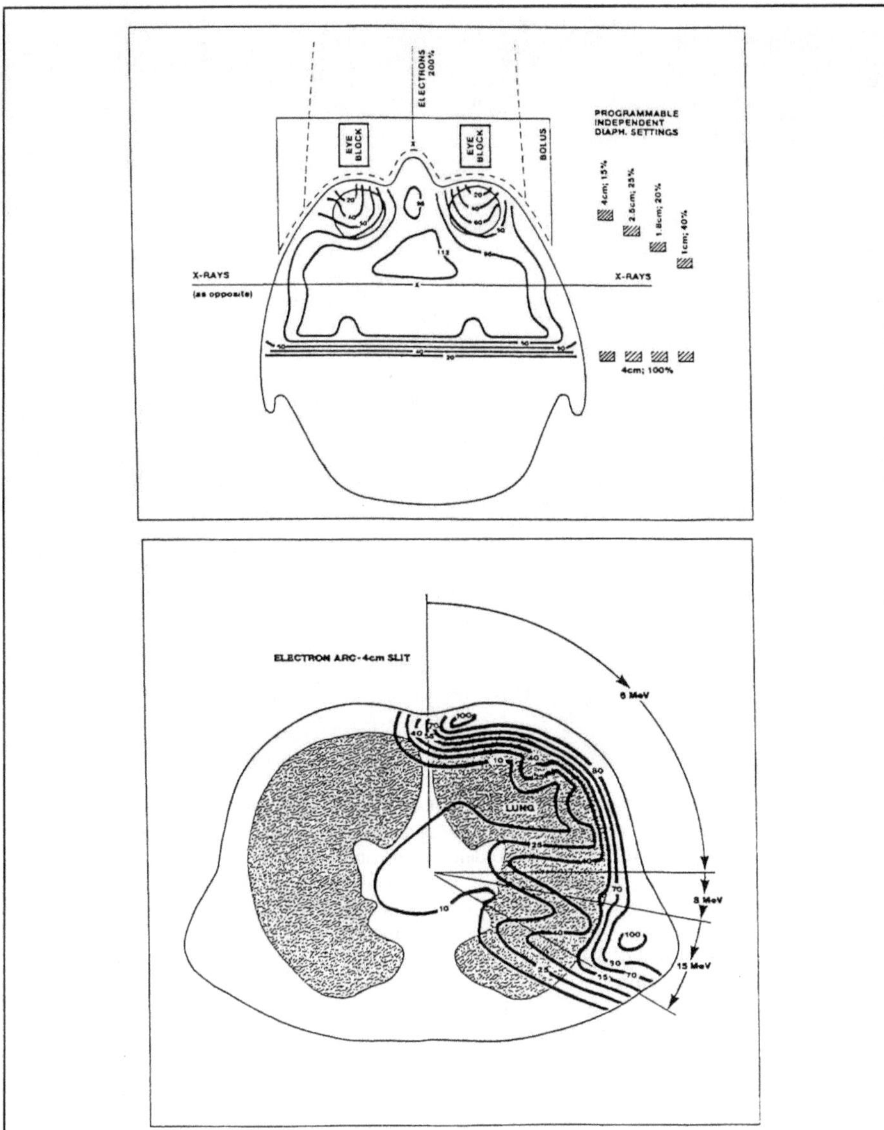

Fig.18.5 Programmable diaphragm : illustration of "Isodosen" dividing for optimal radiation treatment of a patient

[source : courtesy of Philips Medical Systems in *Linear accelerator for radiation therapy (SL18)*]

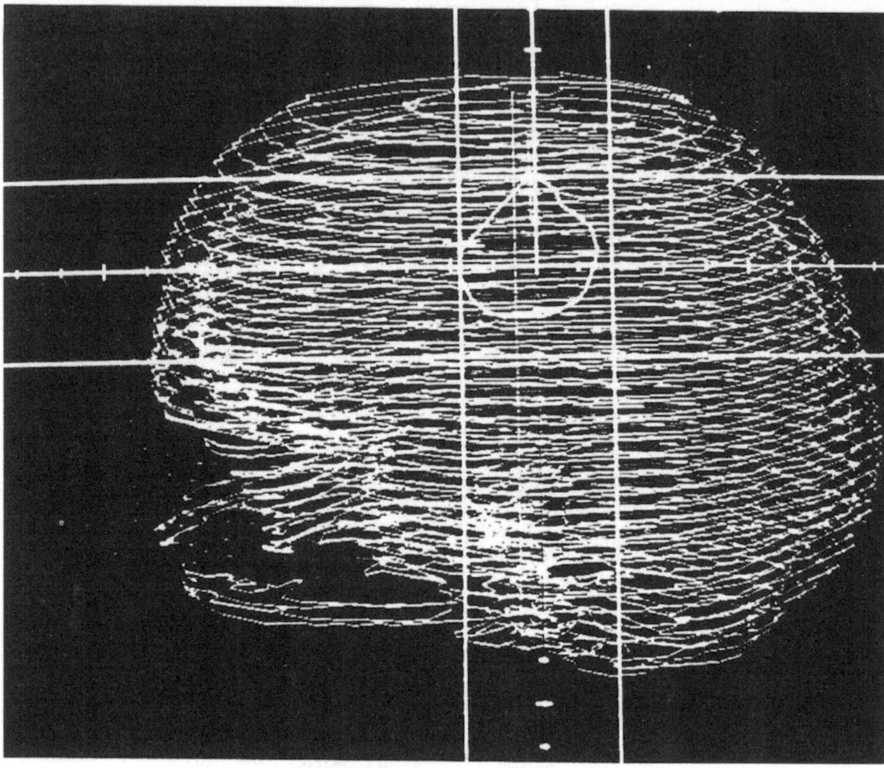

Fig.18.6 Three-dimensional radiotherapy planning: representation on a high resolution display of a 3-D image of the head, based on CT scanning data, taking the patient's volume as well as the tissue density into account. The contour of the tumour and the accurate representation of the expected dose distribution in any transverse, sagittal, frontal or oblique plane can be displayed after calculation, for specific beam settings. The radiotherapy planning system combines diagnostic CT viewing with realistic 3-D treatment planning. The region of interest is indicated automatically.

(Source with permission from Storme G., M.D., hospital of the Free University of Brussels - department of oncology)

18.3.2 Simulation

After the dose planning has been performed, the *simulation* of the patient is started. As the word simulation implies,in this phase one starts to simulate the radiation of the patient. The simulator is a device geometrically identical to the radiation source with the difference that the patient is irradiated with diagnostic X-rays instead of high-energy ionising radiation. The patient is placed on a mobile table around which an RX source circulates axially. The physical parameters based upon those defined in the planning phase are controlled and verified. The result is the final definition of: beam directions, beam size and position of the patient on the table and position of the table in the treatment space.

As it is essential that the patient always lies in an identical position on the table during irradiation, fixation and laser beams are employed, and skin marks are indicated on the patient's body.

18.3.3 Treatment Delivery

Finally, during treatment the machine is adjusted according to prescriptions of beam size, direction, time and all related parameters which are stored in the patient's dose record. This record must be available on-line for authorised persons (physicists, physicians, nurses) as patients are generally seen for check-up by their radiotherapist a long time after treatment. The positioning of the patient is extremely important: the patient always should be in the same position, and this should be verified continuously (e.g. by portal films). Lasers have become a common feature in treatment rooms nowadays to assist in positioning the patient. Computerised portal imaging allows the evaluation of the beam position during treatment. This technique is still under development and is described below.
As part of the general patient appointment system, features such as scheduling, follow-up visits, reminder letters and no-show letters for patients who did not meet their appointment are essential.

18.3.4 Computer-Assisted Therapy Planning

As CT scans (and MRI, etc) generate digital images, accurate diagnostic images of patients could lead to the replacement of entering the patient's contour and the topography of the tumour manually into the treatment planning computer by digitisers (Fig.18.5). This transferred image, called the *portal image*, provides the following advantages :

- Correct patient contour
- Correct location of the tumours, target volumes and surrounding critical organs (spinal cord, etc). By addition of CT image slices the size, total volume and location of a tumour and its exact topographical-anatomical location in space and relation with surrounding organs can be represented. From these data a reliable calculation of the dose distributions (based on geometric dimensions, densities, depth, etc.) can be derived
- It takes into consideration the differences in tissue densities (incorporated in the digital image) related to the dose distribution of radiation.
- Continuously check whether or not the reduction in size of the tumour corresponds satisfactorily during and after treatment (eventually using accurate "shrinking field" techniques)
- Provides the possibility of early detection of tumour recurrence

18.3.5 Portal Images

In some locations the accurate reproduction of the treatment configuration may be difficult or even error-prone. An example is the treatment of abdominal or pelvic tumours. Indeed, the positions of the skin marks used to set up the patient's position and the beam's entries are not fixed with regard to the tumour often located 10 cm or more below the skin or with regard to sensitive tissues. Portal imaging means the visualisation of the exit part of the treatment beam. It allows us to visualise the tumour, sensitive tissues or structures relevant for the positioning during treatment and to correct errors before a significant fraction of the dose is delivered. Portal imaging is probably the most important advance in clinical radiotherapy over the past few years.

HARPER HOSPITAL
RADIATION ONCOLOGY CENTER
PATIENT DOSE SUMMARY

GENERATED
06/19/91
10:11 AM

ID# 910020
NAME: COVA, MARGARET
DOCTOR: IHH
DIAGNOSIS: ENDOMETRIUM;;PO

PORTS	1A	2A	3A	4A	5B
SITES .	PELVIS	PELVIS	PELVIS	PELVIS	VAGINA
MACHINE	20 MEV	20 MEV	20 MEV	20 MEV	HDR
MODE/TECH	P/	P/	P/	P/	H/S
MODIFIERS	CB	CB	CB	CB	UN
DATE	DOSE/SET	DOSE/SET	DOSE/SET	DOSE/SET	DOSE/SET
01/17/91	45/52M	63/67M	36/54M	36/54M	
01/18/91	45/52M	63/67M	36/54M	36/54M	
01/21/91	45/52M	63/67M	36/54M	36/54M	
01/22/91	45/52M	63/67M	36/54M	36/54M	
01/23/91	45/52M	63/67M	36/54M	36/54M	
01/24/91	45/52M	63/67M	36/54M	36/54M	
01/25/91	45/52M	63/67M	36/54M	36/54M	
01/28/91	45/52M	63/67M	36/54M	36/54M	
01/29/91	45/52M	63/67M	36/54M	36/54M	
01/30/91	45/52M	63/67M	36/54M	36/54M	
01/31/91	45/52M	63/67M	36/54M	36/54M	
02/01/91	45/52M	63/67M	36/54M	36/54M	
02/04/91	45/52M	63/67M	36/54M	36/54M	
02/05/91	45/52M	63/67M	36/54M	36/54M	
02/06/91	45/52M	63/67M	36/54M	36/54M	
02/07/91	45/52M	63/67M	36/54M	36/54M	
02/08/91	45/52M	63/67M	36/54M	36/54M	
02/11/91	45/52M	63/67M	36/54M	36/54M	
02/12/91	45/52M	63/67M	36/54M	36/54M	
02/13/91	45/52M	63/67M	36/54M	36/54M	
02/14/91	45/52M	63/67M	36/54M	36/54M	
02/15/91	45/52M	63/67M	36/54M	36/54M	
02/18/91	45/52M	63/67M	36/54M	36/54M	
02/19/91	45/52M	63/67M	36/54M	36/54M	
02/20/91	45/52M	63/67M	36/54M	36/54M	
02/21/91	45/52M	63/67M	36/54M	36/54M	
02/22/91	45/52M	63/67M	36/54M	36/54M	
02/23/91	45/52M	63/67M	36/54M	36/54M	
02/25/91					323/181.5U
02/26/91					323/183U
02/27/91					323/184.5U
02/28/91					323/186U
03/04/91					323/193.5U
TOTAL	1260	1764	1008	1008	1615
PORTS	1A	2A	3A	4A	5B

FOR AREA: 195.3:PELVIS TOTAL DOSE= 5040 cGy
FOR AREA: 184.0:VAGINA TOTAL DOSE= 1615 cGy

Fig.18.7 Dose summary produced for a patient for each area treated and for a specified date range. The cumulative dose for each area treated is given at the bottom.

[source: courtesy of Don Ragan, Ph.D., president, RAMS, Medical Knowledge systems, Detroit 1990)

Due to the high energy of treatment beams, the contrast of bone versus soft tissues is much less with portal images than with diagnostic X-rays. Therefore, computerised image enhancement is often required. Considerable computer power is needed to process these images within a reasonable time to allow routine use of the system. Further developments include the comparison by computer between the portal images and the simulator film and automated decision making.

18.3.6 Future Trends

The trend in computer-assisted therapy planning is obvious, due to the objectives of gaining a high level of accuracy for patient treatment only obtainable by using powerful computer methods (e.g. array processors) and successive refinement calculations to arrive to an optimal isodose distribution (Fig.18.7). Moreover, if we use objects which influence the radiation fields (blocks, wedges, tissue compensators) it can lead to an increase of computation time for each field. Therefore, as is often the case in information processing, one should be aware of the problems that can arise in integrating medical devices from different vendors. It is advisable for the moment (advantageous) to have CT scanners and therapy planning units from the same manufacturer or using the same standards.

19

Pharmacy Information Systems

19.1 Introduction

Inside and outside hospitals, drugs are a mainstay of medical treatment. A great number of functions within a pharmacy lend themselves very easily to computerisation: computer-assisted pharmacy inventory and turnover management, a hospital-wide formulary, on-line medication order entry systems, on-line unit dose distribution systems and on-line recording of drug administrations are the most relevant advantages offered.

"What is it that makes clinical pharmacy different from traditional pharmacy services? That's a question that's been debated for years, and the answer remains unclear. But the profession is taking steps to define clinical pharmacy and what it can offer health care," explains Souhrada [SOU 90].

Although some people claim that the role of the pharmacist as a consultant for advising drug therapy has been reduced considerably and is simplified to supplying the required drugs, controlling and guaranteeing pharmaceutical quality, the clinical pharmacist has specialised knowledge of chemical and physical properties, alternative routes of administration, adverse drug reactions and therapeutic effects of drugs and their metabolic products on the human body [HOE 77]. That is the reason why pharmacists can assist physicians in determining the optimum drug therapy and calculating optimum doses for specific patients.

If we examine the evolution of pharmacy IS in hospitals, we see that the first ones were introduced at the end of the 1960s and were all -more or less- administrative and management oriented for accounting and inventory control purposes. Although most pharmacy IS are often locked out of existing HIS and are limited to direct links with financial systems, patient billing and inventory control, the professional interest of the pharmacists focussed on patient-oriented pharmacy systems (Table 19.1). It was shown that on-line drug administering and inventory control systems (deliveries, return of drugs) can work very well in practice [HOE 90].

In many hospitals, the focus was more on the economics of drug use, and few hospitals take advantage of more than a part of what clinical pharmacy can offer in assisting decisions about drug use.

Other, more medically oriented functions will gradually be added and will result finally in improved inventory control, reduction of the quantity and variety of drugs stored, control (decentralised) of the storage and distribution of medications, better understanding by nurses and physicians, maintenance of a complete up-to-date medication profile per patient (drug utilisation people) and, last but not least, the establishment of an on-line drug formulary providing a broad scope of information on drugs and their interactions, resulting in increased compliance.

Table 19.1 Clinical pharmacy defined; in Hospitals 5 October 1990 (source: ASHP 1987)

Services involving hospital-wide programmes aimed at selection of drug therapy, drug therapy monitoring and education
Examples : - Pharmacy and therapeutics committee and formulary system activities - Medication error monitoring systems - Adverse drug reaction reporting systems - Retrospective drug use review - Drug therapy bulletins or newsletters - In-service education programmes for pharmacists, nurses and physicians
Services that directly gather information from or provide information to patients:
Examples : - Medication histories - Discharge consultations - Patient education programmes
Formalised hospital-wide services, focussing on patient groups or drug types aimed at improving therapy by education prescribers or patients
Examples : - Drug information centres - Pharmacokinetic dosing services - Nutritional support teams - Investigational drug services - Target drug and disease programmes - Medication monitoring clinics - Medication refill and compliance clinics - Cardiopulmonary arrest pharmacy services
Services provided by highly specialised practitioners aimed at select patient populations
Examples : - Critical care pharmacy services - Emergency department pharmacy services - Transplant services - Hematology-oncology services - Pharmacist-managed primary care clinics - Pharmacist-managed speciality clinics

Nowadays, almost all hospitals have installed a pharmacy system and many software vendors provide such systems, ranging from mainframe-oriented to mini-computer-oriented towards LAN systems, to improve the efficiency and cost-effectiveness of pharmacy practice.

A pharmacy system comprises two parts:

- *An administrative oriented inventory system* based on a standard stock control or inventory management system with traditional features such as stock monitoring, stock valuation and pricing, reorder level assessment, overdue reminders to supplies, delivery checks against orders, demand forecasting usage and cost analysis, centralised and decentralised inventory control, invoice checking, stock movements, drug expiry dates

- *An extensive drug delivery and administering system,* that cannot be realised until the former has been introduced successfully.
  Drug delivery is actually labor-intensive, requiring hospital pharmacy staff to print labels (including warnings), to manually select and label drugs, to check the dosage, to register a medication profile, to dispense information, to look for interactions (drug-drug, drug-laboratory, etc.), and possible alternative drugs with advantages and disadvantages, etc.

As the pharmacy system is one amongst many other departments within the hospital involved in patient treatment, this departmental system must be integrated with the HIS (for patient-related functions and data) and with the general ledger (for financial management). Stand-alone "full pharmacy functionality" is no longer sufficient within future hospital systems.

19.2 Functions of a Pharmacy Information System

The main functions of a pharmacy information system are defined and represented herein by means of a data flow diagram (DFD) , a technique described by Gane and Sarson [GAN 79]. In the DFD (Fig 19.1), the flow of data (represented by arrows) through a system is represented on several levels. In the analysis, we recognise external entities represented by double squares (patient, physician, etc.), data stores, represented by open-ended rectangles (medical record, patient data, etc) and data transformations or processes, represented by rounded rectangles (prescribe, dispense, etc.). Each process box will be exploded by refinement into a lower-level, more DFD. Furthermore, data structures and functional specifications are derived from it. In the next secions the main processes are further discussed in detail.

19.2.1 Prescription

New medication orders (drug prescriptions) trigger an initial entry in a computerised pharmacy system. Drug prescriptions can be handled in various ways. The most advisable manner is to integrate medications prescribed on-line by physicians from the ward unit with the patient management system. It increases speed and reduces transcription errors. The medication order is provided with relevant patient data (allergies, diagnosis) for future evaluation. Currently in most hospitals, requests are still made manually and registered on-line by the pharmacy technician. The main tasks within this phase are:

- Prepare drug therapy in accord with the patient medical record
  Single order medication and Compound medication (large volume intravenous parenterals, partial fill parenterals, total parenteral nutrition solutions (TPN))
- Enter order by selecting a specific drug (dose, route, start date and time, expiration date and time)
- Re-order medications by modification of previous orders with minimal effort
- Provide a variety of checks (duplicate medications, allergies, medication control, maximal daily dose)
- Verify authorisation of the user

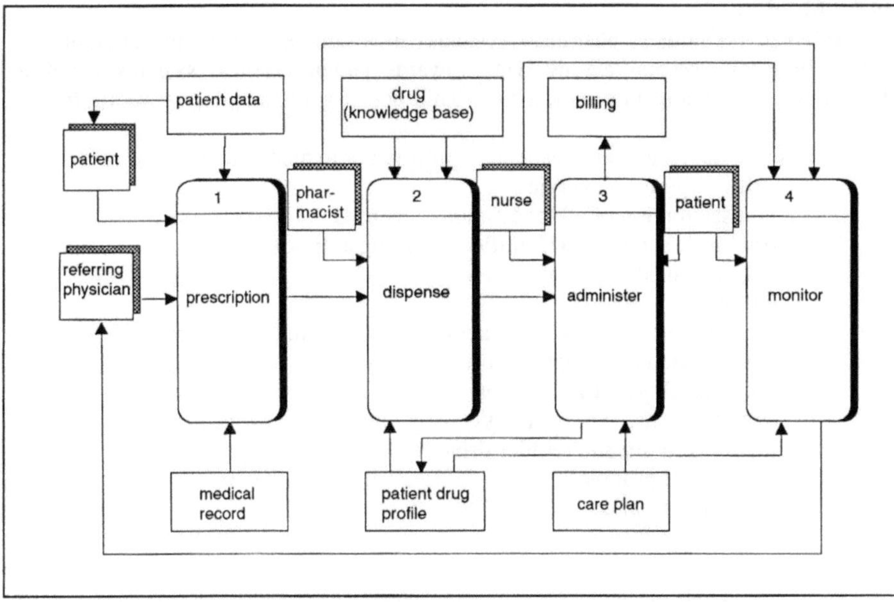

Fig. 19.1 General representation of a pharmacy information system by means of a data flow diagram, following the techniques of C. Gane and T. Sarson [GAN 79]

19.2.2 Dispense

After the requests have been sent (electronically or manually) to the pharmacy, the drugs are dispensed after validation (of the order), update of the stock level and preparation of delivery notes. Main tasks:

- Read the prescription from a pending prescription file
- Check for prescription validity according to the patient medication profile (duplicate orders, drug-allergy detection, drug-drug interactions, drug-laboratory interactions, maximal daily dose)
- Prepare after approval by pharmacist delivery form (print labels, form) and dispense; the delivery form accompanies the distribution of drugs to the wards
- Give advice on the use (administering) of the medication
- Remove medications from inventory as they are dispensed

19.2.3 Administer

At specified moments, medication has to be administered to the patient, covering the following activities:

- Maintain patient drug profile (current and inactive medications)
- Maintain nurse care plan/medication chart
- Notify the billing system of applicable charges (credits, retour) for patients or third-party payers
- Return scheduled doses not administered and discontinued medications back to the pharmacy

19.2.4 Monitor

As explained previously, pharmacy systems- in a similar way to the evolution of (other) hospital systems- are evolving towards patient-oriented systems for drug distribution and therapeutic monitoring. This needs good monitoring tools. In this category is included:

- Observe the patient and respond appropriately to medication alerts:
  - Order expiration overview
  - Transaction log of all medication dispensed
  - Antibiotic screening (identifies receiving antibiotics)
  - Returned medication overview
  - Fill list
- Create drug-use review reports to evaluate drug therapies and to track problems related to suboptimal drug therapy :
  - Too long/short drug therapies
  - Use of expensive drugs if less costly ones are available
- Maintain inventory and reorder drugs:
  - Daily order proposals
  - Usage information
  - Purchase history

19.3 Organisational Aspects of Pharmacy Information Systems

Medications can be delivered in several ways. They can be supplied from the central pharmacy to wards and departments in multiple-dose packs, from which nurses select and administer them to the patient according to the prescriptions of the physician, or they are supplied in a *unit-dose* package for a certain period (typically a day), in which every tablet is enclosed in a plastic protective package identified with name of the medication (eventually by barcode on the back). Although the former approach represents far less work, it suffers from a number of diasadvantages such as waste of drugs and inappropriate administration of therapy. Therefore, the unit-dose system is being used more and more in hospitals nowadays because it provides better control over the patient's drug therapy, although the workload is increased.

In most hospitals, a drug formulary has been established, usually by a steering committee of physicians and pharmacists, which indicates all the drugs with their characteristics available in the pharmacy's inventory. Theoretically, it provides the foundation for guiding clinicians in choosing the safest, most effective agents for treating particular medical problems. The selection of a drug not present in this formulary is "normally" not permitted for prescription in the hospital.

In his article "Drug formularies: myths-in-formation", Rucker and Schiff [RUC 90] discussed the quality of a formulary and the various misconceptions there are. Defining formularies aimed at obtaining a rational drug therapy that minimises cost is a complex procedure; the elements of an effective formulary are indicated in Table 19.2.

Table 19.2 Illustrative comments made by physicians during pharmacy and therapeutic committee deliberations pertaining directly or indirectly to the formulary concept, classified by major theme, 1987-1989 [RUC 90]

[Source : reprinted with the permission from, T.Donald Rucker and Gordon Schiff, Drug formularies myths-in- formation , *Medical Care*, October 1990, Vol. 28N°10, pp 928-938]

---

1. Casual empiricism
    - *I have used this in my private practice for years with good results.*
    - *We want an opportunity to try out this drug for 6 - 12 months to gain some experience using it and see if we like it.*
2. FDA approval implies everyday use for all
    - *The FDA wouldn't have approved it if it wasn't a good drug.*
    - *Patients should not be denied access to any drug approved by the FDA.*
3. Physiology/pharmacology teleology
    - *The physiological data on this drug are impressive (e.g. it is effective in suppressing arrhythmias on 24-h ECG).*
    - *This is a beautifully designed drug that neatly counteracts the pathophysiological mechanisms in this disease.*
4. Interferes with clinical freedom
    - *I'm philosophically opposed to restrictions on a doctor's clinical freedoms; we need education instead.*
    - *Each clinician has his/her own set of drugs that he/she is comfortable with; it's best not to interfere with this with a restricted formulary.*
5. Every patient is unique
    - *Every patient is different and we need a variety of drugs to try.*
    - *We need different drugs to deal with genetic or dietary differences.*
6. Specialist knows best
    - *For this committee to tell infectious disease specialists which antibiotics they should not prescribe is highly presumptuous.*
    - *If cardiology says they need this drug, who are we to question it?*
    - *The committee is just a bunch of non-sub-specialists sitting around making decisions about things they know nothing about.*
7. Education requires experience with a multitude of drugs
    - *By not having access to the newest drugs, our residents are not learning state-of-the-art medicine.*
    - *In the real world, for which we are training our residents, they don't have all of these restrictions.*
8. Widespread use equals drug of choice
    - *This is the most popular agent in this class of drugs; how can we do without it?*
    - *These drugs are widely used worldwide, they are the drugs of today.*
9. Newer is better/newer is safer
    - *The problem with formulary lists is that they're almost immediately out-of-date.*
    - *Any unknown risks are far outweighed by the benefits of this new drug.*
    - *This newer drug clearly has a better side effect profile than the older drug.*
10. Sicker patients need more drugs
    - *We need the drug for patients for whom nothing else has worked and for whom we have no other choice.*
    - *If you were standing in my shoes and a sick patient wasn't responding to a first line drug after 24 h, you'd damned well want other alternatives to try.*
11. Formulary sacrifices patient care to cost control
    - *While we'll probably have to accept drug restrictions due to cost, there is a trade-off in quality each time we do so.*

19.4 Drug Databases

All pharmaceutical products available in the hospital are defined in the drug data-base. In many countries a national drug file exists, containing product information. For the moment no standardisation exists at all between several national drug file systems. A national drug file offers the advantage that the pharmacist can use it to maintain the hospital drug data-base, avoiding too consuming and expensive work for a hospital pharmacist. This drug database system contains multiple information categories:

- Drug identification data
- Stock and purchase administrative data
- Medically related data

The administrative data offer a number of facilities assisting the pharmacist with the tedious administrative work he had to do previously such as automatic drug pricing update, drug ordering by telephone lines, automatic update of the administrative content of the drug database, for accounting and inventory control purposes (storage conditions, packing information, etc.) and management of label texts and a variety of packing sizes (during its manipulation through the pharmacy, the pack size can often be changed).

Apart from the administrative part a number of important medical items are provided. Pharmaceutical products are often referred to by a range of names: the generic (official) name (often quite lengthy, e.g. dextropropoxyphene) and a brand name (proprietary name of manufacturer or trade name), e.g. generic name is diazepam and brand name is Valium (Roche), Alupram (Steinhard), Atensine (Berk) (Fig.19.2). Often a simple mnemonic name is provided for commonly used products, so that they can be easily specified when ordering drugs, e.g. ASP 150 for aspirin in 150 mg-tablets.

In addition, medications are also characterised by a number of other medically important characteristics such as dose forms (injections, tablets, capsules, etc.), strength (10 mg, 5 mg) and finally route in which they are dispensed.

Furthermore, more general information for different users (physicians, nurses) are available [MOL 83] turning a "descriptive drug database" into a "drug information base" :

- Applicability
- Side effects
- Adverse drug reactions
- Drug-drug interaction
- Normal dosages
- Kinetic parameters
- Chemistry
- Administration instructions

19.5 Medication Control

One of the most important functions within a pharmacy system is therapeutic monitoring in order to observe medication administering and to avoid iatrogenic effects and poor administration. Medication control is the process by which the prescription is validated against five criteria: dosage control, contra indications, drug-drug interaction, duplicate orders and patient compliance.

Dosage control is extremely important for drugs characterised by a limited therapeutic scope or by a high degree of toxicity. This implies observation of:

- Age, sex and physiological parameters of the patient
- Previous prescriptions of the same drug
- Administration route
- Medication profile of the patient

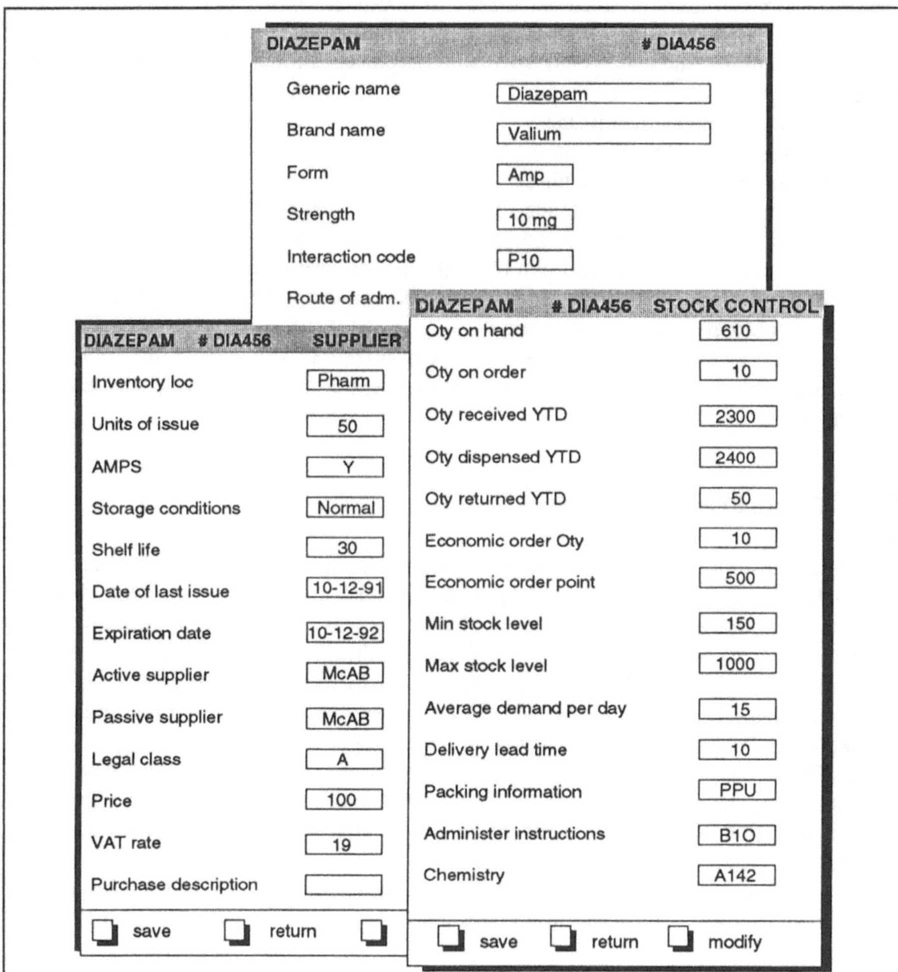

Fig. 19.2 Content of the pharmaceutical inventory control file [University Hospital Brussels (AZ-VUB 1991), Department Medical Informatics]

Contraindications indicate certain conditions under which it is not advisable to prescribe a specific drug. This implies observation of:

- Patient diagnosis
- Administration route

Duplicate ordering especially occurs when identical drugs or drugs belonging to the same pharmacotherapeutic group are prescribed (e.g. when the patient is under surveillance by different referring/ treating physicians).
Usage control/patient compliance indicates whether or not the medication has been administered exactly (time, route of administering).
Drug-drug interaction involves administering a certain medication which will influence the activity of another drug. A drug interaction happens when two or more drugs act together and produce an effect different from the one that should be produced by each drug individually. This effect ranges in severity (from acceptable to life-threatening) and can occur in different phases of the pharmacotherapeutic process:

- In the pharmaceutical phase
- In the pharmacokinetic phase
- In the pharmacodynamic phase

  Comparisons have to be made:

- To which therapeutic (sub) group(s) does the drug belong?
- Is there an interaction between those groups or parts of them?

  It is advisable to sub-divide the drug database by therapeutic classification into main groups and sub-groups.

Drug-laboratory interaction consists of computerized surveillance of microbiology results and antibiotic orders, for surveillance of hospital-acquired infections (see also chapter 31).

19.6 Future Pharmacy Systems

Almost all hospitals have automated pharmacy systems installed at this moment, but only a few have implemented systems that can take advantage of all that clinical pharmacy has to offer. This is about to change, as it will become important to have good methods to analyse the economical and medical aspects of drug use . Some hospitals are currently using an automated dispensing system for drugs placed at the nursing station, providing unit -of- use dispensing and accountability. Other hospitals are exploring facsimile machines placed in a network to send and receive prescription oders [HAR 91]. With more and more drugs entering the market, pharmacy information systems may help pharmacy departments manage increasing demands, reduce operating costs and allocate more time to professional tasks such as drug utilization reviews and increased auditing.
From a clinical point of view, the most interesting features of pharmacy information systems are those that assist physicians and pharmacists in the decision-making process of :

- Prescribing drugs
- Calculating and refining drug doses employing pharmacokinetic models based on the patient's medical history
- Monitoring patients who receive the medication

Existing examples are :

- The MENTOR system developed at Stanford University and designed to monitor drug therapies for inpatients (adverse drug reactions)

- The MEDIPHOR system also developed at the same university and aimed to provide on-line drug interaction information
- The HELP system (3M) assisting physicians in drug- and drug-laboratory interactions

As the quantity and complexity of drug interactions increase, conventional methods (books, literature, microfiche) are no longer sufficient to provide advice in order to improve the quality of health care. Another interesting feature offered by new technologies is the availability of on-line databases over telecommunication lines or rapid-access storage devices (CD-ROM).

An example is Excerpta Media CD of Drugs and Pharmacology from Silver Platter information. This contains more than 900 000 abstracts and citations from 1980 to the present. It provides comprehensive coverage of drugs and the pharmacology literature, including the effects and use of all drugs and potential drugs and the clinical and experimental aspects of their pharmacokinetics and pharmacodynamics. The side effects of drugs are also covered. Drugs are mentioned by trade name.

20

Nursing Information Systems

20.1 Introduction

Although nurses work in almost all health care institutions and represent the largest working group employed by a hospital, the penetration of information technology for them has been minimal up to now. Nursing operations are still largely uncomputerised. In fact, HIS do not involve the real users in hospitals. Nurses, whose salaries account for 30%-40% of a hospital's operating budget, spend 25%-40% of their time performing clinical and especially communication tasks, as indicated by studies in the 1960s. They still use clipboards for recording measurements and observations, although many of these measurements come from automated sources. Repetitive transcription and (telephone) communications are the primary issues to improve the clinical overhead, because nurses spend far too much time on paperwork instead of with the patient.

An important reason to implement a new system and to convert first generation HIS (charge capture system) to a fully integrated clinical IS is to enhance nursing information management. A national nursing shortage looms in many countries. Realising that a shortage of nurses can lead to a reduction in the quality of patient care, we have to place a high priority on nurse job satisfaction. Freeing nurses from the tedium of paperwork can increase their job satisfaction, as well as enabling them to spend more time with their patients and making the nurse's contribution more visible. Currently, a few systems are available which partially support nursing operations. They are in fact extensions of centralised HIS. Examples of this type of architecture are PCS from IBM, TDS from Technicon, HELP system from 3M and SMS (Shared Medical Systems).

Compared with other medical departments within a hospital, nurses these days are faced with an increasing amount of information to manage. Three causes underlying this evolution can be mentioned :

- Medical care has becoming more and more complex and more and more technologically driven and specialised, which results in a more complicated nursing care process. It covers mainly :
  - Observation of vital parameters and symptoms of possible complications
  - Carrying out treatments and nursing care
- The evolution of routine work (where every patient receives the same care) towards a more individual patient care in which a patient is seen as a "whole" (physical, social, mental)
- The transition of an operational attitude towards a more planned and methodical approach

Rather than focussing on the prevention, diagnosis and treatment of the patient's disease (the primary tasks of the medical staff), nurses execute a pre-defined nursing care plan, providing care that patients are unable to perform for themselves and increasing their ability to care for themselves. Nursing approaches nowadays differ widely across Europe, but the past and present situation is characterised mostly by ad-hoc interventions.

Of all the nursing activities, documentation and communication are the most time-consuming. The functions of documenting patient care are in today's sophisticated health care environment almost entirely manual. As nurses form a great part of the human resources of a hospital the challenge for the years ahead lies in finding a way to increase the efficiency and accuracy of documentation and communication and freeing nurses from tedious administrative work in order to provide more time for "real" patient care. (Fig.20.1 represents different phases within the nursing process). A number of automated nursing systems already exist, but most of them are more or less administrative support systems. Many of the existing commercially available ones are single-purpose, stand-alone systems, although there is no other area in a hospital that so begs to be integrated.

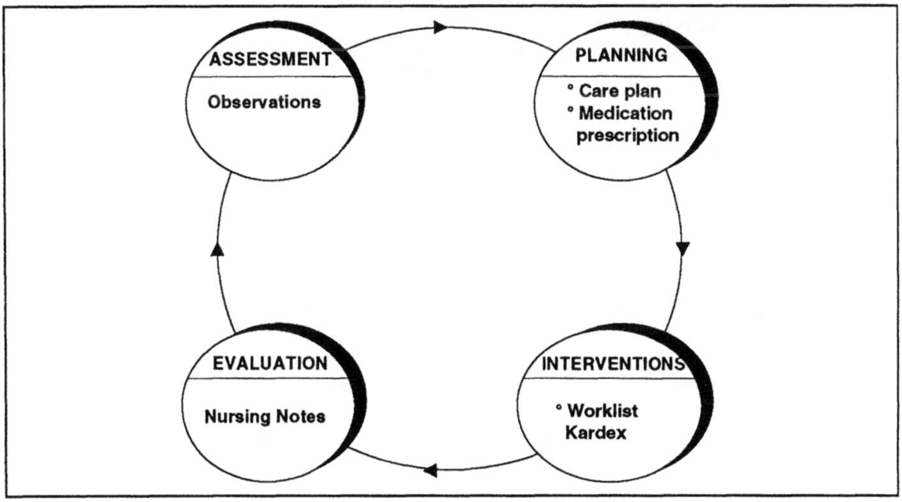

Fig.20.1 Different phases within a nursing process: a conceptual overview

20.2 Objectives of a Nursing Information System

The most important objectives of a NIS can be summarised as having:

- An integrated view of patient data (e.g. integrate nurses and physician orders in the patient care plan)
- Data available from different locations (including bedside entry)
- Control of correctness, validity, safety and confidentiality of information
- Communication with related services
- A user-friendly interface: easy to learn, fast to use, help functions included and homogeneous in appearance
- Planning support activities

20.3 Functions of a Nursing Information System

In defining the information requirements of nursing organisations, a clear conceptual model of the nursing area is needed, describing the most important functions and information requirements that could guide in the design of NIS [MIL 89]. Fig.20.2 represents an entity relationship model of nursing for inpatients. A conceptual information model is proposed based on four important main functions in the clinical and administrative nursing practice, reflecting the real world as close by as possible (Table 20.1). The first area of patient care processes represents individual nurse patient activities and the information derived from them. Emphasis is put on nurse-patient interactions. When these data are consolidated into meaningful information, they form the input for the second category: ward management processes elucidating trends in the need for nursing care and required nursing resources. The third category is concerned with all communication activities surrounding daily nursing activities. The last category focusses on strategic planning and education.

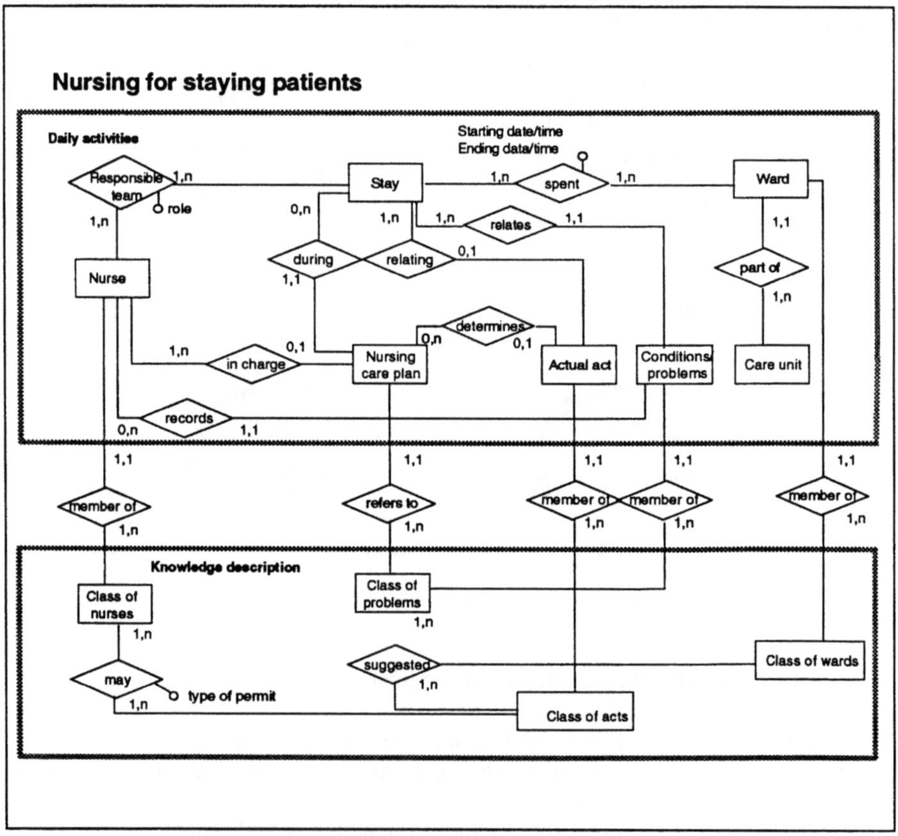

Fig. 20.2 Entity relationship model of nursing for inpatients.
(Source courtesy of Dr. F.M. Ferrara and Prof. A. Van der Werff *RICHE, Consortium*, 1991)

Table 20.1 Main tasks in the nursing care process

Patient care processes	**Main actor : nurses**
Anything done to/for the patient. It can vary from medical treatments (administering medication, fixing bandages, giving a bath) to diagnostic observations. It is the basis for gathering operational information.	
- Patient registration (nurse anamnesis) - Examinations and observations (nursing diagnosis) - Treatments and medication scheduling - Nurse medical record charting - Dietary registration - Patient acuity/ classification (prospective) - Workload assessment - Patient administration (discharge , transfer)	
Ward management processes	**Main actor : nurse manager**
Activities related to the well functioning of the ward unit, to the effective use of the available resources in achieving the specific planned objectives. *It transforms operational information into management-oriented information to assist in the decision-making process.*	
- Quality assurance - Nursing ward unit activity overviews - Staff scheduling (human resources) - Personnel management - Care planning (nurse charting) - Inventory management and supplies - Financial management (budget, patient billing) - Infection control	
Communication processes	**Main actor : nurses**
All activities concentrated on communications about a patient (orders, appointments, talking to the family) and other work-related subjects.	
- Orders (medication, treatments) are integrated in the care plan - Appointment and scheduling - Data review (order status, medical results) - Information transfer to nurses who are coming on duty - All kinds of messages	
Education and research processes	
- Documentation of routine functions and procedures	

20.3.1 Patient Care Processes

This category consists of activities provided for or done in cooperation with the patient.

° *Nursing intake* corresponds to the first interview of the nurse with the patient in which administrative information, general patient health data, social patient data, somatic patient data and particular problems of the patient are written down in the nursing record.

- *Examination and observations* on patients (reactions of the patients, results of measurements) cover a second sub-category of activities, in which the nurse performs a problem analysis and evaluation of the patient's medical condition. This information is composed of assessment data and nursing diagnoses and generates goals reflected in the nurse care plan (= nurse charting).
- *Performing of treatments* or execution of medical orders by nurses. The effects of medical therapeutics provided (medication administering, setting up intravenous lines, watching monitors) are described, including signs and symptoms observed.
- *Patient acuity management* leads to calculating for every patient the level of care required for him/her according to a variety of methods, based on the severity of the illness. It is a system that classifies patients into several levels of acuity in order to distinguish those who need little care from those who require substantial nursing care. The goal of this system is to be able to plan distribution of nursing resources. In addition, besides the estimated nursing time needed for the next shift, the estimated indirect or non-bedside nursing time are calculated in terms of FTE (full time equivalent).
- *Workload assessment* plan contains the patient's vital signs, medication, allergies, past history synopsis and clinical diagnoses, from which a computerised nursing care plan is generated [SMI 89].
- The last activities are related to patient *discharge or transfer movement*: filling out forms, creating nursing summaries, preparing outpatient activities or generating instructions for patients.

20.3.2 Ward Management Processes

These indicate activities necessary to manage the ward unit as an effective organisation unit.

- Starting from the information registered in the first category in conjunction with disease-related data, a nursing care plan is formulated, executed (in the previous phase) and evaluated (quality assurance). This nursing care plan (whether on paper or by computer) is basically a problem-oriented record (POR) describing expected outcomes, interventions and results. Nowadays, production of most care plans is time consuming due to manual processing. They have disadvantages in supporting the nursing process and are inaccessible to research and management.
- Starting with data about the bed census (occupation rate), unit length of stay, number of admissions, patient characteristics, patient acuity data and discharges, the staff schedule is formulated, producing an effective allocation of nursing personnel assigned to the unit.
- Non-nursing activities unrelated to patient care are definition of standard plans (procedure books), protocols and personnel management.
- Personnel management allows for registering information (name, phone number, specialisation areas, assigned rotation, educational history) for each member and reviewing the scheduling. These data help with a variety of functions (performance appraisal, looking for specific skills, used in conjunction with staffing assignments).

- Last but not least, this category also covers materials management and supply activities, to update stock levels and to provide anything for a patient in or outside of the ward unit.

20.3.3 Communication Processes

As nurses spend a great deal of their time on oral or written communications, these activities are very important and cover tasks such as talking about patients with physicians, other nurses, technicians and family.

- *Order processing* is one of the main tasks. Orders are rarely generated at the nursing station, but rather at the bedside or in the corridor. Little information is available at the bedside, and much manual processing is involved there in copying and translating orders, which is time-consuming error prone and quickly out of date.
- *Appointments and scheduling* activities also belong to this category. Results processing, reporting and data review (laboratory test results, radiology results) by means of a terminal are also important.
- *Reporting* about the progress of patients with respect to the care planning to other nurses who are coming on duty is also part of the communication function. A more general mailbox system could be of great help.

Fig.20.3 to 20.5 give a representation of existing nurse sheets as used in the TDS health care system.

```
1S    -0926          TDS HEALTHCARE DEMO HOSPITAL
09/12/89  01:20 PM                    (QAT$$P)                         PAGE 001
====================================
SANDERS, JOHN                      M   57
MR#: 10017572        ACCT#: 50295251
SERV: CARD           1S         100P
MD: CURIE,MARIE           ADM: 09/11/89
DX: ACUTE MYOCARDIAL INFARCTION
====================================                          PATIENT RECORD
SUMMARY: 09/12 12:01 AM TO 01:20 PM                       -PERMANENT CHART COPY-

PATIENT INFORMATION:
 09/12 07:18AM ALLERGY: ERYTHROMYCINS                                          NP
 09/12 07:03AM PRINCIPAL DX:ACUTE MYOCARDIAL INFARCTION 410.9                  MC
 09/12 07:03AM COMPLICATIONS:HEMATOMA RIGHT FEMORAL ARTERY POST CARDIAC
               CATH.                                                           MC
 09/12 07:03AM OPERATIONS/PROCEDURES:CARDIAC CATHETERIZATION --9/12/89
                                                                               MC
 09/12 07:03AM CONDITION: SERIOUS                                              MC
 09/12 07:03AM RESTRICT VISITORS TO IMMEDIATE FAMILY                           MC
 09/12 07:17AM MEDICAL ALERT: CONTACT LENSES                                   NP
 09/12 07:17AM MEDICAL ALERT: REACTION BLOOD TRANS                             NP

NURSING NOTES:
 09/12 06:10AM ACTIVITY- BRP                                                   PM
               BATH- COMPLETE                                                  PM
               AM CARE                                                         PM
               IV SITE CHECKED                                                 PM
               MOUTH CARE                                                      PM
 09/12 10:30AM PRESSURE DRESSING TO RT GROIN DRY AND INTACT                    PM

TRANSFER NOTES:
 09/12 10:30AM PT TRANSFERRED TO 1S, FROM CATH LAB                             PM
               PT CONDITION: STABLE, AWAKE, COLOR PALE....IV IN PLACE
                                                                               PM

VITAL SIGNS OBSERVATIONS:
 09/12 06:00AM CARDIAC RHYTHMS : SINUS TACHY WITH OCCASIONAL PVCS            NP

                                  CONTINUED
```

Fig. 20.3 Patient record is a permanent chart document that composes the legal documentation for all chart entries for a patient made by nursing and ancillary personnel. It contains information from all care-givers for a 24-h period, usually midnight to midnight.

(source Courtesy TDS health care systems - 1991)

```
05/17/91 15:44      (QTO$$P)      PAGE 001 PATIENT WORKSHEET OUTCOME PLAN

                                    F 74 SCU106
  11627320                               SCU1      ADM DATE: 05/15/91
  O  , RIC.     MD           P S  02160281                   07:01     05/17/91
= = = = = = = = = = = = = = = = = = = = = = = = = = = = = = = = = = = = = = = =
ADMITTING DX:
 ACUTE MYOCARDIAL INFARCTION ISCHEMIC MIT

PATIENT CLASS:
05/16/91 CLASS V

PATIENT INFO:
   05/16  SECONDARY DX--S/P CABG X3, MITRAL ANNUROPLASTY
   05/16 DIETARY ALLERGY: NO KNOWN FOODS
   05/16 ADMIT WT-52, STATED
   05/16 ADMIT HT-64", STATED
   05/16 ALLERGY: PENICILLIN
   05/16 ALLERGY: PENICILLIN

VITAL SIGNS/SPECIAL OBSERVATIONS:
    05/16 149.   VS:Q15MIN UNTIL STABLE, THEN Q1H, (SVAI)
    05/16 150.   DAILY WEIGHT 0500, (SVAI)
    05/16 190.   SPECIAL OBSV:--NEUROVASCULAR CHECKS TO RLE Q2/HRS,
                 (SVAI)
    05/16 197.   NOTIFY HOUSE OFFICER OF--BP < 100 OR > 160, TEMP >
                 38.5, UOP < 0.5ML/KH/H X2 CONS. HRS, (SVAI)
    05/16 198.   NOTIFY HOUSE OFFICER OF RESP DISTRESS, (SVAI)
    05/16 199.   NOTIFY HOUSE OFFICER OF FREQUENT DYSRRHYTHMIAS *,
                 (SVAI)

DIET AND FLUID BALANCE:
    05/16 152.   NPO, (SVAI)
    05/16 153.   FOLEY TO GRAVITY DRAINAGE, Q1H UO, (SVAI)

UNIT TESTS/EXAMS:
    05/16 154.   URINE SG, S&A Q6H, (SVAI)
    05/17 238.   BLOOD: GLUCOMETER, Q6H, (SVAI)

HYGIENE/ACTIVITY/SAFETY:
    05/16 151.   BEDREST, HOB UP 30 DEGREES, (SVAI)

PROCEDURES/MISC. ORDERS:
    05/16 160.   CHEST TUBE: 20CM H20, (SVAI)
    05/16 170.   LABS: PANEL 7--HCT/MG/POD#2 EVERY AM X3, (SVAI)
    05/16 171.   LABS: CPK'S--W/ISO EVERY AM X3, (SVAI)
    05/16 175.   KEEP 2U PRBCS ON HOLD FOR 36H POST-OP, (SVAI)
    05/17 254.   LABS: PANEL 7 -CA/MG/PO4/CBC IN AM 5/18, (SVAI)
    05/16 188.   NSG INSTRUCT:INC SPIROMETRY 10X/HR WHILE AWAKE --ONCE
                 EXTUBATED, (SVAI)

MEDICATIONS:
    05/16 161.   MORPHINE SULFATE INJ 2 MG TO 6 MG, IV PUSH, Q1HR, PRN
                 PAIN, HOLD FOR SYS BP <100, (SVAI)
    05/16 162.   VANCOMYCIN 500 MG IN D5W 150 ML INFUSE OVER MINIMUM OF
                 60 MIN. , DOCUMENTED INF. (RENEW:7DAYS) , Q12H IVPB
                 START AT, 0000, START ON 05/17, (05/17/91 0000-..),
                 (SVAI)
```

Fig. 20.4 Part of a patient worksheet and outcome plan, as used in the TDS healthcare system.

(Source courtesy TDS health care Systems - 1991)

```
1S    -0882          TDS HEALTHCARE DEMO HOSPITAL
09/12/89  07:37 AM                  (QAB$$N)                        PAGE 001
==========================================
BAKER, SAMUEL                        M    68
MR#: 10017598        ACCT#: 50295411                  PATIENT CARE SUMMARY
SERV: CARD           1S           106A
MD: PIERCE,BENJAMIN     ADM: 09/11/89
DX: CHF
==========================================
SUMMARY: 09/12 07:00 AM TO 03:30 PM

PATIENT INFORMATION:
        09/11         ADMIT DX:CHF

ALL CURRENT MEDICAL ORDERS:

   NURSING ORDERS:
        09/11   10. ACTIVITY, BEDREST, (BP ).
        09/11   11. POSITION: ELEVATE HD OF BED 30 DEG, (BP ).

   DIET:
        09/11    1. DIET: CARDIAC, SODIUM CONTROLLED: 2000MG (87 MEQ),
                    (BP ).

   SCHEDULED MEDICATIONS:
        09/11    2. LASIX FUROSEMIDE TAB 40MG, #1, PO, Q12H, (09/11/89
                    09AM-..), (BP ).  09
        09/11    3. DIGOXIN TAB 0.25MG, #1, PO, QD, (09/11/89 02PM-..),
                 .  (BP ).  02
        09/12   13. ARTIFICIAL TEARS ARTIFICIAL TEARS (15ML),, 3 GTTS,
                    BOTH EYES, Q4H, WHILE AWAKE, (09/12/89 09AM-..), (MC )
                    .  09 01
        09/12   15. METAMUCIL PSYLLIUM HYDROPHILIC MUCILLOID PKT (LIME
                    FLAVORED), PO, WITH WATER, BID, (09/12/89 09AM-..),
                    (MC ).  09

   PRN MEDICATIONS:
        09/11    8. DALMANE FLURAZEPAM CAP 15MG, #1, PO, QHS, PRN,
                    (09/11/89 10PM-..), (BP ).
        09/11    9. DALMANE FLURAZEPAM CAP 15MG, #1, PO REP X1, (BP ).

   DRUG INTERACTIONS:
        09/11       DRUG INTERACTION: .
                    KALURETICS INCREASE THE EFFECT OF DIGITALIS.
                    DIGOXIN TAB 0.25MG, #1, PO, QD   (09/11/89 02PM-..)
                    ENTERED FOR: PIERCE,BENJAMIN 09/11/89.
                    FUROSEMIDE TAB 40MG, #1, PO Q12H   (09/11/89 09AM-..)
                    ENTERED FOR: PIERCE,BENJAMIN 09/11/89 SEVERITY: 2
                    HANSTEN 4TH: 277 DRUG INTER. FACTS: 249,253

   LABORATORY:
   .#   09/11    6. (IN PROCESS)H&H, TOMORROW, (09/12/89), (BP ).
    #   09/11    7. (IN PROCESS)ELECTROLYTES, TOMORROW, (09/12/89), (BP ).

   RADIOLOGY:
        09/11    4. X-RAY: CHEST, PA & LAT, INDICATION: --CHF, PRECAUTION:
                    OXYGEN, HANDLING: BEDSIDE/PORTABLE, SCHEDULE: STAT,
```

Fig. 20.5 Patient care summary (Kardex) is an automated version of the Kardex, containing such information as diagnosis, attending and consulting physicians, nursing orders, medical alerts, allergies, medications and their schedules and all current orders.It is printed just prior to the beginning of each shift and details the information pertinent to that shift for the nurse assigned to that patient.

(Source Courtesy TDS health care systems - 1991)

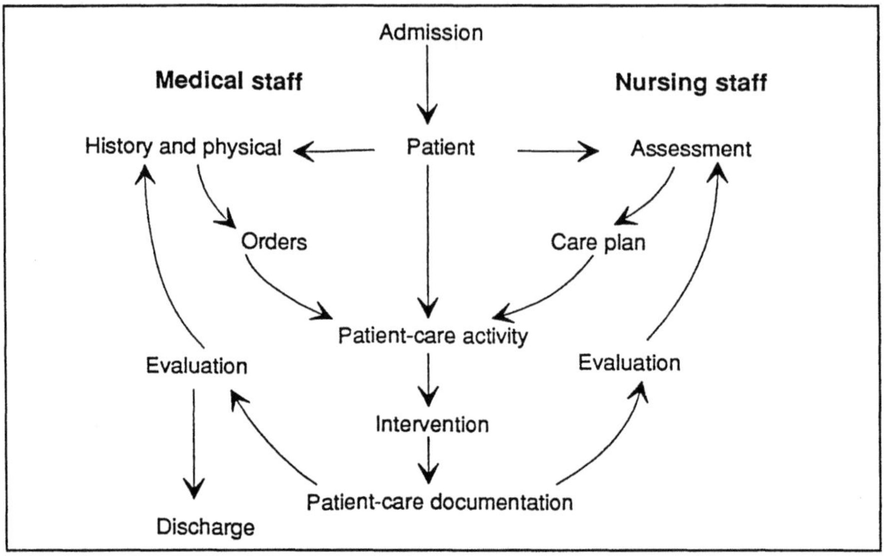

Fig. 20.6 Representation of complementary medical care and nursing care processes. Physicians obtain medical histories, conduct physical examinations, and order medical treatments; nurses assess patients' needs, plan patient care, administer treatments, educate [KOR 84].

(Source Courtesy of Ralph A Korpman, M.D.,Professor, Loma Linda University School of Medicine, and President and Chairman, Health Data Sciences Corporation. Reprinted with permission from Korpman, R.A. Patient care information systems : Looking to the future.Part 4. The changing role of computers in nursing. *Software in Healthcare*, Oct/Nov : 58-64, 1984)

20.4 Bedside Terminals

Especially in inpatient units, the nurse and not the physician is often the primary integrator and coordinator of information and often the primary deliverer and monitor of care [KOR 87], so in establishing a hospital-related computer-stored medical record, the nurse is also one of the primary axes (Fig.20.6). As stated already before, improvement of information registration, nurse documentation and communication with other health care providers is one of the most important objectives for an NIS.
Hospitals are interested in bedside terminals as a tool to enhance nursing productivity. Bedside systems mitigate the impact of an acute nursing shortage. The time spent in indirect patient care, or documentation, occupies nearly half of a nure's patient-centered activities [HEN 90]. In readership serveys conducted [STE 87 ; STE 89] respondents ranked improved quality of care (71 %), immediately behind improved data quality (74 %). A survey conducted in 1990 [STE 91] ranked nurse charting and medication administration at the top (Fig.20.7).

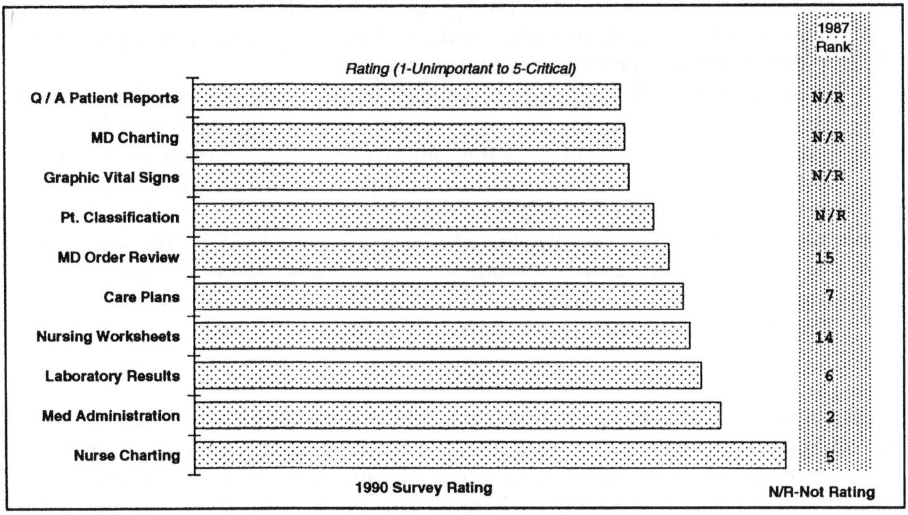

Fig.20.7 Point-of-Care Systems Features [STE 91]
(Source reprinted with permission from Michael F. and Stefanchik, Ph.D in *Point-of-Care Revolution.* Computers in Healthcare, April 1991)

As most information to be gathered is created at the patient's bedside or in the corridor and very seldom at the nursing station, it is obvious that beside terminals will improve productivity and the quality of care and documentation due to:

- o *Better integration of medical and nursing information.* Information is registered immediately when the care is administred and is available at once to other authorised persons, resulting in better documentation (quality assurance, nurse charting, patient care plans).
- o *Better integrity.* Error or incompleteness is prevented by the fact that fewer transcription errors occur, resulting in a more accurate charting
- o *Better quality assurance,* e.g. expansion of medication charting, point-of-care data capture.

User friendliness, as little intrusion as possible into the patient environment and a security system to prevent patient access to some authorised data files are important concepts for a bedside terminal. Nowadays, there are already several companies (Ulticare, IBM, NCR, AT&T, Marquette Electronics, EMTEK, Health Data Sciences, Spacelabs) who are delivering bedside terminals. Various types are in use, depending upon different care environments, each representing different bedside information needs.

We can sub-divide them into the following categories:

- o *Simple stationary terminals* for moderate care environments, where a standard PC (preferrably without hard disc for noise reasons) is advisable
- o *Specially designed terminals* provided with particular characteristies: function keys, screens, robustness, humidity protection
- o *Extended stationary terminals* for high care environments, with specific characteristics: multifunction, windowing, graphical representation, function keys, etc. In fact, they are 386/68030 (UNIX) workstations with extensive capabilities

- *Portable bedside terminals*, although easily transportable and small, are less user friendly and less interactive compared with the previous ones due to the reduced real-time interactive facilities provided.
- *Pen-based bedside computers.* Another concept towards portable bedside terminals could be the use of the pen-based computer. It is probably the most commonly used means of recording information. The computer (Intel 386SX processor) is simply a writing surface (a high-resolution LCD) and a pen (in a package small and easy to carry around) very much like a note pad and a pencil. Instead of first locating the item to be updated on the screen, by entering a keystroke or by double clicking a mouse, with the Note Pad you simply mark the item as with a pencil (manufacturers : NCR, Eden Group). It has the capabilities of covering handwriting into type.

For the moment these devices are more data collection oriented and are suitable to use in combination/complementary with other bedside stations, although it may be expected in the very near future to have real portable bedside terminals with liquid crystal displays and low weight. Transmission of information can be done by hardware interface or by means of radiowave telecommunication in real-time using the same techniques already existant in telemetry. In the Information Technologies Lab at Texas Instruments' Computer Science Center, hand-held devices have been created that perform wireless data transfer using infrared transmission and spread - spectrum transmission [PIC 91].
It is important to stress the fact that for the next decade bedside technology is one of the newest and most dynamic trends in patient care IS. In the study "Bedside technology : a look to the future", the First Consulting Group describes it as " ... *the combination of modern technologies with specific clinical applications to solve medical/clinical problems at the patient level*."

21

Hospitals Financing : Challenges of the 1990s

"No money, no mission"

21.1 Introduction

Hospital financing and the need to control it became one of the major concerns in many countries in the early 1970s to insure better cost and quality control. The aging of population, which is increasing , and technology penetration are the most important reasons escalating health care costs. As often stressed in this book, the financial consequences of implementing new (computing) technologies in hospitals -evolving to high tech organisations- are very important and cannot be studied in depth without considering the economic implications. HIS must not only allow for a better approach to hospital financing but also for an improved knowledge of production efficiency and treatment effectiveness (Fig. 21.1). Hospital management requires medical services to justify everything from staffing to new equipment purchase (i.e. resources acquired). Labor -as always- is the biggest cost in hospitals, represented mostly by nurses. In this chapter we will provide a very general overview of hospital financing in Europe and the USA. Hereafter, we will cover some basic issues of health care economics.

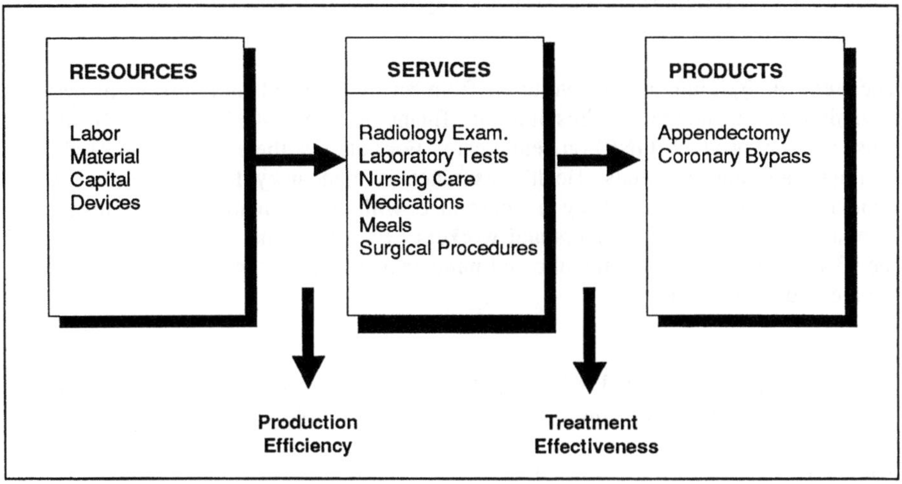

Fig. 21.1 Overview of hospital structure in terms of resources used, services and products delivered.

21.2 Health Care Financing in Europe

European health care systems vary from national health systems to private insurance systems, with additional differences within the systems themselves. One of the actions undertaken in reducing the health care expenditures was reducing the number of hospital beds (Table 21.1), resulting in a substantial decrease in the average length of stay (AVGL) while the number of admissions has increased [WEV 90].
On the other hand, most European countries were studying DRGs for a better understanding of the hospital production, providing a relation between inpatient medical data and financial data in order to improve their healthcare financing mechanisms.

Table 21.1 Changes in number of hospital beds in some countries

Country	1980	1987	Percentage
FRG	707 710	763 687	+ 5%
Belgium	92 436	83 090	- 10%
USA	1 364 500	1 267 000	- 7%
France	597 800	569 184	- 5%
Italy	548 426	441 682	- 19%
Netherlands	173 462	172 650	-
UK	458 000	388 711	- 15%

European financing systems are very different between countries. Moreover, in a given country different financing systems may be established side by side.

The trend in Belgium is the evolution from an open-ended reimbursement system towards a global budget for hospital care financing. In 1987 it spent 7.2% of the gross national product (GNP) on health care. For patients, there is freedom of choice of physicians and hospitals. Health insurance is mandatory for almost the entire population and is managed by a committee with representatives from insurance companies, health care providers and workers. Every Belgian hospital is subject to the 63 law which regulates the allowed number of beds, the types of health care and the methods of operation.

In the Netherlands since 1984, a global hospital budget based on the cost of hospitalization, pharmacy, radiology and clinical pathology laboratories has been defined.
This budget is established on the number of beds, the population served by different medical and hospital disciplines (bed specialisation, etc.) as well as in the way it considers activity forecasts negotiated with insurance companies such as number of consultations, occupancy rate, etc. [WEV 90].
A new system is proposed by creating universal health insurance coverage but allowing people to select between local "sick funds" and other private insurers. Employees and employers split the cost of premium [AND 91].

In the FRG, there is a system that requires employer-employee contributions to sickness funds controlled by the states, varying from 8% to 16% of employee income. The unemployed, disabled, eldery or poor people are covered under social security provisions. Patients have free choice of GPs, specialists and hospitals. Hospitals are paid global budgets according to strict per diem rates.

In France, there exists a disparity between the financing of public and private institutions, with the public sector being poorer off and causing a net shift of physicians from the public sector to private institutions. The French government is making changes in hospital financing, paying more attention to pathologies and nursing care.

Great Britain and Scandinavian countries have established a comprehensive annual budget (negotiated between each region and the central government) in order to control increased activity in health care centres. This global budget is most often related to pay scale increases rather than activities in diagnostic or therapeutic fields.

21.3 Health Care Financing in the USA

The USA has the highest health care cost in relation to their GNP. Health care spending in the United States has topped the $600 billion mark and the cost for all health care services is expected to grow from $663 billion in 1990 to $ 1,003 billion by 1995 (Fig.21.2). Health care expenditures currently consume nearly 12 percent to the gross national product (Fig. 21.3).

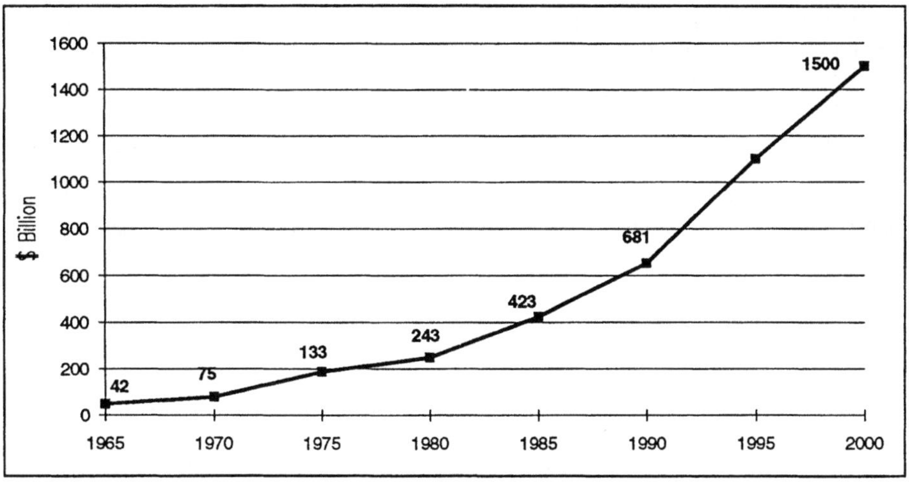

Fig.21.2 U.S. Healthcare Expenditures
(Source Levit Katharina R., Freeland, Mark S., Waldo, Daniel R. "Data Watch", Health Affairs, Summer, 1990, p. 172)

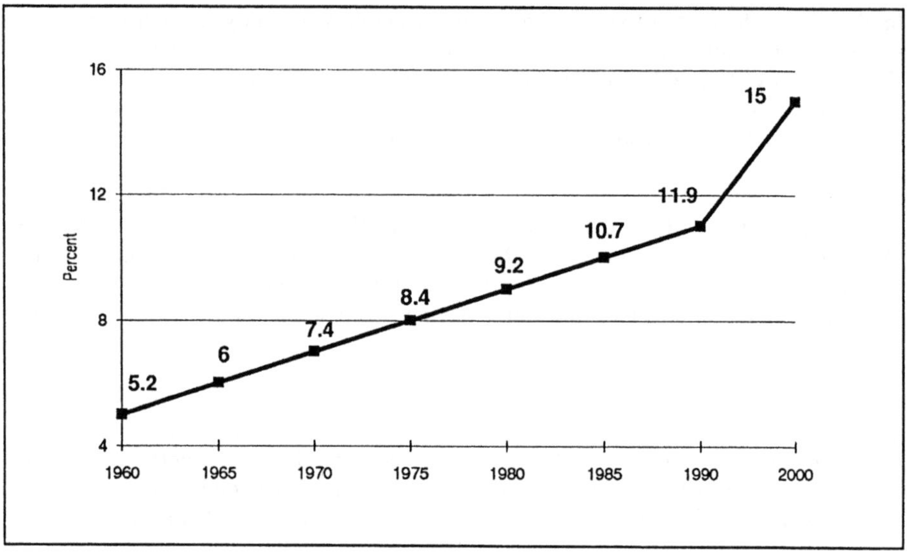

Fig.21.3 Healthcare Spending as a Percent of GNP
(Source "National Health Expenditures, 1986-2000", Health Care Financing Review, Devision of Nat. Cost Estimates, Office of the Actuary, Health Care Financing Administration, Summer 1987, p. 25.)

Health care in the United States may be delivered and financed in a variety of ways. In 1965, congress enacted two major government sponsored programs: Medicare is a Federal health insurance program for the aged and disabled, and Medicaid is a state administered Federal matching program that finances medical services for certain categories of low-income individuals. Prior to October 1983, hospitals were retrospectively reimbursed on the basis of reasonable costs.
However, cost reducing Social Security amendment acts (notably the Tax Equity and Fiscal Responsibility Act, or TEFRA) in 1983 required the Medicare program to pay hospitals on a prospective rate per case irrespective of their costs. This prospective payment system (PPS) was based on the concept of reimbursing for each of approximately 470 diagnostic related groups, or DRGs, a prospectively determined price.

In addition to government sponsored programs, individuals may also be covered by group and service-type plans such as Blue Cross/Blue Shield and so called alternative health care delivery systems. The use of alternative health delivery systems, (organized systems of care that compete the fee-for-service practices), are increasingly encouraged as a means of controlling health care costs both through the utilization and prize side. Patients have reduced freedom to choose health care providers, and providers agree to reduced fee and/or capitated (per patient) reimbursement mechanisms. Health maintenance organizations (HMOs) and preferred provider organizations (PPOs) are the most prevalent delivery arrangements and have been cost effective largely by reducing hospital use. Over the next decade, the share of services purchased through traditional insurance mechanisms will decrease.

21.4 Basic Health Care economics

21.4.1 Cost Versus Quality Considerations

From an engineering perspective the relation cost versus quality (or return on investment, *ROI*) can be illustrated by an S-curve (Fig. 21.4). Moving on the cost (horizontal) axis from left to the right, it represents after the study phase (acquisition phase of new technology) a serious increase in quality until a certain point (*F*) is reached. From this point, a huge investment (cost) is needed to obtain a substantial improvement. This means that a frontier is reached which only could be solved by introducing new technology. It is the objective of every organisation to recognise this frontier and to attain it as closely as possible.

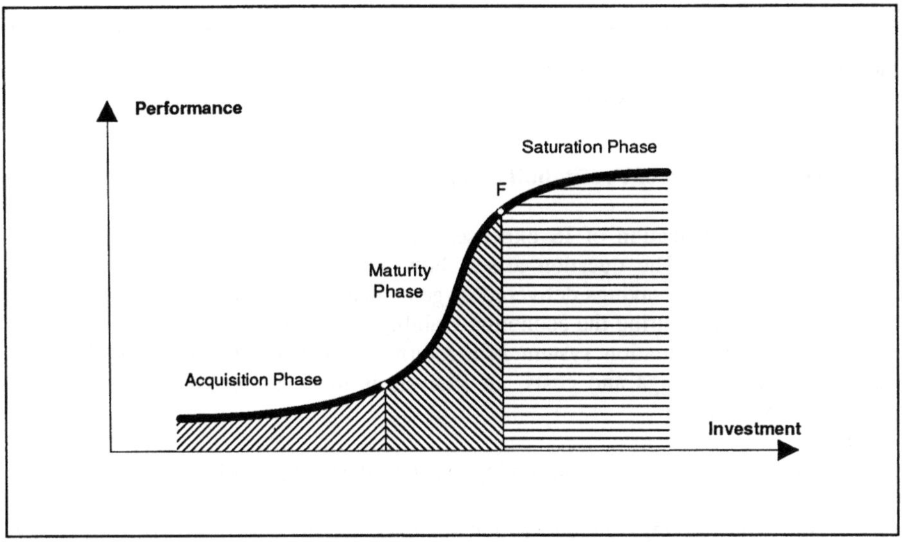

Fig. 21.4 S-curve : introductory period, explosive development period and finally the saturation phase of an innovative technological progress

The penetration of information technology in the health care sector was demonstrated by Nolan at the beginning of the 1980s when he portrayed his six stages of DP growth, from the inception of the computer into the organisation to mature management of data resources by means of an S-curve [NOL 79]. If we continue applying new IT technologies a representation as illustrated in Fig. 21.5 will be the result for the next decade.

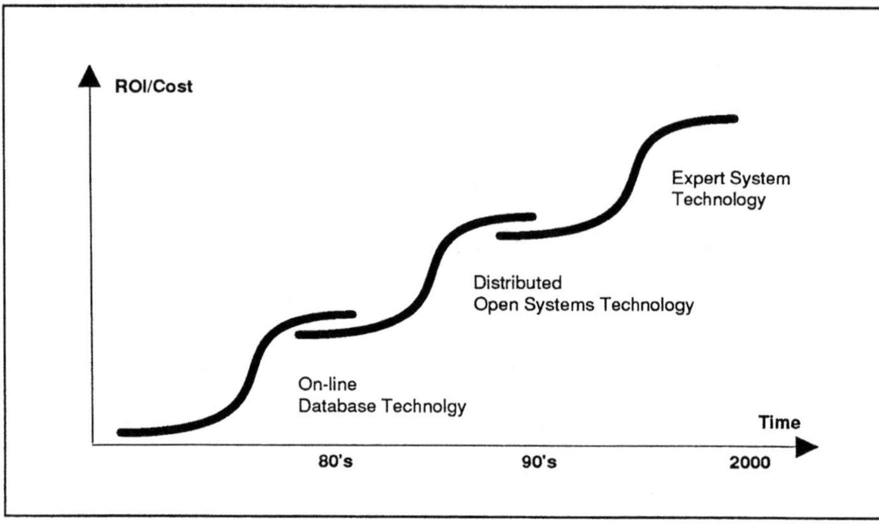

Fig. 21.5 Representation of the impact of different innovative technological processes in the health care environment over time

21.4.2 Determination of Profitability Improvement : *ROI* Analysis

The economic justification of IS expenses has become a very important issue for hospital managers. The question arises, how do we determine and measure the "potential" profits and savings delivered or generated by an IS purchase? A standard business tool for measuring the economic viability of a potential implementation of a new technology/information system is a return on investment analysis (*ROI*). By determination of savings and costs, an analysis is made upon which the strategic planning may be built.

Savings

Savings areas include staff time savings, material saving, equipment savings and revenue enhancements.

- Staff time savings include a transfer of functions previously performed by staff personnel to more or less automated functions. For instance, a complete order entry system can eliminate/reduce the time spent by physicians and nurses on the preparation of medication charts, patient care planning (patient charts), results reporting, Kardex maintenance, etc. Some estimates of the magnitude of this range from 5% to 10% [WIL 90].
- Material savings include all kind of profits as, for instance, reduction of wasted meals, wasted medication, wasted disposibles by optimised information delivery, etc.; this means a revenue enhancement.
- Equipment savings includes improved control of the usability of certain devices (resource utilisation, tracking of equipment security), abolition of some devices (typewriters versus multifunctional terminals; PCs), reduced maintenance costs (quality control), etc.
- Revue enhancements, the other major generated savings from installing comprehensive medical IS may be a more complete and precise registration of

medical procedures performed (therapeutic, diagnostic), generating much faster all outgoing patient bills and reducing length of patient stay.

Costs

The determination of system costs represents the second phase in a ROI analysis. The most important ones are :

- Hardware configuration expenses covering all costs related to the procurement (benchmarks etc.) purchase and installation (electricity, air-conditioning)
- Software expenses covering all costs related to the purchase (software license), installation, maintenance and possible education fees
- Staffing expenses covering the investments in man days (month) to install the system, to adapt the application to the proper needs of the hospital (integration aspects), to train end-users and to assure the daily operation of the computer system.

ROI

The final step in the *ROI* is to consolidate costs and savings and project those estimated figures over a certain time period. In Table 21.2 an example is shown of a completed *ROI* analysis over a period of 6 years for a medium-sized potential user hospital.

Table 21.2 Example of a completed return on investment analysis over a 6-year period provided for a medium-sized hospital. (TDS Healthcare Systems Corporation, 1990)

HOSPITAL X
Medical Information System Return on Investment Analysis

	Net Present Value	Year1	Year2	Year3	Year4	Year5	Year6	Total
Realizable Savings	$8,264,811	$0	$370,000	$2,900,000	$3,000,000	$3,100,000	$3,200,000	$12,570,000
Costs	4,571,556	2,000,000	1,700,000	800,000	400,000	400,000	400,000	5,700,000
Net Annual (Cost)/Savings		($2,000,000)	($1,330,000)	$2,100,000	2,600,000	$2,700,000	$2,800,000	$6,870,000
Cumulative Annual (Cost) Savings		($2,000,000)	($3,330,000)	($1,230,000)	$1,370,000	$4,070,000	$6,870,000	

Internal Rate of Return = 44.69%

These calculations are shown here on an annual basis rather than a monthly basis for simplicity's sake. Note that total costs are $ 5 700 000 and total savings are $ 12 570 000 for the 6-year period. The savings total is comprised of numerous specifically defined savings, each supported by management engineering analysis and approved by the hospital manager in charge (Table 21.3). The net present value (NPV) of the total costs is $ 4 571 556, and the NPV of the savings is

$ 8 264 811 using a 10% discount rate for the value of money. The break-even point for the investment occurs early in the 4th year of the project. The internal rate of return (IRR) for the investment in the computer system is 44.69%.

Table 21.3 How to evaluate the benefits

Tangible issues		
ROI	Determination of	. Staff time . Material . Equipment . Revenue improvements
	Determination of	. Hardware expenses . Software costs . Staffing costs
Intangible issues		
System performance	Capabilities	. Functions available . Long-term issues . Integration features
	Level of end-user satisfac- tion	. Ease of use . Flexibilities . Documentation . Degree of support . Reliability . Implementation
	Technical assessment	. Response time . Integration . Improvement of quality of care

21.5 Main Components of a Financial System

As it is not within the scope of this book the main components of a financial system will be mentioned only briefly. A financial system is composed mainly of the following sub-systems (Fig. 21.6):

The general ledger system is the core of the financial management system and provides in-depth, accurate and timely reports concerning the financial status of the hospital. Trial balance reports, general ledger reports and journal reports are essential features besides other functions, e.g. to consolidate financial reports providing an actual-to-budget analysis, to input journal entries.

The accounts payable system is integrated with the general ledger system and the materials management system and provides payment authorisations, detailed accounts payable reports (e.g. by supplier, by referring service, etc.).

The accounts receivable system is also integrated with the general ledger system, patient management system and charge capture system. It includes all functions necessary to manage (status reports, claims, etc.) patient bills, insurance bills and third party bills. The accounts receivable system provides revenue analysis reports and various on-line functions such as debit and credit adjustments and inquiry functions.

The personnel management system facilitates human resource management by maintaining the complete employee record from the date of hire through retirement (position, skills, education, military history, foreign languages, address, family, etc.) and the complete hospital profile (e.g. department profile: functions of the department, employees, managers, etc.). Some systems also offer the advantage of maintaining on-line applicants with the same system. Finally it is obvious that this system should be integrated with several other subsystems such as payroll and general ledger and should have links with other departmental systems.

The payroll system covers payroll calculations and payment. This system also needs to be integrated with the general ledger system and the personnel managment system.

Materials Management

Materials management can be defined as the management and control of goods, services and equipment from procurement, acquisition, receiving, distribution, processing, inventory control and maintenance up to disposition. It is a very important function in hospitals nowadays, as medical supplies takes a large portion of the hospitals budget. More and more vendors are offering electronic order entry systems to facilitate ordering, reducing paperwork and delivery times and finally decreasing the stock needed.

As in other applications, the requirements for integration of materials management, with sub-systems such as patient billing, accounts payable and accounts receivable are rather high. The end product must be the production of financial and cash reports.

Materials management consists of two cycles, purchasing and processing. The purchasing cycle is composed of the following functions :

- ° Requisitioning phase focussing on the method, selection and quantity of ordering that may be done directly on a terminal
- ° Procurement phase stressing the fact that the "cost in use" is as important as the purchase price
- ° Receiving phase which should be centralised as it is important to verify what is ordered and delivered by the suppliers; receipt of stock must be recorded

The processing cycle covers the following functional phases :

- Distribution phase which is often overlooked in hospital materials management and must be part of an established general policy.
  It covers replenishment of inventory stock, pick lists, etc.
- Processing. Purchasing equipment is one part of a global materials management system, but "tracking" the equipment after installation is even more important. This function is often shared between biomedical engineering, finance and maintenance services and has to look after tagging, locations, servicing history, functional and technical descriptions and evaluation of the equipment.

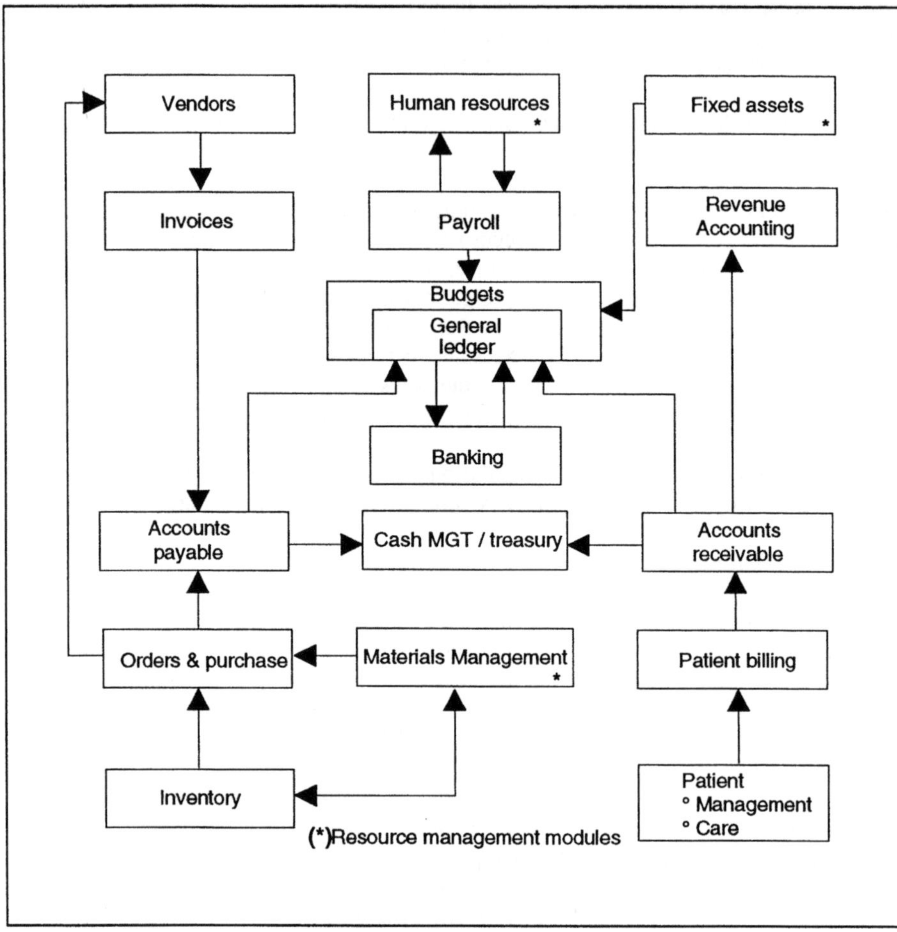

Fig. 21.6 Main components and relationships of a financial management system

- Inventory control through the inventory management system is also an important part in the materials management system. It tracks the quantitity on hand and movement history of each item at each location. The inventory record contains information such as quantity on hand, quantity on order, economic order quantity, expiration date, packaging size and usage history. Medical devices can be classified into some 6000 generic types; an estimated 750 000 or more brands, models and sizes are in use worldwide. As the use of devices is increasing, a classification system for devices not available must be set up.

Decision Support Systems

If the IS is unable to deliver financial as well as clinical data, it is impossible to produce a good executive information system (EIS) in order to make strategic decisions. It is important to stress that "in the minds of executives, EIS is the answer to their prayers. It gives them the information they need to make decisions. In reality, there are no systems that could meet these expectations. Executives haven't defined what they want from EIS. For EIS to work, executives have to have a clear idea about what they want from the system," says Sheldon Dorenfest, president of Sheldon I Dorenfest and Associates, Chicago.

Contracts management involves a wide variety of contracts and monitoring the actual activity or service provided against each contract. Benefits are tracking of contracts and payments.

Case mix management aims to predict practice volumes, analyse trends and forecast the effects of changes in clinical practice by integrating patient information, clinical information and medical information. Examples of output are :

- Cost per patient by treatment group
- Cost per patient by diagnosis
- OR use by surgical procedure
- Actual versus planned patients by treatment group, speciality
- Inpatient admissions and discharges by type, by speciality
- Bed utilisation by treatment group

The budgeting and monitoring module enhances and streamlines the budgeting process by monitoring expenditures versus budget. An example of its output is the production of statistics by budget period at multiple levels.

Medical Computing Applications

Part 3

" When you can measure what you are talking about and express it in numbers you know something about it, but when you cannot express it in numbers, your knowledge is of a meagre and unsatisfactory kind; it may be the beginning of knowledge but you have scarcely in your thoughts advanced to the state of science "

Lord Kelvin

22

Medical Data: Acquisition, Manipulation and Analysis

22.1 Introduction

Nowadays, computers in medicine are often used to capture and analyse signals in real time from different human body sources. The role of computers in signal processing consists of the registration of biomedical signals through data acquisition sensors (transducers), signal transformation, signal improvement (e.g. to obtain a better signal-to-noise ratio, SNR), data reduction/compression, analysis of the signals (feature extraction and pattern recognition) and finally signal classification (Fig. 22.1). In the early days of information processing in cardiology or clinical physiology, the signals were fed into a mini-computer by modem and telephone line or via an intermediate storage device (tape unit, casette recorder). Nowadays, most devices are equipped with their own imbedded microprocessor system. With the emergence of 16 or 32 bit PCs, many data acquisition boards are available for a wide range of bus architectures (XT, AT, EISA, Microchannel, NuBus, Multibus, VME) in contrast to the 1970s when expensive, dedicated equipment was necessary.

In this chapter we only consider those signals created by physiological processes. Whether we are measuring temperature, pressure or compliance, data acquisition is the process of converting one form of energy to another, usually electrical. We put the emphasis on the fact that the concept of capturing and manipulating those signals is almost independent of the source of those signals. Moreover, it is important to stress the similarities between image processing on one hand and signal analysis on the other. Biological processes generate signals, while objects give rise to an image or pattern. In fact, an image is a signal arranged and displayed as a 2D pattern.

The goal of signal processing can be oriented towards prevention (e.g. continuous monitoring in an intensive care unit), diagnosis or evaluation of therapy.

The signal that the system measures may be internal (blood pressure) or on the body surface (bioelectric potentials) or it may emanate from the body (X-ray radiation). The methods used for data acquisition can be invasive (where we "invade" the human body by means of specific transducers) or non-invasive. Finally, examinations can be divided into "passive" and "active" (e.g. stress test). The most important biosignals can be classified in the following categories: temperature, displacement, velocity, acceleration, force, pressure, flow, bioelectric potential, impedance and chemical concentrations.

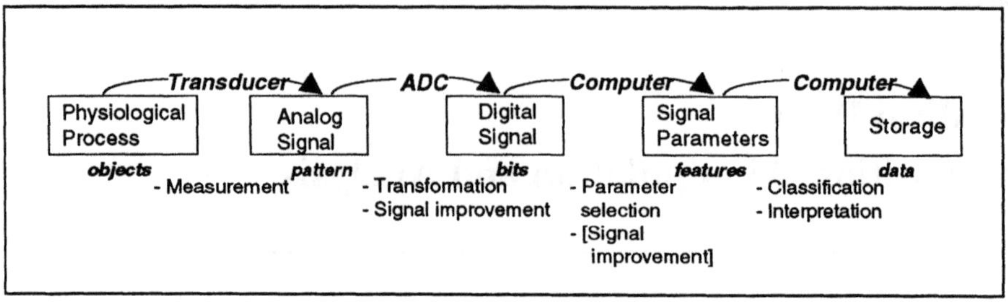

Fig. 22.1 Representation of different stages in signal processing and pattern recognition. Data acquisition involves measuring some physical phenomena. The captured signals must then be "conditioned". Afterwards the signal is converted to a digital form, manipulated and interpreted by the computer. These functions are common to all data acquisition systems

The aim of computer-based physiological signal analysis is to:

- Extract more meaningful information than an ordinary observer can do and to assist the physician in his decision making
- Increase calculation speed and memory size, in order to display the results in "real time"
- Enhance the signal using different enhancement techniques

22.2 Signal Registration

To transform measurements from the human body into electrical signals we need transducers (sensors) which transform the analog signal (sometimes electrical) . Two main problems have to be faced.

First, it is often difficult to bring the transducer as near as possible to the signal source, so the measured signal will be disturbed by signals emanating from other sources, resulting in an increased signal-to-noise ratio (SNR). The transducer is an important element in the registration process of the physiological signal. The emphasis is put on the linearity, frequency range, amplitude range and SNR of the transducer. The type of transducer is dependent upon the physiological signals to be registered, e.g. for ECG registration, transducers are simple electrodes gathering potentials. Other transducers are piezoelectrical transducers, temperature transducers (thermocouples), multi-functional catheters which are able to measure flows and pressures or biochemical parameters.

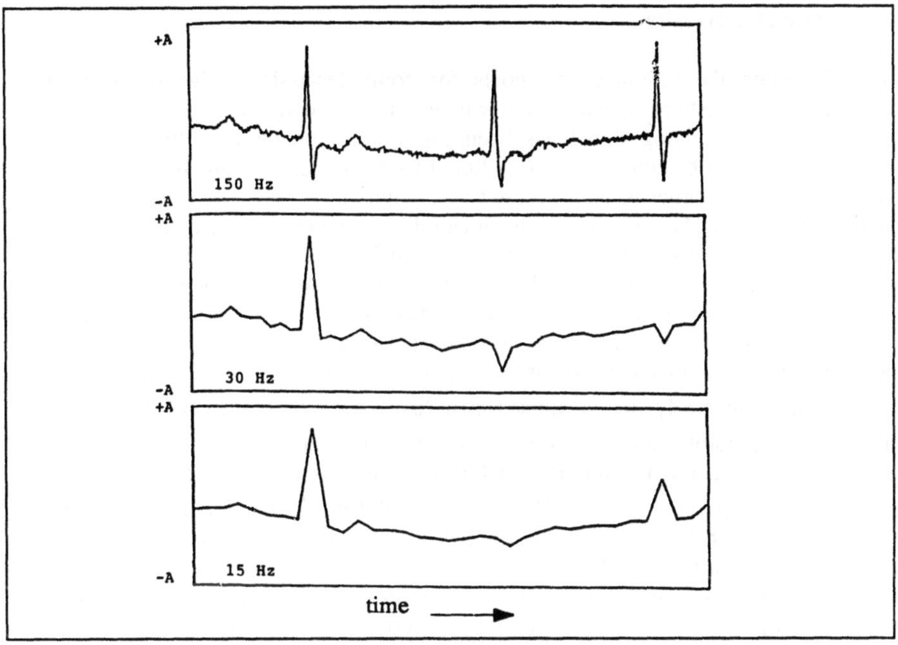

Fig. 22.2 Representation of the impact of different sampling frequencies on an ECG. The sampling frequencies are 150, 50 and 15 Hz. At 15 Hz details disappear. [BEM 89, p 251]

(Source reprinted with permission from Van Bemmel J. and Willems J. in Handboek Medische informatika, Bohn, Scheltema & Holkema, 1989, p.251)

Second, biomedical signals are often non-stationary, and therefore the mechanisms are in many instances not well understood. Only if we have assembled enough a priori knowledge about the signal and its source based on scientific understanding of the process and its behaviour, can we develop effective processing techniques [BEM 83]. Signals in medicine can be divided into [BEM 89] deterministic and stochastic (or statistic) types. *Deterministic signals* can be described exactly and can be further divided into periodic signals (e.g. sinus) or quasi-periodic signals (e.g. ECG, Fig. 22.2) or transient signals (e.g. singular response to an event). *Stochastic signals*, can only be described in statistical terms and are divided into stationary signals, whose characteristics do not change over the time (e.g. EEG signal) and non-stationary signals, which do change in time (e.g. EMG signal).

Prior to signal analysis a model has to be built. This can be physiological, describing the signal source in physiological or anatomical terms; it can be mathematical, reflecting the behaviour in mathematical terms or algorithms; or computational, which is the translation into a computer language of the former models.

22.3 Signal Conversion

After discussing the rationale and goals for computer-assisted signal and image processing, the question is, what shall we instruct the computer to do with these signals? After an analog signal has been captured by means of a transducer, the electrical signal will be converted into a digital form by means of an analog-to-digital converter (ADC) in order to be processed by a computer. The accuracy of the ADC is determined by two factors: the precision and the sampling rate (frequency).
In fact, the precision (resolution) is an indication of how accurately a sample of input signal is represented. The precision is the number of bits used to represent the analog signal. It determines the voltage sensitivity. A 4-bit ADC, for example, transforms an analog signal that varies between -s/2 and +s/2 (e.g. s=1 V), into a digital signal characterised by 16 different levels. A change in a signal of 30 mV will be undetectable. Generally, the quantisation q (n) = $s/2^{n}$ of data can take a finite number of 2^{n} possible values. If we have a 7-bit ADC, and the signal s is 1 V, then the ADC can detect signal differences of 1/128 = 8 mV. If we have a 12-bit ADC and the same signal s (1 V), then the ADC detects signal differences of $1/2^{12}$ = 1/4096 = 2.44 mV, while a 16-bit converter would have a sensitivity of 0.2 mV. Normally, the range of an ADC varies from 6 to 12 bits.
The sampling rate is an indication of how many times (how many samples) the input signal is sampled. If the sampling rate is too low, the representation will be insufficient (Fig.22.3). If the sampling rate is too high, the representation will be fine, but the amount of storage capacity needed will be very large. A fundamental guideline is the *Nyquist sampling theorem* which states that the sampling rate should be at least twice the frequency of the highest frequency component in a signal.

22.4 Signal Improvement

A signal is composed of the real signal of interest and a large amount of parasites (called "noise" and produced by other sources such as electric or magnetic fields of surrounding devices, etc.) and sometimes signals originating from processes other than the one being measured (EEG or respiration in background interfering with ECG) or poor contact (artefact) between transducer and patient. Noise rejection is an important factor in data acquisition applications. So the signal itself has to be improved in order to eliminate those disturbing parasites from the real signal. The aim is to design the transducer in a way to obtain signals with a high SNR. To reduce the effect of noise several filtering techniques can be used.
On the hardware level this is accomplished by shielding, isolation and grounding of cables and devices and not forgetting by improving the transmission modes. Digital signals are less noise sensitive. For transmission over quite large distances, frequency modulation is often used, in which amplitude variations are transformed into frequency modulations.
As it is more convenient and cheaper to modify a program rather than modifying hardware circuits, a lot of "software-driven" pre-processing modules are available nowadays. On the software level, several filtering algorithms can be implemented.
Well-known methods are several transformations (e.g. Laplace, Fourier, Karhunen - Loeve), cross-correlation, auto-correlation and spectral analysis.

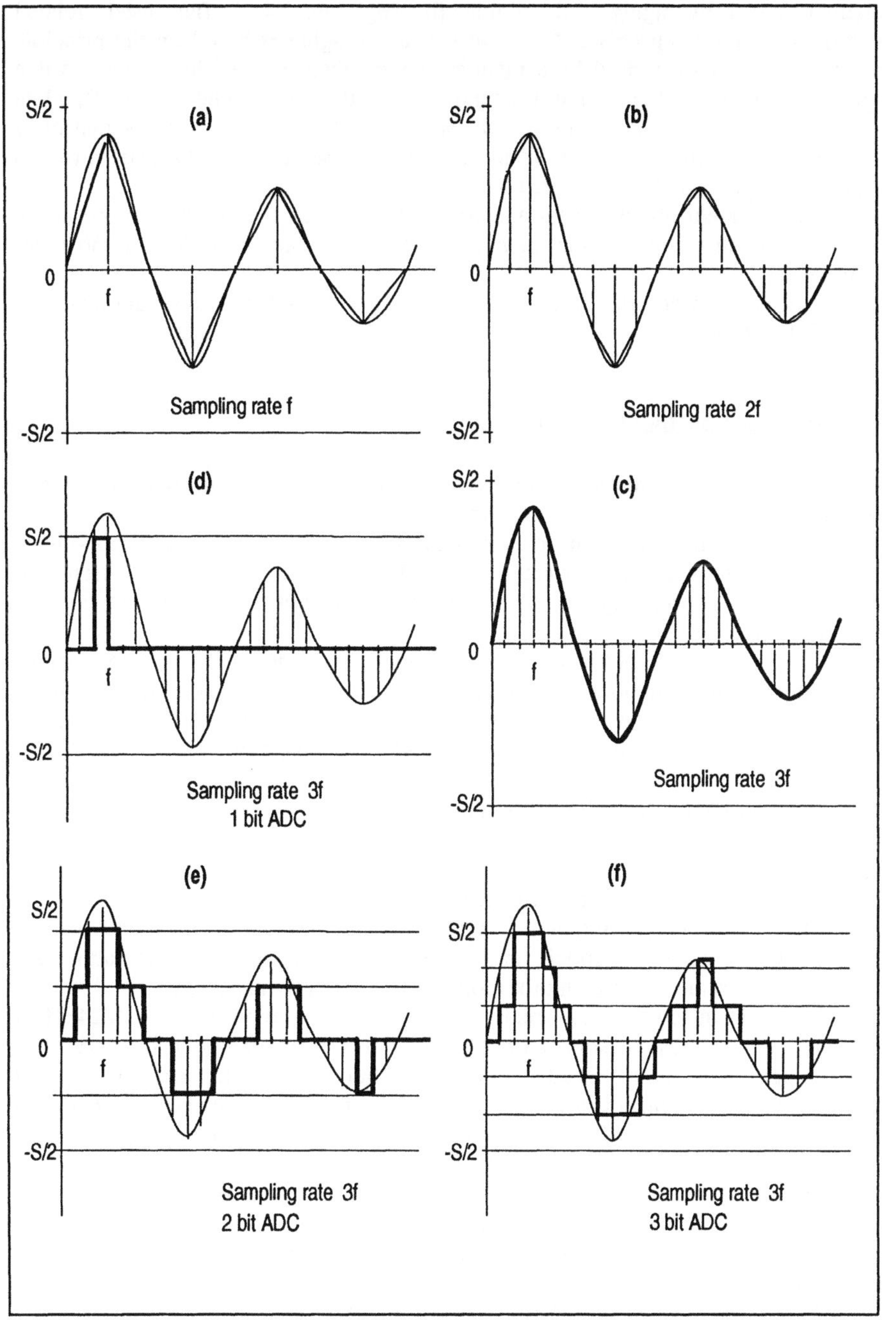

Fig. 22.3 a-f The higher the precision and the sampling rate, the more closely the sampled signal will correspond to the original signal: **a-c** illustrate the effects of an increasing sample rate; **d-f** illustrate the effect of an increasing precision under a constant sample rate

Coherent signal averaging and "digital filtering" are two, often used, related techniques for reducing noise. Coherent signal averaging is based on the principle that as noise is characterised by a random pattern, their average has a lower value than either signal (i.e. the random fluctuations caused by noise tend to cancel), while the average of two identical copies of the same signal is identical to the signal itself (coherent copies will not cancel). If noise is characterised by a regular pattern (60/50 Hz electrical field), it can be filtered out.
Signal improvement affects signal and noise; it decreases the effect of noise at the price of some distortion of the signal. SNR improvements of 30:1 to 50:1 are common.
For a more detailed description of these phenomena several references are available [WIE 85] [BEM 89].

22.4.1 Medical Imaging: Basic Concepts

Medical imaging is a constantly growing field in recent years. In medicine, image (pictorial) data can be of two different types:

- *Computer graphics* for the presentation and interactive analysis of non-image information, such as movement flow, ECG, EEG curves, etc. Here the emphasis is primarily on data structures and not on spatial or contrast transformations.
- *Images* (grey scale or binary) where the emphasis is primarily on spatial and/or contrast transformations, feature extraction, interpretation and enhancement of medical images. Although the data formats themselves are quite simple, operations on image data are very CPU and time-consuming.

22.4.2 Current Image Data Requirements

Typical spatial resolutions are usually of the moderate size of 256x256 pixels to 512x512 pixels, with some important exceptions:

- Digital radiography requires very high resolution images of up to 4096x4096 pixels. In general hospitals, more than 90% of all imaging examinations are X-radiographs, accounting for more than 75% of all images taken.
- The DSA resolution is currently being changed from 512x512 to 1024x1024 pixels. Medical sensors can deliver 8 to 16 bits of amplitude for grey scale images with up to 32-bit overlay capabilities, which increase the required pixel-value storage. Once the images are scanned, they must be managed in an easy-to-use, fast and reliable manner. Digital image data must be retrieved from disks and distributed at high speeds over local area networks with a sufficient bandwidth in order to meet the demanding needs of the physicians.

The functions required by medical imaging include:

- Convolution-type filtering for image reconstruction and restoration (noise reduction, back-projection, etc.)
- Grey level transformations for contrast enhancement (window levelling, etc.) or pseudo-colours
- Geometric transformation for matching different images (warping transformations, mapping of images from different imaging modalities into a common frame of reference, etc.)

- Extraction of quantitative geometrical and statistical data (measurements, ROI statistics, cross-sectional profiles, etc.), arithmetic and logical combination of images, segmentation of images (thresholding, cluster analysis, etc.), computer graphics for facilitating diagnosis and planning therapy (overlay techniques, cine animation, volume rendering, etc.)
- Knowledge-based techniques for the interpretation and analysis of medical images in order to support diagnosis and plan therapy.

There will be an increasing overlap between the computer graphics employed for visualisation and interactive analysis of medical data on the one hand and the functionality provided for scientific visualisation and mission planning on the other.

22.5 Data Compression

After measuring the signals, not all the information contained in the original signal is relevant for feature extractions or pattern recognition. On the other hand, continuous measurement of signals often leads to a requirement for a huge amount of storage capacity. Therefore, one should eliminate the irrelevant details from the signal as early as possible in the processing cycle, in order to improve the efficiency of the procedures to follow. This process is called data compression. It aims to reduce redundancy and unwanted details.
Two important data compression techniques are "thresholding", especially for image processing tasks, and "predictive coding". The former compresses the signal by reducing the amount of data beneath a certain threshold value. Predictive coding is based upon the fact that signal values most of the time do not change suddenly and that therefore the value of a given sample is rather predictable from the immediate past values. Compressed data is still recognisable as a signal.

22.6 Parameter Extraction and Pattern Recognition

In this stage, the parameters or features of a signal with relevance to their analysis are extracted. The set of features, often called "feature vector", is a parametric description of the signal, which is in fact a replacement for the measured signal [SCO87].

Parameter Extraction

The trained physician has the ability when he observes medical signals to extract parameters and patterns in the waveform. The human brain has the ability to bring (structural) order in the chaos that surrounds him.
After acquisition, transformation and compression, the extraction of most relevant features or parameters starts. This phase focusses the attention on the semantic content of the signals. This results in a huge information stream, and in order to avoid excessive storage capacity, redundant information has to be filtered out by a reduction of the signal (e.g. a 25-s ECG provides most of the time, the same information as a 5-s ECG).
The problem is to detect all parameters or contours without too many errors. It is clear that if we have a priori knowledge about the wave form to be analysed we can improve and facilitate the recognition process. In ECG wave form recognition, for

example (P and QRS complex), a process of simultaneous detection and estimation in the ECG is done. First of all, a small part of the wave form is searched for and serves as a first reference point. Based on this, the rest of the signal is registered, and the whole signal can be improved.
Again, we have to stress the fact that quantitative measures from patterns or wave forms have to be based on insight into the behaviour of pathophysiological processes or similar results derived from earlier patients, by the use of a learning population of patterns (e.g. ECG recognition processes). The use of these parameters will be the input for the next stage as well as aids to assist the physician in his medical decision making (diagnosis, future treatment).

Pattern Recognition
As medical decision-making is closely related to classification methodologies, the classification of the "feature vector" into a specific class is called pattern recognition. Several approaches are available nowadays. Some well-known examples are discriminant analysis of parameters, statistical pattern recognition and linguistic approach. On the other hand, it is very important to stress that pattern recognition is strongly influenced by developments in the field of artificial intelligence, following the way human brains perceive and recognise patterns to conceptualise the information that they store. Generally, if one talks about pattern recognition in medicine, it can cover two areas: one puts the emphasis either on processing and recognising images or on arranging specific measured values derived from different objects into groups or clusters.
There are a lot of programs for data analysis and cluster analysis available nowadays for pattern recognition. Cluster analysis is a set of computer procedures which build up or recognise hierarchies or partitions underlying data sets. Data analysis is a series of computer procedures which describe, recognise or identify structures underlying clouds of points. For a more indepth study of this field, we refer to Jambu and Lebeaux [JAM 83] and Van Bemmel [BEM 83].
The main issue here is finding the most convenient classification model and afterwards selecting carefully the parameters upon which the grouping or clustering algorithms will be based. It is interesting to mention that some well-known statistical packages (SAS, BMDP, SPSS) also offer specific tools for clustering purposes. They are all more or less batch-oriented.
Examples of applications in this domain are cell classification, chromosome recognition, trend detection, characterisation of blood cells.

22.7. IEEE (P1073) Medical Information Bus Standard

The medical information bus standard (briefly called MIB) provides a method (backed by a number of suppliers of medical instruments and organisations : Hewlett-Packard, AT & T, Siemens, IEEE, Travenol, Emtek, MIT) for solving the problem of data logging of different medical instruments from different manufacturers to a common interface.
A wide range of instruments used nowadays in hospitals lack a common means for data acquisition and do not even offer computer-addressable interfaces.
From the hardware viewpoint, the MIB is a polled twisted-pair network running at 9600 baud. A bus can have up to 255 instruments attached. Each device is identified

by a number of codes: an ID which identifies each device and common descriptors for each class of machine (i.e. describing the functions and parameters they register). MIB detects automatically whether devices are connected or disconnected.

Types of monitoring instruments for which the MIB was designed to meet these deficiences and needs in communication with patient care IS are:

- Non-invasive and invasive measurement instruments (pulse rate, atrial and ventricular blood pressure)
- Fluid delivery IV pumps and fluid collection devices (chest drainage, urine output)
- Respiratory instruments (ventilators)

The MIB operates under a "master-slave" communications protocol. From the software viewpoint, the master-slave communication protocol is a sub-set of the highly reliable synchronous data link control (SDLC) protocol [GAR 86].

The central device or master communication controller (MCC) polls all the medical instruments and recognises when devices are present or not on the network. A special purpose medical device language (MDDL) has been proposed for message interchange. The slave is the interface between the bedside instrument and the MIB and is called the device communications controller (DCC).

23

Automatization in Cardiology

23.1 Introduction

Developments in Cardiology

In the past15 years there has been a growing interest in techniques that can study the anatomical and mechanical deviations of the heart in a non-invasive fashion. Computers have played an important role in electrocardiology for a number of years. Medical practice has shown an unmistakable trend towards quantification. Computer processing of ECGs has provided an important impulse in this direction. Modern cardiology has become a "high-tech" discipline, comprising a broad fan of applications like ECG and vectorcardiogram (VCG) interpretation, pacemakers, body surface potential maps (BSPM), cardiac imaging (ultrasound, scintigraphy, 3D-MRI), etc.

The Mechanical Heart Function

The heart is a hollow muscle that as a pulsating pump creates and sustains the blood circulation (Fig.23.1). A heart cycle is characterised by two phases :

- *Diastole*, during which the heart is mechanically passive and takes on its maximum size. The aortic and pulmonary valves (AV valves) are closed, preventing back flow of blood from the arteries into the ventricles. The mitral and tricuspid valves open, and blood from the atria flows into the ventricles.
- *Systole* begins after the ventricles are filled completely, the AV valves close, the aortic and pulmonary valves open, and the ejection of blood starts. This cycle is normally repeated 70-75 times/min.

While respiratory frequency is determined from a centre within the brain, the action of the heart occurs autonomously but is modulated by the sympathetic/ortho-sympathetic equilibrium. This means that the source of heart activity lies within the heart itself. The electrical stimulus normally originates in the sinoauricular node (SA) and propogates until it reaches the atrioventricular node (AV). The heart muscle tissue is interwoven with nodal tissue having specific electrical properties and forming the electrical conduction system of the heart. All cells within this nodal tissue can play the role of pacemaker. A number of cells on the right atrium, forming the sinoauricular node (SA node or sinus node), usually fulfil this function.

23.2. The Electrocardiogram

General

The ECG measures the potential differences between a limited number of points on the body surface. A depolarisation or repolarisation wave is propagated in the heart wall, and generates a bioelectrical current that spreads over the entire thorax conductor. By fixing electrodes on standardised locations on the skin, the action potentials of the heart can be measured. The amplitude of the continuously measured potential is noted in one channel (for more electrodes more channels are available), and in this way an ECG diagram is generated (see Fg.23.1). To obtain sufficient information to interpret the ECG correctly, views along several axes of the body are required, by placing multiple electrodes on various parts of the body and measuring the voltage differences between pairs of electrodes. Two systems of obtaining these views are in use today: the 12-lead scalar ECG system and the Frank orthogonal lead vector cardiographic system.

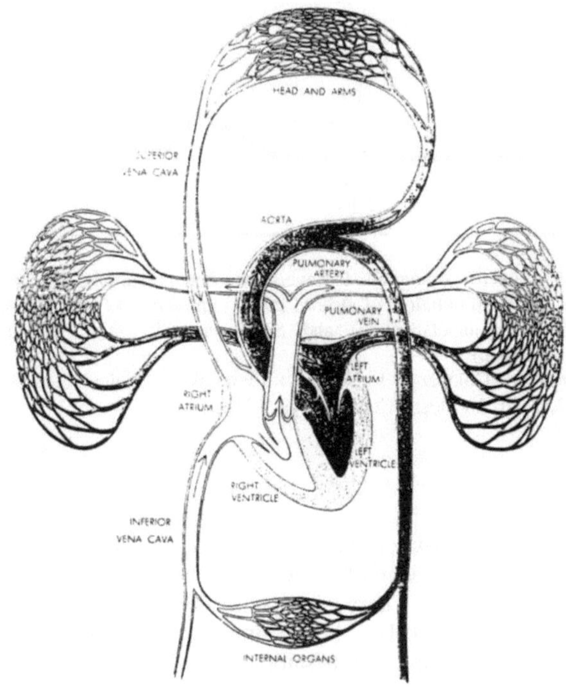

Fig.23.1 Anatomy of the heart and its relationship to the circulatory system is schematically depicted. The arterial blood is represented in bright grey; venous blood, in a somewhat paler grey. The capillaries of the lungs are represented at the left and right; the capillaries of the rest of the body, at top and bottom. The term atrium is now used in preference to auricle [WIG 57].

(source reprinted with the permission of Carl J. Wiggers, in scientific American, May 1957)

Automatic Interpretation and Classification

Computer analysis of ECGs offers important advantages for medical practioners who are less confident about the interpretation. It offers an automated procedure to analyse and process the ECGs in a consistent fashion leading to an improved classification and uniformity in the reporting and archiving (Fig.23.2). At the moment, a number of diagnostic programs exist like the Dalhousie and Pipberger are for the Frank system, the Bonner one for the standard 12-deviations and the Simoen s-program for the ECG registration during a standardised exercise test (XECG). The ECG analysis via a computer can be subdivided into a number of different phases that will be discussed very briefly.

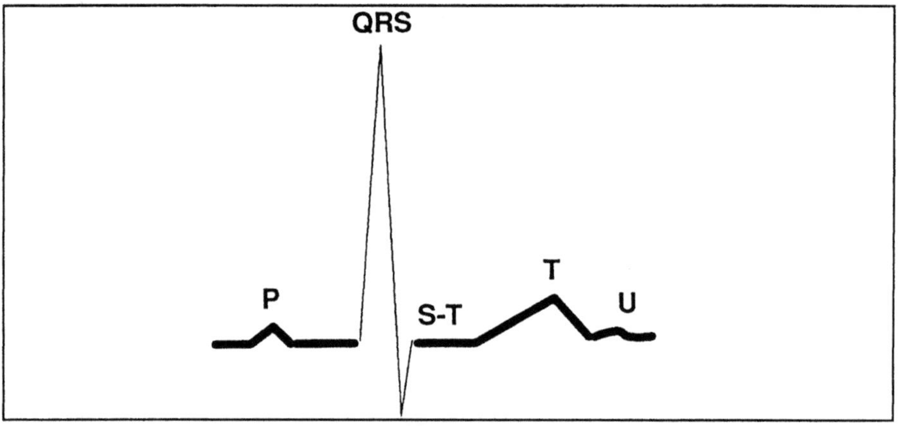

Fig.23.2 Typical electrocardiogram: P wave (atrial depolarisation), PR interval (time span from initial stimulation, of atria to initial stimulation of ventricles), QRS complex (ventricular depolarisation) and ST segment,T wave, V wave (ventricular repolarisation)

(source courtesy of Goldberger E., M.D., : Textbook of Clinical Cardiology, St. Louis, 1982, The C.V. Mosby Company, pp. 125).)

23.2.1 Input

First of all, the identification data of the patient (name, age, sex, weight, etc.) as well as the ECG are registered. Subsequently, the signals are transmitted to the computer by tape, telephone or on-line. These signals are sampled (by an ADC) with a sampling frequency of 250 - 500 Hz. For example an ECG of 5 s (12 leads) has a sampling frequency of 500 Hz and 12 bits/sample ; number of samples is 5 x 12 x 500 = 30 000.

23.2.2 Parameter Extraction and Wave Recognition

In this phase the computer checks the ECG data for the presence of noise and selects only those points which represent the ECG waveform (wave shape). A set of shape, time and amplitude criteria are applied to determine the different regions:

- P wave is the deflection of the ECG tracing representing the depolarisation of the atria (depolarisation is the action in which the normal electrical potential across the cell membrane is reduced by the application of an outside stimulus).
- QRS complex is the deflection of the ECG tracing representing the depolarisation of the ventricles [IBM 74].
- T wave is the deflection in the ECG tracing representing the repolarisation of the ventricles (repolarization is the action by which the cell returns to its normal potential).

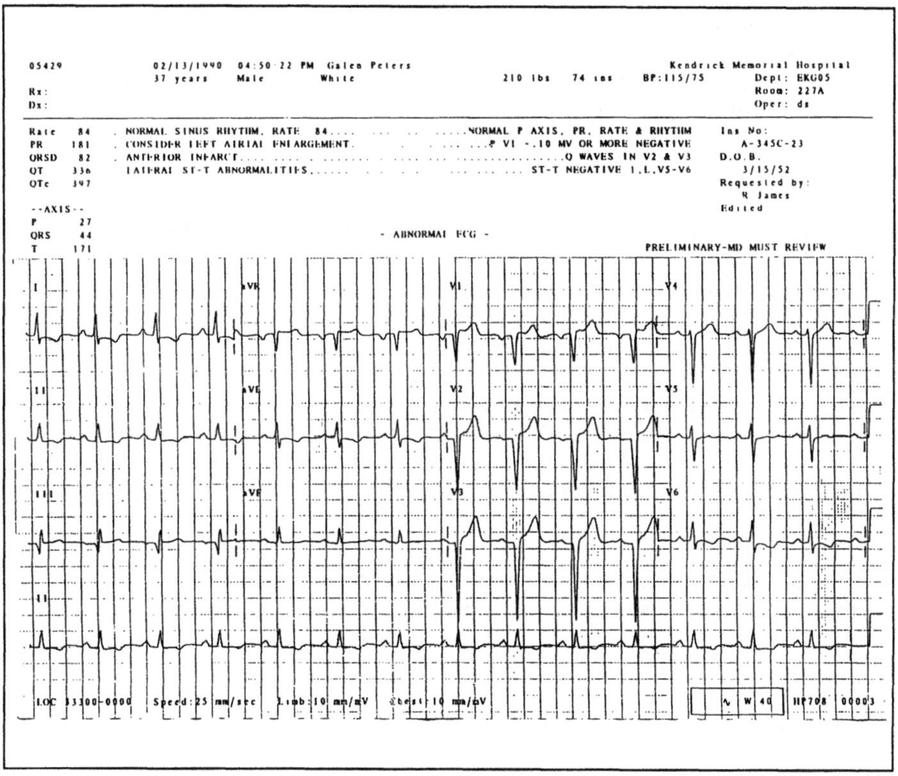

Fig.23.3 Abnormal ECG: interpretative ECG report carrying patient identification, measurements, analysis statements and severity of statement.

(source courtesy of Hewlett Packard Company , Cardiology Business Unit, in *HP PageWriter XL cardiographs*, 1990)

The different wave forms (P, QRS,T) are recognised together with their start and end points. They are also stripped of spurious signals (spikes, hum 50 Hz, noise and artefacts are filtered out). A dominant P-QRS-T-complex is then chosen for contour classification on the basis of a number of selection criteria that are incorporated in an algorithm. Start and end points and as well as the baseline can in this way be determined using a mathematical and statistical methodology. The methods used are developed on the basis of a learning population of ECGs on which human observers have indicated the start and end points of the P, QRS and T waves.

Nowadays, about 15 different systems are operational, of which some are marketed by the industry.

23.2.3. Rhythm and Contour Analysis

A number of parameters are calculated on the basis of which the diagnostic classification can take place.

- Peak amplitudes
- Time duration
- Gradients

Subsequent classification makes use of statistical methods or logical decision trees or a combination of both. Pipberger has performed pioneering work in this area, basing his research on a population of 2 600 patients.

Rhythm analysis considers the regularity of occurrences of the electrical activity of the heart with time. The interpretation of long ECG recordings such as occur in coronary care units (CCU) and ambulatory ECG monitoring is a long and tedious task. By applying a set of criteria, the basic rhythm of the heart and the presence of secondary rhythms or abnormal waves can be determined.
In the case of complex rhythm disturbances most computer programs remain powerless due to on one side the short duration of the measurements and on the other side to the complexity of the problem. Most computer programs can deal with the most frequent rhythm disturbances. Complex problems at this moment must be left to the interpretation of the cardiologist.

Contour analysis uses a representative ECG cycle to determine the orientation of the electrical activity, damaged tissue and other abnormalities of the heart by applying a set of time, voltage and directional criteria.

23.2.4. Output

Finally, the graphical and numerical data are plotted out or printed in the form of a report (Fig.23.3 and Fig. 23.4), after which they are incorporated in the medical file of the patient, which contains patient identification information, rhythm and contour analysis interpretations and other associated measurements. These data can now be archived in the central ECG/VCG database, in order to render comparisons possible. For this option, a centralised computer system is necessary to provide a large storage capacity. It will be clear that, because of the quantity of data and the state of technology of storage media, data reduction must be applied wherever possible.

23.3 The Vector Diagram

The resulting dipole moment of the tissue layer in which the depolarisation or repolarisation is situated at each moment in time is called the *heart vector*. It moves in space according to three loops per heart beat. The activity of the heart can be projected in three perpendicular planes.

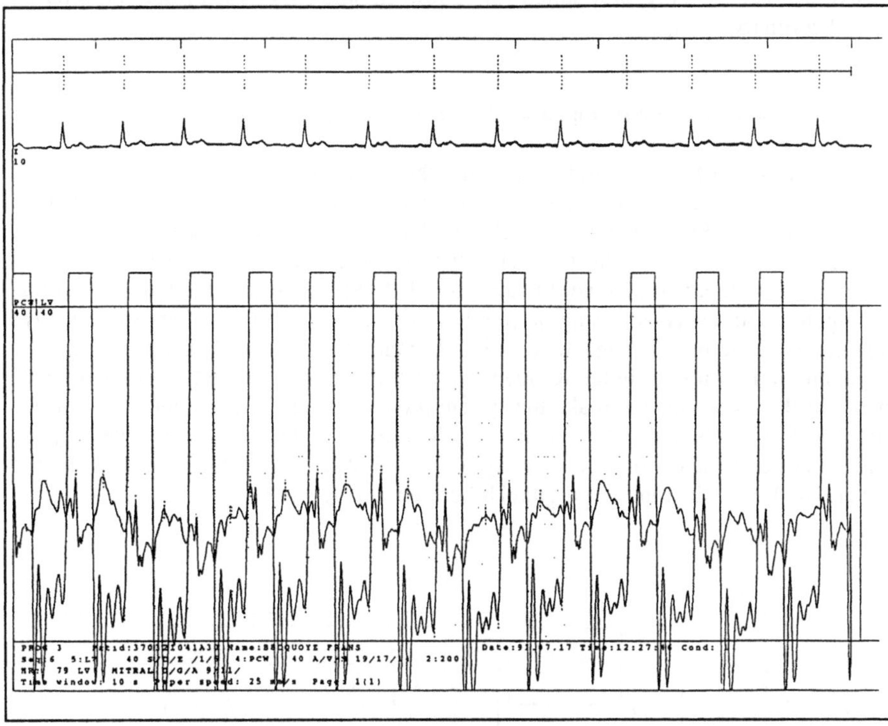

Fig.23.4 Simultaneous pressure recording from capillary wedge pressure (CWP) and left ventricle, mitral gradient 11 mmHg [Micor Siemens]

In vector cardiography the signals from several electrodes are combined, allowing the determination of the action potentials along three principal axes of the body: the tranverse (horizontal) ; (X), coronal (frontal) ; (Y), and sagittal (sagittal) ; (Z) projection planes. In older equipment, the registrations in the three planes are made subsequently. The drawback of this procedure was that the curves were derived from three different heartbeats, making the combination of the three not completely reliable. Currently, the X, Y and Z data from the same heartbeat are stored in real time in the computer memory, increasing reliability and reducing the measurement time. After this procedure the VCG has to be interpreted, a problem considerably more complex than the interpretation of an ECG.

23.4 The Stress Test (Exercise-Electrocardiogram)

For an exercise ECG, the ECG of the patient is registered before, during and after a progressive exercise test, during which the patient exercises on a ergometer, bicycle or running loop. During the conditioned physical stress test the computer stores the data at different stages of the exercise, eliminates interference by applying filtering techniques, extracts parameters and produces reports about the test. This non-invasive test is especially well suited for follow-up studies, or for evaluation after a surgical coronary therapy.

22.5 The 24-h Electrocardiogram (Holter Scanning)

The problem of an ECG examination is that this study only detects permanent heart disturbances. Isolated conduction and/or functions of the heart can only be discovered after very lengthy ECG examination. A long-term ECG or Holter scanning offers a solution for this problem. On a portable tape recorder carried by the patient for a maximum of 48 h, a two-channel ECG is recorded. Subsequently, the tape is read on a computer and analysed using a number of standard criteria that are already programmed. The patient himself can add information by means of an 'event-marker'. Holter monitors with a digital IC memory card are now expected to improve the fidelity of the recording and make the system more compact. The amount of digitised data over 24 h for two channels is about 20 MB, making data reduction necessary as IC memory cards have a limited capacity of 256 - 512 KB [AKI 90]. Fig.23.5 shows a functional block diagram of a digital Holter monitoring system.

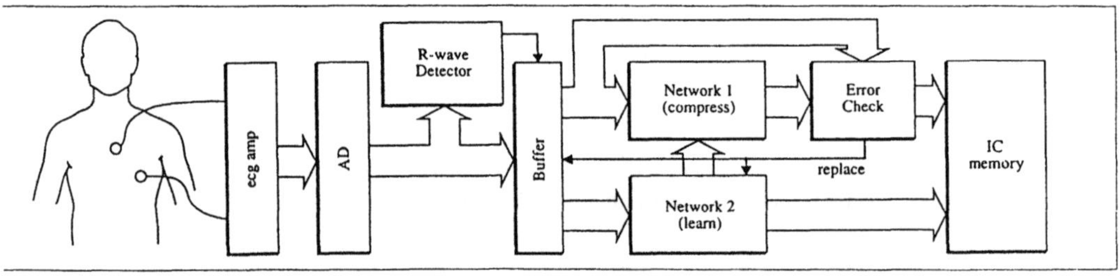

Fig.23.5 The functional block diagram of the digital Holter monitoring system using a dual three-layered neural network. The ECG is measured with two electrodes on the thorax surface and is sampled and digitalized by an A-D converter. The digitized data are sent to the buffer and R-wave detector. The dual three-layer neural networks is implemented on an ANN processor that is composed of digital signal processors. One network is used for data compression and a second is used for learning current signals. The compressed data are stored in IC memory.

(source Akira Iwata, Yasunori Nagasaka, Nobuo Suzumura in *Data Compression of the ECG. Using neural network for digital holter monitor - IEEE engineering in medicine and biology*, Vol. 9 nr. 3, sept 90, p. 53 - 57)

23.6 Body Surface Potential Maps

This consists of a series of graphical or image representations reconstructed by means of recordings using a large number of electrodes (120 - 240) placed on the chest and back of the patient and representing the spatial distribution of the ECG potential differences for the thorax surface or a part thereof. The spatial distribution of the

ECG is traditionally presented as snapshots in the cardiology cycle on maps consisting of equipotential lines (isopotential maps) (Fig.23.6). The huge amount of data is temporarily stored in analog form on tape (frequency or pulse modulation) or fed on-line into a computer system.
Although the debate about the diagnostic information content of these so-called body surface potential maps (BSPMs) (Fig.23.7) as compared with conventional ECGs is still going on and although the research around BSPMs has changed from a measurement problem to an interpretation problem, it is clear that BSPMs are useful when the delivered diagnostic information cannot be obtained through conventional means. For the moment, the use of BSPMs is not widespread. One of their disadvantages is the labor-intensive activitiy when placing a large number of electrodes on the chest of the patient.

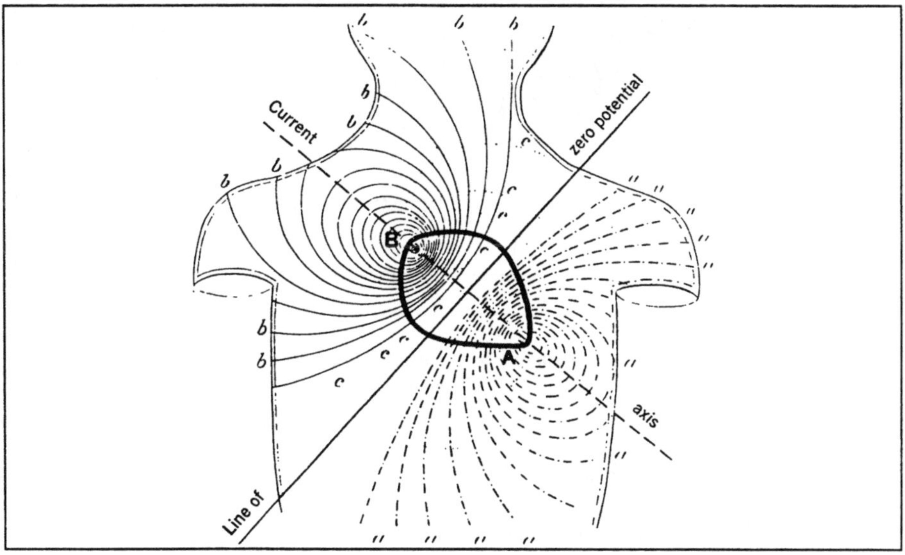

Fig.23.6 Diagram illustrating current distributions and resulting equipotential lines resulting from the ventricular activity of the heart following Wallers
(source from A.C. Waller, 1989. Phil. Trans. Roy. Soc. 180B : pp. 169 - 194)

A modular system for measuring BSPMs has been developed at the Free University of Brussels by Cornelis J., (ETRO division) and at a number of other research centres. In contrast to ECG interpretation, the interpretation of potential maps is mainly qualitatively oriented caused by the fact that the number of cases available is not yet large enough.

23.7 Heart Catheterisation

Heart catheterisation, most often used in the preparation for a surgical intervention, is an invasive procedure during which the cardiologist measures a number of parameters within the heart through a catheter. Pressure and flow transducers are shifted upwards

to the great arteries, the ventricle and the artrium in order to measure the functioning of the cardiac muscle. A visualisation on a computer display unit can assist the physician in analysing the signal and establishing the diagnosis.
Computers can play an important role in this procedure: measuring and representing the graphical parameters, processing them and deriving other parameters such as arterial and venous blood pressure and shunts and stenosis.
A lot of systems are available on the market from well-known companies in this area.

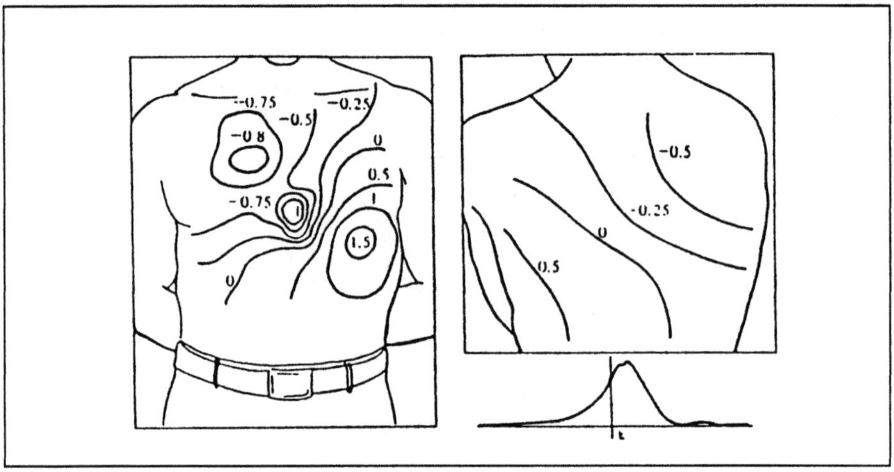

Fig.23.7 Graphical representation of a body surface potential map
(source from A.C. Waller, 1889. Phil. Trans. Roy. Soc. 180B : pp. 169 - 194)

23.8 Pacemaker Technology

The history of heart stimulation is characterised by three stages :

- Temporary pacing using a large external generator
- Semi-permanent pacing using implanted electrodes, connected to a portable external pacemaker
- Permanent pacing using a completely implanted system

The pacemaker system replaces the sino-atrial pacemaker (SAN) and/or also the conduction system transferring the stimulus to the ventricles (in case of a block). A pacemaker system can also be incorporated in a therapy of written deviations as illustrated by the anti-tachycardia pacemaker.
A cardiac pacemaker is a closed electric impulse circuit, consisting of a battery oscillator delivering the current pulse that stimulates the heart (myocardium) via the lead electrode and returns to the battery where the circuit is closed. The electrode can be uni-or bipolar. The tip of the electrode can be placed in the epi- or in the endocardial position in the heart.
The type of pacemaker used defines the frequency of the impulse :

- Demand pacemakers detect the underlying heart rhythm and generate an impulse if the heart rate falls below a certain level.
- Fixed-rate pacemakers send an electric pulse at a predefined rate independently of the heart rate.

Pacemakers are of vital importance to the patient and are therefore submitted to an automatic follow-up by a computer database. Pacing parameters are registered in the database during every patient check-up. The follow-up of these patients is an interesting application for the portable medical record (Smartcard).

24

Automatization in Pneumology

24.1 Anatomy and Physiology

In studying the application of computers in pulmonary function laboratories, there are several aspects comparable with the activities in cardiology (e.g. catheterisation laboratory), although most data acquisition procedures in pulmonary function laboratories are mainly non-invasive. In fact, the computer in the pulmonary function laboratory aims to measure *flows, pressures, volumes, capacitances* and *impedances*. The lung pathophysiology can be rather well described using a mechanical model. The respiratory system can be schematically subdivided into two areas, namely the respiratory passages and the lung tissue (Fig. 24.1).

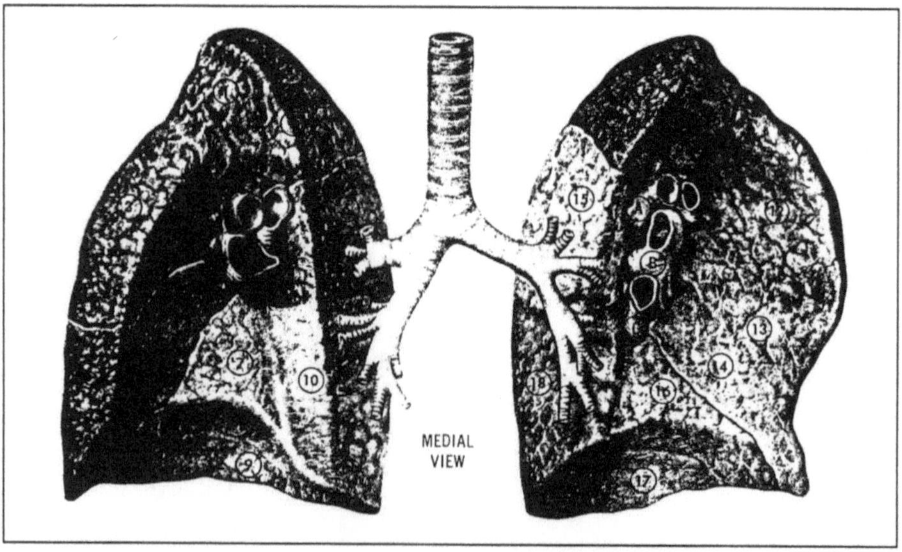

Fig. 24.1 The bronchopulmonary segments. **Lobes of right lung:** *upper* (1, apical; 2, posterior; 3, anterior), *middle* (lateral above; 5, medial) and *lower* (6, superior; 7, medial basal; 8, anterior basal; 9, lateral basal; 10, posterior basal). **Lobes of left lung:** *upper* (11, apical posterior; 12, anterior), *lower division of upper lobe* (13, superior; 14, inferior) and *lower* (15, superior; 16, anteromedial basal; 17, lateral basal; 18, posterior basal)

(source Davis + Geck, *Atlas of Normal Anatomy*; Lederle Laboratories Division of American Cyanamid Company, 1974 [DG 74])

24.1.1 The Respiratory Passages/Airways

The main function of the conducting airways (respiratory passage) is the transportation of gases. During inhalation *(inspirium),* atmospheric air (very poor in CO_2 and relatively rich in O_2) and a variable quantity of water vapour depending on the percentage of moisture in the air are inhaled. In the alveoli, the air is always completely saturated with water. During exhalation (*exspirium*), a mixture of gases rich in CO_2 (6%) and water vapour (6%) and poor in O_2 (depending on consumption) leaves the body. Inhalation is always active and supported by means of the inspiratory muscles (the diaphragm being the most important). Exhalation in rest is almost completely passive, caused by the relaxation of inspiratory muscles and by the elasticity of the lung tissue. During exercise, breathing must be faster, and exhalation becomes active by using the expiratory muscles.

Under normal circumstances, the transport of air occurs very smoothly. Transport can be complicated and requires a larger effort from the respiratory muscles in the case of hindrance by:

- Increased compliance of the thoracic wall (the muscles deform the thorax instead of enlarging it)
- Increased elasticity of the lung tissue (reduced compliance)
- Narrowed respiratory passages (most frequent cause)

The respiratory passages start at the nose, pass through the throat (pharynx), larynx and trachea and subsequently split into the two main bronchi and the five so-called lobar bronchi. These in turn subdivide or split into from two to five so-called segmental bronchi, and so forth. Depending on the level this ramification will take place 16 - 22 times. In the end, there are about 4 000 000 small branches (*bronchioli*).

24.1.2 The Lung Tissue

After the last ramification, the respiratory bronchioli passages split into groups of alveoli. At this level the gas exchange takes place, and O_2 can be brought into the blood circulation, while CO_2 leaves it by gas diffusion through the alveolar-capillary membrane. The pulmonary artery always carries oxygen-poor blood (*venous blood*) in which the O_2 pressure is lower and the CO_2 pressure is higher than in the blood leaving the alveoli. In the alveoli the inverted process takes place thanks to the respiratory motions.

After the gas exchange *arterial blood* (enriched with O_2, and poor in CO_2) leaves the lungs. The total number of alveoli in an adult is estimated to be in the range of 300 - 600 million. Only the air in the alveoli can be used for the gas exchange; the air in the respiratory passages cannot.

24.2 Pulmonary Function Tests

The aim of pulmonary function tests is the determination of the quality of functioning of the respiratory system. Serious defects will always result in a less efficient gas exchange. If the CO_2 and O_2 concentrations in the blood are not affected, we call this a *"compensated insufficiency"* , if they are affected we have a *"decompensated insufficiency*". Pulmonary function tests try to establish at which level the defect occurs.

24.2.1 Spirometry

The lung content is subdivided into a number of different compartments. By definition, we call a compartment that cannot be further subdivided *a volume* and the sum of at least two volumes, a *capacity*. There are four static lung volumes and four capacities (Fig. 24.2). It is not very useful to calculate these eight quantities continuously, since the knowledge of four of them is sufficient to enable derivation of the others.

The four static lung volumes are:

- *Tidal volume* (TV), the gas volume that is inhaled or exhaled with each breath
- *Inspirational reserve volume* (IRV), the maximum volume that can be inhaled starting from the end-exspiratory position of tidal respiration
- *Expiratory reserve volume* (ERV), the maximum quantity of air that can be exhaled starting from the end-inspiratory position of tidal respiration
- *Residual volume* (RV), the gas volume that remains within the lungs after forced exhalation

The four different capacities are:

- *Vital capacity* (VC), the maximum gas volume that can be exhaled after a complete inhalation or can be inhaled after a complete exhalation : VC = IC + ERV
- *Inspiratory capacity* (IC), the maximum gas volume that the patient can inhale from the end-expiratory position that follows a normal tidal exhalation
- *Total lung capacity* (TLC), the quantity of air in the lungs after a maximum inhalation : TLC = VC + RV
- *Functional residual capacity* (FRC), the gas volume in the lungs at the end of a normal tidal exhalation : FRC = ERV + RV

24.2.2 The Lung Mechanics

Using lung mechanics we measure everything that hinders the normal process of gas transport. As in cardiology, the lung pathophysiology can be rather well described using a mechanical model (using mathematical formulas), while the signals measured are low frequency and therefore very well adapted to computer sampling and calculations.

$$P = \frac{V}{C} + \dot{V} \cdot R + \ddot{V} \cdot I$$

elastic forces + resistive forces + inertia

with V, volume; $\dot{V}$, flow; $\ddot{V}$, acceleration, $1/C$, elasticity; R, resistance; I, inertia

Flow resistance is a pressure that must be exercised in order to overcome the frictional resistance in the airway. As the airways decrease in diameter, flow resistance becomes larger:

$$R = \frac{\Delta P}{\dot{V}'} \quad [\text{cmH}_2\text{O/L/s}]$$

Tissue resistance. During inhalation and exhalation, the dynamic resistance of the tissues in the lungs and the thoracic wall must be overcome. Under normal conditions, this resistance is extremely small (less than 10% of the flow resistance). Only in very exceptional situations does this resistance become abnormally high (lung fibrosis).
*Lung and chest wall elasticity.*During respiration, the elasticity of the lung tissue and chest wall must be overcome. The smaller the elasticity, the better the compliance (compliance = 1/elastance). The compliance reflects the change of the lung volume, divided by the exercise pressure (L/cmH2O or L/kPascal).

$$C = \frac{\Delta V}{\Delta P} \quad [\text{L/cmH}_2\text{O}]$$

Compliance and elasticity are static measurements : they are always made at two levels of respiration, but at each of these levels the respiration must stop briefly in order to do so. The flow and tissue resistances are measured during respiratory motion, and in fact this means that a dynamic change is measured.
Inertia. The pressure loss due to acceleration of the gas in the airways is usually so small, it can be neglected.

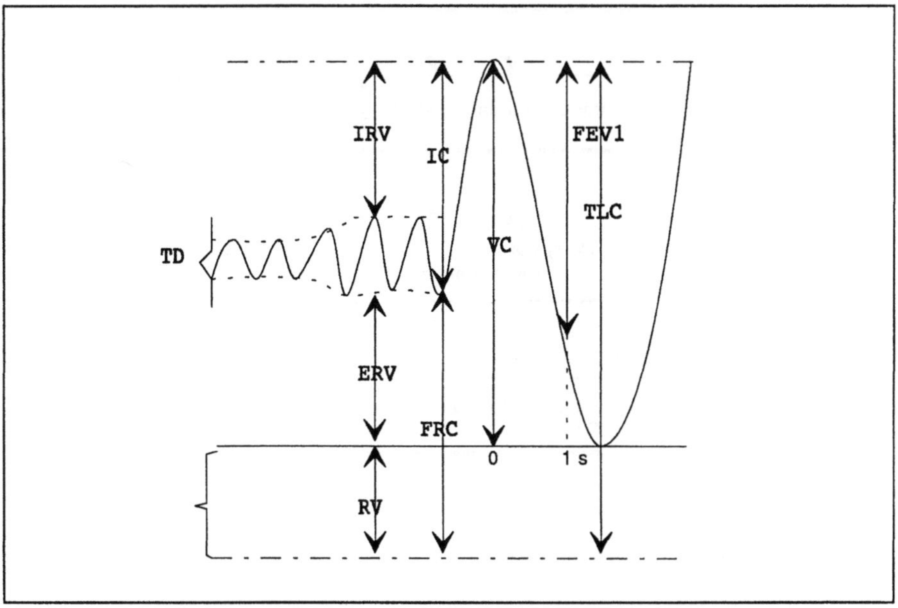

Fig. 24.2 Static lung volumes and capacities: ***VC,*** vital capacity; ***IC,*** inspiratory capacity; ***ERV,*** expiratory reserve volume; ***RV,*** residual volume; ***FEVI,*** forces expiratory volume after 1 s; ***TV,*** tidal volume; ***FRC,*** forced residual capacity; ***TLC,*** total lung capacity

24.3 Pulmonary Function Measurements

During pulmonary function tests, the parameters described previously can be determined by means of spirometry, which gives an idea of the bronchial deviations and problems with the gas metabolism. In some cases, the pneumologist will use an ergometer bicycle in order to determine pulmonary function during physical exercise. Whole body plethysmography to measure static lung volumes and capacities (RV, FRC, TLC) is also implemented through computer processing. Most flow parameters, however, are determined using a *spirometer*. The spirometer registers respiration by measuring the volume of air that enters and leaves the lungs when breathing into a closed system through a tube.
A generic procedure is described as follows (Fig. 24.3). Every day before measurements are to be taken, the instruments need to be calibrated. Afterwards, personal patient data have to be entered into the computer. Then the patient can undergo different measurements.

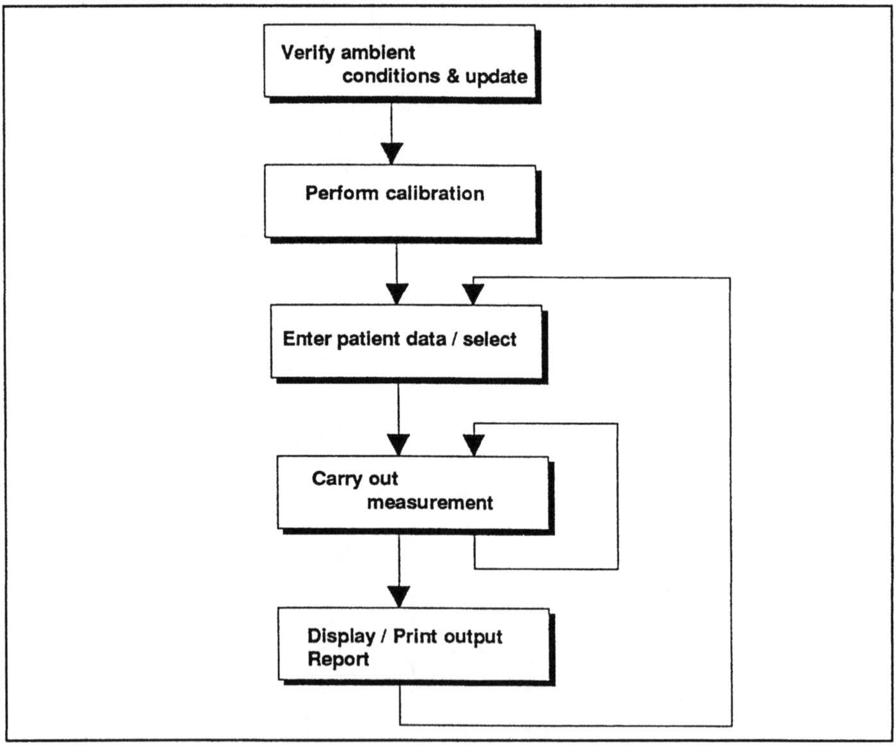

Fig. 24.3 Generic measurement procedure after calibration in pneumology

24.3.1 Spirometry

From spirometry results at tidal breathing we can measure the following parameters (Fig.24.4):

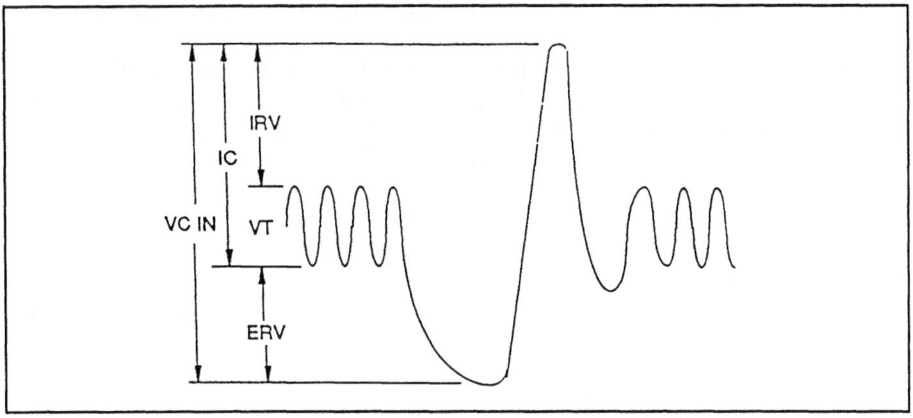

Fig. 24.4 Parameters measured in the spirometry test ***ERV,*** expiratory reserve volume; ***IC,*** inspiratory capacity; ***IRV,*** inspiratory reserve volume; ***VC IN,*** inspiratory vital capacity; ***VC EX,*** expiratory vital capacity; ***VC MAX,*** maximum vital capacity; ***TV,*** tidal volume; ***MV,*** minute volume; ***BF,*** breathing frequency.

24.3.2 Volume Flow Curve

By plotting the breathing parametres, the volume flow curve is created (Fig. 24.5). This test is mainly used for screening, preoperative clarification, diagnosis and surveillance. It includes **FVC,** forced vital capacity; **VC IN,** inspiratory vital capacity; **FEV .5,** forced expiratory volume after 0.5s; **FEV 1,** after 1 s; **FEV 2,** after 2 s; **FEV 3,** after 3 s; **MEF75,** mean expiratory flow at 75% maximal VC; **MEF50,** at 50% maximal VC; **MEF25,** at 25% maximal VC; **PEF,** maximum expiratory flow (peak flow); **FEV1 %I,** in % of VC IN (Fig.24.5).

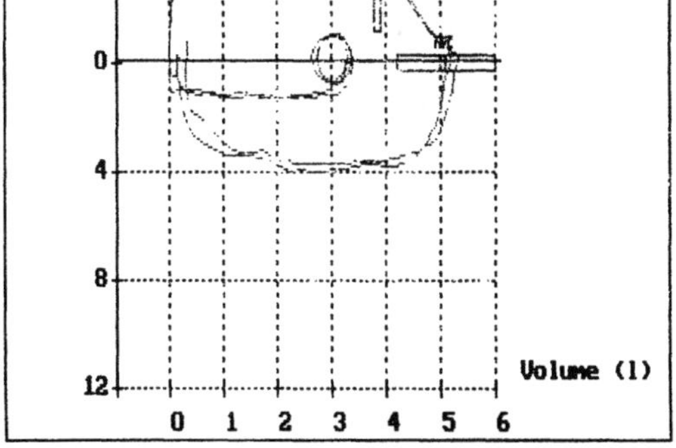

Fig. 24.5 Parameters used in the volume flow curve

24.3.3 Total Lung Capacity, Airway Resistance and Distribution Disturbances

These parameters can be measured by means of a body plethysmograph (Fig. 24.6). The TLC is given by specifying the lung volume subdivisions. The airway resistance is an indication of restricted ventilation with tidal breathing, while determining the distribution disturbances highlights different flow hinderances.

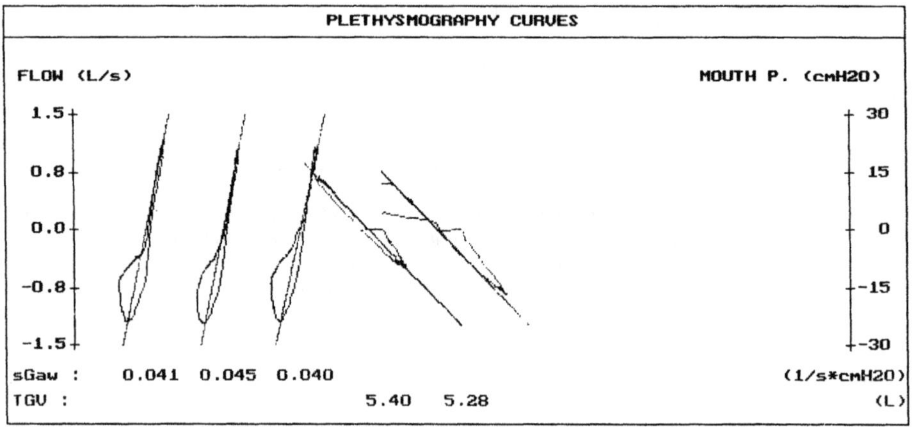

Fig. 24.6 Plethysmography curves

24.3.4 Distribution of Ventilation

The heterogeneity of ventilation is caused by the fact that there exist certain zones inside the lungs at which gas exchange takes place very slowly or by the fact that there are regional differences in the resistance of the respiratory passages. It can be determined by a method based on a single inhalation (SBO2 or single-breath oxygen test). This method is carried out as follows: after a single inhalation of 100% O2, the inhaled gas is distributed in the lungs. During the ensuing exhalation the N2 concentration is continuously measured in the expired gas. Initially, the N2 concentration is zero (phase I, dead space volume), then it rises (phase II) to an alveolar plateau (phase III). In normal subjects, the slope of this plateau, measured between 750 and 1250 ml of expired volume, is less than 2%. When this N2-concentration increases above 2% this can be an indication that certain lung elements are not uniformly filled or emptied, or that a hetergeneous distribution of the ventilation is taking place.

24.3.5 Compliance

Compliance is the reciprocal value for the elasticity of the lung tissue and supplies an indication for all restrictive diseases which increase the elasticity (or reduce compliance) of the lung. Compliance measurements are subdivided into dynamic ones registered during breathing at rest and static ones.

24.3.6 Lung Diffusion Measurements

A measurement of the diffusion capacity (DL) provides the physician with quantitative information on the gas exchange through the alveolar-capillary membrane and the red blood cell membrane. The DL is the quantity of gas (in milliliters) that enters the blood per minute per unit of pressure difference between the gas in the alveolar air and the pulmonary blood (ml/min. mmHg).

In the apnea method, the patient sits erect and inhales maximally from residual volume a gas mixture of air, CO and He or Ne (an inert gas). One of the characteristics of CO is its affinity for haemoglobin (Hb), which is 210 times higher than that of CO_2. At the end of the exhalation, the exhaled gas volume is measured, as well as the dilution of the inhaled gas (Ne or He). From the dilution, the computer can automatically derive DL (Fig. 24.7).

24.3.7 Gas Diffusion Measurement

In theory, this means measuring the speed with which gases are transported through the alveolar-capillary membrane. This depends on a enormous number of different factors:

- *The molecular weight of the gas.* As the heavier the gas , the slower the diffusion. In order to standardise measurement, the same gas (C0) is always used in minimum quantities.
- *The pressure gradient* must be constant to be able to estimate diffusion. That is one of the reasons why CO is used in such small quantities (the pressure in the blood will always be zero because CO is fixed immediately by Hb). When too large quantities of CO are present, in blood back pressure results, which slows down diffusion. In anaemia (lack of Hb), diffusion is slowed down as well.
- *The surface of the membrane.* This is an unknown. One can obtain an approximate idea of the surface through knowledge of the volume. The larger the volume, the better the diffusion. Only in emphysema does the volume increase greatly and the surface decrease (hence the reduced diffusion capacity).
- *The thickness of the membrane.* The thicker the membrane, the slower the gas diffusion. An approximate estimate of diffusion can be made by bringing a quantity of CO, with known partial pressure, into contact with the alveoli for a given amount of time. During the exhalation immediately following this period one measures the quantity of residual CO and calculates the quantity that has been mixed.

The measurement of the reduction in lung diffusion is done by determining the amount of CO taken up per minute and the partial CO pressure in alveolar gas.

$$D_{CO} = \frac{V_{CO}}{PA_{CO}}$$

Two techniques are available : diffusion by single breath method (apnea) and diffusion steady state. The latter has the advantage that it registers diffusion under natural conditions.

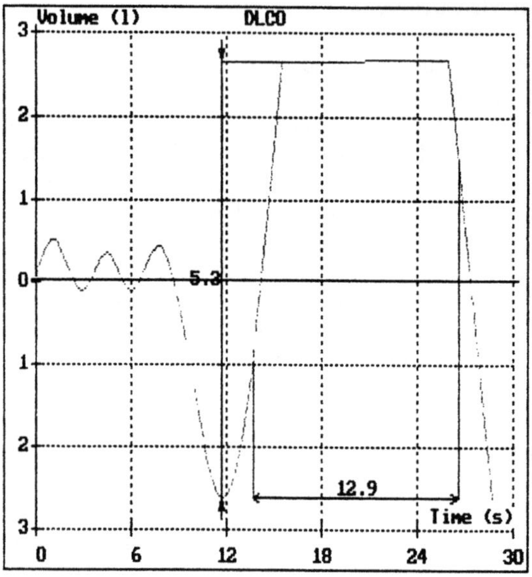

Fig. 24.7 Measurement of lung diffusion using CO

24.3.8 Functional Residual Capacity: Helium Rebreathing

The FRC is the volume of air residing in the lungs after tidal exhalation and is the sum of the ERV and the RV: FRC + IC = TLC. The measurement principle is based on determining the concentration of gas (He) in a space of unknown size (lungs) which decreases the bigger the space volume is. Measured parameters include FRC, FRC% and TLC.

25

Patient Monitoring Systems

25.1 Past and Next Generation Intensive Care Unit Systems

Computers have been introduced into ICUs since the 1970s. These systems were developed by patient monitoring companies (Hewlett-Packard, Siemens, GE, Marquette) and were primarily focussed on the acquisition of vital signs, originating from bedside instruments. They all were characterised by bedside instruments connected to a central departmental mini-computer system, with little computing autonomy at the bedside. Pioneer work has been done by Sheppard on closed-loop control of the patient's fluid balance, by Pryor et al. on broadening the system with clinical staff assistance functions (HELP system) and by Osborn on the continuous monitoring of respiratoıy functions.

Many of these systems installed today have the capability to register vital signs, medications and notes, presenting this information in tabular and graphical formats and making calculations possible. It seems that many of these systems did not fulfil the expectations of the user due to:

- The "people" issue (their inability to change from a manual system they have used for years) is probably the most important factor
- Rigid design and programming cause difficulties in installing requested user modifications
- Lack of integration with the ADT, laboratory and other related departmental systems
- Performance degradation under peak loads
- Less user-friendly interface due to the limited display technology at that time, characterised by extensive hierarchical menu-driven screens. Fancy graphics are perhaps not the "answer to all the world's problems," explains R. M. Gardner. In the LDS Hospital (Salt Lake City, Utah) they have spent lots of time working on graphics interfaces and in many cases have concluded that numerical representation of things like K + and Na + is better than graphical presentation because small changes are sometimes very crucial. They actually made people take plots and write the numerical values on the plot

The success of a computerised ICU depends on many factors: the organisation, the acceptance of the system, its reliability and the integration aspect. The situation nowadays is that most commercial ICU systems are not well accepted (especially by nurses) because of their lack of user-friendliness. The so often claimed advantage of "....nurses who will have more time available for direct patient care..." [BEM 84] seems to be far from the reality. That will change as next generation ICU systems will address a much broader information management problem, clinical as well as administrative and managerial with the help of new technologies: distributed network computing, high bit mapped work stations, RDBMS and graphical user interfaces.

25.2 The Role of Computers in Monitoring

The total management of today's ICUs is a complex task that involves many health care providers confronted with the delivery of a variety of information used in making diagnosis and therapeutic decisions. A typical critical care patient generates each day much medical data that should be transcribed tediously into a paper medical record (Fig. 25.1). In order to improve the productivity of an ICU, the information collected from ancillary services, bedside devices, physicians and nurses has to be streamlined and timely accessed through very friendly and easy-to-learn graphical user interfaces based on the efficient use of advanced windowing techniques in order to produce cumulative, comparable (graphical) reports (Fig. 25.2). Although these information management activities do not have an immediate impact on the patient's illness, they are crucial for the operation of the unit.

Computers installed in ICUs focus on two objectives in order to improve patient care [GAR 86]: integrated patient management and monitoring of physiological parameters. Some vendors are now offering state-of-the-art monitoring systems, in which patient monitoring and clinical monitoring seemed to be integrated (e.g. companies such as HP Care View, EMTEK, Marquette/Clinicomp, etc.). Let us focus on those two kinds of capabilities.

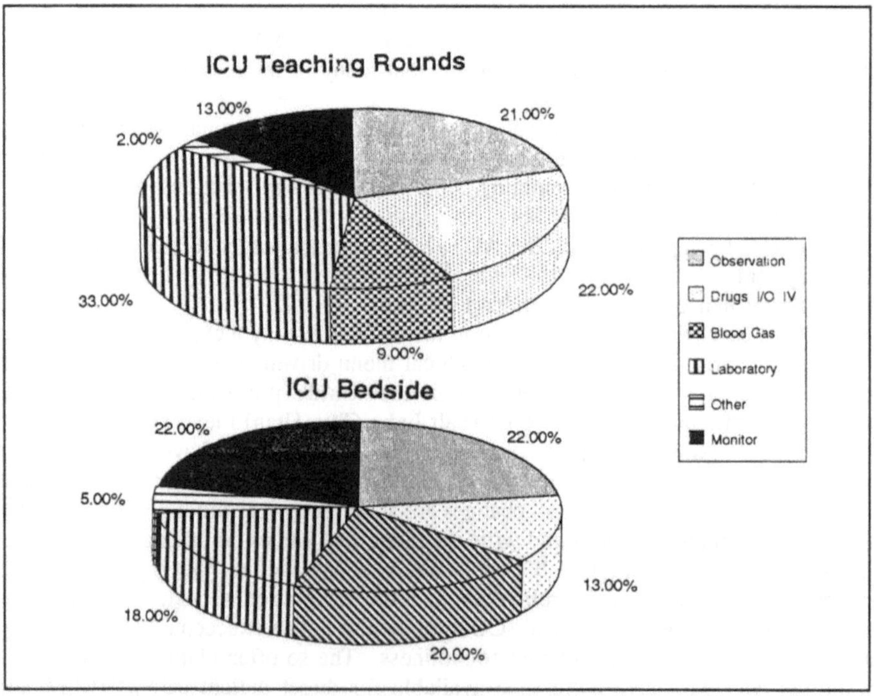

Fig. 25.1 Information used in the intensive care unit [BRA 84]
(Source : reprinted with permission from Bradshaw KE, Gardner RM, Clemmer TP, Orme JF Jr, Thomas F, West BJ. *Physician Decision-Making-Evaluation of Data used in a Computerized ICU.* Int J. Clin Monit Comput 1984; 1:81-91. Gardner RM. Computerized management of intensive care patients. MD Computing 1986; 3(1):36-51.)

25.2.1 Integrated Patient Management

A large variety of information has to be dealt with and displayed in a user-friendly way to assist in critical care management decisions. Important patient data arrive from different locations, services and health care actors and need to be presented in a *broad integrated computerised ICU record* tailored to the need of each user. Few exceptions (e.g. LDS Hospital HELP System) exist in which these administrative, medical and nursing procedures are integrated. Often manual duplicate input is necessary to provide this integration. Fig.25.2 represents the results of a work sampling study [BRA 89] comparing time spent on care, charting etc. before and after implementation of a computer-based charting. The most important features to be provided in an integrated patient management system are:

- *Nursing assessment* helps the nurse to register the condition of various organ systems, by pre-defined choice mechanisms as well as by the introduction of free notes.
- *Nursing care plans* provide a shift-based chronological summary of all tasks that have to be accomplished by nurses for all patients related to that specific ICU. It covers scheduled medications, treatments and nurse activities.

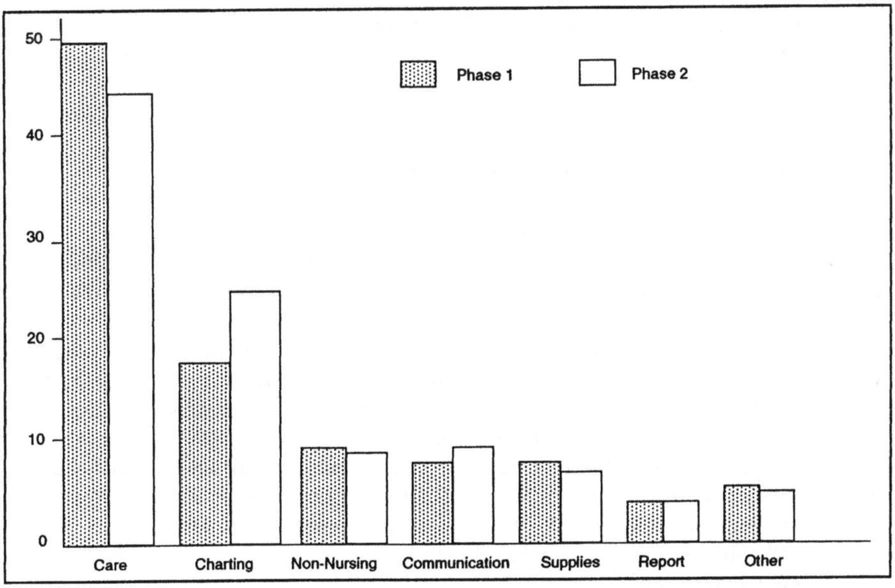

Fig. 25.2 Results of phases 1 and 2 of the work sampling study, conducted before and after implementation of computer-based charting. The study showed a decrease in the percentage of time spent on patient care and an increase in the percentage spent in charting after installation of a computing system. [BRA 89]

(Source : reprinted with permission of Karen, N.E. Bradshaw, Ph.D., Dean F. Sittig, Ph.D. Reed M. Gardner, Ph.D., T. Allan Pryor, Ph.D., and Marg E. Budd, R.N.,M.S. in *Computer-Based data entry for nurses in the ICU*, MD Computing, Vol. 6 nº 5, 1989, pp. 274 -280. [BRA 89])

- *Nursing acuity* provides an "up-to-the-minute" perspective on nursing utilisation per patient in the critical care environment. The estimation of patient acuity is based on time weightings (user-defined acuity points) associated with each performed task.
- *Vital signs and flowsheets* permit health care providers to record and review vital signs data on an hourly or more frequent basis, obtained through bedside instrumentation or entered by physicians or nurses. Graphic trends of vital signs on screen or hard copy are totally automated.
- *Lab results* must be transcribed into the system, instead of being entered manually (phone or printed), so the system has to interface with the laboratory computer system.
- *Order entry and communications* provide the facility for introducing the physician's and nurses orders, which will be duplicated into flowsheets, work lists (task list) and medication lists.
- *Calculations* can be derived from other manually or automatically entered data, e.g. severity of illness indices (such as APACHE II, CIS, etc.), intake/output and cardiac and respiratory functions.
- *Drug administration and fluid balance*
- *Reports* have to be scheduled or printed on demand and customised depending on the type of report desired.
- *ADT* module has to provide a tool to enter each patient's demographic data, history and admitting information, to assign the patient to a bed or to transfer a patient from one bed to another.

25.2.2 Monitoring of Physiological Parameters

Intensive care units (ICU), coronary care units (CCU) and operating theatres (OR) have evolved into one of the most highly computer-intensive areas in a hospital. In such areas, where each patient may generate hundreds of data values per day, the task of managing clinical and physiological data can easily overload traditional record-keeping systems. The real-time monitoring (acquisition, processing, storing, alarms and display) of related physiological parameters of critically ill patients or during the performance of medical procedures is one of the main objectives. As a human is a complex system, effective regulation depends highly on feed-back from important vital parameters, generated by continuous measurements, signal analysis and signal processing (such as the electrocardiogram (ECG), pulse oximeter SaO2, respiratory gases, blood pressure, etc...). A monitor is conceptually segmented in a set of hardware and software building blocks (Fig.25.3):

°signal acquisition	(hardware)
°parameter and signal processing	(software)
°monitor control and data input	(hardware & software)
°display unit	(hardware)
°communication unit	(software)

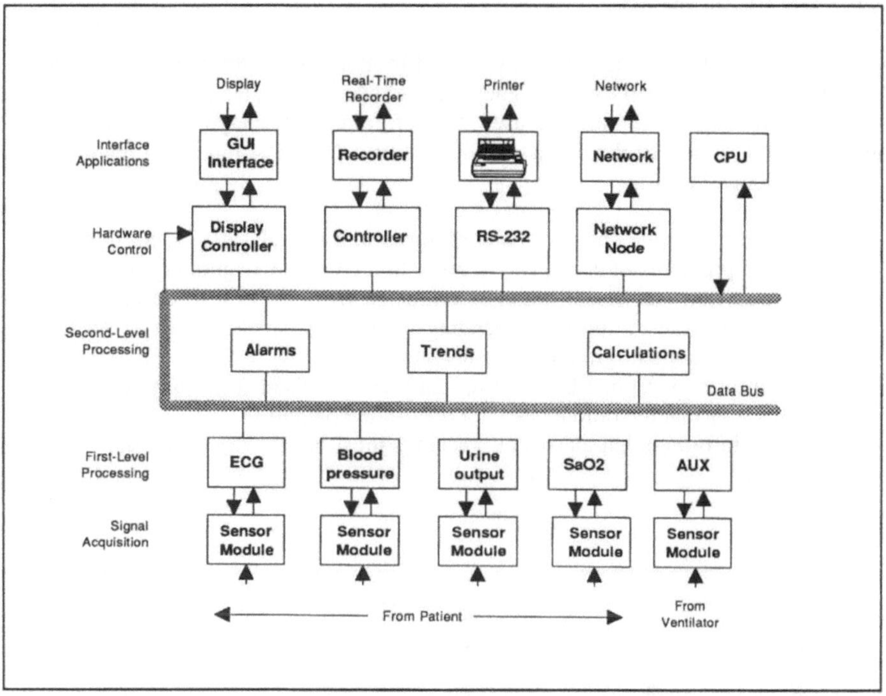

Fig. 25.3 Functional block diagram of a patient monitoring system [WES 91].
(Source: Adapted from Westerteicher C. in *Introduction to the HP component monitoring system*, Hewlett-Packard Journal, October 1991, pp.6-10)

In the past, most functions were performed by a central supervisory mini-computer system, which polled and communicated continuously all signals. Nowadays, with the advances in microprocessor technology, most medical instruments are equipped with multiple microprocessors so that a lot of processing is executed in the medical device at the bedside. By the limited intelligence in the bedside patient monitor, the emphasis of the central departmental monitoring computer is shifted towards more data management functions such as dynamic data management, retrieval (graphical, trends, conditions) and processing. The benefits of the emergence of microcomputer-based monitoring devices are:

- Sophisticated pattern recognition and wave form feature extraction
- Much smarter alarms, instead of previous high/low range values, because of a better signal quality acquisition
- Easier to update by upgrading the software

The ICU departmental computer represents in that way the gateway towards other "externally" located hospital computer systems or departments such as laboratory, admission, radiology and pharmacy.

25.3 The Requirements

Due to the variability of the pathology treated in many units, the requirements upon monitoring systems are very broad. They have to be versatile, adaptable (modular) to every medical situation and easy to use. This offers the advantage that each monitor can be tailored to best fit the patient medical status. The most important features are briefly mentioned hereafter :

- Monitoring systems have to be configured in a modular way according to the medical problems of each patient: arrhythmia module, respiratory module, etc.
- Reproduction and visualisation of extracted features have to be displayed in almost any desired format, depending upon the personal wishes of nurses or physicians: tabular, graphical, trends, etc.
- This information must be retrieved and decentralised (from any terminal) in such a way that the output does not disturb the patient.
- Soft or informational alarms or warnings must be adapted to the status of the patient.

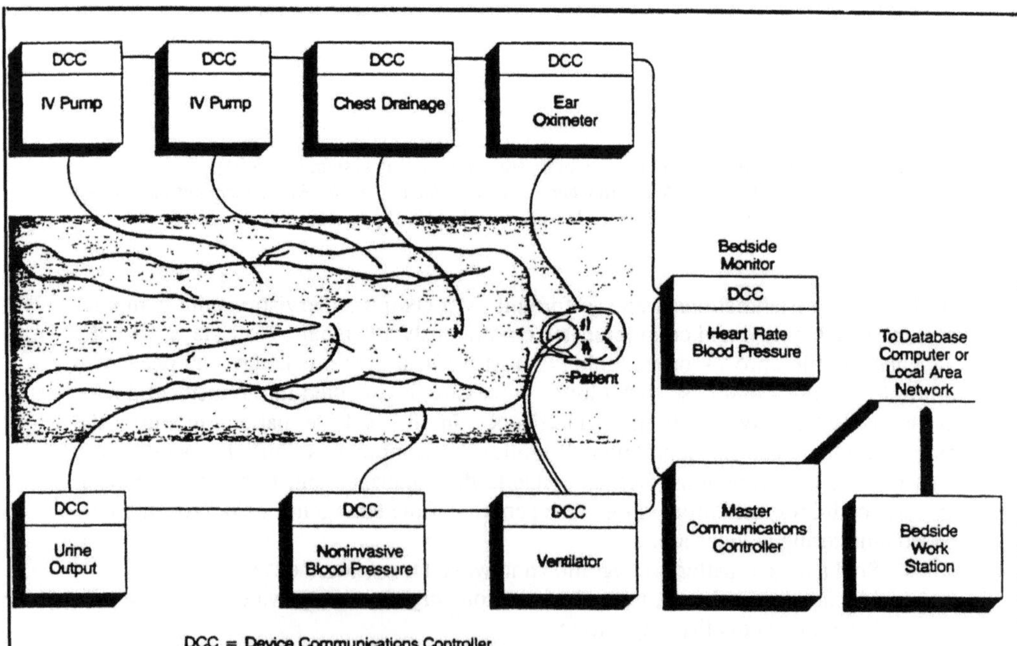

Fig. 25.4 Medical information bus (MIB) data collection in intenvise care unit, from a variety of bedside monitors: *DCC,* device communications controller [BRA 84]

(Source : reprinted with permission from Bradshaw KE, Gardner RM, Clemmer TP, Orme JF Jr, Thomas F, West BJ. *Physician Decision-Making-Evaluation of Data used in a Computerized ICU.* Intl Clin Monit Comput 1984; 1:81-91. Gardner RM. Computerized managment of intensive care patients. MD Computing 1986; 3(1):36-51.)

25.4 Areas and Functions

An increasing number of biosignals (ECG, EEG, blood pressures) are the basis of continuous or intermittent patient monitoring and diagnosis. Future biosensors will include continuous blood gases, chemical and clinical analyses. As is often the case, these biosignals are currently acquired and processed using multiple proprietary monitoring devices, and a standard digital representation for them would facilitate access to the patient's history and aid decisions of clinicians (Fig. 25.4).
Simple monitors display ECG and heart rate. More sophisticated monitors can analyze ECG, note arrhythmias, monitor respiratory status and measure intravascular pressures and arterial and mixed venous oxygen saturation. Computerised monitoring can be found in several areas within the hospital: coronary care, intensive care (monitoring situations during shock), postoperative care, neonatal care, haemodialysis and generally during situations in which the effect of anaesthesia should be controlled (e.g. in the OR during surgical interventions). The functions that may to be monitored in an ICU are (Table 25.1):

Vital signs:
Cardiovascular signals. The system examines each patient's ECG samples for ectopic beats and performs the following measurements:
Heart rate
Cardiac arrhythmias are alterations of cardiac rhythm that disrupt the normal synchronised contraction sequence of the heart and reduce pumping efficiency.
An arrhythmia monitor system is an automated system for the early detection and warning of VPB (ventricular premature beats, sometimes also called PVC or premature ventricular contractions; beats are classified as VPB if they are premature and do not match the shape of the normal QRS complex) and most other premonitory or life-threatening cardiac arrhythmias. A continuous display of the medical status of all patients monitored and visualisation of their trends over the past few hours permits a constant feed-back to the various therapies provided. All VPB types are counted, and the ventricular rate (VR) is derived and eventually displayed. It was discovered after monitoring cardiac patients "preventively" for arrhythmias on a continuous long-term basis that arrhythmias were frequently preceded by less serious dysrhythmias such as VPB, which could be successfully treated by anti-arrhythmic drugs and electronic pacemakers. Some studies show that arrhythmias occur in nearly 80% - 90% of all patients suffering from a myocardial infarction.
QRS shape, identifying the QRS complexes (derived from the heart rate in beats per minute and asystole detection) and providing information for arrhythmia analysis
Ventricular fibrillation as determined by the shape and rate of the signal, looking for round, rolling, low-amplitude waves occurring at a rate of 250 - 300 per minute
Respiratory signals cover respiratory frequencies, volumes, flows and analyses of respiratory gases during exhalation and inhalation (CO/N2 diffusions), from which compliance and other parameters are calculated. The majority of respiration monitoring is done through the technique of transthoracic impedance plethysmography. In this process, a tiny constant current is driven through the patient (ECG lead). As the patient breaths, the change of the electrical impedance across the thoracic cavity is measured. Since the current is constant, a variable voltage waveform is generated. This waveform is processed to determine respiration rate and to detect apnea. Unfortunately, transthoracic impedance varies not only with

respiration but also will mechanical and fluid volume changes in the chest. For example, motion of the patient and even perfusion of the thoracic cavity after each heartbeat can contribute significantly to this waveform. It is the responsibility (quality) of the IS to distinguish a valid respiratory event and the lack of it (apnea).
In the Hewlett Packard 78534A monitor terminal, for instance, the respiration module continuously compares the measured respiration events to QRS events as detected by the ECG module. If a patient stops breathing and a large heart artefact remains, the monitor will detect that these signals are coincident and the respiration alarm will not be inhibited. The amplifier response is also adjusted as a function of the respiration rate. This recognises that as patients breathe more slowly, then they must breathe more deeply in order to maintain the minute volume. It also realises that at high respiration rates the patient will compensate for the proportionally large dead space. These features contribute significantly to artifact rejection.

Fluid management
This consists of measuring fluid losses, e.g. drainage and urine.
In a critically ill patient, the normal mechanisms regulating the complex fluid equilibrium are frequently disorganised. Disturbance of this fluid equilibrium can have an impact on cardiac and pulmonary functions. By measuring the fluid losses, the computer can calculate the necessary infusion rate and gives alarms in case of unbalanced weights. The physician needs help to manage these factors and relies on the measurement of the patient's body weight, height, amount of fluid taken in (oral and intravenous), salt intake and amount of fluid loss (urine, bowel movements, skin). These relations change with activity, temperature, nutrition and administered medications.

Measured data :
Neurophysiology
Brain functions are monitored by carotid flows and pressure, intracranial pressure, EEG parameters and brain maps.
Electromyography (EMG and EEG samples)

Registered data :
Lab results
Drug infusion calculations
Blood gases measurements : arterial, venous, transcutaneous O_2 / CO_2
Medication administering
Temperature (venous, body)
Renal functions (electrolyte loss, clearance of creatinine)
Haemodynamic analysis

Table 25.1 : Overview of biosignals as a basis for continuous or intermittent patient monitoring

Montioring parameters

Cardiovascular and haemodynamic monitoring:

- ° Heart rate
- ° ECG
- ° Systolic, diastolic and mean arterial pressure
- ° Pulmonary artery pressure (systolic, diastolic and mean)
- ° Pulmonary capillary wedge pressure
- ° Central venous pressure
- ° Cardiac output
- ° Stroke volume
- ° Cardiac index
- ° Stroke index
- ° Right ventricular stroke work (index)
- ° Left ventricular stroke work (index)
- ° Systemic vascular resistance
- ° Pulmonary vascular resistance

Continuous electrocardiography:

- ° ECG samples
- ° Trend curves
- ° Arrhythmic events
- ° Heart rate variability
- ° S-T segment deviations

Respiratory parameters:

- ° Inhaled O_2 fraction
- ° Exhaled O_2 fraction
- ° End-total CO_2 fraction
- ° Concentrations of volatile anaesthetics
- ° Arterial O_2 tension
- ° Arterial O_2 saturation
- ° Arterial O_2 content
- ° Mixed venous O_2 tension
- ° Mixed O_2 saturation
- ° Mixed O2 content
- ° Arterial CO_2 tension
- ° Arterial pH
- ° O_2 consumption
- ° O_2 production
- ° Arterio-arterial O_2 gradient
- ° O_2 extraction rate
- ° O_2 delivery
- ° O_2 consumption
- ° Alveolar-arterial O_2 gradient
- ° Venous admixture
- ° Respiratory rate
- ° Tidal volume
- ° Minute ventilation
- ° Airway pressure (peak, mean and end-expiratory)
- ° Dead space
- ° Alveolar ventilation
- ° Lung-thorax compliance
- ° Airway resistance

Respiratory function parameters:

- ° Vital capacity
- ° Total lung capacity
- ° Functional residual capacity
- ° Maximal expiratory flow
- ° Residual volume
- ° Peak expiratory flow
- ° Forced expiratory volume
- ° Lung volume by an indicator gas
- ° CO diffusion parameters
- ° N_2 diffusion parameters

Measured parameters

Stress test:

- ° Samples of ECG
- ° Heart rate
- ° Arrhythmic events
- ° S-T segment deviation
- ° Blood pressure
- ° O2 consumption
- ° Work load

Coronary arteriography:

- ° Coronary arteriographic pictures
- ° Ejection fraction data
- ° ECG samples

Echocardiography:

- ° Samples of echocardiography pictures
- ° Left ventricular dimensions
- ° Right ventricular dimensions
- ° Left atrial dimensions
- ° Dimensions of mitral and aortic valves

Renal function parameters:

- ° Glomerular filtration rate

Neurophysiology

Electromyography

Electroencephalography:

- ° Samples of multi-channel EEG curves
- ° EEG characterisation results
- ° EEG maps
- ° Multi-dimensional brain maps

Sleep laboratory:

- ° Samples of multi-channel EEG curves (up to 64 channels)
- ° Samples from video monitoring of patients
- ° Transcutaneous blood gas monitoring

Registered data (patient demographics)

Pacemaker implantation:

Type of pacemaker
Pace mode
Pulse duration
Current threshold
Voltage threshold
Lead data

Laboratory data (enzymes, electrolytes, haemoglobin):

Blood pressure
Pulse rate

Other parameters:

Central temperature (arterial/venous)
Peripheral temperature
Muscle relaxation
Evoked potentials
Body surface area
Energy expenditure
Nitrogen balance
Respiratory exchange ratio

Fluid data

fluid losses
(Urinary output)

25.5 Computers in Renal Care

The clinical management of patients in renal care departments receiving continuous ambulatory peritoneal dialysis (CAPD) or haemodialysis or treatement after a renal transplantation is characterised by long-term monitoring (over many years) of their medical status, relying on an ever-increasing accumulation of medical data. Moreover, over the past decade there has been an increase in the number of patients treated in such centres. Therefore, the problems of handling huge volumes of alphanumerical data led to the introduction of computerised systems in renal care departments in the early 1980s to solve many of those problems.

Of all the medical data gathered in a renal unit, biochemistry and haematology results represent the greatest proportion. Therefore, connection and integration with the LIS and HIS are clearly necessary, as this reduces or eliminates incomplete recording. The data should be accessible in real time and presented preferably in tabular (medical data against time) and graphical form, either on screen or printed out. Physicians appreciate this [GOR 83], especially for haemoglobin, WBC, systolic blood pressure, diastolic blood pressure, weight, potassium, liver function tests (albumin, bilirubin, alkaline phosphatase).

Modern information technology makes it possible to improve communications within and outside the department, e.g. general practitioners and the European Dialysis and Transplant Association (EDTA) registry. Other benefits that can be realised are statistical evaluations for clinical research, summarised displays of key information and important events in the patient's history, improved monitoring of drug levels, standard letters, etc.

25.6 Processing Wave Forms in Obstetrics

In any department of obstetrics the intrauterine pressure (IUP) and the fetal ECG (FECG) are measured frequently during labour to follow the status of the fetus. The IUP (measured by means of a pressure transducer) measures the action on the fetus, where as the fetal ECG (measured by means of electrodes or if not possible, an ultrasonic or abdominal transducer) is an indication of the reaction of the fetus to different conditions. By means of a computer system, these signals can be recorded for storage, computation and classification of parameters in the patterns present.

Due to uterine contractions, the heart rate of the fetus often changes, and several classification schemes exist to correlate fetal heart rate patterns with certain pathological conditions.

26

Computer-Stored Medical Record Systems

26.1 Medical Records: Present Situation

In a society in which medicine is becoming more and more mobile, it is understandable why a patient medical record originally created as a personal record in a particular "physician-patient" relation imposes difficulties nowadays compared with the past when the terminology, usage and shared information were not critical issues as they were used by only one physician without the need for interchangeability.
Most medical records are still manual and handwritten. Limitations in a handwritten medical record are found by the fact that:

- Information is *not easily retrievable* for optimal medical decision making
- One copy of a paper-based record circulates in a society where care is often given in *multiple locations* by multiple health care providers. Health care information should be time and space distributed.
- Its variability and *lack of standardisation*
- Its fixed and *inflexible representational order*

As this medical record is the central source of data and medical knowledge in the care process of a patient, this document begs to be computerised due to various shortcomings inherent to a traditional paper-based medical record.
However, it has proven difficult to computerise. The reasons for this lack of success and the widespread use are [KUP 90]:

- Too great expectations from users and developers in the attempt to employ immediately all possible benefits obtained from computerisation. What cannot be expressed with a certain level of technology should not be implemented
- The problem of capturing and authenticating data collected by physicians (problem of user interface) or obtained from ancillary systems throughout the hospital, and the homogeneous representation of information in different views
- Lack of agreement between physicians and/or medical specialists on what information must be or should be kept and for how long; cost of support
- Health care information is *huge in volume* (Fig. 26.1), keeps increasing and is *multi-media in form.* Computerised medical record systems are characterised as data-intensive applications. Some entities of this medical record are multi-user in nature (e.g. patient demographic data, lab results, observations), while others are single-user but require highly complex data (e.g. radiotherapy radiation schemes)

Medical data are quite heterogeneous: they include at least 6 kinds:

- *Alphanumerical data,* e.g. administrative data, sex, age, weight, height, laboratory results
- *Subjective data,* e.g. results and interpretations of physical or technical examinations, auscultation, external documents
- *Machine-generated data* (signals), e.g. ECG records, EEG records
- *Image data,* e.g. RX pictures, scans
- *Interpretative comments,* e.g. radiological diagnosis, electrocardiography protocol
- *Derived data,* e.g. graphical documents, flowsheets

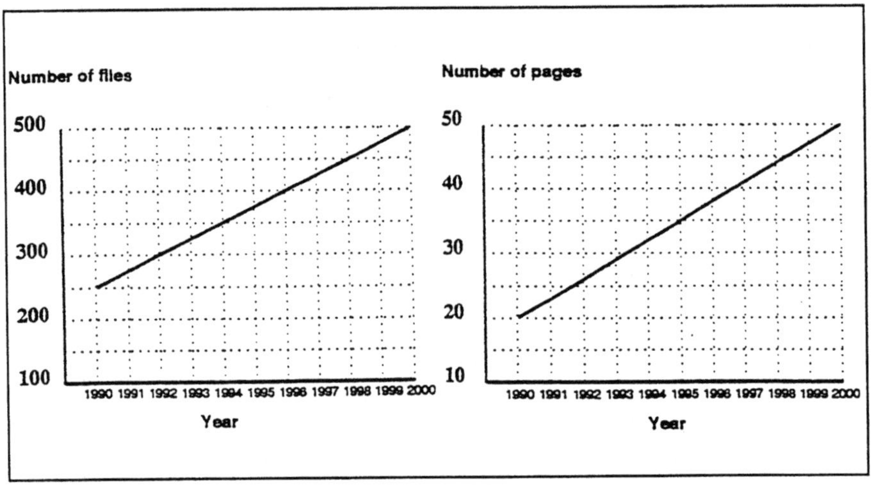

Fig. 26.1 Study conducted by the Erasme Hospital in Brussels (Belgium). This university hospital commands 900 beds, treats 25 000 patients in a year by hospitalisation. The medical information service assures manual and central archives, providing a unique file identification and handled in 1990 a total of 20 000 000 pages

(Source: courtesy of Erasme hospital, ULB, Prof. Dr. De Wever A.)

One definite goal for the near future is the achievement of a *life-long, longitudinal electronic medical record* that includes information of all types (text, wave forms, voice, images and other pictorial information) linking clinical, financial and administrative data (Fig. 26.2). It offers many advantages as opposed to the manual system. McDonald stated [McD 88] that complete computerisation of a medical record is a matter of time, and that in the mean time, hybrid computerised and paper records can have significant advantages over paper-only systems. However, standards are necessary to be able to exchange data from different feeder systems, in order to avoid re-entering of data that may cause errors.
The objectives of a medical record cover three domains [McD 90] :

- It improves *patient care* (i.e. continuity of Care) as it functions as a central source of information for communication between health care providers, covering the patient's history, observations, diagnostic and therapeutic conclusions and a wide variety of unstructured documents and information. Moreover, it will facilitate increased external linkage possibilities with health care providers (such as general practitioners, other hospitals, other specialists) and identify clinical events that need attention. However, it is important to stress that the attitudes towards a medical record differ from country to country, from hospital to hospital, from speciality to speciality and from doctor to doctor.

- It can solve many of the *actual logistics problems* of archiving retrieving, tracing and finding paper-based medical records (Table 26.1). In the medical record important parameters are buried, such as financial and human resources. Therefore the electronic medical record serves as a central information repository for health care policy makers (providers, management) and is a guide for future policies by analysing the past on several levels:
  - Medical audit
  - Quality assurance (quality of care against effective resources used and minimal cost)
  - Operational planning (human and material resources)
  - Correct billing system (third-party)
  - Financial and management planning
  - Classification of patients (DRG, ICD-9-CM, etc.)
  - Legal protection for patient, hospital and physician
- It improves *clinical research* for retrospective and prospective studies based on medical record reviews. It is a basis for analysis, study and evaluation of the quality of care.

26.2 Medical Record Models

Summarising the previous section, a (computer-stored) medical record aims to facilitate and improve patient care and clinical research and has to serve as a financial and legal record. Most medical records today focus on the inpatient medical record, and less attention has been given to the ambulatory medical record, although this is changing as there is a shift towards a less costly ambulatory care of patients. As legal or governement authorities impose new requirements, new technologies enter the scene and it is clear that the function and organisation of the medical record will change in the near future as medicine and health care delivery evolve. The emergence of ambulatory computerised medical records is an example.

However, before implementing an electronical medical record, some important questions have to be resolved:

- *How* can we be assured that the physician's notes are entered into the computer?
- *What* should be stored in a medical record?
- *How* should the medical data be stored?
- *Where* should the data be stored?
- How are we going to face *security* issues?
- On what *medium* should the information be available?

As already stressed before, the most critical challenge in the acceptance and implementation of a computerised medical record is the capturing and authentication of data gathered by physicians. Therefore, the input and output will be discussed briefly.

Table 26.1 Comparison between computer-stored versus manual, handwritten medical records. Computer-stored medical record systems can remedy many of the shortcomings of a traditional system

Traditional medical record	Computerised medical record
Inaccessibility (one user, one location often not always in the same place), parts of the records are geographically widely distributed	Decentralised, simultaneous access all the time
Passive: unable to trigger certain actions	Active: it can trigger certain actions according to the data
Non-standardised information handling	Standardized information storage, increasing legibility; it allows communication between departmental systems and can lead to an improvement of quality assurance
"Manual" linkage	"Increased" linkage with external health care providers
More risks of being incomplete (by lending, less control of completeness)	Can improve completeness by additional checking mechanisms at data entry
No flexible data representation (one representation only)	Flexible representation of data following various "views" tailored to the needs (on individual/patient basis or global)
Time consuming to explore for clinical or financial studies	Excellent basis to conduct clinical and financial studies
No risk of technical failure	Risk of technical failure and unavailability depending on the hardware/software
Lower cost (only entry cost not overall cost)	Higher cost for installation, training and management of the system
Physicians enter handwritten data manually	Probable resistance and fear of physicians of entering data into the computer
Protection, confidentiality ; easy to access	Protection and confidentiality more difficult to maintain (tracking and logging)

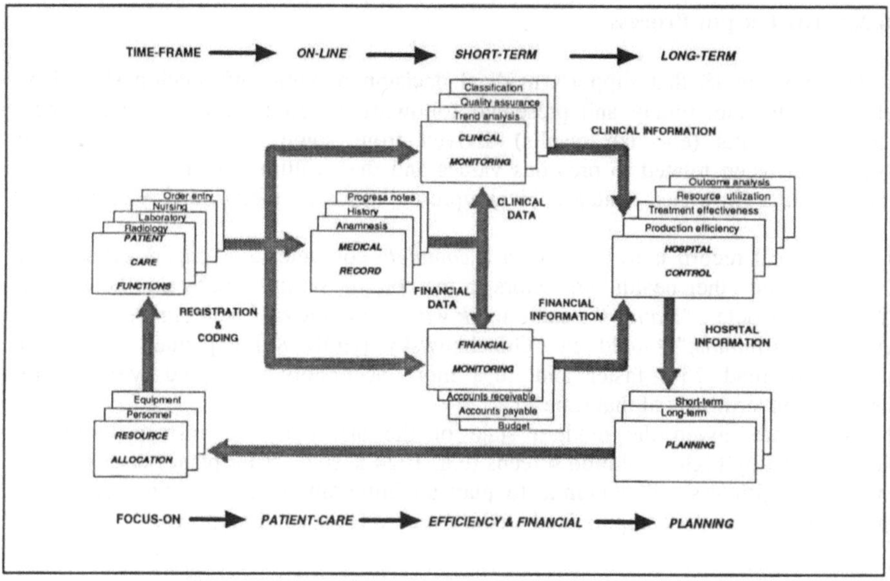

Fig. 26.2 The medical record is the central repository for many health care actors and the foundation for many related activities

26.2.1 The Input Process

A medical record consists of structured (coded) and unstructured (such as free narrative text) data. Structured elements and data are, for instance, laboratory results, drug prescriptions and patient identification data. As already explained in the discussion of result reporting facilities in radiological IS the same mechanisms for collecting information in the medical record are valid: transcription by secretaries of dictated or handwritten reports, coded input or direct input of the physician himself (with stock phrases). The transcription or coding of handwritten physician notes can cause problems due to the illegibility of the text.

The problem in informatics is that the usefulness of data for advanced functions, such as decision support systems, quality assurance and research, increases with the degree to which they are structured. At the same time, one notices that the general user's acceptance of the system tends to be reduced when the degree of the structure is increased [WHI 88], although structuring input data is often a matter of motivation after demonstrating the benefits of the method.

The use of new graphical user interfaces with pointing devices can bridge this widening gap and stimulate physicians to immediate input of all information through display forms *resembling their usual forms as closely as possible.* By reducing free text input as much as possible, combined with user-friendly fill-in screens using code lists, pop-up, pull-down windows and pictorial displays can really lead to an improvement and reduction of resistance towards the general use of a computerised medical record.

26.2.2 The Output Process

In designing an IS that supports medical decision making, information should be reliable, complete, timely and presented following different views. For instance, numerical results (e.g. lab results) derived from some examinations are only meaningful when related to previous values and the evolution of these values over time. Tabular (flowsheet) and graphical representations are therefore very desirable.

If the medical record is to be used in a *complete* computerised "paperless" way by physicians and other health care actors in the coming future is debatable because in 1984 in an article : "*Doing the same work with hardcopy and with cathode ray tube computer terminals,*" Gould and Grischkowsky [GOU 84] explained that paper reports are read 25% faster and 10% more accurately compared with reports displayed on terminals of that time.
It seems that, given the modern state of the art today of bit-map terminals, characterised by high-resolution screens (e.g. 1024 x 1024, 8-bit plane) laser printers and impact printers will continue to play an important role producing temporary specific reports of the computerised medical record for special purposes.

26.2.3 The Storage Process

Electronic medical records rely heavily on data that are too "expensive" to structure and that have not yet been structured by the medical community and are not well suited for tabular structures of existing RDBMS. A computerised medical record can primarily be viewed as a multi-media database in which medical, identification and socioeconomic patient data are stored. Research is carried out in different domains handling multi-media. Two major concepts of how huge the amounts of irregular data to be handled have emerged: the first is to make extensions to the current relational model, the second is to introduce object-oriented databases handling pictures, images, text, etc., as persistent objects.
At present, so-called multi-media databases capable of handling those different kinds of structured and unstructured data are not commercially mainstream.
Thus, we have to face the problems of archiving and presenting information to physicians in a coherent manner, arriving from various "information sources" such as WORM products, CD-ROM products, on-line data bases, external databases, etc.

26.3 The Way Medical Records Are Organised

This section describes briefly the way medical records are organized and their most important components (Fig.26.3)
Nowadays, countries differ in their legal and administrative attitude to the health care record and the way information is organised within it, although diseases and treatments have the same fundamental similarities anywhere. We cannot discuss for instance telemedicine or data exchange to link hospitals with hospitals (eventually across national borders) without defining the architecture of medical records.

The information within the medical record is a cumulative care profile, made up of various records created at each patient encounter, describing the results, resources used, time and location.

The earliest medical records were organised in a "chronological structure". They were real case "histories" [VRI 75]. At this moment, most of the medical records are "*source structured*", and within each source category the information is time sequenced. The medical record is organised by speciality each of which may have a separate file. The physician updates the medical record with observations, progress notes, prescriptions, requests for tests, etc.

The global content of the medical record covers five kinds of informations:

- Demographic patient information (face sheet)
- Physician entered data :
  - Medical history (social history, environmental history)
  - Anamnesis (actual health state problems)
  - Medical procedures to be performed (treatment planning)
  - Admission and discharge diagnoses
  - Progress notes (physical findings)
- Nurse entered data :
  - Nursing anamnesis and diagnosis
  - Medication
  - Observations (nursing notes, vital signs,) acuity of care
  - Nurse planning
- Ancillary departmental records, e.g. radiology, laboratory, pneumology, etc.
- Discharge summary (letter). A resume of the patient's course of treatment including the reason for hospitalisation, significant findings, procedures performed, treatment rendered and the condition of the patient upon discharge (most of its contents is an automatic byproduct of the data above).

Although the importance of registering dated medical events, physicians tend to think problem-oriented and tend to organize a patient's record around the medical problem present at the moment. With each (future) medical encounter, the medical data will be rearranged to facilitate consideration of a new problem [BIS 91]. As Whiting-O'Keefe has stated [WHI 88]:

One fundamental cause of physicians' reluctance to impose structure on their data is that clinicians tend to think of and record clinical data relative to events (e.g., a hospital admission, a pregnancy, etc.) whereas, for most clinical purposes, computers can most usefully manipulate data when they are in a longitudinal structure. If these event-oriented data are to have value when their event is over, they must be mapped into a longitudinal database with medically appropriate linkage relationships and summarization, a difficult task, to say the least [BIS 91].

As manual medical records were composed of chaotic narrative with seemingly instructured components, Weed [WEE 68] proposed more than 20 years ago an alternative to the traditional time-oriented record keeping, recognising the importance of the internal structure of the medical record. Thus, the *problem-oriented medical record* (POMR), whether stored in a computer or on paper, was born. Weed felt that

the patient must be seen as a "whole", including his or her psychological, physical and social problems.
Opposed to the traditional medical record which had a rather 'diagnostic emphasis', Weed stated that more attention has to be given to the patient's problems, which are whatever can be observed as being a difficulty for him or her. This may cover symptoms and signs which cannot be explained without further examinations [ABB 86]. Starting from previous and actual medical data a 'problem list' was created which leads to the **SOAP** (*subjective, objective assessment plan*). After collecting these subjective and objective patient data an assessment of other examinations is initiated, resulting in a new or another plan and in a better "problem specification" afterwards:

(1)

S = subjective data	*What is going on?*
O = objective data	*Numerical lab reports*

↓ ↓

(2)

A = assessment	*What does it mean?*
P = plan	*What to do?*

The reflections on this information are written down in progress notes. However, the Weed system 'helpful in some forms of teaching' has some disadvantages [TIE 90]:

1. There is no clear definition of "problem" like there is no clear definition of "disease" or "diagnosis".
2. It is difficult to assign each finding to one of the problems stated in the problem list.

In 1989 Linnarson and Wigertz [LIN 89] presented a data model in which the clinical database is organised according to the POMR approach.
The top level has 10 categories:

1. Anatomy
2. Organisms
    2.1 Invertebrates
    2.2 Vertebrates
    2.3 Bacteria
    2.4 Viruses
    2.5 Lower plants
3. Medical and social history
    3.1 Medical history
    3.2 Social history
    3.3 Environmental history
4. Symptoms and signs
5. Physical examinations
6. Laboratory and other diagnotic procedures
    6.1 Clinical chemistry

6.2 Bacteriology
6.3 Clinical physiology
6.4 Radiology
6.5 Pathology
6.6 Other diagnostic procedures
7. Diagnosis
8. Medication
9. Therapeutic procedures
9.1 Prevention
9.2 Rehabilitation
9.3 Care
9.4 Medicine
9.5 Surgery
9.6 Physical therapy
9.7 Other therapeutic procedures
10. Health care population characteristics
10.1 Facilities
10.2 Economics

Another model is called the *decision-directed medical record* (DDMR), which relates patient data to clinical decisions, providing information for better patient management and care review.

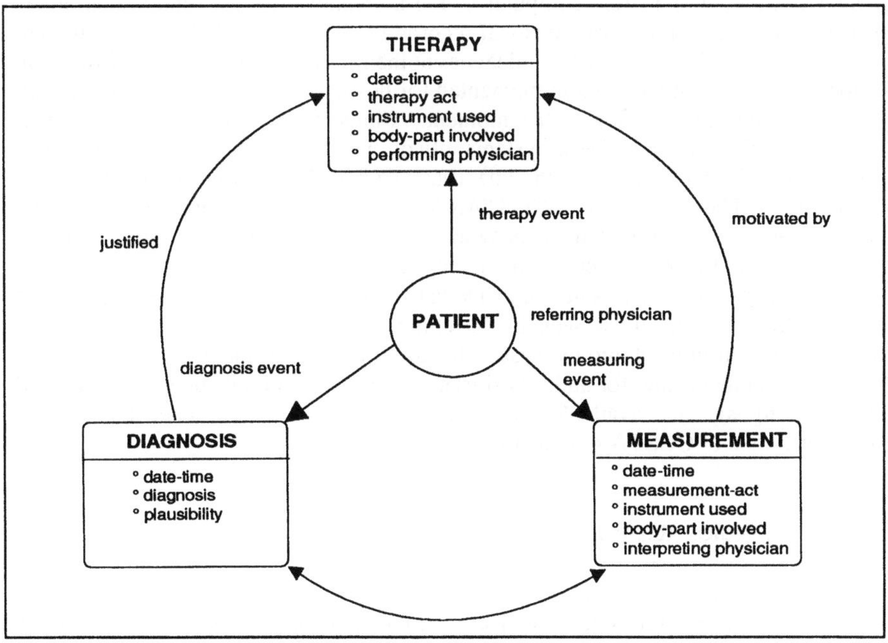

Fig. 26.3 Schematic representation of the most important components and their relationships within the patient medical record

26.4 Computerised Medical Records: Some Examples

In the past decade, several computerised health care records have been implemented. Herein, some well-known medical record systems in Europe and in the USA are briefly described.
All those systems have some features in common. First, they are mixed systems in which data are captured by means of an encounter form, which is printed and delivered to physicians before the patient arrives. Those forms are updated by clinicians, and visit data are entered into the system by clerks. Direct physician/computer interactions did not seem to be very satisfying [KUH 84]. The second common characteristic is that they use a data dictionary for storing metadata (i.e. identification of medical acts, tests, diagnoses, abnormal values, units). Medical data are stored in records which access the data dictionary. There is a benefit of a fixed field medical data relation in using the tools of a RDBMS, but this approach seems to be inadequate for a full medical record system, which has thousands of different clinical data types. Third, the system stores only relevant medical data without details arriving from medical feeder systems in order to reduce information overload. The last common characteristic is time orientation of medical data.

26.4.1 The Computer Stored Ambulatory Record

COSTAR is an acronym for "computer stored ambulatory record" and is one of the most widely used computerised medical records in computer ambulatory health care record, created by Barnett and his colleagues at the Massachusetts General Hospital in Boston (Fig. 26.4). It has been implemented for hospital and family care. More than 100 installations are running at the moment. Finnstar, an adaption of the former system, is used in Finland. These systems rely on the heavy technology of the 1970s. Since its first implementation in the late 1960s COSTAR has been installed in more than 100 sites. The actual version COSTAR V include 5 modules: patient registration, appointment scheduling, system security and data integrity, financial registration and communication of medical records and management reporting.
Prior to each patient's visit, summary medical record reports (diagnoses, results) are printed. After the patient is seen in the clinic, encounter forms completed by the physicians are introduced into the system by administrative personnel. Once entered, they are available on-line for authorised users. COSTAR is implemented in the ANS MUMPS language and available on a variety of hardware environments. Public-domain versions of COSTAR are available.

26.4.2 The Medical Record System

The medical record system of Duke University (TMR) was developed by Stead and Hammond [STE 88] to introduce an electronic medical record.TMR is an information system capable of gathering data about a patient directly into a database during the patient care process by physicians, nurses, technicians and secretaries. Seven data categories are registered by patient:

- Demographic data
- Research protocols, tumour registry information and special patient needs

- Problems and diagnoses
- Time-oriented data
- Studies
- Therapies
- Encounter or admission related data

Several forms of input have been developed; e.g. paper worksheets tailored to the individual patient are printed, to be filled in and registered afterwards, for users who do not like to work with a terminal For other users, interactive data entry through interactive collection protocols or on an item-by-item basis are available. TMR supports three levels of printed reports, varying from rigid and pre-defined to flexible formats controlled by a data dictionary.

TMR is operational on more than ten operating systems and on DEC computers working under the VMS operating system in connection with IBM PCs. TMR uses a proprietary data base management language GEMISCH, supporting different file types (hash file, inverted file, B-tree, direct access, and sequential access file.).

TMR will soon support the ASTM standard (for laboratory data exchange) and HL7.

26.4.3 The Regenstrief Medical record System

The Regenstrief computerised medical record system (RMRS) has been operational at Wishard Memorial Hospital since 1972 (Fig. 26.5). It was designed as a summary medical record to complement and not necessarily replace the paper medical record. It stores medical records for inpatients and outpatients about lab results, progress notes and physical examinations [McD 83]. After patient registration, the computerised medical record includes most of the patient's diagnostic studies, treatments, discharge and visits diagnosis, clinical vital signs and test orders. Laboratory and medication data are fed into the system from the laboratory and pharmacy system. The remaining hand-coded information is entered into the computer by technicians. Reminder messages generated by 1490 rules on behaviour remind physicians about actions needed [McD 84].

RMRS runs on a DEC system. User-oriented command languages permit non-programmers to access and manipulate medical data stored in the Regenstrief Data Base Management System (RDB). They also offer the advantage that the format and content of most reports is created or modified without the need for programmer assistance. The system uses a standard unified dictionary of surgical procedures, nursing procedures, diagnoses and observations. For communication it is using the ASTM-HL7 message format.

The individual patient medical data are stored in sequential, variable length records. The names of drugs, tests and clinical findings are represented within the file as integer codes referring to the dictionary containing the data definitions. In analogy with previous systems, RMRS also generates printed reports prior to the patient's visit. Flowsheet summary, encounter form and quality assurance reports that provide recommendations (medical procedures to be performed, drug therapies, contraindications,etc.) to the physician are pre-printed.

26.4.4 The Summary Time-Oriented Record

The Summary Time-Oriented Record (STOR) was developed at the University of California San Francisco (UCSF) Medical Center in 1980 (Fig. 26.6). It provides a common inpatient and outpatient database. Before each patient visit, STOR prints a patient specific encounter form. The physician uses this form -which includes a medical summary- to register new data during the patient's visit. Afterwards, it is entered into the computer by a secretary.

STOR is based on a central clinical database in which medical data are registered on-line over a local area network (LAN). It covers three functional areas [WHI 88]:

- ° A centralised summary database of clinical patient information
- ° An on-line display system
- ° A computerised ambulatory record

The central computer is a Data General using Meditech's system software MIIS and programming language MIIS (a proprietary dialect of MUMPS). Most of the medical ancillary (feeder) systems have also been developed by UCSF. Via a LAN, all the medical information from departmental systems are fed into the central clinical database.

Terminals located throughout the inpatient and outpatient clinics offer the possibility to access on-line clinical information stored in this database. On-line STOR reports cover pathology, discharge diagnoses, operative notes, cytology, X-ray, nuclear medicine, microbiology, ECG, visit summary, laboratory, demographics, flowsheets, charts and appointment lists.

26.4.5. General state of Computerized Medical Records

Other systems that may be classified as computer-stored medical record systems have been (e.g. HELP, DIOGENE) discussed in previous chapters.

To conclude the status of existing computer stored medical record systems one discovers that most important applications are found in university hospitals, while commercial vendors more or less focus on departmental systems. Most of these existing systems are qualified as centralised systems intended not to replace but to complement the paper medical records, characterized by a lack for flexibility. Next decade computer stored medical record systems will focus on a distributed architecture using knowledge based features (see HELP).

Although there are advantages to a computerised medical record (the system provides good research tools), it does not solve the problem of "information overload". So for the physician who consults the medical record on-line, an automatic summary of the medical record -meaningful clinical events- would be very helpful (Fig. 26.7). Secondly, there is also a risk of data quality decreasing.

Idefix [ZEG 88] is an example of a knowledge-based system that abstracts high-level concepts from low-level data and represents in graphic format the summary to help physicians handle large amounts of information (Fig. 26.8). The medical records come from a sub-set of the Aramis database.

```
                    CASE SUMMARY
PRINTED ON: 5/14/91

PRIMARY PROV: GO        ,J     ,MD                  UN: DEMO-092
IMA-5                                               EXAMPLE,CASE I
LAST SCHEDULED VISIT: 10/29/90
                                                    (M) 54 YRS   (4/6/37)

PERSONAL DATA AND OVERALL HEALTH: (10/29/90)
  LITTLE REGULAR EXERCISE, DISCUSSED AGAIN TODAY.
______________________________________________________________________

HEALTH MAINTENANCE
  RECTAL GUAIAC    NEG                                           10/29/90

ALLERGIES/SENSITIVITIES                              DATE FIRST ENTERED
* DRUG ALLERGY                                                    5/21/90
        LISINOPRIL (RASH).

MAJOR PROBLEMS
  DYSPEPSIA                                                       2/18/87
        S: DOING WELL, ABLE TO TOLERATE 1 FULL REGULAR
           ASPIRIN PER DAY.                       [10/29/90]

  CHEST PAIN                                                     10/29/90
        S: NO FURTHER EPISODES WHATSOEVER, HAS BEEN
           REASONABLY ACTIVE ABOUT WORK.

  HEARING LOSS                                                   10/29/90
        S: /BILATERAL.
        A: WORSE ON (L) THAN ON (R), NO NOISE TRAUMA. DOES
           HAVE OCC TINNITUS.
        P: GIVEN THE NAME OF DOCTOR TO CONTACT FOR HEARING EVAL.

  HYPERTENSION                                                    2/18/87
        S: ASYMPTOMATIC.
        O: BP 190/100.
        A: CONTROL NOT YET OPTIMAL BUT BETTER.
        P: ADD ANOTHER 30 MG. OF NIFEDIPINE XL. CONTINUE
           WITH ATENOLOL.                          [5/21/90]

  SMOKING                                                         2/18/87
        S: CONTINUES TO ABSTAIN.
                                                        [9/2/87]

  OVERWEIGHT                                                      2/18/87
        A: FURTHER GAIN.
                                                        [9/2/87]

  HYPERCHOLESTEROLEMIA                                             3/9/87
        A: FURTHER DISCUSSION TODAY. WILL CHECK CHOLESTEROL


STATUSES:  M/MAJOR    I/INACT    H/HO    R/RO    Y/SP    P/PRESUM
                D/DO NOT DISPLAY    S/SHORT TERM PROBLEM
```

```
EXAMPLE,CASE I  DEMO-092                                          PAGE 2

PRINTED ON: 5/14/91

MAJOR PROBLEMS

           THIS AFTERNOON. HE HAS BEEN TAKING COLESTIPOL ONCE A
           DAY, WILL INCREASE TO TWICE A DAY. ? LOVASTATIN THERAPY
           ON RETURN.                                [9/2/87]

  HEPATITIS                                                       3/9/87
        A: IMPROVED LFT'S. STI[illegible]. DRINKS OCCASIONALLY.
                                                       [7/15/87]

  SITUATIONAL STRESS                                             2/18/87
        S: ANXIETY. EPISODES HAVE NOW LARGELY RESOLVED.
        A: GOOD RESPONSE TO BETA BLOCKER.
                                                       [3/19/87]

  RECTAL BLEEDING                                                2/18/87
        S: 4 YRS AGO APPARENTLY HAD RATHER PROFUSE
           HEMORRHOIDAL TYPE BLEEDING. NONE RECENTLY.

  CAROTID BRUIT                                                  2/18/87
        S: /BILATERAL. ASYMPTOMATIC.

  PERICARDITIS  [S/P]                                            2/18/87
        S: HOSPITALIZED 7 DAYS 15 YRS AGO FOR CHEST PAIN.
           NOW RESOLVED.

SURGICAL PROCEDURES

PAST MEDICAL HX, FAMILY HX, SOCIAL HX, ROS         DATE LAST NOTED
PAST MEDICAL HISTORY:                                            2/18/87
     DRINKS 2 CUPS OF COFFEE PER DAY. NO KNOWN MEDICAL
     ALLERGIES. DRINKS 2 TO 3 MIXED DRINKS PER NIGHT.
FAMILY HISTORY:                                                  2/18/87
     FATHER DIED OF STOMACH CANCER. MOTHER LIVING WITH
     HYPERTENSION.


PHYSICAL EXAMINATION
* BLOOD PRESSURE         120/80                                 10/29/90
                       * 190/100 LEFT ARM SITTING                5/21/90
  WEIGHT                 175                                    10/29/90
                         229                                      9/2/87
* PULSE                * 48 REGULAR                              6/22/87
  HEENT:                                                        10/29/90
      BILATERALLY DECREASED HEARING, ABLE TO HEAR FINGER RUB
      AT APPROX 24 INCHES ON EITHER SIDE, SLIGHTLY WORSE ON
      (L).
  NECK:                                                         10/29/90
      SUPPLE WITHOUT THYROMEGALY OR BRUIT.
  CHEST:                                                         5/21/90
      CLEAR.
  COR:                                                          10/29/90
      I/VI MR MURMUR.
  ABDOMEN:                                                      10/29/90
```

Fig. 26.4 COSTAR, example of a case summary which gives the physician an overview of the patient's major problems, surgical procedures, physical examinations, laboratory tests, medications

(source Dr. O. Barnett, Massachusets General Hospital - Boston 1991)

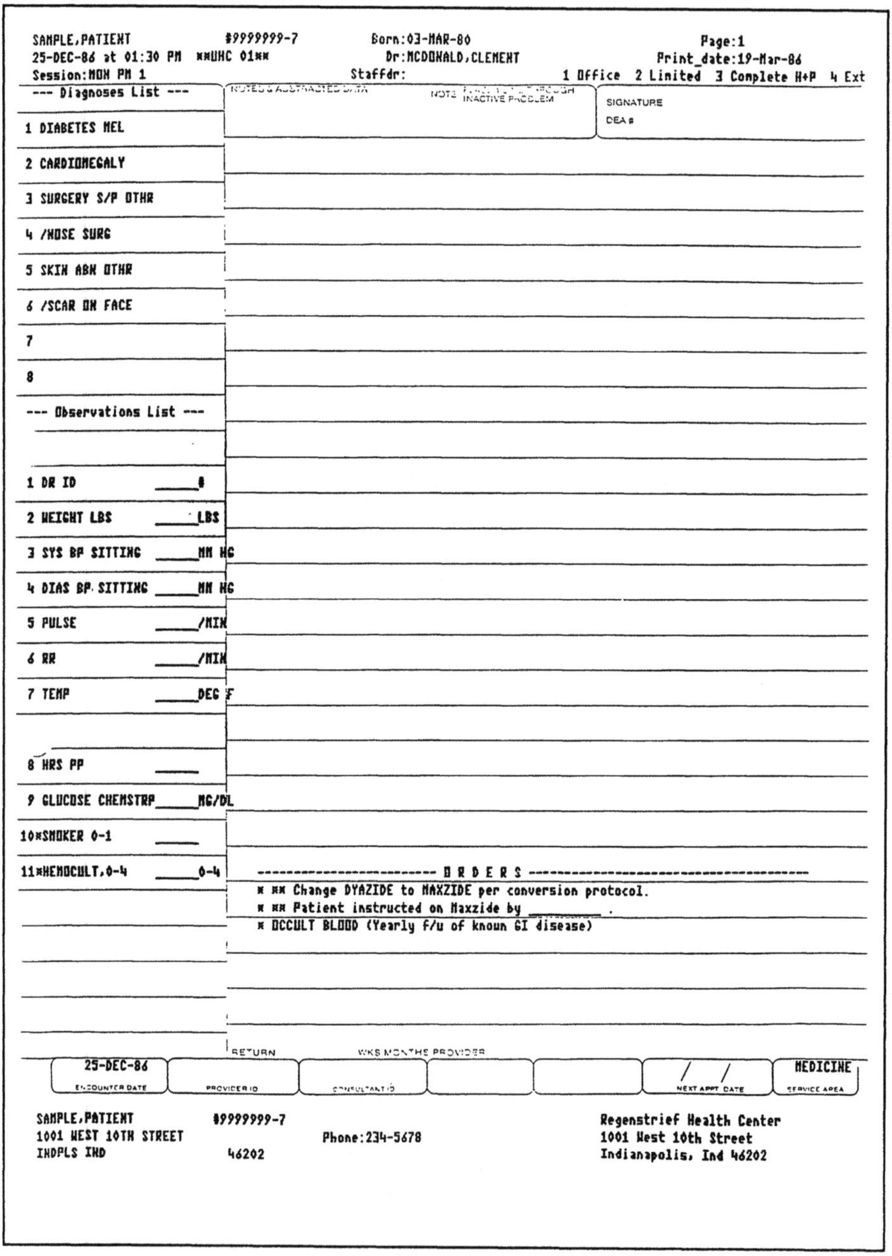

SAMPLE,PATIENT #9999999-7 Born:03-MAR-80 Page:1
25-DEC-86 at 01:30 PM **UHC 01** Dr:MCDONALD,CLEMENT Print_date:19-Mar-86
Session:MON PM 1 Staffdr: 1 Office 2 Limited 3 Complete H+P 4 Ext

--- Diagnoses List ---
SIGNATURE
DEA #
1 DIABETES MEL
2 CARDIOMEGALY
3 SURGERY S/P OTHR
4 /NOSE SURG
5 SKIN ABN OTHR
6 /SCAR ON FACE
7
8
--- Observations List ---
1 DR ID ____#
2 WEIGHT LBS ____LBS
3 SYS BP SITTING ____MM HG
4 DIAS BP SITTING ____MM HG
5 PULSE ____/MIN
6 RR ____/MIN
7 TEMP ____DEG F
8 HRS PP ____
9 GLUCOSE CHEMSTRP____MG/DL
10*SMOKER 0-1 ____
11*HEMOCULT,0-4 ____0-4

------------------------ O R D E R S ------------------------
* ** Change DYAZIDE to MAXZIDE per conversion protocol.
* ** Patient instructed on Maxzide by ________ .
* OCCULT BLOOD (Yearly f/u of known GI disease)

RETURN WKS MONTHS PROVIDER
25-DEC-86 / / MEDICINE
ENCOUNTER DATE PROVIDER ID CONSULTANT ID NEXT APPT DATE SERVICE AREA

SAMPLE,PATIENT #9999999-7 Regenstrief Health Center
1001 WEST 10TH STREET Phone:234-5678 1001 West 10th Street
INDPLS IND 46202 Indianapolis, Ind 46202

Fig. 26.5.a The Regenstrief medical record, first page of an encounter form. On the left side, the diagnoses and observations list are indicated; on the right side, space is provided for the physician to write his notes.

(source Courtesy of C. J. Mc Donald, M.D.)

LONG ROUNDS REPORT For Patient **Wishard Memorial Hospital**

TEST, PATIENT 999999-6

SEX : M RACE : B AGE : 26
WARD : B4 BED# : B402B BILLING# : 2-37533-5
PROBLEMS : 1) ETOH abuse 2) constipation
ALLERGIES : 1) NO KNOWN DRUG ALLE
DIET : CLEAR LIQUID DIET Starting now
PRECAUTIONS : NO SPECIAL PRECAUTIONS
ACTIVITIES : UP AD LIB

ALL TESTS ORDRED :

1) AMYLASE -- Ord 14 OCT 90
2) BLOOD CELL PROF -- Ord 14 OCT 90
3) EKG -- Ord 14 OCT 90
4) HB CORE AB -- Ord 14 OCT 90
5) HBS AB -- Ord 14 OCT 90
6) HBS ANTIGEN -- Ord 14 OCT 90
7) LIPASE -- Ord 14 OCT 90
8) TRIGLYCERIDES -- Ord 14 OCT 90
9) URINALYSIS -- Ord 14 OCT 90

ACTIVE MEDICATIONS :

1) * FOLIC ACID INJ, , 1 mg Inj in first IV fluid bottle QD -- Ord 14 OCT 90, Actv 2 D
2) * IV FLUID ORDERS, , Run D5W-0.9% NaCl at 125 ml/hr. Add 20 mEq KCl to first bottle of day. Add nothing to following bottles. -- Ord 14 OCT 90, Actv 2 D
3) MEPERIDINE INJ, , 50 MG Q4H PRN X2 DOSES -- Ord 15 OCT 90
4) * MOM, , 30 ml PO QHS PRN constipation -- Ord 14 OCT 90, Actv 2 D
5) * MVI INJ, , 10 ml Inj 1XD in first IV bottle each day -- Ord 14 OCT 90, Actv 2 D
6) * PROMETHAZINE INJ, , 25 MG Q4H IVSS PRN X2 DOSES W/DEMEROL -- Ord 15 OCT 90, Actv 1 D
7) * THIAMINE, , 100 MG IN FIRST IV BAG EACH DAY -- Ord 14 OCT 90, Actv 2 D

ALL NURSING SERVICES ORDERED:

1) * VITALS (TPR & BP), , Measure Q SHIFT -- Ord 14 OCT 90, Actv 2 D

* Indicates an Active Orders

STANDARD OBSERVATIONS :
(abnormals are bold, critical abnormals are underlined)

YEAR	1990	1990	1990	1990	1990	1990	1990	1990	1990	1990	1990	1990	1990	1990	1990	1990
DAY-MONTH	15 OCT	15 OCT	14 OCT	13 OCT	08 AUG	08 AUG	29 MAY	28 MAY	27 MAY	26 MAY	25 MAY	25 MAY	25 MAY	14 FEB	12 FEB	12 FEB
HOUR	01:19	06:00	11:08	20:48	18:33	17:49	06:00	06:00	06:00	11:22	23:54	21:41	07:47	06:00	07:31	06:00
AMYLASE	-	83	-	-	-	37	-	-	-	-	-	133 h	29 l	-	-	-
BLOOD CELL PROF																
WBC	-	4.9	-	7.4	-	10.4	8.3	8.6	11.2 h	11.8 h	-	13.9 h	7.7	-	-	-
RBC	-	4.2	-	4.7	-	4.9	3.6 l	3.2 l	3.8 l	4.7	-	4.7	4.8	-	-	-
HGB	-	13.8 l	-	15.2	-	-	11.6 l	10.5 l	12.3 l	15.2	-	15	14.9	-	-	-
HCT	-	39 l	-	43	-	45	33 l	30 l	36 l	44	-	44	44	-	-	-
MCV	-	94	-	93	-	92	94	94	95 h	93	-	93	92	-	-	-
MCH	-	33 h	-	33 h	-	-	33 h	33 h	33 h	32	-	32	31	-	-	-
MCHC	-	35	-	35	-	-	35	35	34	35	-	34	34	-	-	-
CHEM12																
BUN	-	-	-	9	-	9	4 l	2 l	4 l	4 l	-	5 l	11	3 l	-	-
GLUCOSE	-	-	-	91	-	104	89	92	100	108	-	99	95	113 h	-	-
CREATININE	-	-	-	.9	-	.8	1	.8	.9	.8	-	.8	.9	.7	-	-
CALCIUM	-	-	-	9.9	-	-	-	-	-	-	-	-	9.9	-	-	-
PHOS	-	-	-	3.3	-	-	-	-	-	-	-	-	3	-	-	-
URIC ACID	-	-	-	7.5 h	-	-	-	-	-	-	-	-	7.1	-	-	-
CHOLESTEROL	-	-	-	253 h	-	-	-	-	-	-	-	-	268 h	-	-	-

TEST, PATIENT **Page 1** **Date 16 OCT 9'**

Printed 16 OCT 90 11:03AM by WARVEL,JEFF from JEFF2 The Medical Gopher (R)

Fig.26.5.b The Regenstrief Medical Record. *First* page of the patient flowsheet summary. It includes laboratory results, active medications and nursing services ordered.

(Source courtesy of Clement J.Mc. Donald, M.D.)

LONG ROUNDS REPORT For Patient Wishard Memorial Hospital

TEST, PATIENT **999999-6**

(abnormals are bold, critical abnormals are underlined)

YEAR	1990	1990	1990	1990	1990	1990	1990	1990	1990	1990	1990	1990	1990	1990	1990	1990
DAY-MONTH	15 OCT	15 OCT	14 OCT	13 OCT	08 AUG	08 AUG	29 MAY	28 MAY	27 MAY	26 MAY	25 MAY	25 MAY	25 MAY	14 FEB	12 FEB	12 FEB
HOUR	01:19	06:00	11:08	20:48	18:33	17:49	06:00	06:00	06:00	11:22	23:54	21:41	07:47	06:00	07:31	06:00
ROUTINE URINALYSIS (continued)																
1) amorphous l																
BACTERIA UA	occas l	-	-	-	(1)	-	-	-	-	-	occas	-	-	-	occas h	-
1) several																
MUCOUS THREADS»	(1)	-	-	-	(1)	-	-	-	-	-	(1)	-	-	-	(1)	-
1) present																
TRICHOMONAS Spp	-	-	-	-	(1)	-	-	-	-	-	-	-	-	-	-	-
1) present																

(abnormals are bold, critical abnormals are underlined)

YEAR	1990	1990	1990	1990	1990	1990	1990	1990	1990	1990	1990	1989	1985
DAY-MONTH	16 OCT	16 OCT	15 OCT	15 OCT	14 OCT	14 OCT	14 OCT	14 OCT	29 MAY	28 MAY	28 MAY	18 FEB	04 NOV
HOUR	00:07	08:21	15:42	07:48	23:34	15:13	00:56	07:21	07:34	23:41	15:43		
VITALS (TPR&BP)													
TEMP AUTO ORAL	99	98.6	99.4 h	100.4 h	100.4 h	100.2 h	101 h	101.3 h	98.6	-	98.8	-	-
PULSE AUTO	71	68	70	77	94	112 h	101 h	119 h	63	70	-	-	-
SYSTOLIC BP AU»	128	135	136	123	123	134	136	150	151	154	-	-	-
SYS BP SITTING	-	-	-	-	-	-	-	-	-	-	-	150	150
DIASTOLIC BP A»	81	84	83	75	77	84	90	104 h	104 h	99 h	-	-	-
DIAS BP SITTING	-	-	-	-	-	-	-	-	-	-	-	100 h	80
WEIGHT LBS	-	-	-	-	-	-	-	-	-	-	-	-	159

TEST, PATIENT Page 3 Date 16 OCT 9

Printed 16 OCT 90 11:03AM by WARVEL,JEFF from JEFF2 The Medical Gopher (R

Fig. 26.5c The Regenstrief Medical Record. *Third* page of the flowsheet summary. It includes laboratory results.

(source Courtesy of C. J. Mc Donald, M.D.)

NAME: UNIT #: 009 70 BIRTHDATE: 04/09/1914 CLINIC: ARTH
AGE: 71 PHONE #1: DATE: 5-23-85

DATE / CLINIC / PROVIDER			5-23-85 ARTH	8-31-84 TO 9-12-84	8-6-84 ARTH U590	7-12-84 ARTH U590	7-5-84 ARTH U590	6-11-84 ARTH U590	5-7-84 ARTH U590	4-16-84 ARTH U590
PROBLEMS/MANIFESTATIONS	ONSET	UNITS								
30.1 VITAL SIGNS										
18. WEIGHT		LBS	130		129	129	132		128	130
27. PULSE			85		84		90			90
32. RESPIRATORY RATE			24		25	20		19		
19.2 INTERSTITIAL LUNG DIS. (DUE TO #1)	1965		? worse							
22. FATIGUE		0-3	3		3		1.5	MODERATE	MODERATE	MODERATE
23. EXERTION DYSPNEA		0-3	2		1.5		1.5	SAME	SAME	
21. HYPERTENSION		MM HG	160/86		152/84	178/90	120/98	140/94	160/100	158/103
1. SJOGREN'S DISEASE	1958		STABLE							
2. XEROSTOMIA		0-3 SCAL	2		2		2	2	2	2
3. KERATOCONJUNCTIVITIS SICCA		0-3	2		2		2	2	2	2
4. ARTHRALGIA		0-3 SCAL	0		1		1	1	1	1
24. PALPABLE PURPURA			0		0		0	0	0	FEW
14. CRYOGLOBULINEMIA (IGM KAPPA MONOCLONAL)	1984									
8. PERIPHERAL NEUROPATH PARESTHESIAS		0-3	1+ TOES		1	1	2	3	3	3
METAST. ADENOCARCINOMA (PROB. FROM LUNG)	9-12-84									
Hx OF HYPONATREMIA	9-12-84									

THERAPIES	ROUTE	UNITS	5-23-85	8-31-84 TO 9-12-84	8-6-84	7-12-84	7-5-84	6-11-84	5-7-84	4-16-84
3. VALIUM	PO	MG	←		5 MG PRN					
6. CARBAMAZEPINE	PO	MG	←		200 TID		200 BID			200 QD
10. PREDNISONE	PO	MG	←		5 QD		5 QD			5 QD
11. HYDROCHLOROTHIAZIDE (STARTED 1982)	PO	MG	←		100 QD		100 QD	100 QD		100 QD
12. METHYLDOPA	PO	MG	←		250 TID	250 TID	250 TID			

LABORATORY		UNITS	5-23-85	8-31-84 TO 9-12-84	8-6-84	7-12-84	7-5-84	6-11-84	5-7-84	4-16-84
HEMATOCRIT	HCT	PERCENT		41.0	43.7		40.1	41.2	43.8	40.3
WBC COUNT	WBC	K/CUMM		5.5	5.6		5.7	5.1	5.3	4.8
PLATELETS	PLT	K/CUMM		169.0	167.0		155.2	166.0		
SEDIMENTATION RATE	ESR	MM/HR								
CREATININE	CR	MG/DL		1.2				1.1	1.0	
POTASSIUM	K	MEQ/L		4.7	3.7		3.8	3.4	3.8	3.7
PROTEIN ,UR	PRUA			NEG			NEG			
WBCS ,UR	WBCU	/HPF		5-10			2-5			
RBCS ,UR	RBCU	/HPF		10-25			2-5			

Fig. 26.6a The summary time-oriented record (STOR). ***Part A*** is a flowsheet of patient's problems, physical findings, therapies and clinical laboratory data.

(source Quinn E Whiting-0'Keefe, MD; Donald W. Simborg, MD, Wallace V.Epstein, MD; Anne Warger. A computerized summary medical record system can provide more information than the standard medical record. JAMA, Vol 254, no. 9 Sept.6 1985 pp 1185 - 1188)

NAME:	UNIT #: 009 70 AGE: 71	BIRTHDATE: 04/09/1914 PHONE #1:	CLINIC: ARTH DATE: 5-23-8

VISITS / HOSPITALIZATIONS

INPATIENT:	8/31/84 TO 9/12/84	GENERAL MEDICINE
OUTPATIENT:	8/13/84	PHON VISIT
	8/6/84	ARTH VISIT

REPORTS

UCSF	HOSPITALIZATION: DIAGNOSES:	8-31-84 to 9-12-84 1. Adenocarcinoma, metastatic, probably from lung. 2. Sjogren's. 3. Hyponatremia. 4. Chronic globulinemia vasculitis. 5. Hypoxia.	
XRAY	CHEST PA AND LAT:	8-31-84 Interval increase in size of previously noted right upper lobe mass and new pleural effusions and interstitial edema. The findings are most suspicious for primary malignancy in the left upper lobe.	
PHON	VISIT SUMMARY:	8-13-84 ARTHRITIS: CALLED IN TO REPORT GREAT IMPROVEMENT IN LEG CRAMPS ON VALIUM. NOTE FALL IN GAMMA GLOBULIN.	U590
ARTH	VISIT SUMMARY:	8-6-84 IMP: DOING POORLY FOR 2 SOLID WKS. QUALITY OF LIFE = 0 SECONDARY LEG PAINS AND MALAISE. SOME HYPERDEFICATION AND 3 LB WT LOSE. EXAM: NO NODES, NO ABD MASSES, RECTAL NL, STOOL HEME NEGATIVE. LABS SHOW CRYOGLOBULIN ABSENT. COUGH IS WORSE. PLAN: INCREASE TEGRETOL. CXR (?ORDERED). CHECK IEP, CH50, (?BONE MARROW). TRY VALIUM FOR MUSCLE CRAMPS. D/C QUININE.	U590:Z282
ARTH	VISIT SUMMARY:	7-5-84 IMP: MAJOR PROBLEM IS INTERMITTENT GLOBAL MALAISE - INVOLVING ACHING AND NUMBNESS. BUT DOES HAVE GOOD WEEKS AND HAS GAINED WT. LAB NOT ABLE TO DO IEP LAST VISIT SO WILL REPEAT. HAVING 5 FIRM STOOLS IN LAST 2 DAYS. BP EXCELLENT. NO PURPURA. PLAN: CHECK IEP. IF PAIN NO BETTER INCREASE TEGRETOL. CONSIDER BONE MARROW.	U590:Z282
ARTH	VISIT SUMMARY:	6-11-84 IMP: HAVING MORE FREQUENT EPISODES OF PAIN - WHICH APPEARS TO BE THE NEUROPATHIC PAINS. BP IN GOOD CONTROL AND ST IS UP. NO PERAPERA. PLAN: INCR TEGRETAL. CHECK IN 2 WKS AND INCR TEGRETAL IF TOLERATED. CHECK CBC, SMA 6, K+, CA++. REPEAT IEF; IF + FOR MONOCLAUD DO BONE MARROW.	U590:Z282
ARTH	VISIT SUMMARY:	5-7-84 IMP: HAVING SEVERE CALVE CRAMPS AT NIGHT - SOUNDS UNRELATED TO NEUROPATHY. NOTE ADDITIONAL WT LOS. INTERESTED IN TENS. PLAN: TRY QUININE. CHECK U/A, CREAT. WATCH WT.	U590:Z282
ARTH	VISIT SUMMARY:	4-16-84 IMP: GENERALLY IMPROVED. HAD BAD KCS AND MYALGIAS, PARESTHESIAS ONE WEEK AGO BUT NOW RESOLVED. TOLERATING TEGRETOL. B/P BETTER. WEIGHT UP ONE LB. PLAN: CHECK CBC, K+. CONSIDER INCREASE IN TEGRETOL.	U590:Z282
ARTH	VISIT SUMMARY:	3-26-84 IMP: BP BETTER ON HCTZ. TEGRETOL DID REDUCE PAIN BUT HAD GI UPSET OF UNKNOWN CAUSE AND STOPPED TEGRETOL. PLAN: RE-START TEGRETOL. CHECK CBC.	U590:P030

PROBLEMS/MANIFESTATIONS	ONSET	UNITS	LAST DATA	DATE	LOC	PRVD	NEW DATA
13. PAST MEDICAL HISTORY:						J626	
5. PEPTIC ULCER DIS.	1978		NONE	07-27-83	ARTH	J626	
6. ELEVATED C.E.A.	3/83					J626	
11. HX DIVERTICULOSIS	3/83					J626	
34. SURGERIES:						U590	
12. S/P T.A.H.	9/82					J626	

Fig. 26.6b The summary time-oriented record (STOR). ***Part B*** contains short free-text visit notes, free-text summary reports (radiology reports, discharge diagnoses), laboratory results since the last clinic visit, inactive problems and inactive therapies. [WHI 85]

(source Quinn E Whiting-0'Keefe, MD; Donald W. Simborg, MD, Wallace V.Epstein, MD; Anne Warger. A computerized summary medical record system can provide more information than the standard medical record. JAMA, Vol 254, no. 9 Sept.6 1985 pp 1185 - 1188)

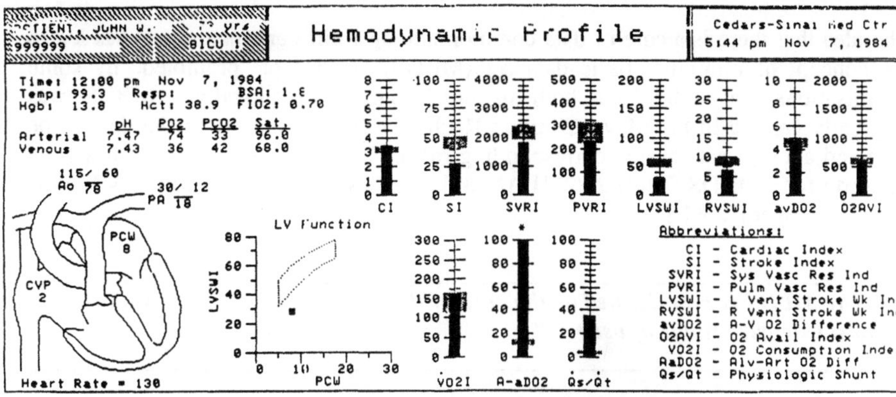

Fig. 26.7 A computer-stored medical record can organise and represent data in special tailored reports and displays of the clinical state of the patient [SHA 88]

(source Shabot MM : *Software for computers and calculators in critical care medicine.* Software in Healthcare, Feb.March 1985,pp 26-39 in *JAMA, june 17, 1988 - Vol 259, No.23 pp 3435 -3439)*

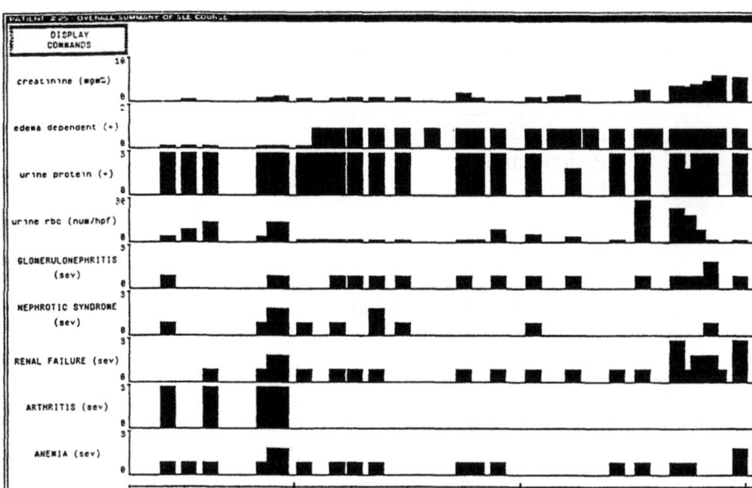

Fig. 26.8 Idefix is a knowledge-based system which generates intelligent summaries from a time-oriented database of patients who have systemic lupus erythematosus (SLE), in order to help physicians handle large amounts of information and avoid overload. Derived entities are given on a severity scale from 0 to 3. [ZEG 88]

(source I. M. De Zegher-Geerts, M.D., Andrew G. Freeman, M.D., Michael G. Walker, B.S., Robert L.Blum, M.D., Ph.D. and Gio Wiederhold, Ph.D. *Summarization and display of on-line medical records.* In *M.D. computing, VOL 5 n°3, 1988* pp 38 - 45)

26.5 Minimum Basic Data Set

The idea that there is a core of data common amongst different institutions has led to the concept of minimum basic data set (MBDS), a concept "promoted" by some organisations and individuals both nationally and internationally. MBDS was originally created in the Mayo Clinic at Rochester (USA), indicating the data to be gathered about a patient and corresponding rules. In Europe a proposition has been put forth for a MBDS (Table 26.2) [LAM 82]. The best known definition of MBDS is given by Roger [ROG 81]:

> ***"The MBDS can be defined as the core of the hospital information, with the most extensive range of usages."***

This was further clarified : "The MBDS was not designed to meet the total needs of any one or all user groups. Each group is therefore free to expand beyond this core to meet its own total data needs."
The information covers patient identification data, ADT-data, identification of the responsible referring physician, examination and treatment data. This collection of data is also known under the name 'uniform hospital discharge set' (UHDS) and is especially relevant for clinical and epidemiological studies.

Table 26.2 Minimal basic data set proposed for the EEC, covering 13 categories. [LAM et al 82]

1.	Hospital identification
2.	Patient number
3.	Sex
4.	Age
5.	Marital status
6.	Area of residence
7.	Month/year of admission
8.	Duration of stay
9.	Discharge status
10.	Main diagnosis
11.	Other diagnoses
12.	Surgical and obstetrical procedures
13.	Other significant procedures

26.6 A Name Is Not Enough: Classification and Coding Schemes

One of the most important fundamentals of medicine today is communication of medical information. In order to exchange and compare data, symptoms, signs, diagnosis and treatments, terminology has to be standardised. Therefore, international classification schemes were composed. A classification is the clustering of terms or concepts into classes which share common attributes, while a nomenclature concerns a list of names in a specified medical domain with the same meaning.

As explained by Blois [BLO 88], the higher one climbs in the knowledge hierarchy, the less descriptions remain exact. For example, the term cancer is higher in the knowledge hierarchy compared with the word atom (for which even no synonyms exist) and has a variety of other meanings such as "neoplasm", "tumour" and "malignancy". Due to the enormous richness in medical terminology the necessity to code each medical term with synonymous terms was recognised very early.
The National Library of Medicine (USA) acknowlegded this type of problem and decided to use a controlled vocabulary for indexing its stored literature citations in its ***medical subject headings (Mesh) system*** [BIS 89].
The first attempts at classification schemes date from 1880, but the first multi-axial form was the ***Systematized Nomenclature of Pathology (SNOP)*** that has been in use since 1965 by American pathologists.
Pathological entities can be described by using a four-dimensional model, indicating :

T	topography	(1)	
M	morphology	(2)	
F	functions	(3)	(physiology)
E	etiology	(4)	(the cause of a disease)

By selection of an item in one of these four classes set up following a pre-defined hierarchy, the pathological state can be described (Fig.26.9).

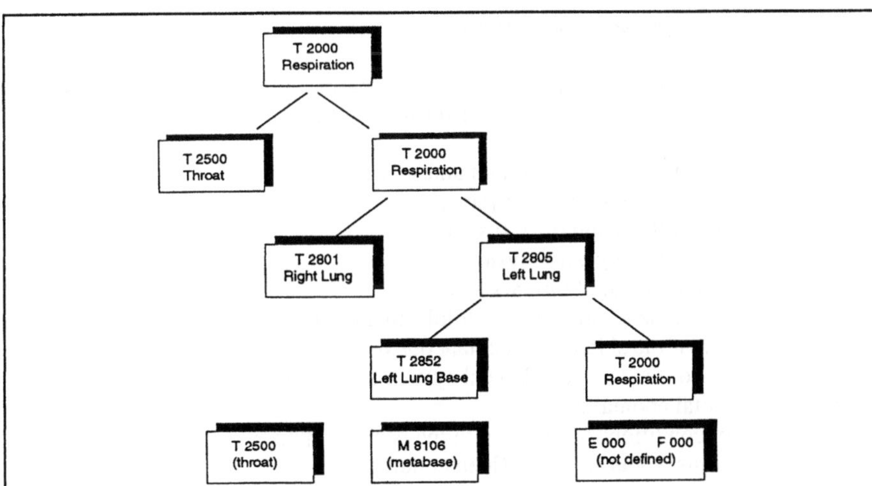

Fig. 26.9 Systematized Nomenclature of Pathology (SNOP) representation

The Systematized Nomenclature of Medicine (SNOMED) classification adds more elements to the previous method, namely :

- P Procedures containing all administrative, medical, diagnostic and therapeutic actions
- D Disease
- O Occupation of the patient

[For definition of terms histology, morphology, physiology, aetiology and topography, see glossary.]

SNOMED is a codification system originally defined for pathologists and consists in that way of the topography, morphology, aetiology, functions, disease, procedure and occupation. Although SNOMED contains more than 50 000 coded terms, it seems not to be used very frequently.

Parallel with this, the World Health Organization (WHO) defined the International Classification of Diseases (ICD). The first ICD, ***Injury and Death*** was established a long time ago and is now in the 10th revision, which is expected to be implemented in 1993. ICD-9 is now in use generally and is the best international norm for hospital record abstracts, mortality statistics, cancer registers and occupational medicine.

This classification system has, however, some well-known shortcomings, as it is felt not to be specific enough or to be incomplete. These limitations gave rise to extension of the classification scheme in some countries. The Commision on Professional and Hospitals Activities (CPHA, 1979) has made a clinical modification (CM, Table 26.3) by extending diagnostic categories and by adding a classification of procedures including surgery. Nowadays, there exist various computer programs on the market to assist physicians in creating their own ICD-9-CM codes.

Table 26.3 Classification of ICD-9-CM (volume 1)

1. Infectious and parasitic diseases
2. Neoplasms
3. Endocrine, nutritional, and metabolic diseases and immunity disorders
4. Diseases of the blood and blood-forming organs
5. Mental disorders
6. Diseases of the nervous system and sense organs
7. Diseases of the circulatory system
8. Diseases of the respiratory system
9. Diseases of the digestive system
10. Diseases of the genitourinary system
11. Complications of pregnancy, childbirth and the puerperium
12. Diseases of the skin and subcutaneous tissue
13. Diseases of the musculoskeletal system and connective tissue
14. Congenital anomalies
15. Certain conditions originating in the perinatal period
16. Symptoms, signs and ill-defined conditions
17. Injury and poisoning
18. Classification of external causes of injury and poisoning
19. Classification of factors influencing health status and contact with health services
20. Morphology of neoplasms

Diagnosis-related groups (DRG, Fetter et al. 1980) is an inpatient classification scheme that groups patients who are medically related by diagnostic, therapeutic and demographic categories with homogeneous costs based on the length of stay and medical activity analysis. The classification scheme and the assignment of inpatients to DRG groups is dependent upon the consumption of resources that vary with the length of stay, the patient's primary and secondary diagnoses at discharge time, (in some but not all cases) patient's age sex and discharge status and surgical procedures performed, resulting in 467 homogeneous diagnosis groups. It has been proven [TIE 89] that the DRG system is not easily transportable to other countries. In several countries in Europe the DRG is under study and evaluation for health care financing. The DRG is divided into 23 sub-divisions (major diagnostic categories, MDC) to which all of the codes of ICD-9-CM have been assigned on the basis of organ system wherever possible (Fig. 26.10). An important consequence is the fact that implementing the DRG requires the use of the ICD-9-CM classification scheme. An obstacle within this context is the fact that the national scheme for procedures and operations is not directly comparable in Europe between countries. A number of software programs for DRG exist on the market. The one that assigns DRG is known as the Automatic Grouping System (AUTOGRP), which clusters information by minimising the distance between observations.

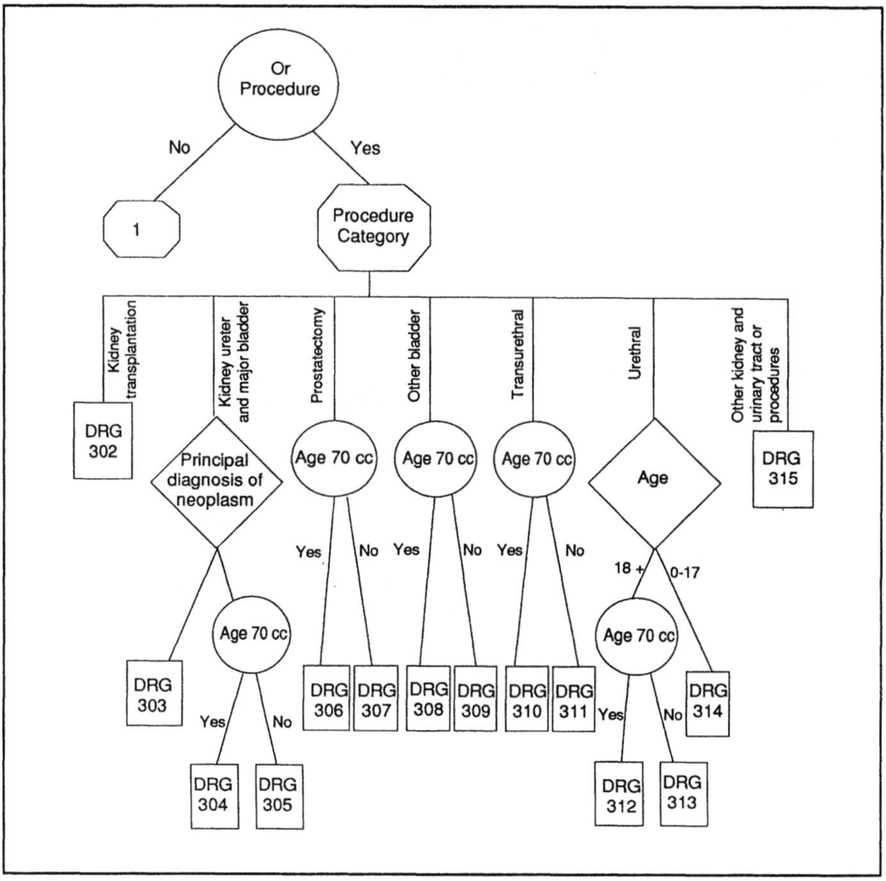

Fig. 26.10 Diagnosis-related groups decision tree for major diagnostic category 11, diseases and disorders of the kidney and urinary tract

(source reprinted with permission from Paul L. Grimaldi and Julie A. Micheletti in *Prospective Payment : The Definitive Guide to Reimbursement* (Chicago : Pluribus Press 1985). pp. 34 - 35. Copyright 1990 by the Foundation of the American College of Healthcare Executives)

The TNM classification is a system for virtual representation of the anatomical extent of malignant tumours at the different stages of their development [TNM-Atlas - 2nd edition]. It is based on the assessment of three indictors, T, N and M: ***T*** represents the extent of the primary tumour, ***N*** is an indicator for spread to the regional lymph nodes and ***M*** stands for the absence or presence of distant metastases. The addition of numbers to these three components (e.g. T1, T2, N0) indicates the extent of the malignant disease.

For example, an oncologist familiar with the TNM classification might describe a patient suffering from lung cancer as "T3 N2 M0". This would indicate :

T3 tumour with a size of more than 5 cm
N2 demonstrable spread to the lymph nodes in the mediastinum
M0 no clinical evidence of distant metastases

Current Prodedural Terminology. As the ICD-9-CM classification is too detailed for general practioners, many physicians in the USA are using the Current Procedural Terminology (CPT) of the American Medical Association (AMA). It consists of a five-digit code (Table 26.4). CPT4 is not used very much in Europe.

Table 26.4 Major categories in the CPT4 coding system
Physicians Current Procedural Terminology ,4th ed (AMA 1988)

CPT4 Coding	Classifications
Anaesthesia	00100 - 01999
Surgery	10000 - 19499
Radiology	70010 - 79999
Pathology and laboratory	80003 - 89399
Medicine	90000 - 99140

Read Codes. The Read Clinical Classification (commonly called the Read Codes) contains a coded nomenclature of 100 000 terms and a synonym list of 150 000 terms and covers the whole of medicine in the detail needed for patient medical records, i.e. diseases, occupations, history/symptoms, examinations/signs, diagnostic preventive and therapeutic procedures, drug administration and DRG. This hierarchical nomenclature uses a five-character alphanumerical code, is organised into classes and is classified by attributes, e.g. aetiology, physiology, anatomy (Table 26.5). Moreover, the Read clinical classification is cross-referenced to and compatible with other classifications such as ICD-9-CM, CPT4 and the British National Formulary (BNF).

Table 26.5 Read classification

LEVEL	TERM	READ	ICD-9-CM
1	Circulatory system diseases	G...	390-459
2	Ischaemic heart disease	G3...	410-414
3	Acute myocardial infarction	G301.	410
4	Anterior myocardial infarct	G301.	410.1
5	Acute anteroseptal infarct	G3011	410.1

Table 26.6 In the area of coding and terminology within health care, many tools for medical semantics are available ranging from nomenclature systems, classification sytems, thesauruses, glosssary, knowledge base and grouper systems. It is important to mention that for procedures standards are still missing. This table represents a non-exhaustive overview of some well known systems. (Modified from [EWO 90])

- ICPM (International Classification of Procedures in Medicine - 1978) has served as a basis for the development other coding systems.
- OPCS-4 (Office of Population Censuses and Surveys : Tabular list of the classification of Surgical operations and procedures - 4th revision)
- ICCS (International Classification of Clinical Services) by CPHA

Category	Purpose	Example	Originator	Topic
Nomenclature	Medical records	SNOMED	CAP	General
		Read Codes	NHS-CCC	General
Classification	Statistics	ICD-9-CM	AMA	Diseases and Procedures
		ICPM	WHO	Procedures
		OPCS-4	UK	Surgical Procedures
		CPT4	AMA	Procedures
		ICCS	CPHA	Clinical Services
Thesaurus	Information retrieval	MeSH	NLM	General
		UMLS	NLM	General
		Malimet	Excerpta Medica	General
	Medical records	THESAM	AP Paris	General
Grouper	Reimbursement	DRG	Medicare	Hospital stay
Knowledge base	Decision aid	MYCIN	Stanford	Diagnosis
		QMR	Stanford	Diagnosis

26.7 The Unified Medical Language

The National Library of Medicine (NLM) USA started in 1986 a multi-year research project called the Unified Medical Language System (UMLS). The aim of the UMLS project is to facilitate information retrieval and provide uniform access from current and future biomedical information databases, including biographical, clinical records and medical knowledge databases. Due to the great variation in the terminology used by different systems, a metathesaurus of biomedical concepts had to be built relating the different resources and nomenclatures (MeSH, SNOMED, ICD-9-CM, CPT4). The UMLS Metathesaurus is viewed as a constantly changing dictionary (because of the volume of information) and represents alternative ways of saying the same thing and alternative ways of saying related things. It is more than a thesaurus because it contains the biomedical concepts of different thesauruses and controlled vocabularies [SPE 89]. In order to relate all these information classes and different meanings, a UMLS semantic network (Fig. 26.11) accompanying the metathesaurus has been built.

26.8 Achitecture of an Electronic Medical Record System

"*A patient file which comes too late is lost !* " is often said. So we must look for an improved way to handle manual medical records and that is where electronic medical records can offer an improvement as well as for other organisational issues. The architectural design of such a system is important. Managing large amounts of data and extracting useful medical information are a hardware and a software problem in the move towards an electronic medical record.

The storage problem.
In the past few years, optical storage technology has made possible applications, especially in the medical (imaging) environment, which were not feasible with magnetic disk technology. It is clear that providing storage is only half the battle, as data have to be moved from the storage device into memory and face several limitations. Besides the storage sub-system latency, one also has to deal with the limitations of the server's bus system, the network communications bandwidth.
Everybody in medical informatics agrees upon the concept of facing the ever increasing need for storage, by means of a layered storage pyramid. At the highest level of the data storage pyramid characterized for its greater speed, you find traditional magnetic media. Then deeper in the network, you have your secondary storage, erasable magneto-optical (MO) drives. Their slightly slower speed didn't matter as much. Finally at the bottom of the pyramid there is write-once optical memory (WORM). Putting all of these together, vendors estimated - one year ago - the hottest market since years.
What do we see today ? Optical technology seems to be stagnant because magnetic media continues to improve, because disks increase in storage capacity, and on the other hand tape provides more and more random accessibility. Technology wise there have been no advances in optical technology in the last year .

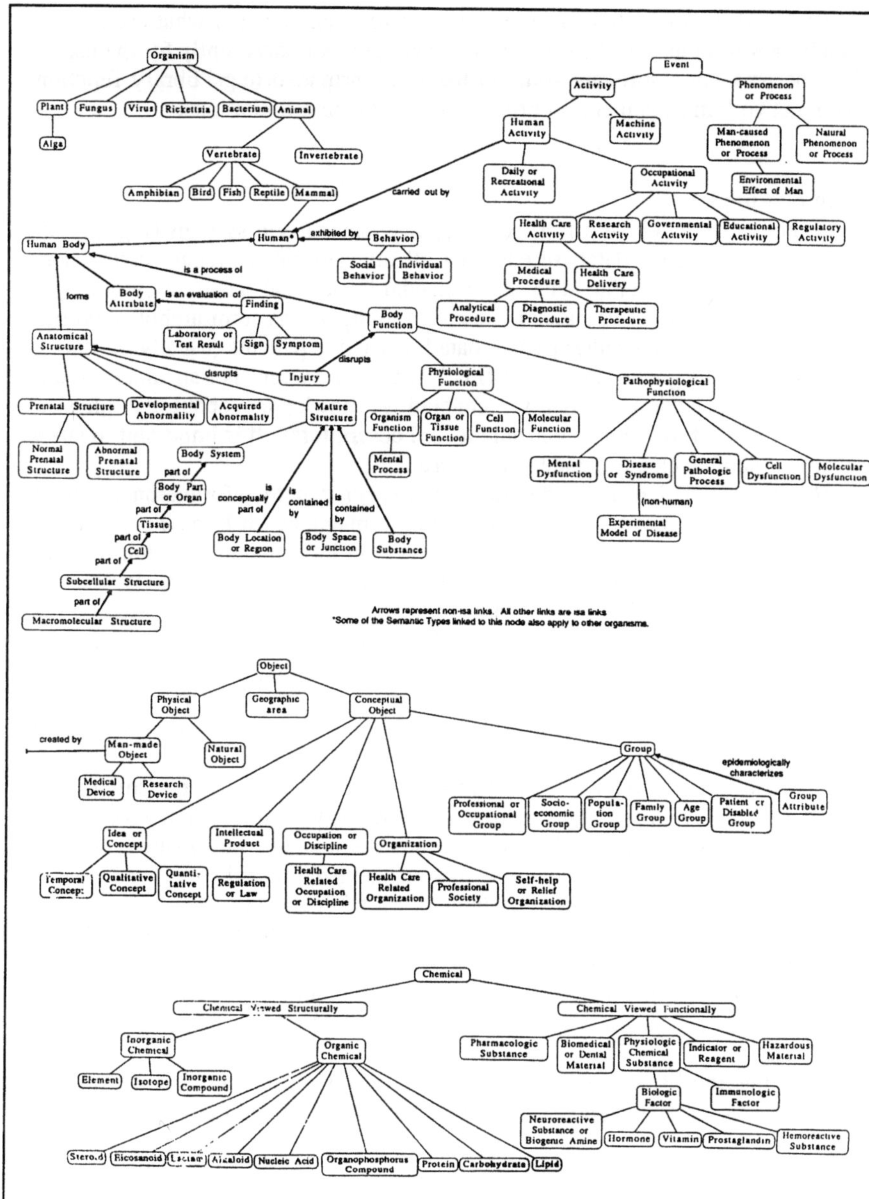

Fig. 26.11 Representation of the Unified Medical Language System (UMLS) Semantic Network [CRA 89].

(source : reprinted with permission from Mc Cray A.T. The UMLS Semantic Network in Kingsland L.C. (Ed), *Proceedings of the thirtceenth Annual Symposium on Computer Applications in Medical Care,* Washington DC, IEEE Computer Society Press, 1989, pp. 506 - 507)

Most vendors offer optical disks as a replacement for magnetic, but what users really want is a library of units and the software to make it work transparently for the user. As often the problem a software solution has to be provided (e.g.: library function, intelligent network management) in order to deal with these limitations.

In search of a model.
An electronic medical archive can be scattered over several sub-systems (Fig. 26.12): one containing the patient database covering all relevant patient identification data, "recent" medical (multi-media) data using standard relational database systems (on fast magnetic disks) for active patients; one containing a long-term archive covering all historic medical (multi-media) patient data for inactive patients (usually on optical storage devices or magnetic tape); and finally one in between, i.e. an index system providing a fast selection mechanism containing knowlegdge about the physical location of patient information (electronic record descriptors). It is important to stress several concepts of an electronic medical record:

- *The hierarchical mult-imedia storage concept,* where information is stored depending on the status (RAM memory, magnetic disk memory, optical memory and tape) after deactivation of certain information. The multi-media aspect is capable of managing different media : alphanumerical data, image data, text data (motion pictures and voice in the future). This is based on one actual economical factor, the availability of low-cost large optical discs, and optical tapes. Within 3 - 5 years, the whole picture may change.
- *The distributed storage architecture* in order to face the huge data transmissions needed across the network, as classic networkings are not adequate enough.
- *The storage manager* responsible for distributing (prefetching) the information over several layers based on a strategy to store recent generated or accessed information on fast storage devices and old information on slow main storage. Knowledge-based management techniques have to be developed to face the issue of optimal information allocation.
- *The parallel architecture* of the archive in order to face the high peak data transmission performance.
- *The communication network* assuring transportation integrity, security and management of information over high-rate networks through appropriate cable systems.

The prefetching mechanism will be a fundamental part in any hospital/medical record, offering acceptable response times by optimising physical transport.

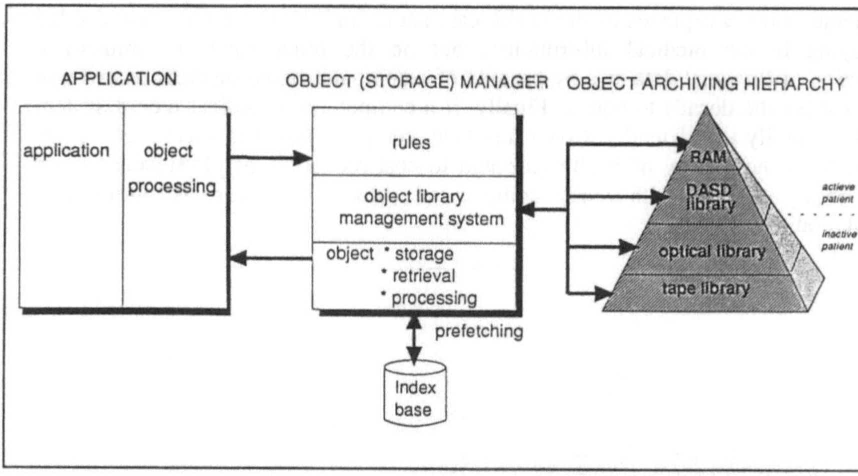

Fig. 26.12 General architecture of a longitudinal electronic medical record system, representing the archiving hierarchy and the storage manager function

The algorithm providing this stage-in and stage-out mechanism will be based upon the information contained in the central HIS database, providing information for patient visits, appointments, localisation, admission and speciality, in order to determine which part of the medical history is expected to be used. For images, the modality, body region and type of examination will be important input parameters.
Once information has been retrieved, the probability for a second retrieval within a short time is higher than before. The transfer (archival) of data between the storage layers can happen on a real-time basis (if information is necessary at once) or on a regular basis (during the night or in the background).
What computer architecture will be suitable as archive manager [multi-processor architecture, fast IO processors (IPI Interfaces), broadband communication bases], will be shown in the future.

26.8.1 Conversion from paper records to Computerized Medical Records: Some considerations

When planning to implement a computerised medical record system, it is essential to integrate the existing paper medical records into the new system (Fig. 26.13).
Several alternatives are possible to convert the existing paper medical record to a digital record by:

- Summarising the "active" old record and entering it into the computerised medical record
- Converting the existing paper record (documents) into digital pictorial information (electronic image) by means of scanning devices (the average of one letter-sized image is about 50 KB)
- A combination of both

Which choice is made depends upon the policy of the hospital. Furthermore, for developing an automated medical record system, it is worthwhile to take into consideration the acceptance of the health care actors and the amount of time needed for keying in the medical information, but on the other hand the immediate production of financial data as a by product of a computer-based medical record will be a must for the decade to come. Finally, if a computerised medical record system provides a really user-friendly driven interface, computer-based medical records can contribute to the quality of health care and to cost reduction, as physicians have a finite ability to deal with many complicated subjects and various information presentations [McD 88].

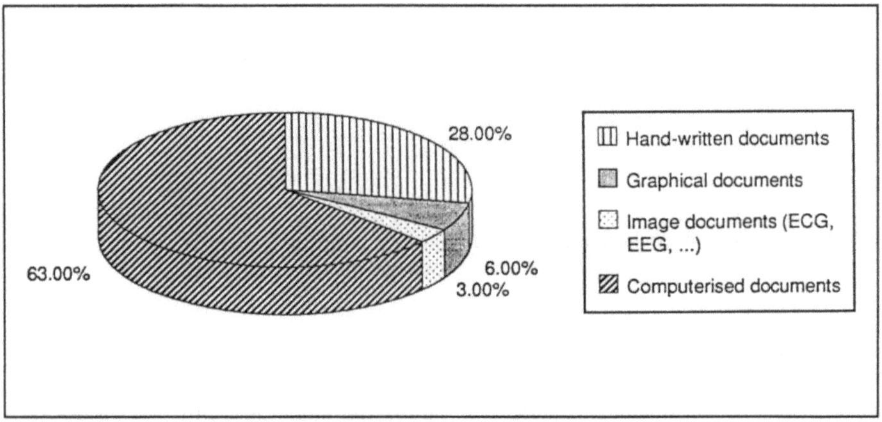

Fig. 26.13 Study conducted at the hospital of the Free University of Brussels in 1990 (AZ-VUB). Documents broken down by type for inpatient medical records (RX images not included) (Department of Medical Informatics, AZ - VUB)

26.9 Bibliographic Retrieval Systems

26.9.1 The Information Overload

We are living in an age of "information overload". There have been almost more books published the past 50 years than in all the previous centuries together. Dealing with that information overload is becoming extremely complex, and the challenge for every person is to read and retrieve only that information which is of interest to him or her and worth reading. As the availability of information is so immense, specific technological tools are used assist people to find the specific information they are looking for.

26.9.2 On-line Database Services

Since the mid-1960s, several technological features have converged to support the development and use of on-line database services, nowadays widespread in many (especially academic) organisations. By using computer terminals and PCs over international telecommunication networks, local access has been provided to several remote computers at far less than the cost of dialling long distance.

During the past few years the role has been widely recognised that on-line database services can play a valuable role in meeting the needs of professionals in hospitals, educational institutions, research centres, etc. The use of such services can help to eliminate duplicative or unnecessary research, transfer new ideas and concepts faster and sustain research activities.
Databases may be classified into referral and source types. The latter contains the original source data.

Some biomedical database systems are described here as examples. For further details, we refer to *On-line databases in the medical and life sciences* published by CUADRA, Elsevier (1987).

Medline

Type: Reference (bibliographic) **From:**National Library of Medicine (NLM)
Subjects: Biomedicine, biotechnology, food sciences and nutrition, health care, pharmaceuticals and pharmaceutical industry, toxicology
Content: Provides access to the world biomedical literature, including research, clinical practice administration, policy issues and health care services. Contains references to articles from 3200 journals published in the USA and about 70 other countries. Also covers chapters and articles from selected monographs through 1981. Author abstracts (from 1975) are available for about 60% of the citations. Corresponds in part to coverage of Index Medicus, Index to Dental Literature and International Nursing Index.

Embase

Type: Reference (bibliographic) **From:**Elsevier Science Publishers
Subjects: Bioengineering, biomedicine, biotechnology, environment, health care, pharmaceuticals and pharmaceutical industry, toxicology
Content: Contains over 2.9 million citations with abstracts of the world biomedical literature on human medicine. Covers anatomy, anthropology, anaesthesiology,biochemistry, bioengineering, cancer, dermatology, developmental biology, drug adverse reactions, drug dependence, drug effects, endocrinology, environmental health and pollution control, forensic science, genetics, gerontology and geriatrics, health economics, haematology, hospital management, immunology, internal medicine, microbiology, neurology, nuclear medicine, obstetrics and gynaecology, occupational health and industrial medicine, ophthalmology, otorhinolaryngology, pathology, paediatrics, pharmacology, physiology, psychiatry, public health, radiology, rehabilitation, surgery, toxicology and urology. Approximately 40% of the citations added to the database each year do not appear in the correspnding printed abstract journals and indices.

Emdrugs

Type: reference (bibliographic) **From:** Elsevier Science Publishers
Subjects: biomedicine, pharmaceuticals and pharmaceutical industry
Content: Contains citations with abstracts to the world literature on drugs corresponds to the pharmacology, Drug Literature Index and Adverse Reactions Titles sections of Excerpta Medica and to citations from those sections contained in EMBASE .

26.9.3 CD-ROM

Another way of dissemination of this information is handled by means of CD-ROM. A CD-ROM is a compact disc (CD) containing about 600 MB or 275 000 pages of information. It is only possible to read this information, and it cannot be altered.

CD Plus Medline from CD Plus
CD Plus Medline is the entire Medline database, covering 1966 to the present (on 7 CDs), Additional On-Disc tools: annotated MeSh, MeSH Tree Structures, Permuted MeSH, MeSH Scope Notes (comprehensive on-line user manual and tutorial), Browse Permuted MeSH for all related terms, Browse Trees (display relevant subheadings that have been applied to MeSH terms). Special features: search full citations, including abstracts with no disc swapping, automatic mapping from natural language terms to MeSH headings, menu and expert modes, emulate NLM, AIM, nursing and dentistry sub-sets, Printoff, SaveSearch, BackSearch features, floating sub-heading searchable, context-sensitive help screens, find similar citations feature.

Drug Information Center from Americal Society of Hospital Pharmacists
This CD-ROM contains detailed information on virtually every single drug entity in the USA. Included are the American Hospital Formulary Service Drug Information Annual, International Pharmaceutical Abstracts (1970 to now) and the Handbook on Injectable Drugs. With this, you receive information on drug indications and uses, contraindications and side effects, drug administration, options, cautions, toxicity and interactions, dosage and regimens, chemistry, stability and pharmacological actions and investigational drugs.

Excerpta Medica CD: Drugs and Pharmacology from Silver Platter Information Inc.
This contains more than 900 000 abstracts and citations from 1980 to the present. It provides comprehensive coverage of drugs and the pharmacology literature, including the effects and use of all drugs and potential drugs and the clinical and experimental aspects of pharmacokinetics and pharmacodynamics. The side effects and adverse effects of drugs are also mentioned. Drugs are listed by trade name.

27

Computer Assisted Clinical Decision Making

" ***Nothing is certain but death and taxes*** ."Benjamin Franklin

27.1 Introduction

One of the most important activities in the health care world is medical decision making. Decisions for selecting an appropriate diagnosis or therapy rely on deductive reasoning, knowledge and experience. It has always been one of our society's expectations 'especially in the field of medicine, which is characterised by a considerable growth of knowledge' to couple "science-fiction" intelligent machines with the complex task of medical decision making. Another important issue in using computers to assist physicians is to reduce the number of errors made in diagnosis by recognising that computer systems do not suffer from human weakness such as fatigue, forgetfulness and failure and therefore perform better at certain moments or in specific environments where specialists are not available [BON 85]. The way a physician carries out a diagnostic or/and therapeutic decision making process can be described by a cyclic act as illustrated in Fig. 27.1.

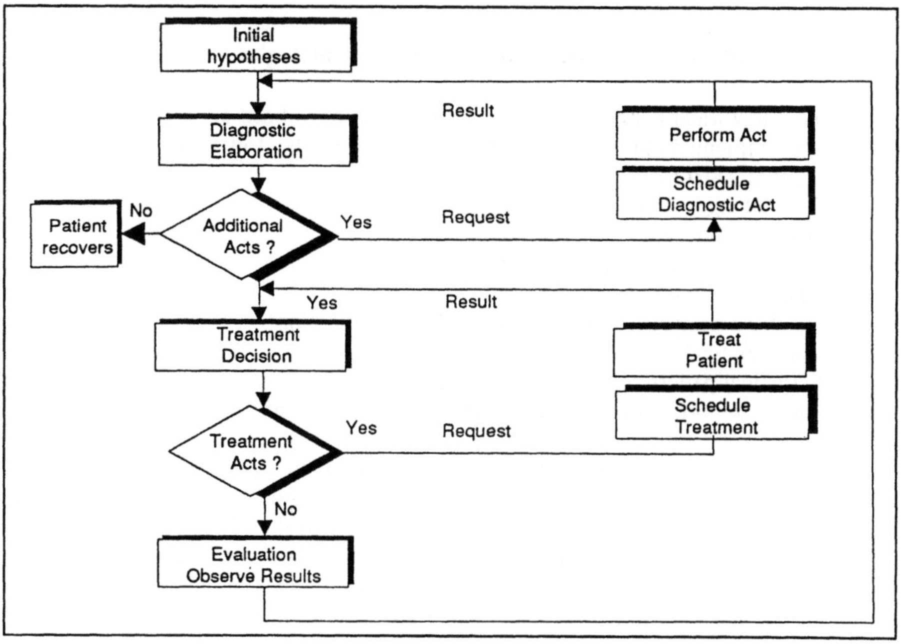

Fig. 27 1 Cycles in medical decision making

In contrast to previous chapters which describe the way in which computers assist medical professionals in clinical decision making by information management and communication (know what), this chapter focusses on the functionality of medical decision making (know how).
According to their function, medical computer systems can be categorised as information management systems, decision support systems or data acquisition systems. The aim of information management systems is to store and communicate all kinds of patient data. Examples include the conventional HIS, RIS and LIS as described earlier. Data acquisition systems are intelligent computer nodes for capturing, processing, monitoring and verifying electronic signals measured by medical instruments derived from patients (monitoring, CT, analysers, etc.).
A medical decision support system (DSS) can be defined as an interactive computer system supporting the physician in clinical decision making [REG 81]. The main objective is to assist the physician, *not to replace* him. As no computer program knows all elements of the patient to be taken into consideration for the decision making, the physician is free to override or adjust the recommendations made by the system. Up to now, several types of DSS have been built with varying success.
These DSS can be split further into consultation systems, monitoring systems and critique systems, following Rennels and Shortliffe [REN 87]. To understand the way clinical support systems assist the health care professional in the diagnostic process, we can characterise them by surveying the underlying computer-based approaches in decision-science methodology.

27.2 Survey of Underlying Decision-Science Methodologies

If we take a historical perspective of techniques that have been applied so far in the design and implementation of DSS, we can mention the following according to Shortliffe, et al. [SHO 79]:

- Clinical algorithms
- Decision theory
- Reasoning with uncertainty (Bayes' theorem)
- Knowledge-based systems
- Database analysis for prognosis and therapy selection
- Mathematical modelling
- Statistical pattern recognition techniques

Only the most important methodologies are discussed here briefly.

Clinical algorithms have been used in conventional computer programs to describe in detail the operations to be executed in a pre-defined order necessary to solve a problem in a very narrow domain. The first attempt in that direction arose in the 1960s as it was the only technique available at that time.As medicine covers a complex domain, clinical algorithms have been rejected by health care providers as too simplistic and too limited for use. There are several other techniques to support decisions discussed hereafter.

27.3 Decision Trees and Decision Tables

- ° Decision trees (flowcharts) indicate in a logical order in a stepwise manner the decisions to be taken (fig.27.2).
- ° Decision tables composed of four sections: the conditions, state of conditions, actions and state of actions. They can be further classified into limited entry, extended entry and mixed entry tables (see also Karnaugh diagrams).

In the following, an example of decision tables is presented. It illustrates the application to therapy decisions in patients with liver metastases of colorectal carcinomas [SCH 89].Eight decision tables with a total of 76 rules were composed. In Table 27.1, the overall resectability decision table is shown. For five conditions, seven decision rules (R1 - R7) were created, specifying two actions (A1,A2) and the decision table to be executed in the next phase.

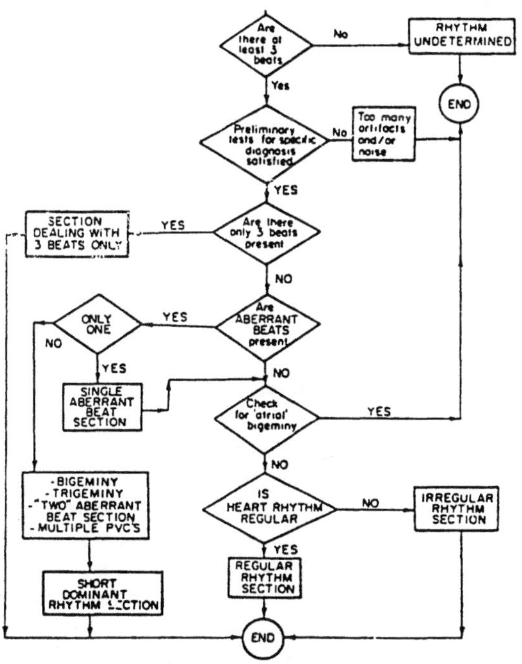

Fig.27.2 Arhythmia analysis by means of a decision tree [BEM 89]
(source reprinted with permission from Van Bemmel J.H., Willems J.L.; *Handboek Medische informatika,* Bohn, Scheltema & Holkema, Utrecht/Antwerp 1989, p. 234)

In medicine and other areas as well, it is accepted that facts and conclusions are characterised by a degree of uncertainty and are often based on incomplete information. Therefore, in the implementation of expert systems, the knowledge representation has to be combined with uncertainties. In this domain of reasoning 'known as plausible or inexact reasoning' there are several schools of thought. One important direction is based on probability reasoning. Four important methods here are [LUC 88]:

- Bayesian method (= probability theory)
- Certainty factor model
- Dempster Shafer theory
- Fuzy Logic (Zadeh)

Table 27.1 Example of a decision table for "overall resectability". EHD , extra-hepatic disease; LM, liver metastases; PT, primary tumour; syn, synchronous; meta, metachronous ; N, No ; Y, yes

(Source Study carried out by the Oncology Department of Surgery, University of Heidelberg, FR and department for Medical and Biological Informatics, German Cancer Center, Heidelberg)

DT5	Overall Resectability	R1	R2	R3	R4	R5	R6	R7
C1	Extrahepatic Disease (EHD)	N	N	-	Y	Y	-	N
C2	Occurrence of Metastases	syn	syn	syn	meta	-	-	meta
C3	Resectability of the LM	Y	N	-	Y	-	N	Y
C4	Resectability of the PT	Y	Y	N	-	-	-	-
C5	Resectability of theEHD	-	-	-	Y		-	-
A1	Set resectability	Y	N	N	Y	N	N	Y
A2	Set Foundation	11	7	5	11	5	9	13
NT	Next Decision Table	Liver Resection	I.a Chemoth.	Systemic Chemoth.	Liver Resection	Systemic Chemoth.	Systemic Chemoth.	Liver Resection

27.4 Reasoning with Uncertainty: Bayes' Theorem

In many expert systems estimates are based on probabilities and use of the Bayesian method, calculating the probability that a patient is suffering from a certain disease as derived from prior information and observations of the relative probability with which certain symptoms occur. The theorem of Bayes is a quantitative method revealing the diagnostic probability p (D/T) using the sensitivity and specificity of a certain test and prevalence of the disease. Starting from the registration of test results for individuals who are suffering from a certain disease and test results for healthy people, we come to the distribution in fig. 27.3 and table 27.2.

Table 27.2 Representation of TP (true positive), TN (true negative), FP (false-positive) and FN (false-negative) results in a population characterised by the presence or absence of a disease

Test result	Disease		
	Present (D)	**Absent (D')**	**Total number of patients with**
Positive (T)	TP	FP	Positive test result
Negative (T')	FN	TN	negative test result
Total number of	Diseased patients	Non-diseased patients	Total population

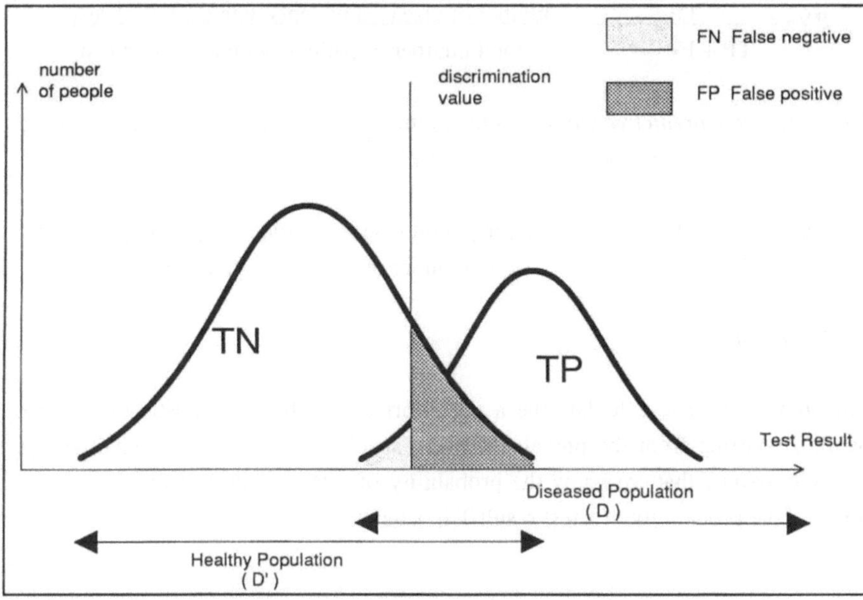

Fig. 27.3 Representation of the distribution of test results in a healthy and diseased population. The displacement of the discrimination value along the X-axis will vary the false- positive and false-negative values for the two populations

Terminology

p (T/D) =sensitivity: probability that a patient suffering from disease D has a positive test result.

$$\mathbf{Sn} = \frac{TP}{TP + FN} = \frac{\text{number of diseased patients with positive test}}{\text{total number of diseased patients}}$$

p(D) -prevalence: the *(a priori)* probability of disease D in the population concerned (a priori means "before we know the result of the test").

p(T'/D') =specificity: probability that a non-diseased patient has a negative test result

$$\mathbf{Sp} = \frac{TN}{TN + FP} = \frac{\text{number of non-diseased patients with negative test}}{\text{total number of non-diseased patients}}$$

p(D/T) =positive predictive value of a test: probability that a patient with a positive test has the disease D (it is also called the diagnostic or a posteriori probability).

$$\text{PV+} = \frac{TP}{TP + FP} = \frac{\text{number of diseased patients with a positive test}}{\text{total number of patients with a positive test}}$$

p(D'/T') =negative predictive value of a test: probability that a patient with a negative test does not have the disease.

$$\text{PV-} = \frac{TN}{TN + FN} = \frac{\text{number of non-diseased patients with a negative test}}{\text{total number of patients with a negative test}}$$

Bayes' Theorem

The theorem is used to calculate the a posteriori probability (diagnostic or posttest probability) starting from the prevalence p(D), specificity p(T'/D') and sensitivity p (T/D). We assume that we know the probability of a test result T if the disease is present and the probability of a test result T in a healthy population.

$p\,(T\,.\,D) = p\,(T/D)\,.\,p\,(D)$ (1)

$p\,(T\,.\,D)$ is the probability that a patient has a positive test result AND the disease

$p\,(T\,.\,D') = p\,(T/D')\,.\,p\,(D')$ (2)

$p\,(T) = p\,(T(D + D')) = p\,(T.D + T.D') = p\,(T.D) + p\,(T.D')$ (3)

Combining Eqns. (1) and (2) gives

$p\,(T) = p\,(T/D)\,.\,p\,(D) + p\,(T/D')\,.\,p\,(D')$ (4)

we know that $p\,(D.T) = p\,(T.D)$ (5)

with Eqn. (1) yields $p\,(D/T).\,p\,(T) = p\,(T/D).p(D)$

$$p\,(D/T) = \frac{p(T/D)\,.\,p\,(D)}{p\,(T)} \quad (6)$$

Substituting Eqn.(4) into Eqn.(6) gives

$$p\,(D/T) = \frac{p\,(T/D)\,.\,p\,(D)}{p\,(T/D)\,.\,p\,(D) + p\,(T/D')\,.\,[1 - p\,(D)]} \quad (7)$$

and finally in terms of prevalence, sensitivity and specificity :

$$\boxed{p(D/T) = \frac{p(D) \cdot S_n}{p(D) \cdot S_n + (1 - p(D)) \cdot (1 - S_p)}}$$

Bayes' theorem has certain requirements in the medical field due to the fact that :

- The probabilities of two illnesses (or symptoms) are assumed to be independent, i.e. the occurrence of one illness does not influence the probability of the occurrence of the other disease, conditions that seldom hold in practice. The approach is valid if illnesses are mutually exclusive and exhaustive (sometimes called "simple Bayes" models). Most current methods of computer diagnosis use this model, as it is expected that without this assumption the complexity of the calculations would become highly difficult to execute.
- The elements of the a priori probabilities (on the right) are rarely known with accuracy, which reduces the global accuracy of the result.
- A third problem occurs when a series of tests are used who are conditionally dependent (i.e. the probability of a particular result depends on the result of the previous test)

27.5 Decision Analysis

In decision analysis, one creates a decision tree representing diagrammatically the clinical alternatives. Such a decision tree contains different nodes. By convention,

- Square boxes define decision nodes, from which multiple lines (i.e. actions or alternatives) leave.
- A chance node is represented by a circle, from which several lines emanate. To every branch of each node, probability estimates are assigned.
  Every chance node is characterised by a number called the "expected value". It is the value that is expected on average for a specified chance event or decision.
- At the end of each branch, the outcome of the corresponding strategy is depicted, (utility values).

In performing a decision analysis, several steps have to be taken: after designing the decision tree and assigning probabilities and outcome utilities (a), expected values in every chance node have to be calculated (b). Subsequently, the alternative with the highest expected value is chosen (c) and finally the decision making process ends with a sensitivity analysis (d). For example, we have two possible medical treatments (A and B) for an illness, and the life expectancy after every treatment is shown in table 27.3:

Table 27.3 Life expectancy following two treatments

Life expectancy (years)	Patients Treatment A	% B
0	10	5
5	70	60
10	20	35

The question arises, which treatment is preferable ? How do we choose ?
Regardless of the choice of the treatment, the patient will have died by the end of the 10th year. So we have to establish a criterion related to a numerical value for choosing among treatments. In this case the criterion can be the duration of life after treatment. This is defined as the Utility and represents the value of a specific outcome to a decision maker [OWE 90]. The associated decision tree is presented in Fig. 27.4.

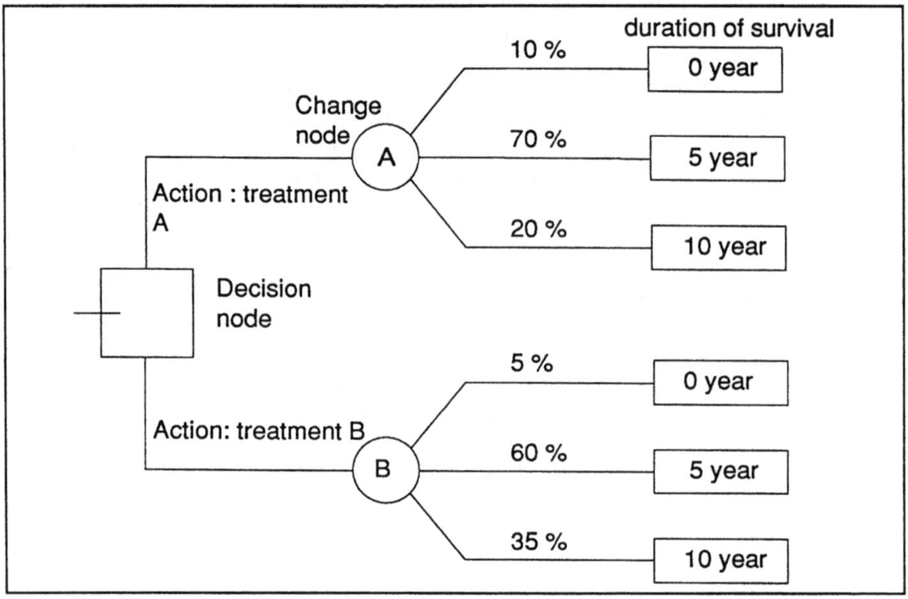

Fig. 27.4 Example of a decision tree representation of surgical intervention given two differnent treatments, A and B

Expected survival for treatment A
= (10 % x 0) + (70% x 5) + (20% x 10)
= 5.5 years

Expected survival for treatment B
= (5 % x 0) + (60 % x 5) + (35 % x 10)
= 6.5 years

The choice of the criterion (Utility) is not always easy, and we also have to take into account the quality adjusted life-year (QALY), a commonly used concept as a measure of utility in medical decision analysis.
For example, a 77-year-old patient (man) has a lump in the prostate and a slight increase of phosphate level. There is a strong suspicion (about 70% probability) of cancer of the prostate. As treatment, prostatectomy is considered. The mortality after surgery is estimated at 1%. The probability for a complete recovery after surgery is estimated at 10%. On the other hand, without surgical intervention, the illness has a progressive course. The likelihood of discovering that the patient is

suffering from prostate cancer can be increased by an early biopsy test. The sensitivity of the test is estimated at 95% and the specificity at 90%. The possible survival outcomes include 'death', 'completely recovered' or 'incurable'. To characterise each outcome accurately, we decide that the utility values for each outcome are "1" for completely recovered, "0.2" for incurable and "0" for death. These should reffect the patient's own evaluations. With this information, the decision tree for this treatment can be created (Fig 27.5).

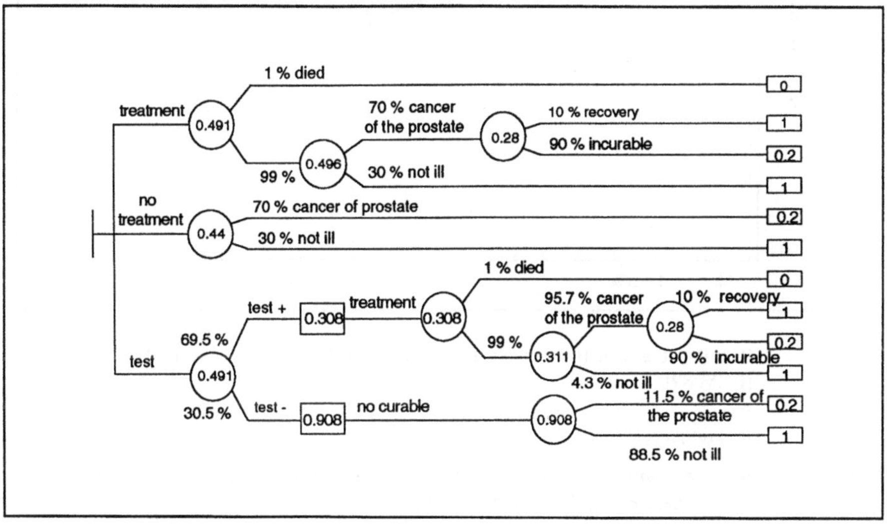

Fig. 27.5 Decision tree for prostatectomy example. Probabilities have been calculated for each branch in each node. The patient's valuations of outcomes (1 ; 0.2 ; 0) are assigned to the tips of each branch of the medical decision tree [BEM 89].

(source reprinted with permission from Van Bemmel and Willems: *Handboek Medische informatica.* Bohn, Scheltema & Holkema, Utrecht/Antwerpen 1989, p. 245)

27.5.1 Sensitivity Analysis

If we examine the results of the decision tree of the previous example, we see that the expected values for immediate treatment and treatment after a positive test result remain the same. The question arises of whether the conclusion will change with modified probability or utility values ?

By modifying the probability at certain chance nodes, we can discover the validity of certain choices and detect the optimal strategy. This technique for testing the robustness of a decision analysis by repeating the analysis with probability and utility estimates within a reasonable range is called sensitivity analysis (Fig. 27.6).

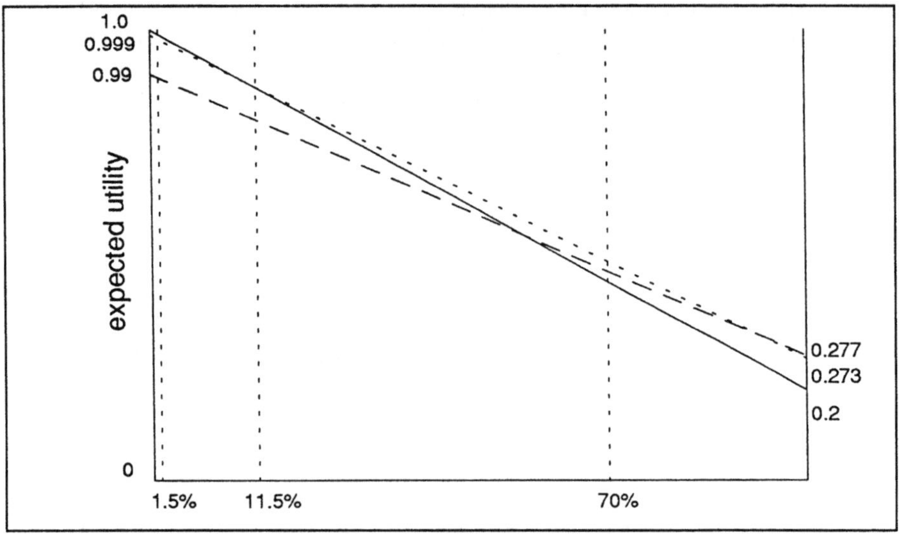

Fig. 27.6 Results of a sensitivity analysis. (a priori probability of cancer of the prostate) [BEM 89]

Strategy _______ : no treatment ; - - - - - - : first make tests ; .... : treat immediately

(Source reprinted with persmission of Van Bemmel, Willems in *Handboek medische informatika*, Bohn, Scheltema & Holkema, 1989, p. 246)

27.6 Artificial Intelligence

Artificial intelligence (AI) is a growing field that covers many disciplines. As a science, essentially part of cognitive science, the goal of AI is to understand the principles that make intelligence possible. As a branch of computer science, it deals with the design of intelligent computer systems involving symbolic (as opposed to numerical) representation of knowledge and its use in problem solving and search [WAH 86]. Nowadays, there is much confusion surrounding terms such as AI, expert systems (ES) and knowledge-based systems (KBS) (Fig.27.7). AI has many different sub-areas [CER 86]:

- Natural language understanding
- Computer vision
- ES
- Search, problem solving and planning
- Theorem proving, logic programming
- Knowledge representation
- Learning
- Miscellaneous (game playing, AI approaches to education, AI tools, speech understanding and other areas).

Just as a HIS can be viewed as a special case of a DBMS, an ES is a special type of a KBS. It embodies knowledge about a particular, generally fairly narrow domain in

partially) of an expert in that domain. The aim of a KBS is to manage a knowledge base, while the goal of an ES is to infer advice or new facts on which to base further actions using specialist knowledge about a finite domain [GRI 88].
ES are a sub-domain of AI as both technologies have the capability to reproduce the human ability to select relevant facts and generate logical conclusions. The difference is however, that in AI the system learns from previous cases (adding or modifying information in the system), while ES do not generate or modify their own KB logic without the help of experts in the relevant field and knowledge engineers.
In recent years, there has been an increasing interest in medical KBS, which will play a crucial role in the next decade as medical knowledge is rapidly changing, expanding and highly specialised and often requires very large amounts of knowledge and data.
As KBS do not suffer from human weaknesses such as forgetfulness or failure in making a diagnosis, and as in some environments or at certain specific moments a specialist (expert) is not available, it is understandable why there were so many expectations towards the development of computer programs to assist with medical decision making.
In contrast to traditional data processing that is engaged in quantitative analysis and numerical or data-processing applications, KB technology concerns itself with qualitative analysis and symbolic reasoning [HAA 87]. (Table 27.4). A physician's knowledge is not mathematical or quantitative, but qualitative . For instance, ES might use the patient's history from the conventional HIS database (= quantitative analysis) to predict a diagnosis or plan medication therapy.
The real problem is to formalise the medical knowledge, to agree on facts in the medical world and to define what is meant by a diagnosis, a prognosis, etc.

The main issue in medical informatics is to interpret data as information and to make sound decisions. Although a lot of work has been done in that domain by important research groups since 1970 (Fig.27.7), most ES developed for the health care environment did not leave their research institutions, and if they did, they were mostly implemented on separate computer systems 'due to their resource consumption and complexity 'with no integration at all with other computers or databases. Because of this, integration of promising KB applications in today's HIS is more the exception than the rule.

Table 27.4 Comparison of knowledge -based (KBMS) versus data-based (DBMS) systems in medicine

	KBMS	DBMS
Analysis	Qualitative	Quantitative
Representation	Representations and use of knowledge	Representations and use of data
Efficiency	resource consuming	provides high efficient management of large volume of data
Use	Use of medical Knowledge for deduction and explanation	Use of medical data for management decision and statistical studies
Functionality	high generic methods of representing data & knowledge	moderate
Models	Knowledge models ° production rules ° frames ° semantic networks ° logic	Data models ° classical file ° hierarchical DBMS ° network DBMS ° relational DBMS
Process	Inferencing mechanism Decision making Heuristic	Repetitive processing mechanism Record keeping Algorithmic

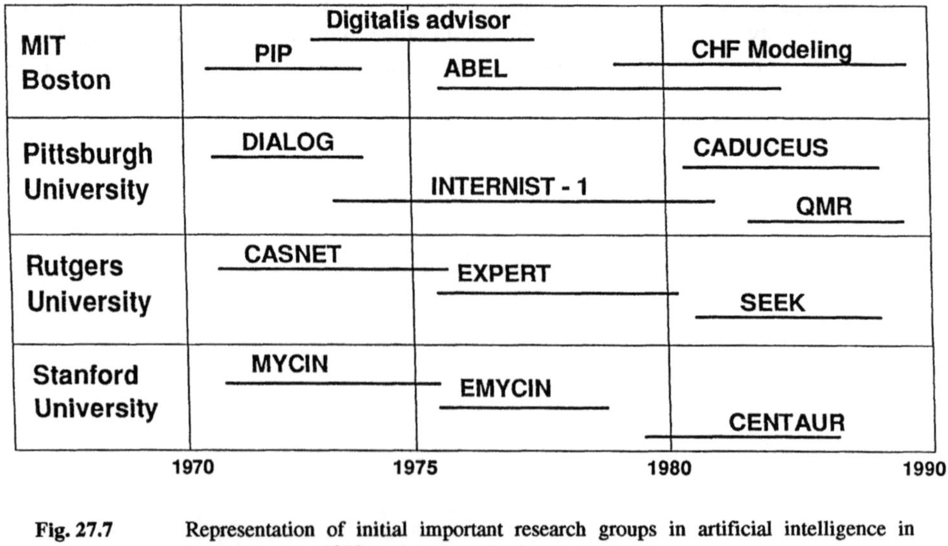

Fig. 27.7 Representation of initial important research groups in artificial intelligence in medicine since 1970, and their medical expert systems.

27.7 Architecture For an Expert System

The architecture of an ES can be presented by the following modules (fig.27.8):

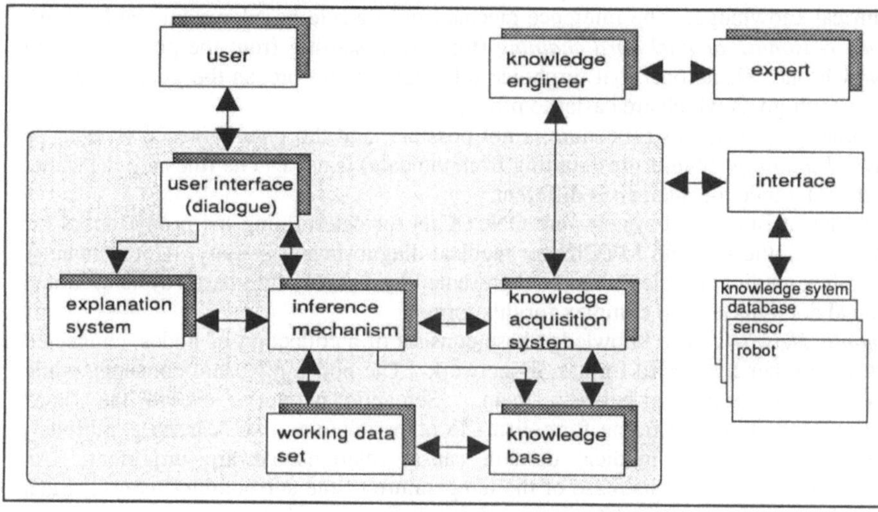

Fig. 27.8 Representation of the general architecture of an expert system

The knowledge base takes the most important place in the system and contains a collection of domain knowledge, while the *inference engine* contains the general knowledge. The inference engine must be interfaced with an *explanation facility* such that a domain expert can interrogate the rules without the help of a knowledge engineer.

According to Rennels and Shortliffe, there are several challenges to be faced in designing KBS. The first is that one has to take into account the huge quantity of information and the richness of knowledge from medical experts to be managed. For example, the QMR knowledge base may contain 250 000 items of knowledge, which took 10 years of collaboration between knowledge engineers and physicians to elicit, test and validate. The laborious nature (build-test-rebuild cycle) of medical knowledge acquisition is commonly ascribed to problems in communication and transfer of knowledge between two experts, one in the medical field and the other in information processing, each speaking "different" languages. The formalisation of medical knowledge is the most difficult one to achieve. A second challenge develops from the fact that medicine has only limited models of the human body or of its diseases. This in contrast to industrial expert systems in which processes are well known and more easily described. The third and most important challenge is to ensure that the knowledge base is designed in a way that can easily be adapted or enlarged to accomodate to the changes in human knowledge. Ideally, this data structure -though hard to achieve- should be independent of algorithms that manipulate this knowledge.

Representing knowledge

Knowledge can be represented in several ways:

Rule-based. The knowledge (base) consists of a collection (= rule base) of production rules (e.g. IF < CONDITION>THEN <ACTION>) and one or several data structures containing medical facts related to that domain (=fact bases). One can say that production rules are most widely used in ES to describe heuristic, theoretical or empirical knowledge. The inference mechanism in a rule based system can be *goal-driven reasoning or backward chaining* (top-down, starting from the possible goals) in which one selects one goal or choice (alternative) and breaks the goal down into smaller sub-goals which are easier to prove.
For other problems this procedure is not possible, and the *data-driven reasoning or forward chaining* (bottom-up , starting from the data) is used. The rules are the same, but the inference mechanism is different.
Examples of rule-based systems are ONCOCIN for determining the proper doses for VAM chemotherapy and MYCIN for medical diagnosis and therapy. Unfortunately, only a few medical problems can be represented by a purely rule-based system. Some medical domains are too complex for this format.
Semantic Network. The knowledge base consists of a collection of nodes, connected with each other by arcs to form a 3D network. The nodes represent concepts, while arcs give the relations between them. Semantic networks extend the "is-a" relationships -as in the frame formalism- to other relations like "causes", "inhibits", "stimulates". In the medical domain causal relationships are important: "An inflammation causes an increase of the temperature of the surrounding tissue". Such networks are often referred to as causal networks in medical applications, as they encode causal relationships among items [GIU 88]. Examples of medical applications are CADUCEUS, CASNET and MEDES. (Fig. 27.9).

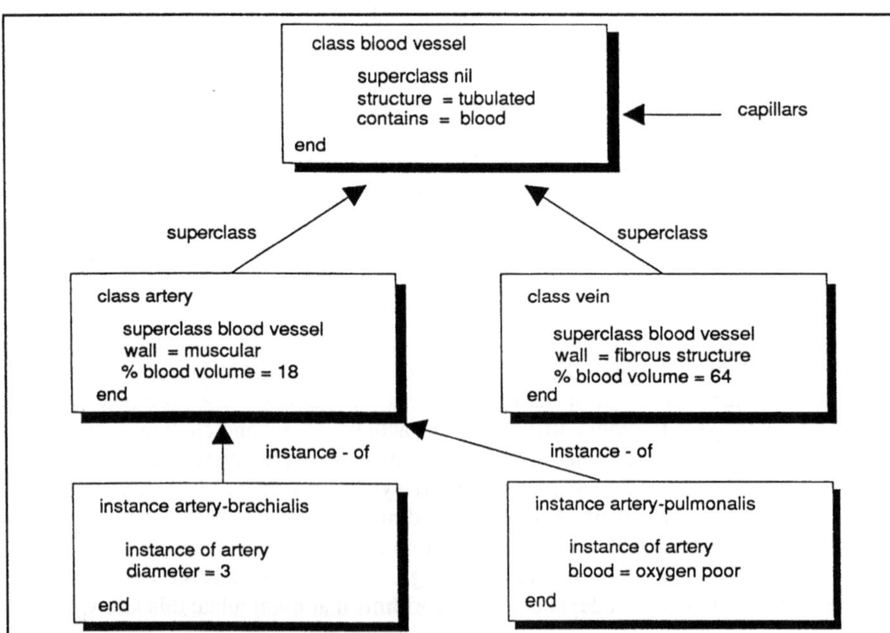

Fig. 27.9 Semantic network example from the vascular system characterised by a hierarchical frame taxonomy

Frames. Frames is another method of knowledge representation introduced by M. Minsky. In frame based ES all knowledge about a concept or an object is grouped into a frame. (Fig. 27.10.) Frames and values can be represented as a generic network. The rules can be represented as a specific type of arc. To transform frames into a semantic network, the different slots of a frame are represented by different types of arcs in the semantic network. This knowledge representation can also be presented as a semantic network. Both knowledge representation mechanisms are characterised by the inheritance concept, by which certain objects through transitivity inherit the properties of (parent/ancestor) objects. Two frame-based systems are CENTAUR and LOOPS.

RULE
To determine the dose of methotrexate administered in VAM chemotherapy in protocols 20-83-1 and 2091:
if: the serum creatinine level (in mg per dl) exceeds 1.5 **Then:** do not give methotrexate

FRAME		
Name: Tularemia		
Symptoms and Signs	Evoking Strength	Frequency
FEVER	0	5
SKIN Lesion Culture Francisella Tularensis	5	4
LYMPH Node Enlarged	1	4
SKIN Ulcer	1	4
EKG Sinus Tachycardia	0	4
TULARENSIS Skin Test Postive	4	3
EXPOSURE To Rabbits.Rodents Small Mammals	2	3
TICK Bite Recent History	2	3
HEADACHE Severe	1	3
Can cause:		
Pyrogenic Shock	1	2
Appendictis Acute	1	1
Predisposes to:		
Endocarditis Acute Infective Left Heart	1	1

Fig.27.10 RULES AND FRAMES are the elements of two approaches to representing medical knowledge. Rules have the form "If condition X, then action Y". When rule-based ONCOCIN (*top*), in determining the proper dosages for VAM chemotherapy, establishes that the "if" part of its methotrexate rule is true, it concludes that the "then" part is indicated. Frames are descriptive details of such objects as diseases and symptoms. In frame-based QMR the disease frame for tularemia has weighted links to various signs, symptoms and other diseases. "Evoking strength" weights reflect the likelihood that the disease is present when a certain symptom is observed: 0 means the symptom is nonspecific and 5 means the disease in the only cause of the symptom. "Frequency" weights, on the other hand, indicate how likely the disease is to give rise to a particular symptom: 1 means it does so rarely, whereas 5 means it does so in almost every case [REN 87,p.152]

(source reprinted with permission from Rennels, G.D. and Shortliffe, E.H. in *Advanced computing for medicine.* Scientific American, Octobert 1987, p. 152)

Predicate calculus. Here knowledge is represented by logical sentences in which predicates occur to define relations or properties [TAL 90] e.g. *If an epileptic patient has partial seizures and carbamazepine does not sufficiently control the seizures, then Valproate sodium may be tried.* This can be written as:

DIAGNOSIS (epilepsy, X)
EPILEPSY- TYPE (partial siezures, X)
DRUG- PRESCRIBED (carbamazepine, X)
SEIZURE-STATUS (controlled, X)
===>
DRUG TO BE TRIED (valproate sodium, X)

Other. The knowledge base is a mixture of both production rules and semantic networks and other possibilities. Examples of medical ES falling in this category are QMR and INTERNIST. QMR uses bitmap data structures (arrays of 0's and 1's) to create a small, fast pattern-oriented ES.

Knowledge acquisition sub-system assists the knowledge engineer and the domain expert with a more user-friendly (graphical) interface for recording and maintaining incrementally rules and parameters in the knowledge base. The absence of this subsystem is nowadays seen as the critical bottleneck in building ES.

An inference engine executes reasoning (invokes rules from the knowledge base) based on the data of the problem applied to the KB to draw inferences or conclusions. In traditional inference engines, data are mostly found in the working memory or from interaction with the user instead of the HIS (operational) database.
The inference engine of the ES uses these rules in the knowledge base to evaluate information about patient treatments and institutional processes from the HIS. There are two approaches for achieving optimal integration:

- The HIS is the system of the user, and special tasks are dedicated to the KBS
- The KBS is the system of the user, and data are retrieved and stored in the HIS

There exists no general way to build an inference engine as it depends heavily on the application domain and the way the KB is designed.
Inference engines (namely for rule-based systems) use forward or backward chaining (or interleaved chaining). The inferencing strategy and the knowledge base are interdependent [BER 89].

Explanation sub-system is an end-user interface that manages consultations between users and the ES during decision-making. It traces the system's progress through the reasoning process and provides, on request, an overview of the logic supporting a decision. Good tracing facilities are essential to allow the domain expert to validate the rule base [JON 90]. If an ES can explain its actions, it will be better accepted by experts in that domain for validation and by non-experts seeking its advice.

A working memory is generally used to store initial and derived data about the case in hand.

Table 27.5 Overview of tasks important Medical Experts Systems perform in medicine

Name	Domain	Action	References
MYCIN	Blood infections and meningitis	Diagnosis	[SHO 76]
CENTAUR	Pulmonary function	Diagnosis	
NEOMYCIN	Diseases causing neurological symptoms	Diagnosis	
ABEL	pH control	Diagnosis	[PAT 82]
SAM	Arterial hypertension	Diagnosis	[GAS 81]
INTERNIST/ CADUCEUS	Internal medicine	Diagnosis	[POP 82]
CASNET	Glaucoma	Diagnosis	[WEI 78]
PIP	Renal disorders	Diagnosis	[PAU 76]
PUFF	Pulmonary infections	Diagnosis, interpretation	[KUN 79]
CRYSALIS	Protein analysis	Interpretation	[ENG 79]
SPHINX	Epigastric pains	Monitoring	[FIE 81]
IRIS	Ophthalmology	Monitoring	[TRI 77]
DIGITALIS	Cardiology	Monitoring	[GOR 78]
ONCOCIN	Cancer	Monitoring	[SHO 81]
MOLGEN	Planning biological experiments	Monitoring	[MAR 77]
VM	Monitoring patients in intensive care	Monitoring, interpretation, control	[FAG 80]
ATTENDING	Anaesthesiology	Tutorial	

27.8 Tools for Developing Expert Systems

One can develop ES with traditional procedural languages such as C or Pascal, or with specific AI languages or with ES shells. Procedural languages will offer you a high degree of independence and flexibility but also involve extensive investment or development (time), while AI languages will improve productivity but sacrifice performance.

Today, there exist a number of AI languages such as Prolog, LISP, SMALLTALK and others to build ES (Table.27.6). They commonly use the technique of recursion.

LISP, which stands for List processing, is the mainstay of AI communications. Prolog, which stands for programming in logic, is based on a sub-set of traditional logic called predicate logic. For a very readable introduction of Prolog, we refer to the classic work by Clocksin and Mellish. The SMALLTALK language is an object-oriented environment.

An ES shell is a domain-independent software tool (empty framework), including an inference engine, an acquisition component for entering rules and sometimes an interface for progresses or file systems. Examples are Cognate, Experfacts, Instant

Expert Plus, Nexpert, KEE, Art, Knowledge Craft, OPSS, EMYCIN.ES shells provide the fastest and easiest way of realising ES, but the more powerful shells are expensive and often "resource consuming".

Table 27.6 Programming tools with models and paradigms

Programming environment	Models and Paradigm	
Prolog	*Logic-based*:	uses predicate calculus
LISP	*Procedure-based* :	uses nested subroutines
SMALLTALK	*Object-oriented*:	uses the object oriented paradigm
EMYCIN	*Rule-based*:	uses IF-THEN rules, providing forward and backward chaining

27.9 Illustrative Examples of Some Clinical Decision Support Systems

27.9.1 MYCIN

The most important medical ES up to now have been developed at Stanford University and at the Massachusetts Institute of Technology (MIT). Stanford is well-known for ES such as MYCIN, ONCOCIN, PUFF and RADIX, while PIP, DIGITALIS ADVISOR and ABEL have been created at MIT. In particular, Shortliffe has made an important contribution with the design of MYCIN (Ph.D. dissertation in 1974).

As MYCIN is of historical interest due to the fact that it was pioneering work in the field of medical ES, it deserves special attention. From its origin until now MYCIN embodied all the features that stand for what ES should be. LISP was the programming language of choice. MYCIN is an expert system in which heuristic knowledge about diagnosis and treatments for infectious diseases is stored. It aims to identify the bacteria responsible and suggests a medication therapy with the required dosage. It computes degrees of certainty to indicate the strength of its conclusions.

In MYCIN the knowledge is represented as production rules of the following form [BUC 84]:

RULE 156	
IF :	1. The site of the culture is blood, and 2. The grain stain of the organism is gram-negative, and 3. The morphology of the organism is rod, and 4. The portal of entry of the organism is urine, and 5. The patient has not undergone a genitourinary manipulative procedure, and 6. Cystitis is not a problem for which the patient has been treated
THEN :	*There is suggestive evidence (0.6) that the identity of the organism is e.coli.*

(**Source** [BUCH 84] Buchanan G.B., Shortliffe E.H. (1984). *Rule-Based expert systems. The MYCIN experiments of the Stanford heuristic programming project.* Addison-Wesley Publishing Co.)

1) Patient's name: (first-last)
** **FRED BRAUN**
2) Sex: *(Questions 1-3 request background patient data.)*
** **M**
3) Age:
** **55**
4) Are there any cultures for Fred Braun which may be related to the present illness, and from which organisms have been grown successfully in the microbiology laboratory?
** **Y**

--------CULTURE-1--------
5) From what site was the specimen for CULTURE-1 taken?
** **BLOD**
=BLOOD *(System corrects typing error.)*
6) Please give the date and time when CULTURE-1 was obtained. (mo/da/yr time)
** **JUN 20, 1977**
The first organism isolated from the blood culture of 20-JUN-77 (CULTURE-1) will be referred to as:

--------ORGANISM-1--------
7) Enter the laboratory-reported identity of ORGANISM-1:
****UNKNOWN** *(Typically identity is not yet known.)*
8) The stain (gram or Ziehl-Neelsen acid-fast) of ORGANISM-1:
** **NEG** *(Preliminary lab results give some clues.)*
9) Is ORGANISM-1 rod or coccus (etc.):
** **ROD**
10) What is the form of the individual organisms (e.g. lancet-shaped for cocci, fusiform for rods, etc.)?
** **FUSIFORM**

(... more questions follow in order to gather sufficient information to infer the identity and significance of the infecting organisms ...)

23) What is the suspected portal of entry of the gramneg rod from the blood culture of 20-JUN-77 (ORGANISM-1) into this sterile site?
** **GI (6)** *(User indicates the uncertainty of his response.)*
24) Is Fred Braun a burn patient?
** **N**
25) Is Fred Braun a compromised host (e.g. alcoholic, sickle-cell-disease, immunosuppressed)?
** **N**
26) Is Fred Braun febrile?
** **Y**

(... after about 50–60 questions, MYCIN prints the diagnostic hypotheses on which therapy will be based ...)

My therapy recommendations will be designed to treat for organisms that are either very likely or, although less likely, would have a significant effect on therapy selection if they were present. It is important to cover for the following probable infection(s) and associated organism(s):

INFECTION-1 is BACTEREMIA

<ITEM-1> E.COLI [ORGANISM-1]
<ITEM-2> KLEBSIELLA [ORGANISM-1]
<ITEM-3> ENTEROBACTER [ORGANISM-1]
<ITEM-4> KLEBSIELLA-PNEUMONIAE [ORGANISM-1]

Fig. 27.11 MYCIN rule-based expert system. Excerpts from a MYCIN consultation. Comments in italics are not part of the actual interaction. User input is shown in bold print [BUCH 84, p. 69]

[Source : Reprinted with permission from Van Melle W. The structure of the MYCIN system in BUCHANAN B.G. and Shortliffe E.H. (eds), *Rule based expert systems,* Academic Press, 1985, p. 69]

The inference mechanism of MYCIN mostly uses backward chaining or goal-driven reasoning, starting with the goal and working backwards:

Goal: Find out about	D
Rule 1:	IF C, then D
Rule 2:	IF B, then C
Rule 3: IF A, then B	

Implicit rule:	IF A, then C
Question: Is A true (?)	

The selection of the therapy is a four-part decision process. To start, the physician must answer the question whether or not the infection is significant for the patient (1). If so, the organism must be identified (or the range of possible identities found) (2). As there are several drugs available, and some drugs are highly useful against certain organisms but not effective against others, a set of potentially useful drugs has to be selected (3). Finally, the best drug for the patient must be selected from the list of possibilities (4).

The third component of MYCIN is the explanation facility, aimed to give the user access to the ES knowledge. As illustrated in Fig. 27.11 the questions put to the systems are explained to the user as completely and understandably as possible.

27.9.2 ONCOCIN Therapy Planning System

The ONCOCIN system is an interactive expert (advisory) system designed to support physicians in their treatment of cancer patients. It deals with cancer treatment *protocols* (a protocol is a pre-defined treatment plan). Each protocol contains detailed information on chemotherapeutic treatments that should be administered to a patient, indicating drug choice dosages and treatment planning (Fig. 27.12). The recommendations generated by the system are based on important clinical events such as the patient's past and current physiological state, laboratory results, concurrent treatment operations and the patient's response to the drugs and/or radiation treatment over a period registered into the system by the consulting oncologist during a visit.

This system is currently being used on an experimental basis in the Stanford Oncology day centre. The most common mechanism to store protocol knowledge is the production rule. Over 900 rules about 35 different treatments are currently included in the ONCOCIN system. The following is an example of a typical rule, translated into English [WAL 87]:

IF	the chemotherapy is B-CEPP, and drugs are to be administered, and serum creatinine > 2.2
THEN	administer 75% of the full dose.

As it would be impractical to redesign ONCOCIN every time a new protocol is implemented, the system is extended with a knowledge-entry system, called OPAL, to enter details of new protocols through a graphical user interface into the system. The aim of this interface was to eliminate the role of the knowledge engineer as go-between for the KB and the physician.

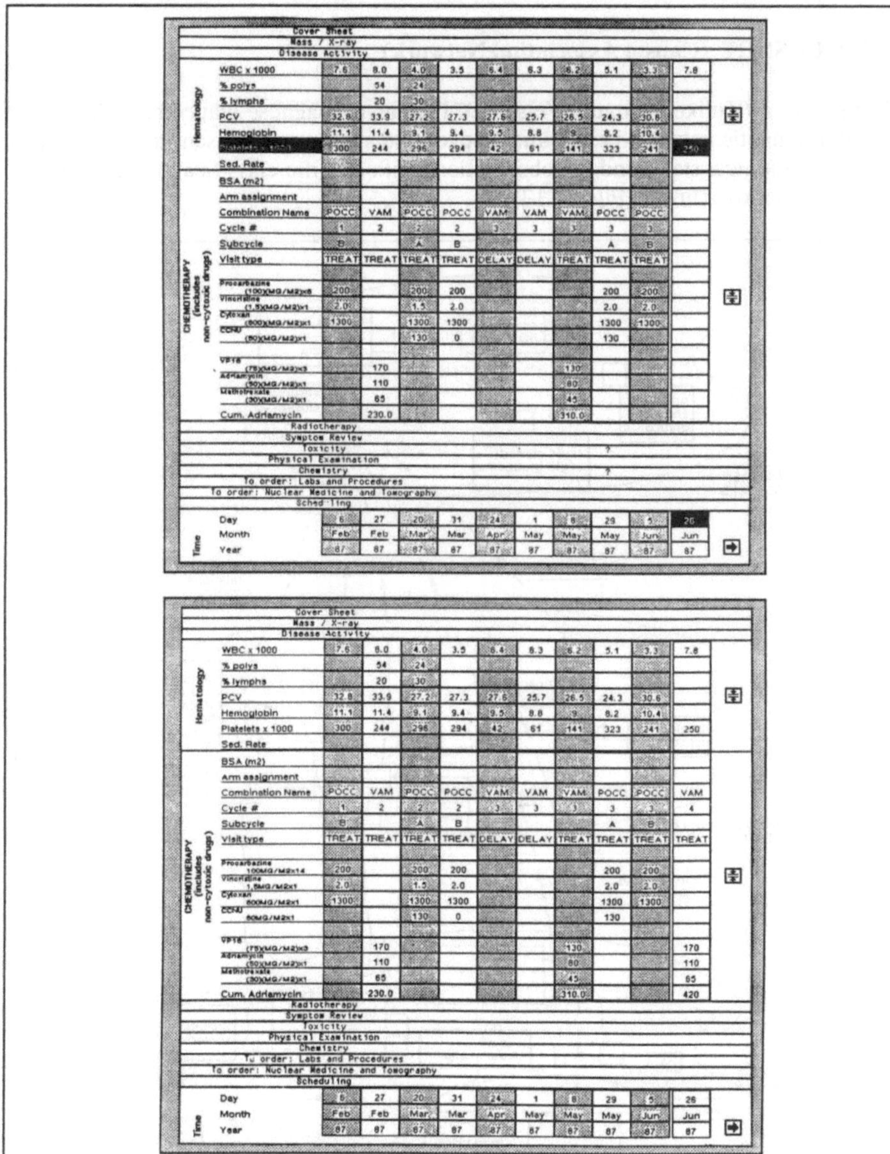

Fig. 27.12 ONCOCIN consults about chemotherapy by way of an electronic spreadsheet, two "snapshots" of which are shown: a data-gathering stage and an advice stage. Windows for haematology and chemotherapy are open; others are available. The doctor enters haematology data for June 26 ***(top)***. Working with these data and with knowledge of the applicable protocol and of the patient's condition and earlier treatment, ONCOCIN applies rules to recommend dosages for the patient's June 26 visit ***(bottom)***; under different conditions the system might have modified the dosages or advised delaying treatment. [REN 87]

(source reprinted with permission from Rennels, G.D. and Shortliffe, E.H. in *Advanced computing for medicine*. Scientific American, October 1987, p. 150)

27.9.3 CASNET (Causal Association Network)

This program (Kulikowski and Weiss, 1971) aims to diagnose glaucomas. It makes use of a semantic network-based, knowledge-base system to represent the illness, the physiopathological states and the observations with specific classification, association or causal relations (links) (Fig. 27.13).

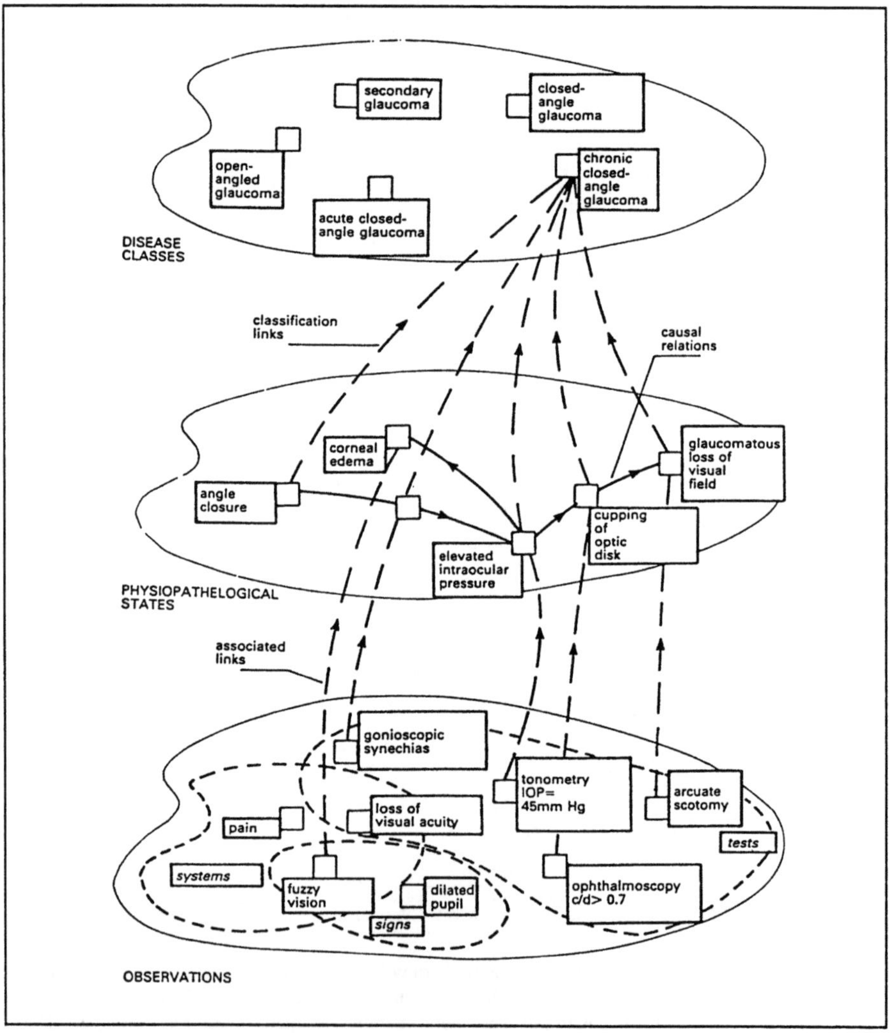

Fig. 27.13 Three-level description of an illness (after Weiss) [BON 85]
(source reprinted with the permission from Alain Bonnet. in *Artificial Intelligence*, InterEdtions, 1985, p. 165)

27.9.4 The HELP System

The HELP System could have been mentioned as an example in many chapters of this book and is a comprehensive HIS that combines medical ES capabilities with other programs that perform administrative, clinical, quality measurement and medical research functions.
Its modular, integrated design and data-driven decision support logic are unique in the industry and enable HELP to provide powerful assistance to clinicians. HELP facilitates clinical research by (1) automatically capturing specified data; (2) weighing the data against pre-established criteria stored in the computer and (3) reporting the results. Information is monitored and reported both concurrently and retrospectively, and study results are achieved quickly, accurately and with little manual interaction.

The concept for HELP (Health Evaluation through Logical Processing) originated at LDS Hospital (LDSH) in Salt Lake City, Utah, in the early 1950s with investigation into the possibility of using computers to assist in early diagnosis of congenital heart disease. This research led to the formation of the Department of Biophysics and Bioengineering at the University of Utah and subsequently to the development of a sophisticated HIS with integrated clinical applications, a central database of patient information and diagnostic, decision-support and alerting capabilities [WEE 90].
Today, HELP is being jointly developed by Intermountain Health Care and 3M Health Information Systems, both based in Salt Lake City. Intermountain Health Care is using the HELP System as part of a project called IHCNet which will electronically link IHC's 24 owned, leased or managed hospitals, the central office, Health Plans (an IHC health insurance subsidiary) and doctors' offices. 3M Health Information Systems is marketing the HELP System to other hospital organisations throughout the USA. IHC and 3M are currently making the necessary modifications and enhancements to enable HELP to operate in a multi-hospital environment. New programs are also being jointly developed to meet the growing demand for automation in the health care industry.

HELP runs on a Tandem mainframe computer that is interfaced to several Charles River mini-computers used as multiplexors and preprocessors. The Tandem mainframe is fault-tolerant. It has multiple processors to prevent a single failure from halting the system, and clinical data are stored on mirrored disk drives to reduce the possibility of data corruption.

The HELP System has clinical and administrative programs such as admission/discharge/transfer, pharmacy, NIS modules (including bedside terminal applications), laboratory alerting, radiology, infectious disease monitoring and others. Patient data are centrally stored in a database that can be accessed by the decision support logic and all programs (e.g. pharmacy, Radiology) in the system. HELP assists with billing functions, inventory control and surgery scheduling and performs other standard HIS functions. However, the HELP System's uniqueness lies in its modular, integrated design and its data-driven decision support logic.
For example, the medical decision logic that drives the HELP System is entered into separate modules. This decision logic is made up of rules and protocols developed by

physicians and other medical experts, who also decide how the modules will interact to simulate the processes they use to assess and implement treatment. This modular and integrated design enables the HELP System to suggest possible diagnoses and methods of treatment for health care professionals to consider in determining the most appropriate course of action (Fig. 27.14).

New modules can easily be added to the system and existing modules edited. HELP is able to accommodate a continually expanding body of medical knowledge, which is necessary for "state-of-the-art" health care delivery and prevents the system from becoming obsolete. This flexibility provides an optimal environment for research activities. HELP automatically collects, organises and reports information from many hospital departments and is readily available for study purposes. Modules can be designed and written to retrieve specific data and calculate and organize it to meet research criteria.

Medical knowledge has been encoded in logic frames (i.e. providing a knowledge base in that way) by collaboration of clinical experts and computers scientists, using a specialised in-house-developed language (PAL). If new patient data enter the system, HELP checks to see whether they match the criteria for invoking the logic decision of an HELP frame.
HELP's decision-support logic is data-driven. This means that patient information is analysed, suggestions for treatment are produced and event-driven alerts generated automatically when new patient data are entered into the system. For example, each time a nurse updates a patient's chart or laboratory test results are recorded, the process of acquiring these new data triggers HELP's decision support mechanism without requiring manual intervention.
The HELP pharmacy module demonstrates the data-driven concept. This module produces alerts for drug-to-drug interactions like most pharmacy systems in the industry. But unlike the others, HELP also checks for drug-lab, allergy, disease, diet, dose and drug-interval. Intermodular capabilities have proven valuable since findings in a 16-month study indicated that only 30% of drug alerts are drug-drug related. Drug-lab interactions account for 45% of alerts. This frequently occurs because a certain medication is acceptable at admission, but over the duration of a patient's stay, their laboratory values change such that the same medication is no longer appropriate. HELP automatically alerts the pharmacy or clinical laboratory as values change.
When a drug is ordered, the HELP System will automatically screen the order, check for adverse conditions and generate alerts. This feature has gained wide acceptance from physicians at LDS Hospitals. A study done in 1988 showed that more than 99% of LDSH physicians comply with HELP's recommendations on drug alerts.

```
Title: Pneumonia diagnosis (7.141.1)
Type: Diagnosis
Author: Peter Haug.
Date: 12/12/86
Message: "<disease_prob (val: #.##)>Pneumonia (history)".
Variables: chest_pain as (DO YOU HAVE CHEST_PAIN?),
        cough as (HAVE YOU HAD A COUGH WITH THIS ILLNESS?),
        fever_or_chills as MAX(fever, chills)
        where fever is (HAVE YOU RECENTLY HAD A FEVER?)
        and chills is (HAVE YOU HAD CHILLS RECENTLY?)
        if Exist (fever) or Exist (chills),
                        •
                        •
                        •
Statistics:     for fever_or_chills with TPR(YES, 0.85:  NO, 0.15),
                and FPR(YES, 0.3:  NO, 0.7),
                for cough with TPR(YES, 0.9:  NO, 0.1),
                and FPR(YES, 0.2:  NO, 0.8),
                        •
                        •
                        •
Evoking Criteria: If chest_pain EQ YES or fever EQ YES or chills EQ YES or cough EQ YES.
Logic:      disease_prob = 0.014.
        If Exist(fever_or_chills) then disease_prob=Bayes(disease_prob, fever_or_chills).
        If Exist(cough) then disease_prob = Bayes(disease_prob, cough).
                        •
                        •
                        •
        If disease_prob LT 0.014 then finish.
Ask:  Patients(fever, chills, cough) Hierarchical.
Urgency: 5/9
Gold Standard: If ICD_pneumonia and pneumonic_infiltrate
References: Harrison's Principals of Internal Medicine. Braunwald E., et al (editors)
Validation: Tested experimentally (DD method)
```

Fig. 27.14 This diagnostic frame (sector) for pneumonia in the HELP system was written with the general-purpose HELP decision editor. The frame is processed if the criterion in the Evoking Criteria field is met. The Ask field indicates which information the frame may collect interactively. The Urgency field indicates the relative urgency of recognising this disease. The Gold Standard field specifies criteria available by the time of discharge that would prove the existence of the disease being modelled. References refers to literature support for the frame, and Validation indicates the degree of evaluation to which the frame has been subjected. [KUP 88]

(Source reprinted with permission from Kuperman, G.J. and Gardner, R.M. *The Help System : A Snapshot in Time*, 1988, LDS Hospital)

HELP knowledge frames developed for event-driven logic on the main HIS computers have also been adapted at the University of Utah for use in a medical educational tool known as Iliad (Warner et al., 1988). Several studies (see, for example, Evans et al.,1986) have demonstrated the beneficial effect of HELP's decision logic on clinical measurements at LDS Hospital.

The HELP system is evolving toward a more distributed architecture, with microcomputers serving as workstations and data being shared over local-area networks. This large project at the University of Utah has been able to show how decision support through integrated data monitoring can bypass many of the traditional barriers to the use of computers for clinical decision support.

27.10 Coupling Database and Artificial Intelligence Technologies: Intelligent Databases

Nowadays, the world is reaching a point of information overload, if we bear in mind the steadily increasing number of scientific and other publications each year and the increasing availability of on-line public and private databases. [In 1980, there were about 500 on-line databases worldwide; for the moment, one estimates the number of on-line public databases over at 3500, without indicating some important proprietary databases.] Often, the possibility to store information greatly exceeds the ability to retrieve information, so information is not used effectively, without worrying where to search and to find the right sources and how to navigate in the file system. For instance, if we want to search for all newborn children within a 1 month period, the IS should give an indication that it is unreasonable to look for these patients on a ward unit of elderly people. As the need is constantly growing and more and more information is stored on-line, it is clear that current database technology is inadequate in most cases. Usually, conventional databases are represented in a three-layer architecture giving a static structure: the user view, the conceptual and the logical model. Each model has tools such as query languages, data models and indexing, with no (or fewer) semantics in the database. It shows that there is a clear need for intelligent databases to achieve the objectives. Because next generation HIS will be medically oriented and have to support the daily activities of health care providers in all areas, KBS can be introduced to support the rules for daily routine work and providing in that way a basis for building up further expertise, for example, intelligent ways of order entry and medication prescription. Therefore, our existing databases have to be expanded with intelligence to sustain medical thinking. One solution is merging relational DBMS with ES technology, enhancing in that way the dynamism of the database by adding reasoning and inference mechanisms. Intelligent databases will be characterised by two components: an object-oriented, deductive database engine and an inference engine which compiles and executes those programs written in extended SQL. One of the greatest expectations for this decade is the integration of clinical databases and medical KBS into a single unified framework.

As integration deserves extra attention and is now on the lips of everybody in the health care environment, there has been an increasing interest in coupling DB and KBS. There are three methods to produce hybrid systems :

- *Enhancing an existing database management system* with deductive capabilities (deductive database)
- *Coupling an existing database management system with an existing ES* tool (DB-AI coupling)
- *Extending an AI programming language* with database management capabilities (enhanced AI systems)

The first approach aims to introduce deductive and other features directly into a conventional relational database system while remaining compatible with the existing declarative ANSI standard. It extends the relational model (which can be viewed as an interpretation of a first order language of logic) to provide deductive databases in which new facts are derived from facts that are explicitly introduced. This is one of the bases for the continuing Japanese fifth-generation project.

The second approach is concerned with interfacing KBS with DBMS. The rule-based systems and databases can be loosely or tightly coupled. Although the most obvious way today to couple DBMS and KBS is a loose coupling strategy, (Fig. 27.15) in which the KBS extracts data from the DBMS, there are limitations due to the limited expressive power of SQL. For instance, if we would like to list the relations between patients (father/mother, parent/child), we find that it is impossible to express the transitive closure of this relationship. Extensions should be made to make the SQL language as powerful as predicate calculus while retaining its declarative nature. It is important to extend SQL and to remain compatible with the declarative ANSI standard, to protect existing developments and not to punish less sophisticated users. As this is currently not the case, nowadays, a loosely coupled system results in excessive data traffic and query processing overhead; on the otherhand, the consistency between the two engines is not guaranteed as there is no synchronisation mechanism (metaphor) between them.

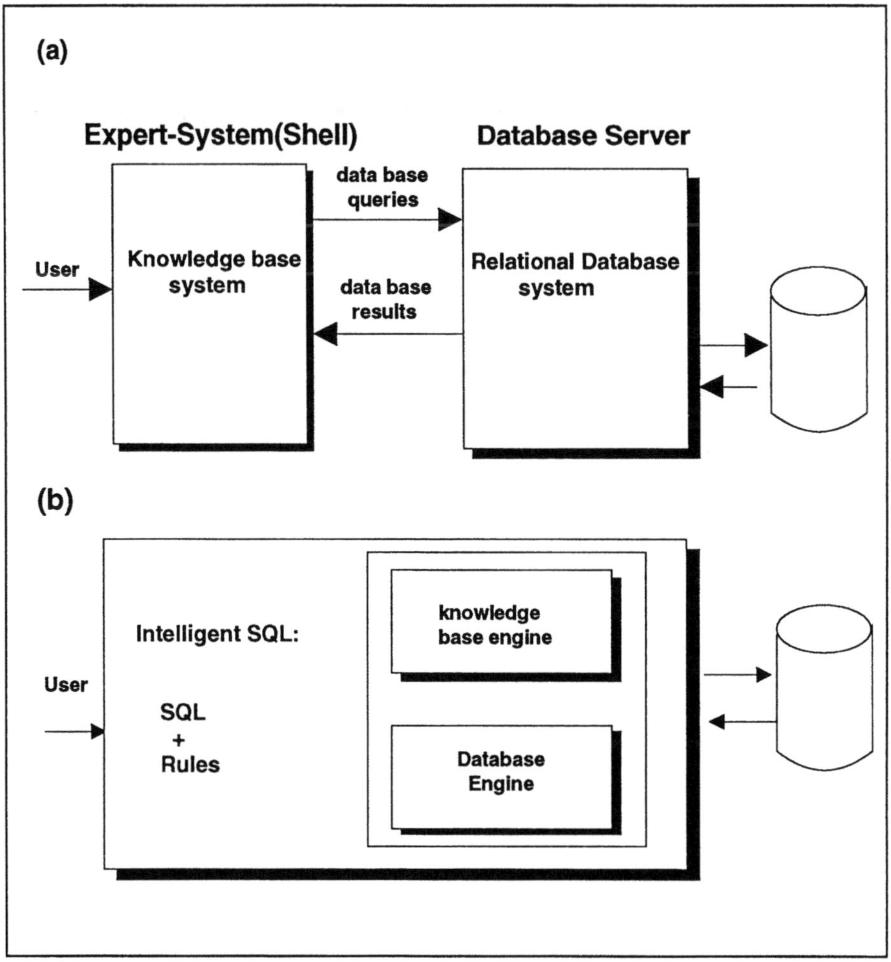

Fig. 27.15 Coupling Database and Artificial Intelligence Technologies:
a Loose coupling strategies: interconnection between a knowledge-based system and a data-base (file) management system
b Thight coupling

One of the arguments for a loose coupling between KBS and DBMS is that these are two substantially different technological domains. Product developers of both domains pursue distinct aims and extending one technology to incorporate aspects of the other might not be so easy. For example, how do you incorporate the features for concurrent access and protection into a tightly coupled system originally based on an AI system?

In the long run, the tight coupling engine will be the favourite choice for many reasons. This strategy executes database calls dynamically during the evaluation of a query. However, two major difficulties have to be solved when using this strategy:

- The complexity of queries, which can be more complex than in conventional database applications
- The huge amount of database calls generated every time the knowledge base requires new facts

The optimisation mechanism must be adaptable.

As described by Khoshafian et al. [KHO 90], an intelligent database engine implements the features of the deductive, object-oriented database model and is characterised by the following architectural components: optimiser, inference engine, transaction manager, meta-information manager, storage manager and multi-media manager.

28

Medical Imaging

28.1 A Concept of Digital Imaging

The aim within health care to gain insight into the human body in a non-invasive way has stimulated -especially in the past 15years- a number of new developments in the areas of diagnostic imaging such as : computed tomography (CT), magnetic resonance imaging (MRI), digital subtraction angiography (DSA) nuclear medicine (NM) and ultrasound (US). These techniques have become possible by the use of advanced computer technology and have given birth to digital imaging, an area that can be expected to embrace conventional radiography in the near future (Fig.28.1a). Under development since 1970, digital imaging represents an image by a large number of pixels (or picture elements). In this form, the image can be stored in a computer memory as a matrix, each element of which corresponds to one pixel (picture element). Each pixel, labelled by its *x* and *y* coordinates, is thus made to correspond to a numerical value (grey scale) related to the intensity of the original image at the position of the picture element. Images that confront us in daily life generally contain more than a million picture elements. New technologies were necessary in order to store and process (e.g. Fourier transform) this kind of image.

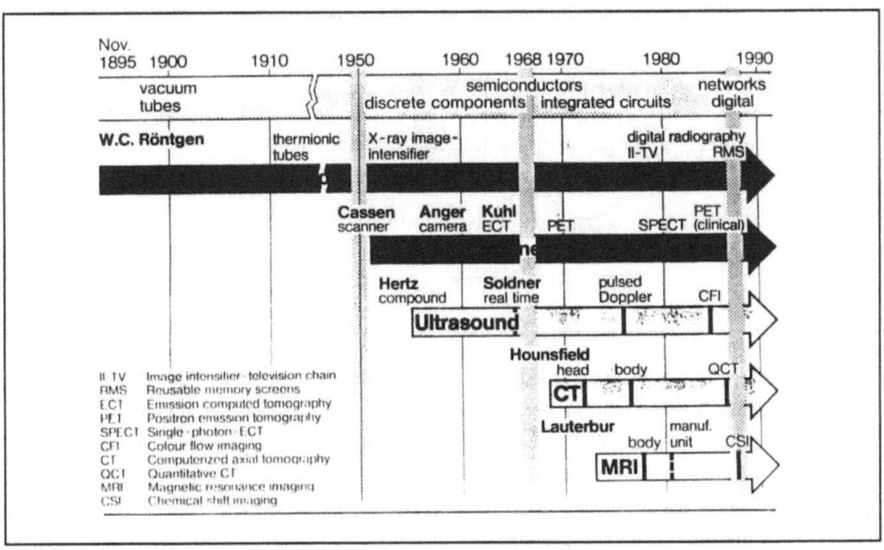

Fig.28.1a Innovations in medical imaging. Overview of the evolution since 1895
(Source: Courtesey of Brueckner E.K., Siemens Medical Systems Erlangen)

Digital imaging entails (in analogy with signal capturing systems) five basic features (Fig.28.1b):

- *The acquisition system* composed of a sensor that converts analog signals emitted by objects into electric signals
- *The analog to digital converter (ADC)*, transforming the analog signal into a digitised 2D array of pixels, each holding a grey level in discrete values from 0 to 255
- *The image (array) processor*, performing manipulation and enhancement (improvement) tasks with those images such as windowing (contrast enhancing, grey level mapping, histogram stretching) which reassigns, according to a user-pre-defined map (look-up table, LUT) other grey values to certain pixels without affecting the original image
- *The digital image communication system*, composed of a high transmission network capable of transporting image data at extremely high speeds (> 100 Mbit/s)
- *The digital storage and retrieval system.* The storage capacity needed for different image modalities is huge, and it is clear that the capabilities of today's technologies are insufficient to manage these image data in such a way that the physician can access them instantaeously.

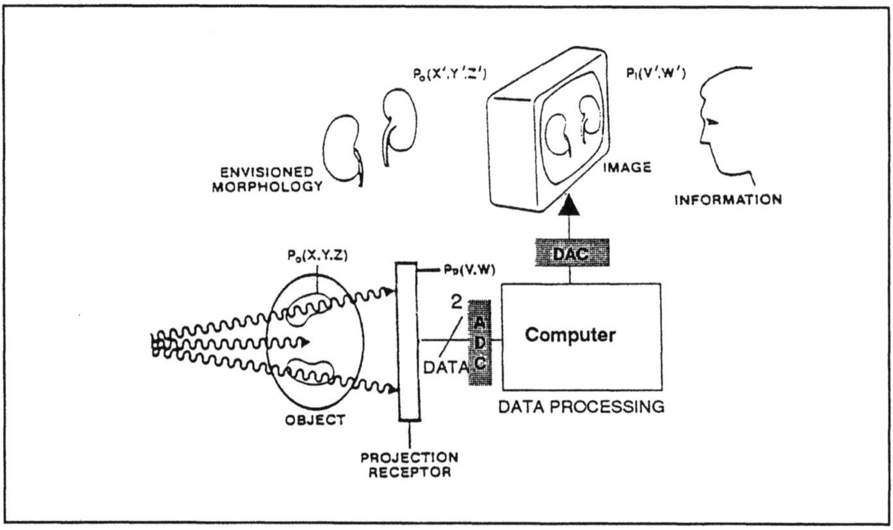

Fig.28.1b Functional diagram of a digital imaging system. In projection imaging, generally a 3D distribution of an object property Po (x, y, z), produces a 2D image Pp (v, w). Through a scanning process, this 2D distribution - after the analog output signal is converted by the ADC into a digital image signal- is sent to a computer, which stores it as a 1D set of data. The display converts the 1D set $P(t)$ to a 2D image with the aid of a DAC converter

Classical Radiology

Classical radiology relies on the superimposition of projected shadows onto a flat detector,which by transformation of the X-photons into light photons generates a visible image. A beam of X-rays is aimed at the region under investigation, and these rays are attenuated to varying degrees, by the different structures, depending on their density and composition. As a consequence, a photographic plate placed behind the organ in the path of the X-rays will register their shadows. Due to differences in the attenuating power of different organs, anatomical details can be visualised. The whole process is governed by the **Law of Lambert-Beer**.
One of the main drawbacks of conventional radiology is the lack of depth resolution. The resulting image is a projection of all structures present between the X-ray tube and the photographic plate. In addition, soft tissues, like brain, liver and kidney, are poorly rendered. In contrast to dense bone, soft tissues are unable to attenuate X-rays to a significant degree, while very small and very large differences in attenuation cannot simultaneously be registered on the photographic plate. In summary, conventional radiology is characterised by the following important drawbacks:

- Many details are lost in the radiographic process due to the superposition of 3D stuctural information on a 2D detector.
- Small differences in X-ray attenuation (1%-2%) by different parts of the body cannot be visualised.
- A large proportion of the radiation is scattered, with an accompanying reduction in the signal-to-noise ratio.

These shortcomings are solved by computed tomography (CT): by collecting projections along a number of different angles of incidence and substituting a detector array for the photographic plate, it is possible to use the collected information in order to reconstruct an image of a thin slice of the body .

28.2 Computed Tomography

28.2.1 The Basic Measurements

In conventional radiology, tissues with significant differences in attenuation are visualised well. The underlying physical law is Lambert-Beer's Law, which describes the attenuation of an X-ray beam on its straight path through an object (I= intensity, μ= linear attenuation coefficient) (Fig.28.2).

From this law, the attenuation coefficients can be derived as follows for a voxel with attenuation coefficient μ and thickness d :

$$\mu = \frac{1}{d} \cdot ln\frac{I}{I_0}$$

For an inhomogeneous object (Fig.28.3) we find:

$$I = I_0 \cdot e^{-((\mu_1 + \mu_2) \cdot d)}$$

or, in general, for a large number of small cubes:

$$I = I_0 \cdot e^{-\int (\mu(Z) \cdot dZ)}$$

Measurement 1 only yields a value for the total attenuation: the sum of

$$\mu_1 + \mu_2 = \mu_s$$

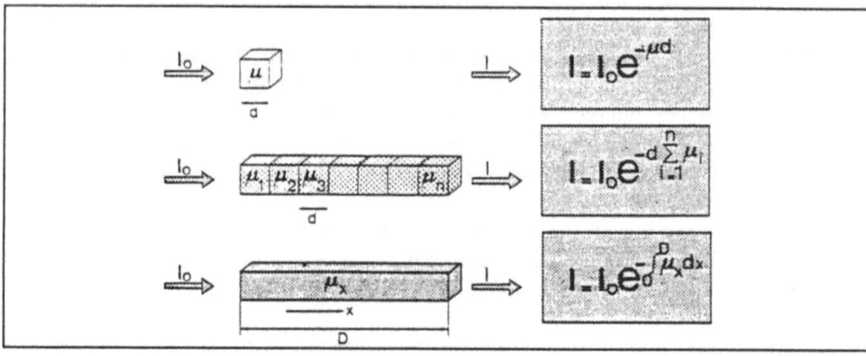

Fig.28.2 Irradiation of a homogeneous volume, characterised by an attenuation coefficient μ and thickness d

In order to determine the value of all the attenuation coefficients, a number of additional measurements are needed, that is, a number of additional irradiations along directions I, II, etc.(during SCAN I and SCAN II) resulting in a number of projections (first-order equations). A set of measurements recorded with beams that are parallel to one another is called a projection of the object in a specified direction. From the measured values a computer can reconstruct the values of all the attenuation coefficients, stated simply, by solving a mathematial problem: of four equations with four unknown variables. The same is true for the four remaining attenuation values. By increasing the number of measurements, it is possible to improve the resolution, which means dealing with a larger number of small cubes (voxels).

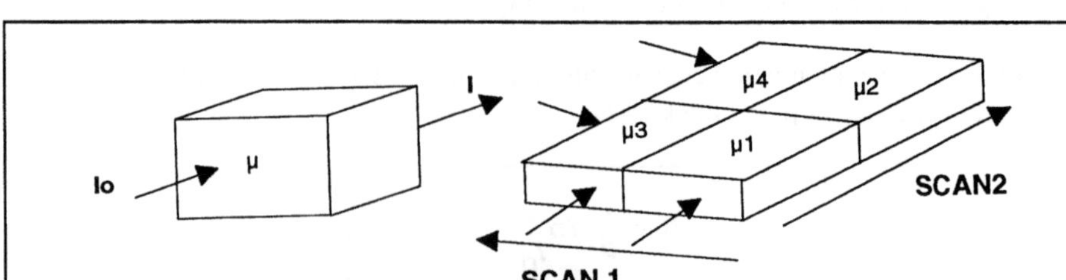

Fig.28.3 Irradiation of an inhomogeneous volume composed of four voxels (volume elements), each characterised by a different attenuation value (μ_1, ...μ_4)

28.2.2 Longitudinal (Linear) Tomography

At the moment, four generations of technical implementations of the CT scanners exist. In 1930, the conventional (longitudinal) tomograph as simplest form of tomography appeared. Although it yielded better results than ordinary projection radiography, it did not completely eliminate the problems listed above (Fig.28.4).

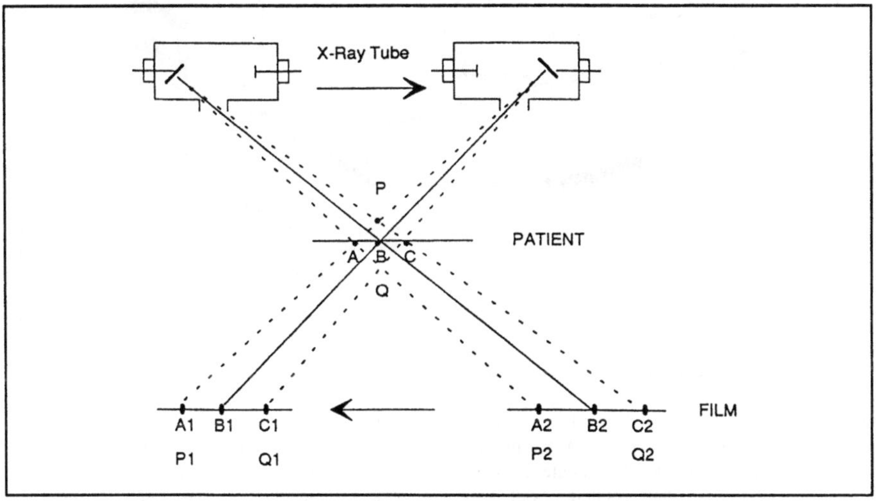

Fig.28.4 Principle of linear tomography explaining how the image of an object in the ABC plane remains in the same place as the film moves in the opposite direction to the X-ray tube. Voxels in position P and Q, are blurred (outside the plane A B C)

28.2.3 Computer Assisted Tomography (CT Scanning)

The advent of computed (axial) tomography, minimising scattering and eliminating superposition effects, finally brought an acceptable solution. The attenuation pattern in a plane is reconstructed on the basis of attenuation measurements along a number of beam directions in this plane (Fig.28.5). In the simplest implementation, a thin beam of X-rays probes through a thin layer and is subsequently measured by a detector positioned on the other side of the body under investigation. Hereby the common problem of superimposition of features within the object in conventional radiography is avoided. During successive measurements, the tube-detector arrangement is first translated along the image plane and then rotated around the axis of the patient until 180° have been covered.

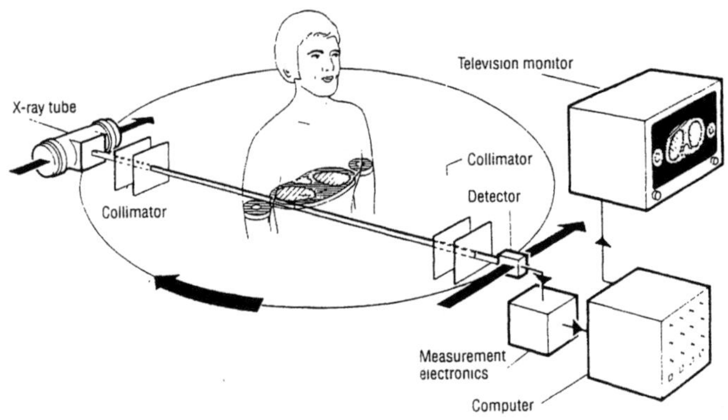

Fig.28.5 Basic representation of a computer tomograph in the simplest design form. The measurement system, consisting of an X-ray tube and radiation detector, is first moved linearly in the slice plane over the entire object cross-section. The measurement system is then rotated about approximately 1° and then a new linear scanning movement performed, etc., until an angle of at least 180° has been traversed. Throughout the entire scanning process, the measurement signal obtained by an X-ray beam approximately the thickness of a pencil is recorded at fixed intervals and transferred to a computer. This computes a 2D distribution of attenuation values corresponding to the object layer from the measurement values, which is finally displayed as a tomogram on a television monitor after conversion to video signals [KRE 90]

(Source Courtesy of Siemens Medical Systems in Krestel E. *Imaging Systems for Medical Diagnostics.* Siemens Aktiengesellshaft, Berlin and Munich, 1990, p. 92)

The main features of a CT scanner are high-power X-ray tube and generator, gantry, couch and detector array. Since the development of CT in 1972, four generations of scanners have been designed (Fig.28.6):

1. *First generation (translate-rotate)*: A pencil beam samples the slice through a number of translation and rotation movements. The rotation about 180° requires an exposure time of 300 s. In each translation a number of measurements is made (e.g. in the EMI CT1000, 160 measurements).
2. *Second generation (translate-rotate)*: A fan beam-detector array probes the slice through translation-rotations in about 20 s for 180°.
3. *Third generation (rotate):* Makes use of a rotating X-ray tube (fan beam) and a rotating detector array. A 360° rotation is executed in less than 5 s.
4. *Fourth generation (rotate):* A rotating X-ray tube (fan beam) is combined with a ring of (more than 1000) fixed detectors. A 360° rotation takes less than 5 s.

	Single-detector	multi-detector	fan beam	fan beam
	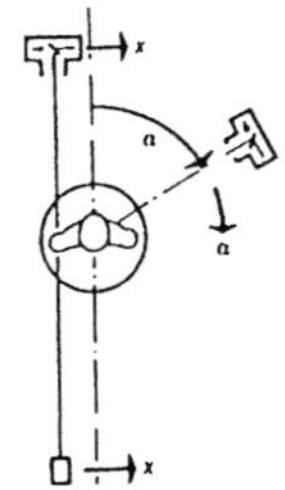	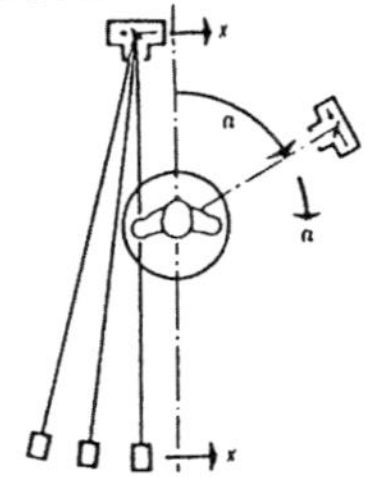	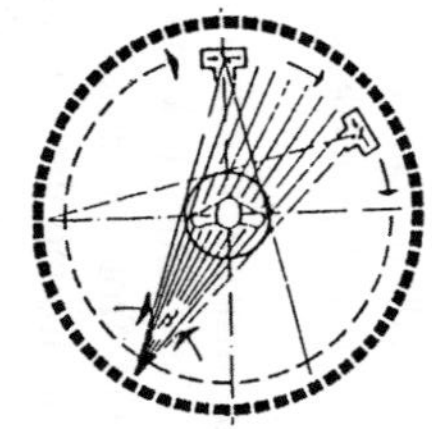	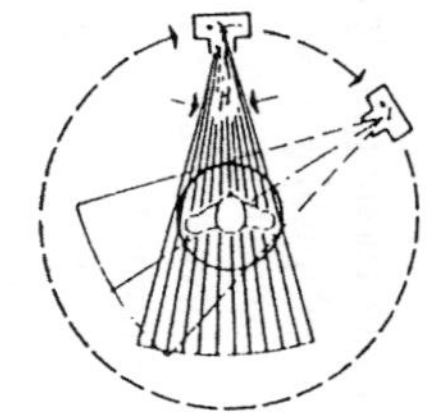
Measuring times	5 MIN The parallel-beam system with only one measurement beam alternately moved in a translational and rotational manner, only poorly utilizes the radiation of the x-ray tube and requires a long measuring time	20 s to 60 s The parallel-beam system with several measurement beams makes better use of the generated radiation, reduces the number of movement steps and therefore cuts down the measurement time	1s to 5 s The ring-detector system has a fixed detector ring; operates with a fanshaped x-ray beam simultaneously covering the entire patient cross sectrion and therefore only requires a rotational movement of the x-ray tube.	1s to 5s The fan-beam system has a multicellular detector system rotating about the patient together with the x-ray tube.
Measuring principle	translation-rotation		rotation	
Detector system	moving single-detector	moving mum-detector	stationary detector array	rotating detector array
X-ray source	continuous radiation			pulsed radiation
			central projection	
Type of projection	parallel projection		center = detector	center = tube focus
Number of projection	number of detectors times number of angular steps		number of detectors in the array	number of radiation pulses
Measured values per projection	number of detector samplings			number of detectors in the array

Fig.28.6 Comparison of four generations of computed tomography scanners

28.2.4 Image reconstruction

In the first generation, scanning was done according to the translate-rotate principle, in which 240 measurements were made for each rotation position. Typically, a set of 42 000 equations with 25 600 unknown parameters had to be solved in order to reconstruct a 160x160 image matrix. Since reconstruction also involved a number of corrections (filter functions), the real need for computer technology to solve this problem is clear. At present, CT scanners make exclusive use of fan beam techniques. Up to 1440 projections are made, which means that the tube-detector arrangement rotates around the patient in steps of 1/4th of a degree. The detector array contains up to 724 detector elements, and more than 1 000 000 measurements are combined to yield a 512x512 image matrix. A specialised image processor is needed to do this in a reasonable time.
For the reconstruction of a 2D image in CT, the computer (array-processor) executes millions of calculations (500 000 equations, containing 160 000 unknown variables); they all start from the set of basic data collected from a series of projections while the source and the detector rotate and translate around the patient. Three methods are in use : the mathematical calculation, the iterative method and the back-projection convolution.

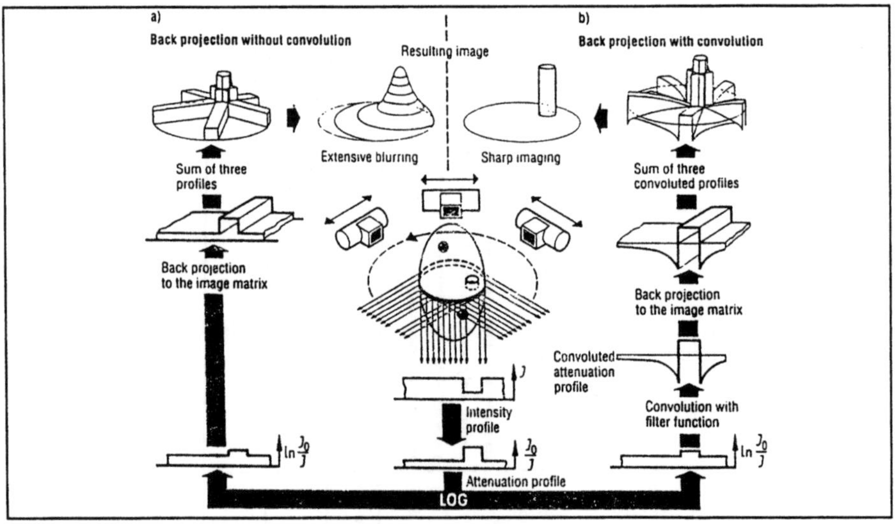

Fig.28.7 Importance of convolution for image reconstruction in CT. The intensity profiles *J* obtained by measurement are converted to attenuation profiles *Jo/J*, where *Jo* is the intensity measured without the object in the radiation path. The attenuation profiles are then converted to logarithms, so that a quantity proportional to the attenuation coefficient is available for further processing. If, as shown in path *a*, the logarithmic attenuation profile is superimposed according to its projection direction, then there would be considerable blurring of the detail to be imaged. Therefore, a specific alteration of the logarithmic attenuation profile is undertaken, as shown in path *b*, by convolution with a suitable filter function. The convoluted profiles exhibit negative as well as positive components, whose contributions to the superposition image exactly cancel the extensive blurring when the filter function is correctly chosen [KRE 90].

(Source courtesy of Siemens Medical systems in Krestel E. *Imaging Systems for Medical Diagnostics.* Siemens Aktiengesellshaft, Berlin and Munich, 1990, p. 96)

In modern machines, only the **back-projection convolution** technique is used. Without taking precautions, the process leads to a blurred image. In order to avoid this blurring, each projection is first corrected (using a convolution algorithm) before being back-projected (Fig.28.7). The mathematical function (kernel) inside the convolution algorithm is usually optimised for each type of examination (head, abdomen, etc.).

28.2.5 Grey-level mapping

In CT, each array element corresponds to the attenuation at the corresponding position in the slice to be imaged. These attenuation values are usually expressed in Hounsfield units as follows:

$$CT_{numbers} = \frac{\mu - \mu_w}{\mu_w} . 1000$$

Where μ_w is the linear attenuation coefficient of water (water = 0, air = -1000, bone ranges from +100 to 1000). With the present state of technology, image signals have a resolution of 10 - 12 bits, and 2048 - 4096 grey levels can be distinguished. CT scanning generates Hounsfield numbers in the range of -1000 to +1000 (actually, -2000 to +4000). As the human eye can only discern 35 grey levels, the *level* (center C) and the *width* of the display can be adjusted to represent any range of the digitized video signals with the maximum contrast resolution on the viewing station. In order to bridge this gap in sensitivity, use is made of the windowing technique: a limited range of Hounsfield units is mapped to the full black-to-white grey scale (Fig.28.8). The **level** and the **width** of the display of the display unit can be changed over the complete range, offering the radiologist the ability to focus his attention on a small region of interest of the image.

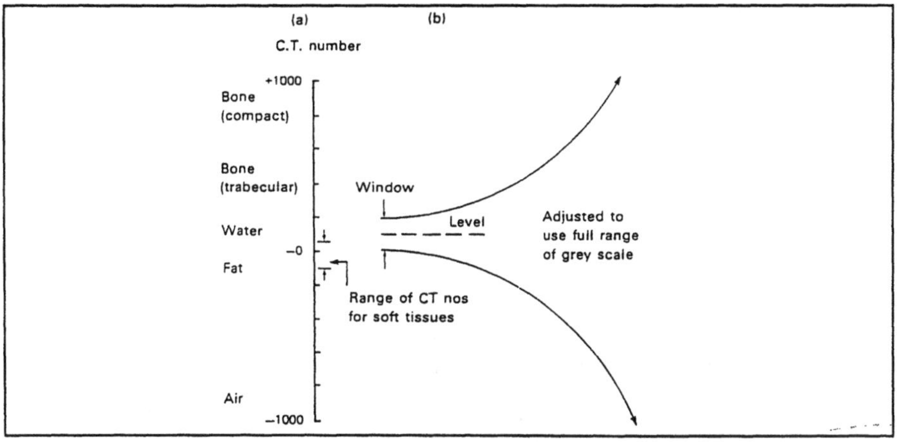

Fig.28.8 The range of CT numbers used (modern scanners may now have higher CT numbers of 2000 or even 4000) and the effect of 'windowing' on the image, allowing as many as 256 shades of grey to be displayed within the selected window

28.3 Magnetic Resonance Imaging

28.3.1 Physical Principles

MRI is a method for acquiring information on the structure and properties of molecules. The measured signal depends on three independent physical parameters: *spin density and two relaxation times, T1 and T2.*
A substance is composed of molecules, themselves built out of atoms, which in turn consist of charged particles: nuclei and electrons. Electrons and some nuclei spin around an internal axis and have magnetic properties: they behave to some extent as little bar magnets. Stable nuclei (e.g. ^{1}H, ^{2}H, ^{13}C, ^{7}Li, ^{19}F and ^{31}P) containing on odd number of protons (or neutrons) produce a magnetic moment caused by the spin of the odd proton (neutron).
In the absence of a magnetic field, the little magnets have a random orientation. As soon as we switch on an external magnetic field, however, the bar magnets take on parallel and anti-parallel orientations with respect to the direction of the field. The orientation parallel to the field has the lowest potential energy, the energy difference between the two orientations being proportional to the field strength. As a consequence, a majority of the nuclei will align with the field, superimpose and result in a macroscopic bar magnet, the magnetisation *M* oriented along the external field.

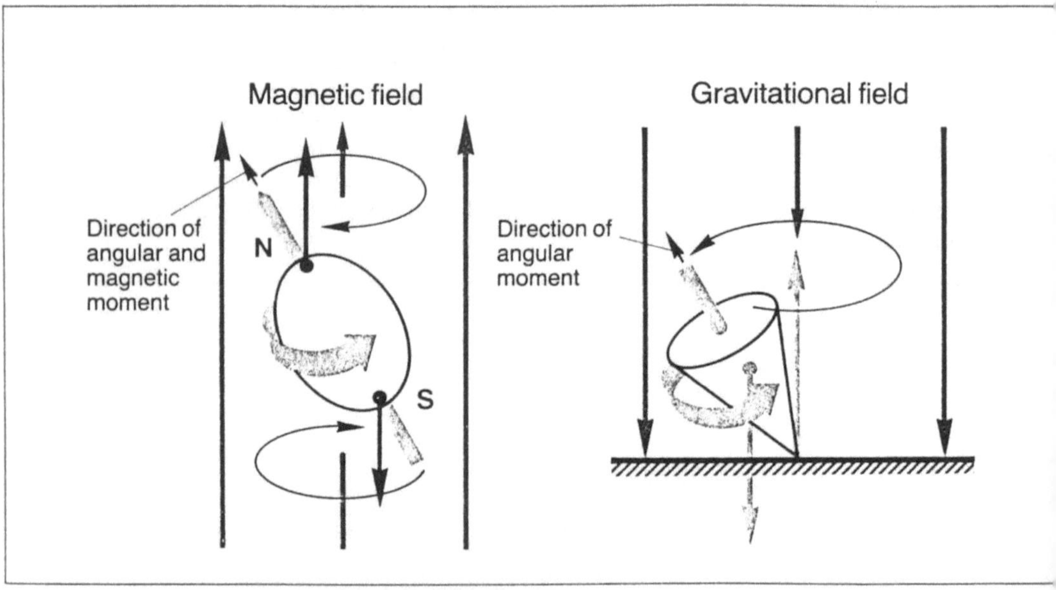

Fig.28.9 Illustration of the similarity between a spinning and precessing top in a gravitational field and a spinning and processing nucleus in a magnetic field [PHI 84]

(source courtesy of Philips Medical Systems in *Principles of MR imaging.* Philips Medical Systems, Netherlands, 1984, p. 9)

Although this orientation will be typical for the equilibrium situation, it is possible to force the magnetisation away from the field direction. In order to accomplish this, we must add energy in the form of electromagnetic radiation, oscillating at a frequency corresponding to the energy difference between the parallel and anti-parallel orientations. This electromagnetic radiofrequency radiation (RF) is produced by a special antenna (coil). Resonant absorption of the RF pulse occurs (hence the name "nuclear magnetic resonance"; E=h.f by *Planck's law*). As a consequence, the magnetisation starts nutating and gains an angle with respect to the direction of the field. As soon as a transverse component of magnetisation exists, it starts a rolling motion (**nutating**) around the direction of the external magnetic field (Fig.28.9 - Fig.28.10).

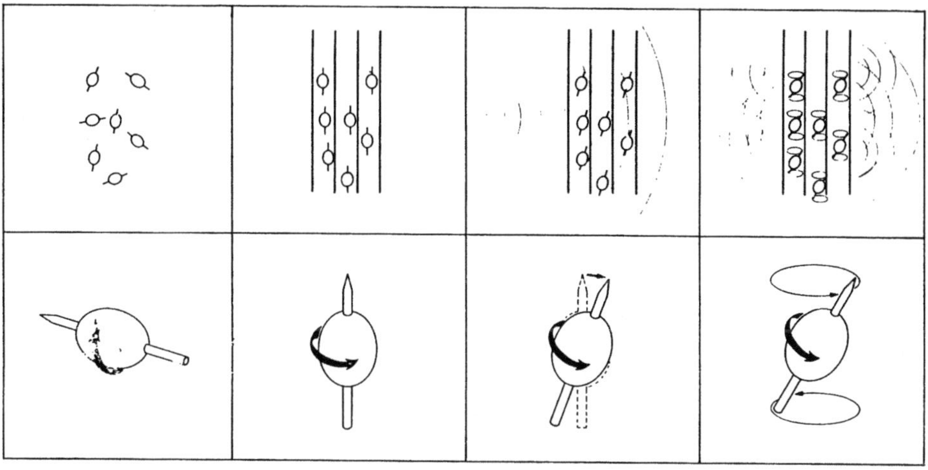

Fig.28.10 Randomly oriented nuclei tend to align with an applied magnetic field, and are shown releasing electromagnetic energy after excitation with radiation at their Larmor frequency

(Source Courtesy of Philips Medical Systems in *Principles of MR imaging*. Philips Medical Systems, Netherlands, 1984, p. 12)

The angular frequency of the precession is given by the *Larmor expression* :

$$\omega = \gamma \cdot \overline{B_0}$$

where. ω is the *gyromagnetic ratio* which is constant for a particular nucleus and Bo is the static magnetic field. In this situation, it is possible to detect the motion of the macroscopic magnetisation through magnetic induction in a conducting loop (coil) in the neighbourhood of the spins.

The nutation during RF excitation depends on the duration and strength of the pulse applied (Fig.28.11). After the pulse is terminated, the transverse magnetisation does not disappear immediately but decays following an exponential law (free induction), while the longitudinal component returns to its equilibrium value, again following an exponential model. After a 90° deviation from the equilibrium orientation (following a "90° pulse"), these two relaxation processes can be described mathematically by(Fig.28.12):

$M_z = Mo \,.\, (1\text{-}e^{-t/T1})$ Longitudinal component

$M_{xy} = Mo \,.\, e^{-t/T2}$ Transverse component ($T_2 < T_1$)

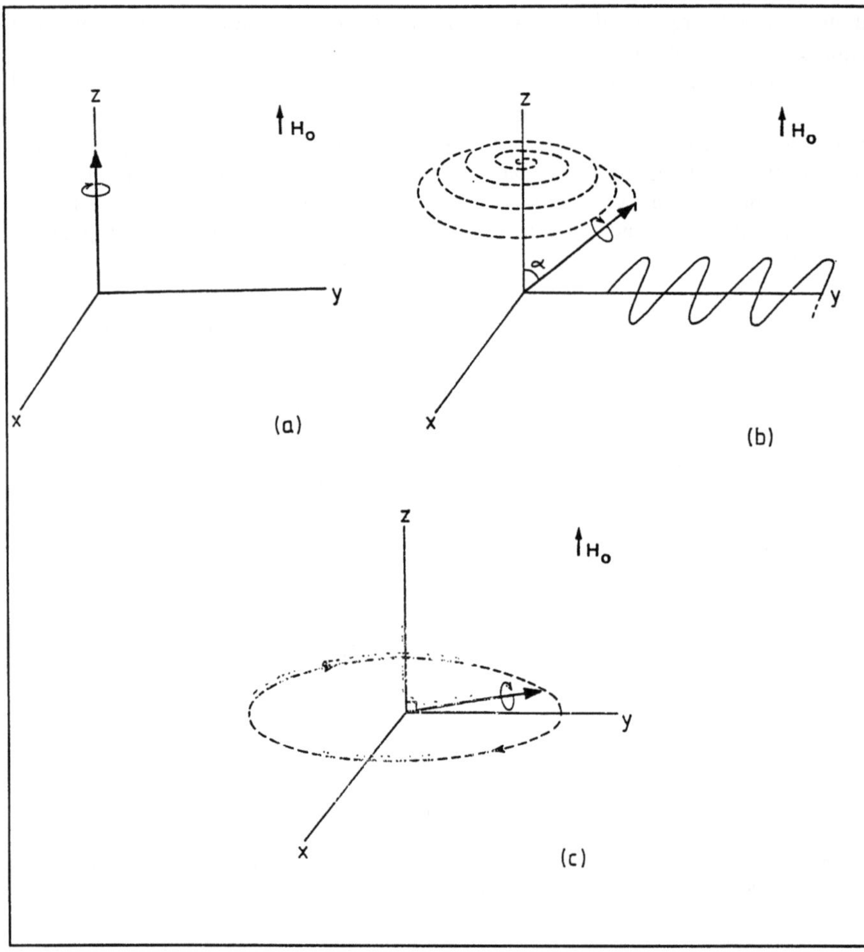

Fig.28.11 a-c Motion of the nuclear magnetisation vector $\bar{M}$ under the influence of the static magnetic field Ho, and the circularly polarised high frequency field. **a** A single proton is aligned in the direction of the external magnetic field. **b** An oscillating magnetic field in the horizontal plane (an RF pulse at the Larmor frequency) causes the nucleus to precess, the angle gradually increasing with time. **c** With a sufficient RF pulse the nucleus can eventually be arrive at 90° to the external magnetic field [KEA 86].

(source Reprinted with the permission from D.Kean, M. Smith *Magnetic Resonance Imaging - Principles and applications.* Butterworth-Heineman Ltd, Oxford, 1986 , p.11)

T_1 is the longitudinal (or spin-lattice) relaxation time and describes how long it takes for the longitudinal magnetisation to return to its equilibrium value after RF excitation. For fat, it is rather short (0.1 s), while for pure liquids, it is long (a few seconds). *T2 is the transverse (spin-spin) relaxation time* and describes how fast any

transverse component of magnetisation decays. It is very short for solids, while for liquids it tends to be long (water has a long T2 of hundreds of milliseconds). The signal which is detected in MRI to compute the images will disappear at a rate equal to 1/ T2.
In summary, we can say that T1 and T2 describe the response of the magnetisation to a non-equilibrium condition created by an RF pulse (Table 28.1).

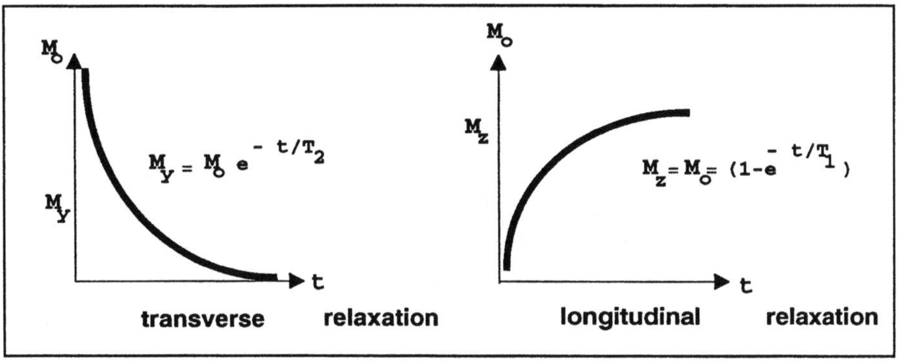

Fig.28.12 Variation of magnetisation in time as a function of relaxation time T_1, T_2

Table 28.1 Typical relaxation times T_1(at 1T) and T_2 [5.7] [KRE 90].

Tissue	T_1 (s)	T_2 (ms)
Muscle	0.73 ± 0.13	47 ± 13
Heart	0.75 ± 0.12	57 ± 16
Liver	0.42 ± 0.09	43 ± 14
Kidney	0.59 ± 0.16	58 ± 24
Spleen	0.68 ± 0.19	62 ± 27
Fat	0.24 ± 0.07	84 ± 36
Grey matter	0.81 ± 0.14	101 ± 13
White matter	0.68 ± 0.12	92 ± 22

(source Courtesy of Siemens Medical systems in Krestel E. *Imaging Systems for Medical Diagnostics.* Siemens Aktiengesellshaft, Berlin and Munich, 1990, p. 146]

28.3.2 Image Reconstruction

In order to reconstruct an image it is necessary to locate all the signals emitted from each pixel. This spatial encoding is performed by introducing differences in field strength (*gradients*) for nuclei that have different positions, and it is possible to label the signals emitted by these nuclei according to their position (per voxel). All MRI imaging techniques are based on this principle. Although several methods of localisation have been developed, only the 2D Fourier method will be discussed here. We will assume the static field to be oriented along the *z*-axis and linear gradients to be available along the three principal axes, *x, y ,z.* In general, the *z*-axis will be parallel to the body axis of the patient. When a gradient along the *z*-direction

is switched on, it is possible to excite selectively the nuclei in a thin slice perpendicular to the z-axis by using an RF pulse of limited bandwidth (Fig.28.13).
As we said before, the Larmor frequency is proportional to the strength of the magnetic field. If we make sure that the field varies linearly along the X-axis of a Cartesian coordinate system, the resonance frequency will depend on the exact position of the volume element along the X-axis. This is illustrated in Fig.28.14.

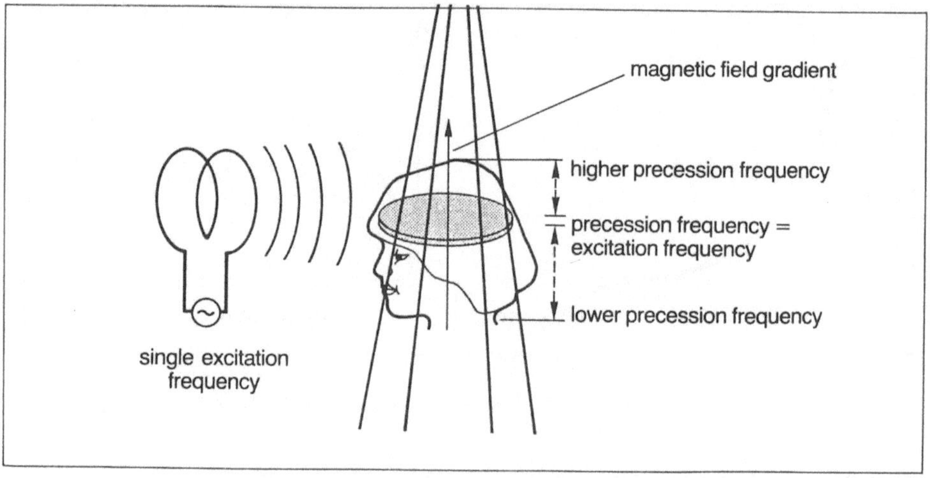

Fig.28.13 In view of the field gradient, nuclei in a plane with a Larmor frequency matching the frequency of the excitation pulse are the only ones excited [PHI 84]

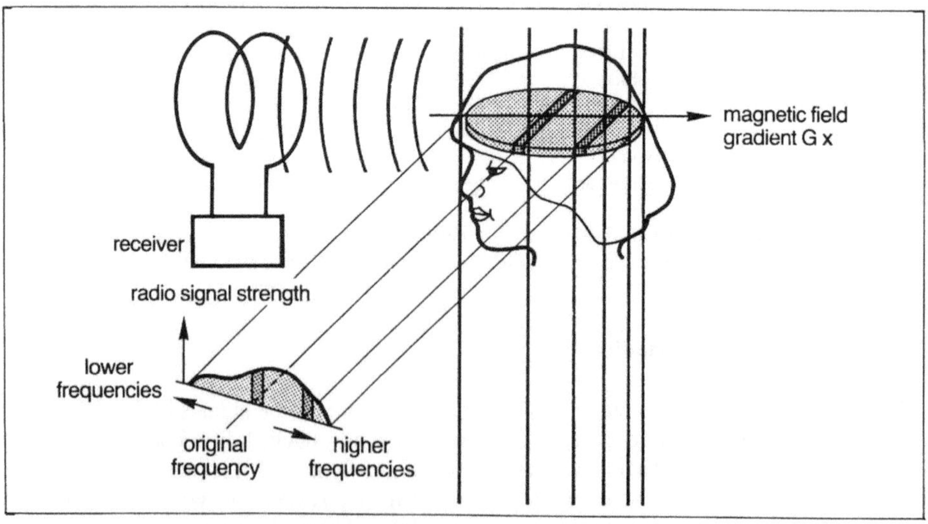

Fig.28.14 The gradient Gx causes the excited nuclei to precess at increasing frequency in direction x. The frequency spectrum of the response signal shown provides a 1D profile of nuclear density in the object.

(source **Fig.28.13 - 28.14** Courtesy of Philips Medical Systems in *Principles of MR imaging*. Philips Medical Systems, Netherlands, 1984, p. 40)

Provided that the gradient Gx = 0, all the voxels will resonate at the same frequency. On the other hand, when Gx is different from 0, all voxels will feel a different magnetic field, and the induced electronic magnetic current will be a superpositon of several frequency components (Fig.28.15, 28.16). By applying field gradients in the different spatial directions, localisation in these directions can be obtained, and as a consequence an image can be reconstructed.Through a mathematical analysis (by means of Fourier transformation) on a computer, the individual signals per voxel can be calculated. The signal is representative for the composition of tissue at the signal origin. For a spin echo sequence, its dependence on tissue parameters can be expressed as follows :

$$S = \rho \cdot e^{T_E/T_2} \cdot \left(1 - e^{T_R/T_1}\right)$$

where ρ is the proton density, TE echo time and TR= repetition time.

Advantages and Drawbacks

The advantages of MRI are :

- It does not use ionising radiation (it is therefore safe).
- Images display a high degree of natural contrast
- It is sometimes possible to detect the technical and physical changes before anatomical changes are visible.
- Images clearly demonstrate soft tissues not visible directly in radiology, and moreover their visualisation is not disturbed by bone artefacts as is frequently the case in CT scanning.
- The spatial resolution is comparable with that of a CT scan (0.5 mm or less), while the contrast resolution (sensitivity) is much greater.
- Images are multi-parametric (density, T_1, T_2, etc.), while radiological images are based on one parameter, the attenuation factor.
- The examination does not require any preparation of the patient (no injection or pre-medication).
- Images can be reconstructed in any plane through the patient (transverse, sagittal or coronal).

The drawbacks are:

- Long acquisition times requiring complete immobility of the patient
- Interference by metallic objects: patients with cardiac pacemakers or ferromagnetic implants cannot undergo MRI examination because of risks of disturbance, heating, etc.
- Moderate spatial resolution
- Complex site planning
- Training required for the radiologists as interpretation of these images is often complex
- Huge investments in terms of infrastructures (location), and personnel (well trained).

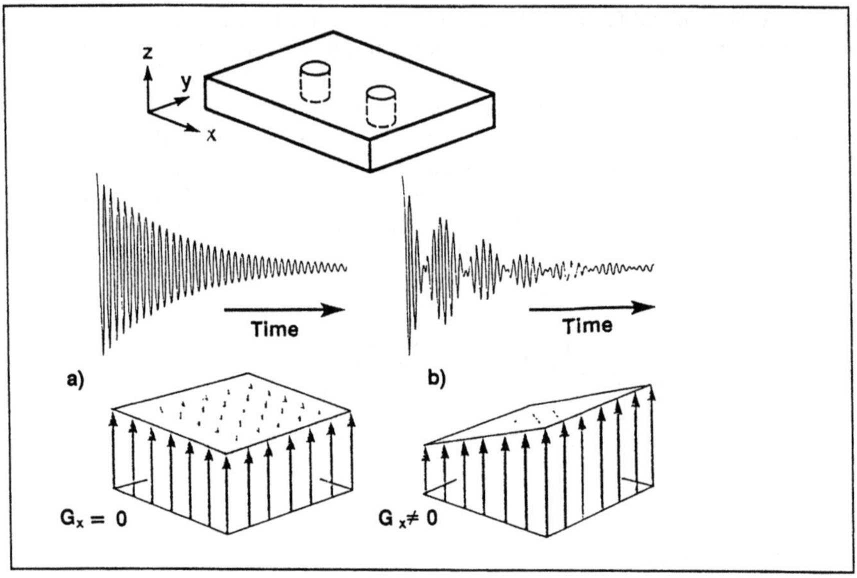

Fig.28.15 ***a*** In the absence of the field gradient ($G_X = G_Y = G_Z = 0$) both samples sense the same field; the free induction decay therefore consists of a single frequency . ***b*** In the presence of a gradient Gx, the two samples sense different fields, resulting in a free induction signal consisting of two frequencies. [GEN 84]

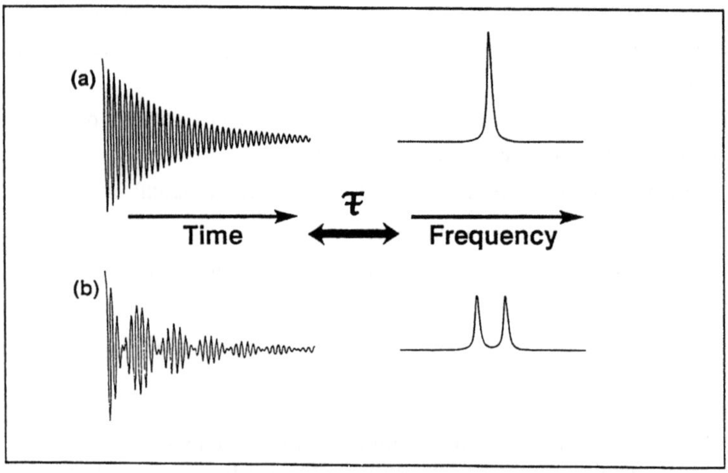

Fig.28.16a,b Free induction decay and its frequency domain analogue for ***a*** single frequency, ***b*** two different frequencies. The symbol τ implies that the two domains are related by a Fourier transformation[GEN 84].

(source **Fig.28.15 - 28.16** Courtesy of General Electric from *NMR. A perspective on imaging.* General Electric Company, 1984,pp11)

The main component of a MRI device is a very powerful superconducting magnet covering the whole body of the patient. Once activated, this type of magnet needs no further electricity. Other elements include: a computer for storing and processing the MR signals, an image console, three sets of orthogonal gradient coils with independent power supplies controlled by the computer system and, finally, an RF emitter and receiver coil for capturing the emitted signals (Fig.28.17).

28.3.3. 3D Imaging

In the past few years, 3D displays based on CT slices have become more and more interesting especially for surgeons and orthopaedists, as this feature offers the advantage of a more detailed view of complex structures. 3D images are summations of 2D representations of a cross-section of the human body, with slice thickness varying from 1 to 10 mm. The principle of 3D imaging is rather simple : images of a number of successive slices in some part of the human body are acquired digitally (through CT scan or through NMR techniques), and these images are then stacked one on top of the other. We then specify to the computer which parts from this stack have to be visible (for instance, weak tissue, skin or bone). These data are displayed on the computer as they would look when irradiated by a light source positioned at a certain location. By the effect of light and shadow a quasi-3D image is created on the screen. This image can be rotated and tilted, allowing us to view the structures from the inside and from the outside. It is even possible to extract certain parts in order to study these separately or in order to look at the internal structure. Many procedures on 3D reconstruction have been published and can be subdivided into two main groups :

- *Surface-oriented* reconstructions are based on the extraction of the contour from each of the many slices in a sequence. 3-D surface-oriented programs run directly on the CT system processors.
- *Volume-oriented* reconstructions are based on the processing of the entire scanning volume. For that purpose, special high-performance array processors are used (e.g. Kontron, Cemax, ARRi, MEK and Pinar).

3D images offer a number of advantages to the different therapeutic specialities within hospitals. Since one can look at all elements from the outside, from the inside as well as under all possible angles, the images are very interesting for surgeons, oncologists and orthopaedists. Information provided in this way can in many cases remove the necessity for explorative surgery. In the future, computer-controlled manufacturing of life-like, custom-made protheses will be prepared on this 3D surface reconstruction. Since one can obtain a lot of data concerning exact dimensions, it is possible to make, for instance, an exact copy of a hip. It is then only a small step to make a completely true copy of the hip, using a computerised milling machine.

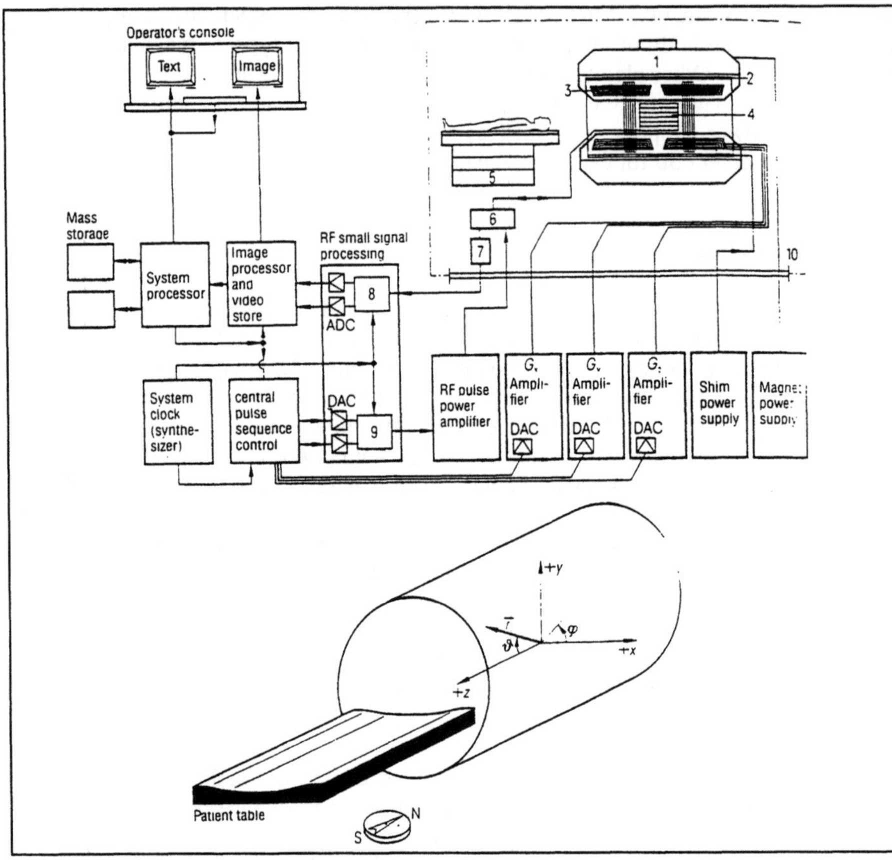

Fig.28.17 *Top,* schematic wiring diagram of an MRI scanning system: ***1***, magnet with cryotank and cryogenic shielding; ***2***, shim coil system; ***3***, gradient coil system; ***4***, RF resonator (antenna); ***5***, patient table; ***6***, transmit-receive switch; ***7***, preamplifier; ***8***, quadrature demodulator with two low-frequency, low-pass filters and ADC; ***9***, SSB modulator with two DACs; ***10***, RF-proof leadthroughs.
below, coordinate system (Cartesian and spherical coordinates) of the gradient coils; definition of field polarity[KRE 90]

(source Erich Krestel. in *Imaging Systems for Medical Diagnostics.* Siemens Aktiengesellshaft, Berlin and Munich, 1990, p. 480)

28.4 Digital Subtraction Angiography

Introduction

Conventional (analog) subtraction angiography is based on the principle of subtracting pre-injection blood vessel images from post-injection images in order to highlight (amplify) the blood vessels, characterised by a low concentration of radio-opaque iodine for the X-ray diagnosis of major vascular abnormalities. In spite of the use of these contrast agents, conventional angiography leads to insufficient contrast to obtain an optimal visualisation of the vessels. In an ideal situation all parts that do not belong to the desired structure under study should display 0 intensity, while the parts that do belong to it should correspond to a different intensity level. Using the substraction method developed by Ziedses Des Plantes in 1934, it is possible to get very near to this ideal situation. This technique is used to image defective heart valves, atherosclerotic plaque or lesions in the blood vessels.

Principle

The subtraction technique is based on following principles. If two photographic plates obtained under identical conditions contain different information at certain locations (during the examination, images are visualised at a rate of 1 or 2 per second before and after the injection of radiocontrast), it is possible to visualise these differences alone by superposition of one negative with the positive of the second photograph (Fig.28.18). In other words, if plate B differs from plate A because it contains an opaque vessel, it is possible to isolate this vessel by superposition of B with the inverse of A. Whereas before classic photography was used to obtain this effect, it is now possible to implement the superposition and inversion in a completely electronic and automatic way through digitisation in order to obtain the result that is automatically displayed on the monitor. The initial image from an angiographic sequence is stored in RAM, and subsequent images are subtracted from this image and displayed continuously on the console and stored on disk (Fig.28.19). In order to realise this, two transformations have to be completed :

- Subdivision of the image into pixels : most commercial systems operate with a 512 x 512 matrix.
- Attributing to every pixel a numerical value that corresponds to the luminance (grey value) of the image at the point concerned (8 - 10 bit).

The features of a DSA system are a high heat-capacity tube to make multiple high-intensity exposures possible of up to 30 frames per sec., a large field image intensifier (14" - 16" cross-section) to cover all the parts under investigation, a television camera, an ADC to digitise the signals from the TV camera and to deliver them to the image processor and finally the image acquisition console. The computer registers the information, forming the basis for subtraction, pixel by pixel, with the advantage that we can further evaluate and optimise the image on the screen.

There are some major differences and similarities between CT scans and DSA. The former one records cross-sectional images, while the latter generates planar images, registered on an intensifier television camera system and reproduced by a cathode-ray-tube, CRT-display. Its contrast resolution (1%) is extremely high, while the spatial resolution is moderate compared with the images produced by conventional radiography.

Advantages of the Subtraction Technique

It presents savings on the following points :

- Duration of the examination (15 - 60 min for one examination)
- Film usage (the potential to visualise the images in real time without waiting for development of X-ray photographs, is of enormous importance)
- A higher resolution (4 - 8 times better in comparison with photographic subtractions)
- Quantity of contrast material needed is considerably lower than in a conventional angiogram.

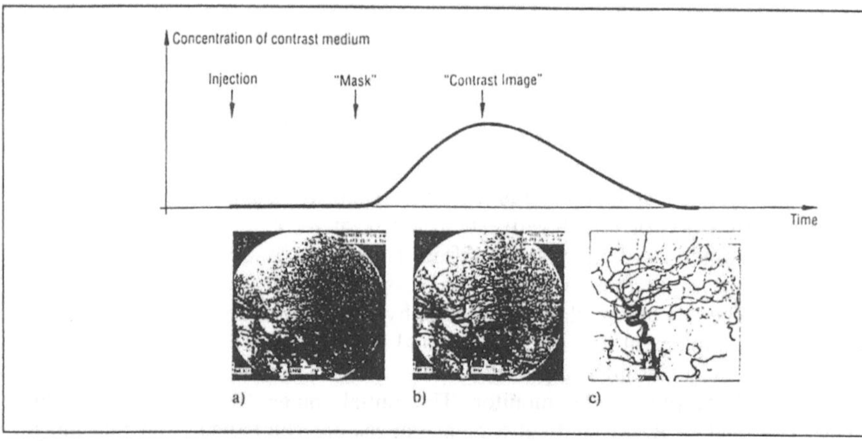

Fig.28.18a-c Evolution over time of the contrast medium with the corresponding images : (*a*) mask, (*b*) contrast image and (*c*) subtraction image [KRE 90]

(source courtesy of Siemens Medical system in Krestel E. *Imaging Systems for Medical Diagnostics.* Siemens Aktiengesellshaft, Berlin and Munich, 1990, p. 370)

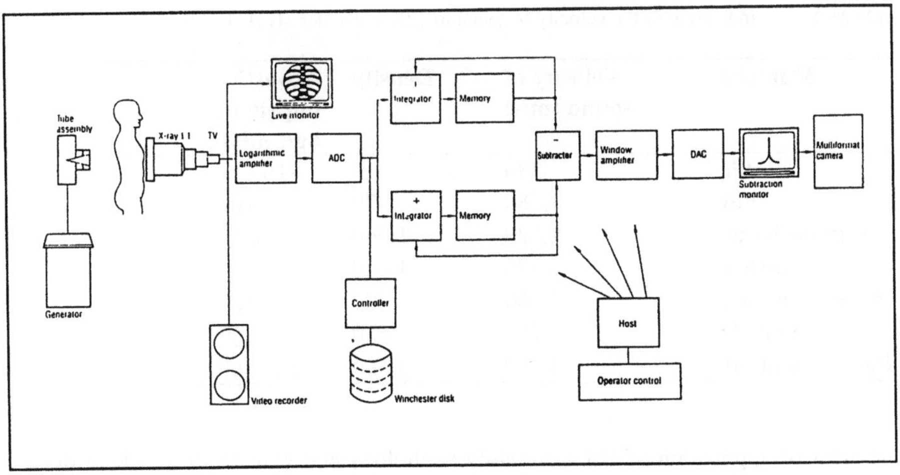

Fig.28.19 Schema of a DSA system with two memories for the contrast image and the mask image [KRE 90].

(source courtesy of Siemens Medical systems in Krestel E. *Imaging Systems for Medical Diagnostics.* Siemens Aktiengesellshaft, Berlin and Munich, 1990, pp. 370 - 371)

28.5 Ultrasound (Echography)

Basic Physical Principles

US techniques are based on the fact that pulses of sound oscillating at a frequency of a few MHz (2.5 - 10 MHz) are capable of travelling through tissue but are nevertheless partially reflected when they meet interfaces between different tissues having different acoustic impedances (ρ_i v_i) in which ρ_i is the density and v_i the speed of sound in the tissue of interest. For the interface between two tissues with acoustic impedances ρ_i v_i, (assumed to be independent of frequency) we obtain for the orthogonal incidence of a beam I_0 :

$$I = I_0 \cdot \left(\frac{\rho_1 \cdot v_1 - (\rho_2 \cdot v_2)}{\rho_1 \cdot v_1 + \rho_2 \cdot v_2} \right)^2$$

From the delays between reflections and the known speed of sound we can determine the distance between successive interfaces and in this way construct the image (Table 28.2).

Table 28.2 Indication of the velocity of sound in different materials [JAC 77]

Material	Velocity of sound (m/s)	Density	Acoustic impedance kg/(m^2s)
Air	330	1.2	416
Fat	1,480	970	$1.36 . 10^6$
Nervous tissue	1,520	1,040	$1.56 . 10^6$
Muscle	1,570	1,060	$1.66 . 10^6$
Bone (compact)	3,600	1,700	$6.12 . 10^6$
Quartz	5,750	2,650	$15.2 . 10^6$
Barium titanate	4,460	5,400	$24 . 10^6$

The areas of application of US are mainly cardiology and gynaecology, where these non-invasive examinations can yield real-time images. In obstetrics, US is the method of excellence for determining the size of the placenta, its position and for testing for extra-uterine pregnancies. It is the only method allowing observation of the unborn child without risks.
Real-time echocardiography by means of B-mode registration, using a multiple element transducer and sequential registration, delivers important qualitative information about the structure of the heart, heart wall, valves, aorta, ventricles and chambers. The M-mode registration, written out as a function of time on a recorder, yields quantitative information.
The sound waves generated by an US generator (transducer) propagate in the form of a beam. In the immediate neighbourhood of the transducer the beam is cylindrical; at larger distances, however, it diverges and takes on the form of a cone (Fig.28.20).

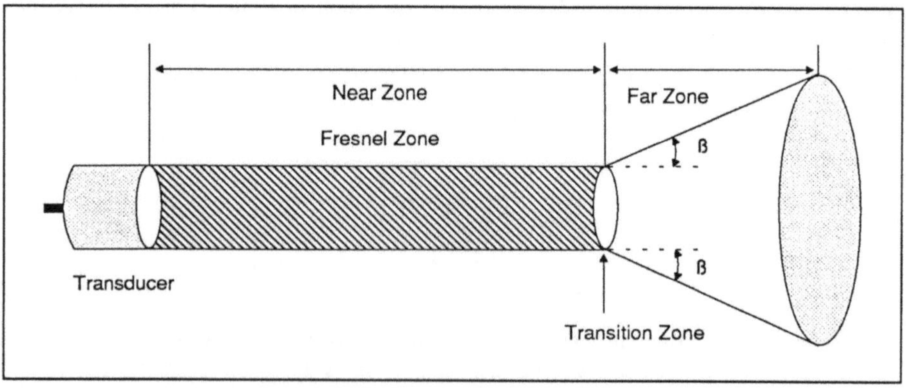

Fig.28.20 Illustration of ultrasound propagation via a transducer

The transducer (consisting of crystals and using the piezoelectric effect) is one of the most critical parts in an US device and plays simultaneously the role of transmitter and receiver. It is clear that the resolving power of this technique improves as the beam becomes narrower. In order to obtain a narrow beam, one can use the principle of phased-arrays already known from antenna techniques. The limitations in resolution are determined by the axial and lateral aspects. The *axial resolution*, defined as that along the axis of the emitted pulse, has to do with the separating potential of a sound beam in the longitudinal direction. It is mainly determined by the length of the pulse train (Fig.28.21). The shorter the pulse length, the better the axial resolution. On the other hand, lower-frequency pulses will penetrate to greater depths, with decreasing axial resolution. A trade-off has to be made between the degree of axial resolution versus the penetration depth. In fact, a variety of transducer frequencies are normally used.

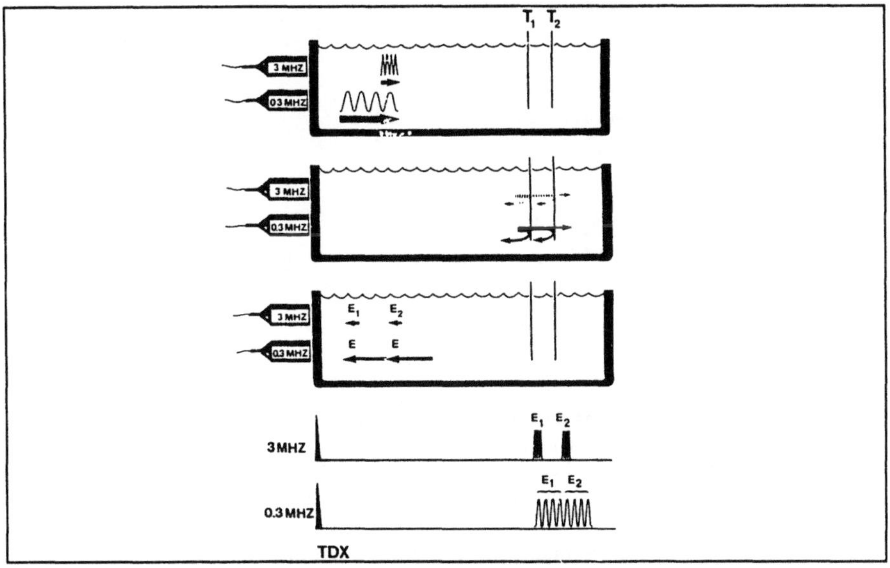

Fig.28.21 Illustration of the effects of frequency on axial resolution . In the *upper most* panel, 2 pulses of 4 cycles each, one from a 3-MHz transducer and one from a 0.3-MHz transducer, are emitted into a test medium. Because of its higher frequency, the pulse from the 3-MHz transducer is much shorter. When these pulses strike two targets, T1 and T2, echoes are reflected at both interfaces. Because of the shorter pulse duration at the higher frequency (3 MHz), separate reflections (E1 and E2) arise from each target and are recorded as distinct. At the lower frequency (0.3 MHz) the pulse length is such that the echoes from T1 and T2 are continuous, and hence these targets cannot be "resolved" as separate [WEY 82].

(source reprinted with the permission from A.E. Weyman. *Cross-sectional echocardiography*. Lea & Febiger, Philadelphia, 1982, p. 12)

A sound wave of 300 kHz, for example, has a wavelength of 5 mm, while one of 3 MHz has a wavelength of 0.5 mm. Points that are situated relatively near to each other cannot be distinguished by a long pulse train.

Another parameter is the *lateral resolution*, which is determined mainly by the width of the beam. In Fig.28.22 we see that the points A1 and A2 can be distinguished, as well as B1 and B2, but it is not really clear what the actual lateral distance between these points is. Finally, the reflections of points C1 and C2 are superimposed and therefore cannot be distinguished.

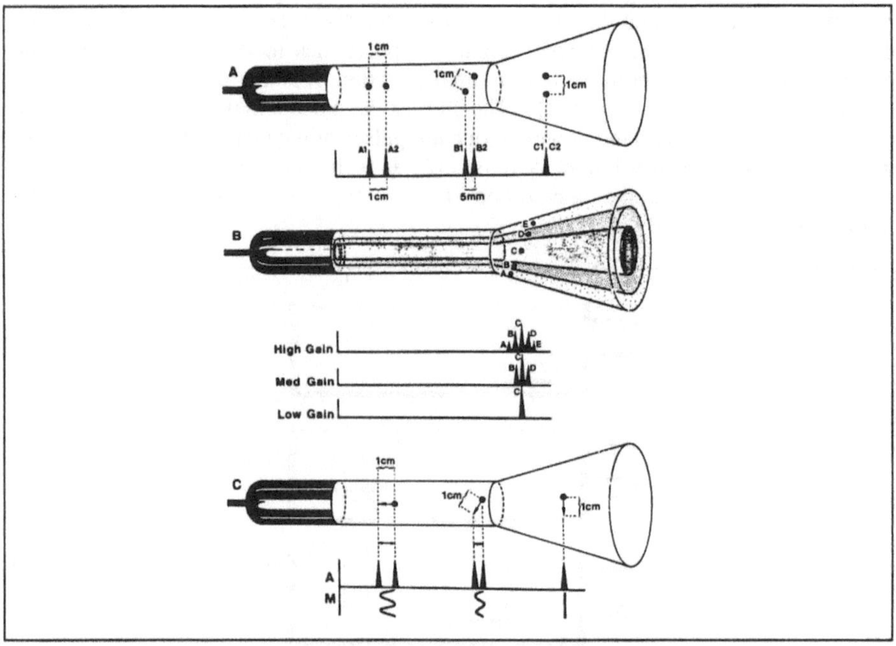

Fig.28.22 a-c Diagram illustrating the effects of beam width and gain on lateral resolution and the recording of off-axis motion [WEY 82]

(source reprinted with the permission from A.E. Weyman. *Cross-sectional echocardiography.* Lea & Febiger, Philadelphia, 1982, p. 14)

Ultrasound acquisitions can be made in 3 modes: A (amplitude), B (brightness) and B-scan and M (motion). In *A-mode*, the echo amplitudes are displayed on a distance base. In *B-mode*, the intensity of the baseline is modulated by the echoes. By carrying out a beam mode registration for each element of a multiple element transducer and writing it out sequentially, it is possible to construct a real time image (Fig.28.23).

The transmitted US pulses are created by a class of crystals that produce ultrasonic waves upon vibration induced by applying an electric field. This is known as the "piezoelectric" effect.

In *M-mode* the registration is made in B mode, but it is recorded as a function of time on a recorder. It is used for a graphical representation of the motion of the reflecting surfaces . This mode is mainly used for cardiological applications (Fig.28.24).

Video techniques that yield high resolution and anatomical images in real time offer a lot of advantages. Depending on the technique used, there are a number of hard copy possibilities, going from instant photographs to videotape.

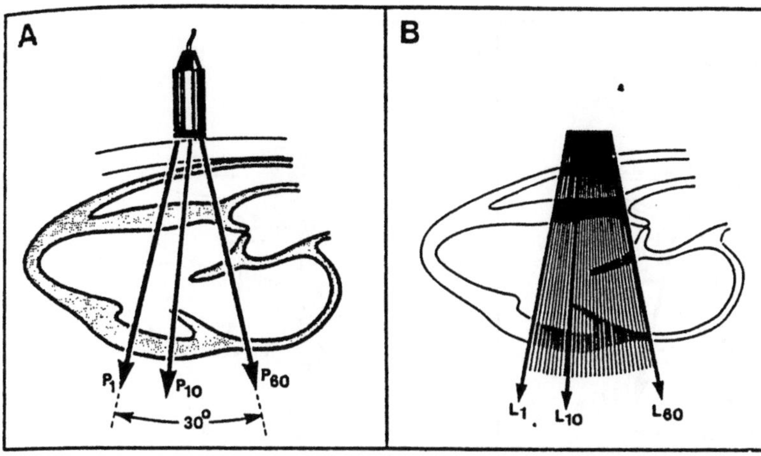

Fig.28.23 A,B Diagram of the method of pulse transmission and image recording and display in cross-sectional format. ***A***, Pulses are continuously transmitted as the transducer is moved in a fixed plane through a 30° arc from the papillary muscles to the left atrium. ***B***, B-mode lines, which correspond to each of these pulses, are recorded and are assembled and displayed in a pattern that corresponds to the pattern of pulse transmission. The first data line (L1), therefore, corresponds to the position of the first pulse (P1), the tenth data line (L10) to the tenth pulse (P10), and so on [Wey 82].

(source reprinted with the permission from A.E. Weyman. *Cross-sectional Echocardiography*, Lea & Febiger, Philadelphia, 1982, pp. 22 - 24)

Doppler Echography

Finally, we mention Doppler echography, in which frequency shifts caused by the motion of substance or interfaces within the tissue are measured (compare with speed traps for cars). The technique consists of aiming US waves at blood vessels through the skin and detecting the return frequency which varies with the blood velocity. If the object or substance (blood) is moving away from the transducer, the frequency (related to the velocity of the moving substance or tissue) decreases, while the frequency increases if the object is moving toward the transducer. Doppler echography is applied in order to obtain velocity profiles (study of blood circulation) or to study heartbeats from a fetus (cardiotocography). Technology is evolving in a direction in which the different possibilities can be combined in the same apparatus using one single transducer, for instance, a combination of B-mode with Doppler. Doppler echography is also applied for investigating the circulation of blood in the brain, arteries in the neck, and abdominal aorta and gynaecological examinations.

Compared with MR angiography, color Doppler is also non-invasive but less expansive.

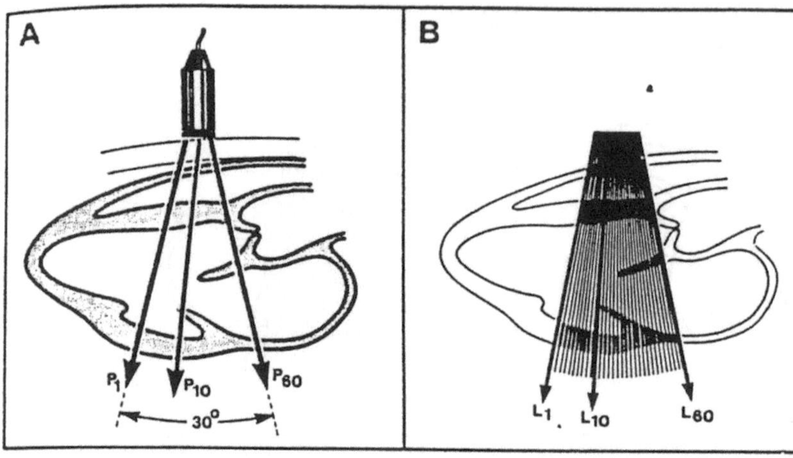

Fig.28.24 Types of echocardiographic displays currently used. To the *left*, an ultrasonic beam is directed through the heart at the level of the mitral valve. In the A-mode format, the distance of the echo-producing interfaces from the transducer is depicted by a series of spikes along the vertical axis of the display. The strength of the echoes from each interface is indicated by the length of the horizontal spikes. In the B-mode format, distance is again depicted along the vertical axis by a series of dots. The intensity or brightness of the dots corresponds to the strength of the reflected echoes. In the M-mode format, the B-mode line sweeps across the face of a cathode-ray tube. Because of the persistence of the phosphor of the tube, the B-mode dots leave a trail as they move. This trail depicts the motion of intracardiac structures relative to time [WEY 82].

(source reprinted with the permission from A.E. Weyman. *Cross-sectional Echocardiography*, Lea & Febiger, Philadelphia, 1982, p. 22)

28.6 Nuclear Medicine

Introduction

Whereas in radiology one usually deals with anatomical information, in nuclear medicine both anatomy and function play important roles. Very small quantities of a radioactive isotope or radionuclide (technetium-99m, indium-113m, etc.) are administered to the patient. By measuring the distribution of radioactivity from the outside of the patient, one can obtain an idea of the form, dimensions and function of the organ in question. The applied dose of radioactivity is very small and decays very rapidly (short half-life). As a consequence, the probability of radiation-related damage is small. Imaging using radioactive pharmaceuticals focusses on the metabolic and physiological function of the organs under study. Nuclear medicine displays these processes (which are dynamic) as time-dependant images, by measuring the variations of the locally detected activity.

We can distinguish two types of clinical radioactive examinations, in vivo and in vitro tests. In an in vivo examination the patient receives a radioactive substance.

In vitro examinations form part of clinical chemistry, and are known as radioimmunoassays (RIA). They concern the assay of samples of human fluids/excreta following injection or ingestion of radioactivity. If a chemical compound has one or more of its atoms substituted by a radioactive atom, the chemical compound is said to be "labelled".

Gamma-cameras and Computers

Nuclear medicine makes use of gamma-cameras converting light photons to electrical pulses and using a large single crystal 250-400 mm in diameter (Fig.28.25). Its central part is a NaI crystal the same size as the image required and characterised by a very homogeneous structure. In the crystal radioactive irradiation (gamma-radiation) generates scintillations. These are detected by a bank of photo multipliers. The localisation of the light flash is registered in a matrix, and by means of arithmetic circuits,the position (x,y coordinates) of the detected photons is determined. The radioactivity of the body is therefore measured in terms of its distribution in time, space and terms of energy spectrum of emitted radiation. At the moments matrices of 64 x 64 or 128 x 128 pixels are being used.

Nuclear medicine images are characterised by low resolution compared with other imaging systems due to the limited amount of radioactive tracer given to the patient and acting as a radiation source inside the patient and emitting photons. Secondly, the radioactive organs emit radiation in all directions. Furthermore, the nuclear medicine sources (liver, bone, kidney, etc.) are volume sources characterised by complex radiation emission patterns [PAT 85].

Computer image processing is not able to restore the resolution but can enhance those images. In order to be able to measure only the activity of a small volume of the organ, multi-hole collimators are necessary, designed to focus at different distances within the body depending upon the organ to be scanned.

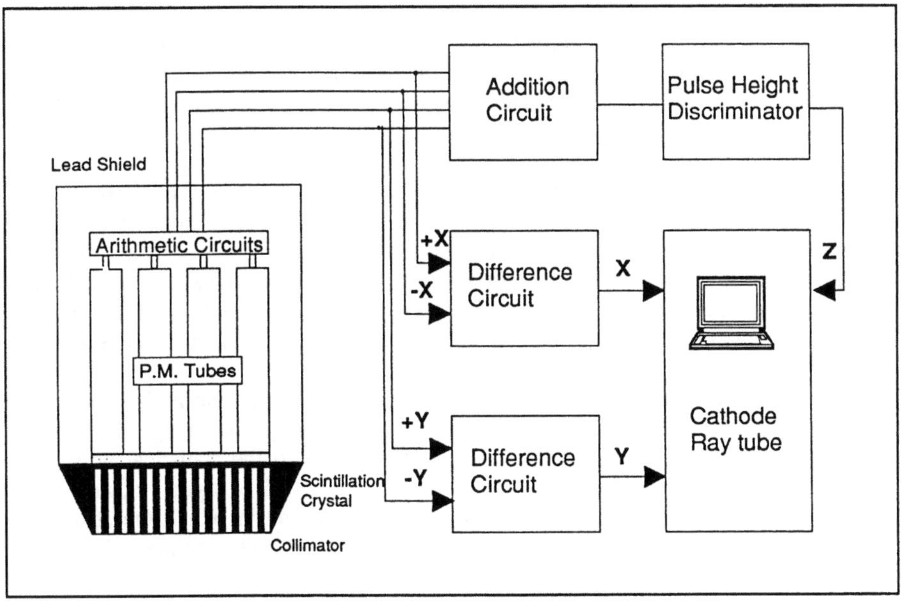

Fig.28.25 Block diagram of a gamma–camera with parallel hole collimation, using a scintillation crystal and photomultipliers

The images can be displayed in colour or black and white. Black and white displays are preferred for diagnostic purposes, because differences in activity are well reflected in a grey scale. Colour displays are usually reserved for parametric images. The distribution of radioactive material is dependent on the form as well as the function of an organ, which explains why nuclear medicine images give an idea of anatomy as well as function. An example of this is a kidney that has lost its filtrating capacity. In this case, the radioactive material will no longer be filtered from the blood and will therefore remain invisible in the kidney.

Dynamic and Static Studies

In nuclear medicine, two types of examination can be distinguished, static and dynamic. In *static studies* one works in the histogram mode, in which incoming data are stored in the central memory as a matrix. New events are added to those already registered. The computer acquires data over a pre-set time or until a pre-set number of counts is reached. The radiation distribution in the organ gives information for the diagnosis. In *dynamic studies* one wants to study information concerning the function of the organ. A number of images covering a certain span of time are recorded in the memory (usually the disc memory). The computer can operate in frame mode or in list mode. In the former, data are accumulated during certain predefined periods and stored in a corresponding frame, which can be reviewed forwards and backwards. In the latter the computer registers the location and the time of occurrence of each event.

Aim of Computer Processing

The main aim of computer processing is to calculate different numerical and graphical information, giving an idea of the function of the organ under investigation. There are two factors that determine the diagnostic value of scintigraphy and for which the computer is necessary :

° *Image Improvement*

Since scintigraphic images contain a relatively limited numer of photons (a few hundred thousand), the images obtained are masked by statistical noise. Due to the limited spatial resolution of the gamma-cameras the images moreover lack sharpness. The noise can be reduced by *spatial filtering*. A useful method is called "*smoothing*", in which each pixel value is replaced by a balanced combination of the values corresponding to neighbouring pixels. Another alternative, for instance, is the use of a Canterbury filter.

By way of an example let us take an original digital recording from an isotopic heart study investigating the function of the heart as a bloodpump. The image shows low-contrast, large pixel-to-pixel variations in intensity due to the statistical noise and recognisable square pixels (Fig.28.26 a),left . In Fig.28.26 b, right, however, an image is shown that its derived from the previous one and in which the structures have been clarified by means of computer processing. The contrast has been improved by using a better grey scale, noises have disappeared by spatial filtering and individual pixel outlines have disappeared through interpolation (we have obviously assumed that low contrast, noise and sharp edges have no relevant diagnostic information in this case).

° *Pattern Recognition*

In scintigraphic imaging the computer is also used in order to recognise metabolic and physiological patterns and for describing this patterns by means of parameters that are diagnostically meaningful.

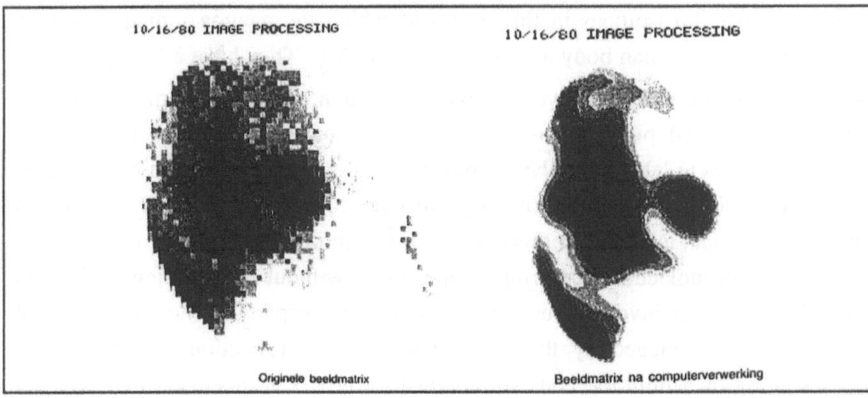

Fig.28.26 Example of computer processing of an image matrix in nuclear medicine (before and after)

Use in Medicine

Brain scanning. Investigations of the brain - one of the first uses to be made of radionuclides and still an important diagnostic tool - result in general in a number of transit times that can be intercompared and in this way yield information about, for instance, an existing obstruction of the blood vessels by sclerosis or thrombosis .

Renography. For investigation of the kidneys, the dynamic examination is very important. It yields a curve (renogram) that describes for a radioactively labelled material (that is not metabolised by the body) brought into the kidneys by the blood how it is filtered out and how the residue is drained away (clearance, a measure for the filtering capacity). A comparison of the left and right kidneys, is possible.

Bone imaging. For the diagnosis of bone tumours, scintigraphy is the method of choice. Using radioactive methylene diphosphate (a material that has a strong affinity for bone), all malignant lesions can be discovered through the increased activity. These lesions can, moreover, be detected before any deviation would be seen on an X ray photograph.

Heart examinations can show inactive wall segments, but it is also possible to follow an injected isotope on its way to the heart ('bolus'). The passage of this bolus can lead to quantitative data like :

° Cardiac output
° Ejection fraction
° Transit times through the left ventricle

Other domains include visualisation of the lymph channels and nodes, lung scans performed as ventilation or perfusion studies, liver anatomy and function by liver imaging,tumour imaging and thyroid imaging.

28.7 Positron-Emission Tomography (PET-Scanner)

Introduction

In PET, also called emission computed tomography (ECT) the activity distribution of a radioactive isotope in a cross-section of the body of the patient is imaged. The technique makes use of a very limited group of radionuclei, namely those that emit positrons. The radio isotopes in this group of which the gamma radiation can be detected outside the human body are ^{11}C, ^{13}N and ^{15}O. They have a half-life of 20, 10 and 2 min, respectively. It is well-known that carbon, nitrogen and oxygen are the building stones of all biochemically important molecules. Hence, the potential of these radioisotopes to label a number of biochemical molecules (like the blood gases, sugars, amino acids and a number of drugs) in order to follow their behaviour within the human organism, is great. In this context, it is important to note that the labelling is carried out on molecules occurring in the body, without the addition of foreign bodies. The molecules involved keep their biochemical properties. The distribution of labelled molecules imaged by the PET scanner is the reflection of biochemical processes going on within the body. In contrast to the CT scanner, the PET scanner does not show anatomical structures (form and extent of the organs) but only the distribution of the radioactive label, that is to say, the functional processes. In this way, it is possible to follow within the patient the metabolism of a certain substance by making snapshots at different moments in time. Whereas the CT scan images density and MRI images water and fat content, PET yields images containing information on metabolism. The different phases of the imaging process involve the following steps :

- Positron emission
- Positron annihilation
- Attenuation
- Scatter
- Detection
- Coincidence counting
- Corrections, reconstructions and quantifications

Nuclei like ^{11}C, ^{13}N, ^{15}O and ^{18}F have a shortage of neutrons and, as a consequence, are unstable. They return to a stable state by the transformation of a proton into a neutron and a positive electron (positron).

During the decay, the positron leaves the nucleus with a high kinetic energy. Under the influence of electrical forces (coulomb forces), it will continuously change direction while emitting electromagnetic radiation, and as a consequence the kinetic energy of the positron, that is to say its velocity, will decrease. As its velocity decreases the probability of a positron colliding with an electron becomes very large and *matter anti-matter annihilation* will take place. In this process, the rest energy of

511 keV of both particles is simultaneously transformed into two gamma rays travelling in opposite directions ($E = mc^2$). The detection of annihilation radiation is based on photon-electron conversion. Two diametrically opposed detectors determine the coincidence of gamma-rays according to place and time (Fig.28.27). A detailed description of the steps necessary can be found in the literature. Software, resembling that of other scanners, processes the signals generated and yields an axial cut through the body. The result is a relatively detailed image of the function of organs and metabolism.

At present, PET cameras remain in the realm of research. They are dependent on a complete infrastructure and can only be used optimally within a multi-disciplinary cooperation. The production of positron-emitting radionuclides and a cyclotron are necessary. The multi-disciplinary environment must consist of a group of physicians surrounding the cyclotron, a group of chemists that take care of synthesising the labelled molecules, a group of electronics and informatics specialists and finally a number of medical people. As mentioned earlier, the half-life of most tracers is very short. That is why all procedures must take place in the immediate neighbourhood of the cyclotron, preferably in the same complex of buildings. Due to the specific infrastructure required, the use of the PET camera has until now remained restricted to a number of large centres, and it can hardly be called a routine diagnostic examination.

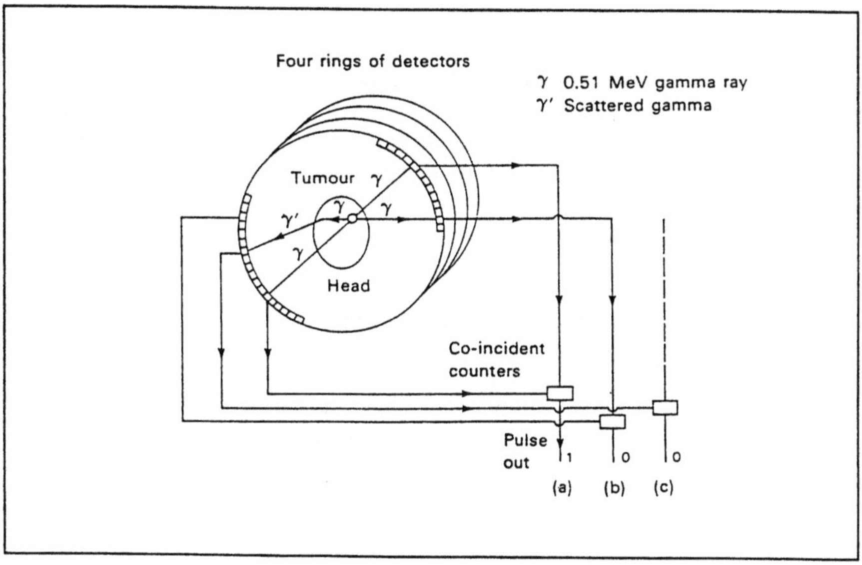

Fig.28.27 Schema of a PET system showing how only the annihilation gamma-rays that are exactly at 180° to each other will produce a pulse from the coincidence counters, e.g. at *a* ; whereas at *b* one of the gamma-rays is scattered, so no pulse is produced; and at *c* the scattered photon is detected but does not have a coincident partner, so no pulse is produced [AIR 88]

(source reprinted with permission from E.G.A. Aird in *Basic Physics for medical imaging*, W. Heineman Medical Books, 1988, p.132)

Application Areas

The application areas of the PET camera cover general medicine and physiology but are specifically directed towards neurology, oncology and cardiology.
In neurology, the PET camera is used for a study of glucose metabolism. Glucose is an extremely important substance for brain metabolism, since the energy requirements within the brain are almost completely fulfilled by the uptake of glucose. Deoxy glucose is administered intravenously, and just like normal glucose it is admitted inside the cells. In contrast to glucose, however, it is not metabolised. A relationship between glucose usage in brain tumours and the degree of malignancy has been shown to exist. As glucose consumption rises, malignancy increases. Another neurological test is the examination of regional perfusion and the oxygen consumption in the brain and the relation between both parameters. In order to study this, a tracer quantity of $C0_2$-gas labeled with 15_O is inhaled.

In cardiology, the PET camera is applied for studying the function of the heart muscle. The uptake of glucose in damaged parts of the heart muscle accords with their metabolic activity and shows whether or not muscle cells are healthy. Information on the local metabolism of the heart muscle is important in order to judge the seriousness of the infarct and the probability of recovery (eventually through a surgical intervention). In badly perfused heart muscles, the uptake and consumption of free fatty acids decreases, as does the glucose uptake.

Another area of application of the PET camera is oncology, where informaton about, the perfusion, rate of growth and biochemical properties of a tumour can be studied. In this context, it is important to know that the availability of oxygen inside the tumour plays an important role in its sensitivity to radiotherapy. Moreover, knowledge about the speed with which tumour cells can proliferate is an important item of information in order to determine the frequency with which radio-or chemotherapy must be administered.

28.8. Future Trends in Medical Imaging Modalities

Non-invasive procedures such as ultrasonography and laser treatments will become more important not only for the safety of the patient but in response to government regulation and to reduce the costs of health care (reduced length of stay, etc).
CT is a mature technology, and old CT equipment is automatically replaced by new. MRI, on the contrary, is a rather new technology and has enormous new market potentials. The situation of MRI is comparable with that of CT 10 years ago. Although the cost of CT equipment is far less than that of MRI scanners (50%), MRI is very suitable for cardiovascular, orthopaedic and abdominal examinations, although images are not available in real time, which is desirable for cardiological imaging.
MRI 3D reconstruction has proven more valuable than CT 3D reconstruction, due to the fact that MRI can distinguish not only tissue and bone (as CT) but also different

types of tissue, fat or lesions or fluids. Therefore, it offers a lot of guidance for pre-surgical planning.

Of all the imaging modalities available, US is increasing in importance fastest, for examinations (due to recent advances in sensor technology) in nearly every region of the body (except for the lungs, intestines and skeleton). Less invasive, less costly, real-time images (compared with CT and MRI) are probably the reason for a growing importance of US in the years ahead, especially in imaging blood flow (Fig.28.28).

US and MRI applications are - particularly in the domain of cardiology- facing competition from PET and single photon emission computed tomography (SPECT). Due to the high investment and multi-disciplinary approach of PET and SPECT, it may be expected that these technologies will not penetrate [SOU 90] in the short term, and PET may be limited primarily to research centres rather than to clinical settings.

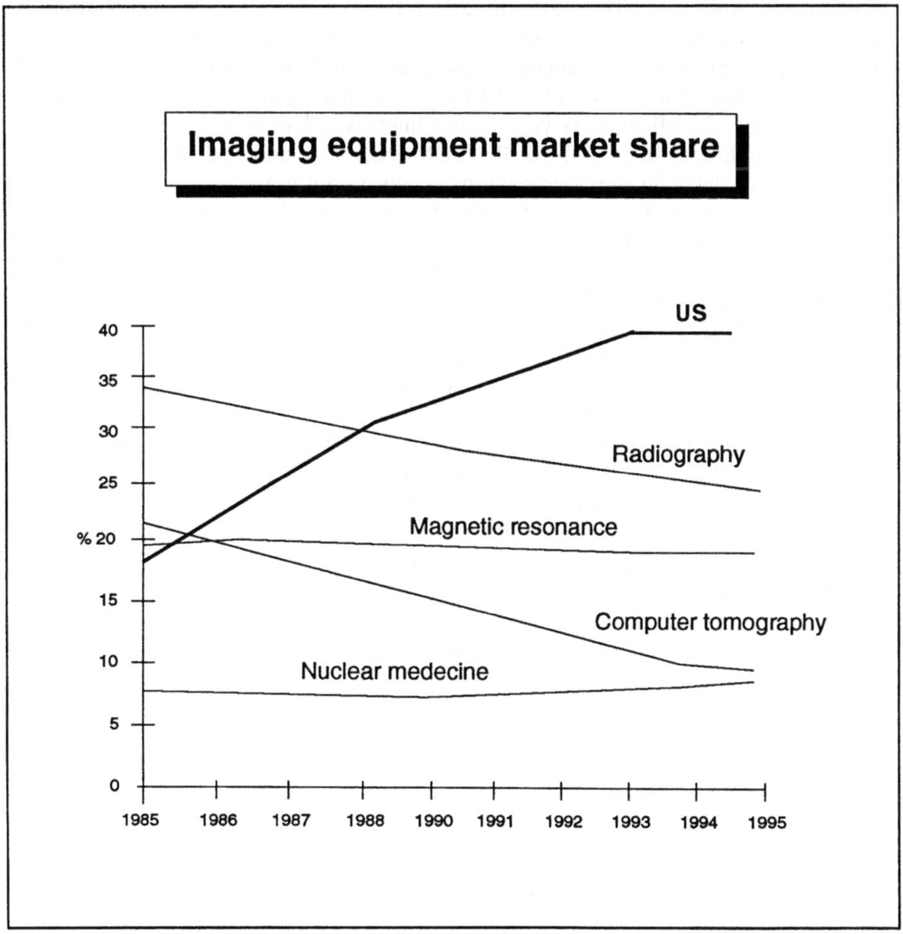

Fig28.28 Imaging equipment market share [SOU 90]
(source Reprinted with permission from Souhrad Laura. Imaging devices shifting uses affect market, MIRC, 1990, *Hospitals*, November 5, 1990, pp. 28-31)

29

Image Management and Communication Systems in Medicine

29.1 Introduction

Image management and communication systems (IMACS) devoted to medical imaging in general are probably the best-known communication systems under development nowadays. They aim to assist the functions of storage, archiving, management and transmission of digital images within an acceptable response time and quality in medical departments. Photographs and film material are forms of image information that require a lot of room for archiving and for which the process of retrieval and classification is very labour-intensive. The increasing use of digital acquisition modalities like CT, MRI, PET, DSA, US, DA, and nuclear medicine (NG) as described in detail in previous sections produce enormous quantities of digitised diagnostic data. In the future, this information is expected to be archived, so that it can be made available locally to authorised users. After image acquisition and digitisation, the next step consists in the distribution of these images through a local electronic network to which stations for the visualisation of these images are connected. An IS consisting of several image databases within a network of image stations allowing on-line transmission, manipulation and visualisation of these images and cooperating with other medical and administrative patient data available within the existing HIS is called IMACS.

Recent advancements in technology such as optical storage, fiber optics, multi-processing techniques, VLSI, high performance communication network, fast (array) processors and high-quality monitors make the implementation of an IMACS feasible in the near future. The expected benefits of the implementation are (Table 29.1):

- Improved access and communication facilities
- Improved diagnostics
- Saving of resources, such as space, film and personnel

The major functions which IMACS offer are:

- Image capture
- Image storage
- Image management
- Image retrieval and communication
- Image manipulation (enhancement, annotation)
- Facilities for research and education

It is important to indicate that 99% of the images are grey-level images, representing morphological information. Colour is only useful for functional information such as blood flow, due to the fact that colour could generate false contours for morphological information when moving from one colour to another.

Table 29.1 Comparison of a conventional film-based management system versus an image management and communication system (IMACS)

Conventional Film-based radiology		IMACS
	Availability	
Films are located at one place at a time (making copies is expensive)		Images are located in image databases available to different authorised users at different places simultaneously
	Investments	
Films are expensive in terms of amount of space and personnel needed		Image databases produce savings in terms of floor space and personnel. IMACS will result in a reduction of the number of X-radiographs, because fewer will be misplaced or lost and therefore unavailable when needed by physicians.
	Information manipulation	
The information on films cannot be further manipulated		Images can be manipulated as users wish without modifying the original image
	Integration	
Patient-related information and image data are stored on different media		IMACS can offer an integrated environment by coupling to HIS and RIS

29.2 Requirements for Successful Implementation

The different requirements for the conceptual design of an IMACS can be studied from different angles of incidence:

29.2.1 Coupling of IMACS with HIS and RIS

It is clear that for the successful implementation of IMACS the systems cannot stand alone, and they should not duplicate data already available in other systems. It is important to stress that the user needs an integrated environment: images from IMACS have to be coupled to examinations from RIS, accompanied by patient-demographic data from HIS and (historical) medical data (previous radiology reports, clinical diagnoses) from the electronic medical record system. Re-entering data can cause errors and needs extra handling. Therefore, patient identification should be performed just before or immediately after acquisition of the image. Integrating HIS and IMACS systems provides at image generation time patient demographic data (patient ID, name, etc.) and examination data by means of the console belonging to

the modality (specialised image station). Moreover, these data are also needed to feed its image management strategy (i.e. the prefetching module), to be completed later on with image-related parameters such as exposure values, number of images made, etc. included in the image file.
Two alternatives are possible here : either one develops both systems separately and solves the integration problem afterwards, or one develops both components as parts of a global HIS concept, an approach that is technically more complex but seems to be the most suitable solution. Yet, the first alternative is usually the one recommended by the manufacturer. In fact, IMACS itself is a subsystem of the electronic medical record system. Integration involves not only requirements on the information side by displaying on an IMACS workstation images together with alphanumerical clinical patient data, but also part of the functionality available in a HIS/RIS system such as order entry, mailing and reporting, appointment and scheduling, etc. In the area of software system tools such as multi-media database software (that will manage a database of images) the requirements in the area of integrity, reliability and protection corresponding to those in classic DBMS theory are of crucial importance.

29.2.2 Image Storage Structure

Digitised images require an enormous storage capacity. Standard resolution of nuclear medicine, CT and MR scans vary from an 256 x 256 x 8 image matrix size in bits (spatial resolution 256 x 256; dynamic range 8 /12 bits) towards a 512 x 512 x 12 matrix . For some DSA systems it is 1024 x 1024 x 8 and for thorax photographs, 4096 x 4096 x10. Taking into account that the pixels can take grey values from 0 (= black) to 4096 (= white), it is clear that huge quantities of data must be dealt with. The problem of archiving and transferring large amounts of data can be solved by parallel connection of many disks (disk arrays are very expensive) or by reducing the amount of data without losing relevant image information. At present, the possibility exists to compress the data through mathematical methods. This process can generate a gain factor between 2 and 3 (maximum 5, for instance, by registering differences between pixel values). In this case, the compression process can be inverted, that it is to say the original image can be reconstructed completely and is called *reversible or lossless compression.*
Data compression maintains data integrity and removes redundancy from a data block without loss of information. For data interchange reasons, all systems involved need the same compression facility (the same hardware/firmware implementation). Two procedures are used: difference value formation and prediction.
Another method, called *data reduction* or *irreversible compression* allows gain factors between 5 and 20, but it has the drawback that information is lost and that the original image cannot be reconstructed faithfully. Irreversible compression techniques are hampered by the slowness of the (de)compression algorithms and the legal issues when reducing the information content of the image. Well known irreversible transform methods, however computation intensive, are the discrete cosine transform (DCT), and the fast cosine transform (FCT).
For primary diagnosis only reversible techniques are suitable, without loss of resolution. For other purposes, irreversible compression techniques are allowable with compression factors on the order 5 : 1 to 20 : 1.

Taking into account the storage capacities needed and regulations concerning archiving duration (X-ray photographs must be available for many years for instance), it becomes clear that classic magnetic storage media (tape, disk, diskette) are completely insufficient and that optical laser disks (eventually used in combination with jukeboxes) form at present the only alternative. Today, the latter systems have a storage capacity of 6 gigabytes and more. Table 29.2 summarises the storage capacity needed per day in a hospital for digital storage of images generated by the examination of 150 patients (= 560 MB/day).

Table 29.2 Summary of the storage capacity needed over 1 year in the University Hospital of Brussels (AZ-VUB) with 700 beds

Image modality	Matrix size	Average study (images)	Bit pixel	MB image	Images year	MB year
X-ray image	1024^2	4	10	5.2	300 000	1 560 000
DSA	512^2	14	8	0.26	13 000	3 280
CT	512^2	25	12	0.4	290 000	116 000
MRI	256^2	25	16	0.13	160 000	20 800
Nuclear medicine	128^2	40	6	0.01	30 000	3 000
Ultrasound	512^2	40	6	0.2	150 000	30 000
Total					**943 000**	**1 733 180**

Images generated by different modalities vary in proprietary formats. The ACR/NEMA format offers the solution by standardising these incompatibilities.
In order to reduce the response time to an acceptable level, it is necessary to classify the images according to the activity profile. By activity, we mean the frequency of retrieval, and a "prefetching" mechanism is necessary to transfer those images before they are requested by the user. This mechanism is based upon information derived from the HIS. Therefore, a three-level structure seems advisable:

- A first layer (to be compared with dead archive) of large memory capacity contains all images. Due to the data volume, the average retrieval time will be longer than normally acceptable (5 - 25 s). Technically, this layer can be implemented using optical disks, which have a large storage capacity (non-erasable or erasable magneto-optical disks).
- A second layer (to be compared with the work archive) is characterised by a smaller storage capacity and faster access to the data. It contains images requiring frequent retrieval activity, for instance, those of patients who are presently undergoing treatment. This layer will make use of classic magnetic disks.
- A third layer consists of the local memory of the image stations themselves, containing a work file for the specialist in order to be able to access and process images very fast.

29.2.3 The Network

As huge amounts of image information (10-100 MB/s) have to be transported, the performance of the network is extremely important and depends on its type, the physical transport layer and its complexity (i.e. number of acquisition units connected to the network).

The LAN allowing transmission and manipulation of the images will play an important role with respect to the required bandwidth. For transporting this enormous amount of information, classic networking is inadequate. New techniques for storage (image reduction, image compression), configuration of image stations (whether or not they should fave local intelligence and local storage capacity), the transmission medium (optical fiber cable, having a large bandwidth-FDDI) as well as the need to have a management system and tools to assure the maximum availability and performance of the network, are necessary in order to provide a useful alternative to present-day systems. For this purpose it is necessary to monitor and analyze network traffic and register this information in a central network management workstation which integrates the information from the several collecting nodes around the network, processes the traffic data and presents it in a user friendly way to the network manager. This will provide us with high-level information on the entire network such as network statistics and network maps (represented either by its true physical topology or by user-defined semantic constraints).

The type of network can be defined by three categories:

- *The bus configuration* represents the most flexible mode of connection, as the information can circulate freely between different acquisition points.
- *The ring configuration* represents a circular architecture and has the disadvantage that if a problem occurs in one point, the whole network can fail.
- *The star configuration* is the best known one; a failure in one element does not interfere with the rest; the central unit controls the whole network and is the weak point. Although very flexible, the cost of the cabling system is quite high.

The physical transport layer covers:

- *telephone cables,* inexpensive but very slow rates of transmission
- *Coaxial cables,* more expensive, better performance
- *optic fibers,* expensive (especially FDDI controllers for the moment), but characterised by extremely high transmission rates (80-200 Mb/s)

The complexity of the network is determined by the number of units connected, access protocols (CSMA/CD, token passing) and the interfaces, as units of different vendors must be connected to the same network (e.g. ACR/NEMA).

Image compression is interesting both for reducing the amount of storage space needed and for reducing the requirements for transmission speed, provided decompression takes place in the workstation. Depending on the purpose of transmission, different reversible or irreversible techniques may be used.

29.2.4 Functional Requirements for Digital Image Workstations

On the lowest level we find the digital image workstation. They become very important for the handling and interpretation of images generated by a variety of modalities. They are the interface between IMACS and the clinical users. As they must cope with images from several modalities, they need to display images having different spatial and contrast resolutions, depending upon the modality and type of examination. Thus, they have to be provided with some important facilities described hereafter.

Handling Facilities

As explained before images may be classified into two types :

- *Static:* for conventional modalities generating large conventional X-radiographs (e.g. thorax) characterised by the huge amount of data they represent and the physical size of the image
- *Sequences* for modalities generating digital images (e.g. CT, MRI,DSA) characterised by the smaller amount of data they represent but the large number of image sequences generated

For conventional modalities, several images on light-boxes are handled manually, replaced, removed, rotated by physicians, almost intuitively and with no training at all. The same functionality has to be provided by multiple workstations with a graphical user-friendly interface and fast response times. For digital modalities, characterised by a high number of images (slices) per study, the user must be provided with two facilities : a "push and pull" mechanism (sequential display) to walk through the stack of images very fast and a panoramic overview (parallel display) of all or some slices, with the possibility to select and zoom in on any image. In fact, the user has to be supplied with a number of manipulation facilities (Fig. 29.1) for image data such as: level and window adjustments, zoom, pan, cine operations and image reconstructions in different planes.

Image Processing Facilities

The next phase in which work stations play an important role is the interpretation and examination of images. The following tools as described previously : zoom-in, zoom-out, inverse, rotate are necessary, but also contrast manipulation, image improvement, quantitative measurements (length, area, density grey level), annotations and comparisons with reference images.
The following computer-aided analysis and interpretation techniques of digital images may be applied grouped as follows [FU 86]:

Point processing techniques, where the value of an input pixel is modified according to some criteria applied to the single pixel. These routines include grey scale windowing, temporal and dual energy subtraction and histogram equalization (smoothing)

Area processing techniques, where the value of a pixel is modified according to some criteria applied to several pixels surrounding this input pixel. These routines include filtering algorithms to enhance edges, sharpening blurred images (e.g. spatial frequency filtering), convolution techniques. (the spatial frequency is the number of times grey level oscillates from black to white over a distance of 1 mm).

Analysis of images, which performs quantitative manipulations on images. Examples are grey level statistics, morphological features extraction, features extraction.

Geometric processing techniques, where the size, shape or orientation of the image is manipulated. (Examples rubber sheet warp).
For more in-depth information on this topic we refer to more specialised readings, such as mentioned above.

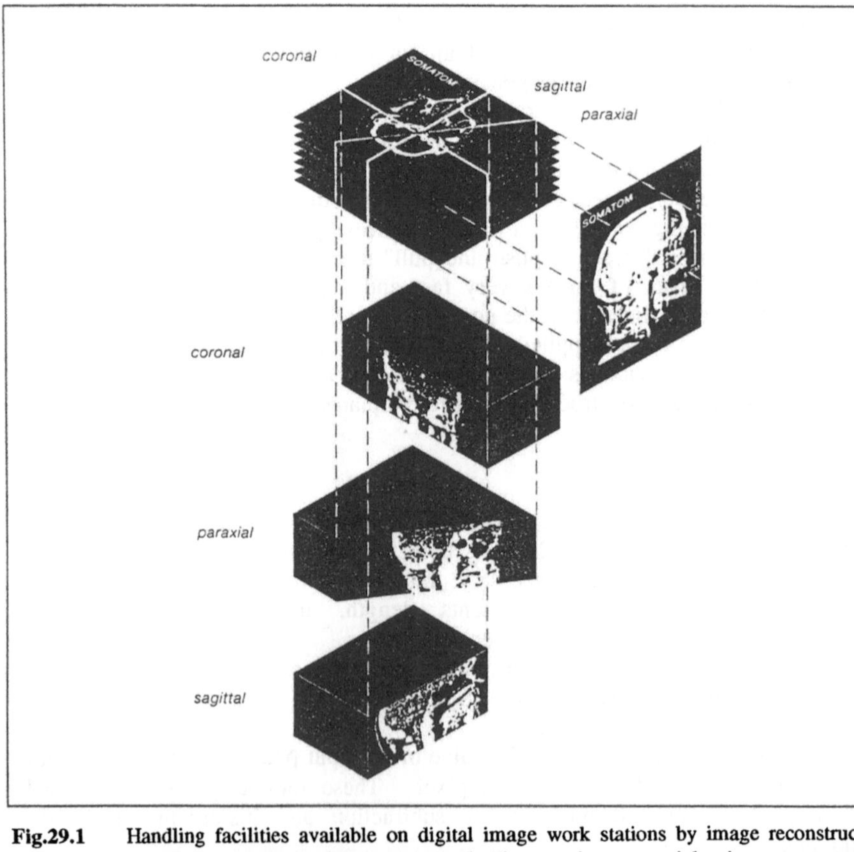

Fig.29.1 Handling facilities available on digital image work stations by image reconstruction provide a sagittal view, a coronal view and a paraxial view reconstructed simultaneously from the stack of contiguous transverse slices (tomograms)

(Source : courtesy of Siemens Medical Systems in Perfect Reformatting with Recon Plus. Siemens Aktiengesellschaft, Erlangen, p.10])

Various types of image processing are available under control of the user (physician, medical engineer, operator).

- **Point transformations (each pixel is transformed independently from the others): arithmetic and logical operations (image additions, subtraction, ORing, ANDing,...), mathematical functions (logarithmic, exponential,...), scale transformation (histogram equalisation).**
- **Global operations: image transforms and encoding (discrete Fourier transforms (DFT), fast cosine transform (FCT), discrete cosine transform (DCT), Karhunen-Loève transforms (KLT), ..., geometrical operations (translation, rotation, geometric corrections).**
- **Noise reduction: by median filtering, smoothing, interpolation...**
- **Edge enhancement with various operators (Laplace, Sobel, Prewitt).**
- **Edge detection and tracking: "low-level" (using local properties in the image) and "high level" (e.g. curve fitting methods using Hough transforms).**
- **Direct segmentation: by multiple thresholding, local histogram methods, clustering methods, methods based on texture analysis.**

Resolution Facilities

An important feature of the image workstation is whether its image quality is sufficient for diagnosis. The image presentation is influenced by a number of variables : its spatial, temporal and contrast resolution (or dynamic range) , display flicker and post-processing (Table 29.3). The ***spatial resolution*** determines the amount of information that the display can contain, defined by the number of pixels, per image area. It is related to the sharpness of the image and is an indication of how well two points that are close together can be distinguished. The ***contrast resolution*** determines the number of bits for every pixel, indicating the number of grey levels (2 to the power of the number of bits used), and provides the ability to distinguish small differences in intensity. Another term often used is dynamic range. With a dynamic range of 8 bits one can determine each pixel value accurate to 1 part in 256 (0.4 %). With a 10 bits dynamic range 1 part is divided in 1024 (0.1 %). The ***temporal resolution*** is a measure of the time necessary to create an image. If one wishes to obtain a real-time environment, a rate of 30 images per second is necessary. Some variables are related to the observer, such as environmental conditions (light), psychological factors and age.

Table 29.3 Comparison of imaging parameters for digital modalities (Mod. = Moderate)

	CT	**MRI**	**US**	**NM**	**DSA**	**Digital X-ray**	**Film X-ray**
Pixels per image	$(256\text{-}512)^2$	256^2	512^2	128^2	512^2	1024^2	2048^2
Spatial resolution	Mod.	Low	Mod.	Low	Mod.	High	High
Contrast resolution	High	High	low	Low	Mod.	High	Low
Radiation	Mod.	None	None	Mod.	Mod.	Low	Mod.
Cost	High	High	Mod.	Mod.	Mod.	Mod.	Low
Portability	No	No	Yes	Yes	No	No	Yes

Table 29.4 provides as example an overview of display classes and accompanying parameters for the radiology department of the University hospital of Brussels [MAT 91]. Based on this classification the minimum requirements can be calculated for image-computers.

Table 29.4 Overview of display classes and accompanying parameters for the Radiology Department of the University of Brussels

M	E	N	S	R	D	T	C	Class
CT	Body	34	21	512	2	30	12	A
	Head	20	15	512	2	30	12	A
MRI	Body	80	13	256	2	40	12	A
	Neuro	128	13	256	3	40	12	E
	Bone	173	25	256	3	55	12	E
	Cardio	19	19	256	4	35	12	C
US	Body	8	4	512	2	20	8	A
DR	Body	8	8	4096	2	15	12	B
DSA	Cardio	400	20	512	4	20	12	C
	Cardio	100	20	1024	4	30	12	C
	Vasc	400	20	512	4	30	12	C
PET	Neuro	20	5	256	2	40	8	D
	Cardio	20	5	256	2	40	8	D

Definition of a 8 tuple (M,E,N,S,R,D,T,C): **M**, modality source {CT,MRI,US,DR,XR,DSA,PET}; **E**, examination {body, head, neurological, cardiac, abdominal, vascular, bone}; **N**, maximum number of images; **S**, maximum number of marked images ; **R**, matrix (n2){64,128,256,512,1024,2048,4096}; **D**, display technique {2,3,4} (depends on acquisition) 2: 2D image (*x,y*) 3: image of a 3D set (*x,y,z*) 4: image in a dynamic 3D set (*x,y,z,t*); **T**, average examination time; **C**, {8,12} contrast resolution in grey level.

29.2.5 User Interfaces

As previously described, the user interface will also play an important role in the acceptance of IMACS by increasing accessibility and convenience.

The user interface will be one of the most critical parts in next generation of HIS in general, especially in IMACS which also have to deal with various types of users with different requirements and lead the end-user in an evolutionary way from film-based image reading habits to digital image-based reading habits (Table 29.5).

In contrast to static user interfaces that function uniformly independently of which physician is working with the system or what task he or she is carrying out, *adaptive user interfaces* will become increasingly important, as they conceptually take into account that workstation users and their tasks vary during run time.

The different categories of physicians (managing radiologists, assistant radiologists, referring physicians, radiological technicians, physicists) have their particular needs, personal preferences and styles, which change over time. This approach demands an iterating design process in cooperation with the end-user (user-driven, user-centred design) in all phases of the project.
User interface research in this domain has been the subject of recent work done by Th. Wendler (Wendler 1989 - 1991 Philips - Hamburg).

Table 29.5 Comparison of classic film versus digital image-based reading habits

Film-based	Digital image based
On light boxes	On image work stations
Easy to manipulate (rotating, repositioning, comparing)	More artificial concepts have to be introduced
Large display space available (parallel viewing of different images possible)	Limited display space (parallel viewing demands several high resolution monitors-expensive)
High spatial resolution, high dynamic range	Better contrast resolution achievable
Manual (slower) access	Automatic (faster) access
Limited image analysis techniques available on the spot	Increased image analysis techniques available such as operation on image sequences and regions of interest

29.3 The Image Workstation

In an IMACS environment image stations can be classified on several levels, depending upon the requirements of every user: modality console, extended image station, multi-modality reporting console, simple (multi-modality) viewing station and multi-modality film output.

- *The modality console* (specialised image station) is the interface between a dedicated acquisition unit/modality (CT, MRI,DSA) and the technical or medical user of this specific modality, allowing the processing of raw data and image manipulations. It must provide the functions to transmit the images to the IMACS.
- *Very advanced image stations* (extended image station) have three functional components namely : local intelligence (e.g. fast array processor), local temporary storage (e.g. disk array storage) allowing simple manipulations (rotation, reflection, panning, etc.) and a high-definition display subsystem (maximum attainable resolution 2K) offering to the end-user an optimal solution in terms of visual perception (non-linearity of the eye with respect to

grey levels, magnification of images without losing the global information of the whole, etc.) and ergonomy (touch screens on which regions of interest can be indicated, softkeys, joysticks, trackballs, mouse, etc.) (Fig. 29.2). They enable sophisticated manipulations and detailed investigations and evaluations of 3D images. These expensive workstations will be used, for displaying high resolution radiologic images, most often in the radiology departement where actual and earlier patient images must be provided for study and reporting. This approach offers the advantage of not burdening the central system too much, while local processing is optimal (retrieval time, presentation, operation).

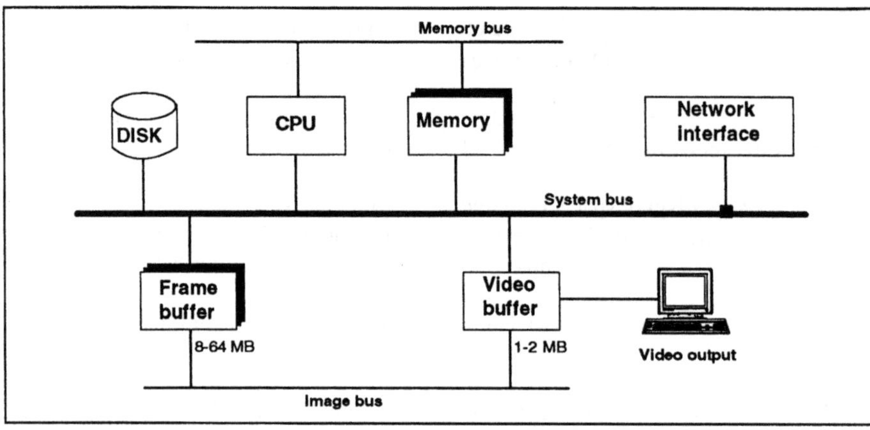

Fig. 29.2 Functional diagram of an Image work station unit and logical image flow: direct access between network interface and fast internal memory, which is necessary for the high quantity of images

- *Multi-modality reporting console* with local intelligence and local temporary storage allows the interpretation and reporting of examinations. Two types are defined in this category. The multiple reporting console displays several images simultaneously on different high resolution image monitors and allows instant transfer comparisons and some simple low-level image operations.
  The other type is the virtual reporting console, which uses panning and scrolling in a large image memory to obtain analogous results with a single monitor. The image roams on the screen just like a microfilm, but instead of moving the head to the left or right, you move the image memory mapping and look at one monitor. It offers the advantage of speeding up the examination because there is no waiting time after selecting the patient file [MAT 90]. Other related functions are contrast modification, text annotation, compression and decompression, fast access to the image archive and reporting tools (link).

- On the last level, the *single viewing (multi-modality) station,* we find monitors for remote viewing applications having a very limited combination of image manipulation functions. These will be found in the therapeutic departments and consultation rooms, replacing the present day light boxes. They are simple to use and not expensive, offer a good spatial resolution and will be available for other IS functions.

29.4 Image Analysis and Diagnostic Quality

29.4.1 Image Analysis

Image analysis is a human perceptual task at which computers currently perform poorly. It is questionable whether computer systems with the help of AI techniques will support imaging analysis in the near future. Image analysis is in fact a pattern recognition process. It consists of four sub-tasks: image enhancement (global processing), segmentation (extraction), feature detection and classification.
The image enhancement (global processing) phase aims to execute specific computations on the image not oriented towards its content, in order to enhance the quality. Examples of such operations are histogram equalisation applied to CT and MR images, filtering algorithms and grey-scale windowing of CT scans. Another facility for image enhancing is provided by means of a *look-up table (LUT)*, which is an aid for producing a (non-linear) effect on the amplitude transmission characteristic. This is realised by conditioning the signal through a ROM or RAM memory.
During the segmentation phase, regions of interest are selected and extracted from the complete image. Edge-detection or region-detection techniques (although not very successful) can be applied.
Finally, feature detection and classification are activities related to extracting parameters from the segmented regions to be used.

29.4.2 ROC Analysis

As the expected benefit of IMACS is improved diagnostics, the question arises, how can we measure the diagnostic quality of IMACS ? A commonly used and well accepted statistical method to evaluate the diagnostic quality of a test is the *receiver operating characteristic* (ROC) curve. Any given point on the curve corresponds to two values: the sensitivity (true-positive value or the likelihood that a diseased patient has a positive test/result) and the false-positive rate (1-specificity) or the likelihood that a non-diseased patient has a positive test/result). Remember that :

$$TP + FN = 1$$
$$FP + TN = 1$$

By varying the cutoff value of a certain test over a specific range, we can calculate the effect on the sensitivity and specificity and plot the values into an ROC curve. It is important to stress that the sensitivity and specificity are two features not directly related to the test alone, but to the test **and** the choice of the cut-off value of the axis. The closer the values of sensitivity and specificity approach the 1, the more the test will reduce the uncertainty about the likelihood of a certain symptom. The steeper the curve rises, the faster an observer makes a correct positive diagnosis.
The advantages of this method are that it helps evaluate a certain test procedure and that it is possible to compare different tests with each other. It has been used in several domains, for instance, in radiology to compare film/screen combinations

(detection of microcalcifications in mammography) and in nuclear medicine to compare various image enhancing procedures (Fig. 29.3).

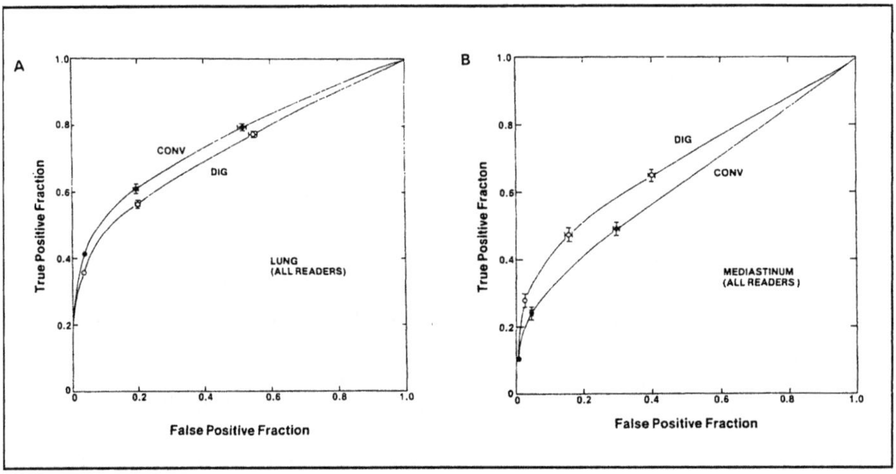

Fig. 29.3 A,B Receiver operating characteristic curves derived from five observers of digital *(DIG)* and conventional *(CONV)* radiographs. **A** The comparison for nodules projected over the lung; slightly more (7%) nodules were detected with the conventional system. **B** The comparison for nodules projected over the mediastinum; here the true positive fraction is 20% greater (at 0.25) with the digital system

(source courtesy R.G. Fraser and G.T. Barnes (1986). Digital radiography of the chest in *Recent Advances in Radiology and Medical Imaging,* N°8 Churchill Livingstone) [FRA 86]

29.4.3 Future developments : Storage Phosphor Films

Storage phosphor screens (similar in composition to intensifying screens) are able to detect X-radiation and store the latent images over a long period of time (sec-minutes). Briefly, this latent storage capacity has been realised by producing electron traps in the band gap through doping. Excited electrons stimulated through radiation fall into those traps. Afterwards, when stimulated by light of a certain wavelength (laser scanner), the stored image information (the electron traps) can be read out digitally (within a few microseconds) (Fig. 29.4).

After the image information is read line by line and following amplification and digitalization, the digital image is transferred to a computer system. Then the residual image is erased. In that way it can be loaded, exposed and read out again (Fig. 29.5). The advantages of these storage phosphor screens are the lifetime of reusability of those screens (several thousand cycles) without the need for films and the high resolution of the images obtained.

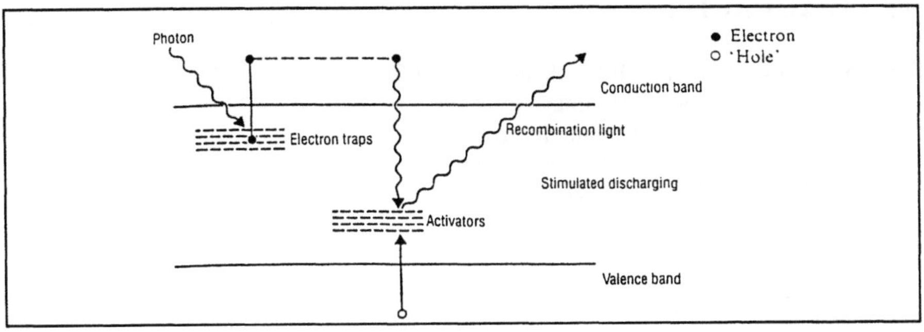

Fig. 29.4 Optical readout (discharging) of the image information from the storage phosphor screen [KRE 90]

(Source courtesy of Siemens Medical system in Krestel E. *Imaging Systems for Medical Diagnostics.* Siemens Aktiengesellshaft, Berlin and Munich, 1990, pp. 283)

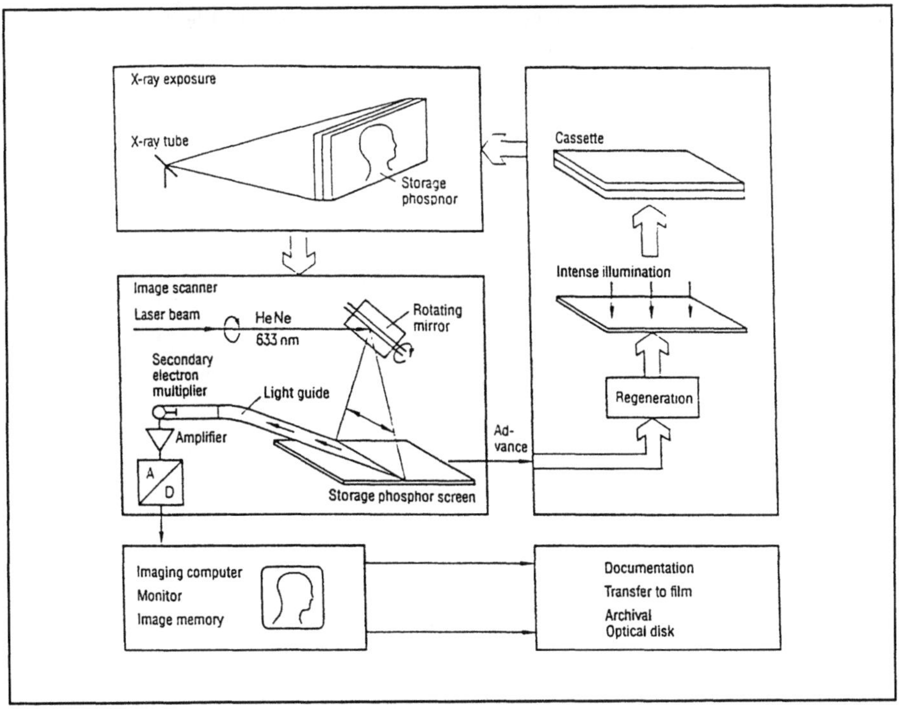

Fig. 29.5 Schematic representation of the sequence of an X-ray exposure with a storage phosphor screen [KRE 90]

(Source : courtesy of Siemens Medical system in Krestel E. *Imaging Systems for Medical Diagnostics.* Siemens Aktiengesellshaft, Berlin and Munich, 1990, pp. 283)

29.5 IMACS Architecture

The main components of an IMACS are (Fig. 29.6):

- High-speed network for image transport
- Work stations for retrieving images
- Modalities which generate the images
- Intelligent network manager
- Interface with HIS
- Interface with RIS
- Storage device
- Laser scanner devices
- Hardcopy units

If the aim is to offer physicians and radiologists images and radiological data at the same time, instead of using classic films, very fast response times have to be assured. As even the most advanced network technology nowadays cannot reduce those waiting times to an acceptable level, other alternatives have to be implemented on the hardware level through a distributed architecture and a layered storage structure and on the software level by a storage manager which is responsible for prefetching certain images as examinations are requested.

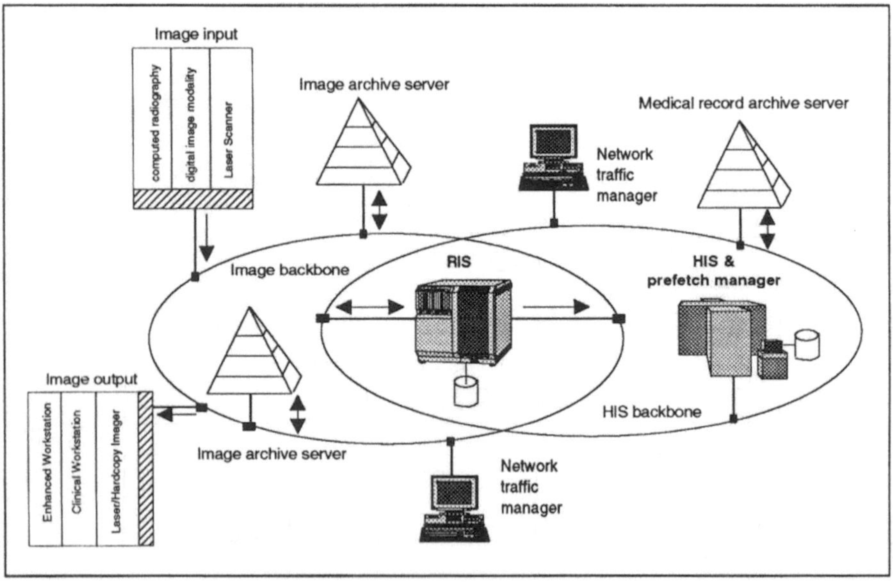

Fig. 29.6 General representation of IMACS architecture. The RIS system can be equipped with two network interfaces and provide gateway services as well.

An IMACS will be scattered over several locations. It is important to stress the following concepts :

- *The hierarchical storage concept,* where information is stored, depending on the status in a multi-layered structure, e.g. on RAM memory, magnetic disk memory, optical memory and tape (after deactivation of certain images)

- *The network manager* to monitor, analyze and register the network traffic
- *The distributed architecture* in order to face the huge data transmissions needed across the network
- *The multi-media aspect* capable of managing different types of data, e.g. image data, text data (motion picture and voice in the future)
- *The parallel architecture* of the image archive comparable with the architecture of electronic medical record systems, to face high transmission peak requests
- *The storage manager* responsible for distributing (prefetching) the information over several layers based on a strategy to store recently generated or accessed information on fast storage devices and old information on slow main storage

The algorithm (expert rules) which has to care for fast retrieval and the reallocation of images in advance contains the following rules:

- Images with an increased probability of being retrieved in the very near future have to be placed in high priority. This can be achieved by transporting images before they are really needed to the fast storage layer (decentralised archives).
- If the image is expected to be retrieved, evaluate HIS and RIS data (referring medical service,previous examinations,age of the examinations, type of the examinations,admission diagnosis).
- Images which are no longer needed have to be placed in low priority (Fig. 29.7).
- Record the location of examination reports and corresponding images.

The image database is organised by patient study, examination and images.The selection of images happens through the use of an intermediate historical file system (pictorial index system) which contains reduced images in low resolution or an alphanumerical index(description) of the required images per patient.

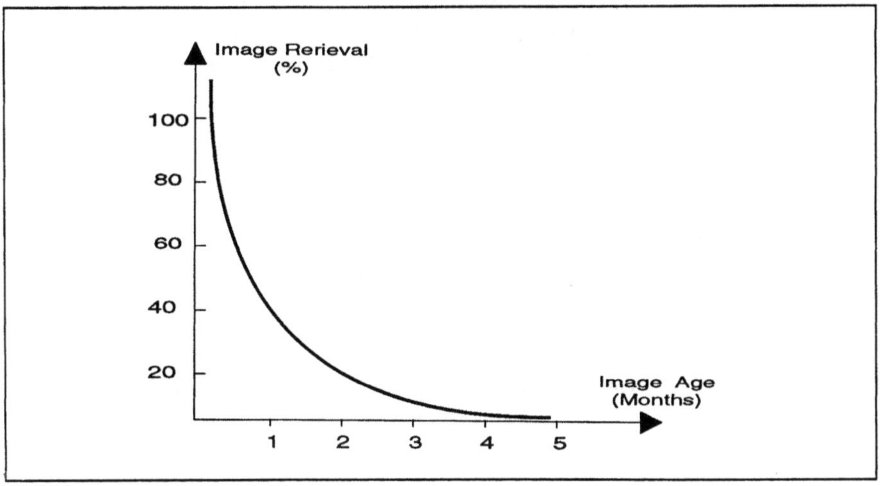

Fig. 29.7 Probability of an image being retrieved over time

The prefetching mechanism will play a fundamental part in IMACS, offering acceptable response times by optimising physical transport. The algorithm providing this stage-in and stage-out mechanism will be based upon the information contained in the central HIS database, patient visits, appointments, localisation, admission, speciality, in order to determine which part of the medical history is expected to be used. For images, the modality, body region and type of examination will be important input parameters.
Once information has been retrieved, the probability for a second retrieval within a short time is higher than before.
The transfer (archival) of data between storage layers can happen on a real-time basis (if information is necessary at once) or on a regular basis (during the night, or in the background).

29.6 Standardisation in Medical Imaging

29.6.1 The ACR-Nema Standard

In order to connect modalities from different vendors, standardisation of communication protocols is necessary. In 1983 the American College of Radiology (ACR) and the National Electrical Manufacturers Association (NEMA) -recognising this problem- formed a joint committee to develop a point-to-point communication protocol (and not a network protocol) that offers the possibility of exchanging digital image information between different [ACR 85] imaging equipment (IE). The ACR-NEMA standard is composed of six layers conforming to the OSI model. As routing functions are not required, the network layer is not included, and the standard defines a point-to-point interface by specifying the hardware interface, a set of software commands and data formats. An image equipment has to be interfaced to the network through a network interface unit (NIU), transforming the specific network protocol into the ACR-NEMA standard (Fig. 29.8). The information for imaging equipment communicated across the ACR-NEMA standard interface is structured in messages, which comprise commands and data. The command group is made up of:

- Normal commands (SEND, GET, MOVE, FIND, DIALOG)
- Disabling commands (CANCEL)
- Check commands (ECHO)

The data group is made up of:

- Identification data
- Patient data
- Image orientation
- Image display
- Image data
- Text
- Overlays

A "*network extension*" (in contrast to the point-to-point connection of the ACR NEMA 2.0. version) will be available soon (Version 3.0). CEN TC251 is also working on this topic and will ensure that this will become an international standard.

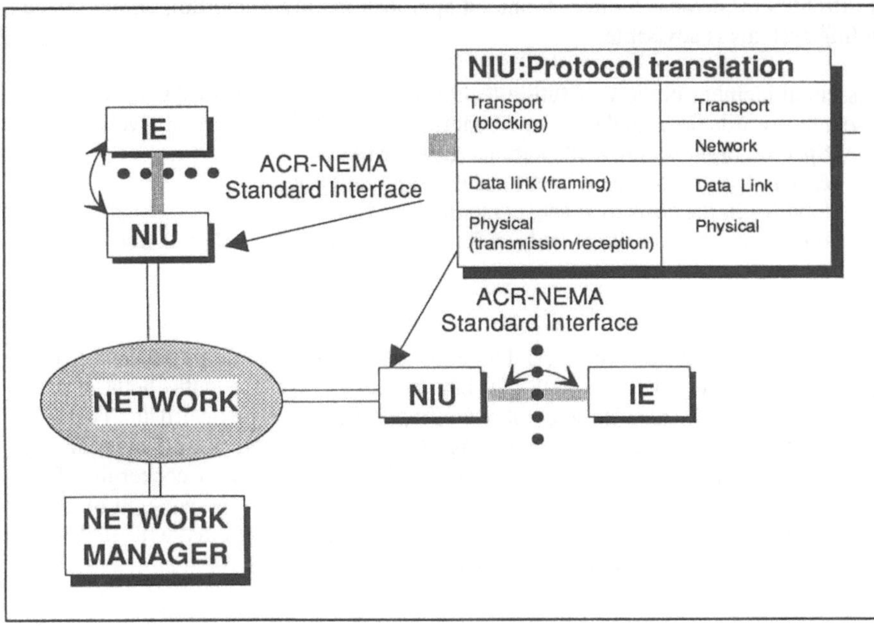

Fig. 29.8 Images sent from the IE via the ACR-NEMA standard interface disappear into an unspecified region. IE, imaging equipment; NIU, network interface unit!

29.6.2 The Standard Product Interconnect

Siemens and Philips formed a joint group to develop the ACR-NEMA conforming Standard Product Interconnect (SPI), fulfilling the minimum requirements of the ACR-NEMA standard. Its main features are:

- The data elements are more precisely defined (layers 6 and 7)
- The application layer protocol is organised into a set of "services" (Image Management, IMS; Public Storage Services, PBS; Export Service, EXS; Configuration Service, CFS)
- For WORM media, uniform data file and directory formats are specified

29.7 The Future of IMACS : Perspectives and Conclusions

It is clear that conventional films will not disappear very soon, making the beginning of the era of all-digital-image systems. Although the importance for medical practice of IMACS is growing, many technical and human engineering problems have still to be solved. Nowadays, the large-scale implementation of IMACS is financially too expensive and technically not yet feasible.

Instead, partial IMACS are being implemented in a multi-disciplinary approach at various locations in Europe (University hospital of Brussels AZ-VUB Fig.29.9; University hospital of Geneva; University Hospital Marburg), which will provide necessary guide-lines for the technical and organisational implementation of large-scale IMACS in the near future. A phased approach mainly supporting digital image handling systems is advisable.

An essential element in view of future technical developments of IMACS prototypes is research towards the actual costs and benefits of the system on several levels:

- Specific organisational adaptations for an IMACS
- Efficiency improvement in clinical care and radiology
- Savings in the costs of space, personnel and film
- Impact of the transition from a film-based system to a digital image-based system

The integration aspect deserves special attention. An IMACS can only succeed if it is integrated with the HIS and RIS. It has points of contact with both system components. The RIS handles appointments, reporting and statistical data. The HIS deals with patient data, billing and archiving of the medical data, as well as prodiving an index to the IMACS. The IMACS provides image information concerning RIS examinations about patients registered in the HIS. In analogy to the creation of other system components (for instance, laboratory, OR), these systems will first (for simplicity) have to appear on the market separately.

Effective integration requires standardisation, necessary to interface heterogeneous image processing equipment from different manufacturers. NEMA (National Electronics Manufacturer's Association, USA) and the ACR (American College of Radiology, USA) have taken the initiative for a standard that is already supported by the majority of manufacturers. The standards cover image data and interfacing to the network and to other equipment. Worthwhile to be mentioned is also the PAPYRUS image format, based on an extension of the ACR-NEMA standard [RAT 91].

Finally when talking about future IMACS projects the situation is much comparable with the discussions and expectations of office systems 10 years ago, when people predict the emergence of the paperless office. What did we achieve? What was promised? Therefore talking about the filmless hospital of tomorrow, let's be serious it should be more realistic to argue about the usage of less films. We are very confident that IMACS research and development have passed the initial exploratory phase but on the technical side there is still a lot of research and development to be done before delivering a large-scale, real production system such as:

- Network traffic control (high-speed image networking)
- Intelligent prefetching management system
- Multimedia database
- Assistance of AI techniques to support imaging diagnosis

Requirements with respect to image quality, work station features (adaptive user interfaces) and overall IMACS performance still need to be defined.

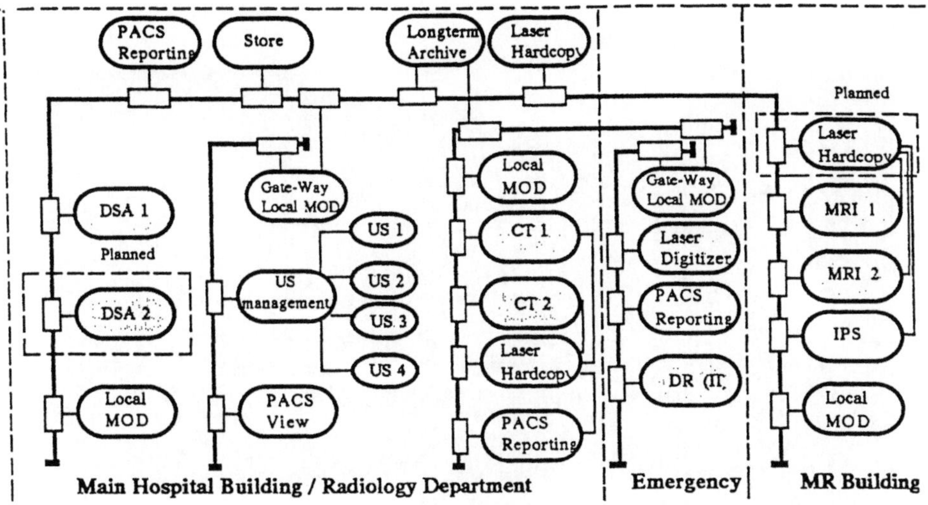

Fig. 29.9 PACS architecture at the University Hospital of Brussels (VUB 1991). The CT-PACS consists of two CT units (Siemens), a prototype three 1kx1k screens reporting station (Siemens), local storage and archiving possibilities (2 Gbyte). A hardcopy unit (3M) is shared by the 2 CTs and the reporting console. The MR-PACS section consists of two MR units (Siemens), two powerful image-processing stations with array processors, local storage, shared hardcopy (3M) and archiving possibilities (3.2 Gbyte). In the emergency department the PACS consists of a laser digitiser (Dupont), a two 1kx1k screens reporting console (Dupont) and a prototype DR (II) (CGR-GE) system based on image capture on the image intensifier tube. Evaluation studies are being carried out for the emergency-PACS, with promising medical results but with technical problems at the level of integration of patient identification on the laser scanner and at the throughput of a set of images.
The DSA (Philips) system is integrated in the network, and a logical step will be the connection of the DSA (Siemens) which was installed early in 1990. This will result in the creation of a DSA-PACS section, with local storage, reporting and hardcopy units.
The ultra sound management application allows the user to archive, retrieve and manipulate echo images. Examinations can be compared locally. The system allows the retrieval of the echo images together with the report. It is based on standard Macintosh hardware and allows the connection of up to four US units

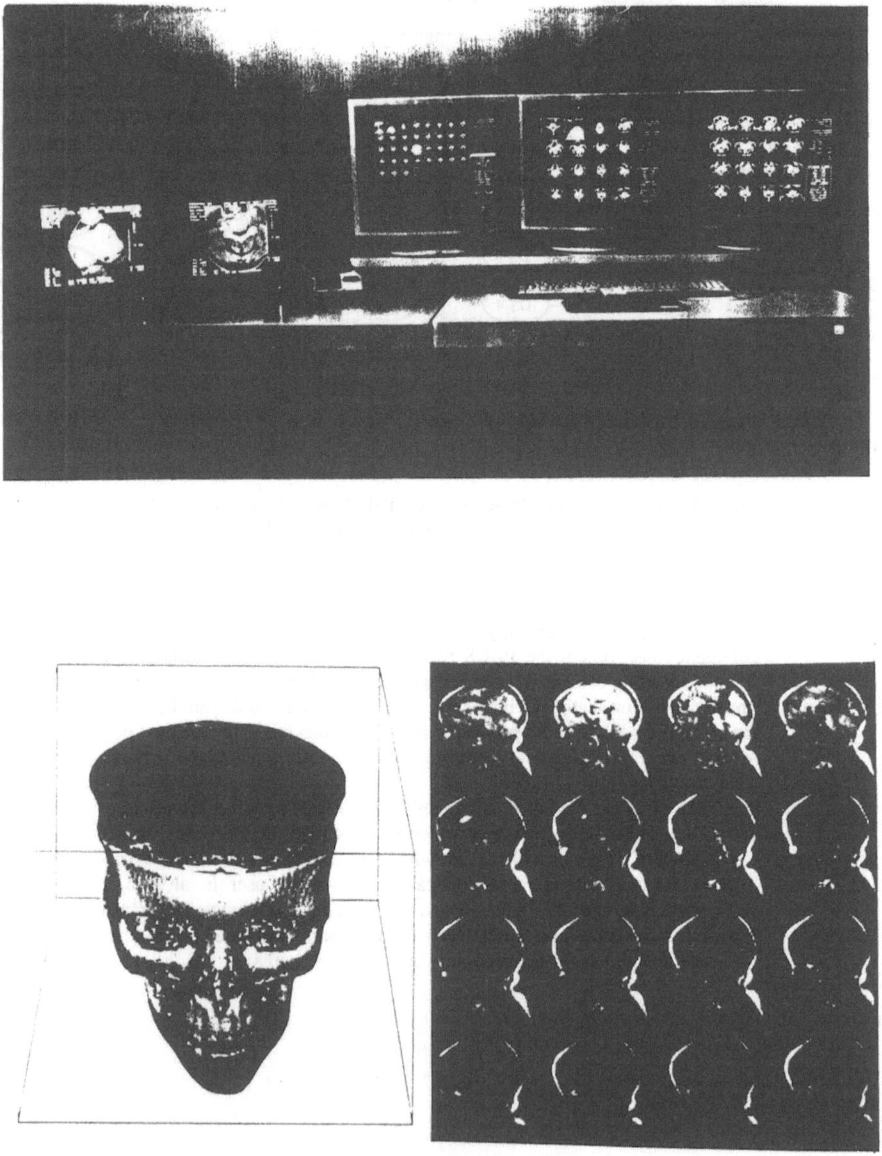

Fig.29.10 (a) Multi modality reporting console (MRC) at the CT-PACS reporting section of the university hospital of Brussels (VUB). At the left, two real-time monitors for communication with the two CT-rooms are installed. The MRC is a 3 screen 1kx1k prototype console from Siemens. (b) 3D-Bone presentation of the head for MR images. (c) Head 3D-MRI set (128 slices).

(Source courtesy of Osteaux M.,M.D., hospital of the Free University of Brussels department of Radiology)

30

The Era of Telemedecine

"Healing from a Distance"

30.1 Setting the Communication Scene

Nowadays, medical care and medical data are produced at many locations: hospitals, general practitioners, nursing homes, ambulatory health care centers, patient home, etc. Patients with varying disabilities are often homebound and need constant surveillance there, because if assisted they could lead better or normal, social and economically productive lives. As patients request more and better health care services, care will have to be provided more and more where the patient wishes (or resides) rather than in health care institutions. Instead of moving the patient to the health care institutions, as it is today largely the case, therapy and diagnostic procedures will be brought to the patient in some situations.

There is an increasing demand for better communications between health care providers, health care institutions and related health care establishments (insurance companies, legal authorities) for two reasons:

- The increased mobility of health care providers and patients
- Health care is becoming very specialised and delivered by a team of health care providers (often at various locations) who need to share information. The "one to one" relationship that existed in the past between a physician and a patient is being replaced by a "one to many" relationship.

Despite boundaries, distances and systems heterogeneity communication between health care information systems will become very essential. The era of telemedicine is revealing. In the telecommunication area, hospitals lag behind other industries. There is a great difference in maturity between, for instance, banking applications and health care, although hospitals have higher telecommunications needs compared with other businesses. This market segment will be of great importance to telecommunications vendors in the near future (Fig. 30.1).

Although hospitals are just starting to implement LANs or integrate computer systems within their own walls, they are already facing a growing pressure for data exchange inside and outside the institution, and an increasing demand for communication of already digitalised data. New techniques and telecommunication facilities like integrated broadband communications (IBC), wide area networks (WAN), metropolitan area networks (MAN), offer new facilities for improving communications in the health care sector to create an internationally integrated health care environment. Computer networks will provide connection facilities for a broad range of health care actors (hospitals, general practioners, pharmacists, dentists, preventive care institutions, public authorities, suppliers of health care products, banks). It is necessary to make a distinction between interhospital and intrahospital communications. For the former, LANs can be used, while for the latter we need WANs or MANs.

Because information exchange deals with patient information, special measures have to ensure the patient's privacy. All physicians fear that somebody might look in their files. Besides cost and cultural aspects, the most limiting factor for telemedicine might be security of the data. The danger of privacy violation is real in those countries in which applicable legislation is still not available. Thus, communication through electronic messages is preferable over direct database access.

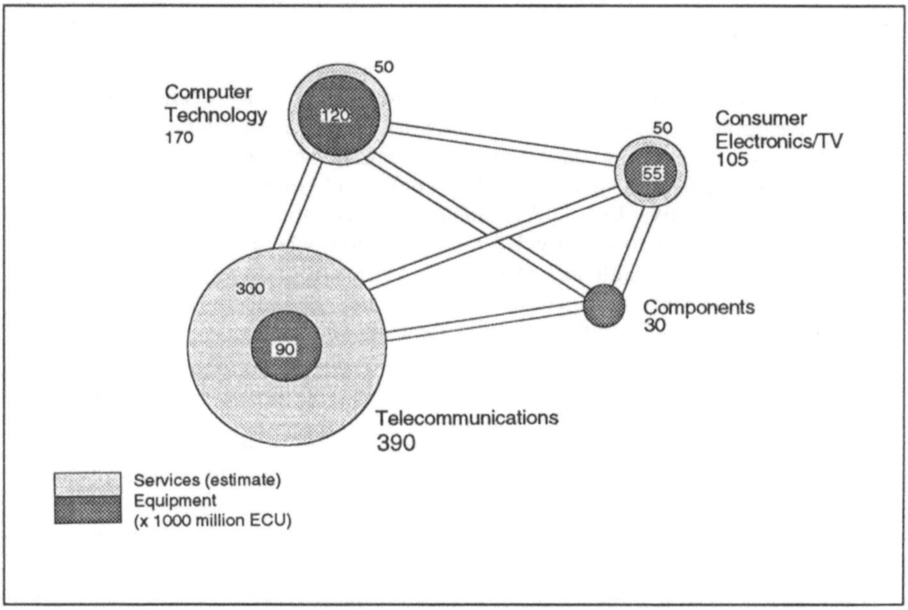

Fig. 30.1 Technology world markets
(source : studies of the Commission of the Europeen Communities,1990)

Telemedicine is the integration of two well-established disciplines, medicine and telecommunication. The overall functional definition of telemedicine is: *the investigation, monitoring and management of patients and the education of patients and health care staff using systems which allow ready* ***access to expert advice and relevant patient information****, no matter where the patient is located.*

This means that patients will be treated in a familiar environment with additional facilities, e.g. clinical findings are interpreted by experts located at remote centres of excellence, even transcending national boundaries if necessary.

Technical elements that will contribute to telemedicine are not only network facilities but also patient data cards (PDC) that can facilitate medical data transfer and information exchange. Its infrastructure creates a lot of advantages:

- Medical expertise can be brought (wherever present) to remote areas where there is a lack of skilled personnel.
- It will give the opportunity to exchange information on special cases.
- It offers fast access to retrieve and update medical patient data.
- It offers an educational potential for patients and health care providers.

Some specific telemedicine applications are:

- *Teleradiology,* which offers the possibilities for image transmission including non-standard image formats,very high resolution,error-free transmission and short transmission times
- *Homedialysis,* which offers the facility to monitor patients centrally from a nephrology unit
- *Teleconsultation,* which uses telecameras to allow professionals at different locations to consult each other
- *Teleanalysis,* which tests the validity of blood and urine tests executed at remote laboratories
- *Teleobstetrics,* which offers the possibility of monitoring, fetal heart signals and newborn vital signs at home
- *Teleencephalogram,* which transmits EEG signals from remote hospitals into a neurology centre
- *Telecardiology,* which looks at the transmission of ECG signals from different locations into a cardiology centre

To achieve this goal standards for the acquisition, semantic content, organisation of the information, format (such as ACR-NEMA and Papyrus for images) and encoding, transmission and interpretation of medical data are obviously needed. For the moment, several European standardisation bodies are working in the medical domain of telecommunication standards.

In telematics we may indicate the priority of different application domains as follows:

1. Clinical pathology laboratories
2. Radiology (communication of text protocols)
3. Hospital discharge summaries
4. Messages from the pharmaceutical industry (information on new drugs)
5. Access to literature and knowledge bases in medicine
6. Image communications

30.2 Communication Between Health Care Providers

30.2.1 Wide Area Networks. Integrated services Digital Network (ISDN)

If information is transmitted over large distances the use of public digital service (PDS) communication networks is required. Communication networks are based on *circuit switching, message switching* or *packet switching*. Circuit switching establishes a communication path prior to starting transmission, while in message switching (also called a store and forward system to a switching center) no complete path is established. A packet switching network subdivides messages into small packets, and transmits them packet-by-packet. It is also a store and forward system, where each packet is stored in nodes on the network.

The ISDN standard is based on packet switching, capable of transmitting two 64 Kb/s B-channels and one D-channel at 16 Kb/s for signaling rates. ISDN, although not yet available everywhere, will play an important role in the telecommunication area in the near future. It covers a set of standards for a common link between networks and their users, which will enable the user to communicate with any node (mainframe databases, specialists) and give them access to voice, data, video facsimile, telex and other communication methods.

30.2.2. X400 MHS: An Introduction

Electronic data interchange (EDI) and the message handling system (MHS) aim to facilitate the transfer of electronic mail and are only concerned with the delivery of messages from computer to computer. The ISO and CCITT has developed a set of protocols for MHS known as X400. EDI and X400 standards have been developed independently, although both are concerned with communications at the application level. X400 is a MHS concerned with the communication, transport and delivery of messages (Fig. 30.2). The two logical components of an X400 MHS are:

- *User agent (UA)* is the part of a user's system which acts on behalf of a single user, handling all the protocols for interacting with the rest of a MHS.
- *Message transfer agent (MTA)* is a device which stores a message and then forwards it onto the next MTA or to the destination user (UA). The MTA can be compared with a post office, a UA with a mailbox.

The X400 is characterised by an envelope, which is used to transfer the message, and the contents, which is the information. The rules for communication are defined by three protocols : P1 for the communication between MTAs, P2 for the contents of a message (body, header), and P3 for the communication between UA and MTA.

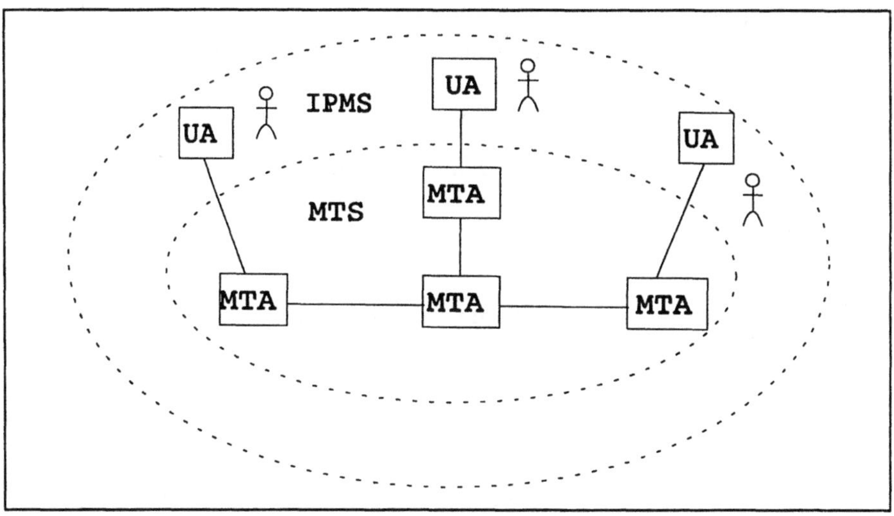

Fig 30.2 Conceptual representation of a X400 system. ***UA,*** user agent; ***MTS,*** message transfer system (the communication system which carries messages from sender to the recipicient's UA); ***MTA,*** message transfer agent; ***IPMS,*** interpersonal messaging system

MHS offers the following facilities to the user:

- Message delivery and submission
- Basic access security between a UA and a MTA
- Delivery time control (i.e. delivery can be deferred to a given time)
- Delivery of a message to multiple recipients
- Notification of delivery or non-delivery
- Submission and delivery time stamping

- Trace information on the path taken by a message
- Probe message for testing message paths
- Message encoding conversion (e.g. Teletex to FAX)
- Security (encryption of data)
- Message store
- Interworking with the X500 directory service standard

30.2.3. A Basic Introduction to EDIFACT

EDIFACT is the acronym for electronic data interchange for administration, commerce and transport (Fig. 30.3). It contains the automated exchange of predefined and structured data, for some "business" purpose, among information systems of two or more parties. The EDIFACT syntax is subdivided into a number of functional groups, delimited by an interchange header and an interchange trailer. Each functional group contains a number of messages, which in turn contain a sequence of data segments (a logical grouping of data elements, equivalent to a record).

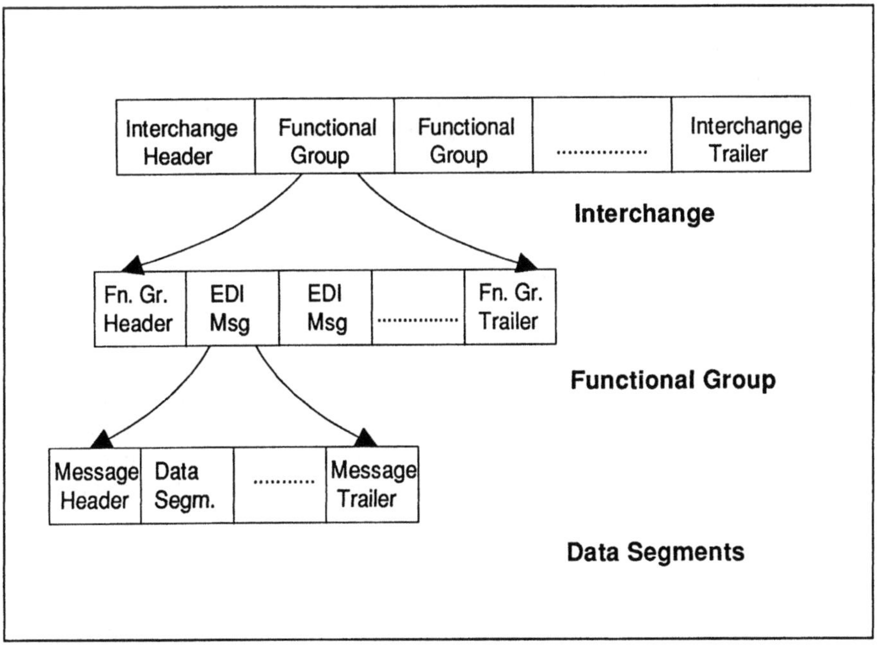

Fig. 30.3 Example of an EDI message

30.2.4. ASN.1

ASN.1 is the acronym for abstract syntax notation one and takes a place in the 6th layer of the OSI reference model. To be able to represent data structures in an unambiguous way for exchange between two entities is the aim of ASN.1. FTAM,

X400 and ODA (open document architecture) are based upon it. In ASN.1, every data element is defined by its type (through a numerical code: integer, boolean, bit string, octet, string, etc.), length (bytes) and content. The content in turn can contain another data element (nesting). By applying standard encoding rules of the ASN.1 data definitions, a standard way of representing a structure as a machine-independent bit stream for interchange purposes can be obtained. The basic encoding rules (BER) allow any ASN.1 type to be encoded into a string of octets in a machine-independent manner.

30.2.5 Open/Office Document Architecture

Open/Office Document Architecture (ODA)is a standard developed to exchange multi-media (text, image, graphics) office documents. A document is a structured set of information, defined by a logical structure (interrelationships of the components) and the layout structure. These structures offer two alternative and complementary views of the same document, logical (as a view of chapters, sections) and layout (as a view of frames of text, graphics). Under a contract with the Norwegian Telecommunication Administration (NTA) a reference model for health care information, processing and communication and its implementation in ODA has been defined [HAN 90]. It has to be stressed while ODA offers more advantages in the health care sector compared to EDIFACT (it provides the possibilities to transport data and images), it demands far more infrastructure and investments compared to implementing EDIFACT. So obvious in the long term both standards will be used.

30.3 Applications

30.3.1 Important Health Care Actors

Nurses

New nurse call systems (instead of ringing a bell or flashing a light as exists currently in hospitals) which have the capabilities to track the locations of nurses and to let them communicate orally and in written format (i.e. computerised data collection at patient bedside) with physicians, patients and computers will be of great importance. The systems will have to be integrated into existing phone and computer networks.

Physicians

By using a telecommunication infrastructure (network or a telemedicine WAN), medical results from hospitals will be communicated and accessible on-line by network stations for authorised physicians and general practitioners, in the first phase alphanumerical results and later on images. In addition, this infrastructure can also be used for communication of prescriptions, requests for admissions, etc.

Administrators

The network serves (as is the case already in some countries) also as a communication vehicle for administrative documents with insurance companies, legal authorities, etc.

30.3.2 Some Applications of Telemedicine

Telecardiology (Cardiophone)

A company in The Netherlands (Cardio-Control, Rijswijk) has developed an ECG transmitter which makes it possible to transmit for an expert opinion a full 12-lead ECG to the hospital or to a cardiologist in less than 1 min. They had developed three different types of cardiophones for use in different situations by general practioners, by the patient (6 extremity leads) or in the ambulance (portable FM transmitter and receiver). All Cardio-Control ECG transmitters have a unique built-in code, which makes it possible to locate the transmitter with the ECG receiver developed by the same company (that can also be coupled to a PC for page format printing and storage).

3 I Project

In 1985 the Academic Hospital Maastricht, The Netherlands, with a grant received from the Dutch Ministries of Health Care and Economic Affairs set up the 3I Project (acronym for Inter-Institutional-Information Exchange Project) which aims to investigate the possibilities of interfacing heterogeneous IS in primary and secondary care by means of electronic communication.

After a preparatory study, a feasibility study was undertaken to design the standard electronic messages for providing communication facilities in an environment of hospitals, GPs and pharmacists. Messages [HAS 90] composed in the EDIFACT standard are deposited by the sending application in the mailbox of the receiving system. At a convenient time, these messages are loaded by the receiving system, translated and shown to the user. The application can archive the information after a single key stroke by the user.

Teleradiology

University or large hospitals could communicate with remote X-radiography facilities by transmitting the X-radiographs to the central hospital for diagnosing and storage. The results and interpretation of the images could be sent back. Another application domain is the use of *"mobile units"* with complex diagnostic modalities (CT,MRI,etc), which could transmit the information to university hospitals in order to benefit from their knowledge and experience. This could happen through normal telephone lines or by microwave links when modem telecommunication infrastructures are not available. Experiments are being carried out in some places in Europe (Berlin, Montpelier, Geneva).

Clinical Laboratories (EUCLIDES)

It is well-known that there is an urgent need nowadays to provide a clinical laboratory data exchange standard between independent and heterogeneous MIS. Various experiments have been carried out using proprietary message formats and less efficient communication facilities, resulting unfortunately in a proliferation of incompatible solutions. EUCLIDES (European clinical laboratory data exchange standard), an AIM project addresses this area and provides an open modular standard solution, freely available to all, and unbiased towards any manufacturer's hardware or software [DEM 90].

EUCLIDES focusses on the data exchange problem in a three-pronged approach:

1. The message transfer mechanism
2. The message syntax
3. The medical coding systems used within the message.

   Moreover, the EUCLIDES system offers through the EUCLIDES BRIDGE a user-friendly software solution for interfacing with existing local systems at both the sender's and receiver's ends.

Four areas for its application have been defined:

1. *Patient-related data,* two-way routine transmission of laboratory messages (orders,requests, results) between remote computers in medical offices, hospitals and laboratories (hospital, university and private laboratories)
2. *Control-sera related data,* transmission of data for external quality assessment programmes
3. *Test-related data,* use of the EUCLIDES coding systems (test codes, test units, methods and equipment in clinical laboratories) to interface analysers with laboratory computers
4. *Laboratory-related supervision data,* forwarding of anonymous and aggregated data to public authorities for financial analysis and budgetary control at local, regional and international levels

EUCLIDES uses two distinct classes of messages :

1. System messages, e.g. for the transfer of metadata (e.g. syntax specifications)
2. Data messages containing laboratory-related information (L.R.I., e.g. a test report)

EUCLIDES adopted MHS, which is a set of specifications known as the CCITT X400 series of recommendations, designed to guide the system implementor towards achieving a complete, secure and open messaging system.

EUCLIDES is intended to cover the following branches of clinical pathology: clinical chemistry, toxicology, haematology, immunology, haemostasis, microbiology (bacteriology, serology) but *not* anatomopathology. The vectors of the coding system are :

1. Tests
   - ° analytes
   - ° procedures
   - ° function tests
   - ° ratios
2. Specimens
   - ° specimen types
   - ° specimen locations
   - ° specimen collection procedures
3. Laboratory procedures
   - ° basic (analytical) methods
   - ° reagents
   - ° temperatures
   - ° equipment
4. Units
   - ° denominators
   - ° numerators
5. Kinds of quantities

6. Coded comments

Telemed

Telemed is an application pilot (R 1086) of the RACE (research and development on advanced communications) programme of the EC. It is a multi-disciplinary collaboration of health care actors, computer scientists and telecommunication professionals. The work undertaken in this project its aim is to study the application domain of physicians communicating over IBC. Integrated broadband communications comprises four objectives:

- Remote expert consultation
- Radiological image reference database (IRDB)
- Transfer of patient data and images
- Special needs for security, accuracy and integrity of the record data

In Montpelier (France) and in Florence (Italy) a radiological image reference database is being developed for teaching and care applications. Medical images stored in the IRDB will be available on-line across national boundaries over 2 Mbits telecommunications lines for physicians located in Barcelona (Spain), Montpelier, Florence, Geneva, Heidelberg and Berlin, using a retrieval language close to the medical natural language.

Between Leeds, Rotterdam, Berlin and Patras patient data, laboratory results and cardiac images will be transferred by broadband links for remote image processing and expert consultation.

Other developments done or underway are [RAT 91]:

- Definitions of standards in image format and image communication (called the PAPYRUS format, based on an extension of the ACR-NEMA image communication standard)
- Standardisation of a dictionary of descriptive and anatomical nomenclature for images
- Requirement specifications for image manipulation and management software
- Video conferencing and PACS-to-PACS communication have been carried out in Berlin (FRG), Tromsö and Lund (Norway).

31

Computerised Surveillance System for Nosocomial Infections

31.1 Introduction

Nosocomial infections result in increased patient suffering and raised cost of medical care. Effective infection control programs can reduce the number of nosocomial infections and thus improve the quality of patient care. The first step in the elaboration of a program for the prevention and control of nosocomial infections is the institution of a surveillance program. Although wards at high risk and factors that may influence the occurrence of nosocomial infections are described in the literature, there is a need for specific nosocomial infection surveillance data in each hospital. Once a baseline rate is established for the different sites of infection and nosocomial pathogens, trends can be observed in time, and outbreaks or small clusters of infections can be detected rapidly. Surveillance data can also be used to motivate health care workers to adhere to established procedures; if the data are discussed at regular intervals with all personnel involved in patient care, the awareness of the problem of nosocomial infections and thus the willingness to cooperate in prevention programmes are activated.

Several different approaches to the collection of data for a surveillance program have been described. An ideal method for data collection should be both sensitive and specific and, last but not least, not too labour-intensive. Many are based on prospective or retrospective review of patient records. An effective system was described by Wenzel [WEN 76]: the Kardex search system limited review to 65% of all charts and yielded a sensitivity of 82% - 94% as compared with a review of all charts. Still, for this approach the infection control nurse required 18 - 25 h a week in the 560-bed hospital.

The effective use of computer-based decision analysis has been demonstrated [LAR 89] by assisting the monitoring of patients undergoing non-emergency surgery with respect to indications for perioperative antibiotic use, timing of antibiotic administration and postoperative infectious complications.

At the LDS Hospital in Salt Lake City, a computerised infectious disease monitor has been developed to inform personnel when a patient becomes infected under one of the following conditions [EVA 85]:

- A hospital-acquired infection
- An infection at a normally sterile body site
- An infection due to a bacteria with an unusual antibiotic sensitivity pattern
- An infection for which the patient is not receiving an antibiotic
- An infection that could be treated with a less expensive antibiotic

- An infection which is required by law to be reported to state and national health authorities
- Those patients receiving prophylactic antibiotics for too long a period

31.2 CASE : University Hospital of Brussels

In Belgium, the Infection Control Officer has in addition to an infection control task many other activities and cannot spare that much time for surveillance. In the University Hospital of Brussels (AZ-VUB) a system based on reports from the microbiology department was developed [LAW 90]. The microbiology lab is computerised and integrated with the HIS, making the development of computer selection programs possible. The general procedure is as follows.

Selection of Microbiology Results for the "Nosocomial Infections" List

Every morning all newly available microbiology results are introduced into the computer by the technologists. Immediately thereafter, a selection program for nosocomial infections is started by the computer. The criteria used for this selection are summarised in Fig. 31.1: in a first step all "negative" cultures are discarded, while for the remaining results selection depends upon current and previous hospital admissions and culture dates. In a second step an attempt is made to eliminate results that represent contamination or incorrect sampling techniques; here the selection criteria used differ from specimen to specimen. Besides the result from cultures, data from direct examinations are also taken into account. Finally, a "nosocomial infections" form is printed, listing all patients that could present with one or more nosocomial infections. Patients are ordered according to ward number. An example of part of a daily "nosocomial infections" listing is given in Fig.31.2. Apart from the microbiology result(s) (direct examination, culture and antibiogram, indication of previous identical isolations), the most recent leucocytosis and RBC sedimentation rate is included as well. For surgical patients, the date of surgery is stated.

About 20 patients appear daily on the list, and each patient is listed twice (mean). In general 10% of all admitted patients will appear on the "nosocomial infections" list.

Verification and Validation of the Crude Data of the "Nosocomial Infections" List

The list is viewed daily by the Infection Control Officer who validates the data after a visit to the wards where each case is discussed with the ward physician and/or the head nurse. A standard set of written definitions of nosocomial infections for the different body sites is used. In doubtful cases, the microbiologist is consulted as well. For outpatients, the patient record is consulted. On average, 1 of every 3 listed patients has a nosocomial infection.

Treatment of "Nosocomial Infections" Data

A secretary is responsible for the input of all validated nosocomial infection data into a PC. A specific infection control software is used. Denominator data are down-loaded from the HIS computer into the infection control database. Demographic data (patient name, record number including age and sex, admission number and date, ward, discharge date) are down-loaded once a week, and more specific data (such as surgical data, date and type of surgery, name of the surgeon(s), duration of surgery, other risk factors, prophylactic antibiotics) once a month.

Analysis and Use of Data

Once a year, graphs depicting rates for the four major sites of nosocomial infections (urinary tract infections, surgical wounds, pneumonia and blood-stream infections)

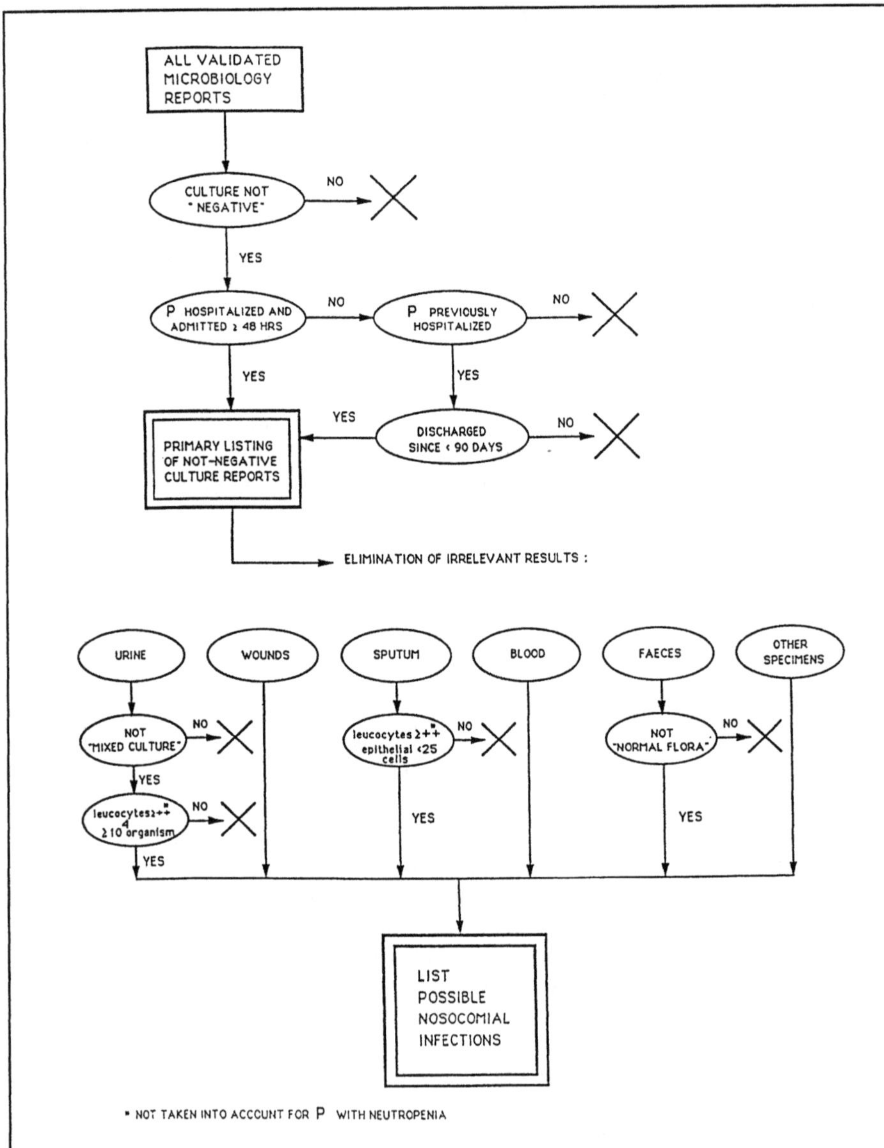

Fig. 31.1 Selection of microbiology results for the "nosocomial infections" list

for the different departments and nosocomial pathogens per site are discussed in the Hospital Hygiene Committee and with each department head. For comparison, the rates of the previous year are represented as well. Further analysis is performed for bloodstream infections and for infections in ICU patients. More detailed analysis is carried out for surgical wound infections : once a year, all department heads of the different surgical sub-specialities receive a booklet with the percentage of wound infections for different groups of interventions (37 in total), the surgeon-specific wound infection rates for clean operations as compared with the rate for all surgeons performing the same type of operation, and a summary of relevant information for each patient who suffered from a wound infection. These results are also discussed during a "postoperative wound infection" lunch.

Specific graphs are generated more often for rotavirus infections on the neonatal and paediatric wards, for MRSA and for any other multi-resistant organism or infection that might represent a problem at a certain moment. Selected graphs and tables are used frequently for the motivation and training of personnel.

31.3 Discussion

It is clear that the sensitivity of the system depends on the policy of collection of specimens for microbiological analysis, on the quality of the specimens and on the microbiological analysis. It also depends on the type of microbiological criteria used for selection on the "nosocomial infections" list : for example, taking into account only sputum specimens yielding one or two microorganisms in the culture and discarding all "normal mouth flora" reports will lead to under-reporting of nosocomial pneumonia. Selection of purulent specimens is a better approach. The specificity of the computer list is acceptable: 1 of 3 patients listed appear to have a nosocomial infection.

The daily ward rounds of the Infection Control Officer (about 6 h a week) necessary for confirmation of the microbiological results with the condition of the patient are useful for other purposes, e.g. ward nurses have the opportunity to discuss hygienic problems at the same time.

Finally, it is also necessary to recognise the importance of another type of error [EVA 86], occurring with inappropriate antibiotic use by sometimes overlooking or misinterpreting microbiology test results. It is valuable to integrate the microbiology system with other departmental systems such as pharmacy and medical records to monitor antibiotics use in hospitals.

************ AZ-VUB MICROBIOLOGY LABORATORY ************ 28-11-91

NOSOCOMIAL INFECTIONS

WARD : 32
****

Patient : V.J. **File nr. :** A420318VY00E **Previous surgery :** 08-10-91

Dates of admission : 22-11-91 19-11-91
Dates of discharge : 26-11-91 20-11-91
Admission numbers : 1595628 1591002

Wound coccyx Collection date : 26-11-91 ACC : SM8446 RL : 21018
Previous date with id. result : 16-10-91 fistula of coccyx

Streptococcus species

PEN	AMP	CFZ	NET	AMI	TOB	GEN	HRG	TET	ERY	CLI	VAN
S	S	S	S	S	S	S	S	S	S	S	S

Direct exam.: white cells : + red cells : epith. cells : G+cocci : G-bacilli :

Haemato : white cells : 4.8 date : 27-11-91 ESR : 71 date : 29-10-91

Patient : V.A. **File nr. :** B150821VH00L **Previous surgery :** 0- 0- 0

Dates of admission : 19-11-91
Admission numbers :158958A

Urine Collection date : 25-11-91 ACC : SM8428 RL : 20026
Previous date with id. result : 20-11-91 urine

Klebsiella pneumoniae

AMP	TEM	CFZ	CFU	CTR	AZT	NET	AMI	TOB	GEN	TRI	FUR
R	S	S	S	S	S	S	S	S	S	S	S

NAL	NOR
R	S

Candida albicans

Direct exam.: white cells : +++ red cells : epith. cells : G+cocci : G-bacilli :

Haemato : white cells : 6.1 date : 27-11-91 ESR : 46 date : 25-10-91

Fig.31.2 Daily nosocomial infections listing. Not all antibiotics mentioned above are printed on the microbiology labreport.

(Source reprinted with the permission of Prof. Lauwers S. M.D. department of microbiology A.Z.-VUB.)

Hospital Information Systems in the Years Ahead

Part 4

"What we do not understand, we do not possess."

Goethe

32

Hospital Information Systems: The Future is now!

32.1 Coping with Technology: The New Environment

The health care sector finds itself on a double-edged sword: how do we balance an increasing demand for providing high-quality health care while reducing ever rising health care costs? In order to solve this problem, it is clear that technology will be the symbolic battlefield for the next decade where this widening gap between decreasing funds and increasing costs will be debated. As technology is at the same time part of the solution and part of new problems (ethical issues, maturity), the questions arise, is it better to offer patients access to medical breakthroughs in spite of financial investments, or is it preferable to put the emphasis on less costly, lower-tech approaches because they can benefit a greater percentage of the population [BER 90]?
In the health care sector, heavily involved in the collection and communication of huge quantities of multi-media information, up to now HIS failed to demonstrate a real utility in the clinical environment and were not universally recognised as a useful medical system. HIS will play a more important role, are becoming the "neural system" of the hospital, are big business and will represent therefore an increasing market share for vendors in the next decade. If we take a look at the past and future of these systems, it is generally accepted that first generation HIS focussed primarily on automating more administrative functions, starting with financial systems, and delivering medical data as a "byproduct". When hospital managers rely only on financial statements, they lose sight of the operational possibilities. Therefore, hospitals are looking for new strategies to make IS more cost-effective, delivering financial data as a "byproduct" of medical information.
For the next generation of HIS, the architecture and conceptual requirements will be characterised by a shift in professional orientation (Table 32.1).

32.1.1 Conceptual Requirements

From Administrative-Centered Systems to Patient-Centered Systems
Most hospitals have computerised systems for financial, ADT and other major administrative functions. A HIS must not only allow for a better approach to hospital financing but must also deliver an improved knowledge of hospital pathology. This can be realised by building up the IS from the patient's bedside towards patient care and point of care systems. Patient care systems are necessary to improve the hospital's operations. One way to achieve this is installing bedside terminals, thus improving accuracy in tracking patient information. If data are entered at the source (i.e. bedside), information becomes more efficient and accurate. Several vendors nowadays provide bedside terminals.

Table 32.1 Next generation of HIS: representation of shifts in professional orientation in order of importance.

FROM		TO
Administrative-centered systems	-->	*Patient-centered systems* ***era of patient care and point of care***
Technology driven	-->	*User driven* ***era of user interface***
Islands	-->	*Integrated systems* ***era of communications***
Proprietary driven	-->	*Standard driven* ***era of standards***
Data driven	-->	*Knowledge base driven* ***era of intelligent data bases***
Centralised systems	-->	*Distributed systems* ***client-server era***
Home-grown systems	-->	*Vendor-made systems*
Monopoly	-->	*Competition*
National	-->	*International*

Therefore, by recognising the real user in the hospital, one of the most challenging items in health care is to develop a real-time accessible medical record and make medical data exchange feasible by tracking inpatients and outpatients. Nowadays, it is a time-consuming task for a physician to collect and analyse data in paper-based medical record systems. In view of the small number of staff versus the large number of patients to be treated, medical data should always be available and easily accessible, represented in different ways at various locations.

Participants in the electronic medical record of tomorrow will be:

- The patient, who stresses primary care and data communication
- The general practitioner, who needs communication, decision support and evaluation tools
- The specialist, who needs communication, decision support, evaluation and auditing tools
- The nurse in the centre of this universe, whose role should evolve towards more specialisation and professionalism, and who also stresses communication needs and decision support systems
- The hospital board, who need management support and regional communication

From Technology Driven to User Driven

In contrast to first-generation HIS, which were rather technology driven and whose information requirements were often defined by technical experts rather than hospital experts, next generation HIS will be driven by a user-centered design process. Most health care users are not trained to use computer systems. An approach to overcome this obstacle cannot be achieved by refining current IS working practices but must be based on the real understanding of health care users and their needs. Software

engineers and vendors need to change their attitude and must react more on a user-centered basis (recognising the users' needs) than on a technical basis. Acceptance and usefulness of IS -what it is all about- depend on their user interface friendliness, which should be consistent and intuitive, making the system easy to learn with response times that are short.
Nowadays, most human-machine interfaces are static and modal, i.e. they operate uniformily, regardless of the end-user who is working with the system. Future user interfaces must be adaptive and in contrast dynamic, taking into account the user profile. The GUI is not merely a nicety but a true necessity. How much screen resolution and windowing is required for an effective user interface and workable electronic medical record depends on many issues. New iterative modelling techniques will play an important role in translating and adapting as smoothly as possible the dynamically changing user requirements. As a consequence, system design must start with an in-depth study of users' "information requirements" as a continuous guideline during the design and implementation phases. The old equations: *automation = mass production* and *mass production = restricted user flexibility* are no longer true. Automation and flexibility are no longer mutually exclusive.

From a Centralised Architecture to a Distributed Achitecture
The urgent necessity to downsize organisations illustrates clearly the age-old discussions between centralized control and departmental autonomy caused by the emergence of new technologies.
No hospital over a certain size can operate effectively in a centralised way. The decision makers at the centre are too far away from the individual users/departments and their needs. Decomposing the IS into several domains has become an essential part of every successful organisation. Every system is embedded in a larger system and is differentiated from its environment by a "boundary". This boundary is not always easy to identifiy and changes continuously. For instance, in medicine the radiology boundaries were fairly clear till 1945 . After that, the appearance of new digital technologies came to influence the monolithic speciality of radiology by sub-specialisation and dissociation into independent specialities, such as nuclear medicine, US, cardiology and vascular diagnostic techniques, radiation oncology, etc.
This is the reason why a high level study of a hospital's information needs and setting of priorities are necessary. To achieve this breakdown, several methodologies are available.

The emergence of the microcomputer has had a tremendous effect on mainframe and mini-computer use in hospitals. Especially in the hospital world, mainframe-based systems will continue to lose their market share due to their comparatively high cost, as well as the dissatisfaction among some users. For small hospitals, there will be a shift from mini-computers to supermicro or intelligent work stations as servers; for large hospitals, there will be a shift from mainframe to (super) mini computer systems servers driven by the need for higher returns on investment. About mainframes there are two schools of thought: one predicts the end of the mainframe era others contends that the mainframe will always reside . In fact the answer is nor black or white but can be declared by the changing role of the mainframe. Mainframes will become less important and function more as a long-term information repository, instead of

frequently accessed, data-intensive, database servers. On-line transactions will be handled by less costly and more effective (better price/performance) mini-computers or workstations.
For performance reasons, as databases grow and make heavy demands on storage capacity, they will also be distributed, and multi-media databases emerge as a natural successor of distributed database systems. Effective cultivation of a distributed architecture creates its own (other) problems, allocating downwards some responsibilities and shifting (vertically, horizontally) necessary information for managing the hospital as a "global company".
The trend in HIS is clear, a shift from monolithic systems towards network computing systems with physicians in satellite offices and ancillary departments (laboratories, radiology). In fact, we are *evolving from centralised multi-purpose systems* **or** *distributed single purpose systems* **to** *distributed multi-purpose systems.*

From Chaos to Integrated Systems
Like other industries, hospital computerisation is often characterised by "islands of automation", in which applications run on a variety of large and small computers. Some computer systems are dedicated to a single application. As a result, patient information is often scattered among different systems in different locations with little or no transfer of information from one system to the next.
As medicine today contains many specialities, communication requirements are growing in exponential relation to the rate of sub-specialisation in health care. This is mostly is driven by the emerging technological evolution and in turn results in less cohesion and degradation of medical care. As the patient remains the same and wishes to be seen as a whole, integration on the operational level (=patient care) and informational level (=patient data) must be assured. Hospital users are increasingly demanding a coherent IS rather than the collage of disparate systems that they too often find today. Complaints about "data diarrhoea", too many facts, are common. Again, the integration of the user interface deserves attention as we are confronted with a chaos of different software systems, various hardware systems and multi-media data (medical data, images and knowledge).
If users wish not to deal with different incompatible systems, a communication vehicle (protocol) on the technical level and integration (standards) on the logical level are needed.

The most important trend of the past years was the convergence between data communications and telecommunications. This has been driven on the user side by the proliferation of high-performance workstations in a distributed environment and on the technical side by the emergence of multi-media technologies, and has led to an increased demand for packet switched networks with improved bit rates and response time. Therefore, one must realise that (tele)communications -socially and economically already the most significant area of information technology- are also of importance for the health care sector, as it will provide the facilities to link physicians and hospitals. Generally, the network will control communications between multiple software and computer systems in order to solve the urgent need to let software and hardware systems "talk to each other". Communication systems will be connected with a common backbone and move information to the health care users who need it. Networks will span all *actors,* resulting in improved information access and providing expert guidance for new or infrequent users, access to high-tech medical instruments and better managerial assistance. As technology makes the world smaller, health care quality is often determined by the speed and flow of information in order to exploit existing available potential performance to the full. As most hospitals are currently not familiar with LAN technology, they are now facing a new challenge : managing WANs and MANs: *the era of telemedicine is coming.*

From Proprietary-Driven Systems to Standard-Driven Systems

Integration implies standards. Due to the fact that the present tower of Babel of incompatible hardware, software and communications services cannot provide a stable foundation for meeting future needs, standardisation has become a crucial issue in the development of HIS. Interoperability of heterogeneous sub-systems is a prerequisite. The battle for integration and thus standardisation will continue. *Especially in Europe,* the popularity of Open systems increase, because of relevant accompanying advantages: *scalability, interoperability and portability.* Open systems architecture provides the facility of integrating heterogeneous sub-systems into a unified HIS.

From Data -Driven to Knowledge Base Driven

Medicine is one of the fields in which up to now a lot of KBS and ES have been developed. Technically speaking, all existing KBS take individual, isolated approaches and lack a common framework for the representation of medical knowledge. These systems were mostly designed in scientific centres, but none of them has found a market. They also lack a user-friendly interface, which makes them difficult to use for physicians and nurses; moreover the systems are isolated and not integrated. Therefore, it is most advisable to agree upon how medical knowledge should be represented and how to interface these KBS with other systems.

From Home-Made Systems to Vendor-Made Systems

Nowadays, every person has to do more than there are resources available. In particular, the hospital world has become so complex in the last decade that being an expert both on hospitals and on technology is virtually impossible. As the next generation medical systems will be comprehensive and complex, it is not advisable from an economical point of view to built a complete HIS alone, since investment in education for new technologies and medical informatics "know-how" is no longer feasible. It is clear that the number of home-made HIS will decrease, while the number of transportable, general purpose, software packages from several niche vendors will increase. Self-designed software tend to have higher maintenance costs over the long term. Whether to buy or to develop depends upon several criteria such as integration aspects, functionality, etc.

For small hospitals (200 beds or fewer) there is a real problem nowadays, as on the one hand they have insufficient funds to afford a system that meets their needs, while on the other the systems that are affordable do not have all the necessary features they require.

"Everything out there is either too big or too cumbersome to handle" [HAR 90].

Larger hospitals will spend more in this area of data processing, and most of this budget will go for personnel and applications.

The choice of a system will be influenced by four criteria: efficiency, quality, management support and accessibility

From Monopoly to Competition
For the next decade hospitals will be less committed (loyal) to one software and hardware vendor, as they search to improve their return on investment and aim to be more cost-effective. As a result, the number of hospitals using one single software and hardware vendor will decline, because software will be designed more and more in an "open" environment. The question arises if large existing HIS vendors will be able to remain the origin of interesting software facing this new paradigm.

32.2 Giving the Renovation a Chance

The Evolutionary Approach
Although it is a fact that technology can solve our problems, one should be aware that the implementation of new technology often causes problems and takes longer than predicted. A change of system can be effected in two different ways: by a gradual process of evolution or by radical revolutionary shock treatment. However, as explained before, to start something new it is not sufficient to give up the old.
Technology transition across an entire discipline is something that takes time, more than a few months. To understand fully the concepts and philosophy behind it takes a certain time. Installing new technology not only requires a conversion from existing older systems (which represent in fact huge amounts of invested time, and thus money!) in a smoothly technical way with as little human resistance as possible, but also a conversion of philosophy in the minds of people, which is perhaps the most difficult thing to achieve. This is strongly related to the creativity of human beings. Every human being tries to explore new ways. Creativity is something that doesn't happen from 9 to 5, it is the result of continuous work day in and day out, during weekends and at night. Creativity happens as individuals work closely together. But it is even more difficult to transform creativity into innovations. *It needs an environment which accepts innovation.* In the business world most ideas do not even have a chance to grow.

When Leonardo da Vinci invented the parachute he was a visionary; when almost 2 centuries later André Garneron succeeded in descending with a parachute, he was an innovator. Although he did n't invent anything, he made somebody else's dream possible by conquering all material problems lying between the concept and realisation.

The Most Valuable Aspect: Human Resources.
Most technological tools that can assist hospitals to reduce their costs, improve their return on investment and improve their care quality are already available. It is clear that the personnel -including the Chief Information Officer- will play an important role in planning and installing this more complex technology.

Hospital executives are looking for three basic qualifications in data processing managers: familiarity with information technology, management skills and the ability to communicate with different kind of users. Very often, hospitals hire DP managers for their technological expertise without considering that the technical and organisational sides should form an amalgam. As there was a limited population growth during the 1960s and 1970s, there are not enough young people to enter the DP world. In the long run, non-technical people have to be involved and will have a positive effect by cross-fertilising.
With the increasing importance of medical systems in the years ahead, people with a health care qualification and thorough understanding of health care organisations are becoming increasingly valuable as Chief Information Officer. Some hospitals hire physicians with expertise in information technology, who have a broad insight into the needs of clinicians.
"You just can't move in from manufacturing, retail, banking or the insurance industry and understand how to organize and develop systems for hospitals," says Henry Wagner, president and CEO of the Jewish Hospital HCS, Louisville. *"I think a person has to have a dozen years of experience before he or she can begin to understand how medicine is delivered".*

Writing this book about discovering the future and observing trends and facts in hospital information systems gave me a sense of disillusionment: won't the future be what it was supposed to be? What did we achieve? What was promised?
Let's be serious : the future of next generation HIS is now !

R. Van de Velde

GLOSSARY

Acuity The level of patient care required, calculated by a variety of methods.

Administrative data All data necessary to run the hospital or the service.

Admitting diagnosis The diagnosis established at the time of admission, which served as the primary basis for patient admission to the hospital.

Aetiology The cause of a disease.

Algorithm A precise statement of a method of calculation. It can sometimes be expressed conveniently in a programming language.

Analysis A test connected to a sample (sample + test = analysis).

Anatomy The science of the macroscopic body structures.

Animation Use of computer graphics in simulations or to generate images for motion pictures.

Antecedent ° A premise; the IF and AND parts of a rule.
° The past medical / surgical history of a patient

Apgar Score An index of newborn health status computed from measurements taken at 1 and 5 min after birth.
Heart rate, respiration, muscle tone, reflexes and colour are each rated on a scale of 0-2, and the sum of the five component scores forms the index.

Architecture A framework from which applications, databases and workstations can be developed in a coherent manner, and in which every part fits together without containing a mass of design details.

Assertion A true proposition, a fact.

Attribute A property associated with an entity or an object.

Audit The tracking of who has accessed and/or used resources and the resources which were accessed or used.

Authentication Method to establish security services by means of simple or extensive authentication. There are two kinds: data origin authentication and peer entity authentication.

Authorisation The granting of rights, which includes the granting of access based on access rights.

Backward chaining Reasoning from observations to conclusions; proving a presenting hypothesis from rules; sometimes called goal-directed inferencing. In this approach, the expert system begins with a goal and successively examines any rules with matching conclusions. The unmet conditions of the antecedent are extracted from each plausibly applicable rule, and these conditions are then defined as new goals. The backward-chaining control procedure then shifts attention recursively toward the new goal, terminating when the top goal has been reduced to a set of satisfied sub-goals. For example, assume that the hypothesis to be proven is that "X is a bird". In a backward-chaining system, an applicable rule with a matching conclusion would be, "If X can fly, then X is a bird." The new goal is to prove that X can fly. An appropriate rule for this sub-goal might be, "If X has wings, then X can fly." This process continues until the hypothesis is either accepted or rejected by the inference engine.

Baseband A communication sytem in a LAN that handles one signal per communication line at time. The maximum transmission rate for baseband systems is 10 MBPS (slower than broadband sysems).

Bit map Bit pattern in memory that corresponds to the pixel pattern on a computer screen, each pixel being represented by one or more bits.

Bit-mapped display A display screen divided into a grid of pixels, each associated with a value indicating the intensity of the pixel.

Bridge Protocol-independent devices for interconnecting different LANs at the Data Link Layer.

Broadband A communication system in a LAN that can handle more than one signal per communication line at a time. The maximum transmission rate for broadband systems is 180 MBPS (faster than baseband systems).

Brouter Device that simultaneously routes packets using Network Layer protocols and bridges traffic at the Data Link Layer.

Cache A high-speed memory, logically residing between a central processing unit (CPU) and main memory, that holds data the CPU is most likely to need for upcoming operations.

Cache miss rate The number of times that an operand needed by the CPU is not found in cache memory and therefore a measure of cache algorithm performance.

Case mix Grouping of patients according to disease categories with homogeneous costs, following a scoring system using mean values by hospital, in relation to the means obtained from national statistics.

Certainty factor The confidence factor; the level of confidence or validity associated with data, rules or conclusions. The degree of certainty is usually represented by a numerical value from 0.0 (minimum certainty) to 1.0 (maximum certainty). For example, the rule "If X is a bird, then X can fly (0.9)" states that if an object is a bird, then the assertion that the object can fly will be correct 90% of the time (not all birds can fly).

Circuit-Switched Network A network that establishes a temporary physical circuit, which is maintained until it receives a disconnect signal.

Client A machine that employs the resources delivered by a server machine.

Client-server model Model of a distributed application process in which various activities are carried out by different entities. The client is that entity which requests a service. The server is that entity which provides the service.

Clinical support system System used by ancillary services to manage their internal processing control.

Co-morbidity A pre-existing condition which will, because of its presence with a specific principal diagnosis, cause an increase in length of stay by at least 1 day in approximately 75% of the cases.

Coding Transforming verbal descriptions of diseases, injuries and procedures into numerical designations.

Complex-instruction-set computer A computer whose CPU is designed to run a large number of often lengthy built-in instructions that support higher-level languages. (See also reduced-instruction-set computer).

Computer security Ensuring that unauthorised people do not obtain access to computer systems to find out, alter or destroy information.

Conceptual model Has the objective of describing the organisation, the information it manages and the performed activities, through criteria and models not dependent on specific technological contexts.

Confidentiality The property that information is not made available or disclosed to unauthorised individuals, entities or processes.

Cryptography The discipline which embodies principles, means and methods for the transformation of data in order to hide the information content, prevent undetected modification and/or prevent unauthorised use.

Data flow diagram A graphic representation of a system in which data sources, data links, storage and processes performed on data are shown as nodes, and the logical flow of data is shown as links between the nodes.

Data integrity The property that data has not been altered or destroyed in an unauthorised manner.

Decision support system Any computer-based support of medical, managerial, administrative and financial decisions in health using knowledge bases and/or reference material.

Departmental system System that supports a specific departmental functional activity within a health care environment but which could also work as a stand-alone unit.

Device In the context of medical informatics, device designates any biomedical equipment that generates information on the patient or therapeutic equipment that can be actuated by such information.

Diagnosis The act of identifying a disease from its signs and symptoms.

Diagnosis-related groups An inpatient classifications scheme which categorises patients who are medically related with respect to diagnoses and treatment and who are statistically similar in their lengths of stay. (DRG)

Digital image A digital image is a 2D array of positive integers f (x,y), where $1 <= x <= m$ and $1 <= y <= n$; n,m,x,y representing numbers of rows and columns. For any given x and y, the small region in the image represented by the coordinates (x,y) is called a picture element, or pixel, and f (x,y) is its corresponding functional value.

Digitisation Digitisation is a process that quantises or samples analog signals into a range of digital values. Digitising a picture means converting the gray scales in the picture into a digital image.

Direct-access storage device An electronic system for storing data on-line on magnetic disk.

Discharge summary A resume of the patient's course of treatment including the reason for hospitalisation, significant findings, procedures performed, treatment rendered and the condition of the patient upon discharge.

Double buffer A duplicate frame buffer that allows a new image to be constructed off-screen in one frame buffer while a different image is being viewed in the other buffer; smooth animation effects result from continually interchanging the buffers.

Dynamic range The range of a signal's amplitude compared to the maximum noise level ; in the case of a CRT display, determined by the number of gray levels at each pixel.

Electronic Data Interchange It contains the automated exchange of predefined and structured data, for some "business" purpose, among information systems of two or more parties.

Electronic Mail The electronic generation, transmission, and display of correspondence and documents.

Expert system A computer program that embodies knowledge of a particular domain in conjunction with inferencing mechanisms that enable them to use this knowledge to advise, analyse, categorise, communicate, consult, design, diagnose, explain, explore, forecast, form concepts, identify, interpret, justify, learn, manage, monitor, plan, present, retrieve, schedule, test and tutor.

Expert system shell A domain-independent software tool for building expert systems. Minimally, a shell includes an inference engine, some means of entering rules or examples and some means of using the system in a consultation mode. The better shells also provide a variety of tools that can be used in maintaining and debugging the knowledge base and for interfacing with external programmes and data. An expert system shell provides an empty framework into which you must add rules and facts.

Extended industry standard architecture An extension for 80386 and later processors of the ISA bus for PC-compatible computers that provides compatibility with earlier ISA systems. (See also Industry Standard Architecture) (EISA)

Fibre distributed data interface A network based on the use of optical fibre cable to transmit data in non-return-to-zero, invert-on-1s (NRZI) format at data rates of 100 megabits per second. (FDDI)

Flicker A repetitive variation in luminance in a CRT display.

Forward chaining Drawing conclusions from data, often termed data- or stimulus-driven. In expert systems using a forward chaining inference strategy, a rule is triggered when changes in working memory data produce a situation that matches the rule's antecedent component. For example, assume that the rule "If X is a bird, then X can fly" has been fired. The conclusion "X can fly" resides in the working memory. Next, the inference engine searches for a rule of the form "If X can fly, then ..." If such a rule is found in the knowledge base, then its conclusion is placed in working memory, and the process continues until the original hypothesis is verified or denied.

Frame One refresh cycle of a raster display image or one full display of information; 30 frames/s is considered real time.

Frame buffer An area of memory that represents the screen. When an application writes to this memory, it displays on screen.

Frames A method of knowledge representation used by some expert systems instead of, or as a supplement to, rules. Frames can be thought of as objects with slots or place holders for particular values. For example, a particular frame might have slots for patient's age, sex and diagnosis.

Gateway Internetworking device that operates at the Transport Layer and above, of the ISO/OSI network model.

Graphical user interface The combination of windowing display, menus, icons and a pointing device.

Graphics The creation of images by the expansion and display of compact geometric primitives.

Graphics primitive Basic display element; line, segment, point, letter, number, marker.

Grey level value The functional value f (x,y) of a pixel (x,y) is called the grey level value (or grey level), a non-negative integer. It can range from 0 to 255 (8 bit), 0 to 4095 (12 bit), depending upon the digitisation procedure or the radiological object used. These radiological image grey levels correpond to some physical properties of the structures in the object. For example, in an image obtained by digitising an X-ray film, the grey level value of a pixel corresponds to the optical density of that specific area of the film. In the case of X-ray computerised tomography (CT), the grey level value corresponds to the relative linear attenuation coefficient of the tissue, and in magnetic resonance imaging (MRI), it corresponds to the magnetic resonance signal response of the tissue.

Grouper Computer software (programme) which assigns DRGs based on the following factors: age, sex, principal and secondary diagnoses, procedures and discharge status.

Histology The science of microscopic tissue structure.

History and physical Written findings of the medical history and physical examination of the patient including: chief complaint, details of present illness, relevant past, social and family histories, inventory by body systems, and prenatal history, if applicable.

Holter Device for the 24-h recording of an ECG signal on a magnetic tape and its subsequent visualisation and analysis on a reproduction unit.

Homonymy Relation between designations and concepts in which identical designations represent different concepts.

Icon A graphical symbol displayed on a computer screen to represent, by analogy, a function performed by resident software; for instance, a wastebasket for material to be deleted

Image acquisition The process of creating digitised images from analog data; also known as image capture. The image acquisition process requires a device that samples the physical attributes of an object or scene that originates from the real world. An example of an image acquisition device is a scanner, which measures the physical attribute of light.

Image data A continuous, linear vector of values of a digital image. Files that contain image data are also called bit-map files because they contain information about the image as a series of bits.

Image exchange format The logical data format used for "image" exchange and storage.

Image manipulation Processing function like rotation, centre, window which do not change the content of the image.

Image pre-fetching In a PACS system based on current information technology a multiple layer storage structure is needed to contain all the images. Such a structure comprises large but slow optical disk archives (low level) and fast but small internal memory buffers (high level). Image retrieval from the slow archive through the PACS network would take much time. Acceptable response times can only be achieved when images are pre-fetched from the low level archive to the high level local buffer before they are actually requested.

Image processing Image processing encompasses the complete process of working with digitised images, including capture, manipulation, processing and output onto video display devices and printers.

Image size The dimensions of an image are the ordered pair (M,N), and the size of the image is the product *m* x *n* x *k* bits where *k* equals the grey level range. In case of CT, this is 256x256x12 bits, 312x312x12 bits; 512x512x12 bits. A 14"x17" radiological film digitised to 10-bit size measures about 2000x2400x10 bits.

Imaging equipment Global term for image acquisition unit like CT, MRI, US.

Induction The process of creating general rules from specific examples; reasoning from particulars to generals. Experts systems that make use of programming by examples, e.g. SuperExpert, use induction to create a rule base from specific examples.

Industry standard architecture (ISA) The name given to the bus architecture developed by IBM for the AT version of its personal computer. (See also extended industry standard architecture)

Inference engine The mechanism, usually provided by an expert system shell, for using the information in a knowledge base. Most inference engines use rules to reason either forward (from observations to conclusions) or backward (from a hypothesis toward observations that might lend support to or refute the hypothesis).

Inheritance The propagation of a property through successive generations.

Interface A common boundary between two associated systems across which information may flow.

Knowledge base The task- or domain-specific information that must be supplied when creating an expert system. A knowledge base is usually composed of rules and facts but may also be composed of frames, objects and other forms of knowledge representation.

Learning bridge A bridge that adaptively creates a table of addresses for both sides of the network it is bridging, and forwards only those packets destined for the "far" side of the bridge.

Lighting model Simulates the effect of light falling on objects in 3D graphics.

Linker A computer program used to create a single run-time programme from two or more independent, compiled modules.

Local Bridge A bridge directly connecting two distinct, but physically-close, LAN segments into a unified network.

Local Talk Defines the Physical and Data Link Layer characteristics of AppleTalk network protocols. It is a 230 kbps carrier-sense, multiple-access, collision avoidance protocol.

Loop A portion of computer code that is performed iteratively until certain criteria described in the program are met.

Major diagnostic categories Broad classifications of diagnoses. There were 83 MDCs (coding system oriented) in the original DRGs, and 23 MDCs (body system oriented) in the revised set of IDC-9-CM. (MDC)

Medical data All data concerning the medical state of the patient such as measured physiological data, therapeutic data and medical patient records.

Medical record A written memory of all information about a patient, constantly updated.

Menu A list of command options currently available to the computer user.

Message An information object which contains address information and content, also assembly of characters and sometimes control codes, that is transferred as an entity from an originator or one or more recipients.

Message authentication Ensuring that a message is genuine, has arrived exactly as it was sent and came from the stated source.

Modality Refers to particular medical "imaging equipment" whereby an image is produced.

Modem An acronym for modulator/demodulator. A device which enables data to be transmitted over long distances without error.

Monitoring Any kind of system keeping watch on one or several physiological parameters.

Mouse A device whose motion across a desktop or other surface causes an on-screen cursor to move.

Multi-modality workstation Man-machine interfaces which simultaneously handle images of different modalities, e.g. CT, sonography, ultrasound.

Neoplasm A new growth of tissue serving no physiological function.

Nomenclature System of terms which is elaborated according to pre-established naming rules.

Nosocomial infection A hospital-acquired infection.

Object A functional entity which has a state and a defined set of operations to access and modify that state. Objects can interact with one another.

Object class A set of objects possessing the same logical and functional properties.

Object database management system A database management system built to store and retrieve objects rather than simple data types

Object identifier A value (distinguishable from all other such values) which is associated with an information object. (An information object is a well-defined piece of information, definition or specification which requires a name in order to identify its use in an instance of communication.)

Object-oriented programming A technique for writing programs in which data representing objects or elements of the system and a code defining the legal operations on the object data are packaged together in modules.

Open system A computer system which complies with the requirements of OSI (Open Systems Interconnection) recommendations in its communications with other computer systems.

Operative report A resume of the surgery performed including description of findings, technical procedures performed, specimens removed, pre-operative diagnosis, post-operative diagnosis, and name of primary surgeon and assistants.

Order entry A sub-system as part of a HIS containing all the functions to communicate and manage medical orders for inpatients and outpatients to various medical services.

OSI Model Open system Interconnect is a model for data communication created by ISO (International Standards Organization) consisting of seven layers of protocols.

Packet-Switched Network A network in which data is transmitted in units called packets. The packets can be routed individually over the best available network connection and reassembled to form a complete message at the destination.

Patient A patient is often a global concept of the real patient and its associated data descriptions and actions.

Patient record A record containing all related patient identification, administrative and medico-administrative data.

Pattern recognition An automatic or semi-automatic signal processing function to recognise given definite patterns, which can be either normal or abnormal pathology, to assist diagnosis.

Physical address A binary address that refers to the physical location of information stored in memory (for instance a disc drive).

Physiology The science which studies organ function and metabolism.

Pixel Abbreviation for picture element; the smallest resolvable and addressable segment of an electronic display.

PostScript A text and graphics language created by Adobe Systems to drive laser printers and used in some display interfaces.

Primitive Basic display element, such as point, segment and alphanumerical character.

Principal diagnosis The diagnosis which most substantively accounts for the reason the patient was admitted to the hospital.

Principal procedure The procedure performed for definitive treatment rather than for diagnostic or exploratory purposes or which was necessary to take care of a complication. It is most related to the principal diagnosis.

Privacy The right of individuals to control or influence what information related to them may be collected and stored, by whom and to whom that information may be disclosed.

Procedural language A language that is designed to execute efficiently pre-defined procedures or algorithms. BASIC, C , PASCAL, FORTH and FORTRAN are all procedural languages. When working with a procedural language you tell the program how to solve a problem : you specify a procedure. When working with a non-procedural language, such as Prolog, you specify what is to be done (what problem is to be solved) but not how to go about solving it.

Prospective payment system A payment method in which hospital rates are set prospectively (before services are rendered) and are based upon expected classes and volumes of patients.

Protocol Set of rules and conventions that govern an orderly exchange of information.

Protocol converter A device that changes one computer or communications protocol into another.

Quality assessment Assessment is the act of detecting and measuring the difference between efficacy and effectiveness that can be attributed to care, including variations across regions and people. In practical terms, it is the measurement of the technical and interpersonal aspects of medical care.

Quality assurance This is the formal and systematic exercise of identifying problems in medical care delivery, designing activities to overcome the problems and carrying out follow-up steps to ensure that no new problems have been introduced and that corrective actions have been effective. The ultimate objective is to improve the outcome of all health care in terms of health, functional ability, patient well-being and consumer satisfaction.

Quality of care Degree of excellence of care in relation to actual medical knowledge, identified by quality tracers based on outcomes of care, as well as on structure and process recommendation provision that conveys advice or guidance.

Reduced-instruction-set computer A computer in which the instruction set is simplified and minimised for rapid execution by specially designed hardware. (See also Complex-instruction-set computer) (RISC)

Reimbursement, cost-based The amount of the payment based on the costs to the provider of delivering the service. The actual payment may be based on any one of several different criteria.

Relational database A database in which data elements are organized into relations viewed as rows in tables.

Reliability A measure of a software system of how well it provides the services expected of it by its users.

Repeater Device that operates at the Physical Layer of the OSI model to amplify and/or translate the data signal between different media; usually used to extend the physical length of a network.

Retrospective payment system Payment to providers by a third-party carrier for costs or charges actually incurred by subscribers in a previous time period.

Rotate Transform a display or display item by revolving it around a specific axis or point.

Rule base The production rules used by an expert system; the set of rules specific to the problem at hand. Each rule has two parts, the permise and the conclusion. The rule base, together with applicable facts, forms the knowledge base in a rule-based expert system.

Rule-based system A particular type of expert system in which the knowledge base is composed of domain-specific rules. Rule-based systems are expert systems, but expert systems are not necessarily rule-based.

Scale Size transformation made by multiplying or dividing coordinate dimensions.

Scroll bar A graphical construct, consisting of a rectangular box and a position marker, used in conjunction with a mouse to position an image, table or text in view.

Security policy A set of rules that specify the procedures and mechanisms required to maintain the security of a system, and the security objects and security under the purview of the policy.

Semantics Meaning of symbols and codes.

Server A machine that provides resources to the network.
A machine that employs these resources is called a *client* . A machine may be both a server and a client.

Small computer systems interface An industry-standard, high-speed interface for second-level storage systems. (SCSI)

Smart cards Small computer embedded in a card with the size of a credit card that can hold substantial amounts of information.

Software portability The ability to execute a program on a variety of computers.

Sub-system A part of a system that provides a particular service, but the service is only meaningful within the scope of the system.

Subnet Portion of a backbone partitioned/segmented by repeaters, bridges or routers.

Telemedicine Systems that allow the transmission of biological signals at a distance for diagnostic or therapeutic purposes.

Telemetry Transmission by radiowaves of biological signals (the most common is the ECG signal).

Test The method of analysis. An executed test delivers an analysis result.

Token ring Token passing access method with a ring or star-wired ring topology using 4Mbps or 16Mbps transmission rates.

Transformation Geometric alteration of a graphics display, such as scaling, translation and rotation.

Translate Shift a display item across the display surface to a new location.

Treatment The total of services rendered to a patient in order to cope with a specific problem.

Trusted software Software code believed to be safe because it is functionally correct, i.e. it does what it was designed to do and nothing more, and it enforces its correctness on programmes that run under it (as in the case of an operating system).(Based on text in US Trusted Computer System Evaluation Criteria Orange Book)

User interface Method of interaction between users and information systems. This includes graphical user interface (GUI), dialogue model, particular devices and general ergonomy features.

Validation The formal approval of analysis results.

Virtual address A binary address issued by a CPU that refers to the location of information in a primary level of memory, such as main memory; the physical address is changed to the virtual address.

Virtual instrument An instrument whose general function and capabilities are determined in software. (VI)

Widget A special class of an object supported in the window toolkit. Generally this is a window object that has a special function. Examples are menu widgets and button widgets.

Window An area of a workstation screen in which a task or application runs.

Worklist A list of samples which still have to be performed for a certain test.

Workstation A term used to mean more powerful computer than a PC. It is a device that has data input and output and local processing capabilities and is operated by a user.

X.25 Recommendations developed by CCITT that define a protocol for communication between packet-switched Public Data Networks and user devices in the packet-switched mode.

X.400 The international standard for a store-and-forward message handling system in a multivendor environment.

X/Open An independent consortium of international computer vendors created to develop a multivendor Common Applications Environment (CAE) based on de facto and international standards.

Zoom To cause the "viewing window" of the image to take in a smaller or larger part of the image.

ACRONYMS

Two D Two-dimensional (images)
Three D Three-dimensional (images)
AAMSI American Association for Medical Systems and Informatics
ACEMB Annual Conferences on Engineering in Medicine and Biology
ACM Association for Computing Machinery
ACMI American College for Medical Informatics
ACR American College of Radiology
ADT Sub-system of a HIS, fulfilling the functions of patient admission, discharge and transfer
AEMB Alliance for Engineering in Medicine and Biology
AFIPS American Federation of Information Processing Societies
AFNOR Association Francaise de Normalisation
AIM Advanced Informatics in Medicine
AMA American Medical Association
AMIA American Medical Informatics Association
ANSI American National Standards Institute
AOW Asian and Oceanian OSI Workshop (located in Japan)
API Application programming interface
ASCII American Standard Code for Information Interchange
ASN.1 Abstract syntax notation one
ASTM American Society for Testing and Materials
BNF Backus-Naur form
BSI British Standards Institution
CAD Computer-aided design
CAM Computer-aided manufacturing
CAP College of American Pathologists
CAV Constant angular velocity
CCITT International Telegraph and Telephone Consultative Committee
CCITT The Consultative Committee International Telegraph and Telephone which recommends worldwide telecommunications standards.
CD-ROM Compact disc read-only memory
CEC Commission of the European Communities
CEN Comité Européen de Normalisation
CENELEC Comité Européen de Normalisation Electrotechnique
CIS Clinical information system; information system that manages clinical data to support patient care and medical decision making

CLV Constant linear velocity
CPT4 Current Procedures and Terminology, 4th edn.
CR Computed radiography is based on laser-stimulated luminescence detection. It uses an image plate (IP) consisting of fine phosphor crystals which are photostimulatable. This enables it to store X-ray energy in a quasi-stable state
CSMA/CD Carrier-sense multiple access/collision detection
CT Computed tomography; radiographic technique based on tomographic reconstruction of body slices using digital data processing of radiation intensity measured by detectors
CTS Conformance Testing Service
DBA Database administrator; manager of the database
DBMS Database management system
DDA Distributed database architecture
DF Digital fluoroscopy
DIN Deutsches Institut für Normierung
DIS Draft International Standard
DP Draft proposal
DR Digital radiography; an image acquisition process which yields radiographic images in digital form
DRG Diagnosis-related groups; method to define case mix taking into account about 480 diagnosis categories and procedures coded with ICD-9-CM grouped by homogeneous costs, proposed in 1980 by the Yale School of Management
DSA Digital subtraction angiography
DTA Distributed transaction architecture
ECG Electrocardiogram
ECMA European Computer Manufacturers' Association
EDI Electronic data interchange
EDIFACT Electronic data interchange for administration, commerce and transport
EEG Electroencephalogram
EFMI European Federation for medical informatics
EFTA European Free Trade Association
EMEDI European Medical EDI Group
EN Européene norme (European standard)
ENV European Norme Vorausgabe (European prestandard)
EPHOS European Procurement Handbook for Open Systems
ESPRIT European Strategic Programme for Research in Information Technology
ETSI European Telecommunications Standard Institute
EUCLIDES European Clinical Laboratory Data Exchange Standard
EWOS European Workshop on Open Systems
FDDI Fibre distributed data interface
FTAM File transfer access and management
GKS Graphical kernel system; an ANSI/ISO 2-D graphics software standard
GOSIP Government OSI Profile

GUI Graphical user interface
HCIS Health care information system; general medical information systems covering any part of the health care delivery organisation
HIS Hospital information system
HISCC Hospital Information Standards Coordinating Committee
HL-7 Health level 7
ICD International Classification of Diseases
ICD-9-CM International Classification of Diseases, 9th Revision, Clinical Modification; statistical classification of diseases consisting of a limited number of categories to encompass the entire range of morbid conditions and a statistical classification of surgical and non-surgical procedures
IEC International Electrotechnical Commission
IEEE Institute of Electrical and Electronic Engineers
IEEE 802 Institute of Electrical and Electronic Engineers standards for LAN interconnections. IEEE 802.1 defines network interfaces and methodology for internetworking and network management. IEEE 802.3 defines a 10Mbps bus topology. IEEE 802.5 defines token ring at 4 and 16Mbps at the Physical and Data Link Layers.

IFIP International Federation for Information Processing
IFMB International Federation for Medical and Biological Engineering
IM Imaging modality
IMACS Image management and communication systems; describes an advanced image-based medical information system. The system can manage varieties of medical images and is capable of retrieving and displaying alphanumerical information from the conventional medical information system or facilitating information transfer by sound. The IMAC system could have many configurations, ranging from a single module capable of supporting a small medical operation to a network of modules shared among major medical centres. IMACS covers the total hospital, and PACS is more radiology restricted
IMIA International Medical Informatics Association
IPS Image processing station; unit for advanced image processing and manipulation
ISCAMI Integrated systems for computer-assisted management and manipulation of medical images
ISDN Integrated Services Digital Network
ISO International Organization for Standardisation
ISP International Standardized Profile
ITSTC Information Technology Steering Committee (of CEN, CENELEC)
JISC Japanese Industrial Standards Committee
JTC1 Joint Technical Committee 1 (of ISO and IEC)
KBS Knowledge-based system
LAN Local area network
LIS Laboratory information system
MAN Metropolitan area computer network

MBDS Miminum basic data set
MDDL Medical device data language
MEDIX Medical Data Interchange Committee (I EEE P1157)
MEDLARS Medical literature analysis and retrieval system
MEDLINE An on-line version of MEDLARS
MHS Message handling system
MIB Medical information bus
MIPS Medical Image Procuring Standards (Japanese version of the ACR/NEMA standard)
MIS Medical information system
MIT Massachusetts Institute of Technology
MR Magnetic resonance
MRI Magnetic resonance imaging; modality which operates with a high magnetic field and generates images illustrating the differences in magnetic properties of the atoms in a patient
MTA Message transfer agent (X.400)
MUMPS Massachusetts General Hospital Utility Multi-programming System
NEMA National Electrical Manufacturers Association
NIU Network interface unit
ODA Office document architecture
ODIF Office document interchange format
OEM Original equipment manufacturer
OOM Object-oriented model uses a distributed set of objects to represent a (health care) information system. Objects are representations of real and conceptual entities and can have attributes and actions
OOP Object-oriented programming
OSI Open systems interconnection; concerned with the exchange of information between open systems (and not the internal functioning of each open system). It is concerned only with the interconnection of systems. All other aspects of systems, which are not related to interconnection are outside the scope of OSI. OSI is concerned not only with the transfer of information between systems, i.e. transmission, but also with the capability to interwork to achieve a common (distributed) task
OSTC Open Systems Testing Consortium
PACS Picture archiving and communication systems. The acronym comes from the first Society of Photo-Optical Engineers (SPIE) conference and workshop on PACS for Medical Applications, held in January 1982 at Newport Beach
PAS Patient administration system (ADT)
PDS Public digital service communication network
PET Positron emission tomography
POSIX Portable operating system interface

PPS Prospective payment system; payment of health care by setting payment rates before the care is provided, rather than basing it on actual costs, and paying for hospital stays as a "bundle", thus removing any financial reward for long stays or expensive services

PSTN Public switched telephone network

PTT Post, Telegraph and Telephone Administration

RACE Research in advanced computer electronics

RICHE Réseau d'Information et de Communication Hospitalier Européen

RIS Radiological information system

RISC Reduced-instruction-set computer

RS232 Hardware standard for serial communication (most of the modem instruments)

SAMS Society for Advanced Medical Systems

SCAMC Symposium on Computer Applications in Medical Care

SCM Society for Computer Medicine

SI Système Internationale

SIGs Special interest groups

SNA System network architecture (IBM)

SNOMED Systematized Nomenclature of Medicine

SOGITS Senior Officials Group on Information Technologies Standards

SPARC Sun's proprietary RISC microprocessor implementation

SPECT Single photon emission tomography

SPI Standard product interconnect

SQL Structured query language

TCP/IP Transmission Control Protocol/Internet Protocol is a set of protocol standards at the Transport (TCP) and network (IP) Layer that conforms to U.S. Department of Defense standards.

UA User agent; acts on behalf of the user in an application process

UMLS Unified medical language system

UNIX Trademark name for AT&T's operating system

US Ultrasound

VAR Value added reseller

WAN Wide area network

W
A
N Wide Area Network connecting devices and LANs situated over geographically- dispersed locations, over common carrier or private telecommunication facilities.

WG Working group

WHO World Health Organisation

WORM Write-once read many times optical device

X.11 An industry standard for workstation window software from the MIT consortium of vendors and supported by many hardware and software vendors

XWindows Developed by MIT (Project Athena) funded by DEC and IBM

REFERENCES

1. The Current Healthcare System : In a State of Transition

[BAR 90] Barber B, Asbjorn O et al.(1990)
The six safety first principles of health information systems. E C AIM Requirements Board, March 14 : pp. 1 - 6

[COL 88] Collen M (1988)
HIS Concepts, Goals and Objectives
In : Bakker A et al. (eds) *Towards new hospital information systems.* Elsevier (North-Holland), Amsterdam, pp. 3-10

[ING 90] Ruge I (1990)
The growing influence of microelectronics on telecommunications. *Siemens Review*, Fall 1990 : p.16

3. The Genesis of Hospital Information Systems : A look at the Past and the Future

[FRE 91] Frenkel, K.N. 1991
An interview with Fernando Jose Corbato. *Communications of the ACM*. 34 (9), pp 82-90

4. Concepts of Computer Systems

[MUG 84] Mumps User Group (MUG) (1984)
in : *MUG 13th annual meeting, questions and answers.*

5. Standardisation in Medical Informatics

[ACR 88] National Electrical Manufacturers Association (1988) ACR - Nema 300:*Digital Imaging and Communications.* Nema Report, Washington DC.

[AND 90] Anderson Consulting (1990) *Hospital of the future - news.* Brussels, Q3 : pp. 1 - 6

[ANS 91] Cornish SI (1991) *Proposal for the formation of an ANSI healthcare informatics standards planning Panel* ANSI document, June 7

[DEM 90] De Moor GJE, Tran Q (1990) *European standardisation activities in medical informatics.* CEN TC 251-Report, Gent

6. Most Important Trends in the 1990s

[BIR 91] Birsfelder M (1991) *Das Gelbe vom Ei.* IBM object-orientation symposium, July 22-26, 1991 La Hulpe, Belgium

[FRA 90] Francis B (1990) Serving up vertical software. *Datamation,* Sept 1 : pp.45 - 48

[NOE 89] Noehr C, Bernstein K (1989) Can HIS be developed without organizational change? The creative potential in user participation. In : Barber B, Cao D, Qin D, Wagner G, (eds) *Medinfo '89,* Elsevier, Amsterdam, p. 337

[NOR 86] Norman DA (1986) Cognitive engineering. In : Norman DA, Draper S (eds) *User-centred system design:new perspectives on human-computer interaction.* Erlbaum, Hillsdale, pp. 31 - 36

[SEA 90] Seacerd RC (1990) User interface management systems and application portability. *Computer,* IEEE Computer Society, Oct : pp. 73 - 75

[WEN 91] Wendler T (1991)
Digital image workstations. In : Osteaux M et al. (eds): *A second generation PACS concept.* Springer, Berlin, Heidelberg, New York

7. Modelling Health Care Systems

[BRO 88] Brooks F (1988)
No silver bullet. IEEE, *IEEE Software,* April

[CHE 80] Chen PP(1980)
*Entity-relationship approach to systems analysis and design.*North-Holland, Amsterdam

[COA 91] Coad P, Yourdan E (1991)
Object-oriented analysis, 2nd edn. Yourdan, Engelwood Cliffs

[DAV 88] Davis AM (1998)
A taxonomy for the early stages of the software development life cycle. *J System Software* 8 : pp. 297 - 311

[DEM 78] De Marco T (1978)
Structured analysis and system specification .Prentice-Hall, Englewood Cliffs

[HEN 90] Henderson - Seller B, Edwards JM (1990)
The object oriented systems life cycle. *Communications of the ACM* 33 (9) : pp. 142 - 159

[MAR 86] Martin J (1986)
Information engineering, vols.1,2. Savant Research Studies, Lancashire

[MEY 88] Meyer B (1988)
Object-oriented software construction. Prentice-Hall, Englewood Cliffs, p.354

[MUR 90] Murphy EE (1990)
Software R & D : from an art to a science. IEEE, *IEEE Spectrum,* Oct : pp. 44 - 47

[WIN 87] Wintraecken JJVR (1987)
Informatieanalyse volgens NIAM. (Information analysis following NIAM). Academic Service, Schoonhoven

[WIR 90] Wirfs-Brock R, Wilkerson B, Wiener L (1990) *Designing object-oriented software.* Prentice-Hall, Englewood Cliffs, pp. 8 -9

8. The Make or Buy - Decision

[CAR 87] Carney GA (1987) Planning for acquisition of a radiology information system. *Administrative Radiology Journal,* 5 (5), Glendale

9 Computer Safety in Health Care Systems

[GIS 89] GISA, German Information Security Agency (1989) *IT-security criteria : criteria for the evaluation of trustworthiness of information technology (IT) systems.* Bundesanzeiger, Cologne

[WIN 89] Van Winkel JC (1989) *The phenomenon of computer viruses reviewed.* NGI, Amsterdam

10. Architecture of a Hospital Information System

[CEN 91] European Standardisation Committee (CEN) Technical Committee 251 (Medical Informatics) (1991) *Directory of the European standardisation requirements for healthcare in informatics and programme for the development of standards.* CEN/TC251, version 1.1 - 3, March 1991

[CLA 87] Clayton DP, Delaplaine KH, Jensen DR et al. (1987) Integration of surgery management and clinical information systems. In : Stead W (ed) *Proceedings of the 11th symposium on computer applications in medical care.* Computer Society Press (Washington), pp.393 - 395

[COA 91] Coad P, Yourdan E (1991) *Object-oriented analysis.* Yourdan, Englewood Cliffs

[EHL 91] Ehlers CT, Schillings H, Pietrzyk PM (1991) *His and integration in reprints of the proceedings of trends in modern hospital information systems.* Scope - Design - Architecture. IMIA Working conference, Göttingen, pp. 45 - 52

[JAC 89] Jacobeus M (1989) Trends in bar code scanning. *Auto ID Today* : 6 pp 5 - 7

[KEY 88] De Keyser L (1988) Deductive database technology for KB-HIS. In : Bakker et al. (eds) *Towards new hospital information systems.* Elsevier (North Holland), Amsterdam, pp. 273 - 278

[STE 85] Steinbauern D, Wedekinf H (1985) Integritaetsaspekte in Datenbanksystemen. *Informatik Spektrum* 8 : pp. 60-68

[VEL 87] Van de Velde R (1987) Subject databases for hospital information systems. The patient appointment system. In : Serio A, O'Moore R, Tardine A, Roger FH (eds) *Proceedings medical informatics Europe 1987.* Springer, Berlin Heidelberg New York, Vol 2 : pp. 593 - 604

[VEL 89] Van de Velde R (1989) *Ziekenhuisinformatiesystemen (Hospital information systems).* Academic Service, Schoonhoven

[WIE 81] Wiederhold G (1981) *Databases for health care.*, Springer, Berlin Heidelberg New york

11. The Patient Management Systems

[BRI 88] Bright R (1988)
Smart cards : principles, practice, application.
Horwood, Chicheskr, p 170

[KRI 91] Krieger D, Burk G, Sclabassi RJ (1991)
Neuronet. *Computer*, March 1991 : p. 52

[SCH 90] Scherrer JR (1990)
An integrated hospital information system in Geneva. *MD Computing*(2) : p. 81

[VEL 91] Van de Velde R. (1991)
Overview of an architectural approach to the development of the A.Z.-VUB distributed clinical Information system. In : Adlassing KP, Grabner G, Bengtsson S, Hansen R (eds) *Proceedings medical informatics Europe 1991.* Springer, Berlin Heidelberg New York

12. Order Entry and Result Reporting Management Systems

[PRO 88] Prokosch HU, Pryor TA (1988)
Intelligent data acquisition in order entry programs. In : Greenes RA (ed) *Proceedings of the 12th symposium on computer applications in medical care.* SCAMC, Computer Society Press, Washington, pp.454 - 458

13. Patient Appointment and Scheduling

[DAV 67] Davis AY (1967)
Systems analysis and design of outpatient department.
Appointment department and information systems, Unit Hospital Fund of New York

[HOL 67] Holston CA (1967)
Central appointment system for outpatient clinics. *Hospital Management,* Oct. : pp. 65 - 71

[PET 84] Peterson GF (1984)
PCS/ADS resource and appointments scheduling system. International Customer Executive Program, IBM

[SCH 73] Schuling J (1973)
Het afspraak-spreekuur (Appointment hours). *Hospital Research Project,* Report n° 4, June 1973

[VIS 78] Vissers JMH (1978)
Wachttijden in de polikliniek (Waiting times in the outpatient clinic). *Medisch Contact,* pp. 500 - 503

[ZWI 81] Zwieten-Edelenbos HJ (1981)
Afspraakplanning als onderdeel van een totaal ziekenhuiscommunicatie- en informatiesysteem (Appointments scheduling as part of a complete hospital communication and data system). *MIC 81,* Proceedings MIM-VMBI

14. Operating Theatre Management Information Systems

[BAL 89] Ball MJ, Hannah KJ, Gerdin Jelger U, Peterson H, (1989)
Nursing informatics. Where caring and technology meet, 2nd edn. Springer, Berlin Heidelberg New York

[BAR 87] Barbie F, Fumagalli F et al. (1987)
Design requirements for an operating room management information system. In : Seri OA, O'Moore R, Tardine A (Eds) *Proceedings medical informatics Europe 1987,* vol 1 : pp.479 - 486

[BER 89] Berg CM, Lassone D (1989)
Operating room information systems software. In : Ball MJ, Hannah KJ, Gerdin Jelger U, Peterson H (eds) *Nursing informatics,* 2nd edn., Springer, Berlin Heidelberg New York, pp. 146 - 160

[HAR 90] Hard R (1990)
O.R. system investments offer hospitals financial gains. *Hospitals,* June 20 : pp. 60-61

[KRI 91] Krieger D, Burk G, Sclabassi RJ (1991)
Neuronet, *Computer,* March 1991 : p.50

[TOR 90] Toro MJ (1990) in Kenny GNC (ed)
Automated anaesthetic records. Baillière Tindall, London, pp. 17 - 35

15. Automation in Nutrition

[BIJ 82] Van Bijl K, Van Spengen B (1982)
A meal distribution system in an integrated hospital information system. In : Moore et al. (eds.)*Proceedings medical Informatics Europe 82,* pp 48 - 50

[IBF 81] Information Bureau for Nutrition (1981)
Automatische verwerking van informatie voor de voedingsdienst (Automatic data processing for the food supply department), vols. A, B. The Hague

[PLU 84] Pluyer-Wenting ESP, Groningen LEW, van Bijl K (1984)
Computer-based system for daily individual menu choice by patients in hospital: development, implementation and application. In : (eds) *Proceedings medical informatics Europe* 84. Springer, Berlin Heidelberg New York

[SWI 82] Swieringa I (1982)
Automatische verwerking van informatie in de voedingsdienst (Automatic data processing in the food supply department). *MIC 82,* Proceedings MIM-VMBI

[WHE 84] Wheeler LA, Wheele ML (1984)
Review of microcomputer nutrient analysis and menu-planning programs. *MD Computing.* 1 (2)

16. Laboratory Information Systems

[ALB 80] Albert A, Vitek PJ (1980)
An approach to comprehensive validation of laboratory data. *Proceedings of the 3rd annual WAMI meeting* May 80. Annals of the World Association for Medical Informatics, pp.473 - 479

17. Radiology Information Systems

[GAN 79] Gane C Sarson T (1979)
Structured systems analysis. Prentice Hall, Englewood Cliffs

[GRE 90] Greenes RA, Brinkley JF (1990)
Radiology systems. In : Shortliffe EH, Perreault LE,- Wiederhold G et al. (eds) *Medical informatics. Computer applications in health care.* Addison-Wesley, Reading, pp. 324-365

[LEH 73] Lehr L, Lodwick G, Nichilson B, et al. (1973)
Experiences with MARS (Missouri Automated Radiology System). *Radiology* 106 : pp. 289 - 294

[MAN 73] Mani R, Jones M (1973)
MSF. A computer-assisted radiology reporting system. *Radiology* 108 : pp. 587-596

[MAT 89] Matheus R(1989)
Picture archiving and communication systems : a digital image management system. *MIM News,* 1: pp. 38 - 44

[MAT 90] Mattheus R,Van den Broeck R,Osteaux M(1990)
Differentation and requirements of image-computers in a clinical PACS environment. In : *Integrated systems for computerized management and manipulations of medical images.* Lecture notes in medical informatics. Springer, Berlin Heidelberg New York

[VEL 87] Van de Velde R (1987)
Subject databases for hospital information systems. The patient appointment sytem. In : Serio A, O'Moore R, Tardine A, Roger FH (eds) *Proceedings medical informatics Europe 1987.* Springer, Berlin Heidelberg New York, Vol 2 : pp. 593 - 604

[VEL 91] Van de Velde R (1991)
Radiological information systems.In : Osteaux M et al. (eds) *A second generation PACS concept.* Springer Berlin Heidelberg New York

[WHE 79] Wheeler PS, Gitlin IN (1979)
Computers in radiology : a viewpoint of pitfalls and payoffs. In : *Proceedings of the 6th conference on computer applications in radiology,* June 18-21. IEEE Computer Society Press Washington, pp.1 - 4

18. Oncology Information Systems

[AIR 88] Aird EGA (1988)
Basic physics for medical imaging. Heinemann Oxford

[BLU 86] Blum BI (1986)
Clinical information system. Springer New York

[DAH 85] Dahlin H(1985)
Computer assisted radiology (computer assisted radiation therapy). In : Lemke HU, Rhodes ML, Jaffee CC, Felix R (eds), *CAR '85,* Springer, Berlin Heidelberg New York, pp. 337-351

[ENT 89] Enterline JP, Lenhard RE, Blum BI (eds) (1989)
A clinical information system for oncology. Springer, Berlin Heidelberg New York

[FUS 89] Fusi IS et al. (1989)
Three dimensional radiotherapy planning system with enhanced visual supporting capability. In : Burber ZE (ed) *MEDINFO 1989.* North-Holland, Amsterdam, pp. 422 - 426

[LEN 84] Lenhard ER, Blum BI, Mc Calligan EE (1984)
An information system for oncology. In : Blum BI (ed) *Information systems for patient care.* Springer, Berlin Heidelberg New York, pp. 385 - 403

19. Pharmacy Information Systems

[GAN 79] Gane C, Sarson T (1979)
Structured systems analysis. Prentice Hall, Englewood Cliffs

[HAR 91] Hard R
Managing the pharmacy becomes more complex
Hospitals, Sept 20 : p. 54

[HOE 77] Hoelen AG (1977)
EDP in the pharmacy at the Radboud Hospital Nijmegen. In : Wagner G (ed) *Laboratory information systems. Hospital pharmacy systems.* Schattauer, Stuttgart : pp. 83 - 90

[HOE 90] Hoelen J (1990)
Pharmacy planning and organizational growth. In : O'Moore R, Bengtsson S, Bryant JR, Bryden JS (eds) *Medical informatics Europe '90.* Lecture notes in medical informatics. Springer, Berlin Heidelberg New York, pp. 369 - 372

[MOL 83] Molenaar GCC, De Moel J, Veth AFL (1983)
A drug information system as part of a hospital pharmacy information system. In : Van Bemmel JH et al. (eds) *MEDINFO 83.* North-Holland, Amsterdam : pp. 156 - 159

[RUC 90] Rucker T, Schiff DG (1990)
Drug formularies Myths-in-formation. *Med Care* 28 (10) : pp. 928 - 938

[SOU 90] Souhrada L (1990)
Economics and pharmacy. *Hospitals*, Oct 5 : pp. 52 - 56

20. Nursing Information Systems

[HEN 90] Hendrickson G (1990
Journal of nurse administrators 20 (3), p. 31

[KOR 84] Korpman RA (1984)
Patient care information systems: Looking to the future. Part 4. The changing role of computers in nursing. *Software in Healthcare*, Oct/Nov : pp. 58-64

[KOR 87] Korpman RA (1987)
Using the computer to optimize human performance in health care delivery. *Arch Pathol Lab Med,* 3 pp.637 - 645

[MIL 89] Miller E (1989)
A conceptual model of the information requirements of nursing organizations. In : Kingsland LC (ed) *Proceedings of the 13th annual symposium on computer applications in medical care (LA,CA).* IEEE Computer Society Press, Washington, pp. 784 - 788

[PIC 91] Picone J.,Wheatley B., Lews R. (1991)
The hand-held, voice controlled terminal: Medical information interface of the future. *Computers in health care,* August : pp. 40-47

[SMI 89] Smith CR et al. (1989)
Integrated computerized clinic flow sheet for nurses and physicians. In : Kingsland LC (ed) *Proceeding of the 13th annual symposium on computer applications in medical care (LA, CA).* IEEE Computer Society Press, Washington, pp. 839 - 843

[STE 87] Stefanchik MF (1987)
Bedside terminal data entry, *Computers in Healthcare,* November : p. 57

[STE 89] Stefanchik MF, Cohen P (1989)
Point-of-care faces cost challenges, *Computers in Healthcare*, December : p. 38

[STE 91] Stefanchik MF, Michael F (1991)
Point-of-care revolution, *Computers in Healthcare,* April : pp. 19 - 24

21. Hospitals Financing : Challenges of the 1990s

[AND 91] Anderson HJ (1991)
Looking abroard for changes to the U.S. health care system in hospitals, May 20, pp. 30 - 35

[HCF 87] "*National Health Expenditures, 1986-2000*", Health care financing review. Devision of nat. cost estimates. Office of the Actuary, Health Care Financing Administration, Summer 1987, p. 25

[NOL 79] Nolan RL (1979)
Managing the crises in data processing in *Harvard Business Review*, March April : pp. 115 -126

[WEV 90] De Wever A (1990)
The financing of hospitals in Belgium : challenges of the nineties. In : O'Moore R, Bengtsson S, Bryant JR, Bryden JS (eds) *Medical informatics Europe '90.* Springer, Berlin Heidelberg New York

[WIL 90] Williams Bob (1990)
How to do an ROI? *Healthcare Informatics,* February

22. Medical Data : Acquisition, Manipulation and Analysis

[BEM 83] Van Bemmel JH (1983)
Pattern in signal in medical informatics, Amsterdam, 10 years review. Department of Medical Informatics, Free University of Amsterdam, pp. 67 - 74

[BEM 89] Van Bemmel JH, Willems JL(1989)
Handboek medische informatica. Bohn, Sheltema and Holkema, Utrecht

[GAR 86] Gardner RM (1986)
Computerized management of intensive care patients. *MD Computing* 3 (1) : pp. 36 - 51

[JAM 83] Jambu M, Lebeaux MO (1983)
Cluster analysis and data analysis. North-Holland, Amsterdam

[SCO 87] Scott PD (1987)
Making sence out of complexity : methods for processing waveforms and images. In : Anbar M (ed) *Computers in medicine.* Computer Science Press, New York, pp. 88 - 104

[WIE 85] Wiederhold G et al. (1985)
Processing biological data in real time. *MD Computing* 2 (6) : p. 16

23. Automatisation in Cardiology

[AKI 90] Akira I, Yasunori Nagaska, Nobuo Suzumura (1990)
Data compression of the ECG using neural network for digital holter monitor. *IEEE Engineering in Medicine and Biology* ,Sept : pp. 53-60

[GOL 82] Goldberger E (1982). *Textbook of clinical cardiology.* Mosby, St Louis, p. 125

[IBM 74] IBM (1974)
Health care support/electrocardiogram (ECG) Analysis program, general information manual, 2nd edn., New York

[WAL 89] Waller AC (1889)
Philos Trans R Soc Land (Biol), 180 : pp. 169 - 194

[WIG 57] Wiggers CJ(1957)
The heart. *Scientific American,* May '57, Freeman, San Francisco

24.Automatization in Pneumology

[DG 74] Davis + Geck (1974)
Atlas of Normal Anatomy; Lederle Laboratories Division of American Cyanamid Company, p 26

25. Patient Monitoring Systems

[BEM 84] Van Bemmel JH, Pronk RAF (1984)
Trends in computers in anesthesiology. In : *Computers in anesthesiology*: pp. 293- 311

[BRA 84] Bradshaw KE, Gardner RM, Clemmer TP, Orne JF Jr, Thomas F, West BJ (1984)
Physician decision-making-evaluation of data used in a computerized ICU. *Int J Clin Maint Comput* 1 : pp. 81 - 91

[BRA 89] Bradshaw KE, Sittig DF., Gardner RM, Pryor TA, Budd ME (1989)
Computer-based data entry for nurses in the ICU. *MD Computing,* 6 (5) : pp. 274 -280

[GAR 86] Gardner RM (1986)
Computerized management of intensive care patients. *MD Computing* 3(1) : pp. 36 - 51

[GOR 83] Gordon M, Venn CJ, Gower PE, De Wardener HE (1983) Experience in the computer handling of clinical data for dialysis and transplantation units.
Kidney Int 2A4 : pp. 455-463

[WES 91] Westerteicher C. (1991)
Introduction to the HP component monitoring system, *Hewlett-Packard Journal,* October : pp.6-10

26. Computer stored Medical Record Systems

[ABB 86] Abbott W (1986)
Information technology in health care. Kluwer, Lancaster

[BIS 89] Bishop CW (1989)
A name is not enough. *MD Computing,* 6 (4) : pp. 200 - 206

[BIS 91] Bishop CW. (1991)
A New Format for the medical record. *M.D. computing,* 8 (4) : pp. 208-215

[BLO 88] Blois M (1988)
Medicine and the nature of vertical reasoning.
N Engl J Med, 318 : pp. 847 - 852

[BLU 84] Blum BI(1984)
Information systems for patient care. Springer, Berlin Heidelberg New York, pp. 210 - 211

[CRA 89] Mc Cray A (1989)
The UMLS semantic network. In : Kingsland LC (ed). *Proceedings of the 13th annual symposium on computer applications in medical care.* IEEE Computer Society Press, Washington, pp. 503 - 512

[EWO 90] *EWOS-Report* (1990)
CEN 1990, p. 17, version 3.10

[GOU 84] Gould J, and Grischkowsky (1984)
Doing the same work with hard copy and with cathode ray tube computer terminals. *Hum Factors, 26 :pp. 323 - 338*

[GRI 85] Grimaldi PL, Micheletti JA (1985) in :
Prospective payment : the definitive guide to reimburusement. Pluribus, Chicago, pp. 34 - 35
Copyright 1990 by the Foundation of the American College of Healthcare Executives)

[KUH 84] Kuhn I, Wiederhold G et al (1984)
Automated ambulatory medical record systems in the US. In : Blum BI (ed) *Information systems for patient care.* Springer, Berlin Heidelberg New York Verlag, pp. 199 - 218

[KUP 90] Kuperman GJ, Garoner RN (1990)
The impact of the HELP computer system on the LDS hospital paper medical record. In : *Proceedings of the 14th annual symposium on computer applications in medical care.* IEEE Computer Society Press, Washington, pp. 673-677

[LAM 82] Lambert PM, Roger F (1982)
Hospital statistics in Europe. North-Holland, Amsterdam

[LIN 89] Linnarson R, Wigertz 0 (1989)
The data dictionary - a controlled vocabulary for integrating clinical data bases and medical knowledge bases. *Methods Inf Med* 28 : pp. 78 - 85

[McD 76] McDonald CJ (1976)
Protocol-based computer reminders, the quality care, and the nonperfectability of man. *N Engl J Med* 295 : pp. 1351 - 1355

[McD 83] McDonald CJ, Blevins L et al. (1983)
Regenstrief medical record system.
J Med Systems 7

[McD 84] Mc Donald CJ, Hui LS et al (1984)
Reminders to physicians from an introspective computer medical record. A two-year randomized trial.
Ann Intern Med, 100 : pp. 130-138

[McD 88] Mc Donals CJ, Tierney WM (1988)
Computer stored medical records : their future role in medical practice. *JAMA* 259 : pp. 3433 - 3440

[McD 90] Mc Donald, CJ Barnett OG (1990)
Medical record systems. In : Shortliffe EH, Perreault LE, Wiederholt G (eds) *Medical informatics. Computer applications in health care.* Addison Wesley, Reading, pp. 782-218

[ROG 81] Roger FH (1981)
The minimum basic data set for hospital statistics in the EEC. Office for official Publications of the EEC, Luxembourg

[SHA 88] Shabot MM (1988)
Software for computers and calculators in critical care medicine. *JAMA* 259 (23) : pp. 3435 - 3439

[SPE 89] Sperzel D, Tuttle M (1989)
Updating the UMLS metathesaurus : a model.
In : Kingsland LC (ed) *Proceedings of the 13th annual symposium on computer applications in medical care.* IEEE Computer Society Press, Washington pp.488 - 493

[STE 88] Stead W, Hammond WE (1988)
Computer-based medical records : the centerpiece of TMB. *MD Computing*5 (3) : pp. 48-61

[TIE 89] Tielemans L (1989)
Het medisch dossier (The medical record). Lecture notes, Free University Brussels - Faculty of medicine

[VRI 75] De Vries R (1975)
Useful elements of POMR - a Report of experience. *Med Rec* 16, (6) : pp. 13 - 17

[WEE 68] Weed L (1968)
Medical records that guide and teach. *N Engl J Med*: (278) : pp. 593 - 600 and pp. 652 - 657

[WHI 85] Whiting-O'Keefe QE, Simborg DW, Epstein WV, Warger A (1985). A computerized summary medical record sysem can provide more information than the standard medical record. *JAMA* 254 (9) : pp. 1185 - 1188

[WHI 88] Whiting - O'Keefe QE, Whiting A, Henke J. (1988)
The stor clinical information system. *MD-Computing*, 5 (5) : pp. 8 - 21

[ZEG 88] De Zegher-Geets I.M., Freeman A. et al.(1988)
Summarization and display of on-line medical records *M.D. Computing*, 5 (3) : pp. 38, 45

27. Computer Assisted Clinical Decision Making

[BEM 89] Van Bemmel JH, Willems JL (1989)
Handboek medische informatica. Bohn, Scheltema and Holkema, Utrecht, p. 245

[BER 89] Bergeron B, Locke S (1989)
The Macintosh in medicine. *MD Computing*, 6 (2) : pp. 100 - 111

[BON 85] Bonnet A (1985)
Artificial intelligence. Promise and performance. Prentice-Hall, Englewood Cliffs

[BUC 84] Buchanan GB, Shortliffe EH (1984)
Rule-based expert systems. The MYCIN experiments of the Stanford heuristic programming project. Addison-Wesley, Reading

[CER 86] Cercone N, McCalla G (1986)
Artificial intelligence : underlying assumptions and basic objectives. In : *Computers for artificial intelligence applications.* IEEE Computer Society Press, Washington, pp. 12-22

[CLO 87] Clocksin WF, Mellish CS (1987)
Programming in logic, 3rd edn.
Springer, Berlin Heidelberg New York

[ENG 79] Engelmore RS, Terry A (1979)
Structure and function of the CRYSALIS system.
In : *Proceedings of the 6th international joint conference on artificial intelligence,* Tokyo, pp. 250-256

[FAG 80] Fagan LM (1980)
VM : representing time-dependent relations in a clinical setting. PhD dissertation, Heuristic Programming Project, Computer Science Department, Stanford University

[FAG 85] Fagan LM, Kunz JC, Feigenbaum EA, Osborn JJ (1985)
Extensions to the rule-bases formalism for a monitoring task. In : Buchanan BG, and Shortliffe ED (eds) *Rule-based expert systems.* Academic, New York, p. 400

[FIE 81] Fieschi M (1981)
Aide à la décision en médicine : le système SPHINX. Application au diagnostic d'une douleur épigastrique.
Medical dissertation, University of Marseille

[GAS 81] Gascuel O (1981)
Un système expert dans le domaine médical.
Dissertation, University of Paris IV

[GIU 88] Giuse NB et al. (1988)
Computer assisted multi-center creation of medical knowledge bases. In : *Proceedings of the 12th annual symposium on computers in healthcare.* IEEE Computer Society Press, Washington, pp. 583 - 589

[GOR 78] Gorry GA, Silverman H, Pauker SG (1978)
Capturing clinical expertise : a computer program that considers clinical responses to digitalis.
Am J Med, pp. 452-460

[GRI 88] Grimson Jane B (1988)
Knowledge-base approach to hospital information systems. In : Bakker et al. (eds) *Towards new hospital information systems.* Elsevier, North-Holland, Amsterdam : pp.265 - 271

[HAA 87] Haas IL (1987)
The integration of data and knowledge base systems : activities in ESPRIT. In : *Entity-relationship approach : ten years of experience in information modelling.* Proceedings of 5th international conference on ER approach,Nov 1986. North Holland, Amsterdam, pp. 9 - 21

[JON 90] Jonkers V (1990)
Proposal for a regulations expert system architecture. Notes, Free University Brussels

[KHO 90] Khoshafian S, Parsaye K, Wong KTH (1990)
Intelligent database engine. *Data Base Programming and Design.* 3 (7) : pp. 56-65

[KUN 79] Kunz JC, Fallat RJ, McClung DH, Osborn JJ, Votteri BA, Nii HP, Aikens JS, Fagan LM, Feigenbaum EA (1979)
A physiological rule-based system for interpreting pulmonary function test results. In : *Proceedings of computers in critical care and pulmonary medicine,* pp.375-379

[KUP 88] Kuperman GJ and Gardner RM (1988)
The help system : a snapshot in time. LDS Hospital

[LUC 88] Lucas PSF, van der Gaag (1988)
Principes van expertsystemen. (Principles of expert systems). Academic Service, Schoonhoven

[MAR 77] Martin N, Friedland P, King J, Stefik M (1977)
Knowledge-based management for experiment planning in molecular genetics. In : *Proceedings of the 6th international joint conference on artificial intelligence, Tokyo,* pp. 882-887

[OWE 90] Owens KD, Sox CH (1990)
Medical decision making : probabilistic reasoning in medical informatics. In : Shortliffe EH, Perreault LE (eds) *Computer applications in healthcare.* Addison-Wesley, Reading : pp. 70-116

[PAT 82] Patil R, Szolovits P, Schwartz WB (1982)
Modeling knowledge of the patient in acid-base and electrolyte disorders. In : Szolovits P (ed) *Artificial intelligence in medicine,* Westview, Boulder

[PAU 76] Pauker SG, Gorry GA, Kassirer JP, Schwart, WB (1976.
Towards the simulation of clinical cognition : taking the history of a present illness by computer. *Am J Med,* 60 : pp. 981-996

[POP 82] Pople HE (1982)
Heuristic methods for imposing structure on ill-structured problems: the structuring of medical diagnosis. In : Szolovits P (ed) *Artificial intelligence in medicine.* Westview, Boulder

[REG 81] Reggia SA (1981)
Computer assisted medical decision making : a critical review. *Ann Biomed Eng,*9 : pp. 605 -619

[REN 87] Rennels DG, Shortliffe HE (1987)
Advanced computing for medicine. *Sci Am,* Oct : pp. 146 - 153

[SCH 89] Schwarz V, Hohenberger V, Köhle, CO, Schlag P (1989)
Setting up a decision support system with decision tables. *Methods Inf Med,* 28 (3), : pp. 126 - 132

[SHO 76] Shortliffe EH (1976)
Computer-based medical consultations - MYCIN. Elsevier, New York

[SHO 79] Shortliffe EH, Buchanan BG, Feigenbaum EA (1979)
Knowledge engineering for clinical decisison making : a review of computer based clinical decision aids.
Proc IEEE 67 : pp.1207 - 1224

[SHO 81] Shortliffe EH, Scott CA, Bischoff MB, Campbell AB, Van Melle W, Jacobs CD (1981)
ONOCOCIN, an expert system for oncology protocol management. In : *Proceedings of the 6th international joint conference on artificial intelligence,* Tokyo, pp. 876-881

[TAL 90] Talmon JL (1990)
Knowledge-based systems, concepts, methods and techniques. In : Pretschner DR, Urrutia B (eds) *Knowledge-based systems to aid medical image analysis.* Commission of the E.C., DC Science, Research and development, pp. 11 - 12

[TRI 77] Trigoboff M, Kulikowski C (1977)
IRIS, system for the propagation of inferences in a semantic net. In : *Proceedings of the 6th international joint conference on artificial intelligence,* Tokyo, pp. 274 - 280

[VRI 87] De Vries PR (1987)
Cycli in medical decision making. In : de Witte SSSC, Kwee AYL (eds) *Kennissystemen en medische besluitvorming.* Samson, Amsterdam, p. 41

[WAH 86] Wah B, Ili G (1986)
Introduction to artificial intelligence applications. In : *Computers for artificial intelligence applications.*
IEEE Computer Society Press, Washington, pp. 1 - 4

[WAL 87] Walton JD, Musem MA, Combs DM, Lane CD, Shortliffe EH, Fagan LM (1987)
Graphical access to medical expert systems. III. Design of a knowledge acquisition environment. *Methods Inf Med,* 26 : pp 78 - 88

[WEE 90] Weed M (1990)
Systems for quality management and cost reduction.
Intermountain Health Care

[WEI 78] Weiss SM, Kulikowski CA, Safir A, Amarel S (1978)
A model-based method for computer-aided medical decision making. *J Artif Intell* 11 : pp. 145-172

28. Medical Imaging

[AIR 88] Aird EGA (1988)
Basic physics for medical imaging.
Heinemann, Oxford, p.132

[GEN 84] General Electric (1984)
A perspective on imaging.
GE Company, p.11

[JAC 77] Jackson B, Webster JG (1977)
Medicine and clinical engineering. Prentice-Hall, Englewood Cliffs

[KEA 86] Kean D, Smith M (1986)
Magnetic resonance imaging.
Butterworth - Heinemann, Oxford, p.11

[KRE 90] Krestel E
Imaging systems for medical diagnostics. Siemens Medical Systems, Berlin

[PAT 85] Patton DD (1985)
Computers in nuclear medicine. In : Hunter TB (ed), *The computer in radiology,* Aspen , Rockville, pp. 178-205

[PHI 84] Philips Medical Systems (1984)
Principles of MR imaging. Philips Medical Systems, Netherlands, pp. 9, 12, 39, 40

[SOU 90] Souhrada L(1990)
Imaging devices shifting uses affect market,MIRC. *Hospitals,* Nov 5 : pp. 28-31

[WEY 82] Weyman AE (1982)
Cross-sectional echocardiography.
Lea and Febiger, Philadelphia

29. Image Management and Communication Systems in Medicine

[ACR 85] ACR-NEMA (1985)
American College of Radiology. National Electrical Manufacturers Association ACR-NEMA.
Digital imaging and communications standard : ACR-NEMA standards. ACR-NEMA, Washington, Publ no. 300 - 1985

[FRA 86] Fraser RG, Barnes GT (1986)
Digital radiography of the chest. In : *Recent advances in radiology and medical imaging,* no. 8 Churchill Livingstone, Edinbourgh

[FU 86] Fu Tao-Yi, Hayworth Mark (1986)
The digital image : its structure, storage and transmission in : Hunter Tim B. ed. *The computer in radiology, Aspen publication,* pp.94-120

[KRE 90] Krestel E, (1990)
Imaging systems for medical diagnostics. Siemens Medical Systems Berlin, p. 283

[MAT 91a] Mattheus R, Osteaux M, Van den Broeck R
Differentation and requirements of image-computers in a clinical PACS environment.
In : Demongeot J & Sousa Pereira A (eds) *Integrated system for the management and manipulation of medical images*, ISCAMI 1, Springer, Paris Berlin Heidelberg New York, pp. 36 - 45

[MAT 91b] Mattheus R, Ottes FP, Bakker AR, Osteaux M
HIPACS : Hospital integrated Picture archiving and communication systems. An R & D effort of the EC.
In : Huang et al. (eds) *Picture archiving and communication systems (PACS) in medicine.* NATO ASI series, vol. F74. Springer, Berlin Heidelberg New York, pp. 325 - 331

[RAT 91] Ratib O, Ligier Y, Appel R, Scherrer JR
PAPYRUS : a portable image file format.
In : Huang et al. (eds) *Picture archiving and communication systems (PACS) in medicine.* NATO ASI series, vol. F74. Springer, Berlin Heidelberg New York, pp. 91 - 94

[WEN 91] Wendler T (1991)
Digital image workstation. In : Osteaux M et al. (eds) : *Hospital integrated picture and communication systems. A second generation PACS concept.* Springer, Berlin Heidelberg New York

30. The Era of Telemedecine

[DEM 90] De Moor GJE (1990)
EUCLIDES: European clinical laboratory data exchange standard (AIM-project : A 1033).
Department of Medical Informatics, State University Hospital Gent

[HAN 90] Hannemyr G, Belsnes D, Hanseth 0, Larsen H, Moller-Pedersen B (1990)
A reference model for health care information processing and communication, and its implementation in ODA.
Contract with the Norwegian Telecommunication Administration (NTA), Sigurd From, Sigbjorn Health Care System and valuable comments. Norwegian Computing Center , Jan 25

[HAS 90] Hasman A, Arnou G, Van Kesteren AC, Ament I (1990)
The 3I-project-electronic data interchange in the Netherlands. In: *Proceedings of the 14th annual symposium on computer applications in medical care.* IEEE Computer Society, Press, Washington (1990)

[RAT 91] Ratib O
Telemed project. In: Huang HK et al. (eds) *Picture archiving and communication systems (PACS) in medicine.* NATO ASI series, vol. F74. Springer, Berlin Heidelberg New York, pp.335 -336

31. Computerised Surveillance System for Nosocomial Infections

[EVA 85] Evans SR, Gardner RM, Bush AR, Burke JP, Jacobson AA, Larsen RA, Meier FA, Warner HR (1985)
Development of a computerized infectious disease monitor (CIDM). *Comput Biomed Res*, 18: pp. 103 - 113

[EVA 86] Evans SR, Larsen RA, Burke JP, Gardner RM, Meier FA, Jacobson JA, Conti MT, Jacobson JT, Hulse RK (1986)
in: *Computer surveillance of hospital-acquired infections and antibiotic use*. JAMA, 256 (8): pp. 1007-1011

[GOR 83] Gordon M, Venn CJ, Gower PE, De Wardener HE (1983) Experience in the computer handling of clinical data for dialysis and transplantation units. *Kidney Int* 24: pp. 455-463

[LAR 89] Larsen RA, Evans SR, Burke JP, Stanley L, Pestotnik RP, Gardner RM, Classen DC (1989) Improved perioperative antibiotic use and reduced surgical wound infections through use of computer decision analysis. *Infect Control Hosp Epidemiol,* 10 (7): pp. 316 - 320

[LAU 90] Lauwers S, De Smet F, Van Zeebroeck A, Van de Velde R (1990) *Description of computerized surveillance system for nosocomial infections in a Belgian teaching hospital.* 2nd International Conference of the Hospital Infection Society, London, 2 - 6 Sept '90

[WEN 76] Wenzel RP, Osterman CA, Hunting KJ, Gwaltney JM (1976) Hospital-acquired infections. Surveillance in a university hospital. *Am J Epidemiol* 103: pp. 251-260

32. Hospital Information : The Future is Now !

[BER 90] Berman S (1990) The 1990s : the critical decade for medical technology *QRB,* 16 (6): pp.200-201

[HAR 90] Hard R (1900) Small hospitals work to expand IS functions. *Hospitals,* Febr 5: p. 73

SUBJECT INDEX

ECT INDEX

26,

Printing: Mercedesdruck, Berlin
Binding: Buchbinderei Lüderitz & Bauer, Berlin

MIX
Papier aus verantwortungsvollen Quellen
Paper from responsible sources
FSC® C105338

If you have any concerns about our products,
you can contact us on
ProductSafety@springernature.com

In case Publisher is established outside the EU,
the EU authorized representative is:
Springer Nature Customer Service Center GmbH
Europaplatz 3, 69115 Heidelberg, Germany

Printed by Libri Plureos GmbH
in Hamburg, Germany